RURAL AMERICA IN PASSAGE: Statistics for Policy

Dorothy M. Gilford, Glenn L. Nelson, and Linda Ingram, *Editors*

Panel on Statistics for Rural Development Policy
Committee on National Statistics
Assembly of Behavioral and Social Sciences
National Research Council

NATIONAL ACADEMY PRESS
Washington, D.C. 1981

NOTICE: The project that is the subject of this report was approved by the Governing Board of the National Research Council, whose members are drawn from the councils of the National Academy of Sciences, the National Academy of Engineering, and the Institute of Medicine. The members of the committee responsible for the report were chosen for their special competences and with regard for appropriate balance.

This report has been reviewed by a group other than the authors according to procedures approved by a Report Review Committee consisting of members of the National Academy of Sciences, the National Academy of Engineering, and the Institute of Medicine.

The National Research Council was established by the National Academy of Sciences in 1916 to associate the broad community of science and technology with the Academy's purposes of furthering knowledge and of advising the federal government. The Council operates in accordance with general policies determined by the Academy under the authority of its congressional charter of 1863, which establishes the Academy as a private, nonprofit, self-governing membership corporation. The Council has become the principal operating agency of both the National Academy of Sciences and the National Academy of Engineering in the conduct of their services to the government, the public, and the scientific and engineering communities. It is administered jointly by both Academies and the Institute of Medicine. The National Academy of Engineering and the Institute of Medicine were established in 1964 and 1970, respectively, under the charter of the National Academy of Sciences.

Library of Congress Catalog Card Number 81-84160
International Standard Book Number 0-309-03175-3

Available from:

NATIONAL ACADEMY PRESS
2101 Constitution Ave., N.W.
Washington, D.C. 20418

Printed in the United States of America

PANEL ON STATISTICS FOR RURAL DEVELOPMENT POLICY

JAMES T. BONNEN (Chair), Department of Agricultural Economics, Michigan State University
WALT T. FEDERER, Biometrics Unit, Cornell University
GLENN V. FUGUITT, Department of Rural Sociology, University of Wisconsin
WAYNE A. FULLER, Department of Statistics, Iowa State University
JOHN FRASER HART, Department of Geography, University of Minnesota
DARYL J. HOBBS, Office of Rural Development, University of Missouri
JOHN MOLAND, Jr., Center for Social Research, Southern University
HARRY V. ROBERTS, Graduate School of Business, University of Chicago
ALVIN D. SOKOLOW, Institute of Governmental Affairs, University of California, Davis
RAYMOND J. SUPALLA, Department of Agricultural Economics, University of Nebraska
CONRAD TAEUBER, Center for Population Research, Georgetown University
MARTA TIENDA, Department of Rural Sociology, University of Wisconsin
LUTHER TWEETEN, Department of Agricultural Economics, Oklahoma State University

DOROTHY M. GILFORD, Study Director
GLENN L. NELSON, Consultant
LINDA INGRAM, Research Assistant
CAROLYN A. CARROLL, Research Assistant
THELMA L. NEAL, Administrative Secretary

COMMITTEE ON NATIONAL STATISTICS

CONRAD TAEUBER (Chair), Center for Population Research, Georgetown University
OTIS DUDLEY DUNCAN, Department of Sociology, University of Arizona
STEPHEN E. FIENBERG, Department of Statistics, Carnegie-Mellon University
JEAN D. GIBBONS, Department of Management Science and Statistics, University of Alabama
ZVI GRILICHES, Department of Economics, Harvard University
CLIFFORD G. HILDRETH, Center for Economic Research, University of Minnesota
J. STUART HUNTER, School of Engineering and Applied Science, Princeton University
NATHAN KEYFITZ, Center for Population Studies, Harvard University
LESLIE KISH, Institute for Social Reseach, University of Michigan
HOWARD LEVENE, Department of Mathematical Statistics, Columbia University
PAUL MEIER, Department of Statistics, University of Chicago
INGRAM OLKIN, Department of Statistics, Stanford University
EDWARD R. TUFTE, Department of Political Science, Yale University

CONTENTS

PREFACE

The Panel on Statistics for Rural Development Policy was established by the National Research Council in response to a request from the Farmers Home Administration of the U.S. Department of Agriculture. Our overall charge, as conveyed in our name, was to assess the current quality and availability of data for rural development policy. We were asked to make recommendations for improving those data.

Specifying the statistics needed for rural development policy is a more difficult task than might first appear. Until recent decades, rural development was commonly understood to be the development of agriculture. As science and technology transformed U.S. agriculture and as rural communities have grown, however, farming has accounted for a declining portion of the employment and economic activity in rural areas. In the 1970s, the net migration to metropolitan America ebbed, and a reverse flow to the countryside is now bringing new economic activity and greater diversity to rural communities. What rural development means or should mean today has become a difficult and often contentious question. Indeed, what is meant by "rural" cannot be clearly conceptualized or statistically defined. Discovering the appropriate statistical data base for rural development policy under these conditions is a rather brisk challenge.

It was necessary for the panel to understand the enormous diversity of rural communities and the complexity of public policies and programs affecting them. As detailed in the report, a multifaceted strategy was followed to collect information about programs and the perceptions of decision makers at various levels of government about rural development problems and data needs. One rather remarkable insight was provided by reading the hundreds of letters received from county and substate regional officials on their perceptions of rural development issues: an impressive amount of bitterness and cynicism about federal and some state programs that affect rural communities. Many rural officials believe that inappropriate but well-intended federal (and state) decisions have eroded their communities' integrity and capacity for self-determination. One is left with a profound feeling that the social contract underlying American federalism has evaporated. The sense of independence and community that has been so strong in rural society is now threatened.

The data requirements for most rural development policies arise in the context of this disordered structure of federalism. Contention and uncertainty make a good statistical base difficult to specify but simultaneously enhance its social value. This is the setting within which the Panel on Statistics for Rural Development Policy undertook its task.

The panel's report is the effort of many people. The panel was established under the auspices of the Committee on National Statistics of the Assembly of Behavioral and Social Sciences. Edwin D. Goldfield, executive director of the committee, provided administrative guidance, good-natured encouragement, and support to panel and staff. Margaret Martin, the committee's former executive director and currently senior research associate, had the staff responsibility for the establishment of the panel. Conrad F. Taeuber, chair of the Committee on National Statistics and member of the panel, devoted many thoughtful hours of attention to the panel from the earliest phases to the final review of its report.

Vincent P. Rock, director of the policy staff of the sponsoring agency, the Farmers Home Administration, followed the panel's deliberations and was an intellectual stimulus to the panel and staff. His respect for the independence of the panel was appreciated. Sara Mazie and Jeffrey Soule of the policy staff were cheerfully responsive to the questions and requests of the panel and staff.

We acknowledge with gratitude the assistance received from the many other organizations and individuals who cooperated in informing the panel about conditions and problems in rural America. Kenneth L. Deavers, director of the Economic Development Division in the U.S. Department of Agriculture, was immensely helpful in providing data, analysis, and advice. Special thanks are due John Cornman, director of the National Rural Center, and his staff for their unfailing interest and support. Irma Elo, director of the Center's data needs and capacity building program, was especially helpful in arranging a workshop with the Washington representatives of a number of national organizations with interests in rural development. We also owe a considerable debt of thanks to the hundreds of people who responded to our letter survey of 465 sample counties. They provided us with a view of what it is like on the firing line of rural community development.

No panel with a task as complex and as difficult to focus as ours could perform its duties well without an excellent, well-managed staff. We are uniquely indebted to our staff director, Dorothy M. Gilford, who developed much of our intellectual strategy, organized and managed a very complex set of activities, and diplomatically but firmly nudged us on to meet our deadlines. Her intellectual contributions are embedded in every phase of our work. Her role and those of consultant Glenn Nelson and research assistant Linda Ingram are reflected in their designation as editors.

During the early months of the panel's work, Margaret Fulton, administrative secretary, prepared the letters sent to state extension directors and to 671 people at the local level. After June 1980,

Thelma L. Neal, administrative secretary, was responsible for the growing volume of typing as well as the word processing of successive versions of the report. She cheerfully undertook any task requested by panel members or staff.

We are also indebted to a special consultant, Brady Deaton of Virginia Polytechnic Institute and State University, who redrafted and further developed Chapter 10 in a very timely way, thereby helping keep the panel on schedule for the report. Carolyn Carroll, originally a consultant to the panel and later a research assistant, made major contributions to Chapter 8 and assisted in collecting information and in coordinating the redrafting and editing of progressive versions of the report. Eugenia Grohman, associate director for reports of the Assembly, was responsible for editing the report and made valuable suggestions about its structure. Elaine McGarraugh, editorial assistant, helped prepare the manuscript for publication.

Finally, I wish to express my profound appreciation to fellow panel members for their willingness to devote long hours and their special knowledge to the development and writing of the report. They have worked together well and patiently, a critical element in so multidisciplinary an enterprise. Everyone reading the report will appreciate Fraser Hart's willingness, beyond his responsibilities as a panel member, to apply his literate style and years as an editor to convert some of our more opaque utterings into bright and readable English. I should point out also that two rather original statistical ideas developed by panel members Wayne Fuller and Walt Federer can be found in Appendixes G and H.

JAMES T. BONNEN, Chair
Panel on Statistics for
Rural Development Policy

1

RURAL AMERICA: KNOWN AND UNKNOWN

INTRODUCTION

Half a century ago the American countryside differed from the city in nearly every way. Country people lived longer, had larger families, worked on the land rather than in shops and offices, wore different kinds of clothing, ate different kinds of food, went to different kinds of schools and churches, read different newspapers, and voted for different politicians. The stereotypes of the city slicker and the country bumpkin were exaggerated, and, like most stereotypes, tinged with malice, but they were based on widespread experience because urban and rural life-styles were so completely different.

Today, those life-styles have become so similar that the old distinctions between urban and rural have become blurred and fuzzy. The automobile has emancipated rural people from the land and released urban people from the city. Many of the people who live in the country today do so out of choice, and they are quite as much at home, when need be, on the sidewalks of the city as they are on the furrows of the land. Some country dwellers are refugees who have fled the city and elected the luxuries of peace, quiet, and open space. But these luxuries, like all others, have their price; those who dwell in rural areas must pay the cost of space and endure the problems of distance.

Although the people of rural America are becoming more difficult to distinguish from their urban cousins, the effects of space and the presence of most of the nation's forests, mines, and farms will always keep them slightly different. Rural people live farther apart than urban people, and they pay a price for their extra elbow room. It costs more to provide them with telephones, electricity, water, and other services that require home delivery. Rural people must travel farther to reach stores, schools, hospitals, libraries, and other service establishments. Many rural areas have too few people to support the levels of services that many city people consider essential. The concept of rurality once had significant economic, social, and political associations, but today the concept of rurality has become primarily, albeit not entirely, geographic: one of the still distinctive features of rural areas is the distances that separate the homes of rural people.

Until recently, the concept of rurality represented a whole bundle of closely interrelated economic, social, and political traits. This tight interrelationship enormously simplified the task of policy makers and analysts because so many variables could be used interchangeably. Today the bundle has come apart, and the individual traits that once were closely associated under the broad rubric of rurality are now almost completely unrelated.

The disintegration of the "rural bundle" has left two awkward legacies. First, every person has a firm, and often emotional, notion about what rural really is, and people cling to the term even though they know that it has become nearly meaningless. Some Americans, for example, still think that all rural people are farmers, or vice versa, but nothing could be further from the truth. Foresters, miners, storekeepers, and other nonfarm people have always been a part of the population of many rural areas, even though the Bureau of the Census did not officially distinguish the nonfarm component of the rural population until 1920. Nonfarm people made up only 38 percent of the total rural population in 1920 (Bureau of the Census 1974), but had mushroomed to 82 percent of the rural population by 1970 (Bureau of the Census 1979). One can identify obvious polar extremes of urban and rural--midtown Manhattan clearly is urban, for example, and a corn field in Iowa is patently rural--but things begin to come unstuck when one tries to agree on a single definition and establish one discrete boundary in the fuzzy middle ground, where a value that is critical in terms of one criterion may have little or no significance in terms of others. All attempts to develop a common definition of rurality have been unsatisfying. Rural-urban is clearly a continuum, not a dichotomy.

As a second awkward legacy, the disintegration of the "rural bundle" of traits has created difficulties for policy makers, program managers, analysts, and all collectors and users of statistical data for rural areas, however those areas are identified. The federal government has decided, as a matter of principle, that all citizens have the right to some specified level of human services; special efforts have been made to identify rural people and rural areas that have been served inadequately in the past, but different programs have used widely different definitions of rural. The problem becomes most obvious for programs that transfer federal and state funds to local units of government. These programs must establish statistical criteria of eligibility, and they often use the best available data to do so, but even the best data are inadequate and outmoded when they are based on concepts about a bundle of rural traits that has long since disintegrated into unrelated components.

The national ignorance about rural areas stems in part from the fact that such areas have long been out of fashion in American society. The massive movement of millions of rural people to urban areas during the twentieth century has been one of the great migrations of human history, and most Americans, including those responsible for collecting data on our society, have been fascinated by the phenomenon of metropolitan growth. Nonmetropolitan areas have been dismissed as residual, or they have been treated superficially.

A few scholars have tried to call attention to the fact that many rural areas in some regions were gaining population, albeit at a slower rate than metropolitan areas (Hart and Salisbury 1965, Hart 1974) and that a similar trend seemed to be occurring nationally (Beale 1969, 1974, 1977, Beale and Fuguitt 1978, Morrison and Wheeler 1976). In fact, since 1970 the nonmetropolitan areas of the nation have been growing more rapidly than the metropolitan areas. Preliminary counts from the 1980 census show that nonmetropolitan counties grew in population by 15.4 percent from 1970 to 1980, compared with a 9.1 percent increase for metropolitan counties and a 10.8 percent increase for the country as a whole (Beale 1981).

The population turnaround has made headlines, and there is a growing national awareness that rural America has been changing rapidly into a new and very different society. Entirely new questions are being raised about the nature of these changes and the future of rural life, but answers are hard to obtain, partly because of the inadequacy of the current data base. Relatively little is known about the rural nonfarm population and the activities that sustain it, and data for small areas and for local units of government are especially inadequate. More than half of the 39,000 local units of government in the United States have a population of less than 1,000, and 70 percent have a population of less than 2,500 (Bureau of the Census 1979). These units have limited capacity for developing their own data bases, and census data for small areas are also limited. The United States has one of the world's finest census operations, but censuses are taken infrequently, and census publications have focused on the places with most of the people and the places to which people seemed to be moving.

There is a limited capability to track systematically what is happening to rural society, except in the most aggregate sense, and thus little ability to describe many problems concretely or to develop policy to deal with those problems. Numerous rural areas, including some quite remote from large cities, are among the most rapidly growing in the United States. The lack of ability to understand that change and to provide coherent policy direction can have costly consequences. Rural America is not just the residual left behind by the urbanization and industrialization of the United States; more than a quarter of all Americans live in rural areas. The rural economy is growing in scale and diversity, and it plays an important role in the decentralization of national economic activity and population now taking place. Formulation of effective public policies to contend with the major problems of rural America requires an appropriate data base.

The need for particular attention to the data base for rural areas derives both from the increasing diversity of rural values and from the inherent physical characteristics of rural society. Rural and urban people largely share the same concerns for meeting basic human physical needs and providing a social environment conducive to developing the potential of each person. The values of rural and urban residents have tended to converge over time, although some differences persist and even grow (Larson 1978). Further convergence seems likely as migration between urban and rural areas continues on a large scale and as new technologies reduce the cost of exchanging information between rural and urban areas. However, one effect is an increasing diversity of values among rural people. The mixing of rural with urban values, life-styles, and vocations is generating vitality, change, and growing conflict over the current state and future path of rural communities.

Differences between rural and urban problems, policies, and data requirements have important roots in demography and in the geography of places. Population density, size of settlement, distance to services, resource base, and physical environment are prime characteristics that distinguish rural from urban areas. These and related features have major effects on problem definition and should influence policy design and program implementation.

The statistical system of this country gives inadequate attention to the unique problems of people in rural areas, and consequently it serves the nation--urban as well as rural people--poorly. For standard metropolitan statistical areas, data are provided by surveys such as the annual housing survey and the monthly current population survey, but the primary source of data for rural areas is the decennial census. Many rural problems are therefore ignored or ill-defined, policies are misdirected, and programs are mismanaged. The resulting inefficiencies and inequities are, and should be, concerns of informed citizens in both urban and rural areas.

The next section of this chapter describes rural America, placing particular emphasis on trends with major policy implications. The third section examines the general features of rural data problems. The definition of these problems flows from a discussion of discrepancies between actual and desired conditions in rural areas. The fourth section identifies the agencies that are in the best position to initiate needed changes; those agencies are the principal audience for this report. The final section of this chapter briefly reviews the remainder of the report.

RURAL SETTING

Many forces shape rural society. The Panel identified seven major factors that have particular importance for the design of data needed by policy makers and others concerned with rural problems: the convergence of urban and rural culture; the uniqueness of rural areas; the heterogeneity of rural areas; interdependence; conflict about growth; a changed notion of planning; and the capacity of government.

Convergence of Urban and Rural Culture

Advances in transportation and communication technologies have progressively reduced the spatial and cultural isolation of rural life from urban influences. Rural people read the same newspapers as urban people, watch the same television programs, use the same goods, and, to a large extent, receive the same public services. Rural children study the same textbooks as urban children, and they are taught by teachers who attended the same colleges as urban teachers. Although jobs in natural-resource-based industry (especially farming, forestry, and mining) once dominated rural employment, the jobs in rural areas seem to be moving toward an urban pattern. As rural and urban life involve more shared experiences, the views of the world held by rural and urban people are clearly converging, and most signs point to even further convergence in the future. Rural people will become increasingly indistinguishable from urban people on the basis of employment, consumption patterns, political beliefs, and lifestyles.

All policy actions, rural or urban, are responses to a perception of an unwanted divergence between "what is" (the perceived state of the world) and "what ought to be" (prescriptive beliefs). Common cultural experience tends to increase the degree to which people have a shared view of "what is." Such a convergence does not imply greater policy consensus, but rather a trend toward a similar distribution of values and knowledge of the world. Policy makers who address the question "What do citizens desire?" will find the distinction between urban and rural less helpful than in the past.

Uniqueness of Rural Areas

Space and distance are unique features of rural areas that will continue to differentiate them from urban areas, and they are integral parts of nearly all rural problems. Both public and private institutions evolve differently in response to the problems and potentials of open space and low population densities in rural areas. Governmental units serve smaller numbers of people, businesses operate on a smaller scale, transportation costs are a larger consideration, and the cost of land is less important--to cite but a few of the more important rural-urban differences related to space and distance.

The relationship of rural residents to natural-resource-based industries continues to be important, despite the faster relative growth of manufacturing, trade, and service employment. Industries such as agriculture, mining, and forestry are tied to locations with appropriate soil, mineral, or climatic characteristics--and will always be unique to rural life. Each industry, in turn, imposes particular features on the social environment. In addition, the rhythm and style of rural life are often closely tied to the season of the year, the biological cycles of plants and animals, and the vagaries of weather. Urban life, in contrast, proceeds largely in an environment created by people and reproduced in a similar manner in numerous locations.

The unique features of rural and of urban settings create differences in their problems and policy needs. These differences are rooted in the geography of places, will not disappear over time, and are a prime motivation for a study of rural data needs. Many of the institutions and procedures in current information systems were designed with little or no consciousness of rural-urban differences and, in the worst cases, were designed almost exclusively for urban areas, with rural tacked on as a residual. Frequently the lack of data for rural areas is an unintended consequence of using a sample design that, for a fixed cost, minimizes the sampling error for national or state estimates of the main variable of interest. Such designs will concentrate on large cities and sample few people in sparsely settled areas, and estimates for such areas are then not published because of large sampling errors.

Heterogeneity of Rural Areas

Rural people, environments, and communities differ greatly. Varying climates and resources have led to regional specialization along economic lines, for example, so there is wheat in the Great Plains, corn and hogs in the corn belt, cotton and soybeans in the Mississippi Delta, timber in the western mountains, and coal in parts of Appalachia and the Great Plains. The current decentralization of manufacturing, trade, and service industries into rural areas has added diversity to long-standing variations growing out of natural-resource-based industries. Manufacturing employment especially has grown rapidly in parts of the rural South. Some rural areas, particularly those with large numbers of retired persons, have become increasingly dependent on transfer payments. Recreation services are a mainstay of many rural economies in areas with attractive scenery, lakes, and mountains. Each particular pattern is associated with the distinctive characteristics of the population, such as age, occupation, proportion of in-migrants, and other social and economic characteristics. These differences are, in turn, associated with variations in values and in understanding of the "what is" of the world. The reverse migrations, bringing highly varied urban life-styles, add to this growing diversity.

The heterogeneity of rural America implies a compelling need for statistics on small rural areas if the growing number of important policy conflicts are to be resolved with a minimum of damage to community. Public programs are premised on particular needs. These needs must be measured if the programs are to be effective, and current statistics for rural areas often do not permit such measurement. Growing areas are aggregated with declining areas, rich areas with poor, agricultural with nonagricultural areas, and urban fringe areas with remote hinterlands. The widespread disenchantment of citizens and local officials with federal and state programs designed and administered on the basis of such aggregated statistics is understandable.

Interdependence

The economic specialization of enterprises and of regions has produced a nation, and indeed a world, in which rural people and communities are dependent on others. Rural regions are not even independent in food production. Urban centers depend on rural areas for foodstuffs, but at the same time, they are vital markets and sources of inputs to rural enterprises. National policies impinge directly on the welfare of rural enterprises and communities. Finally, rural development policy, like all other national policy, must take cognizance of global interdependence. Rural society is greatly affected by such things as rainfall in the Soviet Union and its impact on the price of grains; the ability of OPEC nations (Organization of Petroleum Exporting Countries) to restrict petroleum exports and raise energy prices; trade negotiations affecting the prices of imports and exports; and U.S. immigration and border patrol policies with respect to Mexico.

The point has been reached where "there is no separately manipulatable rural society" (Daft 1972:4). Local rural markets and social organization have become so integrated into the evolving urban social order that no conceptual framework or development policy for rural areas can have a unique geographic basis. City and country have too many economic and social structures and problems in common. Some policies and programs recognize this interdependence, but many still focus on rural or urban with little regard for the effects of each on the other.

Conflict About Growth

Over the past decade people have increasingly asked "Growth for what and for whom?" Pursuit of a few aggregate measures, such as a larger gross national product, higher per-capita income, and full employment, is viewed as not only narrow-minded but sometimes dangerous. New technologies that would have been welcomed by people in an earlier time under the banner of "progress" are now often viewed with suspicion or hostility. For example, chemical additives in food are a cause for concern, as are environmental pollutants, and local people in many areas continue to express opposition to nuclear power plants.

Rural development is affected in many ways by the changing attitudes toward growth. People are moving to rural areas in search of amenities even at the expense of decreased income (Fuguitt and Voss 1979). Current rural residents are often apprehensive about growth, fearing the loss of both physical and social amenities (Doherty 1979). They also wonder who will benefit from growth--landowners, "main street" proprietors, wage earners, or the new in-migrants. "Growth policy" is better characterized as "anti-growth policy" in many communities, ironically but perhaps not surprisingly, just as nonmetropolitan areas are experiencing a reversal of past declines in population. Although the current administration is committed to reverse the drift toward an "anti-growth policy," at the local community level the trade-offs are specific and fewer so the conflict between proponents of growth and those opposed to growth is intense.

A story in _The Washington Post_ by Eugene L. Meyer (1980:Bl, B7) describes the situation in Jefferson County, West Virginia, 60 miles northwest of Washington, D.C.:

> The West Virginia panhandle, once a sleepy backwater, is fast becoming Washington's newest bedroom suburb.
>
> The Washington commuter boom . . . has begun to change the political and cultural complexion of Jefferson County. . . . Countywide, natives still hold all the elected offices but Republican newcomers have created at least the potential for two-party politics in a county completely dominated by Democrats since the Civil War.
>
> With the influx of outsiders have come scattered subdivisions and . . . stormy debates over lack of zoning and basic services of government that are taken for granted in the D.C. area but are alien to this region.
>
> "These people come up here from Montgomery and Fairfax because of the low tax rate, and they immediately demand all the services they had down there," complains Henry M. Snyder Jr., president of the county commissioners.
>
> Despite the 47 percent growth spurt of the 1970s--from 21,280 to 30,300 people--Jefferson County still is small. . . . But if the trend continues unabated, many natives and newcomers alike fear, the special rural qualities that both groups enjoy could disappear. Current projections anticipate 45,000 residents by 1995.
>
> . . . a dairy farmer (commented), "There is plenty of land in this county that can be developed without hurting the agricultural industry. Unfortunately, agricultural land is the easiest and cheapest to develop."
>
> "You know we can't stop progress," said Bill Henshaw, the seventh generation of his family to farm the West Virginia panhandle, "but we gotta have some control. How we're gonna do it I don't know because in this society of ours the government shouldn't dictate what you do with your property . . ."

A bumper sticker on a Shepherdstown, West Virginia, jeep says it all: HELP PRESERVE THE EASTERN PANHANDLE--SHOOT A DEVELOPER.

The inability to monitor many of the desired qualities of life is at the core of the anti-growth movement. Existing measures of the quality of life are partial and inadequate. So long as official measures of growth are limited largely to demographic and financial data, people will understandably view growth with concern and uncertainty. Better measures of the many dimensions of the quality of life--especially the availability of suitable employment, the quantity and quality of public services and their effects, physical amenities, and the social environment--would aid in clarifying the debate about growth and in resolving conceptual questions concerning relationships among the dimensions. The task of developing better measures of the quality of life will not be easy. Measures suitable for comparing different geographic areas with unique features (such as rural and urban) are especially difficult to conceptualize and implement.

Marked differences among areas in natural amenities and in man-made goods and services have implications for quality of life. (In many cases, a trade-off exists between particular features of the natural and social environments, and the trade-off is unique to each individual. For example, one individual who likes both science and the out-of-doors works in a remote field station while another who likes both things chooses to work in an urban university setting.) Identifying and quantifying the trade-offs is difficult because the availability of many amenities is highly and inexorably correlated with geographic location or the rural-urban spectrum. For example, the pleasure of living in open space is inconsistent with regular access to the ballet, and the convenience of walking to work in a densely populated area is inconsistent with having the land for a private vegetable garden. Physical and economic constraints will forever prevent the introduction of certain amenities, goods, and services into some communities. Rather, policies must often seek to provide equivalent packages--albeit _not_ identical packages--to meet the basic needs of people and communities in different settings.

Changed Notion of Planning

The proliferation of planning activities at all levels of government makes it difficult if not impossible for a complete accounting of all such activities. A recent review by the ACIR (Advisory Commission on Intergovernmental Relations 1978) of planning at the federal level identified between 30 and 40 programs that provide funds to state and local governments for planning assistance. ACIR estimated that a minimum of 150 federal programs require formal plans. In addition, ACIR estimated that federal programs have led to about 2,000 regional planning organizations, which include a large number of units at the state and local levels. Although most of these planning efforts apply to both rural and urban areas, a few are unique to rural areas.

The idea of planning as a form of regulation is usually resisted in rural communities. Planning activities have not proved an adequate response to public worries concerning growth and change, at least as planning is traditionally and typically practiced. As Wilkinson (1978:119) notes:

> Much of the agenda of public action in many small towns is now set by employees of state and Federal agencies. The result is a more vigorous assault on some public problems than formerly, but an emphasis on public relations rather than on genuine citizen participation, and with very little coordination of efforts, resulting in interagency competition and discontinuities in projects.

Citizens are demanding that planning be a participatory process rather than a public relations exercise. Subject matter experts, once entrusted with many planning responsibilities, are now looked upon with suspicion. People are demanding that governmental institutions be more open and information more accessible.

Role of Government

Social and economic changes have transformed the structure and the role of federal, state, and local governments. Every level of government has acquired new functions, most of them regulatory, and public subventions and services have grown immensely. There has been a growing dependence of state governments on the federal government, and an even greater growth in the dependence of local units on state and federal levels of government. The proportion of general revenues of city governments with populations of less than 50,000 that came from the federal government increased from 5.8 to 12.3 percent between 1972 and 1977 (Bureau of the Census 1974, 1979). In 1977, 24 percent of all state revenues and 39 percent of all local government revenues were transfers from other levels of government (Bureau of the Census 1979).

In spite of this growth of transfers, federalism is in disarray, with no clear division of labor; it is an uncoordinated mixture of programs in which accountability and even purpose are often hopelessly confused (Advisory Commission on Intergovernmental Relations 1980, Walker 1978). Unanticipated and unintended impacts of public programs loom large, sometimes rivaling stated objectives in importance (Vaughan et al. 1980). The side effects of federal expenditure and taxation programs on the geographic distribution of growth, although not well understood, are a major issue in the debates over the need for, and the appropriate form of, national policies on rural and urban development. The Advisory Commission on Intergovernmental Relations recently blamed Congress for the chaos, and the states are pressing hard for reform through the National Governors Conference and the National Conference of State Legislatures (*The New York Times*, August 25, 1980:1).

Underlying the disarray in the institutions of government in rural areas is a fragmented political scene. Rural values and social views dominated state legislatures and the U.S. Congress for many decades without any special organizational effort. The massive migrations to the cities and the "one man, one vote" decisions of the Supreme Court ended that dominance, which, in most states, was not replaced by any very effective organized effort. Thus, the rural counties, townships, and cities are not now well organized and are not represented in most states or at the national level. Public policy is the product of effective political power, and rural society does not now seem to have an effective political voice (Daft 1972). Farmers have long been joined together in general farm organizations and commodity groups, and those organizations were once viewed as representing rural people; but now farmers and their families constitute only a small proportion of the rural population, and their economic interests are quite different from those of other rural people. There will be a political vacuum in rural America until rural units of government form an effective political coalition. Growing economic and social vitality and return migration will eventually make this vacuum intolerable at the same time that it creates a potential political base of some consequence.

Inadequate and misused information plays a major role in creating what ACIR (1980) labeled a "crisis of confidence and competence." For small rural areas, the data elements used in formulas for allocating grants-in-aid, such as population, unemployment, and per-capita income, are often only crude estimates. The data required of local officials in applications for grants from state and federal agencies are a major cause of frustration; local people believe many of these data are irrelevant due to measurement errors and lack of timeliness.

The problems of data often translate into inequitable treatment of people and communities. Systematic errors in estimates will lead to systematic inequities. While such systematic patterns may exist, the panel believes that the problem for people and communities in rural areas is more commonly random errors in various estimates. This is particularly true of the estimates used to distribute revenue sharing money in the years between censuses. The disturbing result is that the population of rural areas with rapid population growth tends to be underestimated while the population of areas with declining populations tends to be overestimated. Similar people and similar communities are thus treated differently in governmental programs. While the overly generous and excessively parsimonious cases balance out in the aggregate, data problems lead to considerable inequity within the population. In addition, the data needed for analyzing the effects of governments on the welfare of people and communities are often missing or of poor quality.

NATURE OF RURAL DATA PROBLEMS

Two important unifying themes emerge from this examination of the current rural setting. These themes, which form the context for the remainder of this report, are the ill-defined nature of the problem of rural development and the need to consider rural development as part of development of the whole society.

Rural Development: An Ill-Defined Concept

Rural society today exhibits such complex dimensions that the concept of rural lacks clarity and resists quantitative efforts at definition. It is a concept evolving from human experience that, by consensus, is accepted as having meaning, but one that cannot be defined precisely. The idea of development also presents many similar difficulties. Thus, "rural development" is inherently ill-defined conceptually.

In addition to conceptual vagueness, factual knowledge of rural areas has important gaps. The expense of collecting statistics for small, sparsely settled areas on a regular basis has led to a data base composed of yearly statistics for large aggregations of rural areas, interspersed with detailed census data only every 10 years. The aggregated data are often misleading because of the heterogeneity of rural areas. The values involved in prescription ("what should be") for rural development are also at issue. The heterogeneity of rural areas, the political fragmentation of rural people, the ferment surrounding growth and planning, and the lack of any focus within government for rural issues have so far prevented the building of any consensus on rural America.

Finally, the operational aspects of development policy are not well understood. Linkages between the tools available to government and the variables impinging on the quality of citizens' lives are well defined only in cases where the chain of causation is direct and short. Indirect effects of programs, commonly believed to be significant in the aggregate, are largely a mystery in terms of causal chains and magnitudes. Thus, there are significant voids in knowledge about the values of rural people as well as knowledge of "what is," "what should be," and how to move from the current to the desired situation.

Diverse philosophies characterize the question of appropriate national policies for rural development. One view holds that the federal government should focus on human resource and job development programs for <u>people</u>. According to this view, local citizens in a community should retain the decision authority for the selection of level and mix of community services and infrastructure. The rural dimension of this approach is that many human resource and job-related problems have a higher incidence in rural than urban areas. Programs addressing these problems are thus relatively more important in rural than urban areas.

Another view focuses on <u>areas</u>, that is, on directly increasing development, economic activity (frequently with a concomitant increase in population), in a rural area relative to what would have occurred in the absence of public policy. The industrial and infrastructure development programs of the Farmers Home Administration and the Economic Development Administration are major examples of this view. A third view holds that a unified national rural development policy is neither politically feasible nor socially desirable because of citizen desires for local self-determination and of heterogeneity among rural areas.

The purpose of the panel was not to make recommendations on the nature of rural development policy, but rather to recommend improvements in the statistical foundations for research, policy analysis, and program implementation. The panel takes no position on the appropriate overall public policy for rural development. We recognize, however, that we must be aware of current conditions and anticipate future changes insofar as they influence the need for data.

Rural development will continue to be an ill-defined concept at the state and federal level for the foreseeable future. Many individual rural communities will make different types of community decisions on their problems and needs. These decisions will go largely unnoticed at state and federal levels except for casual and sporadic attention and will not add up to a national policy in any conventional sense. A relative emphasis on programs for people versus area programs will probably not be clear. The problems and recommendations discussed in this report, however, characterize rural data regardless of any specific policy.

The direction of policy is especially difficult to discuss as this is written at a time when the Reagan administration is proposing major budget revisions in several functional areas. In some cases the future existence of programs is in doubt. Under a scenerio in which the federal government relinquishes more responsibility to states by the use of block grants consolidating federal program funds, the panel would not change its recommendations for improvement of data for rural areas. It is likely, however, that federal and state governments will continue to respond to some specific needs with specialized programs that are not well coordinated.

In this policy environment, the provision of information must be flexible, accessible at the local level, and usable at state and federal levels. Heterogeneity of conditions among areas and changes in conditions over time demand flexibility. Local decision makers must have access to data and to producers of data if they are to have information needed to solve local problems and to meet state and federal requirements. Federal and state decision makers require data that are comparable over areas in order to make efficient and equitable allocations and to design appropriate programs. Producers of data must have access to users if producers are to be responsive and effective in providing for major data needs. These requirements involve cooperation in the development and management of data bases across many organizations at federal, state, and local levels of government. In a highly decentralized set of institutions, a system-like performance can be achieved only if there is a clear purpose and if a major investment is made in the coordination of common functions across those institutions and in the development and implementation of common statistical standards.

Rural Development: Part of the Whole

The United States does not have and should not develop a comprehensive "rural data base" or "rural data system" separate from the information systems for other parts of the county. Rural and urban society are slowly merging in many respects. The interdependence of rural and urban people causes the actions of each group to affect the other. Similarly, policies designed to meet the needs of rural people have ramifications for urban residents and vice versa.

Rural areas do have unique features, however, as well as considerable heterogeneity. There are good reasons to ask whether rural citizens are ill-served by current data systems.

The implication of these two related points is that the panel had an impossible task: the review of all data systems for accurate and equitable treatment of rural people and communities. The panel established priorities in order to place bounds on its task, which retained an imposing scale even after it was pared down to subjects clearly and directly related to the quality of life of rural people.

AUDIENCE

The intended audience for this report consists of decision makers who need, generate, and use data. The Farmers Home Administration (FmHA), the sponsor of the study, is a key agency because of its financial resources and network of personnel at county, state, and federal levels. The Economic Development Administration (EDA) and the Department of Housing and Urban Development (HUD) also have major financial resources and sizable staffs. Another key network of people and programs is the Cooperative Extension Service, which concentrates on information dissemination and collection and education rather than on delivery of physical goods and services. The report may also be of use to state rural development committees, which have recently been formed in many states. University researchers and their professional associations with an interest in rural policy are another audience of critical importance.

Producers of data comprise an important part of our intended audience. Agencies at the federal level include, but are not limited to, Bureau of the Census, Bureau of Labor Statistics, Economics and Statistics Service, several agencies in the Department of Health and Human Services, and the Department of Education.

There are also many other important readers. These include elected officials and their staffs at all levels of government who control the funding of statistical programs. Providing resources on a timely and adequate scale is clearly crucial to improving the rural component of information systems. Additional audiences for this report include other state and local officials as well as citizens and citizen groups. Substate and multistate regional planning and economic development agencies are also important.

Finally, some of the many diverse users of rural data will find our extensive documentation of sources of information (Appendix E) to be useful. The panel and its staff found this documentation was an important and necessary part of their task, and we are pleased to share the results.

FRAMEWORK OF THE REPORT

A framework is needed within which data problems can be identified and remedies suggested. The framework for rural development policy, however, is not obvious. The relevant programs are diverse and often uncoordinated.

The framework adopted by the panel evolved from three interrelated approaches. First, one can approach rural development policy by identifying the programs having rural development as their intent and by identifying people and agencies having responsibility for administering institutions, programs, and policies in rural areas. The data problems of these users are a guide to needed changes in information systems. The process of identifying and contacting contemporary users of rural data is described in Chapter 3, and their characteristics and purposes are discussed in Chapter 4. Their needs were a primary influence on the work of the panel. However, stating that "rural development is what rural developers do" is not satisfying intellectually, nor does it contribute much insight into future needs.

A more challenging and potentially more insightful avenue is to give theoretical and empirical content to the term "rural development." This was attempted in the other two elements of the panel's approach. The second major thrust was to define the concept of rural, which was considerably more difficult than the uninitiated person might expect. The reality and the perceptions of rural have changed considerably over time, and in Chapter 2 we attempt to define the concept of rural operationally.

The third line of inquiry was to define the concept of development. After wandering down some dead-end paths, examining the ideas of other analysts, and engaging in heated but stimulating debates, the panel arrived at the definition expressed in Chapter 2. The panel defined development in terms of broad prescriptive goals, i.e., a concept of "what ought to be" rather than as a theoretical construct or in programmatic terms. Others have come to the same conception (e.g., Copp 1972).

Although the three approaches are definitely related and often complementary, they do not yield a well-integrated, internally consistent view of rural development. The linkages between observed policies and the concepts of rural and development are not always clear, and at times the policies and concepts appear to conflict. The panel, however, could find no better framework for an applied, multidisciplinary study of data needs for rural development policy.

The structure of our report follows from our framework. Chapters 2 through 4 expand the concept of rural development, with much attention to institutional issues: Chapter 2 establishes the scope of the study by presenting operational definitions of "rural" and "development" in a manner consistent with their use by policy makers; Chapter 3 describes the information-gathering procedures of the study; Chapter 4 identifies the various data needs of different levels of rural development policy makers, analysts, and administrators.

Chapters 5 through 11 discuss specific data elements and procedures organized by development goals. Demographic data, which are fundamental to policy in all areas, are covered in Chapter 5. Chapters 6 through 11 consider the data needs in housing, health, education, community facilities, economic development, and natural resources. Each chapter describes what data are needed and what data are available. The panel made an explicit decision to treat agricultural data needs in the context of the data needs for all rural industries and economic activities. Agricultural concerns are found primarily in the chapters on economic development (10) and on natural resources and energy (11). (More extensive descriptions of the available data sets can be found in Appendix E.) Chapter 12 presents general strategies for solving some of the data problems identified in Chapters 5-11.

Throughout the text, underlined sentences identify data that are needed but not available and not covered by our recommendations; these data gaps are also listed at the end of each chapter for the convenience of the reader.

Finally, Chapter 13 presents a summary of the panel's findings, the data gaps considered by the panel to be most important, and the panel's recommendations.

REFERENCES

Advisory Commission on Intergovernmental Relations (1978) The Role of Federal Planning Assistance Programs in National Growth and Development. Background paper prepared for the White House Conference on Balanced National Growth and Economic Development. Washington, D.C.

Advisory Commission on Intergovernmental Relations (1980) A Crisis of Confidence and Competence. Report A-77. Washington, D.C.: U.S. Government Printing Office.

Beale, C.L. (1969) Hearings Before the Ad Hoc Subcommittee on Urban Growth of the Committee on Banking and Currency. U.S. House of Representatives. Washington, D.C.: U.S. Government Printing Office.

Beale, C.L. (1974) Rural development: population and settlement prospects. Journal of Soil and Water Conservation 21(1):23-27.

Beale, C.L. (1977) The recent shift of United States population to nonmetropolitan areas, 1970-75. International Regional Science Review 2(2):113-122.

Beale, C.L. (1981) Rural and Small Town Population Change, 1970-80. ESS-5. Economics and Statistics Service. Washington, D.C.: U.S. Department of Agriculture.

Beale, C.L., and Fuguitt, G. (1978) The new pattern of nonmetropolitan population change. Pp. 157-177 in K.L. Taeuber, L.L. Bumpass, and J.A. Sweet, eds., Social Demography. New York: Academic Press.

Bureau of the Census (1974) Statistical Abstract of the United States: 1974. Washington, D.C.: U.S. Department of Commerce.

Bureau of the Census (1979) Statistical Abstract of the United States: 1979. Washington, D.C.: U.S. Department of Commerce.

Copp, J.H. (1972) Rural sociology and rural development. Rural Sociology 37(4):515-533.

Daft, L.M. (1972) Toward a possibly practical framework for rural development policies and programs. Southern Journal of Agricultural Economics 4:1-8.

Doherty, J.C. (1979) Public and private issues in nonmetropolitan government. Pp. 51-101 in G.V. Fuguitt, P.R. Voss, and J.C.

Doherty, eds., Growth and Change in Rural America. Washington, D.C.: Urban Land Institute.

Fuguitt, G.V., and Voss, P.R. (1979) Recent nonmetropolitan population trends. Pp. 1-47 in G.V. Fuguitt, P.R. Voss, and J.C. Doherty, eds., Growth and Change in Rural America. Washington, D.C.: Urban Land Institute.

Hart, J.F. (1974) The spread of the frontier and the growth of population. Geoscience and Man 5:73-81.

Hart, J.F., and Salisbury, N.E. (1965) Population change in middle western villages: a statistical approach. Annals of the Association of American Geographers 55(1):140-160.

Larson, O.F. (1978) Values and beliefs of rural people. Pp. 91-112 in T.R. Ford, ed., Rural USA: Persistence and Change. Ames, Iowa: Iowa State University Press.

Meyer, E.L. (1980) Peaceful invaders: West Virginia panhandle attracts commuters with low tax rates and a pastoral life style. The Washington Post, November 17.

Morrison, P.A., and Wheeler, J.P. (1976) Rural renaissance in America?: the revival of population growth in remote areas. Population Bulletin 32:1-26.

Vaughan, R.J., Pascal, A.H., and Vaiana, M.E. (1980) The Urban Impacts of Federal Policies: Volume I, Overview. R-2206-KF/HEW. Santa Monica, Calif.: Rand Corporation.

Walker, D.B. (1978) A new intergovernmental system in 1977. Publius 8(1):101-116.

Wilkinson, K.P. (1978) Rural community change. Pp. 115-125 in T.R. Ford, ed., Rural USA: Persistence and Change. Ames, Iowa: Iowa State University Press.

2

WHAT IS RURAL DEVELOPMENT?

WHAT IS "RURAL"?

No single concept or definition of "rural" dominates in policy formulations, analytic work, or popular literature. While the lack of consistency is frustrating, most of the diversity is a legitimate reflection of the multidimensional character of rural life. But this diversity does not imply that the many definitions are arbitrary matters that can be approached casually. Indeed, the multidimensional nature of rural is precisely why its definition and the resulting implications for the rural data system must be approached thoughtfully and with special care.

Programmatic Definitions

Even a brief look at the _1980 Catalog of Federal Domestic Assistance_ (Executive Office of the President 1980, hereafter cited as _1980 Catalog_) reveals several examples of definitions of rural. The Farmers Home Administration (FmHA) uses a variety of eligibility criteria for different programs. The rural housing loan program is for all places with a population of less than 10,000 and also for those places with a population of 10,000-20,000 that are not in a standard metropolitan statistical area (SMSA) (_1980 Catalog_:26). Eligibility for the FmHA water and waste disposal systems program is limited to areas not including a city or town with a population of more than 10,000 in the latest decennial census (_1980 Catalog_:32). Applicants for the FmHA program of business and industrial loans must be located outside of cities with a population of more than 50,000 and also outside of the surrounding densely populated urbanized area (_1980 Catalog_:35). The Rural Electrification Act defines rural as areas outside of places having a population of more than 1,500 (_1980 Catalog_:66).

Programs focused on urban problems implicitly define rural as the residual ineligible areas. These definitions also vary a great deal, as exemplified by the following two cases. The formula grants awarded in the community development block grants/entitlement grants program of the Department of Housing and Urban Development go to central cities in SMSAs, to other cities in SMSAs with populations of more than 50,000, and to "urban counties" (1980 Catalog:522). The definition of an "urban county" includes the stipulation that the county "has a combined population of two hundred thousand or more (excluding the population of metropolitan cities therein) in such unincorporated areas and in its included units of general local government" (U.S. Code, Title 42, Section 5302). The Urban Park and Recreation Recovery Act administered by the Department of the Interior requires that local governments meet one of three criteria to be eligible: 1) central city of an SMSA, 2) cities and townships with populations of at least 40,000, or 3) counties with populations of at least 250,000 (U.S. Department of the Interior 1979).

Analytic Definitions

A variety of common concepts of rural are used in the collection and reporting of statistics. This discussion sets forth the basic concepts. (The detailed, lengthy definitions can be found in Appendix A.)

The urban population as defined by the Bureau of the Census includes people in "incorporated or census designated places of at least 2,500 population at the most recent national census" plus those in "urbanized areas" (see below) (Federal Committee on Standard Metropolitan Statistical Areas 1979:44). Census Bureau definition of the rural population includes all people not classified as urban.

The standard metropolitan statistical area (SMSA) is a commonly used concept necessary in defining areas. Throughout this century large cities have spread into the surrounding countryside, leading to large metropolitan areas with a high degree of social and economic integration. A metropolitan concept using counties as building blocks is desirable because of the wide variety of statistical data that are available for counties. In general, SMSAs include counties with cities or twin cities having a population of at least 50,000 plus adjacent counties having evidence of metropolitan character and integration with the central city counties. The county or counties of an urbanized area having a population of at least 100,000 can also be designated as an SMSA regardless of the population of the largest included city. (In New England, townships are used instead of counties.) Nonmetropolitan areas include all counties not within an SMSA--a total of 2,485 of 3,097 U.S. counties.

Urbanized areas are defined by the Bureau of the Census in census years in order to provide a better separation of urban and rural populations in the vicinity of larger cities than is provided by SMSAs. Because counties are used as building blocks for SMSAs, SMSAs can include rural areas that have few commuters to the central city. Thus, the Federal Committee on Standard Metropolitan Statistical Areas (1980:351) has defined urbanized areas in the following way:

> The urbanized area criteria generally define a boundary based on a population density of at least 1,000 persons per square mile,

but also include less densely settled areas such as industrial parks, railroad yards, and so forth, if they are adjacent to dense urban development. Under the 1980 criteria, an urbanized area must include at least one incorporated city and have a total population of at least 50,000.

Most urbanized areas are contained within SMSAs. Some urbanized areas do not qualify as SMSAs, and portions of urbanized areas may extend into non-SMSA counties.

A classification scheme introduced in 1975 by Hines, Brown, and Zimmer (Hines et al. 1975) in a U.S. Department of Agriculture (USDA) study has received a positive response from several analysts. This classification distinguishes metropolitan counties by size of SMSA and has the advantage of classifying nonmetropolitan counties on two dimensions: "the aggregate size of their urban populations and their geographic proximity to metro areas" (Hines et al. 1975:3). Thus, it characterizes rural areas with more specificity than other classifications, which merely place them in a residual category. It also has the advantage of locating counties on a nine-point urban-rural scale rather than dichotomizing them. The scheme has been used in other USDA studies (e.g., Ross et al. 1979) and in academic studies (e.g., Martin 1977). The National Rural Center has recommended that this classification be used by the Bureau of the Census (personal communication from John M. Cornman, president of the National Rural Center). The Bureau of the Census has adopted a similar classification of metropolitan areas for 1980 using total metropolitan population cutoffs set at 1,000,000, 250,000, and 100,000 (Federal Committee on Standard Metropolitan Statistical Areas 1980). To the best of the panel's knowledge (as of January 1981), the Bureau of the Census has not taken similar steps to implement the classification for nonmetropolitan areas.

The following description of the scheme comes from the original work by Hines, Brown, and Zimmer (1975:4); the number of counties in each group is based on SMSA designations as of 1973 using population counts as of 1970. This distribution will be revised when 1980 census counts and SMSA designations become available.

I. Metropolitan (SMSA) counties:
   1. Greater metropolitan--counties of SMSAs having at least 1 million population (175 counties):
      a. Core counties--counties containing the primary central city of greater metropolitan areas (48 counties).
      b. Fringe counties--suburban counties of greater metropolitan areas (127 counties).
   2. Medium metropolitan--counties made up of SMSAs of 250,000-999,999 population (258 counties).
   3. Small metropolitan--counties made up SMSAs of less than 250,000 population (179 counties).

II. Nonmetropolitan (non-SMSA) counties:
   4. Urbanized adjacent--counties contiguous to SMSAs and having an aggregate urban population of at least 20,000 residents (191 counties).

5. Urbanized not adjacent--counties not contiguous to SMSAs and having an aggregate urban population of at least 20,000 inhabitants (137 counties).
6. Less urbanized adjacent--counties contiguous to SMSAs and having an aggregate urban population of 2,500-19,999 inhabitants (564 counties).
7. Less urbanized not adjacent--counties not contiguous to SMSAs and having an aggregate urban population of 2,500-19,999 inhabitants (721 counties).
8. Totally rural adjacent--counties contiguous to SMSAs and having no urban population (246 counties).
9. Totally rural not adjacent--counties not contiguous to SMSAs and having no urban population (626 counties).

Since the above classification was first published, Calvin Beale and David Brown of the Department of Agriculture have introduced a useful modification (Beale 1977, Hendler and Reid 1980): Counties that are physically adjacent to SMSAs but that had less than 1 percent of the employed population commuting to the SMSA in 1970 are changed from the "adjacent" to the "not adjacent" categories.

Contrasts Among Definitions

Nonmetropolitan counties, using the area definitions as of 1977, included 27 percent of the nation's population in 1977. Nonmetropolitan residents numbered 58 million, metropolitan residents numbered 159 million, and the U.S. population totaled 216 million (Bureau of the Census 1979b). The proportion of the total U.S. population living in nonmetropolitan counties has decreased in recent years for two reasons. First, a steady expansion of the land area encompassed by SMSAs has led to redefining many previously nonmetropolitan residents as residents of SMSAs. From 1950 to 1974 the nonmetropolitan land area shrank from 93.0 percent to 86.2 percent of the U.S. total (Bureau of the Census 1978). Approximately 21 percent of the growth in SMSA population from 1960 to 1970 was a result of including 5 million people in SMSAs in 1970 who would have been in nonmetropolitan counties based upon 1960 designations (calculated from Bureau of the Census 1971). From 1970 to 1977 the impact of new designations was even more dramatic. In 1977, more than 15 million people lived in SMSA counties that were non-SMSA counties in 1970, and these people accounted for 72 percent of the population growth of metropolitan areas over that 7-year interval (calculated from Bureau of the Census 1978 and 1979b).

The second factor affecting the distribution of people between metropolitan and nonmetropolitan counties is the growth rate within counties. Until 1970 the population growth rate within SMSA counties exceeded that of non-SMSA counties. Using metropolitan designations as of 1974, the population in metropolitan counties increased 26.3 percent in 1950-60 compared with only 3.0 percent in nonmetropolitan counties, and in 1960-70 SMSA counties grew 17.1 percent, while non-SMSA counties grew 4.4 percent (Fuguitt and Voss 1979). But from 1970 to 1975, population growth of 4.1 percent in the same (1974 designated) metropolitan counties was less than the 6.6 percent growth in nonmetropolitan areas. Using the 1970 definition of SMSA counties (a change required because of the nature of the published data), the increase in metropolitan population of 0.7 percent from 1975 to 1978 is significantly less than the increase of 5.6 percent in nonmetropolitan areas (calculated from Bureau of the Census 1976). Thus, the increasing proportion of the population residing in SMSAs since 1970 is more appropriately viewed as the result of a conversion of non-SMSA counties to SMSA status rather than a continuing population growth within established SMSAs.

Using the Census Bureau definitions of rural, urban, and urbanized residences yields a different picture than the contrast between nonmetropolitan and metroplitan counties emphasized above (see Table 1). The comparisons are made for 1970 for reasons of data availability. The terms rural, urban, and urbanized are used throughout this paragraph as defined by the Bureau of the Census (see above). Rural areas contain virtually all (98.5 percent) of the land area in the nation; nonmetropolitan counties-those outside SMSAs--encompass a smaller but still sizable 89.1 percent of the land area. Rural areas, however, contain fewer people than do nonmetropolitan areas: 30 percent of rural residents live in SMSAs, while 41 percent of nonmetropolitan residents are urban dwellers. Another important

TABLE 1. Land Area, Population, and Density of Urban and Rural Territory, by Metropolitan and Nonmetropolitan Status, 1970.

Residence	Land Area: Total (1,000 sq.mi.)	Land Area: Percent of U.S.	Population: Total (millions)	Population: Percent of U.S.	Population: Per Sq. mi.
TOTAL	3,540.0	100.0	203.2	100.0	57
Urban	54.1	1.5	149.3	73.5	2,760
In urbanized areas	35.1	1.0	118.4	58.3	3,376
Other urban	19.0	0.5	30.9	15.2	1,623
Rural	3,485.9	98.5	53.9	26.5	15
Inside SMSAs	387.6	10.9	139.4	68.6	360
Urban	NA	NA	123.0	60.5	NA
Rural	NA	NA	16.4	8.1	NA
Outside SMSAs	3,152.4	89.1	63.8	31.4	20
Urban	NA	NA	26.3	13.0	NA
Rural	NA	NA	37.5	18.4	NA

NA - not available
SOURCE: Bureau of the Census (1979c:18).

dimension is that 18 percent of farm families lived within SMSAs in 1978 (Bureau of the Census 1979a). The average population densities in urbanized and urban areas are about 9 and 8 times as great, respectively, as the density in metropolitan areas. The terms rural and nonmetropolitan or urban and metropolitan should not be used interchangeably, yet this practice exists even in the highest level policy discussions within the federal government (e.g., Deavers and Brown 1979).

Conclusions

There is no single or even multiple definition of rural that is completely satisfactory for all purposes (Hathaway et al. 1968, Duncan and Reiss 1956). Attempts to define rural deal with many variables or dimensions of rural life from which one can conclude several things. Absolute either/or distinctions between rural and urban are nearly useless. Variables with several points of division are better than dichotomous variables because the variation within dichotomous groups turns out very frequently to be greater than the variation between groups. For example, an urban town containing 3,000 people has less in common with an urban city containing 300,000 people than it does with a rural town (Census Bureau definition) containing 2,000 people. Continuous variables also provide users with an opportunity to adapt the definition more readily to varied uses of the data.

Despite the difficulty one faces in developing a practical definition of the idea of rural, it is a real part of people's experience. Thus, it is a term in common use that is useful and broadly understood because of common experience. It is, however, not a term that can be defined in a unique, conceptual, or empirical manner that has general applicability. (Some of the same difficulty is encountered with the idea of urban.)

The simple dichotomous distinction of rural-urban is frequently a trap. Rural development cannot be achieved by planning for and allocating rural resources only, or by dealing only with rural social structures. The same may be said about urban development. Any institutional view of important rural problems reveals a planning and delivery structure that involves both rural and urban social systems and resources. Whether one works at the intensive or extensive end of population distribution over geographic space, one must plan for and use the social systems and resources of the entire society. The degree of economic and social interdependence inherent in the society today makes any other approach inappropriate.

Still, there are major differences between urban and rural areas. If there were not, the distinction, even as a broad term of common use, would lack utility. Clearly, demographic variables are different in low-density settings. The problems of development and provision of services in rural areas have distinctly different characteristics--e.g., higher overhead or administrative costs. The nature and organization of the economic bases are different, and transportation and communication functions are more critical to overcoming the cost of space. These and other differences in the needs of rural people and their communities have to be recognized for successful development to be possible in a rural setting.

The following definitions are used in the remainder of the report. "Rural" with no modifiers is used as a concept that is accepted as having meaning, but that cannot be defined precisely; it broadly characterizes a certain type of environment. (When the Census Bureau's definition of rural is used, we will so indicate.) All other terms describing groupings of people or geographic areas are used in a manner consistent with their technical definitions. For example, the terms metropolitan, nonmetropolitan, and urbanized areas are used as defined in the previous section.

Since no single definition of rural is feasible or desirable for use in all situations, data should be organized in a building block approach. The basic building blocks of the data base should facilitate aggregation in a manner consistent with a variety of definitions of rural. The county is the most commonly used geographic unit for reporting small-area data across a wide spectrum of programs and subjects. These data need to be compatible with data on the rest of society. However, current reporting practices are highly variable and often frustrate rather than facilitate aggregation and comparison. The recommended coding procedure would facilitate aggregation in a manner consistent with a variety of definitions of rural.

> Recommendation: The panel recommends that federal and state data be recorded with a county code to permit tabulations for individual counties and groups of counties.

It is especially important for federal agencies awarding grants or contracts to include the county code in their records. The difficulties of defining rural should not be allowed to result in inequitable treatment for--or among--the rural population. Inequities are more likely to occur when "rural" is defined as the residual remaining after delineation of urban. The quantity and quality of statistical measures for the general population and for specific target groups should be comparable for rural and urban areas. More specifically, the level of aggregation with respect to the size of the population groups for which statistical measures are available should be approximately the same for rural and urban areas.

An important step toward the goal of equal statistical treatment of rural and urban people would be the identification and use, for statistical purposes, of standard statistical areas in states with large nonmetropolitan populations. All too often, discussions of data requirements focus on the need for reliable estimates for states and the larger standard metropolitan statistical areas (SMSAs) but ignore the same need for finer partitions within the nonmetropolitan areas of some states for analytical purposes. To cite an important example, in a proposed redesign of the Current Population Survey, the National Commission on Employment and Unemployment Statistics (NCEUS) (1979) makes its recommendation in terms of state totals, SMSAs with a population of 1 million or more, eleven major central cities, and balances of states where large SMSAs are disaggregated. The recommendation does not mention partitioning nonmetropolitan populations within a state when these are large, i.e., 2 million or more, in order to approximate the 1 million standard in non-SMSAs.

The NCEUS did recognize "the need to take rural areas into account" (NCEUS 1979:96) elsewhere in its report, and the recommendation that geographically disparate but functionally similar rural areas be aggregated has analytic merit. It ignores, however, the use of the statistics for policy decisions involving governmental units within such aggregations, especially in allocating resources.

The response of the Department of Labor to the NCEUS report was to improve labor force estimates for the 125 largest SMSAs rather than only for the 35 largest satisfying the NCEUS's criteria, at some sacrifice in quality for the 35 largest (Stein 1980). The Department's response to the weaker recommendation on rural concerns was a qualified one: "Accepted subject to solution of technical problems" (Stein 1980:13). If consideration of rural areas is not reinforced and strengthened, the outcome will be less than equitable treatment for the large nonmetropolitan populations in states such as New York, Pennsylvania, Ohio, Illinois, North Carolina, Georgia and Texas. Examples other than the Current Population Survey could also be cited.

The important general point is that the sampling and reporting units for nonmetropolitan people should reflect the same level of disaggregation provided for metropolitan people. The panel recognizes that this idea has been considered before (e.g., see the brief discussion of substate statistical areas, Vlasin et al. 1975), but feels that the concept has not yet had the serious examination that it warrants.

Recommendation: The panel recommends that the Statistical Policy Division in the Office of Management and Budget develop and implement a system of standard statistical areas (an extension of the present set of SMSAs) to encompass the entire geographic area of the nation.

Designation of standard statistical areas (SSAs) encompassing the entire geographic area of the nation would provide continuous, inclusive, and systematic data based on boundaries that would be changed less frequently than the presently relaxed SMSA criteria. The SSAs would be delineated in cooperation with states, conforming where possible to substate planning and development districts, but encompassing more than one such district when necessary to meet the statistical reliability standards now used for SMSAs. Delineations would take into account nodal and homogeneous area considerations as they are used in the designation of substate districts. The procedure would preserve the building block approach for county data differences within rural SSAs as well as among rural and urban SSAs. If continued use of the label "SMSA" were deemed useful for a more urban subset of the SSAs, the more rural SSAs could be titled standard rural statistical areas (SRSAs).

WHAT IS "DEVELOPMENT"?

Rural development, either as concept, process, or strategy, has varied meanings for different areas, communities, groups, and individuals. For some, it may mean encouraging population and economic growth in rural areas--providing jobs, increasing income, or expanding local business. For others, it may be addressing basic human problems--poverty, illness, ignorance, malnutrition, and substandard housing. For still others, it may be a matter of preserving and enhancing natural and human-made amenities in the small community setting--clean water and air, landscaping, historical structures, and recreational opportunities.

A discussion of the goals of rural development provides a framework for a consideration of data requirements. The panel explicitly rejected the notion of formulating a ranked set of development goals. While each goal in the set presented here is widely viewed as a worthy objective, people attach different weights to each goal, and such differences are an important element of the growing heterogeneity within rural America. Thus, communities in similar environments often adopt diverse policies due to the different weights they place on various goals. In addition, the priorities that communities attach to goals vary with differences in culture, resources, and geography, and they may also shift over time. A changing technological and social environment invariably makes it harder to achieve some goals and enhances the attainment of others. An appropriate policy response is required, i.e., some goals receiving more emphasis and others less, to move toward the balance desired by local communities and governing units. To avoid duplication, a number of functional problem areas, e.g. regulation, are also handled in the broader context of the various goals of development.

The goals presented here do not arise from any one source. Dudley Seers' "necessary conditions for a universally acceptable aim--the realization of the potential of human personality" (Seers 1977a:2; see also Seers 1977b) was the starting point in the panel's initial discussion of goals. But more than anything else, these goals reflect the panel's common perception of the problems and hopes of rural life. We see development as involving the well-being of people and their communities. As such, it is a concept that includes ends and means, both goals and the process of moving towards those goals. These are comprehensive and general categories, almost more assumptions than goals. Being implicit in the human condition, they are not unique to the rural areas of America; rural people and their communities share a common destiny with all America and do not expect more or deserve less than others in society.

Two separate but interrelated sets of development goals are apparent. On one hand, we have several discrete areas involving specific human and community needs--basic needs such as food and shelter, economic security, education, public services and facilities, and the management of natural resources. On the other hand, there are also fundamental values that condition the manner in which the more specific objectives are pursued. Standards of equity and community self-determination are such underlying values, which we call conditioning goals, that easily become goals in their own right.

Specific Development Goals

Basic human needs A basic human need is simply enough food to survive. At a slightly lower order of priority is the need to conquer malnutrition. Other essentials are shelter, clothing, health, and safety. The deprivation that is associated with the failure to command the basic necessities of life must be defined initially in physical terms, but eventually in psychological terms as well. Obviously there are differing levels of perceived need since fundamental concerns about hunger and malnutrition or basic shelter are not to be compared with the inability to eat at an expensive restaurant or live in a penthouse.

Economic security and social worth Economic prosperity is a goal at all levels of society. Although economic well-being is manifested in variables such as income and consumption levels, the usual focus is on increasing the supply and quality of jobs. Employment opportunities are vital to the well-being of individuals and areas. Lack of employment opportunity often results in absolute physical deprivation, underutilized human and other resources, and high rates of out-migration from the affected areas. Employment provides fulfillment of far-ranging wants, from basic necessities to self-enrichment for the individual and from paved streets to cultural development for the community. To monitor basic employment opportunities with appropriate statistical data is to monitor the heartbeat of rural communities and areas.

Productive activity has dimensions other than those that produce money income, including study, raising children, volunteer work, and homemaking, to name only a few. People contribute to society in many ways, and the sense of fulfillment and independence that comes with socially meaningful work is a major component of individual self-respect.

Education Education is a gateway to many desired things in life. It is a means for obtaining and improving employment, social and occupational mobility, cultural appreciation, and self-understanding. The attainment of educational goals is sought, in part, through formal classroom activity in elementary and secondary schools, vocational institutions, and colleges and universities. In addition, institutions such as libraries, art galleries, and museums provide important opportunities for learning. Even so, most cognitive learning occurs through experience, most of it on the job.

Community services and facilities Community services and facilities are also recognized goals since they provide common benefits that individuals and families find difficult or impossible to create for themselves. This category includes a range of public services and facilities, such as water supply, solid and effluent waste disposal, law enforcement, fire protection, parks and recreation, highways, and social services. Local governments generally provide these services, although the role of private providers--including voluntary citizen associations--is of particular importance in rural communities. For some services, including communications, electrical power, and commercial transportation, the public sector often does not supply the service directly but represents public concerns through extensive regulation of rates, service, and profits. People in rural areas increasingly refuse to accept fewer and inferior services than found in other areas. While urban standards are not always explicitly followed, in part because they are sometimes quite inappropriate, the goal is to overcome barriers of accessibility and cost of services while preserving rural amenities.

Natural resource management Natural resource management is another important dimension of rural development. Some argue that good stewardship of the environment is a primary goal, i.e., a worthwhile end in itself. Others, probably a majority, regard resource management as an important means of achieving many of the other specific development goals. In either case, the relationship between natural resource management and economic development is particularly significant. Primary economic activities such as forestry, mining, and agriculture--as well as activities such as tourism and recreation--depend very much on the existence of natural resources and how they are used. Also of considerable importance in rural areas is the relationship between resource management and the cost or availability of community services, such as water supplies and recreation. Energy availability and the impact of energy development on rural communities are important factors in rural life.

Conditioning Goals

Equity Equity in how the resources and opportunities of a society are shared is a goal that conditions how other goals are attained. Goals concerned with the total supply of desired commodities cannot be pursued in isolation. Development is also a matter of distribution, of how access, costs, and benefits are spread among individuals, groups, communities, and regions.

Equality of opportunity is an especially important facet of the goal of equity. Equal opportunity is in part a function of the equitable provision of the specific goods and services discussed above. Food, shelter, clothing, health care, education, and on-the-job experience are investments in human capital which provide long-term opportunities as well as short-term benefits. Attitudes about physical and social characteristics such as race, sex, ethnic origin, and handicaps are also important determinants of equal opportunity. Such attitudes are often difficult or impossible to measure directly, even from careful analysis of important outcomes such as hiring and promotion practices, wages, and residential patterns, although they may affect various aspects of achieving rural development goals.

Part of the impetus for this report comes from a concern about the relative position of rural America in the nation as a whole. The need for fairness is implicit in any effort to compare rural and urban segments of the country. But for rural development purposes, the issue of equity has just as much significance--if not more--for differences within rural America. Many open-country and small town localities have as great or greater extremes and diversities of income, class, and other characteristics as some big city neighborhoods and suburban communities. The how and why of these differences--these inequalities--must be understood if they are to be dealt with in an equitable manner.

Self-determination There is a long tradition in American society of self-determination, the strong belief on the part of communities that they maintain essential freedoms and a high quality of life only to the extent that they are able to control their destinies. The process aspect of development is at work here--the identification of problems, the building of agreement in determining goals, and the implementation of programs. Self-determination is enhanced by the small size and consensual characteristics of rural communities, but it is impeded by outside pressures and demands, the fact that small towns are especially vulnerable to the policies and practices imposed by other levels of government, and by broad economic forces. How does a town retain any sense of community and direction in the face of the increasing interdependence and national scope of modern social and economic institutions? Given the frequent clash of local values and national standards, there are never easy answers to that question. Autonomy is an illusion. But self-determination will persist as a precious value for all people as it relates to their shared beliefs and desires.

Summary of Goals

Attainment of all the above goals is of course impossible. First, some are competitive with others, necessitating trade-offs. Achieving equity in the distribution of certain economic and political resources, for example, may conflict with a community's majority values and thus with the need to maintain a strong degree of self-determination. In this sense, policies and standards set at national and state levels of government may be at odds with the values of small communities and their desire for autonomy. Second, there is the necessity of relying on human institutions for the translation of goals into action, a process that is imperfect at best. Third, no consensus exists on an appropriate weighting of the goals.

Additional information on goals and the disparities between goals and reality as perceived by people in rural areas would be useful. The most direct and immediate impact of improved information would be to affect policy makers' decisions. The more important result, however, would be to stimulate a better informed dialogue among all people concerned with rural development. Effective problem definition and policy formation in rural development depends as much on a more stable and confident belief regarding "what should be" as on better information regarding "what is".

Community surveys are employed in a majority of states, usually with technical assistance from development specialists or other agency personnel of the Cooperative Extension Service such as program specialists in area agencies on aging and in state government community development agencies. The methodology for doing such surveys typically involves linking technical expertise with volunteer assistance from the community. Analyses of the results are increasingly thorough and sophisticated as the cost of computerized data processing falls. A number of states, e.g., Illinois, Kentucky, and North Carolina, have instituted statewide sample surveys of opinions, including beliefs about values and perceptions of issues. These are designed so the results can apply to the areas and communities from which data are gathered as well as being aggregated for use at a state level. The value of such surveys is that they produce relatively inexpensive data that are uniquely applicable to individual communities. Communities find such surveys, when properly designed, useful not only in determining levels of satisfaction with existing services but also in establishing priorities for future community projects. Survey results have been used frequently to provide evidence in support of efforts to obtain funding for community projects. Surveys are especially valuable in ascertaining perceptions of issues and values of groups without vocal leadership in established political channels, which often includes minorities and poor people in rural areas.

An interesting example of what can happen when local ideas of "what should be" are not considered comes from Maine. State vocational education planners had a white elephant on their hands when they failed to take into consideration the deep-rooted values and traditions of the rural people of the state. The state built a $1.5 million regional vocational center in Hancock, Maine, as part of a state plan for vocational education. Today, the " . . . center sits empty because leery citizens have failed to support it." People in Hancock County have traditionally earned their income from the sea or the land, and they prefer the independence of self-employment to being trained to work for others. These rural people are also apprehensive about consolidated schools because their life revolves around community-based organizations (Rosenfeld 1980).

Considering the remoteness of federal relative to local officials and the greater heterogeneity of rural areas encompassed by federal relative to local policy, the survey tool found useful at a local level should be even more valuable to decision makers at the federal level. Oversampling of minority and economically disadvantaged populations might also prove useful.

National data on perceptions of both factual and value issues are needed periodically. While the information should be focused on fundamental policy choices, the aim should be to clarify broad trade-offs rather than to evaluate specific programs. The Economics and Statistics Service (ESS) in the Department of Agriculture is an appropriate agency to provide overall guidance to this task.

The setting of goals is a worthwhile enterprise. At a maximum, it is an expression of the belief in human potential. At a minimum, it is a way of establishing targets and benchmarks, providing both the means of measuring progress and of establishing appropriate policies and programs. We have a more modest purpose. The setting of goals suggest the scope and character of rural development needs. Goals help answer the question--"Data for what?"

DATA GAP

1. Periodic national data on perceptions of both factual and value issues.

REFERENCES

Beale, C.L. (1977) The recent shift of United States population to nonmetropolitan areas, 1970-75. International Regional Science Review 2(2):133-122.

Bureau of the Census (1971) Social and economic characteristics of the population in metropolitan and nonmetropolitan areas: 1970 and 1960. Current Population Reports, Special Studies P-23, No. 37. Washington, D.C.: U.S. Department of Commerce.

Bureau of the Census (1976) Population profile of the United States: 1975. Current Population Reports, Series P-20, No. 292. Washington, D.C.: U.S. Department of Commerce.

Bureau of the Census (1978) Social and economic characteristics of the metropolitan and nonmetropolitan population: 1977 and 1970. Current Population Reports, Special Studies P-23, No. 75. Washington, D.C.: U.S. Department of Commerce.

Bureau of the Census (1979a) Household and family characteristics: March 1978. Current Population Reports, Series P-20, No. 340. Washington, D.C.: U.S. Department of Commerce.

Bureau of the Census (1979b) Population profile of the United States: 1978. Current Population Reports, Series P-20, No. 336. Washington, D.C.: U.S. Department of Commerce.

Bureau of the Census (1979c) Statistical Abstract of the United States: 1979. 100th ed. Washington, D.C.: U.S. Department of Commerce.

Deavers, K.L., and Brown, D.L. (1979) Social and Economic Trends in Rural America. White House Rural Development Background Paper. Washington, D.C.: U.S. Department of Agriculture.

Duncan, O.D., and Reiss, Jr., A.J. (1956) Social Characteristics of Urban and Rural Communities, 1950. New York: John Wiley and Sons.

Executive Office of the President (1980) 1980 Catalog of Federal Domestic Assistance. Office of Management and Budget. Washington, D.C.: U.S. Government Printing Office.

Federal Committee on Standard Metropolitan Statistical Areas (1979) The metropolitan statistical area classification. Statistical Reporter 80(3):33-45.

Federal Committee on Standard Metropolitan Statistical Areas (1980) Documents relating to the metropolitan statistical area classification for the 1980s. Statistical Reporter 80(11):335-384.

Fuguitt, G.V., and Voss, P.R. (1979) Growth and Change in Rural America. Washington, D.C.: Urban Land Institute.

Hathaway, D.E., Beegle, J.A., and Bryant, W.K. (1968) People of Rural America. 1960 Census Monograph, Bureau of the Census. Washington, D.C.: U.S. Department of Commerce.

Hendler, C.I., and Reid, J.N. (1980) Federal Outlays in Fiscal 1978. Rural Development Research Report No. 25. Economics, Statistics, and Cooperatives Services. Washington, D.C.: U.S. Department of Agriculture.

Hines, F.K., Brown, D.L.. and Zimmer, J.M. (1975) Social and Economic Characteristics of the Population in Metro and Nonmetro Counties, 1970. Agricultural Economic Report No. 272. Washington, D.C.: U.S. Department of Agriculture.

Martin, P.L. (1977) Public service employment and rural America. American Journal of Agricultural Economics 59(2):275-282.

National Commission on Employment and Unemployment Statistics (1979) Counting the Labor Force. Washington, D.C.: U.S. Government Printing Office.

Rosenfeld, S. (1980) Shaping a rural vocational education policy. VocEd 55(March):17-21.

Ross, P.J., Bluestone, H., and Hines, F.K. (1979) Indicators of Social Well-Being for U.S. Counties. Rural Development Research Report No. 10. Washington, D.C.: U.S. Department of Agriculture.

Seers, D. (1977a) The meaning of development. International Development Review 19(2):2-7. (First published in 1969, International Development Review 11(4).)

Seers, D. (1977b) The new meaning of development. International Development Review 19(3):2-7.

Stein, R.L. (1980) National commission recommends changes in labor force statistics. Monthly Labor Review 103(4):11-21.

U.S. Department of the Interior (1979) Urban park and recreation recovery program eligibility. Federal Reporter 44(196):58088-58094.

Vlasin, R.D., Libby, L.W., and Shelton, R.L. (1975) Economic and social information for rural America: priorities for immediate improvement. American Journal of Agricultural Economics 57(5):900-909.

3

DISCOVERING WHAT CONCERNS RURAL AMERICA

The panel and its staff undertook a variety of activities to obtain information on policy issues and data gaps at national, state and local levels. The panel was particularly concerned with trying to get an understanding of issues and data problems throughout the wide variety of rural areas in the country, and so we undertook a letter survey of more than 600 people in a random sample of 465 counties. This chapter describes the survey and presents the major findings. (Appendix B contains complete details of the survey and the findings.) This chapter also briefly describes the Panel's other information-gathering activities, including interviews and workshops.

LETTER SURVEYS OF STATE AND LOCAL RURAL DEVELOPMENT PEOPLE

For the letter survey, a random sample of 465 counties was selected. Lists of names of people knowledgeable about rural development in the sample counties were supplied by the state extension directors and the state rural development coordinating committee chairmen. From these lists of names, obtained for all 50 states, 691 individuals were selected to receive requests for information. (See Appendix B for the sampling procedure and for examples of the letters mailed to the state and local contacts.)

The state contacts suggested many local people to whom we sent the request for information. A large number of these people were either associated with regional planning agencies or were local extension agents, but there was a broad range of types of offices. When the number of names available for a region was large enough to allow some choice, the guiding principle was diversity of official positions. Our goal was not to quantify the frequency of need for data but rather to find the scope and depth of detail of data required for rural development policy. (Tables B-5 and B-6 provide a summary and a detailed breakdown of the types of local contacts made in each state and region.)

The panel wishes to stress that although the original sample of counties was a carefully designed random sample, the process for obtaining names of individuals in the counties undoubtedly introduced biases of many types; we do not claim that the sample of 691 local people contacted by mail or the 258 who responded to the letter survey constitute a random sample of people active in rural development in the United States. The respondents do, however, constitute a cross section of 258 people active in rural development. Tables B-7, B-8, and B-9 give a summary of response rates by metropolitan status/urban orientation of county, by region, and by official position of local contact.

The local contacts were asked to discuss current issues in rural development in their county, to identify data gaps they had encountered in their rural development activities, and to provide copies of recent documents that were related to rural development issues and that used data. Varying amounts of information were received from the respondents. Many people sent long letters discussing data needs and rural development issues and included copies of their local plans. Only crude analyses of the responses are appropriate because of nonresponse bias and other biases introduced in the lists provided by states. In the discussion below the raw data are used without weighting for strata sampling rates or for nonrespondents.

The Issue Scheme

The panel did not begin its work with a list of the most important issues in rural development, or even with a list of issues. Rather, the panel began by asking the state contacts to provide information on the most important issues for rural development in the state. The responses were coded into an issue scheme that the panel believes represents the important aspects of development. That issue scheme has seven major categories and many subcategories.

For the letter to the local people, the panel sent only the list of seven major categories. The local responses not only repeated many of the subcategories that we had in hand from the state respondents, but also added new ones. The result was a far-ranging list of issues about rural development that frames much of our subsequent work and the outline of this report. The full issue scheme, as it developed from the state and local responses to the survey, is presented below.

I. Provision of Adequate Human Maintenance Services
- A. Housing
  - 1. Elderly
  - 2. Low income
  - 3. Siting problems
- B. Medical
  - 1. Elderly
  - 2. Need emergency services
  - 3. Need doctors
- C. Elderly
- D. Handicapped
- E. Unspecified

II. <u>Improved Education and Job Training</u>
- A. Primary and Secondary Education
  - 1. Adjusting to declining enrollments
  - 2. Failure of school administration
  - 3. Dropout rate
  - 4. Juvenile delinquency
  - 5. Drugs
  - 6. Overcrowded classrooms
- B. Post-Secondary Vocational and Technical Training
- C. Leadership Training for Adults
- D. Unspecified

III. <u>Provision of Adequate Community Facilities and Services</u>
- A. Water
- B. Sewer
- C. Solid waste disposal
- E. Transportation
  - 1. People
    - a. Roads
    - b. Innovative systems
    - c. Rail
    - d. Air
    - e. Hard to cut gas use
  - 2. Commodities
    - a. Road
    - b. Rail
- F. Community buildings
  - 1. Senior citizens centers
  - 2. Youth
  - 3. Day care center
  - 4. Migrant workers
- G. Recreation
- H. Law enforcement
- I. Bridge repair
- J. Repair, renovation, or replacement of facilities
- K. Different service management alternatives
- L. Improved understanding of the financing of services where population is dispersed
- M. Problems because of increased population
- N. Problems because of dispersed development
- O. Growth of single issue constituencies has risen threshold of "adequate"
- P. Unspecified

IV. <u>Encouraging Economic Development</u>
- A. Aid existing businesses in the local community to continue and expand
- B. Stop regulating business
- C. Attract new business to the community
  - 1. Provision of industrial park or other facility
  - 2. Recover investment in industrial park
  - 3. Community promotion
  - 4. Agriculture - related

D. Manage economic growth through appropriate planning and institutional change
E. Manage economic (and population) decline through appropriate planning and institutional change
F. Encourage in-state processing of in-state products
G. Small farm aid and development
   1. Improved productivity on existing commercial farms
   2. Farm credit (interest rates too high)
H. Tourist trade and recreation development
I. Develop existing retail and service sectors
J. Protect existing retail and service sectors from competition of nearby metro areas
K. Improve tax structure
L. Get rid of unfair competition of tax loss farmers
M. Need jobs
   1. Need employment diversification
   2. Need jobs using appropriate technology
   3. Young people are leaving
   4. Youth unemployment
N. Need adequate technical staff or T.A. to carry out rural development projects
O. Must be nonexploitative (of resources)
P. Unspecified

V. <u>Improved Natural Resource Management and Conservation</u>
A. Land
   1. Planning to accomodate competing needs (e.g., residential, industrial, agricultural, recreational, natural)
      a. Preservation of agricultural land
      b. Deciding what level of government should control land
      c. Need zoning
      d. Payments to land owners to provide incentives for desirable land treatment practices
      e. Distant preservationists force local inhabitants to bear financial losses (for replacement and repairs)
   2. Conservation, including prevention of erosion
B. Water
   1. Quality, including efforts to restrict pollution from sediment, human waste, animal waste, industrial waste, and agricultural chemicals
   2. Flood control
   3. Irrigation
   4. Scarcity
C. Air quality
D. Wood land management
E. Coastal resource management
F. Energy
   1. Conservation
   2. Understanding and adjusting to changes brought about by higher costs of energy
   3. Alter negative feelings toward nuclear and coal

4. Alternative sources
5. Dealing with impactof energy development
6. Unspecified

VI. Improved Political and Social Environment
A. Understanding of how to impact representative government at the local, state, and federal level
B. Understanding of how citizens in a community are impacted by programs administered at the local, state, and federal level (public policy education)
C. Modifications of political institutions and the consequences, including the implementation of more comprehensive planning
D. Nature of regulations (environmental, safety, health etc.) and their impacts
E. Strengthen local government
1. Administration
2. Aid local planning
F. Better federal, state, and local relations
1. Reduce government interference in local affairs
2. Better understanding of federal and state tax structure
G. More public involvement in rural development
H. Preservation of items and sites of historical importance
I. Understanding of the forces which led to today's society - locally, regionally, nationally
J. Understanding of the interdependencies between a local community and the rest of society which imply both opportunities and constraints for local initiatives
K. Understanding of how citizens and groups in a community are impacted by change and how their differing values and backgrounds cause them to react differently (new migrants have different values)
L. Too much of both
M. Unspecified

VII. Resolving Financial Problems
A. Improved awareness of grant opportunities
1. Need grant specialist
2. Need to encourage assistance of state and federal legislators
B. Improved ability to respond quickly and adequately to opportunities
1. Grants cost too much
2. Grants are not appropriate to needs
3. Federal grant requirements and mandates are oppressive (too bureaucratic)
a. Professional services
b. Davis-Bacon
c. Environmental Impact Statements
4. Federal grant requirements cause local structure changes (e.g., special districts)
C. More equitable treatment by agencies of local community proposals

   1. Allocation criteria favor or urban areas
   2. Federal and state governments are undependable
   3. Not enough funding for all projects - government should target funds better

D. Prefer to keep money locally
E. All grant money should be without requirements
F. Self-sufficiency is a virtue
G. Need federal funds
H. Coordination of federal funds
I. Inflation
J. Lack of resources
K. Low or declining tax base
   1. Do not own land
   2. No commercial industry

L. Reduce taxes
M. Interest rate ceilings on municipal bonds are too low
N. Bond issues put burden on fixed income people
O. Special districts are in debt
P. User charges are too high

State Findings

Issue responses were obtained from our one or two contacts in 45 of the 50 states. There was no limit to the number of issues that each person could mention. Some state respondents mentioned no issues; others, as many as 10. If, for example, a need was expressed for both air and rail transportation, it was counted as two responses under the broad category, "provision of adequate community facilities and services." (The responses, tabulated by region, are shown in Appendix B, Tables B-3 and B-4.)

The most striking pattern in the responses is the diversity. The state respondents identified 99 issues or subcategories of issues. The issue most frequently menioned (65 times) was improved natural resource management and conservation, with land, energy, and water (in that order) being of more concern. Three issues--economic development, adequate human maintenance services, and adequate community facilities and services--were all mentioned more than 40 times. The human maintenance services most frequently mentioned were housing and medical services. Surprisingly, food was mentioned only once, and then in a reference to the need for improvement in the local delivery system for food stamps. Transportation of people was the most frequently cited issue under "provision of adequate community facilities and services." Issues mentioned fewer than 25 times were political and social environment, financial problems, and education and job training.

Local Findings

Overall, respondents from totally rural counties, whether adjacent to an SMSA or not, most frequently expressed concern about adequate community facilities and services, economic development, and financial problems. The respondents from metropolitan counties expressed most concern about natural resources management and conservation and with the political and social environment. (Table B-10 presents a summary of the rural development issues listed by respondents according to metropolitan status/urban orientation of county.)

The provision of adequate community facilities and services, especially water, sewer, fire protection, roads and recreation facilities, were high on the list of issues from local respondents (See Table B-11). There was much concern about financial problems, including the lack of resources, the need for federal funds, and a declining tax base. County respondents indicated that federal agencies should treat local community proposals more equitably and that the allocation criteria now favor urban areas. The county responses also indicated that federal grant requirements and mandates are oppressive and that the grants programs are frequently not appropriate to the needs of nonmetropolitan counties. Respondents expressed a wish to encourage economic development by attracting new industry and diversifying employment.

For the county respondents land use planning and conservation were also important issues. The respondents expressed interest in the protection of agricultural land and the problems of small farms. A need was expressed for additional post-secondary vocational and technical training. The provision of housing and medical care also ranked high, perhaps related to the growth of the numbers and proportions of elderly people in many rural areas.

The reports received from state and local officials contain abundant information about the immediate issues faced by the action, planning, and extension agencies. The people at the county level are oriented to specific issues, probably to some extent to what is feasible given the limitations of public opinion and funds. The list of issues should not be read negatively, i.e., failure to list other issues may reflect the temporary situation of the respondent, who is concerned with what needs to be done today and tomorrow--problems for the day after come later. The most striking finding of the county responses is their great heterogeneity.

Some of the differences in responses were related to regional area or to status of population change. Adequate community facilities and services were mentioned most frequently by respondents in the Middle Atlantic, South Atlantic, East South Central, and West South Central regions. New England, Pacific, and East North Central respondents were most concerned about improving natural resource management and conservation. Financial problems were listed as the leading issue in the West North Central and East North Central regions. (The regions are Census Bureau classifications; see Table B-12 for a list of the states in each region.)

Respondents from counties experiencing a population decline were most concerned about economic development and adequate community facilities and services. Respondents from high-growth counties were most conerned about adequate community facilities and services and financial problems. Respondents from slow-growth counties also mentioned economic development and financial problems most frequently. (Tables B-12 and B-13 provide summary tabulations of the issues by region and by 1970-75 county population change. Detailed tables similar to Table B-11 are available from the panel.)

In addition to listings of issues, the letter responses contained 373 comments about data needs, which included 136 comments expressing the need for more frequent or more disaggregated population data (see Table B-14). In fact, nearly half (171) the comments pertained to population data, followed by comments about data for employment (55), housing (47) and natural resources (28). It can be inferred from the letters that better coordination is needed between federal and local agencies in regard to data needs. Better organization at the federal level would prevent the federal agencies from requiring nonexistent information from the local agencies. Too often, federal programs call for information that can be supplied only by a federal agency, for example, the Census Bureau.

The panel's letter to county people also asked them to send documents relating to rural development. In all, 618 documents were received. Many of the documents are federally funded plans, and others are applications for federal funds, but there are also several surveys, ordinances, brochures, and data directories. These documents are classified in Table 2 by functional category.

Appendix D contains a complete bibliography of these items by functional category, a brief description of the characteristics of the documents received, and some examples of the more interesting types of data they contain. Both the documents and the letters have been used extensively in preparing this report.

TABLE 2. Documents Received from Survey Respondents

Category	Number
General Development	177
Economic Development	118
Land Use	94
Housing	62
Community Facilities	55
Natural Resources	41
Health	22
Social Services	21
Transportation	14
Recreation	14
TOTAL	618

OTHER INFORMATION-GATHERING ACTIVITIES

Consultations at the National and Local Levels

A large number of people with responsibility for rural development policy at the national and local levels were consulted during the course of our study. The objectives of the interviews were to obtain various perspectives on rural development policy, to identify uses of available data, to identify data problems, and to elicit suggested procedures for solving data problems. The people with whom we consulted represented nine federal agencies and five nongovernmental organizations:

Federal Agencies
- Congressional Budget Office
- Department of Agriculture
  - Economics and Statistics Service
  - Farmers Home Administration
  - Program Planning and Budget Office
- Department of Commerce
  - Economic Development Administration
  - Office of Federal Statistical Policy and Standards (now, Statistical Policy Division in the Office of Management and Budget)
- Department of Housing and Urban Development
- Department of Labor
- Domestic Council (Executive Office of the President)

Nongovernmental Organizations
- Advisory Commission on Intergovernmental Relations
- National Association of Towns and Townships
- National Commission on Agriculture Land Use
- National Rural Center
- Urban Institute

Workshop of Regional and State Planners

After responses to the panel's letter survey about data needs and problems had been received from states and counties, a small invitational workshop of regional and state planners was held. The workshop had four objectives: 1) to review the problems or issues in rural development programs for which data are needed; 2) to discuss the uses of data in rural development policy planning and decision making; 3) to obtain the views of state and regional program planners on data needs, data problems and information systems relevant to rural development policy and programs; and 4) to discuss current and future trends in rural development policy and related data needs and problems. The names of workshop participants were suggested by panel members, by staff of the National Governors Association who were involved in a state agency survey of data needed for economic development, by the staff of the Council of State Planning Agencies, and by the staff of the National Rural Center. (See Appendix C for a list of participants.)

During the workshop discussion the participants stressed that for policy analysis, the need for improved methodology for short-term (three years) projections is greater than the need for data. The need for an indicator, possibly a quality-of-life indicator, to evaluate rural development programs was mentioned. Several participants commented that the states and substate regions have the capability to use data, but that smaller areas, especially rural communities, lack library resources and the staff to use data. Texas has tried to tailor a program to help local governments use data, but they show interest only when growth becomes a crisis. Several participants agreed that the lack of uniformity in the data required by federal programs is creating problems for small communities. It was pointed out that the special neighborhood counts that the Bureau of the Census is offering to cities but not to counties puts the counties at a disadvantage. Participants also identified the shortage of capital investment in rural areas and the inability to trace the flow of private capital as problems. The workshop discussions and follow-up materials received from participants are reflected in this report.

Workshop of Rural Interest Groups

Staff of the National Rural Center offered to convene a workshop of representatives of rural interest groups to consider issues similar to those discussed in the workshop of regional and state planners. Groups represented at this meeting included the National Rural Center, Rural America, National Rural Electric Cooperatives Association, and the National Association of Towns and Townships, among others. (See Appendix C, list of participants.)

The discussion concerned rural issues and related data needs. One important rural issue identified was the targeting of federal funds; time-series data are particularly important for targeting. Participants suggested that better data are needed to track where federal funds go. They also noted that the enforcement of equal opportunity and affirmative action legislation would be aided by data on employment by race in rural areas. On energy, one approach to the current problem would be to identify the effects of the energy shortage on rural commuting; thus, trend data on commuting are needed. Economic development and the export of low-wage jobs to foreign countries were identified as continuing concerns in rural areas. It was suggested that more data on multiple job holding, credit availability, and capital flows are necessary to address these concerns.

The unit of analysis for which data are maintained was also a topic of discussion at the workshop. Participants suggested that towns and townships and labor market areas, as well as counties, would be useful units. They noted that different federal agencies use different geographical codes and that these differences hinder rural analysis. Some of the concerns expressed by participants at both workshops are reflected in this report.

4

USER CHARACTERISTICS AND PURPOSES

Collecting information and processing it into statistical data are extremely expensive operations. Some users can afford to collect and process their own data, but most users must rely on some data that have been produced for a purpose other than that to which the user plans to put them. Such second-hand data, even though they may be the best available, seldom are completely satisfactory, but they might be made far more satisfactory to users at only slight additional cost if the producer had a better idea of user needs. An ideal statistical information system would ensure a regular flow of information between producers and users of data; the users would keep producers informed of their needs, and the producers would generate data that would satisfy the widest range of users.

At present, information flows too much in a single direction, from producers to users, and users have too little input to the data production process. The needs of different types of users of data for rural areas and the ways in which they use these data must be examined before we can propose improvements in what can now be described only loosely as an "information system."

USER GROUPS

The development of better statistical information for rural development policy must be based on an appreciation of the different needs of different user groups. These needs vary with the groups' priorities and areas of responsibility. While nearly all groups seems to agree on the general goals of rural development, different groups of data users do not agree on the relative importance of each goal, and their data needs may vary accordingly. For example, nearly everyone agrees that more jobs, higher pay, and less pollution are all desirable goals, but it is not easy to achieve consensus on priorities among these goals.

Different users also vary in their expertise and in their areas of responsibility. Local officials, for example, know more about the streets and roads in their communities than do state and federal officials, but state and federal officials are in a better position to evaluate disparities between communities in order to allocate resources equitably. No government official at any level knows as much about the demand for hammers and nails as the man who makes his living selling hardware.

The value of data as well as their design arises out of use. We have identified eight broad categories of data users who seem to have different characteristics and different data needs.

Persons Responsible for Local Development

Local officials need timely data for such small areas as counties and subdivisions of counties. Some of these data may be obtained from external sources, such as the Bureau of the Census, but many must be developed locally from administrative records such as school enrollments, building permits, utility connections, and assessed property valuations. Local officials may also need data that can be presented to state and national officials, who must compare their area with other areas in deciding where to allocate public funds and locate public facilities.

Private users at the local level have many of the same needs and sources as public officials. The developer of a shopping center, for example, needs much of the same information as a local zoning board or planning commission and must also be able to compare local areas with each other.

<u>Officials responsible for districts, states, or regions</u> Officials responsible for a wide range of potential development projects must have continuous timely data that cover a large area but can be used to examine local detail. They must be able to evaluate needs, allocate resources within the area, and measure the changes that result.

<u>National officials</u> National officials need data that permit comparisons across broad areas, with enough small-area detail to permit assessment of needs and monitoring of changes.

<u>Legislators and legislative staffs</u> Elected officials may need data for areas ranging from the entire country to states, congressional districts, and counties. They also need data on the small areas that would be affected by a proposed project, such as the construction of a dam. They must have continuous and timely data that reflect current developments and that can be used to assess future needs.

<u>Private developers at the county, state, or national level</u> Financial institutions, manufacturers, other business people, and nonprofit organizations that promote rural development all have data requirements similar to those of other groups. Their needs, however, most closely resemble those of national officials. These organizations may also be active users of data pertinent to the specific areas of individual projects.

Persons affected by a development project People who will be affected by a development project must have enough current data to evaluate the impact of that project.

The public Data that permit problem identification and project evaluation are needed by civic groups such as service clubs, public interest groups, chambers of commerce, professional organizations, parent-teacher associations, farmers' organizations, cooperative extension organizations, the League of Women Voters, and conservation organizations. The news media need information that will enable them to report on the progress of rural development projects.

Researchers and evaluators The higher education system in a state may have research organizations that are concerned with rural areas. Regional and national research units, private research groups, and individual scholars are also concerned with rural development. All require broadly based and timely data that can be used to identify needs, to evaluate projects, and to test hypotheses about development.

DATA USES

The uses of data depend on the decisions that users must make, the characteristics of the users, and the limitations of the data. We focus primarily on uses of data for public policy at various levels of government, but satisfying the needs of government for information will also satisfy many of the needs of private groups.

Federal Uses

The major purposes for which data are used at the federal level include resource allocation, problem definition and policy formulation, program evaluation, requests for appropriations, program compliance, and research.

Resource allocation Allocating resources to people or institutions in accordance with legislated statistical criteria is a major use of data. The controversy surrounding the 1980 census is a vivid reminder of the importance of data in allocating federal funds. (Numerous jurisdictions have brought suits challenging the alleged undercount in their areas.) More than $122 billion, one-fifth of all federal obligations in fiscal 1979, were allocated by use of statistical formulas (Emery 1980). The degree to which funds are effectively targeted to legislatively recognized need is a function of the quality (accuracy and timeliness) of the underlying data. Systematic bias for or against any subgroup (e.g., rural relative to urban residents, or low-income people relative to other people) is especially undesirable.

Resource allocation procedures vary among programs. The Farmers Home Administration uses formulas based on selected measures of need to allocate program funds (for the housing, business and industry, and community programs) to states. States are advised to use criteria similar to the federal measures of need in allocating funds to substate districts and counties, but the states are currently free to adopt the procedures they believe most appropriate. District and county offices, in turn, have considerable flexibility in allocating funds. In decentralized programs such as these, the data needs for allocation purposes vary a great deal by governmental level. At the federal level, estimates for states may suffice for many decisions while progressively more detailed data are needed as one approaches the local end of the spectrum of decisions.

General revenue sharing has an allocation procedure in which the federal government deals directly with local as well as state units of government. Estimates of population, per-capita income, tax effort, and intergovernmental transfers are used to allocate revenue sharing funds directly to approximately 39,000 general purpose governmental units (Bureau of the Census 1980). About 19,000 of these units have less than 1,000 people, nearly 13,000 have less than 500, and about 7,000 have less than 250 (National Research Council 1980). Allocations to these units require detailed data.

Eligibility for federal funds is often predicated on satisfying statistical criteria. In order to be eligible for programs of the Economic Development Administration, for example, governmental units must fulfill certain distress criteria based on unemployment, family income, and other data. Population thresholds determine whether a jurisdiction may be a prime sponsor of a Comprehensive Employment and Training Act (CETA) program or is eligible for programs of the Farmers Home Administration and the Department of Housing and Urban Development. The administering federal agency for each of these programs needs a list of jurisdictions that are eligible or some means of quickly verifying eligibility when applications are received. Finally, many federal programs, such as the food stamp program, define eligibility in terms of individual people or families. The administering agency requires some way of verifying whether the individual satisfies the eligibility criteria.

Problem definition and policy formation The identification of problems entails comparison of a credible description of the current situation with the desired situation. Needs are typically determined through the political process, although direct survey data are useful on many occasions. For example, a pilot study of community facilities sponsored by FmHA is a first step in an attempt to obtain baseline data on existing community facilities in rural areas. In addition, the federal government requires data series to monitor progress toward the achievement of goals.

Policy formation often requires considerably more data, and more structured data, than problem definition. Ideally, policy makers would like to know which variables under their control (e.g., taxes, subsidies, government workers, laws) have the maximum net positive impact, taking into account any negative side effects of a proposed policy. Causal relationships between policy variables and problems must be hypothesized and tested. The linkages are often complex, and data must be collected on numerous intervening variables. This aspect of policy formation is, in many respects, applied research.

The manner in which data are collected, reported, and defined can constrain problem definition and policy formation. A notable example is the lack of an adequate concept and definition of underemployment, a condition prevalent in many rural areas. (This subject is covered in more detail in Chapter 11). Unemployment is another concept with definitional and measurement problems. Studies (cited in Chapter 11) indicate that unemployment is a better measure of distress in urban labor markets than it is in rural labor markets. Despite the urban bias of unemployment statistics, their ready availability leads to their widespread use in problem definition, policy formation, and policy implementation, even for rural areas.

Program evaluation Program evaluation is essential if policy makers are to understand the intended and unintended effects of policies as a prelude to modifying them. Most programs are designed to create changes; data series that reflect the degree of change are essential for program evaluation. The data necessary for program evaluation often include numerous intervening variables as well as variables indicating policy actions and effects on the target population. The evaluation of specific programs usually entails more particular data sets than are required for monitoring progress toward broad development goals. Since multiple programs contribute to the attainment of such goals, movement toward or away from the goals is often difficult or impossible to associate with individual programs in the absence of careful monitoring of intervening variables.

Lack of a uniform definition of rural among federal agencies has unnecessarily frustrated evaluations of the federal impact on the geographic distribution of growth. In all agencies, the people we interviewed, especially those in USDA, EDA, and HUD, expressed discouragement at the multiple programmatic definitions of rural. The resulting problems in aggregating data and comparing programs make it difficult to coordinate and to assess overall economic development policy. Of course, each agency must administer its programs in accordance with the law, and Congress will not and should not be constrained unduly by statistical conventions, but the current confusion within the federal government is hardly justified. Although no single definition of rural is feasible or desirable, project records could and should include the county of location. Comparisons and assessments of the cumulative geographic impacts of the development programs of agencies such as FmHA, HUD, and EDA could then use a common aggregation scheme starting from the county building blocks.

Recommendation: The panel recommends that a standard classification of nonmetropolitan counties relating to level of urbanization (in the spirit of the Hines et al. (1975) classification) be developed for use in program analysis and evaluation at each level of government. If possible, the county classification should be supplemented by a distinction between urban and rural areas within counties.

The Statistical Policy Division, which has the federal responsibility for establishing statistical standards, should take the lead at the national level in initiating and coordinating discussion and in overseeing implementation.

Requests for appropriations The use of data in budget preparation is closely related to problem definition, policy formation, and program evaluation. Budget processes, however, warrant special mention because they demand quantitative assessment. Data are needed that describe the total resources available, the distribution by population subgroup of the tax burden, the extent of needs, the impact of a change of funding for each program, and the values placed on further attainment of goals.

Program compliance Data used to determine program compliance must typically be gathered outside normal program administration channels if they are to be unbiased and thus credible. Although monitoring compliance is an important function, it is particular to each program rather than a general policy issue; hence, the panel did not examine it.

Research Research needs are a major stimulus to data collection and dissemination. Applied research is particularly critical in the early development of policy, when the answers to the questions of "what is the problem" and "what data are needed" are difficult, far from obvious, and invariably incomplete. Applied research attempts to identify and solve problems. Researchers need data on the variables relevant to the problem, but "relevant" is not a static concept. As researchers gain new insights, they need new data to test fresh hypotheses. The new data, in turn, yield further insights--sometimes confirming and sometimes refuting hypotheses--and the process is repeated. People who provide data and researchers who use data should communicate regularly on their problems and needs.

Interchange among researchers and data providers is especially important in rural development, which is not a mature field of study in which the concepts are well defined and reasonably stable. The field is in ferment, and uncertainty and fundamental change are expected. In addition, isolation causes providers to collect data on outmoded and irrelevant concepts, and it causes researchers to misunderstand the data they use for testing hypotheses. The primary researchers at the federal level working comprehensively on rural development are in the Economic Development Division of the Economics and Statistics Service of the Department of Agriculture. These researchers have the good fortune of organizational promixity to the data procedures. The panel knows of no other research group in the federal government with a similarly comprehensive mandate in rural development research.

State Uses

The uses of data at the state level parallel the uses at the federal level. These uses include some that are federally mandated, mostly as evidence in support of funding from federal sources. Many state and local officials believe that federal program administrators exercise too much control and leave too little discretionary authority for state and local administrators. Two local officials articulated this view as follows:

> There is one major ingredient that has been lacking in the modern concept and need in rural development, and it has been overlooked by many legislators and agency personnel, but it is generally well recognized by local people in the rural communities and counties of the nation. . . . For rural development to be a viable major and continuing force, it must capture the spirit of local people, harness local energies in harmony, and be directed by local people who come to know better than anyone else their own problems, their capabilities, and their own priorities [Wisconsin Cooperative Extension Service].

> As long as the Federal government reflects our society's conscious and unconscious bias toward centralization, there will be no really effective rural program [Hot Springs County, Wyoming].

Such critics base their argument, in part, on the premise that state and local officals are better informed of developmental needs and possibilities than their federal counterparts. Some critics suggest that federal efforts to develop more disaggregated data in order to direct more aid from Washington to smaller jurisdictions will not lead to a successful development strategy. They argue that data are not a good substitute for informed experience.

States have developed their own statutory data collection and reporting systems for some substantive concerns. Education affords a particularly good example. State departments of education are responsible for collecting extensive data on public education. Such data are the primary basis for the formulation of state legislative requests and formula allocations to schools. This function is especially important because public education depends far more on state than on federal support. State data collection systems will continue to play an important role, but greater comparability of data across states would facilitate program evaluation and research. Comparisons of state policies are a rich source of ideas for improved policies. Much research on rural development is conducted in state colleges and universities, so fruitful interaction among policy makers, data providers, and researchers is possible at the state level as well as at the federal level.

Substate Regional Uses

During the past two decades, an important substate structure of quasi-governmental units has emerged at the multicounty regional level. These units include councils of governments (COGs), many of which serve also as regional planning commissions and regional review bodies for federal grants as stipulated by a directive of the Office of Management and Budget (OMB). These units also include human development corporations, vocational centers, health systems agencies, and agencies on aging; older examples include FmHA district offices and soil conservation districts. The role of substate regional units varies greatly among and even within states. These units have sometimes been resisted by local officials, who fear that they may replace county governments; frequently, however, substate units are welcomed as a source of expertise needed by local officials.

The substate regional units are usually more involved in facilitating the work of other governmental units or in resource allocation than in program administration. Providing the evidence necessary for funding requests is an important use of data at this level. Often the required data are not available for local areas and can be provided accurately only at considerable cost. A regional official observed:

> When small rural communities apply for financial aid, from HUD and EDA especially, the grant applications require statistics to be provided on housing, employment, income for subunits (local areas) that are not supplied in the Census. Housing surveys can be done and employment data extrapolated but often the costs are too high considering the chancy nature of most grant applications [Northeast Florida Regional Planning Council].

Similar comments were made by many other substate regional officials. For example:

> One of the largest statistical problems our organization has observed, and this applies to both an urban and rural setting, is the requirement of the Federal government to utilize data, particularly in formulas, for which there is no accurate source. The "expected to reside" criteria required by HUD in housing programming is a very good example [Richmond Regional Planning District Commission].

This kind of criticism is so widespread that it suggests a functional deficiency in national capacity for local area planning. One local planning official complained about:

> . . . too much planning and too much information at the multi-county and state level and the complete lack of planning and good data at the community level. The federal "plans" being developed are regurgitations of the same secondary

sources of data (U.S. Census, etc.), with no effort to generate needed primary data that is community specific [Southeastern Arizona Area Cooperative Extension Service].

Some funding requests are prepared exclusively by staff of the substate regional units, and the staff assist local officials in preparing other requests. The staff are more knowledgeable than local officials about data sources, contacts among data providers, and grantsmanship procedures. In many states, regional unit staff are among the first people to whom local officials turn with questions of data availability, as these comments indicate:

> Equity and improved access for local communities seeking state or federal funds has fallen on the shoulders of our agency for many of the smaller rural communities. We developed a reputation as a "grantsmanship center" which is now difficult to relegate to a lower priority in comparison to our regional planning goals and policies [Arrowhead Regional Development Commission, Minnesota].

> . . . we, as a Council provide many of the required statistics for McCormick County through cooperation with other agencies. We have not experienced nor do we anticipate any difficulty in obtaining these kinds of statistics [Upper Savannah Council of Governments, South Carolina].

Many of the data in funding requests are included because of federal and state requirements rather than because of any belief by local or substate regional unit officials that the data are genuinely useful in problem identification and policy formation. In other words, local and regional officials often use one set of information to identify goals, problems, and the desired policy responses, but are required to supply a different set to federal and state agencies in order to get needed funds. The letter survey of local officials revealed considerable dissatisfaction with federally imposed data requirements and much cynicism concerning the quality of the information provided. Federal programs are often viewed as uncoordinated and ill-designed, and federal agency personnel as largely unaware of rural problems and appropriate policies.

> I suggest the first priority for national policy would be to recognize the diversity among rural areas. People in large urban centers seem to have some sort of vision of "rural" areas as consisting of either corn and hog farmers in Iowa or seedy characters loafing around a fallen-down shack cracking "Hee-Haw" jokes. Every state in the country has rural areas. I would suggest key differentiating factors would be (a) economic base mixture, e.g., farming, mining extraction, forest products, fisheries, tourism; (b) whether the economy is declining, stable, growing normally, or growing rapidly; and (c) distances to major urban centers. The different

> characteristics of rural areas would indicate that national statistics could be broken out in various subcategories that might be more useful for planning and development agencies [Lincoln-Uinta, Wyoming, Association of Governments].

> Small communities and rural areas in our region have historically been unable to compete with the larger cities and metropolitan areas where the population and votes are. . . . The present approach by the federal government, in most cases, is to redesign large city and metropolitan programs to fit rural needs. It does not work effectively. Specific federal programs for rural areas should be developed to meet their urgent needs [Sixth District Council of Local Governments, South Dakota].

> There is a very definite feeling that urban areas eclipse rural areas in seeking funding. While the six counties in the Middle Peninsula have received a considerable amount of funds, there is also a feeling that in many cases the effort is not worth the results. Requirements attached to many federal programs are often inappropriate for rural counties [Middle Peninsula Planning District Commission, Virginia].

Although regional staffs frequently know more about data availability and grantsmanship than local officials, they are more aware of general data sources than of specialized sources.

Planning is another important activity of the substate regional units that requires the use of data. Much planning is stimulated by the requirements of state and federal agencies rather than by local governments. For example, the guide for developing an overall economic development program (Economic Development Administration 1977:1) begins by stating that "The Overall Economic Development Program (OEDP) is a locally initiated planning process . . ." Just a few lines later, however, the federal requirement is made clear:

> EDA approval of the initial OEDP document, the first report submitted by the district, is a prerequisite to official action by EDA on designation of the district and its selected economic development center or centers. Designation confers eligibility upon the district and its center or centers for public works and business development projects.

Many other examples could be cited. Much of the planning and the use of data related to planning that are required by outside forces is viewed as nonproductive by local officials, although it is necessary to provide access to needed funds.

Planning may also be a genuine response to local and substate needs. Regional unit staffs have considerably more flexibility in the type of data incorporated in these plans than in plans required by external governments. Federal and state agencies often desire comparability among substate and local plans, and thus often give little credence to locally produced data. Planning staff, however, often must collect local data when plans are developed for local purposes.

Local Uses

Local uses of data include preparing funding requests and planning. Local governments rely on generalists and have the least capacity to handle the myriad requirements of state and federal agencies. Local rural governments have limited expertise for planning and for developing grant applications, as these comments indicate:

> Access to information about funding has been improved through various state programs, however, the ability for municipalities to have (and afford) the technical and professional expertise to develop an approvable application for state or federal funding is limited [Columbia County, New York].
>
> . . . because urbanized areas are able to attract the personnel qualified to write successful grants and because grant selection is often based partly upon previous program successes, such areas appear to have greater access to state and federal funds [Coconino County, Arizona].

> Recommendation: The panel recommends that application and reporting forms required by federal and state agencies be standardized to the extent possible and that the instruction sheet provide references to data sources when the form requires data from federal statistical publications.

Some progress has been made in standardization, such as adoption of a common form by FmHA and EDA for proposals for water and sewer systems, but much more should be done. The Academy for Contemporary Problems (1977) came to the same conclusion in a study sponsored by the Commission on Federal Paperwork. Differences in the forms used by FmHA, EDA, and HUD for similar programs (e.g., housing, business subsidies, and community facilities) are difficult to defend. Coordination could be effected by leadership from the Statistical Policy Division in the Office of Management and Budget.

Grantsmanship and planning in response to outside programs represent only a small part of data uses at the local level, however. Local government officials, community leaders, and ordinary citizens can use timely and reliable information on the key characteristics of their communities, including population totals, age and socioeconomic composition, migration, and public services and revenues. Data on such characteristics serve a number of community purposes. In addition to aiding specific policy and program objectives--projecting public service demands, for example--the data contribute to more general understanding of local conditions and trends. Time-series data can show how and why a community changes. Data can enable one to make comparisons with other communities and regional or statewide averages. For these and other purposes, local users need more than the statistical data provided by federal agencies such as the Bureau of the Census. Useful data can come from local sources such as the administrative records of state and local governments, community surveys, and the records of utility and finance agencies. It must be emphasized that rural government officials, who usually work part-time and are generalists, do not require comprehensive data "systems" as much as easy access to small amounts of relevant, clear, and meaningful information.

Examples of State Information Systems

Many states have, or are developing, state information systems for a single program area, such as land or natural resource management, or for several program areas. Some respondents to the letter survey mentioned useful state systems, and three examples are described below.

Minnesota Analysis and Planning System The Minnesota Analysis and Planning System (MAPS) is a computer-based information system designed for storage and retrieval of socioeconomic data. Established in 1967, MAPS provides secondary data to local planners, regional commissions, and other public and private users. Information about available data resources is disseminated to county Cooperative Extension offices and to other potential data users. MAPS staff support the state data center concept being implemented by the Bureau of the Census.

Data available through MAPS include the censuses of population and housing for 1960 and 1970, Bureau of Economic Analysis income and employment data, economic censuses, annual housing surveys, surveys of income and education, and files from state records. State record files include a large human services data base and socioeconomic data by legislative district. A file is usually acquired or developed only after it has been requested by a user; the initial user of a data set will generally bear a large portion of costs.

The most frequent types of requests that could not be serviced satisfactorily were for census-type data for years since 1970 and for energy-related data. Requests for mean or median income data by minor civil divisions were particularly common. Although MAPS does not estimate data for small geographic areas on the basis of data from larger aggregates, some state agencies have made such estimates.

Development Information System for Kentucky The Development Information System for Kentucky (DISK) is a computerized information system for community development and planning. It is part of a statewide computer network established by the College of Agriculture of the University of Kentucky. The network includes computer terminals in extension offices throughout the state. Information in the system is available to county and city officials, planners, interested citizens, and extension personnel.

The information system is organized around thirteen subject areas: population; employment; agriculture and farm management; education; income; industry and commerce; health and safety; housing; government; land use; natural resources, energy, and environment; recreation; and transportation and communications. The following are four examples of questions that can be answered about counties: What is the age distribution and how has it changed in the past decade? What is the unemployment rate for a given year? What is the population projection for a given year? How many farms with sales of $2,500 and over existed in 1969 and 1974, by size class?

Maine State Planning Office Data Base The State Planning Office in Maine has established a data base organized around 493 towns. Statistical reports prepared on a monthly basis include such topics as socioeconomic characteristics of counties and regions, income assistance statistics, and profiles of economic indicators for the state.

The data base was constructed primarily from records of state agencies. Officials in the State Planning Office worked with other state agencies to try to coordinate data collection efforts and to include significant questions. For example, data on income assistance programs for each town were obtained from the records of the Department of Human Services. Population data are derived from the 1970 census and from the Division of Research and Vital Records; population estimates showing changes by county groups are computed by the State Planning Office. Housing data are derived in part from information in food stamp records. Data on social problems and social change are obtained from the Maine Department of Educational and Cultural Services and the Maine Department of Public Safety.

Conclusion

The three above examples of state information systems are exemplary. More generally, the panel's review of the current information network for rural development reveals a pressing need for better linkages among the parts. In fact, the linkages and coordinating institutions are either missing or so poorly developed that the terms information "system" or "network" hardly apply. The recent conclusion of the Advisory Commission on Intergovernmental Relations that "contemporary federalism is in serious disarray" (quoted in Beam 1980:6) applies to rural development with special force. Institutions that are responsible for decisions must be linked from local through federal levels of government before one can specify a coherent rural development policy data base.

Our recommendations address the more important institutional problems in information systems for rural development.

Recommendation: The panel recommends that each state develop or designate a lead institution (or institutions) in the state to facilitate local government access to state and federal statistical information, if no such institution currently exists. The panel further recommends that the federal government encourage use of the statistical service centers by providing general financial assistance and, in addition, that federal program agencies fund the centers to maintain the local and state data bases necessary for application to their programs.

Only publicly available statistical aggregates, not confidential information, would be maintained. The services of these centers should include, although not be limited to, providing information on data sources, disseminating statistics, and preparing tabulations on request. The center itself should not produce statistics in order to avoid bureaucratic conflicts in the statistical system.

Recommendation: The panel recommends that the Federal Information Locator System (FILS) be developed as rapidly as possible with an expanded mission to provide public access to federal data sources.

The FILS is presently designed to serve internal federal government purposes (clearance forms), not user needs, so additional information on data characteristics would have to be added to FILS. It should also be combined with several user services, which might include serving as a central contact point for those seeking information on data availability and sources, preparing annual guides to federal statistical sources, and maintaining a computerized bibliography of major regional and local data collection efforts. If the Office of Management and Budget (which now operates FILS) is not considered the appropriate location for such a data user service, it could be located elsewhere as long as an interactive computer link to FILS is provided. To do otherwise would lead to major duplication of files that are partly identical.

Recommendation: The panel recommends increased representation of local and regional users of information on federal statistical advisory committees.

Recommendation: The panel recommends that the federal government take a more active role in the coordination of statistical activities and in developing and promulgating common definitions and other statistical standards that are appropriate for implementation at the federal, state, and local levels.

Recommendation: The panel recommends that each state designate or develop an organization for managing the state's role in statistical coordination and in establishing and implementing statistical standards if such an organization does not now exist.

Some states may find that placing this responsibility for management within the state statistical service centers recommended earlier is an advantageous arrangement.

The information network for development policy, rural and urban, should recognize the complementary roles of local, substate, state, and federal governments. The network should facilitate communication of data needs from users to data producers and of information on potential uses of existing data from producers to users. The network should facilitate comparisons and linkages among data sets at the local and state level. It should not be designed and administered solely as a means of disseminating data from producers to users. Without an effective two-way linkage of users and producers of data, maintaining policy relevence in information systems is impossible, and statistical resources will not be efficiently used.

A variety of people can be connected through a well-designed information system. The directors of the statistical service centers could be encouraged to be entrepreneurs in attracting clients from state, regional, and local government and from the private sector. A special effort could be made to serve rural-oriented groups such as Cooperative Extension, Farmers Home Administration, and associations of county and township officials and planners. There are doubtless urban planning needs of equal specificity and urgency that could also be served.

The statisticians and analysts within the system should inform users about available data and should design relevant display formats for them. They can also act as intermediaries between producers and users of data. Since users express their needs and frustrations primarily to analysts, they, in turn, can transmit the users' data frustrations and needs (e.g., timeliness, quality, disaggregation) to the producers.

The data management professionals in the centers should deal directly with users. They should be able to respond to users' requests quickly and accurately and to help users define their needs more precisely. They can also aid users unaccustomed to data analysis by designing relevant display formats. They are also in a position to inform producers of data of needed improvements in the formatting and coding of data. The use of on-line computer dissemination of data bases will increase interaction among users, producers, analysts, and managers of data bases.

State statistical service centers should maintain many different kinds of statistics in one location, in order to provide users with one-stop service. The collection of data bases at each service center would evolve in accordance with the needs of users in that state. For example, the service center might acquire data series from state agencies on education, tax receipts, social welfare expenditures, and community facilities. The National County Data Base developed at the Center for Social Data Analysis, Montana State University, is an example of an excellent basic file for a state service center and in many cases can be a convenient continuing source of data. Also, Donnelley Marketing has a proprietary residential data base that might be useful. (See Appendix E for more information about both of these data bases.) The centers should be able to refer users to other sources when the center does not have the needed information. The service center professionals must be responsive, but not captive to any single agency, level of government, or data source. The federal government should supply, at no cost to the service center, an initial package of data about the state (such as the censuses of governments, population, housing, agriculture, and manufactures; personal income data by source; agricultural production and prices; labor market data; and county business patterns).

The federal government should also provide important supporting services to the information network. It can act as a central contact point, providing guidance for those seeking information; see Bryant (1977) for a more detailed statement of the need for this service. The panel supports the concept of a central inquiry service that was recommended in the report of the President's Reorganization Project for the Federal Statistical System (1980) as well as continued development of the Federal Information Locator System (FILS). The <u>Directory of Federal Statistics for Local Areas: A Guide to Sources, 1976</u> (Bureau of the Census 1978) should be regularly updated for rural areas (as it is for urban areas) and given wide circulation. <u>Federal Information Sources and Systems: A Directory</u> (U.S. General Accounting Office 1976) is also useful in identifying and cataloging information sources. <u>City Data: A Catalogue of Data Sources for Small Cities</u> (Carroll et al. 1980) catalogs 272 sources of data through which quality-of-life characteristics of the smaller U.S. cities can be measured. It should be noted that many of the data sources are available only for cities of 50,000 or 25,000 or 10,000 and larger.

The rural component of information systems should reflect the varying objectives of different programs. Federal programs designed to guarantee minimum levels of health, economic security, and other needs require a detailed data base for targeting expenditures and for evaluating whether funds are being distributed to the target populations. The federal government should maintain a data base for small areas and update it annually. It should contain highly disaggregated series on population, per-capita income, and vital statistics. For other program areas state and local officials are in a better position to make accurate assessments of local needs and to set priorities. Examples of such program areas are roads, public utilities, business subsidies, and certain kinds of public services such as recreation and public safety. In these cases the federal data base need extend only to the state level, which requires fewer resources than accurate small area estimates.

Many programs and data systems are appropriately left to state and local governments, but there are advantages at state and national levels in the use of standardized definitions and procedures. The ability to make comparisons and to aggregate state data facilitates analysis. The standardization function can be performed most effectively at the federal and state levels in a broad and continuing dialogue between users and producers of data from local, state, and federal levels. At the state level, as at the federal level, this responsibility should be lodged in a program-neutral organization with government-wide responsibilities, such as the state statistical service center. Developing and implementing statistical standards is a consensus-building process. It should be open and should be managed in a way that respects the many difficult decisions on use and production of data at each level of government.

Finally, the service centers, with federal agency assistance in maintaining the necessary data base, would be able to supply local users quickly and cheaply with a package of data needed for commonly used grant and loan request forms. This package would reduce costs and lift part of the burden of grantsmanship from local officials. Overall, the data base could evolve into an excellent basic file for state and local rural development planning.

CONSTRAINTS IMPOSED BY REPORTING BURDEN

In the next several chapters, many data needs are identified, but there are few recommendations for additional data collection. The panel is well aware of the burden imposed by data collection, which is especially difficult for small rural communities and governments. The panel's constraint also arises from its sensitivity to the fact that to achieve the same level of quality in data collection for small areas as for large areas in a national or state sample, the sampling rates would have to be higher; this presents problems, not only of greater budget costs, but often also of respondent burden. Government statisticians have long been concerned about the burden on respondents of providing the data required by statistical inquiries. This concern has been expressed in various efforts to eliminate duplication; to develop uniform classifications, definitions, and standards so that data from different sources are comparable; and to design increasingly efficient sampling methodologies. Most recently, this concern has been addressed by the Commission on Federal Paperwork, the Office of Federal Statistical Policy and Standards, and the President's Reorganization Project for the Federal Statistical System. The Paperwork Reduction Act of 1980 moved the Office of Statistical Policy and Standards from the Department of Commerce back to the Office of Management and Budget in the Executive Office of the President (where these functions were located prior to 1977); it is now the Statistical Policy Division in the Office of Information and Regulatory Affairs in OMB.

The Commission on Federal Paperwork (1977) found that while statistical inquiries constitute a small part of the total reporting burden placed on the public by government inquiries, the completion of statistical reports for the executive agencies of the federal government by individuals and businesses requires a vast amount of time. In its report, Information Value/Burden Assessment (1977), the Paperwork Commission suggested that even justifiable requests for information can result in an excessive economic and psychological burden. For example, excessive decentralization and the lack of intergovernmental cooperation and data exchange cause needless duplication.

On the other hand, the Paperwork Commission also suggested some managerial guidelines that would enhance the value of existing data, thus minimizing the need for additional data collection. If there is more critical analysis of the level of comprehensiveness of information that is needed and if data are shared, the burden of data collection could be lessened.

The Office of Federal Statistical Policy and Standards (OFSPS), which has long been responsible for improving the gathering, analysis, and dissemination of statistical information, supported many of the ideas developed by the Paperwork Commission. In its report (1978), A Framework for Planning U.S. Federal Statistics for the 1980's, the OFSPS suggested that continual scrutiny be given to the problems of statistical reporting burden, especially for voluntary statistical surveys where the respondent does not directly benefit. The report noted that reporting burden could be counterproductive (p. 340):

> While it is true that all citizens benefit from improved statistics which make it possible to have enlightened policy, it is often difficult, in a specific case, for the respondent to appreciate the value of his contribution. Consequently, if overall governmental demands for information are viewed as excessive, the voluntary statistical inquiries are likely to be among the first to be ignored, especially in comparison with those reporting burdens associated with applying for a Federal grant or benefit or with required reporting on the use and application of such a benefit.

The cabinet-level Statistical Policy Coordination Committee established by Executive Order in 1977 has also examined the problems of the management of statistical information in the federal government. A subcommittee of this committee suggested that the scope and content of the statistical data system is poorly defined and that large amounts of data now produced by the federal government are under-utilized for public and private understanding of problems and issues.

The subcommittee recommended, in a memorandum entitled, "The Planning and Budget Process For Federal Statistical Information Programs" (Statistical Policy Coordination Committee 1980), that an inventory of statistical activities be developed to define more adequately the scope of the federal statistical system. This integrated data system of statistical activities would include all statistical data production and analytical activities. The sub-committee recommended that data collections be multiple in purpose, that administrative data systems be used as much as possible in lieu of separate data collection, and that collected data be made more useful by means of accounting and analytic constructs. The sub-committee's point of departure for its deliberations was the recommendation of the President's Reorganization Project for the Federal Statistical System (1980).

Thus, influenced by the direction taken in the federal government, the panel has scrutinized especially carefully all ideas requiring the collection of new data. As a result, many of the panel's recommendations are concerned with the management, coordination, and use of existing data and have been formulated so that further burdens are not imposed on the public and so that the evolving data base for rural development policy has the coherence and compatibility needed to serve its many varied users.

REFERENCES

Academy for Contemporary Problems (1977) Impact of Federal Paperwork on State and Local Governments: An Assessment by the Academy for Contemporary Problems. Report prepared for Commission on Federal Paperwork. Washington, D.C.: U.S. Government Printing Office.

Beam, D.R. (1980) Forecasting the future of federalism. Intergovernmental Perspective 6(3):6-9.

Bryant, W.K. (1977) Rural economic and social statistics. Pp. 408-420 in G.G. Judge, R.H. Day, S.R. Johnson, G.C. Rausser, and L.R. Martin, eds., A Survey of Agricultural Economics Literature, Vol. 2. Minneapolis, Minn.: University of Minnesota Press.

Bureau of the Census (1978) Directory of Federal Statistics for Local Areas: A Guide to Sources, 1976. Washington, D.C.: U.S. Department of Commerce.

Bureau of the Census (1980) Population and per capita money income estimates for local areas: detailed methodology and evaluation. Current Population Reports, Series P-25, No. 699. Washington, D.C.: U.S. Department of Commerce.

Carroll, S.J., Caggiano, M.N., McCarthy, K.F., Morrison, P.A., and Quint, B. (1980) City Data: A Catalog of Data Sources for Small Cities. Santa Monica, Calif.: Rand Corporation.

Commission on Federal Paperwork (1977) Information Value/Burden Assessment. Washington, D.C.: U.S. Government Printing Office.

Economic Development Administration (1977) Guide for District Overall Economic Development Program. Washington, D.C.: U.S. Department of Commerce.

Emery, D. (1980) Distributing federal funds: the use of statistical data. Statistical Reporter 80(8):213-214.

Hines, F.K., Brown, D.L., and Zimmer, J.M. (1975) Social and Economic Characteristics of the Population in Metro and Nonmetro Counties, 1970. Agricultural Economic Report No. 292. Washington, D.C.: U.S. Department of Agriculture.

National Research Council (1980) Small-Area Estimates of Population and Income. Panel on Small-Area Estimates of Population and Income, Committee on National Statistics, Assembly of Behavioral and Social Sciences. Washington, D.C.: National Academy Press.

Office of Federal Statistical Policy and Standards (1978) A Framework for Planning U.S. Federal Statistics for the 1980's. Washington, D.C.: U.S. Department of Commerce.

President's Reorganization Project for the Federal Statistical System (1980) Improving the federal statistical system. Statistical Reporter 80(8):197-212.

Statistical Policy Coordination Committee (1980) The Planning and Budget Process for Federal Statistical Information Programs. Committee records maintained by the Office of Federal Statistical Policy and Standards, U.S. Department of Commerce.

U.S. General Accounting Office (1976) Federal Information Sources and Systems: A Directory. 1977 Congressional Sourcebook Series. Washington, D.C.: U.S. Government Printing Office.

5

DEMOGRAPHIC DATA

Planners and managers can hardly turn around without needing some kind of demographic data on the number, age, sex, race, ethnicity, family status, education, occupation, fertility, mortality, or migration of the people in their areas. They need to know the numbers of persons and households and how those numbers may change in order to plan for public facilities such as water and sewer systems, and they need good demographic data to document their requests for the funding of such facilities. They need to know the numbers of children in order to provide sufficient schools and teachers. They need to know the number of elderly people, and whether they live alone, with someone, or in an institution, in order to provide facilities and practitioners for appropriate health care. They need to know the numbers of people with low incomes, and the numbers of racial and ethnic minorities, in order to provide assistance for members of targeted groups. They need to know the size and character of the labor force in order to plan for economic development; further information about numbers of commuters, orientation of commuting, and travel times may be crucial to such planning. As one respondent wrote:

> . . . the county has had problems in determining an accurate population count. The Commissioners have hired a consultant to prepare a Capital Improvements Program for the County, the Town, the School Board and the Hospital Board. In embarking on this project, the consultant has had difficulty in establishing the current population for these jurisdictions [Teton County, Wyoming].

The primary source of demographic information is the decennial census of population, which in principle is a complete count of individuals and households. The census provides data for each governmental unit, such as states, counties, townships or their equivalents, and incorporated places, and for some nongovernmental areas, such as the densely settled fringes of cities of 50,000 persons or more, unincorporated places of 1,000 persons or more, and specially designated areas. Data are not provided for unincorporated places of less than 1,000 persons, for the densely settled fringes of cities with less than 50,000 persons, or for sparsely settled areas of "open country." Users, however, may be able to compile their own data for some small areas that do not correspond to governmental areas. Information from the 1980 census, for example, is available for five-digit zip code areas, for special districts in some states, and for census enumeration districts.

A panel member, in an interview with a Cooperative Extension Service district director and a regional and urban planning consultant in Wisconsin, learned that the area surrounding the incorporated village of Hayward (county seat of Sawyer County, population 1,456 in 1976), contains more people than Hayward, yet there is more information about Hayward than the surrounding area. This creates problems not only for the people in Hayward, but also for those in the surrounding area. People in the surrounding area use Hayward facilities, such as the library, a home for the elderly, and the fire station, but Hayward officials, in applying for grants, are unable to provide data about surrounding population to justify their claims of need and potential use because population figures for that area are not available. Consequently, the facilities are crowded and overused.

It would be unrealistic to try to make all data available for all areas, especially since serviceable estimates for small areas often can be derived from census data for larger areas. Data on education, occupation, income, and other social and economic characteristics of the population of small areas were expanded in the 1980 census, which increased the sample proportions to 50 percent in minor civil divisions of less than 2,500 population. In the 1980 census, for the first time, the question about Spanish/Hispanic origin was asked of the entire population, rather than of merely a sample, and more detailed information about this group (the second largest minority in the United States) will be available at county and subcounty levels.

The panel did not identify any perceived need for types of demographic data that are not already available through census and periodic surveys, but there was considerable concern about tabulations available for small areas and timeliness of the results, is discussed below. Also, more small-area data are needed from the results of sample surveys. Data from national surveys, such as the current population survey (CPS), should be provided for regions and states, for rural and urban areas, for metropolitan and nonmetropolitan areas, and if at all possible, for other nonmetropolitan substate units. The panel realizes that this might require a type of sampling different from the cluster sampling now used in the CPS in order to obtain estimates with the least variance. Other sampling methods could be developed, or rural samples could be cumulated over the course of a year to provide annual data. The expense of obtaining larger samples from rural areas could be partially defrayed by eliminating some of the smaller SMSAs from the sample.

Many respondents said that more consistent definitions among agencies would facilitate their preparation of grant requests. One respondent from the Missouri Valley Extension Area complained that definitions of the elderly population, the economically disadvantaged, and of rural, nonurban, and urban are not comparable across sources, and another wrote:

> We are responsible for administering senior citizen programs in a largely rural area. . . . Because of the age group classifications used by the Census Bureau we experience difficulty relating age, income, housing etc. in order to define elderly needs statistically. This is aggravated by the fact that federal programs differ in the age groups which they consider as eligible elderly [North Central New Mexico Economic Development District].

For some purposes, the elderly population includes all persons 65 years old or older, but for other purposes the age limit may be 60, 55, or even 50. For some purposes the classification of an area as urban or rural may use the Census Bureau cutoff point of 2,500 people, but for other purposes rural includes all places with fewer than 50,000 people. Some programs use the official poverty line of the federal government, but others use 75, 125, 150, or even 200 percent of that figure as an upper limit. Some of these differences are based on legislation, but others are merely based on agency regulations. The panel concludes that it probably would not be realistic or even desirable to try to impose uniform definitions and classifications on all agencies, but greater consistency obviously would be desirable.

This is not an exclusively rural problem in that any official change would affect planners in all locations. People involved in rural development are affected disproportionately, however, in that they are less likely to have available the variety of publications necessary to provide requested data on, e.g., the number of elderly defined with different threshold points.

A large number of respondents asked for disaggregated social and economic data for small areas; they were apparently unaware that the data requested are already available, although in machine-readable form on computer tapes that are difficult for nonspecialists to find and to use. For example:

> Perhaps the greatest difficulty we have with statistics . . . lies in the fact that this county is part of a three county SMSA and U.S. Census combines data pertaining to [all three]. It would help if we could isolate [our] county data from the . . . SMSA data [Top of Alabama Regional Council of Governments].

Although not all the detailed tabulations for SMSAs are available for individual counties within the SMSA, extensive census data are published for individual counties. Another respondent wrote:

> It would be extremely helpful if the [Census Bureau] would provide the type of detailed information and data for communities of 1,000-2,500 population with respect to all population characteristics . . . that they do for places of 2,500-10,000 population [Upper Explorerland Regional Planning Commission, Iowa],

apparently without realizing that these data are already available from the Census Bureau on computer tapes. Still another respondent wrote:

> Our county covers 2,000 square miles, approximately the same size as the state of Delaware. One of our problems is not being able to get statistics below the county level. We would like to establish a data base by zip code. There are 18 zip code areas within the county. Much of the available data on county services is available by these zip codes areas [Merced County, California].

Such a comment reflects a serious deficiency in the data dissemination system, because much census information for five-digit zip code areas is available on computer tapes. These tapes obviously require translation into printed form before they will be useful to many of the people on the firing line. These responses reinforced the panel's decision to recommend the establishment of statistical service centers in each state.

The establishment of statistical service centers should also help to reduce the time gap between the collection of data and their availability, which was a common concern of data users:

> [Census data] are often becoming outdated by the time of publication. This is particularly true of the decennial census. I fully understand the enormous cost factor in gathering and publishing accurate county-level data. However, for fully effective program planning at the local level, such information is necessary [Greenup County, Kentucky].

> How nice it would be to have current (within two or three years) data [Piedmont Planning District Commission, Virginia].

The time gap between collection and availability could be reduced appreciably by the ability of the centers to convert census data from machine-readable form into printed tabulations that can be used by nonspecialists.

Timeliness of data availability was associated with frequency of data collection in the minds of many users, and the two together were the most commonly expressed concern of data users. The data of the 1980 census will satisfy many needs, but they will also reveal the flaws of estimates based on the census taken 10 years earlier, and reliance on the 1980 census in the latter years of the decade will be equally misleading. A panel member reporting on an interview with a Cooperative Extension Service district director and a regional and urban planning consultant in Wisconsin summarized their comments as follows:

> Demographic data are fairly comprehensive, but they are not timely enough. Complete census counts, which are obtained every 10 years, are not helpful for local officials who must plan and

> cope with change on a year to year basis. To the extent that significant changes (i.e., the population turn-around) occur during the intercensal period, then projections and estimation procedures are at best approximations. As an example, the "Planning for the 80's" activities in the northeastern part of the state which have taken place during the latter part of 1979 were forced to rely on 1970 census data.

Many respondents to the letter survey expressed such views:

> Our problems in obtaining certain forms of data are typical of most county planning departments. We could use census counts at greater frequency and more information on the social and economic characteristics of very large and unincorporated places [Saginaw County, Michigan].

> In this day and age, a ten year span between up-to-date information on population, etc. is quite a while but I also realize that the economics of it [do not] warrant doing a census more often. We do have a county by county enumeration [estimate] each year by census that is helpful as far as total population is concerned but it doesn't include specifics that are needed in planning work [Trego County, Kansas].

> The only information that is lacking is up-to-date information from the census. It would be appropriate, from our standpoint, that you request the federal government to have a five year census instead of their current ten year census. We know that this has been discussed but was dropped due to budget restraints [Mower County, Minnesota].

> The only data available is the decennial census. This information is very valuable but is outdated within three or four years. An interim census every 5 years would provide valuable more up-to-date information on population, housing, and income [Northeast Missouri Regional Planning Commission].

The overwhelming need of local users for accurate data for small rural areas is a compelling argument for recommending a complete mid-decade census in 1985, as required by 1976 legislation.

> Recommendation: The panel recommends that the mid-decade census of population and housing be implemented at the earliest possible date--in 1985 if possible--as required by 1976 legislation. If the mid-decade effort takes the form of a large sample survey rather than a complete count, the panel further recommends that the sample be large enough to permit direct estimates or good regression estimates for all counties, the basic building blocks of the data system.

Local officials discovered their need for a mid-decade census in the latter part of the 1970s when they had to use a variety of local sources to develop population estimates. These estimates need to be recalibrated periodically against the benchmark provided by a complete census count, and 10 years is too long to wait for a recalibration.

Many respondents expressed a need for estimates of the current numbers and characteristics of specific population subgroups at the county and subcounty level and for projections of future trends. For example:

> Most of the need for estimated data between censuses . . . is for small units in specific categories (i.e., 1977 population estimates of people sixty-five plus) [Southeast Extension Area, Missouri].

Many data sources can be used to estimate the nature and rate of change of the elements of population change in small areas. Comparison with earlier censuses provides useful information. The numbers of births and deaths are reported annually by county (except in Massachusetts, where they are reported by towns). School enrollment may indicate changes in the total population. Estimates of population change can also be obtained by examining changes in the housing inventory, in retail sales, in water consumption, in telephone connections, in automobile registrations, in total employment, and in wages paid; however, users of such indicators must realize that they may reflect developments other than population change. Changes in the number of housing units in an area, for instance, can be used to estimate population change only by taking into account changes in the vacancy rate and in the number of persons per household. The average size of households in the United States declined by 0.3 persons between 1970 and 1980, in part because of a rapid increase in the number of persons living alone.

Administrative data, such as records of the number of families on welfare or of those receiving food stamps or other benefits, may indicate changes in administrative procedures and policies rather than changes in the target populations. Yet population estimates have been based on such data in the absence of better information. The different needs of different users are reflected by the fact that planners might use these data to estimate total population change, whereas the actual increase in the numbers of families on welfare may be more critical information for human service workers.

The preparation of population estimates and projections is a complex and difficult task that is best left to experts. Any population projection, whether made by a local, state, or federal agency or by a private consultant, should be accompanied by a clear statement of the assumptions on which it is based and of the reliability of the data that were used in making it. High priority should be given to the evaluation and refinement of methods for making estimates and projections for specific population subgroups in small areas, such as the elderly and minorities, using the 1980 complete count census data as a benchmark.

Professionals often are dismayed by what they perceive as the poor quality of do-it-yourself estimates and projections that local officials are forced to make in the absence of better data, but some of our respondents complained acrimoniously about what they perceive as the cavalier rejection of their estimates by federal agencies:

> The various federal agencies will not accept local and state population estimates and projections [Southeastern Utah Association of Governments].

> Many Washington agencies insist on using the 1970 census data (or the last decennial count). In areas with rapid population growth, these numbers do not represent a true picture--yet federal grant allocations are determined by these numbers. I would think that one of the major policy issues regarding national statistics would be to get the entire federal establishment to recognize current statistics established by local and state governments as valid [Lincoln-Uinta Association of Governments, Wyoming].

Since 1970 the Bureau of the Census has prepared periodic estimates of the population of nearly 39,000 counties, municipalities, and other governmental units that are eligible for the general revenue sharing program (GRS). Most of these estimates have been prepared in cooperation with a state agency designated by the governor. The validity of these estimates, especially those for small places, has been challenged during the latter part of the decade.

Realistic estimates require good local knowledge, and an organizational challenge arises from the need to improve the highly variable quality of ad hoc estimates produced by local users without falling into the trap of a set of "official" national estimates based on a single standard methodology that ignores local variations. Close cooperation between local, state, and federal agencies is needed in preparing population estimates and projections. The technical skills necessary for preparing them seldom are available at the local level, and there are strong arguments for having comparable estimates and projections for all civil divisions made by a single state or federal agency, with the understanding that these estimates would be accepted at all levels of government. As one respondent noted:

> . . . it would be helpful to have one state agency do population projections for all civil divisions which are uniformly accepted and used in the region [Mississippi River Regional Planning Commission, Wisconsin].

The current federal-state cooperative program of population estimates provides a good working compromise that permits some variation in the variables and methods that are used in individual states (see Appendix E). A similar program for local estimates has recently been launched, and the Office of Federal Statistical Policy and Standards (now, Statistical Policy Division), which was recently moved to OMB and is located in the Office of Information and Regulatory Affairs, was working on a standard for local projection for federal investments in community facilities prior to the move.

A panel member, reporting on an interview said that:

> . . . a great variety of data sources were used by the agencies. The sources of data used were not confined to "standard" sources. It depended on policy needs. The emphasis of the agency is on locally generated data . . . including private firms, banks, construction and real estate firms and local "knowledgeables." There is even some reliance on local impressions--as a credibility check on standard sources. At this level, comparability and equity are not major considerations, accuracy is far more important. Little accuracy is attributed to aggregated statistics, especially as this region's population and economy are changing rapidly (about 25% population increase between 1970-75) [Sierra Planning Organization and Sierra Economic Development District, California].

All population estimates and projections, by definition, are based on imperfect data, and the errors for specific subgroups, such as the elderly, minorities, the handicapped, and children of school age, may be aggravated by problems of census undercount and inadequate data on migration.

The inadequacy of migration data is probably the weakest link in making population estimates and projections for local areas. The number of births and deaths is known from registration data, and the people who were counted in 1980 will be 10 years older in 1990, but good data are lacking about the people who have moved into and out of the area. Improvements are needed in the direct measurement and indirect estimation of migration flows into and out of small areas. Migration affects both the number of people and their characteristics. To cite but a single example, in-migration of the elderly seems to have been a major cause of population growth in some counties that grew rapidly in the 1970s, but it will not be known for certain until the benchmark data provided by the complete counts of the 1980 census are available.

Migration is a major factor in population change in most areas. It is influenced by many factors. Changes in employment opportunities in the local area, and in areas within commuting distance, may have significant effects. Unemployment in a distant industrial center may encourage former residents to return to rural communities. The impact of return migrants was illustrated in a panel member's report of an interview:

> . . . there is a real need for demographic information in larger counties like Dane and LaCrosse. This is not as important for planning in a small county, given that the numbers of old-timers and newcomers are not as great. Even Richland County, which has net outmigration, has a few people moving in and the case loads

> are going up. A survey made in the county showed that most of the people moving in, however, were returned migrants who originally came from Richland County [Richland County Department of Social Services, Wisconsin].

American society is increasingly mobile, but census data on migration and on commuting are more difficult to analyze than data on other population characteristics because both the area of origin and the area of destination must be considered. The number of people who lived elsewhere 5 years ago is available for counties, along with other sample data, but the number and characteristics of out-migrants (those who lived in the area 5 years ago but lived elsewhere at the time of the census) are not available for counties in regular census publications. Data on commuting are even sparser.

The Bureau of the Census published a report on 1960-70 migration streams between State Economic Areas (Bureau of the Census 1972), and on migration by county in 1965-70 by age, sex, and race (Bureau of the Census 1977). Gross migrant data for counties and for intercounty streams from the 1980 census will be available on computer tape. The Census Bureau also has unpublished county data on commuters in 1970 that should prove useful when compared with 1980 data. The unpublished form of these data increases the need for state and substate data service centers, which could make the data available in a form useful at the local level.

In early panel discussions, concern was expressed about the effect of potential undercount in the 1980 census on the quality of data for rural states. The panel feared that the Census Bureau might overreact to urban mayors' concern about central city undercount at the expense of data quality for rural areas. Thus in a letter to the director of the Census Bureau (National Research Council 1980a), the panel expressed concern about possible undercount in rural areas and suggested ways to reduce the undercount. The Census Bureau's response assured the panel that the plans for the 1980 census were designed to reduce the undercount in rural as well as in urban areas.

Since plans for publications and tapes from the 1980 census were to have been completed prior to release of the panel's report, the panel made recommendations on census products in another letter report (National Research Council 1980b). This letter report on recommendations for increasing the availability of data from the 1980 census for rural areas, was sent to the director of the Censu Bureau on April 18, 1980. It provides background on rural data needs and includes recommendations pertaining to two planned Census Bureau publications: the Volume II report on the farm population and the Volume II report on the metropolitan and nonmetropolitan populations. It also contains recommendations about two tape files: Public Use Microdata Sample File and Summary Tape File 4.

The recommendations for the two Volume II reports pertained to details of table content and structure. As of this time (May 1981) the Census Bureau has not completed the table shells for the two reports.

In regard to the tape files, the panel recommended that a Public Use Microdata Sample File differentiating United States regions and divisions by metropolitan and nonmetropolitan residence be made available. The panel has been informed that there will almost certainly be a file that indicates SMSA and non-SMSA areas nationwide. There are also tentative plans to identify regions, divisions, and most states. The file would identify most large SMSAs individually so that data users could classify these areas by size. The panel's recommendation for a size-of-place distinction and identification of counties outside of but adjacent to SMSAs will not be adopted.

Summary Tape File 4 will either provide summary levels by county for urban, rural farm, and rural nonfarm or they will be derivable. It will therefore be possible to determine the characteristics of persons of different races, Spanish/Hispanic origin, and ancestry groups by residence areas, as the panel recommended.

DATA GAP

1. Improvements in direct measurement and indirect estimation of migration flows into and out of small areas.

REFERENCES

Bureau of the Census (1972) 1970 Census of Population. Subject Reports DC(2)-2E: Migration Between State Economic Areas. Washington, D.C.: U.S. Department of Commerce.

Bureau of the Census (1977) Gross migration by county: 1965 to 1970. Current Population Reports, Series P-25, No. 701. Washington, D.C.: U.S. Department of Commerce.

National Research Council (1980a) Letter Report on Undercount in Rural States. Panel on Statistics for Rural Development Policy, Committee on National Statistics, Assembly of Behavioral and Social Sciences, National Research Council, Washington, D.C.

National Research Council (1980b) Letter Report on Recommendations for Increasing Availability of Data from the 1980 Census for Rural Areas. Panel on Statistics for Rural Development Policy, Committee on National Statistics, Assembly of Behavioral and Social Sciences, National Research Council, Washington, D.C.

6

HOUSING

When President Roosevelt made his famous statement about one-third of the nation being ill-housed, ill-clad, and ill-nourished, rural areas accounted for a disproportionate share of the persons and families in that third. By the late 1970s, it might seem that the housing problems of that time have largely been resolved. A rural home without electricity is rare today. Houses that lack some or all plumbing facilities account for only about 7 percent of all housing in nonmetropolitan areas (U.S. Department of Commerce 1979), while as recently as 1950, more than 50 percent of housing in such areas lacked these facilities (Bird and Kampe 1977). Occupancy that involves more than one person per room is considered crowded: in 1977, about 5 percent of housing units in nonmetropolitan areas were crowded (Bureau of the Census 1979); in 1950 the figure was 19 percent (Bird and Kampe 1977). Clearly, conditions have improved and many people have benefited. But, characteristically, the situation improved less rapidly in nonmetropolitan than in metropolitan areas, and the current situation in nonmetropolitan areas is significantly worse than in metropolitan areas.

Although there is no generally accepted standard for the quality of housing, indicators such as the presence of full plumbing, private complete kitchen, and absence of breakdowns in plumbing or electrical service show clearly that rural residents have more lower-quality housing than urban residents.

In 1975, nonmetropolitan areas still included nearly two million housing units that were dilapidated or that lacked plumbing facilities. The occupants of such dwellings included a disproportionate share of blacks, Hispanics, the elderly, and families with low incomes (Bird and Kampe 1977). Rural housing units with plumbing facilities had more plumbing breakdowns than urban housing units. The available data also reflect inadequate maintenance of many rural housing units. In Georgia, for example, two-thirds of all housing that is dilapidated or lacks plumbing facilities is located in rural areas (Georgia Department of Community Affairs 1980).

Blacks are less likely than whites to share in the improvements that have been made in housing, although a higher proportion of nonmetropolitan blacks (51 percent) than whites (42 percent) own their housing free and clear (U.S. Department of Housing and Urban

Development 1979). Blacks accounted for about 7 percent of all housing in nonmetropolitan areas in 1977, but their housing accounted for more than 25 percent of all units lacking some or all plumbing facilities and 22 percent of all crowded housing in such areas (Bureau of the Census 1979). The housing of nonmetropolitan blacks is almost four times more likely to contain some defects than the national average.

In part, the upgrading that has occurred in recent years has been the result of a large volume of new construction. During the 1970s, the number of new housing units in nonmetropolitan areas exceeded the increase in the number of households, thereby making it possible to remove some older substandard units from the overall housing inventory and to accommodate the population growth. Mobile homes accounted for about one-fourth of the new housing units in nonmetropolitan areas (Bureau of the Census 1979). Mobile homes and other factory-built housing are especially attractive to residents of nonmetropolitan areas because they are affordable to persons and families with relatively low incomes.

While 80 percent of all U.S. households are estimated to be able to find living accommodations for no more than one-fourth of their income, only 74 percent of rural households have this cost ratio. Because of the scarcity of savings and loan institutions in nonmetropolitan areas, loans for housing construction are less available there than in metropolitan areas. Although about 60 percent of rural homeowners in 1976 had mortgages, only one fourth of these involved some form of federal aid (Bird and Kampe 1977).

FARMERS HOME ADMINISTRATION

One of the major program forces influencing the quality and availability of housing in rural areas has been the housing program operated by the Farmers Home Administration (FmHA). In recent years, six programs have provided loan or mortgage money (and subsidized loans) for new construction, rehabilitation, and site development: Sections 502 (rehabilitation or new construction loans); 504 (home repair loans); 515 (multifamily loans); 514/516 (farm labor housing loans/grants); and 523 (self-help housing project operation).

Housing funds have been allocated to states through formulas established by the director of the Farmers Home Administration. These formulas have included six variables: the state's percentage of national rural population; the state's percentage of national rural population living in substandard dwellings, defined as those that lack complete plumbing or are crowded; the state's percentage of national rural population with incomes below poverty level; a cost indicator based on average cost of new dwelling and site, factored by population; the state's percentage of national rural population 62 years of age and older; and the state's percentage of national rural households with incomes between $15,000 and $20,000 (Farmers Home Administration 1980). State FmHA directors are required to submit comprehensive housing plans each fiscal year. In the plan, the state director must present a strategy for targeting resources within the state based on formula factors and weights similar to those used nationally to allocate funds to states. Deviations from the formulas are permitted when necessitated by the state's unique situation. For example, in Montana, the funds allocated for multifamily housing project loans cannot be divided among districts since no one area would have sufficient resources for a project.

While the FmHA's policies generally are based on targeting resources to distressed groups, developing cooperative arrangements with other agencies, and inducing private investment (U.S. Department of Agriculture 1979), a respondent to the panel's letter survey has also suggested, discursively, some policy directions for FmHA:

> Region VIII HUD has no Rural Homestead program [like the urban homestead program]! Why not? Why not FmHA homesteading? This is the age of phone, car, and TV. Folks in rural places have same needs and standards as urban America.
>
> Be very nice if HUD and FmHA housing was completely equitable. Costs a great deal to truck in materials for a new house . . . rural new homes are very similar in costs to a new city house.
>
> FmHA should target huge numbers, 1000's, of 502 and other housing here in Energy Impact States and their rural places. FmHA should provide a schedule for these well-paid energy workers to enable home and mobile home ownership. One good program would be to provide for owner-occupied-to-manage 4-plexes, 8-plexes for rental income. Satisfy a great need in rural places [Custer County, Montana].

Review of state plans and conversations with state and national FmHA staff have revealed several factors that affect the success of the housing programs. One factor related to the accomplishment of FmHA goals is articulation between programs. For example, funds from the business and industry program cannot be used for sewer and water in developing communities; as a result, housing cannot be developed in these areas. (Funds can be spent in a developing area only if it will be settled in 4 years or if failure to fund a project will jeopardize the existence of the community.)

Other problems affecting the success of the housing programs are the financing of projects and the costs of individual houses. One FmHA official recently noted that there are too many promises of "better" money, i.e., money that need not be repaid: grant funds are available from government agencies to finance projects (e.g., the small cities program of the Department of Housing and Urban Development) for which FmHA provides only loan funds. Requests for FmHA loans are often submitted simultaneously with grant requests to other agencies.

Land and construction costs and interest rates have made FmHA-assisted homeownership for very poor families impossible. Because the annual payments on principal, interest, taxes, and insurance are likely to exceed 20 percent of a low-income family's adjusted income, an FmHA subsidized 502 loan at 1 percent cannot always be made (although if a family has been paying more than 20 percent for housing, this rule is relaxed). A South Dakota FmHA official made this comment on the rising cost of housing:

> We have a two-county area where the impact of energy development and transportation has made it near impossible for the local low and moderate income family to have a new home. Because of the in-migration of high-salaried families, lot costs and construction costs have risen dramatically because of competition for the limited supply available.

Local building and zoning codes also affect the ability of FmHA programs to reach target groups. While these codes ostensibly protect farmland, they in fact limit the sites on which low and moderate income housing can be situated.

In talking with a panel member, the FmHA administrator in a midwest state expressed concern over his ability to direct loans to minorities. He felt that block building of houses (i.e., several houses built in a single subsection) was leading to a lack of participation by blacks in home building programs. Blacks appeared to be building in metropolitan areas and were shunning block housing in rural areas, primarily because the latter have largely white populations. FmHA administrative data and the Annual Housing Survey can be used to inquire about the extent of this problem nationally.

Review of state plans and conversations with state and national FmHA personnel have thus revealed several factors that affect the success of housing programs. Although some of the problems do involve questions of data or statistics, these problems are minor compared with the administrative and programmatic problems.

DATA SOURCES, NEEDS, AND GAPS

Data on rural housing by county are included in the reports that will be issued in 1981-83 based on the 1980 census of population and housing. The reports will include information on characteristics of housing units, such as number of rooms, the presence of plumbing, crowding, the presence of amenities such as air conditioning, telephone, and electricity, and for nonfarm housing, information about value or rent and mortgage debts. Vacancy rates, housing deficiencies, and some housing costs will also be included. Special tabulations are planned relating to the housing of senior citizens and disabled persons in rural areas. Special tabulations are also planned on the housing of members of minority groups and on the housing of persons living alone. Tabulations are to be provided for places with populations of 2,500-10,000 and for rural farm and rural nonfarm areas. Separate tabulations will supply data for Indian reservations. Some limited data will also be provided for places with populations of 1,000 to 2,500. These tabulations will relate information from the census of population to that from the census of housing. The information will be available in the form of computer tapes as well as in printed reports, facilitating the preparation of special tabulations for areas that differ from the standard census areas. Compilations for river basin areas, conservation districts, development areas, and other special areas can be prepared with relative ease through the use of the summary and other public-use tapes that will become available as the data collected in the 1980 census are tabulated.

The annual housing survey (described in Appendix E) provides information on changes in the housing inventory and on the characteristics of the housing stock. This annual sample survey yields estimates for the nonmetropolitan areas in each of four regions, Northeast, North Central, South, and West. It does not provide data for small areas like the jurisdictions of most planning or development agencies. One important aspect of the annual housing survey is the attempt to account for changes in the inventory due to new construction, the subdivision or consolidation of units, conversion from residential to nonresidential use and vice versa, and the removal of housing units by fire, demolition, abandonment, or other loss. The published reports show data for rural farm and nonfarm units and also for rural units in and outside SMSAs.

The census of housing and the annual housing survey are concerned with housing units, i.e., a house, an apartment, or a group of rooms occupied or intended for occupancy as separate living quarters, and vacant units are included. The count of housing units does not include group quarters, which are defined as living arrangements for institutional inmates or other groups containing five or more persons not related to the person in charge. No information is collected about the housing provided by institutions, boardinghouses, military barracks, college dormitories, hospitals, convents, or monasteries. Although bunkhouses or camps for migratory agricultural workers are group quarters, they <u>are</u> included on the survey form used in the housing inventory.

In addition to the basic housing data sources, some of the letter survey respondents have felt a need to develop their own housing data. For example, officials in Greenup County, Kentucky, felt that they were better served by generating their own statistics concerning the number of vacant dwellings and housing conditions. Another local official described a similar effort:

> Presently, the Council of Governments is employing a regional housing programmer who is conducting a house to house analysis of housing conditions and including economic data. These survey activities are being targeted to those communities which have been identified as having the most critical needs for improvement with a potential for stabilization and economic revitalization. These documentation efforts will lead to the development of a regional housing initiative that will serve to better compete with our metropolitan counterparts for needed financial assistance. This planning project is being financed with a grant from the Rural Development Service/FmHA - Section

III, and local in-kind contributions [Southwest Nebraska Council of Governments].

State and local agencies concerned with rural development have submitted a number of housing plans to the panel, some of which provide examples of locally available data about rural housing. Building permits, demolition permits, assessment records, water and sewer connections, residential electric service records and other indicators of the number and location of housing can be used to monitor local situations.

Clearly the factors used by FmHA to allocate funds nationally and to target resources within a state require reliable data. Data used by FmHA to allocate funds nationally come from the decennial census and from modifications or adjustments to census data made by agencies such as the Economics and Statistics Service of the U.S. Department of Agriculture.

State FmHA offices use data from a variety of sources. The only requirement made by FmHA nationally is that the data be such that equitable decisions can be made. The sources of data used include the decennial census, updates of census data made on the basis of more current within-state data, the annual housing survey, special surveys (e.g., those conducted by an area planning commission as a part of their needs assessment or planning process), and data collected by state agencies (e.g., on water quality, unemployment, income). The available data do not always seem to be adequate. During an interview, one FmHA employee in Oklahoma expressed concern about measures of substandard housing for the housing loan program.

<u>Information is needed on the types and availability of financing for housing purchases or renovations, on local regulatory programs such as building codes and zoning that affect the supply and location of housing, and on the use and impact of housing subsidy programs for low-income and other groups.</u>

Respondents specified these additional data needs and units of analysis:

> One statistic that is needed is the number of property owners (homeowners) in a community compared to renters. Who really carries the burden of paying real estate taxes that support general obligations and pay for local government? In determining need for single family housing, we find no statistics that would indicate who is in the market for housing [Clay and Marion Counties, Arkansas].
>
> . . . it would be helpful to know housing needs for the area. This would be useful in targeting both individual housing funds as well as multi-housing funds [FmHA District Office, Georgia].

An official in Coconino County, Arizona, requested similar data--number of full-time occupancy housing units, number of substandard units, and rent as a percent of income--for specified unincorporated areas. Since small-area data on ownership and occupancy are available only in the decennial census (in some cases special tabluations may be required), local surveys as needed are probably the best way to obtain this information. (An excerpt from a local housing survey can be found in Appendix D.)

DATA GAPS

1. Types and availability of financing for housing purchases or renovations.
2. Local regulatory programs, such as building codes and zoning, that affect the supply and location of housing.
3. Use and impact of housing subsidy programs for low-income and other groups.

REFERENCES

Bird, R., and Kampe, R. (1977) 25 Years of Housing Progress in Rural America. Agriculture Economic Report No. 373, Economic Development Division, Economic Research Service. Washington, D.C.: U.S. Department of Agriculture.

Bureau of the Census (1979) Urban and rural housing characteristics for the United States and regions, annual housing survey: 1977, Part E. Current Housing Reports, Series H-150-77. Washington, D.C.: U.S. Department of Commerce.

Farmers Home Administration (1980) Memorandum to FmHA State Directors on FY'81 State Management Plans. U.S. Department of Agriculture, Washington, D.C.

Georgia Department of Community Affairs (1980) Growth and Change in Rural Georgia: Issues and Opportunities. Atlanta, Ga.: Georgia Department of Community Affairs.

U.S. Department of Agriculture (1979) Rural Development Progress, January 1977-June 1979. Office of the Secretary. Fifth Report of the Department of Agriculture, Washington, D.C.

U.S. Department of Housing and Urban Development (1979) How Well Are We Housed?: 5. Rural. Office of Policy Development and Research. Washington, D.C.: U.S. Department of Housing and Urban Development.

7

HEALTH AND NUTRITION

There are two major concerns regarding rural health: the distribution of providers, facilities, and services for health care; and the health status of the population. From the standpoint of community action, the first of these concerns has been greater because providing adequate health care services is necessarily a community goal or objective.

Thus, a priority of rural communities has been to attract physicians and other health care providers and to make available facilities necessary for the provision of comprehensive health care. The health systems agencies (HSAs) have brought professional health planners into service across the country. These professional planners know the data sources, and they are able to obtain access to them. Through the HSAs, any rural community attempting to enhance the quantity and quality of health care services has access to both the data and the technical assistance of the HSA staffs.

The health status of the population, however, tends to be as much or more a consequence of the actions of individuals and families. Four different contributors to the health status of an individual can be identified:

Individual: Engages in actions and behaviors, such as adequate exercise, avoiding habits that contribute to deterioration of health, and following recommended practices and behaviors for preserving health.

Family: Influences nutrition and stress and socializes health-preserving habits.

Community: Provides for the control of infectious diseases and other debilitating conditions through proper public health measures including sanitation, safe drinking water, and the reduction of environmental hazards and accidents.

Providers of health care: Contribute to the *restoration* of health; but there is little that providers can do to overcome negative effects of the actions of individuals, families, and communities.

There is a growing emphasis on preventive health care and health maintenance rather than an exclusive focus on the provision of health care services. Existing data sources tend to be more adequate vis-a-vis identification of problems and supporting initiatives to enhance health care than they are with regard to health status. Generally, systematic data are lacking on the nutritional status of the population, the prevalence of hypertension, and the prevalence of potentially debilitating but correctable conditions among children. Such data are often collected in special studies but are not integrated into a more comprehensive data base on the health status of the population.

The most striking fact about health data is their abundance. Many data sets and systems exist and many more are in progress. The key data problems seem to be not the need for more data, but who should control and have access to which data and how they should flow from the point of acquisition to other government levels. In regard to data needs, either the data exist or the institutions to collect and disseminate them are in place.

The discussion of health data in this chapter has three sections: determining health status; the distribution of health resources; and health planning. The first two sections deal largely with data collected at the national level and used in national policy. Health care in rural areas is an increasingly important subject at the federal level. The third section deals with two topics that must be considered in effective health planning--access and identification of shortage areas--and with the mechanism for local health planning.

HEALTH STATUS OF PEOPLE IN RURAL AREAS

Federal Data Collection Efforts

At least six ongoing federal surveys and inventories collect data relevant to health and nutrition (described in greater detail in Appendix E).

Basic vital statistics Basic vital statistics come from required records of live births, deaths, fetal deaths, induced terminations of pregnancy, marriages, and divorces or dissolutions of marriages. Registration of these events is a local and state function, but uniform registration practices and use of the records for national statistics have been established over the years through cooperative agreements between the states and the National Center for Health Statistics (NCHS) and its predecessor agencies.

Vital statistics followback surveys Followback surveys, which include information on mortality, natality, and infant mortality, extend the range of information normally included on the vital records. The mortality surveys contain questions on hospital utilization, diagnoses, operations performed, and other information concerning a patient's final year. The natality surveys collect information from mothers who had live births during a given year, from the attendant at birth, and from the hospital where the birth occurred. They include data on medical and dental care, radiological treatment, smoking habits, and health insurance of the mother, and on sources of medical care and health status of the mother and infant. The infant mortality survey includes questions on hospitalization of the infant who died. These surveys provide national estimates.

National health interview survey This annual survey of the civilian, noninstitutionalized population contains questions on disability days, physician and dentist visits, acute and chronic conditions, long-term limitation of activity, and all hospital episodes in the 12 months preceeding the interview. The data are available for four regions and by place of residence: SMSA central city, SMSA noncentral city, non-SMSA nonfarm, and non-SMSA farm.

National health and nutrition examination survey This continuing survey, conducted since 1971, is concerned with the collection and utilization of data that can be obtained only by direct physical examination, clinical and laboratory tests, and related measurement procedures. Specially trained teams of interviewers and examiners collect these data from individuals. The data are of two kinds: prevalence data for specifically defined diseases or conditions of ill health; and normative health-related measurement data that show distributions of the total population with respect to specific parameters such as blood pressure, visual acuity, or serum cholesterol level. Four types of nutritional data are included: dietary intake; hematological and biochemical tests; body measurements (which are especially important in connection with infants and children for whom growth may be affected by nutritional deficiencies); and various signs of high risk of nutritional deficiency.

National hospital discharge survey This survey is the principal source of information on inpatient utilization of short-stay hospitals. The survey provides information on the characteristics of patients, the length of stay, diagnoses and surgical operations, and patterns of use of care in hospitals of different sizes and ownership.

National ambulatory medical care survey This survey samples physicians and their patient visits. The survey obtains such information as referral, length of time since the onset of the problem, diagnoses, diagnostic and therapeutic services, seriousness of the condition, and disposition.

Analysts seeking to establish the relative or absolute health status of people in rural areas have found these data inadequate for several reasons, including the problem of defining rurality, the difficulty of defining medical trade areas,[1] and the lack of comparability of data from physical examinations.

Urban-Rural Differences

Analysts have had difficulty in establishing the absolute or relative health status of people in rural areas. Along with data problems, there is also the problem of deciding which indicators are best for describing overall health standards. Measures of mortality, disability, self-perceived health status, and incidence of diseases have all been used. In various urban-rural comparisons, the use of different indicators results in different outcomes. Thus, it is difficult to say for sure whether the health of the nonmetropolitan population is worse than that of the metropolitan population, and even more difficult to say that "ruralness" causes the differences. Distinct rural-urban differences appear to reflect differences peculiar to the type of life and work in rural areas. For example, farm equipment injuries are obviously more prevalent in rural areas. Since many differences show a consistent pattern but are not large, perhaps there are no big differences in rural and urban health (Copp 1976).

Most data on infant and maternal mortality rates, which are used internationally as a surrogate for health status, suggest that rural populations have slightly higher rates, even after controlling for various socioeconomic factors (Rosenblatt 1979, Copp 1976). The rural-urban differences in chronic conditions are slightly more difficult to interpret. Data from the Natonal Center for Health Statistics show that chronic illnesses are more prevalent among people in rural areas than among those in urban areas (Rosenblatt 1979). Rural dwellers, however, are less disabled by acute conditions than are urban dwellers.

Analysts do not know whether rural people have fewer and less severe illnesses or whether they are less willing to restrict their activity when they are ill (Rosenblatt 1979, Copp 1976). Progress in medical care has resulted in more people surviving formerly fatal illnesses but surviving with some form of disability. Therefore, improved medical care both decreases and increases disability (Ahearn 1979).

In the past, age-adjusted death rates for all ages for the United States as a whole have been somewhat lower for nonmetropolitan than for metropolitan counties. In recent years, however, rates for metropolitan counties have declined more, so there is uncertainty as to the magnitude and direction of this difference at present (Sauer 1976).

A great deal of work has been done on the development of health status indexes. While additional conceptual development is still needed, there now exists a body of health status measures that can be used to assess health outcomes (Ericksen 1979). Because single indicators are generally suspect, various composite health indexes have been developed. One for which a rural breakdown exists is comprised of three indicators: the infant mortality rate, the age-standardized mortality rate, and the age-standardized mortality rate of deaths due to influenza and pneumonia. This composite index shows that the health of metropolitan residents is better than that of nonmetropolitan residents. Specifically, areas that are totally rural had the worst health status, and fringe counties of metropolitan areas measured best on the index (Ahearn 1979).

Two approaches have been suggested to try to determine various aspects of rural health status that go beyond urban-rural comparisons. Copp (1976) suggests that important rural subpopulations be analyzed, while Sauer (1976) suggests that the variable of geographic location be analyzed. Both of these approaches may be necessary to understand fully the health characteristics of rural people.

The major determinants of health status are intrinsic, stemming from the interaction between an individual's biological potential and the surrounding environment in which the person lives. Thus, the demographic characteristics of given population groups may be very powerful in predicting the health status of the members of the group. Copp has identified a number of predominantly rural subpopulations that probably have disproportionately critical health needs, including: southern rural blacks, Chicanos, Appalachian and Ozark whites, the aged, migrant workers, illegal aliens, and residents of environmentally polluted areas, of highly dispersed settlements, of the metropolitan hinterlands, and of communes. These rural subpopulations with critical health needs share certain common characteristics: they tend to have low incomes, to be powerless, and to be looked down on because of race, culture, or life-style. They tend to embody values that are held in low esteem--age, color, rootlessness, poverty, or presumed immorality. Most of these subpopulations cannot be separately identified with present statistical information, and yet their health needs exceed what would be expected from statistics on the rural population in general.

THE DISTRIBUTION OF HEALTH RESOURCES

The health problem that was mentioned most often by the respondents to our letter survey was the lack of a doctor. While additional data will probably not solve this problem at the local level, the distribution of physicians generally has been studied and addressed at the national level.

Health Resources Data Sets

At least three data sets exist that detail the health resources (facilities and personnel) available nationally (described in greater detail in Appendix E).

Area resource file This data set, which is updated annually, contains county-level data on health personnel, facilities, and training, as well as economic, utilization, expenditure, and environmental data. The file uses input data from other computer systems and translates printed materials into a form suitable for computer processing.

National master facility inventory This is a comprehensive file of the facilities (hospitals, nursing homes, and residential schools and treatment centers) in the United States that provide medical, nursing, personal, or custodial care on an inpatient basis. Mail surveys and the collection of directories and lists of new facilities from state licensing agencies, voluntary associations, and other appropriate sources are used to keep the file current.

National nursing home survey This survey, which uses the national master facility inventory as a sampling universe, was conducted in 1974 and 1977. Several types of questionnaire are used to obtain data on the facilities, workers, and residents. Data are collected on nursing home characteristics, services, and staff; major cost components of nursing home operations; and resident health. A purpose of the survey is to interrelate facility, staff, and resident data to examine the relationships among utilization, services offered, charges, and costs.

Distribution of Personnel

In general, there is a strong negative relationship between the total number of physicians and the degree of rurality of their place of practice. Some studies show a nearly linear positive relationship between population size and physician supply--physicians cluster where there are the most other physicians. This relationship also holds for physicians involved only in patient-care activities, those not in patient-care activities, and for hospital-based physicians and office-based specialists. The one exception is with office-based general practitioners. Other primary care physicians--specialists in internal medicine, pediatrics, general surgery, and obstetrics/gynecology--are more abundant in urban than in rural counties. Their relative abundance is sufficient to give urban counties a decided edge in the total number of primary care physicians (Cordes 1976).

The pattern is the same for other types of medical personnel. For osteopaths, for example, the number per 100,000 population in metropolitan areas was 4.7 and in nonmetropolitan areas was 3.4 in 1975. However, osteopathic physicians are more evenly distributed across the nation than other physicians although they are a relatively small group (Ahearn 1979). Osteopaths have more limited practice opportunities and frequently practice in rural areas.

Although these aspects of physician distribution are well known, there have been some important changes in this distribution over time. In the 1960s, governmental attention at the federal and state levels focused on the doctor shortage, and it was thought that increasing the aggregate supply of doctors could improve the supply of physicians in underserved rural areas. However, Rushing and Wade (1976) suggest that this has not happened. In 1959, there were 74 counties without an active nonfederal physician; the figure grew to 98 in 1963 and to 126 in 1968. In 1971, 133 counties did not have an active federal or nonfederal physician in patient care. Although the types of physicians included in the tabulations vary (in the 1950 census all employed physicians except those in the armed forces are included while the 1971 figure includes federal and nonfederal physicians in patient care only), the number of counties with no physicians clearly and consistently increased over the 21-year period. And this was a period in which the overall physician/population ratio increased.

Thus, a single general conclusion should not be drawn about physician personnel in rural areas. Conclusions will vary depending on the type of physician, the period of time examined, how the units of analysis are aggregated, and what comparisons are made (Cordes 1976).

The distribution of mid-level health personnel other than physicians is also particularly important to rural areas. These mid-level practitioners include MEDEX (retrained former service medical corpsmen), nurse practitioners (retrained nurses), and physician assistants (trained de novo). A recent survey indicates that mid-level health personnel (excluding nurse practitioners), over half of whom are in family or general practice, are distributed more evenly in the United States than are physicians. Almost half of them (46.1 percent) practice in areas with less than 50,000 population (with almost half of these in communities with less than 10,000 population). However, the number of mid-level health personnel practicing in areas with less than 250,000 population declined about 10 percent from 1974 to 1978, with a corresponding increase in the percentage practicing in big cities (Perry and Fisher 1980).

Since the use of mid-level health personnel is fairly new, there are several aspects of it that have not yet been evaluated. These include the problems of medical supervision, community acceptance, and, until recently, the lack of reimbursement under federal insurance coverage programs (Decker 1977). Moscovice and Rosenblatt (1979) gathered financial and productivity data on a small sample of geographically isolated mid-level practitioner operations in order to determine the production, efficiency, financial break-even point, community size effects, and overall economic viability of such operations. They found that initial costs are quite high but suggested that good management and experience may reduce them.

Given that there are fewer physicians in rural than in urban areas, and given that this probably means there is a shortage in rural areas, a great deal of research has attempted to determine what affects the location decisions of physicians. For example, a recent study in Missouri found that rural and urban physicians' ideas about the advantages and disadvantages of their respective locations seemed to be based on earlier socialization and attachment to specific life-styles rather than on specific aspects of the practice of medicine (Hassinger et al. 1980). If more were known about these variables, perhaps the location decision could be influenced by the federal government and local communities in order to benefit rural areas.[2]

Distribution of Facilities

A nationwide survey to obtain an overview of hospital needs, which brought to light the deficiencies of rural areas, was first conducted as part of postwar planning during World War II. In 1945 the U.S. Public Health Service published the first national survey of hospital bed supply in relation to population in all counties, along with theoretical proposals for action needed to achieve rural-urban equity. Health service areas were defined in which peripheral (rural), intermediate, and base hospitals should ideally exist (Roemer 1976).

This laid the technical basis for the National Hospital Survey and Construction (Hill-Burton) Act of 1946, which provided grants to states to subsidize hospital construction in areas of greatest need as determined by surveys in each state with design of a state master plan. The law and regulations under it required that a ranking of priorities be established through which areas of greatest deficiency from the optimal standard of bed need would get assistance first. Inevitably that requirement meant that the maximum aid went to building hospitals in rural districts. Largely because of the Hill-Burton influence, the hospital resources of rural America have been greatly improved, both in quantity and quality. Between 1946 and 1966, the disparity in bed supply between predominantly rural and predominantly urban areas was largely eliminated.

In 1976 there were 495 U.S. counties without a community hospital. While there are more community hospitals per capita in nonmetropolitan areas than metropolitan areas, these hospitals are generally smaller. Thus, there are more hospital beds per person in metropolitan than in nonmetropolitan areas. Nonmetropolitan hospitals are also generally older, less likely to be accredited, and lacking in specialized services. The American Hospital Association reports that the assets per bed for metropolitan hospitals are $39,998 compared with $26,804 for nonmetropolitan hospitals (Ahearn 1979). Overall, however, the distribution of hospitals does not reflect the large rural-urban differences in distribution of physicians.

Nursing homes are another type of facility that is important in rural areas. While there are more elderly people in highly urbanized areas, their proportion is higher in rural areas. In 1974, the highest proportion of elderly persons (13 percent) was in totally rural nonmetropolitan counties, and the smallest proportion (8 percent) was in the suburban fringe counties of SMSAs (McCoy and Brown 1978). At virtually the same time (1975), however, there were 479 nursing home beds per 100,000 population in metropolitan areas, compared with 407 in nonmetropolitan areas (Ahearn 1979). This distribution may apppear to be inequitable, but it must be noted that the urban elderly are much more likely to live alone than their rural counterparts, for whom various home-care arrangements may reduce the need for nursing homes (McCoy and Brown 1978). (The Area Resource File--a county-level health data set described in Appendix E--contains data on the number of nursing homes, nursing home beds, and nursing home residents by county.)

HEALTH PLANNING

Access

Access is an important but complex topic in any discussion of equity in health care. For any given patient, access to health care can be measured only in a complicated manner by assessing such factors as knowledge, finances, geography, timeliness, and sociocultural acceptability. While there are many definitions of access, most of them seem to have timely utilization as a common denominator (Duggar 1978). Aday and Anderson (1975), who have done the most extensive work in attempting to define access, have developed several indicators to measure this concept, such as regular source of care, travel time, appointment versus walk-in status, office waiting time, use of emergency room for primary care, health status, and satisfaction with care. Using several available national data sets, they found that rural and inner-city residents were most disadvantaged in regard to access as measured by these indicators. There are, however, no county data on access to health care variables, including ability to pay.

While the indicators are numerous and diverse, there have been problems in developing indices that combine several of them. Various combinations of the indicators, such as travel and waiting time, may not be easily interpreted nor easily translated into policy decisions about health care services (Aday and Anderson 1975).

More recent data on several access indicators (see Koch 1978) suggest that rural areas remain slightly disadvantaged. Metro area residents had relatively more physician visits (5.3) per person per year than nonmetropolitan area residents (4.4) in 1975. The percentage of the population having at least one physician visit during the 12 months prior to being interviewed shows that 75.9 percent of the metropolitan population had one or more visits, compared with 73.0 percent of the nonmetropolitan population. The average visit lasted only 12.8 minutes in nonmetropolitan areas, compared with 15.8 minutes in metropolitan areas (Ahearn 1979).

Dental care, a major component of primary care, is often viewed as elective, and relatively large differences exist among income groups in its utilization. A higher proportion of lower-income persons, along with less availability of dental services, may explain the lower utilization of such services in nonmetropolitan areas.

Other measures of access to health care include whether an individual has a regular source of care, appointment waiting time, travel time to care, ability to obtain a walk-in visit, and office waiting time. A 1975 nationwide survey found that rural farm residents had the least access when access was measured by the last three of these five measures (Ahearn 1979).

On some measures, however, rural people use hospitals more than urban people. For example, in 1975, the percentage of the population with one or more periods of hospitalization was 10.3 for metropolitan areas and 11.6 for nonmetropolitan areas. Differentials by place of residence, although not large, are consistent across age groups. This differential may be related to the greater prevalence of low incomes in nonmetropolitan areas. Hospitalization is known to be inversely related to income for several reasons, including less access to preventive and primary health care. Another determining factor may be the greater distance nonmetropolitan people must travel to obtain care. Thus, a patient may be hospitalized to avoid repeated long trips and to assure prompt attention if it is needed (Ahearn 1979).

Identification of Shortage Areas

One of the most important components of federal programs aimed at alleviating geographic maldistribution of health resources is the identification and designation of those specific areas that are in need of health personnel. The earliest health personnel shortage area designations were mandated by 1965 legislation providing for cancellation of repayment of the educational loans of health professionals if they served in shortage areas. The regulations provided for the designation of shortage areas on the basis of specific ratios of several types of practitioners (e.g., physicians, dentists, nurses, pharmacists, veterinarians) to population, applied to county-level data. Special consideration was allowed for county or subcounty areas exhibiting inaccessibility of medical services to the residents of the area, age or incapacity of practitioners, or particular local health problems. New criteria were established in 1971 designating shortage areas for various specialties (e.g., physicians, optometrists, podiatrists). Most designated areas were entire counties since data were most readily available at the county level. The physician shortage area list accounted for roughly two-thirds of all U.S. counties (Lee 1979).[3]

One weakness of the area designation process was its dependence on county data. The use of county data is appropriate if the county is a reasonable medical service area. In some states (largely in the west), however, rural counties are too large geographically to represent service areas, and in southeastern states rural counties tend to be too small to be considered independently (Lee 1979).

The worst shortcoming of the shortage designations, however, was their reliance on the physician/population ratio. While this measure tends to overdesignate rural areas (or at least underdesignate urban areas), it is generally considered to be very flawed. Cordes (1976) suggests a number of problems:

> <u>Productivity</u>: Physician/population ratios do not reflect possible differences in productivity among physicians and groups of physicians.
>
> <u>Quality</u>: Physician/population ratios are insensitive to quality considerations.
>
> <u>Population characteristics</u>: Physician/population ratios typically assume that populations are the same with respect to their needs

for physician services and to the quantity of physician services demanded, an assumption that is often invalid.

Accessibility: While physician/population ratios measure how many physicians are present in a designated geographic area, they tell little about the ease with which various groups may draw upon their services.

Physician and population mobility: Physician/population ratios for a particular geographic area assume that the area is a closed system. This is a reasonable assumption at the national level but not among smaller geographic units. The fact that physician/population ratios do not take account of either physician or population mobility may be their greatest limitation.

Georgaphic size, contiguous areas, and population density: Variations in these three factors have important implications related to the problems of accessibility and mobility.

On the last point, Cordes (1976:73) gives an example to illustrate the effect of geographic size:

> . . . assume the unit of analysis is the county. In inventorying the physician-population ratio for all U.S. counties, it can be seen that Owyhee County, Idaho, and Robertson County, Kentucky, have the same number of physicians per 100,000 population--namely zero. Owyhee County is 6,100 square miles and Robertson County is 101 square miles. Although neither county would be a good place to become ill, most of us would probably prefer Robertson County without knowing anything else about the two counties.

A county without a physician may not have a shortage of physician services if surrounding counties have easily accessible services. Thus, the ratio for a particular area may incorrectly express service adequacy.

Another problem with this measure is that it does not take nonphysician providers into account and thus may exaggerate the lack of personnel in certain areas (Jaggar 1978). Also, the measure is "lumpy," that is, a small change in the number of physicians, especially when the unit considered is the county, can change the ratio enough so that the shortage classification is markedly altered although actual availability of medical care has not changed for most residents. The sensitivity of the measure to small changes is an important concern since many of the directories from which physician location data are obtained are not accurate or current, e.g., physicans sometimes maintain their licenses in places where they do not usually practice.

The concept of medically underserved populations began with the Health Maintenance Organization Act of 1973, which required that funding priorities be given to health maintenance organizations (HMOs) serving "medically underserved populations." (The concept of medical underservice is broader than that of health personnel shortage since it relates to populations not receiving adequate health care for whatever reason, while the personnel shortage designation is aimed only at identifying health personnel shortages.) A four-variable model was selected. The score generated by this model was called the "index of medical underservice" (IMU) and was evaluated for all U.S. counties. All counties or subcounty areas with values below the median were designated as medically underserved areas (Lee 1979).

The medically underserved area (MUA) designation avoids some of the pitfalls of the physican/population ratio by including three indicators other than the (primary care) physician/population ratio: infant mortality rate, which is an indicator of health status; the percentage of the population over age 65, which is an indicator of probable increased needs and demands for health care; and the percentage of the population below the poverty level, which is an indicator of economic access barriers and higher needs for health care. The MUA designation procedure does not, however, involve any efforts to define rational noncounty service areas or to take into account conditions in contiguous areas (Lee 1979).

The index of medical underservice has frequently been critized by health service researchers. Wysong (1975) has noted that there is no single definition of the concept of medical underservice--although the concept is closely associated with both access and health status, both of which are commonly used--so the four-variable model is a rather arbitrary choice of measure. In fact, underservice may be defined in at least three ways (Wysong 1975:130):

1) Number of services available relative to the average number of services in some specified area;
2) Number of services available relative to the demand for services in a particular areas;
3) Number of services available relative to the need for services.

Which of these, if any, the IMU is measuring is not clear.

In addition, the IMU does not measure a single dimension, but expresses relationships among population size, availability of services, socioeconomic characteristics of communities, and health status. Although these relationships have been studied, they are not completely understood and may vary from area to area (Wysong 1975).

The IMU is now used for purposes of community health centers and other service programs. For example, it is used, often in combination with the list of critical health personnel shortage areas, for implementation of grant funding under the urban health initiative and rural health initiative/health underserved rural area programs.

The Health Professions Educational Assistance Act of 1976 (P.L. 94-484) represents another attempt to designate health personnel shortage areas, but its aims are broader. (One of the aims was to include more urban areas.) This designation includes the following, from Lee (1979):

(1) Separate criteria for each type of health personnel are used.
(2) For each of these personnel types, there are three basic criteria:
    (a) For designation of a geographic area, the area must be defined by an appropriate travel time to care.
    (b) For most types of care, a modified population-to-practitioner ratio is still the basic indicator used. However, for those personnel types for which the available data support such adjustments, either the population or the number of practitioners may be adjusted to reflect special needs or limitations, respectively.
    (c) Personnel in a contiguous area must be considered, specifically: the travel time to reach them, whether they are already overused, and whether there are barriers (e.g., cultural) to their use.
(3) Particular population groups, such as Native Americans and migrants, may be designated as "shortage areas," even though the entire geographic area in which they reside does not qualify.

Lee (1979) has five major issues related to the most recent designation of medically underserved or medical shortage areas. First, the National Health Service corps program was originally designed to place physicians in places (largely rural) where there were few or no physicians. The broader criteria for manpower shortage (which take into account factors other than physician/population ratios) have, however, allowed this program to be used to place physicians in subsections of physician-rich metropolitan areas. Lee suggests that better reimbursement methods or insurance programs would be a more appropriate way of meeting urban medical needs.

Second, while the criteria do work well to designate most areas with personnel shortages, some rural areas, where the population is both small and highly dispersed, have trouble meeting the population standard. That is, one physician may be on call day and night to be available for all people within a geographically large area.

Third, the data base for determination of a shortage needs to be improved substantially. <u>There are a large number of variables important to the identification of shortage areas for which data are not now available, such as: waiting time; percent of emergency room visits used for primary care; geographical origin of patient; and Medicaid reimbursement (to identify poverty populations).</u> The identification of surrogate variables (perhaps available from census data or other common data sources) may be desirable. The surrogates could be used to represent factors that would better identify health personnel shortage areas.

Fourth, there is little difference left between the concept of "population with manpower shortages" and that of "medically underserved populations." Two shortage area designation systems persist, however, one for specific health personnel programs and another for more general community health services programs. Perhaps there should be one set of criteria for each type of health service (i.e., primary care, dental care, vision care, etc.), with the areas meeting those criteria eligible for all types of federal programs relating to that health service. The panel believes this situation warrants the attention of the Statistical Policy Division.

Finally, Lee notes the difference between needs and demands for care. The criteria for shortage designation, as they stand, represent a compromise between the two, since the key population-to-practitioner ratio is basically a need factor, but the population is modified to reflect demands for and utilization of services.

While the various criteria for shortage area designation direct, or are designed to direct, the allocation of more resources into rural areas than they would otherwise receive, the actual designations may not be all that useful. Gittelsohn (1979) looked at several indices of resource use and health status in three different types of areas in Vermont: medically underserved areas (MUAs), critical medical shortage areas (MSAs) and amply served areas. He found that MUA and MSA residents use medical services at about the same rate as residents of amply served areas and that outcomes, as measured by mortality, are similar. Because of this, he believes that the entire concept of medical underservice and the designation criteria must be seriously questioned. Kleinman and Wilson (1977) also found no difference in number of physician visits between residents of the two types of areas. This calls into question the relationship between lack of physicians and shortage of service. These indices may be useful ranking mechanisms but may not be useful in developing policies for correcting the underservice (Jaggar 1978).

> Recommendation: The panel recommends that such Public Health Service agencies as the Health Resources Administration and the Health Services Administration devote further effort to the development of a definition of health service scarcity and to research on measures of this concept.

Substate Health Data Needs: Health Systems Agencies

The National Health Planning and Resources Development Act of 1974, P.L. 93-641, created a national network of local health systems agencies (HSAs) to be responsible for health planning and resource development throughout the country.

The major functions of an HSA include: collecting and analyzing data related to health planning; establishing a health system plan; developing an annual implementation plan; making grants and contracts from an area resources development fund; making recommendations to the relevant state agency on the need for new institutional health services proposed to be offered in the area and on the appropriateness of existing health services; and recommending to the Department of Health and Human Services approval or disapproval of proposed uses of certain Public Health Service funds (Rubel 1976).

An HSA can be either a nonprofit private corporation or a public agency operating under the auspices of a unit of general-purpose local government or a public regional planning body. Every HSA must have a governing body composed of consumers, providers, and local government representatives. The overall purpose of HSAs is to improve the health of residents in their areas by increasing the accessibility, acceptability, continuity, and quality of health services while restraining increases in the cost of health services and preventing unnecessary duplication of health resources.

A major goal of HSAs is to increase access to health care. By means of the health systems plan, the annual implementation plan, the regulatory capability, and the area resources development funds, the agencies will be able to guide improvements in the health care system at the local level and, in particular, in rural areas (Martin 1975).

The HSAs are supposed to cover the United States and must represent certain demographic, economic, and geographic criteria. One requirement for designating HSAs specifically relates to rural areas (Peterson 1976:11):

> The boundaries of a health service area shall be established so that . . . any economic or geographic barrier to the receipt of (health) services in nonmetropolitan areas is taken into account. The boundaries of health service areas shall be established so as to recognize the differences in health planning and health services development needs between nonmetropolitan and metropolitan areas.

This requirement reflected congressional concern that nonmetropolitan or rural areas be ensured fair and equitable treatment in the designation of areas. It has the effect of moderating the requirements relative to the population of nonmetropolitan areas and the range of health services and facilities in them (Peterson 1976).

Approximately 15 percent of the health service areas (about 30) are exclusively nonmetropolitan or rural in character: they do not include any SMSA, however small, in whole or in part, within their boundaries. Most HSAs are probably congruent with substate planning and development districts, i.e., they encompass one or several such districts in their entirety (Peterson 1976).

In regard to data, HSAs are directed to assemble and analyze the data concerning (Health Resources Administration 1977): 1) the status (and its determinants) of the health of the residents of the health service area; 2) the status of the health care delivery system in the area and the use of that system by the residents of the area; 3) the effect of the health delivery system on the health of the residents of the area; 4) the number, type, and location of the area's health resources, including health services, manpower, and facilities; 5) the patterns of utilization of the area's health resources and; 6) the environmental and occupational exposure factors affecting immediate and long-term health conditions. (Appendix F contains examples of local data development.)

Fitzwilliams (1979) has criticized the use of HSAs as units for national health planning, giving special attention to the problems that this can cause in rural areas. After examining the arithmetic means for several variables for HSAs in 10 census regions and also examining within-region HSA variation, she suggests that the range for many variables is so large that the units could not be a suitable basis for planning. In addition, many HSAs with small populations or large land areas have little money in relation to needs. When an HSA has a very large land area, data collection costs increase greatly.

Fitzwilliams (1979:10) suggests that many of the measures now used are misleading:

> The use of aggregated data can be particularly dangerous to the interests of rural people regarding the specifics of health care delivery, as this masking tendency may convince decision-makers and planners that a particular goal has been adequately achieved. It is not uncommon to hear people say "90 percent of the population is within 20 minutes driving time of a certain kind of facility." Yet the 10 percent who are further than a 20-minute drive away may represent 100,000 people with no available public transportation.

Wennberg and Gittelsohn (1973) have also documented that health care information on small areas leads to different health planning decisions than more aggregated data. They compared decisions based on 13 hospital service areas to those based on more aggregated units. Use of the smaller units would have reversed several of the decisions (to increase beds and other facilities). The panel recognizes that aggregate data are a general problem for rural areas because of their heterogeneity. One way to alleviate this problem is to provide distributional measures in addition to measures of central tendency (see Chapter 13).

DATA GAPS

1. County data on access to health care variables, including ability to pay.
2. Shortage area data on waiting time, percent of emergency room visits used for primary care, geographic origin of patient, and Medicaid reimbursement (to identify poverty populations).

NOTES

[1]The patterns people follow in their health-seeking behavior seldom coincide with geopolitical boundaries or with the trade areas for goods and services.

[2]Two different types of research strategies, both with limitations, have been used in attempts to isolate the factors influencing where a physician chooses to locate (Cordes 1976). One is

that of asking physicians why they are practicing where they are or of asking students, interns, and residents what factors they will look for in a practice location. The other is the correlation of the physician/population ratios of geographic areas with various characteristics (e.g., social, economic, and demographic factors) of these areas.

[3]As shortage area criteria were being developed for loan repayment, other criteria were being developed for use in identifying areas eligible for placement of National Health Service Corps personnel. Because this program was to operate only in "critical" shortage areas, more stringent criteria (smaller physician/population ratios) were selected (Lee 1979).

REFERENCES

Aday, L., and Anderson, R. (1975) Development of Indices of Access to Medical Care. Ann Arbor, Mich.: Health Administration Press.

Ahearn, M.C. (1979) Health Care in Rural America. Agriculture Information Bulletin No. 428. Economic Development Division, Economics, Statistics, and Cooperatives Service. Washington, D.C.: U.S. Department of Agriculture.

Copp, J.H. (1976) Diversity of rural society and health needs. Pp. 26-37 in E.W. Hassinger and L.R. Whiting, eds., Rural Health Services: Organization, Delivery, And Use. North Central Regional Center for Rural Development. Ames, Iowa.: Iowa State University Press.

Cordes, S.M. (1976) Distribution of physician manpower. Pp. 56-80 in E.W. Hassinger and L.R. Whiting, eds., Rural Health Services: Organization, Delivery, And Use. North Central Regional Center for Rural Development. Ames, Iowa.: Iowa State University Press.

Decker, B. (1977) Federal strategies and the quality of local health care. Pp. 200-214 in A. Levin, ed., Health Services: the Local Perspective. Proceedings of the Academy of Political Science 32(3). New York: Academy of Political Science.

Duggar, B. (1978) Access, Coordination, and Utilization of Rural Health Care: Evaluation and Research Issues. Paper prepared for the Workshop on Directions in Rural Health Evaluation and Research. National Center for Health Services Research, Annapolis, Md.

Erickson, P. (1979) Rapporteur report: health status indexes--methods and concepts of application. Pp. 275-276 in The Public Health Conference on Records and Statistics. DHEW Publication No. (PHS) 79-1214. Office of Health Research, Statistics, and Technology, National Center for Health Statistics, Public Health Service. Washington, D.C.: U.S. Department of Health, Education, and Welfare.

Fitzwilliams, J. (1979) Unmasking Problems in Rural Health Planning. Rural Development Research Report No. 111. Economics, Statistics, and Cooperatives Service. Washington, D.C.: U.S. Department of Agriculture.

Gittelsohn, A. (1979) Uses of health data in health planning. Pp. 28-34 in The Public Health Conference on Records and Statistics. DHEW Publication No. (PHS) 79-1214. Office of Health Research, Statistics, and Technology, National Center for Health Statistics, Public Health Service. Washington, D.C.: U.S. Department of Health, Education, and Welfare.

Hassinger, E.W., Gill, L.S., Hobbs, D.J., and Hageman, R.L. (1980) Perceptions of rural and metropolitan physicians about rural practice and the rural community, Missouri, 1975. Public Health Reports 95:69-79.

Health Resources Administration (1977) The Cooperative Health Statistics System: Its Mission and Program. DHEW Publication No. (HRA) 77-1456. Public Health Service. Washington, D.C.: U.S. Department of Health, Education, and Welfare.

Jaggar, F. (1978) Health Manpower for Rural Areas: Evaluation and Research Issues. Paper prepared for the Workshop on Directions in Rural Health Evaluation and Research. National Center for Health Services Research, Annapolis, Md.

Kleinman, J.R., and Wilson, R.W. (1977) Are medically underserved areas medically underserved? Health Services Research 12:147-162.

Koch, H.K. (1978) The National Ambulatory Medical Care Survey: 1975 Summary. DHEW Publication No. (PHS) 78-1784. National Center for Health Statistics. Washington, D.C.: U.S. Department of Health, Education, and Welfare.

Lee, R.C. (1979) Identification of health manpower shortage areas and development of criteria for designation. Pp. 35-41 in Public Health Conference on Records and Statistics. DHEW Publication No. (PHS) 79-1214. Office of Health Research, Statistics, and Technology, National Center for Health Statistics, Public Health Service. Washington, D.C.: U.S. Department of Health, Education, and Welfare.

Martin, E. (1975) The federal initiative in rural health. Public Health Reports 90:291-297.

McCoy, J.L., and Brown, D.L. (1978) Health status among low-income elderly persons: rural-urban differences. Social Security Bulletin 41:14-26.

Moscovice, I., and Rosenblatt, R. (1979) The viability of mid-level practitioners in isolated rural communities. American Journal of Public Health 69:503-505.

Perry, H.B., and Fisher, D.W. (1980) The Present Status of the Physician Assistant Profession: Results of the Association of Physician Assistant Programs' 1978 Longitudinal Survey of Graduates. Association of Physician Assistant Programs, Arlington, Va.

Peterson, R.L. (1976) The designation of health service areas. Public Health Reports 91:9-18.

Roemer, M.I. (1976) Historical perspective of health services in rural America. Pp. 3-25 in E.W. Hassinger and L.R. Whiting, eds., Rural Health Services: Organization, Delivery, and Use. North Central Regional Center for Rural Development. Ames, Iowa.: Iowa State University Press.

Rosenblatt, R.A. (1979) Health and Health Services. Paper prepared for the Future of Rural America Advisory Group. Institute for Research in Social Science, University of North Carolina.

Rubel, E.J. (1976) Implementing the National Health Planning and Resources Development Act of 1974. Public Health Reports 91:3-8.

Rushing, W.A., and Wade, G.T. (1976) Community structure constraints on distribution of physicians. Pp. 106-120 in E.W. Hassinger and L.R. Whiting, eds., Rural Health Services: Organization, Delivery, And Use. North Central Regional Center for Rural Development. Ames, Iowa.: Iowa State University Press.

Sauer, H. (1976) Risk of illness and death in metropolitan and nonmetropolitan areas. Pp. 38-55 in E.W. Hassinger and L.R. Whiting, eds., Rural Health Services: Organization, Delivery, and Use. North Central Regional Center for Rural Development. Ames, Iowa.: Iowa State University Press.

Wennberg, J., and Gittelsohn, A. (1973) Small area variations in health care delivery. Science 182:1102-1107.

Wysong, J.A. (1975) The index of medical underservice: problems in meaning, measurements, and use. Journal of Health Services Research 10(2):127-135.

8

EDUCATION

Rural schools show the same diversity as other rural institutions and services. They range all the way from one-room little red schoolhouses, which are still used in a few rural areas, to large multi-grade consolidated schools that serve communities or even entire counties. This discussion of rural education is divided into four sections: issues in rural education; rural education and rural development; types of data needs; and available data.

ISSUES IN RURAL EDUCATION

Demographic changes can have a tremendous impact on schools. Areas of rapid population growth must provide for large numbers of new students and adapt to the new ideas, expectations, and values of in-migrants. Two respondents expressed their concern about increased school enrollments:

> The town of Evanston, Wyoming is becoming heavily impacted by coal, oil, and gas exploration and production. It is projected that 2,000 families will move into this area within the next three years (1980-1983). This of course will create problems not only in the community facilities, but also the school system [Uinta County, Wyoming].

> . . . the county has had problems in determining an accurate population count. . . . it would be extremely helpful to have data on the types of people purchasing in the county; specifically if they have school-aged children, if they are purchasing for speculation purposes, if they plan to live in the county year around, etc. . . [Teton County, Wyoming].

Areas with declining populations, however, must cope with surplus facilities, decreased public interest in the school system, and limited resources. As a midwestern respondent notes:

> [The high schools] are faced with declining enrollments and increased costs and at the same time complying with regulations

> to maintain their classification. Therefore, it is quite difficult to offer a quality educational program (Chariton County, Missouri).

Population decline may lead to school consolidation, but the decline is only one of many factors in the national consolidation trend. In 1931-32 the United States had 127,531 school districts and 232,750 elementary schools, of which 143,391 had only one teacher; in 1972 the nation had 16,960 school districts and 64,945 elementary schools, and only 1,475 had one teacher (National Center for Education Statistics 1980a). By the fall of 1979, the number of school districts had decreased to 15,929; 98 percent (15,625) of the districts operated schools; children in the other 304 districts generally were sent to nearby districts (National Center for Education Statistics 1980c).

School consolidation, encouraged by legislation in many states, was an effort to rationalize the system. Larger schools were considered more efficient, although Fox (1980), in a review of more than thirty studies, concluded that per pupil school costs have a U-shaped average cost curve and that economies were strongly related to such factors as transportation costs and the quality of education. Economies of scale, transportation costs, and declining enrollments have suggested conflicting answers to the question of appropriate school size.

School consolidation virtually eliminated what had been a unique rural institution--the one-room country school. Schools changed not only in size and in location, but in patterns of organization, curricula, and operating philosophies. The school disappeared as a central institution from many small communities, and rural schools were incorporated into a national system of education that has been labeled "the one best system" (Tyack 1974).

Rural areas have less access to educational opportunities and lower levels of educational attainment than urban areas (Fratoe 1978). However, if adjustment is made for socioeconomic and racial background, achievement test scores for residents of different kinds of communities may not differ significantly (Jencks et al. 1972). Although the achievement differences may disappear after adjustment for socioeconomic background, they remain a matter of concern. Other differences may not disappear, and the question of how to allocate resources remains (Tweeten 1979).

The ascriptive (i.e., citizenship, leadership, and personal adjustment) dimensions of schooling have received much less attention than the cognitive dimensions. Rural schools may perform well in the ascriptive areas considering the value structure of rural communities.

Rural education has special problems with resources. For example (Georgia Department of Community Affairs 1980:60):

> On a per-pupil basis, rural education is more expensive because fixed costs of administration, equipment, facilities, and support services are divided among fewer pupils. However, with few exceptions actual per-pupil expenditures are lower in rural counties than in urban and suburban counties.

A midwestern respondent also expressed concern about cost:

> The education and job training (VTAE) are quite adequate. It is the tax cost to pay for each that is the problem [Iowa County, Wisconsin].

There is a continuing debate about the effects of the pattern of consolidation on "rural development." Advocates argue that bringing rural schools into the "the one best system" expanded the range of alternatives for rural youth and prepared them better for more education or for migration, either of which improved the economic well-being of the student. Opponents say that consolidation removed the institutional basis of community life in many rural areas, introduced an educational emphasis insensitive to community and area needs, and encouraged the migration of young people to urban areas. Rosenfeld and Sher (1977:41-42) have argued that:

> Rural-school reform had significant effects on community life in rural America. By transferring control from the community to hired professionals, the traditional sense of involvement, intimacy, and identification existing between rural parents and their schools was diminished. By inauguration of a formalized, standardized, and urbanized education system, the traditional continuity between rural education and rural life was weakened. And by inculcating rural children with urban values, urban aspirations, and urban skills, the reformers encouraged <u>outmigration</u> while discouraging the preservation and improvement of traditional rural schools and communities.

Some respondents also expressed concern about the migration of locally educated young people, such as the following:

> . . . the 70's was a turning point for our area. For 70 years we raised children, the most valuable resource, and exported them gratis. One child through high school carries the equivalent monetary investment, approximately, as the value of the house in which the respective child lives.
>
> Rearing of youth for export to outside job markets is a tremendous wealth depleting process. To the extent that population growth rates exceed employment opportunities within the area, both the area and the individuals are economically benefited by their migration. It must be borne in mind that money invested in rearing these children (feeding, clothing, educating, recreating, transporting, etc.) is diverted from productive capital investment in the area; and youth leave for employment outside the area usually just as they reach the productive age, carrying this capital investment with them. An opposite effect upon the economy is felt when livestock or goods are sold out of the area and money is returned and used for reinvestment, payment on debts and so forth [Licking River District, Kentucky].

Education is the greatest item of public expenditure in most rural areas, but it is seldom considered explicitly as an agent of rural development because local decision makers control so few operational aspects of the school system. Integration into the state system of public education and the uniformity of professional training, curriculum, and organization leave little control in the hands of local people. Public education in the rural community, if it were a relatively self-controlled entity with its own standards, decision-making criteria, and systems of generating and reporting data, could be a potent force for rural development.

One of the greatest challenges facing rural education today is to strengthen and make explicit its link with community economic development. Solutions must go beyond concentrated training opportunities such as CETA programs. Training, and vocational training in particular, must be tailored to meet community needs and it must be coordinated with a comprehensive plan for economic development (Rosenfeld 1980).

The importance of coordinating vocational training with economic development is clearer than strategies for doing so. Rural conditions, program policies, economies of scale, and funding procedures may make coordination difficult. For example, small businesses might be one of the chief sources of employment in a rural community:

> The rural development issue most important to Glascock County, in my opinion, would be encouraging economic development. The bulk of the work force goes outside the county to find jobs. A small sewing plant, a produce canning plant, nursing home, and a small lumber mill are the major employers in the area [Waynesboro, Georgia].

The skills and knowledge that the Small Business Administration considers important to small businesses are taught in distributive education; students in welding classes learn nothing about the financial management or marketing needed in a welding business. The vocational agriculture model, which includes business management and operation, may be appropriate for many of the other subjects taught in rural vocational schools. As one respondent noted:

> Improved education and job training is considered by far our most awesome obstacle to development. In many cases the lack of education deters the desire for compatible development. For those who wish to initiate development within their rural areas, the lack of education does not provide them with the ability to secure development [Chattahoochee and Clay Counties, Georgia].

Some of the special problems encountered by rural areas in linking vocational training and job opportunities are described by the Georgia Department of Community Affairs (1980:65):

Better coordination is particularly important (and also more difficult) in rural areas where students may receive training in skills which can be used only in industries located elsewhere.

The traditional focus on training for profit-oriented enterprises largely ignores the potential for training in how to organize cooperatives which can provide jobs as well as essential services to the community. Examples are agricultural co-ops for storage and marketing of local small farm produce, or processing plants for canning, freezing, or freeze-drying of raw materials.

Particularly in rural areas, where employment opportunities are more limited, cross-training in skills is needed. For instance, few jobs may be available for a rural student with a certificate in plumbing. However, if he or she also had some knowledge of carpentry, electricity, or small motor repair, opportunities to work in maintenance, rehabilitation, and remodeling of houses and businesses might be found.

There are particular problems for the "working poor" in rural areas, where half the poor hold jobs. These people could benefit from education and training programs that would improve their earning power. They have a special need because, as jobholders, they are not eligible for most welfare programs.

Some states have successfully linked vocational education and development. Extensive state networks of vocational-technical institutions have been established in North Carolina and South Carolina to train prospective employees for industries moving into, or already in, the state (Appalachian Regional Commission 1979).

Nonmetropolitan areas receive far less federal financial assistance than metropolitan areas for employment training and vocational education: per-capita federal outlays in 1978 were $44.8 in metropolitan areas and $14.8 in nonmetropolitan areas (Hendler and Reid 1980:8). However, nonmetropolitan areas receive slightly more federal funding per capita than metropolitan areas for elementary, secondary, and adult education: per-capita federal outlays in fiscal 1978 for elementary, secondary, and adult education were $22.5 in nonmetropolitan areas and $18.4 in metropolitan areas.

Although some argue that increased data collection and centralized rural data information systems are needed to identify rural education needs (Parks and Sher 1978), the responses to our letter survey indicated that few of the perceived data needs of development relate directly to education.

TYPES OF DATA NEEDS

There is a lack of data on rural schools and rural education. The National Center for Education Statistics (NCES) currently reports most data on the basis of school size, but does not report education data on any basis that permits inferences about rural education. Staff at NCES, in response to an inquiry, stated that there was little demand for such a distinction, and an attempt to define rural schools would pose difficult problems. The last NCES survey of rural education was a city-suburban-rural survey made in 1956; that survey defined rural schools as schools in rural counties.

Appraising the contribution of the education system to the quality of life of rural people requires data on schooling inputs and on outputs. In general, data on inputs, such as expenditures per student, teacher salaries and qualifications (academic degrees, experience, etc.), class size, school size, and curriculum, are more comprehensive than are data on outputs, which include retention (or dropout) rates, age-grade retardation, incidence of post-secondary schooling and educational attainment. One respondent noted:

> We need more statistics to tell us how serious the school dropout problem is and to tell us what happens to students after high school. That is, what percentage enter college, vocational training and the like. We need this by local school districts, but also for the state and the nation [Ashley County, Arkansas].

The NCES national longitudinal studies described later in this chapter provide most of these statistics at the national level.

The data collection efforts of federal agencies are designed not only to satisfy federal policy-making needs, but also to serve potential users ranging from local school districts to offcials at the federal level. In order to identify deficiencies in education data for rural areas more fully, we distinguish among the various actual and potential users of data pertaining to public education:

Federal and state education agencies These agencies administer programs that operate through the public schools. Since these agencies are primarily responsible for initiating data collection efforts and have statutory responsibility to collect data, existing data are probably adequate, in the opinion of these agencies, for administering, implementing, and evaluating existing programs. If data were not sufficient, they would initiate further data collection efforts.

Researchers Scholars are never fully satisfied with available data. Additional data are needed in a number of areas, such as the effects of school consolidation and the ascriptive dimensions of education.

Federal and state policy makers New public education initiatives during the 1980s will be generated from analysis of existing data about public education. Outputs are an important recurring question: What is the return of investment in public education? Who benefits and how much? More valid data relevant to such questions could lead to legislative and policy initiatives.

Local education agencies Local schools are the primary suppliers of public education data, but most data are supplied at the request of state and federal agencies. These data satisfy some, but not all, of the needs of their own planning and administrative functions. Local education agencies could benefit from additional output data, and they need data pertaining to changes in the social, economic, and demographic characteristics of the areas they serve. As one respondent noted:

> School districts and other units of government need more up-to-date information on migration, population characteristics, etc. for planning purposes [Searcy County, Arkansas].

In order to plan, local school districts need projections of student enrollment, data on the local tax base, knowledge of public expectations of education in the locality, and similar information that is not usually considered education data.

Rural development planners and decision makers Public schools typically represent the largest category of public investment in rural communities, and schools are an important agency of social and economic development. Information about the costs and benefits of public education should be included in local and regional social and economic development plans. Some respondents noted the importance of education planning to rural development:

> An adequate supply of skilled labor is difficult to obtain in areas with an economy that is subject to extreme cyclical variation such as Coconino County. There is no full-time Community College program available in the Flagstaff area, limiting the local labor pool's access to technical training opportunities. The local university has not been able to bring its professional programs to as mature a level as the universities located in the urban counties of Arizona. Clearly, improved educational and occupational training activities would result in a long-term benefit to Coconino County [Coconino County, Arizona].

> Our county public school system has over-crowded classrooms in some schools and insufficient school population to support the schools in other communities. Long range planning for improvement in the school system is hindered by the constant turnover in county political leadership [Lee County, Virginia].

> There is a need for more college graduates in agriculture with rural backgrounds to meet the needs in agricultural education and agri-business positions. High school students need to be made more aware of the potential in the field of agri-business requiring a baccalaureate or higher degree in agricultural specialization [Martin County, Minnesota].

There is little evidence that planners and decision makers have much information about public education and its impact. There is a lack of data on schooling for the appropriate jurisdictional level, especially data on outputs, e.g., retention (or dropout) rates, age-grade retardation, incidence of post-secondary schooling and educational attainment.

These five categories of users have been arrayed on a spectrum from "most use" to "least use" of current education statistics. In general, existing data, with the major exception of performance or output data, are more or less sufficient to meet administrative needs, but new policy directions are likely to be stimulated by additional data. There appears to be little systematic use of available data in many local planning and development activities. Local schools could benefit more from district socioeconomic data, and local rural development efforts could benefit from additional data on local school costs and benefits. Both of these needs are more a matter of improving access to existing data rather than collecting new data.

AVAILABLE DATA

The Bureau of the Census and the National Center for Education Statistics in the Department of Education routinely collect data on education. Other agencies may sponsor special studies and prepare reports on certain aspects of rural education. For example, the Economic and Statistics Service in the U.S. Department of Agriculture published a series of rural development research reports, some of which focus on education. One recent report, Rural Education and Rural Labor Force in the Seventies (Fratoe 1978), discusses schooling inputs (i.e., resources, staff) and outputs (i.e., school achievement) and the relationship between each and labor force participation.

Directory of Federal Agency Education Data Tapes

The Federal Interagency Consortium of Users of Education Statistics, organized in 1975, has attempted to coordinate education data collection. The Directory of Federal Agency Education Tapes describes each study or data collection activity, the methodology, and the population for tapes from agencies such as the National Institute of Education, Office of Civil Rights, National Science Foundation, Bureau of the Census, and National Center for Health Statistics.

National Center for Education Statistics

The National Center for Education Statistics collects data on several areas of education and publishes numerous reports derived from the data. NCES also publishes a Directory of Computer Tapes in which the survey area, years, variables, etc. are outlined for NCES tapes (National Center for Education Statistics 1980b).

Elementary and secondary education In cooperation with state education agencies, NCES collects and compiles statistics on elementary and secondary schools, students, staff, and financial characteristics. These data are collected annually for public schools and quinquennially for nonpublic schools. The data on the universe of public and nonpublic schools are found in the "common core of data." Common core of data school items include the name and address of the school district, type of curriculum, fall school membership by grade, the number of high school graduates, the numbers and types of teachers and other school staff by sex and age, revenues from federal, state, or local government sources, and total capital outlays and expenditures.

Data on public and nonpublic schools are made available by NCES in several ways, including computer tapes, reports such as *Statistics for Public Elementary and Secondary Day Schools*, and the *Digest of Education Statistics*. Data are also collected and reported biennially on the financing of elementary and secondary education and in particular, on the degree to which equalization of resources among districts has been achieved. Special surveys are occasionally conducted to provide general statistics on the characteristics of students, graduates, and staff that cannot be easily obtained from information collected by the state agencies. Among these are "fast response" surveys and special studies on demand for teachers and language minorities and bilingual education.

Statistics may be reported by school size or district. A number of years ago, NCES attempted to obtain maps of all school districts in the United States so that census data could be derived for school districts. Because maps were frequently not available for districts with fewer than 300 students, those districts were excluded. A tape is now available from NCES providing both data collected by NCES from school districts and data from the 1970 census data for the school districts with enrollment over 300.

Higher education The Higher Education General Information Survey (HEGIS) provides statistical information on equality of access to college, the financial status of private colleges and universities, and shifting enrollment patterns. Special studies on recent college graduates, adult education participation, and race and ethnicity supplement the survey.

Adult and vocational education Information on adult education is obtained from individual participants (on demographic characteristics, employment, reasons for taking courses, subject) and from institutions delivering different forms of adult education (e.g., non-credit, home-study, community organizations, 2-year institutions). The vocational education data system (VEDS) provides information on total enrollment, enrollment by occupational field, staff, financing, and employer-student follow-up.

National longitudinal studies The national longitudinal studies program involves periodic examination of the educational and occupational attainment, aspirations, attitudes, and motivations of high school graduates to provide on-going descriptive information about the transition from school to work. The first panel surveyed is a sample of approximately 20,000 members of the high school senior class of 1972. The second panel is a sample of the sophomore and senior classes of 1980 and is referred to as the high school and beyond study.

Learning resources NCES collects data on: libraries, their staff, collections, holdings, services, cooperative loan arrangements, facilities, and expenditures; the availability and use of television and other communication technologies in elementary, secondary, and higher education (jointly sponsored with the Corporation for Public Broadcasting); museums including type, programs, staff, holdings, and financing.

Three summary publications drawing on many NCES surveys and other data sources are prepared annually by the Statistical Information Office of NCES: The Condition of Education, the Digest of Education Statistics, and Projections of Education Statistics. The Condition uses a framework of social indicators to provide statistics on American education with tables, graphs, and supporting text. The Digest provides a compendium of information on education from preprimary to graduate school. Projections presents historical trends, enrollment projections, expenditures, staff and graduates for 10-year periods.

Although considerable data about enrollment, staffing, services, and facilities are collected, it is not now possible to identify or separate rural and urban districts; it is possible only to separate districts in metropolitan counties from those in nonmetropolitan counties.

Recommendation: The panel recommends that codes for rural-urban location of school district be recorded with all school district data (pupil, personnel, curriculum, finance, and facilities) to facilitate comparison of resources available to rural and urban school districts. The National Center for Education Statistics is the appropriate organization to implement this recommendation.

A first step would be to use the county classification scheme recommended in Chapter 4. Since a county may have more than one school district, a more refined alternative would be based on the size of the largest place in the school district. When the school district mapping project has been completed, the Bureau of the Census will be able to provide data by school district. The census data could be used to classify school districts on a rural-urban continuum or by the largest place in the school district. Ultimately it would be desirable to classify schools on a rural-urban continuum. Policy issues on school finance and the equitable distribution of resources could be clarified if the recommended codes were available. Data on rural schools rather than on districts would be more useful for addressing some policy issues, but classification of schools would be difficult and would impose an additional burden on the schools.

National Institute of Education

The National Institute of Education (NIE) sponsors the National Assessment of Educational Progess, a sample survey that collects information concerning the knowledge, understanding, skill, and attitudes of four age cohorts. Data are available for rural schools (see Appendix E).

Bureau of the Census

The Bureau of the Census collects information on education in several ways. The decennial census reports on years of school completed, school enrollment, and school type cross-tabulated by variables such as age, sex, race (and poverty status in some cases) for states and substate political jurisdictions. The October current population survey provides statistics on enrollment in schools by age group and also on educational attainment (for people 25 years of age and older) by sex and race. The survey of income and education, based on personal interviews with 151,000 households, was conducted by the Census Bureau in 1976 and provides data on language spoken, school enrollment, educational attainment, and poverty or welfare status. The census of governments collects finance data for school districts and counties (see Appendix E).

U.S. Department of Labor

The Bureau of Labor Statistics collects and publishes data on the work force, including educational level (see Appendix E).

DATA GAP

1. Data on schooling for the appropriate jurisdictional level, especially data on outputs, e.g., retention (or dropout) rates, age-grade retardation, incidence of post-secondary schooling and educational attainment.

REFERENCES

Appalachian Regional Commission (1979) A Report to Congress on the Continuation of the Appalachian Regional Commission, 1979. Washington, D.C.: Appalachian Regional Commission.

Fox, W.F. (1980) Relationships Between Size of Schools and School Districts and the Cost of Education. Technical Bulletin No. 1621. Economics, Statistics, and Cooperatives Service. Washington, D.C.: U.S. Department of Agriculture.

Fratoe, F.A. (1978) Rural Education and Rural Labor Force in the Seventies. Rural Development Research Report No. 5. Economics,

Statistics, and Cooperatives Service. Washington, D.C.: U.S. Department of Agriculture.

Georgia Department of Community Affairs (1980) Growth and Change in Rural Georgia: Issues and Opportunities. Atlanta, Ga.: Georgia Department of Community Affairs.

Hendler, C.I., and Reid, J.N. (1980) Federal Outlays in Fiscal 1978. Rural Development Research Report No. 25. Economics, Statistics, and Cooperatives Service. Washington, D.C.: U.S. Department of Agriculture.

Jencks, C., Smith, M., Aeland, H., Bane, M., Cohen, D., Gintis, H., Heyns, B., and Michelson, S. (1972) Inequality. New York: Basic Books.

National Center for Education Statistics (1980a) Digest of Education Statistics 1980. Washington, D.C.: U.S. Department of Health, Education, and Welfare

National Center for Education Statistics (1980b) Directory of Computer Tapes. Washington, D.C.: U.S. Department of Education.

National Center for Education Statistics (1980c) Early Release, December 17, 1980. Document 80-129. U.S. Department of Education, Washington, D.C.

Parks, G., and Sher, J.P. (1979) Imaginary Gardens? Real Problems: An Analysis of Federal Information Sources on Rural Education. Las Cruces, N.M.: ERIC Clearinghouse on Rural Education and Small Schools.

Rosenfeld, S.A. (1980) Shaping a rural vocational education policy. VocED 55(March):17-21.

Rosenfeld, S.A., and Sher, J.P. (1977) Panaceas and policy. Pp. 11-42 in J. P. Sher, ed., Education in Rural America: A Reassessment of Conventional Wisdom. Boulder, Colo.: Westview Press.

Sher, J.P., ed. (1977) Education in Rural America: A Reassessment of Conventional Wisdom. Boulder, Colo.: Westview Press.

Tweeten, L. (1979) Rural Education and Rural Development. Paper presented at the National Seminar on Rural Education, May 29-31, 1979. Sponsored by U.S. Department of Health, Education, and Welfare and U.S. Department of Agriculture, Washington, D.C.

Tyack, D.B. (1974) The One Best System. Cambridge, Mass.: Harvard University Press.

9

PUBLIC SERVICES AND COMMUNITY FACILITIES

INTRODUCTION

There is great variation among rural communities in the quality and quantity of services received. When measured by national, i.e., urban-based, standards for specific services and facilities, rural areas overall probably have inferior services, although there is some evidence that the gap is narrowing (Deavers and Brown 1979, Rainey and Rainey 1978, Stocker 1977).

An underlying question is whether national standards should ever be the main reference in guiding decisions for rural communities. Some minimal standards for quality and availability of services are undoubtedly justified for certain dimensions of health and safety, such as clean water and air. But in many programs attention to the specific needs, desires, and capabilities of rural people must lead to qualifications of urban-based criteria. This is especially necessary for programs in which methods of service production and delivery differ greatly between urban and rural areas, making it difficult to use the same measures of quality and quantity. As one respondent complained:

> . . . not only for this region, but in all parts of the U.S., many communities are facing unreasonable standards for water treatment and sewer discharge, placed upon them by the Federal Government [Upper Explorerland Regional Planning Commission, Iowa].

Likewise, it makes little sense to apply city standards of fire fighting or of park acreage minima to small towns and open country areas.

Another problem in measuring the adequacy of services is that they are perceived in a very subjective way. One respondent discussed the difficulties this presents:

> We have found that even in a relatively small study area there is no shared perception of "adequate." In discussing wastewater treatment, water supply, fire protection, police protection, or transportation improvements, the perception of adequacy rests on

> the needs of the client group. Adequate transportation for handicapped and senior citizens is programmatically quite different from adequate transportation for a young family. The growth of single interest constituencies seems to have increased the threshold of adequacy to new heights even in rural areas [Livingston County, Michigan].

NATIONAL DATA NEEDS

Issues and Decisions

Establishing, funding, and delivering public services and facilities is the primary job of local governments and other community-based agencies, with less responsibility for state governments and regional organizations. Washington's role is much more limited, but it has expanded rapidly as local programs have become more intertwined with federal goals and policies. Starting with the economic and social development legislation of the 1960s and marked especially by the Rural Development Act of 1972, recent administrations and federal legislators have looked more closely than before at rural services. In this national scenario, community services and facilities are seen as major tools for enhancing local economies and lives, so a number of federal grant programs help to fund the capital and operating activities of local agencies. Other national policies are intended to influence the ways in which services and facilities are provided in both urban and rural communities, by applying standards of equal protection, affirmative action, and occupational health and safety.

Grant programs draw the most attention. While big cities and metropolitan areas receive the bulk of grant money, federal aid to small towns and nonmetropolitan areas increased greatly in the past decade. The enactment of general revenue sharing (GRS) in 1972 was a key development for local governments in rural communities. Other major federal grant programs of benefit to such communities that started or were enlarged in the 1970s include the programs of the Farmers Home Administration (FmHA), Economic Development Administration (EDA), Environmental Protection Agency (EPA), and Department of Housing and Urban Development (HUD). Including general revenue sharing, these programs distributed more than $12 billion in grants and loans to local agencies for public services and facilities in fiscal 1978. About 27 percent of this amount--$3.4 billion--went to communities in nonmetropolitan areas (Hendler and Reid 1980).

The characteristics (availability, quality, financing, etc.) of services and facilities themselves are not the major criteria by which funds are distributed. Allocation decisions, whether in entitlement or block grant programs that employ standard formulae or in more discretionary programs that rely on "softer" sets of data, are based primarily on such factors as population, income, employment, age, and housing conditions (see, for example, Grassberger 1978). There are some exceptions, to be sure, including the local tax effort element in the GRS program, effluent discharge conditions in the case of EPA grants for wastewater disposal systems, and the absence of the pertinent facility in the case of FmHA loans and grants for public water supply and wastewater systems. National agency administrators who review grant applications in the more discretionary programs may pay some attention to documentation of service conditions and needs, but in these cases too, the allocation emphasis seems to be on demographic and economic measures of local need.

Allocations for specific programs implement more basic policy decisions. The billions distributed to local governments and other agencies are really national investments in community infrastructures (Deavers and Brown 1979). What are the criteria that guide these investments? There is little in the way of unified national policy behind the many programs. Federal priorities and policies seem to shift often, and the aid programs for rural communities were established at different times, are administered by separate cabinet agencies, and have varying objectives. One planner we interviewed told this illustrative story:

> We have problems in shifting federal criteria and how this affects our ability to put together programs. One example is an old bowling alley at Kings Beach (Lake Tahoe area) . . . it was taken over by the state and then leased to the public utility district [a local public entity in an unincorporated area that operates water, sewer, and recreation programs]. They sought a grant to fix up the place and turn it into a useful public facility which went through our agency. We submitted a grant application to Seattle [regional EDA office]. They said the emphasis that year was on senior citizens. I think because they were impressed by a program in downtown Oakland and assumed everybody else should have been in the same boat. So we redid the application with this in mind. But then the priorities changed again . . . the new emphasis became energy conservation . . . I think because the national EDA people had become enamored with a solar energy and conservation demonstration in Minnesota. So we revised our application again and made the project a model of energy conservation. But all we wanted to do from the very start was renovate the building so that it could be used by various groups in the community [Sierra Planning Organization and Sierra Economic Development District].

A rural community may obtain funds for a given project from more than one source. Funds for a sewer treatment plant, for example, could be obtained from any one of four different federal grant programs, depending on how the proposed project can be matched with particular economic or social objectives. The public works grants of EDA are intended to stimulate local economies, HUD is interested in improving low-income and moderate-income neighborhoods with its community development block grants, EPA wants to clean up the nation's streams and lakes with its wastewater management grants, and FmHA is concerned generally with improving rural life in its water and wastewater disposal loans and grants (U.S. Department of Housing and

Urban Development 1978). Such duplication, often deplored by critics of the federal grants system who worry about waste and counterproductive efforts, may not be all bad from the viewpoint of rural communities seeking aid.

In dealing with the distribution of federal funds, decision makers in the national government are faced with a number of continuing issues. One has to do with the proper mix in community investments between economic development and human development. Should grant programs emphasize the support of local projects that help to create jobs, or should the federal priority be on public services and facilities that benefit households? Should the federal government subsidize services to small communities what are havens for middle-class people from nearby high-cost urban centers? There is also concern with the problems of local growth and decline. Should federal funds be directed to the infrastructure needs of rapidly growing communities and away from declining towns? Such a shift would subsidize urban-to-rural migration and increase the growth rate of fast-growing areas.

Finally, there is the perennial issue of national priorities versus local values, a conflict only partly resolved in the 1970s by the decentralization of federal aid through the creation of block grant programs. It is in the rural communities where local values and practices are most at odds with national policies. For example, a Kentucky respondent complained that the Davis-Bacon Act, which requires prevailing urban wage rates to be paid for work on federal projects in rural areas, is expensive and unfair. Yet the dependency on outside resources for the funding of public facilities has increased the most in the past decade in these same communities. Political circumstances largely dictate the resolution of national-local issues on a program-by-program basis, but data on the quality and quantity of services and facilities in rural communities can contribute to the design of changes in investment policy. At least, national decision makers should know how current programs affect the distribution and availability of services and the economic development of rural communities.

Data Requirements

Most individual services are organized in combination, and their quantity and quality are the result of political and administrative arrangements that differ from community to community. Various data are required in order to determine the effect of institutional arrangements on services and facilities. Knowing how well rural communities are served requires, first, basic information on public services and facilities. To what degree are particular services provided or not provided in rural communities? What is their quantity? What is their quality?

While the numbers and other measures are important, their meaning for national policy purposes is limited without some reference to goals and objectives. If the objective is to identify the needs of rural areas and the gap between existing and desirable service patterns, establishing reasonable standards is necessary. Ideally, standards that are applied to specific services should combine minimal necessities with a realistic interpretation of how much can be accomplished in rural communities with likely local, state, and national resources.

A higher level of analysis would require the ability to relate straightforward measures of output to the characteristics of communities and subcommunity populations. Communities with good services and facilities may still contain large numbers of unserved people, which may be a matter of limited access--physical, economic, or social--rather than the absolute absence of a service or facility. Existing facilities in rural areas, such as hospitals, may be underutilized because of location, ignorance, or organization. As to variation among rural communities, population centers such as county seats have more than their share of facilities while other county areas are relatively underserved.

Local governments are the mechanisms through which needs and preferences at the community level are translated into policies. The major data issue in this area is improving the ability of decision makers and researchers to differentiate among various types of local government situations. As of 1977, there were 54,000 such units--including counties, municipalities, townships, special districts, and school districts (Bureau of the Census 1978). Most of course are very small units, serving either small population centers, country areas without a population center, or a combination of both.

Traditionally the concern of scholars and others has been to demonstrate the diseconomies associated with small size and to promote the reorganization of rural governments into larger and presumably more efficient units (Committee on Economic Development 1966, Bish 1977, Fox 1980). More recently the emphasis has shifted to enhancing the capacity of rural governments as a compensation for limitations of staff and expertise (Grosenick 1977, Sokolow 1979, Deavers and Brown 1979). There is enormous diversity among rural governments, and in order to understand them, information is needed on: how local governments are organized, particularly the administrative arrangement of units without chief executives; the performance of local governments in making policy; expenditures as related to size and function; public service responsibilities by type of local government; and how service responsibilities are shared with other kinds of providers, including individual households, voluntary associations, and private firms.

There is a widespread impression that public services in rural communities are underfinanced because of limited wealth and taxing abilities. To what extent do rural communities lack the fiscal capacity to support needed services and facilities? Is limited capacity largely an artifact of revenue sources that imperfectly reflect actual community wealth? Or is limited taxing capacity more nearly a reflection of unwillingness rather than capacity to tax? Answers to these and related policy questions can be provided only by accurate and comprehensive data about the sources, levels, and burdens of public revenues. Data on taxes and other revenues serve a number of other uses as well, including the measurement of economic effects on individuals and groups, the determination of location and other business decisions, and the allocation of federal and state funds. Revenue data should be available for various levels of community, from the county level down to the smallest taxing or governmental jurisdiction. For each important revenue source, information is needed on coverage, rates, and yields.

Tax data for use in assessing the general welfare should probably be collected on a county basis and include: type of tax (income, sales, real property, personal property, mineral severance, etc.); tax rates; and the total amount of money collected under each tax. Tax data for use in assessing the relative attractiveness of an area as a business location might include all of the items for assessing general welfare, as indicated above, plus those taxes that are collected from business firms but not from individuals. Included in this category would be state and local excise taxes and corporate income tax rates. It is important to recognize that the complexity of the administration of tax management to the firm, i.e., its bothersome nature, may be more significant than the level of the tax in deterring business and industry locations.

What tax data are necessary for formula funding depends on the objectives of the funding program of interest and, thus, it is difficult to anticipate data needs. Formula funding, such as general revenue sharing, often includes local tax effort as one determinant of the allocation. The inclusion of local tax effort appears to discriminate against communities that provide services through volunteers rather than through the public sector (Lederer and Badenhop 1976).

The property tax deserves special attention, both because it is the single most important revenue source for most local governments and because it is administered by thousands of counties, townships, towns, and other local governments in complex and confusing ways. Much of the complexity comes from diverse assessment practices in separate (even neighboring) jurisdictions, with the result that there are wide fluctuations from one community to another (and between different parcels in individual jurisdictions) in how well actual values are reflected in assessments (Stocker 1977).

Service charges and fees, increasingly being used by local governments to reduce their reliance on taxes, carry redistributional implications. Decisions to depend more heavily on such revenues are often justified by the need to allocate the costs of services to those who use them, but the movement from general taxes to specific charges often increases the relative burden-- and reduces the benefits of government--for poorer people.

A third major source of funds for local governments, including those in local communities, is intergovernmental grants and transfers. What are the consequences for local government of increasing reliance on state and federal funds? To what extent are particular communities and local services and facilities subsidized by the nation as a whole? Knowing how grant programs affect local public economies is important information for national decision makers.

Major Data Sources

The census of governments Conducted and published at 5-year intervals, the census of governments is the most comprehensive source of information relating to the organization, finances, and employment rolls of governments in the United States. The emphasis is on local governments--counties, municipalities, townships, school districts, special districts-- although some data items are also presented for national and state governments (see Appendix E for more detail). A related and less detailed source of information on local governments is the annual report on finances and public employment published by the Bureau of the Census.

Throughout the several volumes based on the census of governments, data are presented according to several common classifications--by national summary, states, SMSA groups, individual SMSAs, county areas; and by population or enrollment (school districts) size of groups of jurisdictions. Most of the data represent virtually complete enumerations of local governments, although there is some underreporting among small local (and presumably rural) governments.

Federal outlay data Because of the interest in tracking federal expenditures, two agencies now publish data on national government outlays. Reports of the Department of Agriculture (USDA) aggregate these data for four categories of metropolitan areas and six groups of nonmetropolitan areas nationwide (see, for example, Hendler and Reid 1980). They are compilations based in turn on county-level compilations prepared annually by the Community Services Administration (CSA) (see, e.g., Community Services Administration 1979). The data are presented both according to general function (e.g., physical investment, community facilities) and specific program (e.g., community facilities loans, FmHA).

Nearly all federal expenditures are included in the USDA and CSA reports, although for many programs estimates of county-level spending--rather than actual counts--are presented. The inclusion of program identification numbers from the Catalog of Federal Domestic Assistance (Office of Management and Budget 1980) in the USDA and CSA tables permits the analysis of grants to local governments for improving public facilities. The CSA reports are disaggregated down to individual counties and cities of more than 25,000 population.

Other outlay data Other sources of outlay data include the specialized reports of public agencies. HUD and EDA publish information on their annual grants to local governments, including individual recipients and amounts. The amount of general revenue sharing funds allocated to individual cities, counties, and townships, as well as the pertinent formula factors of population, income, and tax effort, are published by the Treasury Department. Regional or area offices of other federal agencies prepare less formal reports on the grant activities in their jurisdictions. Some state governments issue more comprehensive reports on a range of public finance items--expenditures, revenue, debt, assessed valuations, tax rates, etc.--for local government units. For example, the controller of California publishes annual reports on the financial transactions of cities, counties, and special districts.

National rural community facilities assessment study The FmHA has recently undertaken a comprehensive, systematic national effort to assess the status of rural community facilities, and the pilot study has been completed (see Abt Associates 1979, 1980). This pilot study collected extensive information about the quantity and quality of 44 different types of facilities in 12 functional areas. Based on the outcome of the pilot study, the FmHA (as of late 1980) is sponsoring a $5.5 million national survey of 1,000 communities, a sample size adequate to yield good estimates of facilities for the nation and for six size categories of communities. FmHA is seeking funding assistance from other agencies to expand the total sample size to 2,346 communities, which would yield good estimates at the state level. A goal of producing reliable estimates for substate units would require a still larger sample, which is not considered feasible in terms of funding.

The objective of this study is to guide future investment actions of the national and state governments in rural areas. Thus it will include an assessment, by state and size and type of community, of the extent to which facilities meet "minimum performance standards" in each functional area. To establish these standards--really performance "criteria" rather than absolute nationwide standards (which could suggest urban biases)--the advice of experts in each of the functional areas was sought.

Data Shortfalls

Aggregation and disaggregation The quinquennial census of governments, the major source of national information on local governments, contains far less about rural than about urban patterns of public finance, the most widely used information on governmental activities. Much more detail is presented for larger and more urban units of governments, both aggregated to national and state summaries and disaggregated down to individual SMSAs and large governments. Obviously there is far more interest in metropolitan than in nonmetropolitan patterns among users of federal statistics, in light of the 3:1 metropolitan-nonmetropolitan population ratio nationally. And users of rural area data do not have a statistical category comparable to the SMSA, for which more government data are reported than for any other geographic unit.

Short of achieving full comparability with urban data, data from the census of governments could be presented in ways to increase knowledge of rural governmental patterns. Summary nonmetropolitan data are needed for selected finance and employment items for which SMSA totals are already tabulated. Since "nonmetropolitan" is a residual category at the national and state levels, this would be a relatively modest burden on existing computation and publication procedures. Further disaggregation would be more difficult. It is certainly not feasible to demand national published data for each of the many thousands of small local governments, considering the enormous expense of preparing such tabulations and the limited interest in this information. A good compromise would be to extend the standard statistical area (SSA) concept to the entire geographic area of the nation, including rural areas, as recommended in Chapter 2. It would be desirable to have public finance and other data for individual SSAs, ideally in a separate census of governments volume similar to the Local Government in Metropolitan Areas publication.

Some consideration should also be given to the tabulation and presentation of data according to other geographic categories. Although useful for many statistical purposes, a category such as the SSA does not distinguish among different types of rural communities. It would be useful to break down community finance and public service data by incorporated or unincorporated status, a classification that recognizes basic governmental differences. Data by population size of village or city are also needed.

Public finance data More is known about public finance than about any other aspect of governments in the United States. Readily available in quantitative form, such data are used as the major indicators of governmental inputs (revenues) and outputs (expenditures). Yet economists and others note that finance data have serious limitations as measures of public services (Ostrom 1977, Deavers and Brown 1979).

On the input side, revenue figures are only approximate indicators of how the burden of supporting a government is shared. While it is possible to make some inferences about the distribution of costs (comparing general fund sources with service charges, for example), the data do not indicate how specific revenue sources are spread among income or other groups. On the output side, expenditures are seldom adequate measures of the performance of public agencies or of the quality of the services they produce. They are also of limited use in the evaluation of program effects simply because they do not reveal much about the beneficiaries of the various kinds of expenditures.

Overcoming these limitations requires the development of other, more qualitative measures of services and governmental performance. But some tinkering with finance data is possible. As applied to rural governments, improvement is needed in regard to local property tax information, including assessments, rates, and collection. A community's property tax base is frequently taken to indicate its relative wealth and capacity to fund services, both often misleading interpretations because of variations in assessment practices, the tendency to undervalue properties, and the inclination, in rural areas especially, to limit tax rates.

While data on property taxes may overestimate the poverty of many rural communities, data on expenditures and on government employees often underestimate the actual resources that go into public services. Some economists have noted that relatively low salaries are paid to public employees in small communities and that extensive use is made of unpaid or part-time personnel in certain programs, thus reducing the demand on public funds (Stocker 1977, Hitzhusen 1977).

There is some indication that voluntarism is relatively more important in small than in large communities, although the supporting data are very weak (Hitzhusen 1977). One possible consequence is that rural areas receive less than their fair share of general revenue sharing funds since the allocation formula includes local tax effort, which, because of voluntarism, is not comparable with metropolitan tax efforts. The lack of reliable data on volunteer efforts in support of community services warrants increased attention. National decision makers should consider this in the design of future programs.

Extending the FmHA study Trend data on the adequacy of rural public services and facilities are needed. Such data could be collected by the national rural community facilities assessment study if it is institutionalized and made a periodic event--perhaps at 5-year or 10-year intervals--using the same sample of communities. This possibility was implicit in the FmHA's original plans, although the panel recognizes that future efforts probably will depend on the usefulness, administrative ease, and cost of the initial study. The study is now confined to the description of physical facilities--buildings and equipment--and thus does not cover such factors as the operation and financing of services, public versus private sector responsibilities, and community attitudes and service preferences. Perhaps such items could be piggybacked on the basic study in future, periodic surveys. An alternative strategy would be to use the identical sample for surveys on other topics. In either case, the accumulation of separate but interrelated sets of data for the same communities would provide a valuable information source for those concerned about rural community services.

STATE AND LOCAL DATA NEEDS

Issues and Decisions

The diversity of uses and users of data on public services and community facilities is considerably greater at state and local than at federal levels. State governments establish broad policies for their rural areas, and set the service, regulatory, and revenue powers of their local governments. Regional agencies--a fairly new development--strive to improve the economies of their rural areas; engage in land use, transportation, and other forms of planning; and seek intergovernmental coordination. Local governments and other community agencies have the immediate job of delivering services, constructing and maintaining facilities, regulating some public behavior, raising revenues, and representing their constituents. Business firms take account of public infrastructures, land use policies, and taxes in their locational and investment decisions. Above all, rural residents--voters, taxpayers, consumers of service, advocates of particular changes, supporters of the status quo, etc.--deserve clear and accurate information on the adequacy of public programs in their communities and regions.

A measure of the importance of public services to local decision makers is that this topic was mentioned much more frequently than any other general issue by the local people who responded to our letter survey (see Appendix B). Second place went to the related topic of resolving financial problems, with emphasis on obtaining grants. Public service and financial problems were usually mentioned together, as these representative comments demonstrate:

> Local governments in rural areas find it almost impossible to generate the necessary revenue to provide any major capital investment for a needed service such as water or sewage. Inflation has taken its toll and set the rural area efforts back tremendously to the extent now that no major financial undertaking can be accomplished without federal or state assistance [Carter County, Missouri].

> Installment or improvement of utility systems is needed in many rural communities. However, limited sources of financial asssistance or the financial inability of the municipalities, especially those with an elderly age structure, to make any investments frequently impede the adequate provision of utility services [Broome County, New York].

Higher-than-average growth rates have exacerbated these problems in some areas, as these respondents noted:

> . . . certain unincorporated areas of [our] county are urbanizing at a greater rate than the area's largest city. This has resulted in an unprecedented demand for county services. Due to the county's size (18,500 square miles), delivery of such services are quite expensive [Coconino County, Arizona].

> . . . our three-county jurisdicton is experiencing a rate of growth which is approximately three times that of the state average and consequently the provision of an adequate public utility and facility infrastructure is essential to: (a) an adequate rural lifestyle; (b) the continuation of our economic prosperity; and (c) our ability to channel future growth in an orderly manner . . . [South Central Illinois Regional Planning and Development Commission].

A common political problem in growing communities is the reconciliation of two coincident but distinct preferences--the demands for urban services and for the protection of rural amenities--as these officials noted:

> . . . almost 1/3 of the county is considered to be rural . . . many of these new rural dwellers came from the urban areas and once there they realized that the conveniences that they took

> for granted were not available. Then follows the pressure via complaints--roads too narrow, no curb and gutter, distance too great for shopping convenience, well not able to keep up with demand, septic system produces foul odor or does not function properly . . . the list goes on [Baltimore County, Maryland].

> Within the county the political balance has slowly shifted from being a farmer-dominated Board of Commissioners to one in which there is a fairly even balance now between the newcomers and the long-term farm community residents. The newcomers, while fleeing the high taxes of Lansing still demand the minimum levels of services to which one grows accustomed in urban areas. They tend to be urban and heterogeneous in values and lifestyles. Newcomers are viewed as liberals in Clinton County, but could not make it through the door into a good liberal cocktail party in East Lansing or Ann Arbor. Clinton County farmers and other long-time residents tend to retain more of the 19th century conservative values, resent welfare programs, believe people should earn their own way, and are opposed to raising taxes to provide services for the southern part of the County into which the new residents are moving [Clinton County, Michigan].

Many of our respondents addressed the specific problems of seeking federal and state funds--the local costs involved, undesirable grant requirements and mandates, and the inequities of proposal review and fund allocations. The following are some representative comments about federal fund allocations:

> Even when a federal attempt is made to "allocate" assistance under a given program between urban and rural applicants, the former typically receive 80% of the funds with the remaining 20% thrown into a highly competitive "discretionary pot" which is susceptible to political influence and never close to sufficient, given the "rural demand" as depicted by the number of requests submitted [South Central Illinois Regional Planning and Development Commission].

> In nearly all federal programs, the funds are allocated based upon need and project impact for the number of persons that will be served. . . . It is difficult for rural communities to compete under these grant conditions [Upper Explorerland Regional Planning Commission, Iowa].

> Because these communities are small in population and have difficulty in generating the local match required by most grants, their access to grant programs is diminished. If in the era of a balanced federal budget, "bigger bang for the buck" becomes the measure justifying federal aid, we can expect sparsely populated rural areas to bear a proportionately greater burden in funding reductions [North Central New Mexico Economic Development District].

> The whole system of getting state and federal funds at the local level is stupid. If you are good at "B'Sing," have taken the latest course in "grant writing," pay a consultant a fat fee or worse yet, a percentage, are of the proper political party at the time, have an influential congressman or representative in your district, then your chance of success is almost assured. However, after you get it, you find out the red tape and compliance requirements make you spend more than you've got. Kindly note that "need," necessity," etc. do not really seem to be criteria [Ross County, Ohio].

Rapidly growing areas, in particular, have a need for current data in order to obtain equitable allocations. Several planners in the "sun belt" who responded to our survey complained that various granting agencies, such as HUD and EPA, rely on the 1970 census for population figures; this practice discriminates against rural counties whose growth has occurred more recently.

A very different type of grant issue was brought up by some respondents, however, who were worried about the corrosive effects on local self-determination of excessive reliance on outside funds:

> . . . over the years I have watched community leaders gradually turn from their own limited resources to the grantsmanship approach to community development. Grants have been a significant factor in the progress of rural areas but the developing attitude tends to eliminate those options of local people using their own ingenuity and resources to solve some of their problems [Searcy County, Arkansas].

> . . . [There is] too much emphasis on getting the federal dollar. . . . [We need] more education on how to be self reliant. There is a place for federal money but let's stop making people dependent [Macon and Ralls Counties, Missouri].

This emphasis on getting outside money and investments may reflect the particular orientation of our respondents who deal often with government programs in trying to get grants.

For most public officials in rural communities, especially elected officeholders, the majority of decisions involve internal matters. Local officials normally face such questions as the following:

- Are specific capital improvements (expanded sewage treatment facilities, a new city building, additional park acreage, etc.) needed? If so, what about capacity or size, financing, location, and specific features?
- What incremental changes in existing service levels are desirable or possible in the annual budget process?
- How can services and facility costs be reduced? What are the efficiencies and economies possible under various organizational and program changes, such as consolidation, outside contracting, intergovernmental cooperation, employee reassignments, etc.?

- What does the community need--or what does it want--in the way of changes in service levels, new facilities, or reduced taxes?
- How can needs and demands be projected to take account of population growth, decline, or other community changes? How do these developments relate to service capacities, replacement needs, and fiscal abilities?
- Who benefits from particular service changes? Who pays?
- What about externalities? To what extent does the community pay for and produce services that are consumed by outsiders without like return?

As rural communities grow and become more heterogeneous, answers to these and related questions are less easily reached. Hardest of all with diverse populations is the identification of community "needs" and their translation into policies and programs, since local decision makers are dealing with values and preferences rather than neutral engineering standards.

Data Requirements

What do local decision makers and others need to know in order to make budgetary and program decisions about public services and facilities? Considering both the objective and subjective aspects of community service issues, a minimal list of data requirements includes:

- Basic information on the existing capacities, levels, and costs of services and facilities and the value given the services and facilities by community members.
- The general patterns of service use and nonuse within different types of communities.
- The quality of system performance.
- Information on the need or demand for service and facility changes, including the source of the need--replacement of dated facilities, state or federal standards, community growth, increasing expectations and desires, etc.
- Data on alternative methods of constructing, organizing, delivering, and financing services and facilities.

Data Sources

Most systematic data sources of nationwide scope are practically useless to a decision maker in a rural community who is confronted with service problems or demands. He or she will find little, if any, immediate application for the public finance and employment statistics published by the census of governments. While interesting, federal outlay data are hardly a help to understanding local problems and developing solutions. A respondent commented on this divergence between national data sources and local problems:

> Leadership in small communities complain[s] of the never ending "public plans," "public hearings," "advisory boards," etc. required by federal agencies. The same individuals, on the other hand, complain of the lack of good data and the lack of good planning at the local community level. So the interesting situation exists of too much planning and too much information at the multi-county and state level and the complete lack of planning and good data at the community level. The federal "plans" being developed are regurgitations of the same secondary sources of data (U.S. Census, etc.) with no effort to generate needed primary data that is community specific [Graham County, Arizona].

Where can local officials or citizens obtain information applicable to the public service problems and opportunities of their community? Surprisingly, there are a great many different kinds and sources of information (Doeksen and Schmidt 1977). The key is in being resourceful--in ferreting out and making use of nonconventional and unpublished sources, such as:

- A local government's own records--budgets, revenue projections, administrative reports, etc.
- Community public opinion surveys, which cover attitudes and preferences about local services and facilities.
- Reports and materials gathered by such business-oriented groups as chambers of commerce, banks, and public utilities.
- Background data and projections prepared by regional planning agencies.
- Data collected by state government agencies in particular functional areas, such as traffic and road condition information developed by departments of transportation and information on local property assessment practices available from departments of equalization and finance.
- Evaluations of local public services prepared by outside professional agencies, such as the fire ratings issued by insurance associations.
- Standards for local services and facilities, as prepared by national groups, including those developed for the FmHA study of rural community facilities.
- Comparative data on public services in other communities, and information on new methods of organization, delivery, and financing as compiled and distributed by state associations of local governments.
- Information on the practices and experiences of nearby communities.

Data Problems

With such a varied set of data resources, the main problem for decision makers in rural communities is collecting and using the information.

Limited staff, time, and expertise mean that local officials and others seldom approach these tasks with assurance. There is much thrashing around. National and state agencies should provide assistance, such as information manuals that identify sources of data and suggestions as to how they may be applied to different purposes. Such assistance is already provided to rural communities by the Cooperative Extension Service and other agencies in some states.

Recommendation: The panel recommends that the Statistical Policy Division initiate and coordinate the development of manuals to assist local officials and planners in the acquisition and analysis of data.

It is important to recognize the limitations, as well as the potential uses, of certain types of data. Opinion surveys, for example, can be wonderful tools in helping local officials to identify community preferences. But they can also result in misleading information. A common failure of many surveys is that they reveal what services people desire without indicating the level of priority or commitment (Dillman 1977).

Quite another problem is the processing of too much data--the widely identified issue of surplus paperwork. For rural decision makers especially, data can become a burden as well as an advantage. The two principal illustrations involve the frustrations of meeting the paperwork requirements of grant programs and the frequent reports all local governments have to file. Both demands are imposed by higher levels of government. As a midwestern planner noted, obtaining intergovernmental funds is "far too cumbersome and bureaucratic to effectively serve the people that the programs were intended to benefit."

DATA GAPS

1. Summary nonmetropolitan data for selected finance and employment items for which SMSA totals are already tabulated.
2. A breakdown of community finance and public service data by incorporated or unincorporated status and by population size of village or city.
3. Local property tax information including assessments, rates, and collection.
4. Reliable data on volunteer efforts in support of community services.
5. Trend data on the adequacy of rural public services and facilities.

REFERENCES

Abt Associates (1979) National Rural Community Facilities Assessment Study: Pilot Phase. Preliminary Assessment Plans: Executive Summary. Cambridge, Mass.: Abt Associates, Inc.

Abt Associates (1980) National Rural Community Facilities Assessment Study: Pilot Phase. Final Report. Cambridge, Mass.: Abt Associates, Inc.

Bish, R.L. (1977) Public choice theory: research issues for nonmetropolitan areas. Pp. 125-140 in National Conference on Nonmetropolitan Community Services Research. Washington, D.C.: U.S. Senate Committee on Agriculture, Nutrition, and Forestry.

Bureau of the Census (1978) 1977 Census of Governments. Vol. 1, Governmental Organization. Washington, D.C.: U.S. Department of Commerce.

Committee on Economic Development (1966) Modernizing Local Government. New York: Committee on Economic Development.

Deavers, K.L., and Brown, D.L. (1979) Social and Economic Trends in Rural America. White House Rural Development Background Paper. Washington, D.C.: U.S. Department of Agriculture.

Dillman, D. (1977) Preference surveys and policy decisions: our new tools need not be used in the same old way. Pp. 259-275 in National Conference on Nonmetropolitan Community Services Research. Washington, D.C.: U.S. Senate Committee on Agriculture, Nutrition, and Forestry.

Doeksen, G.A., and Schmidt, J.F. (1977) Community service research needs of local decisionmakers. Pp. 343-354 in National Conference on Nonmetropolitan Community Services Research. Washington, D.C.: U.S. Senate Committee on Agriculture, Nutrition, and Forestry.

Fox, W.F. (August 1980) Size Economies in Local Government Services: A Review. Rural Development Research Report No. 22. Economics, Statistics, and Cooperatives Service. Washington, D.C.: U.S. Department of Agriculture.

Grassberger, F.J. (1978) A Typology and Review of Federal Categorical Grant-in-Aid Formulas in Fiscal Year 1975. Formula Evaluation Project, National Science Foundation, Preliminary Report No. 2. Rochester, N.Y.: Center for Governmental Research, Inc.

Grosenick, L.E. (1977) Grass roots capacity building and the intergovernmental system. Pp. 107-181 in National Conference on Nonmetropolitan Community Services Research. Washington, D.C.: U.S. Senate Committee on Agriculture, Nutrition, and Forestry.

Hendler, C.I., and Reid, N.J. (1980) Federal Outlays in Fiscal 1978: A Comparison of Metropolitan and Nonmetropolitan Areas. Rural Development Research Report No. 25. Economics, Statistics, and Cooperatives Service. Washington, D.C.: U.S. Department of Agriculture.

Hitzhusen, F.J. (1977) Non-tax financing and support for 'community services'. Pp. 43-53 in National Conference on Nonmetropolitan Community Services Research. Washington, D.C.: U.S. Senate Committee on Agriculture, Nutrition, and Forestry.

Lederer, T.H., and Badenhop, M.B. (1976) Voluntary effort as a tax substitute in the revenue sharing allocation formula. Southern Journal of Agricultural Economics 8(1):217-220.

Office of Management and Budget (1980) 1980 Catalog of Federal Domestic Assistance. Washington, D.C.: U.S. Government Printing Office.

Ostrom, E. (1977) Why do we need multiple indicators of public service outputs? Pp. 277-286 in National Conference on Nonmetropolitan Community Services Research. Washington, D.C.: U.S. Senate Committee on Agriculture, Nutrition, and Forestry.

Rainey, K.D., and Rainey, K.G. (1978) Rural government and local public services. Pp. 126-144 in T.R. Ford, ed., Rural U.S.A.: Persistence and Change. Ames, Iowa.: Iowa State University Press.

Sokolow, A.D. (1979) Local governments in nonmetropolitan America: capacity and will. To appear in A.H. Hawley and S.M. Mazie, eds., Understanding Nonmetropolitan America. Chapel Hill, N.C.: University of North Carolina Press.

Stocker, F.D. (1977) Fiscal needs and resources of nonmetropolitan communities. Pp. 25-41 in National Conference on Nonmetropolitan Community Services Research. Washington, D.C.: U.S. Senate Committee on Agriculture, Nutrition, and Forestry.

U.S. Community Services Administration (1979) Geographic Distribution of Federal Funds. Springfield, Va.: National Technical Information Service.

U.S. Department of Housing and Urban Development (1978) Community Development Block Grant Program: Directory of Recipients For Fiscal Years 1975-1977. Washington, D.C.: U.S. Department of Housing and Urban Development.

10

ECONOMIC DEVELOPMENT

INTRODUCTION

Economic development in its broadest sense means improving the quality of life. In this chapter, emphasis is on the level and the distribution of income that, among other factors, influence quality of life. Income can be the means for acquiring not only the essentials of life but also better housing, community services, cleaner air and water, and recreational and aesthetic amenities. Nonetheless, the inadequacy of income alone to measure well-being is recognized.

Economic development depends on natural resources, institutions, and human resources (attitudes as well as talents). Savings and investment in the context of efficiently combining resources to produce the mix of commodities desired by society leads to accumulation of human and material capital. The result is economic growth that affects the level and distribution of income. The entire process is coordinated by the political and price systems. It is in this coordinating role that economic development data have their principal application. To monitor performance, it is essential to measure income and to trace the behavior of labor and capital markets, flows, and outcomes. Data requirements for such an effort are outlined in this chapter. Before turning to these requirements, however, we review briefly selected current issues in economic development.

CURRENT ISSUES IN ECONOMIC DEVELOPMENT

Many current issues in economic development relate to economic adjustment, which for many rural communities has meant decline and for other rural communities has meant rapid growth. As people move to rural communities to seek a better way of life, these communities are faced with social and economic adjustments to maintain and improve the quality of life. The major causal factors of economic development among the social and economic forces underlying change must be identified. Appropriate measures of the magnitude and quality of these factors can then be formulated as a basis for effective public and private decisions.

Many community leaders have developed projects intended to attract manufacturing plants, stimulate local economic activity, and provide jobs for local residents. Success in such policies includes more jobs, reduced out-migration, higher incomes, an expanded tax base, better public and private community facilities, improved services, and enlarged markets for local goods and services. Some of these new jobs, especially the better-paying skilled and managerial positions, may be claimed by outsiders to the resentment of local people, who continue their old job for the same pay. While newcomers may bring fresh leadership and create a climate of optimism, these changes may introduce social tensions that abate only with time. Dislocation of people, unequal income gains, environmental degradation, and other negative elements of development are often not well understood, though there is a growing body of research about them. A recent collection of papers from the North Central Regional Center for Rural Development (1979), for example, provides insight into methods of impact analyses.

For eastern Oklahoma, Shaffer and Tweeten (1974) show substantial net economic benefits to the community as a whole from industrial development. However, some segments of a community, such as municipal government, frequently experience net revenue losses because of concessions made to incoming firms. Summers et al. (1976) contend that the lowest income groups in the local economy may not benefit from new industrial growth, and Youmans (1977) cites evidence that the industrialization of rural communities may have a negative impact on the rural elderly.

Research has shown that the changes resulting from industrial development will vary by the type of industry, the type of community, and the demographic characteristics of the community residents (Deaton and Landes 1978, Grinstead-Schneider and Green 1978, Kuehn et al. 1972, Ross and Green 1979, Summers et al. 1976). Frequently initial employment is in low-wage, labor-intensive industries, but a change from labor-intensive, low-wage industry to capital-intensive (human and material), high-wage industry is characteristic of economic progress.

A better understanding is needed of who benefits from different kinds of development and who does not. Good demographic, economic, and social indicators are necessary to monitor rural development and to gauge the changing quality of rural life. All levels of government need to be aware of the local impact of national policies and local investment decisions. The impact includes the "trickle-down" or secondary and tertiary effects of public decisions on the poor or underemployed, which can alter the growth rates and distributional consequences of local decisions. It should be recognized that development of one area may be matched by decline of others; in some situations, however, out-migration may be desirable.

These issues have been raised to provide perspective on the current availability of the data required to assess and guide economic development. The remainder of the chapter discusses more specific components of the inputs into and consequences of economic development, focusing on: the availability of data for public decision making; its reliability and completeness for the tasks of public policy formation and implementation; and alternative approaches to the acquisition of appropriate data.

INCOME MEASURES

Economic growth can be described in a general way as the process of combining the resources of society in a more productive fashion over time to satisfy more fully the wants of society. Income is the most broadly recognized, albeit severely limited, indicator of the level of attainment of the productive processes of society. Economic development possesses inherent functional and spatial distributive consequences which feed back into the productive process with significant implications. Much of the impetus of this report comes from a concern about the relative income position of rural America vis-a-vis the nation as a whole and about the relative well-being of the low-income and underemployed residents of rural America. In other words, how have rural areas and disadvantaged rural people fared in the development process?

Sources of Data

Income data for the population of small areas can be found in four principal sources: the decennial census of population and housing; Bureau of Census postcensal estimates of per-capita income; Bureau of Economic Analysis estimates of personal income; and Internal Revenue Service tabulations of gross (taxable) income. Each series has unique features and is described and briefly evaluated below.

Decennial census of population and housing The information on income obtained in the decennial census is collected on a sample basis. Income estimates are thus not available for the very smallest areas, but they can be computed for areas with a population greater than 2,500. Income is defined as money income, which is the sum of: earnings (including losses from own farm or nonfarm operation); social security and public asssistance payments; supplemental security income; dividends, interest, and rent (including losses); unemployment and workmen's compensation; government and private employee pensions; and other periodic income.[1]

As in most household surveys, underreporting of income is believed to be a problem. Independent estimates are of course difficult to compute and often of uncertain quality themselves. Estimates of money income in 1976 computed from the current population survey (a household survey using more highly qualified interviewers than used by the decennial census) yielded an estimate of underreporting of 10 percent for CPS total money income compared with independent sources (Bureau of the Census 1978b). The range of the discrepancy computed for individual items was considerable: only 3 percent for wage and salary income, a huge 62 percent for interest income, 20 percent for farm self-employment income, and 11 percent for social security and railroad retirement income. While wages and salaries generally account for 71 percent of total income, they are a smaller proportion of total income in areas in which farm self-employment income is a major part of total income. Hence, in such areas, underreporting of self-employment income creates the largest part of the downward bias to per-capita income statistics.

The principal problem with the decennial census data is their infrequent availability. The data are a rich and widely used source of information, but they become badly outdated as the decade wears on. Numerous local users, as noted in Chapter 5, expressed the need for more up-to-date information on income comparable to the census figures.

Bureau of the Census postcensal estimates of per-capita income

Stimulated by the need for small-area data in order to implement the general revenue sharing legislation passed in 1972, the Bureau of the Census now computes annual estimates of population and per-capita income for approximately 39,000 general purpose local jurisdictions. In 1975, 85 percent of the jurisdictions had a total population of under 5,000, and about 36 percent had a population of less than 500 (National Research Council 1980). Since the objective of these estimates is to update the decennial census income figures for postcensal years, income is also defined as money income for this series.

The postcensal estimates have been a subject of major interest. Since these data are used in the allocation of large amounts of federal money, people are very concerned with the accuracy of the estimates. The postcensal estimates are also receiving greater attention as they become more widely used in a variety of ways by analysts in state and local governments, private organizations, and academic institutions. Finally, the methodology for making annual estimates for a very large number of small local places is relatively new and untried and was largely developed after the general revenue sharing law was enacted. The primary sources used in making postcensal estimates have been the estimates of the Bureau of Economic Analysis and the Internal Revenue Service, which are discussed below. There has been a widespread concern, especially among Census Bureau officials, that there may be sizable errors associated with the postcensal estimates. Because of these and other concerns, the Census Bureau and the Office of Revenue Sharing sponsored a study of small-area estimates (National Research Council 1980). The role of small-area estimates in the context of rural development policy is discussed in Chapter 13.

Bureau of Economic Analysis estimates of personal income

The Bureau of Economic Analysis (BEA) of the Department of Commerce constructs annual estimates of personal income by county (described in more detail in Appendix E). The personal income series is based on administrative rather than census or survey data, and personal income is defined somewhat differently than money income. For example, personal income includes the value of in-kind income that is not included in money income, but it excludes items such as employee contributions for social insurance, regular contributions for support received from persons who do not reside in the same living quarters, and income received from roomers and boarders residing in households that are included in money income.

The BEA series is widely used and has many positive characteristics. The internal consistency of the series is desirable for comparisons, analytic work (especially economic models), and other applications. The extensive use of administrative data enables much detailed data to be produced for small areas at a relatively low cost. The alternative of using a survey of sufficient size to generate these data at a county level on an annual basis would be prohibitively expensive.

However, the BEA series also has several negative characteristics. Due to the nature of the construction of the series, measures of the errors inherent in the procedure cannot be computed, such as can be done for a sample survey. A frustrating feature of the series for research requiring county-level data for rural areas is the large incidence of suppressed cells that are required to avoid disclosure of confidential information. In practice, many users must devise their own procedures for estimating these missing observations before a new series can be used. Also, this method produces gross totals that cannot be matched to the characteristics of the population. Another problem is the lack of consistency across programs and across data sources.

Internal Revenue Service tabulations of gross income The Internal Revenue Service (IRS) has tabulated adjusted gross (taxable) income and other summary information from tax records by county for 1972 and 1974 (Internal Revenue Service 1977a, 1977b). County data for 1976 will be published in 1981, and publication of 1979 data is also planned. The county volumes are special reports from the statistics of income series. The annual reports in this series have only state breakdowns (as described in Appendix E). The IRS work, like that of the Census Bureau on postcensal estimates, was made possible--and stimulated--by the General Revenue Sharing Act. Since filing address may not be the same as residence address, taxpayers were asked in 1972 and 1975 to indicate their county of residence on their tax returns as an aid to implementing general revenue sharing. The question was repeated on the 1980 tax returns currently being processed. The county where the farming or other economic activity is carried on, however, may be neither the filing nor the residence address.

Adjusted gross income computed for federal income tax purposes differs from the concepts and coverage of money income and of personal income. For example, persons and families with small incomes need not file tax returns. Certain types of income, such as veterans' payments, social security benefits, and relief payments are excluded from income tax coverage; in some rural areas such income makes up a major portion of total income. Deductions of items such as moving expenses and business losses affect adjusted gross income differently from other definitions of income. The tax concepts of income, deductions, and depreciation, among others, are not comparable with the concept of personal income used in the national income accounts. Small independent proprietors, such as farmers, use such a diversity of accounting methods that calculations of income from tax records are not performed on any uniform basis. Finally, since some income tax returns are filed as separate returns and others as joint returns, the income reporting unit may be either a family or a person, resulting in inconsistent estimates of income per observation.

It is desirable to have annual Internal Revenue Service data on adjusted gross income by county of residence. This information is useful for a wide variety of purposes, but is especially valuable for analyzing the impact of federal fiscal decisions on small areas. The data would be more valuable if made available on an annual basis rather than only in selected years. Analysts can now use these data as benchmarks, often extrapolating to unpublished years by some rule-of-thumb relationship to BEA personal income or Census Bureau postcensal estimates of money income. Such extrapolations are difficult and of poor quality for areas with volatile incomes, such as rural areas with large agricultural or mining sectors.

Cost-of-Living Differences Among Regions

Meaningful comparisons of economic well-being among communities, regions, and program target groups require that wages, salaries, income, net worth, transfers, outlays, taxes, and other dollar indicators be expressed in comparable units. Often this means deflating series for the cost of living among regions and sectors. Meaningful measures of labor, industry and capital market performance also require data adjusted for cost-of-living differences among regions and sectors.

Even after adjusting for cost-of-living differences, however, a number of complications arise because of the differential utility levels reflected by a given dollar income level. For example, the existence of large numbers of Appalachian migrants in the labor forces of Cincinnati, Dayton, and Detroit may imply significantly lower levels of well-being because of psychic costs to the migrants associated with the urban residence. Therefore, the wage differential between these urban centers and their rural hinterland may be severely misleading indicators of well-being (Deaton et al. 1977, Hoch 1979, Deaton 1979). This example illustrates the complications inherent in any attempt to estimate interregional cost-of-living differentials.

Because cost-of-living data are not available for rural areas, wages, salaries, income, and net worth have usually been compared among rural and other areas without adjusting for differences in costs of living. Lack of cost-of-living data cloud comparisons of labor utilization efficiency and equity among regions, sectors, and industries. Currently, adjustments are made for the cost of living in estimating the extent of poverty: the poverty threshold for rural farm households is 85 percent that of urban households. That is, 85 percent of the income of urban households represents comparable real income for rural households. In the 1960s, when the numbers of people in poverty were first computed, the poverty threshold for rural households was 70 percent that of urban households. These figures never had a sound theoretical or statistical base, however, because consumption patterns, preferred market baskets, and market-nonmarket trade-offs vary across communities.

In estimating a cost-of-living index for rural areas, there are two key determinations: the goods and services to be included in the market basket, and price data to weight items contained in the market basket in deriving an overall cost-of-living index. Market basket differences among income classes within a geographic area may be as important as geographic differences per se. Inflation clearly is more damaging to low-income people than to higher-income people, who are more likely to own their homes and can invest in inflation hedges.

The Statistical Reporting Service (SRS) of the Department of Agriculture formerly used a mail survey to gather quarterly price data from 5,000-6,000 respondents in rural areas. This survey was dropped in 1976 because the computed rural cost of living followed a temporal pattern similar to the metropolitan consumer price index (CPI). Initial benchmark weights for a rural market basket are potentially available based on data from the consumer expenditure survey conducted by the Bureau of Labor Statistics (BLS) in 1972-1973 and from the SRS survey in 1973. The BLS sample contained approximately 1,000 rural respondents, and the SRS sample contained 2,500, for a total 3,500 responses relevant to nonmetropolitan areas.

The Urban Institute recently examined the feasibility of constructing a rural cost-of-living index (Holden et al. 1979). Although the urban market baskets constructed by BLS reflect no differences in consumption patterns due to geographic differences and relative prices, the use of a fixed market basket for all rural areas raises a number of questions because of differing prices and preferences among rural areas. Nevertheless, based on a sample of families from the 1972 consumer expenditure survey, researchers concluded that the use of the urban market basket in rural areas may not seriously distort cost-of-living estimates. These results were regarded as tentative and in need of further analysis.

The Urban Institute proposed a method of constructing a cost-of-living index for rural areas similar to that now used by the BLS in urban areas. Costs would be held down by reliance on BLS methodology, instruments, and data to the extent possible. This method entails two surveys: a household survey to provide data on types and location of retail outlets used by rural residents, and a retail outlet survey to provide data on the prices paid by rural residents for a broad range of items. For rural surveys, a stratified random sample of counties would be drawn that is representative of the diversity of rural areas as to region, population characteristics, and distance to metropolitan area. Cost of data collection could be reduced by use of cluster samples and existing urban price data to the extent possible.

A principal purpose of rural cost-of-living data would be to establish initial differences in costs among rural areas and between rural and urban areas. These differences are expected to change only slowly over time, thus the cost of living would not need to be estimated for rural areas each month as for urban areas. Benchmark cost-of-living estimates could be updated less frequently, perhaps annually. Adjustments could be made from month to month according to changes in the urban consumer price index.

To acquire the appropriate data to compare income and wealth among target groups of the rural population and to determine the efficiency and equity of existing allocations of private and public funds, it is essential that the cost of living be measured for rural areas.

Recommendation: The panel recommends that the Bureau of Labor Statistics provide an annual index of cost-of-living differentials between each of eight to ten rural areas and selected urban areas.

Economics of the Household

As new social science theories and constructs emerge, old measures of behavior and consequences become outdated. Perhaps the most recent example of this phenomenon in economics is the "new household economics." When the family unit becomes the primary focus of conceptualization and observation, measurements must be altered to capture the behavior of the unit. This process yields observed results that have caused substantial rethinking of some fundamental economic notions.

Of immediate concern in this section are the implications of household dynamics for income and cost-of-living estimates. Lazear and Michael (1980) recently pointed out that comparison of per-capita income among households of different structures requires judgment about the relationship between real income and family size. As Lazear and Michael observed, this creates problems in comparing per-capita incomes when data are obtained for household units or for only a subset of household members, such as wage earners. Determining real income equivalence among households is very difficult because the size, structure, and environment of the household affect the rate of transformation between nominal income and service flows derived from goods and services purchased with the income. As applied to the household unit, the consumption of goods and services will vary as a result of three factors: family goods, or public goods, within the family context, such as electric lights, art works, and security locks; scale economies gained by quantity discounts on large purchases or reduced excess capacity due to indivisibilities, such as telephones, showers, and television sets; and complementarity in the use of goods due to specialization in household duties (Lazear and Michael 1980).

These observations suggest that analyses of household economic behavior may provide new interpretations relevant to comparing income and utility across families. At the same time, this approach draws attention to the need for highly disaggregated data on household behavior and longitudinal analyses of household dynamics. Studying such behavior will require in-depth sample surveys and panel studies such as the surveys of consumer finances of the Survey Research Center, University of Michigan, and the current population surveys of the Bureau of the Census. The 1% continuous work history sample of the Social Security Administration (briefly described in Appendix E) may provide a means of studying family dynamics over time if it is modified to include more comprehensive data on the entire family unit. The strengths and weaknesses of the continuous work history sample and examples of its use are discussed by Stolnitz (1972).

The significance of the internal economies of the household for aspects of public policy is clear in the work of Lazear and Michael (1980). They constructed new equivalence scales based on different rates of consumption and use by household size, environment, and structure, and they compared their equivalence scale with the Orshansky scale for estimating poverty classes for a sample of 13,000 households from the 1961 BLS consumer expenditure survey. Their scale revealed that a substantially higher percentage of single or older persons is estimated to be below the poverty line (Lazear and Michael 1980). The one-person household required a relatively larger per-capita income to be as well off as a multiperson household. Such findings have implication for rural-urban income comparisons when family size differs.

LABOR MARKETS

Socioeconomic development is related to human resource contributions and rewards. That is, people are not only an important resource for achieving socioeconomic development, they are also the ultimate objective or end of development. Government has assumed responsibility for providing critical statistics used by private individuals, firms, and public agencies in appraising and improving labor market performance. These statistics must be conceptually sound and precise to be of maximum benefit in diagnosing and treating the socioeconomic ills of rural and urban areas. For rural Tennessee, Deaton and Landes (1978) found that labor force entry and exit of household members was the single most important determinant of the distribution of family incomes among families of new industrial workers. This complex relationship between the family and employment activities in rural communities may have important implications for development policy as it relates to labor markets and public services.

Data that could reflect some of these patterns are difficult to obtain. Information on employment by family composition is collected in the decennial census, the CPS, and similar surveys, but necessary tabulations would be elaborate and usually are not available for small areas. Those sources give only limited information on multiple job holding by individuals. The census data include the principal occupation pursued during the census week, though it is possible to get evidence of other activities (e.g., farming self-employment) through the classification of sources of income during the preceding year. Some CPS reports deal explicitly with multiple job holding and classify individuals by two of their different occupations if they have more than one. The census of agriculture has reported off-farm work by farm operators since 1930, and in more recent censuses has also included classifications by family nonfarm income.

Primary surveys are essential to provide new information about rural labor markets. For example, a recent survey of 541 households in four counties in Virginia revealed that one-third of the labor force held more than one income-producing job (Bryant et al. 1980). Of these jobs, 25 percent were in crafts industries and 17 percent were in farming.

As the census is currently designed census data do not reveal sufficient information. More attention should be given to the measurement of multiple job holding and the tabulation of the employment of all family members in family units. Designing necessary data tabulations will be complex, and no doubt detail will have to be sacrificed for small areas, but such tabulation of increasingly complex family and work structures will be of value to research and policy.

Policy Perspective

Jobs provide the principal means through which human labor is combined with capital and managerial ability to create the goods and services enjoyed by society. The ability of the economy to provide jobs to able and willing workers is a critical test of a nation's economic strength. The relative lack of appropriate jobs for the available supply of offered skills signals potential problems for the economy. The resulting conditions of unemployment and underemployment suggest two problems: resources are not being effectively used and consequently the economy's productive potential is underutilized, a problem in economic efficiency; and some people experience economic hardship or deprivation, a problem of economic equity. There is a wide array of federal expenditures and public programs targeted for areas that experience high rates of unemployment, the assumption being that the unemployment rate is an accurate indicator of the need for social welfare and job programs. In discussing these issues, the equity and efficiency aspects of the problem must be kept as conceptually distinct as possible for analytical clarity. Obviously, they become hopelessly intertwined in reality.

Unemployment Data

The single set of statistics most widely used to allocate public expenditures to support job and related programs is the official unemployment rate. Unemployment is officially defined as persons

16 years of age and over who were unemployed in the survey week but who want to work (i.e., they have actively sought work in the past four weeks) as a percent of the civilian labor force 16 years of age and over.[2]

Government allocations among geographic areas are increasingly tied to formulas, and in 1976 some $16 billion of federal funds were allocated according to criteria of employment or unemployment (Norwood 1977). For example, the unemployment rate is used to allocate funds to rural area development under programs of the Comprehensive Employment and Training Administration of the Department of Labor, the Economic Development Administration of the Department of Commerce, and the Farmers Home Administration (business and industrial loans) of the Department of Agriculture.

Estimates of the number of unemployed and the unemployment rate are made every month for more than 6,000 areas. The areas include the 3,100 counties in the nation, some of which are combined into 283 SMSAs, and approximately 2,600 subcounty areas. Labor force and unemployment estimates in only ten large states and two substate areas (Los Angeles and New York City) are sufficiently reliable to be used directly from the monthly current population survey (Goldstein 1979). Unemployment for other states and areas is computed by the BLS "handbook method"[3] and other means. In general, the reliability of estimates decreases as the density of population decreases; estimates are least reliable for the most rural counties. Korsching and Sapp (1977) did a comprehensive personal interview survey of rural Gadsden County, Florida, from which they computed an unemployment rate of 20 percent compared with an official unemployment rate of 9.2 percent. Their estimate of total employment was close to the official estimate, which suggests that the discrepancy arose from a difference in the estimate of the number of unemployed people seeking work.

The current population survey (CPS) collects information each month from a sample of households and business establishments. The survey data are supplemented with data on unemployment insurance and taxes and information from other sources. The number of households interviewed in the CPS is so small that data for the rural population cannot be satisfactorily disaggregated to the state and county level, and increasing the sample size to achieve acceptable sampling error at the county level would entail prohibitive cost. There is also a quarterly survey by the Economics and Statistics Service (ESS) of the Department of Agriculture that collects data on employment and wages of hired agricultural workers from a probability sample of farm operators and agricultural employers. However, place-of-residence data collected from households cannot be linked with place-of-work data collected from establishments, and the CPS does not use the same definitions and concepts as the ESS survey.

Comparability of data sets is further hindered by the lack of any generally accepted definition of "rural." The concept of "employment" also poses problems. Farm and forest workers have never been fully employed in the sense of a 40-hour week and a

50-week year, because work on the land, unlike work in offices and factories, is related to rhythms of the land. Since self-employed persons need devote only one hour of work to their enterprise during the survey week to be defined as employed, any farmer, however minor the farming operation or major the unemployment from another job, would likely be defined as employed by that definition. These self-employed workers probably should be treated as a separate and distinct population for both analytic and policy purposes. The balance of the rural nonfarm labor force in some respects may be conceptualized as a dispersed subset of the urban labor force.

Seasonality of farm work may significantly affect the Census Bureau estimates of the farm labor force. A report of the USDA (Economic Research Service 1974) pointed out that the 1970 census reference week was in March when activity on many farms and in farm-related industries in the northern states was dormant or slow. Therefore, the census estimates may have significantly underestimated the farm labor force. The 1969 census of agriculture reported 2.7 million farm operators, of which more than 1.0 million worked 100 or more days off the farm. Thus, in the 1970 census of population, most of these 1 million primarily off-farm workers reported their occupations as other than farm operators (Economic Research Service 1974). Also, during 1970, 69 percent of the hired farm workers were employed on farms for less than 75 days. The 1970 decennial census would probably not have classified these workers as engaged primarily in farming since they were most likely not working on farms during March.

Employment and Earnings, published monthly by the Bureau of Labor Statistics, reports a host of data relating to employment, unemployment, hours, earnings, labor turnover, and the like for most states and a number of metropolitan areas. Although metropolitan totals subtracted from state totals potentially give nonmetropolitan figures, this procedure is too gross and inaccurate to be of much value in appraising labor market performance in rural areas. Monthly labor market data in _Employment and Earnings_ come from two main sources: a survey of business establishments to determine labor employment, layoffs, earnings, and hours; and the CPS, which provides comprehensive data on characteristics related to employment and underemployment of individual household members.

The National Commission on Employment and Unemployment Statistics (1979) recommended that the CPS be expanded by 42,000 households to enable labor force estimates to be made on a more disaggregated basis and to improve the statistical quality of all published estimates. Expanded monthly samples would not produce acceptable coefficients of variation for rural areas, but aggregation of survey data to an annual basis holds promise. If the establishment survey and CPS were expanded, prospects would be bright for improved benchmark data for the "handbook method" as well as for annual labor force statistics for substate areas and rural multistate regions. It is not now possible to estimate precisely the geographic areas and demographic groups for which labor force data could be provided with acceptable reliability.

Most states are divided into substate multicounty planning districts; unfortunately, county groupings may differ by programs and agencies so that a number of substate delineations exist without standardized boundaries. In a number of states, standardization has proceeded far enough so that a single set of substate districts has become widely accepted in area delineation as well as being the focal point for rural planning. The districts are a compromise between the high cost of data for small areas and low cost for large areas. Aggregations are sometimes too great, as one respondent noted:

> All too often state efforts to provide [intercensal] data are structured solely for the convenience of state supported programs and consequently have little utility for [substate] plans. For example [the state] prepares computerized employment projections annually but does so for substate configurations which range in size from a four county area to a twenty-seven county area. When a planner or elected official attempts to discern the implications for his community from state employment projections which lump the southern one-third of the state together as a single unit, he becomes quickly frustrated [South Central Illinois Regional Planning Commission].

Federal data agencies should work closely with states to report statistics for established substate districts when disclosure or accuracy problems preclude reporting data for counties (or for towns and small cities).

The National Commission on Employment and Unemployment Statistics (1979) suggested the possibility of aggregating data for multicounty units on a functional rather than a geographic basis. A rural labor market typology that would group functionally similar areas (such as mining, agricultural, isolated nonindustrial) would be developed. But areas that are functionally similar according to one criterion may be quite diverse according to another.

Given the increasing utilization and standardization of substate district delineations, these boundaries provide the best basis for moving to a single system for all federal statistics. The single system should be worked out in close cooperation between county, state, and federal governments. Many labor and other statistics are too costly to gather for every rural county. Hence, substate standard statistical areas, recommended in Chapter 2, are needed as sampling and reporting units for rural statistics, which are too costly to compile for counties and too aggregated at the state level.

Unemployment rates reported for rural areas fail to measure the degree of underutilization of human resources (Nilsen 1979, Tweeten 1978), especially in economically depressed rural areas, for four reasons: relatively immobile potential workers have not sought gainful employment or are discouraged and no longer seek gainful employment because of chronic lack of local job opportunities; rural workers face few employers so that the costs of additional active search exceed the possible gains more quickly than for urban workers;

workers classified as employed are often underemployed since the incidence of seasonal work and self-employment is high; and the incidence of jobs covered by unemployment compensation is low. One respondent pointed out other problems in counting the unemployed:

> There are difficulties in obtaining accurate estimates of population and unemployment statistics in the rural villages due largely to the subsistence life style. If the major population of a village uses trapping, hunting, and fishing as their major source of income, it is difficult to include them in an unemployment statistic. Also, in the villages that have been exposed to a cash economy, if the members of the village have been out of work long enough they do not qualify for unemployment insurance and once again are not counted as being unemployed [Fairbanks Town and Village Association for Development, Inc., Alaska].

Rural workers may terminate their active job search earlier than metropolitan workers because they need little time to survey work opportunities. Knowledge of new opportunities is likely to come from friends and relatives in a rural environment where informal labor information systems predominate. This reliance on informal sources of job information and the lack of unemployment insurance in many rural occupations dampens enthusiasm for registering for unemployment compensation or for jobs at the public employment security office, which may be far away. In rural counties, where unemployment compensation claims rather than a sample survey are frequently used to estimate unemployment, the result is an underestimation of unemployment. A respondent cites additional problems in obtaining local employment data:

> In our economy, continuous monitoring of industrial job opportunities is necessary due to substantial fluctuations in these statistics. The [state] Employment Security Commission is unable to provide planning agencies with these data for reasons of confidentiality. Local manufacturers are all too often reluctant to participate in a data-gathering program because they do not want to divert minimum staff to yet another government survey or to disclose data that might be used against their perceived best interest [Livingston County, Michigan].

Reassessment of Unemployment Concepts and Data

The conceptual basis for unemployment statistics was established in the 1930s when each family tended to have no more than one breadwinner and when income alternatives to earnings from employment were few. At that time, unemployment meant economic hardship. The relationship between unemployment and economic hardship is less distinct today. Many of the unemployed today are secondary or tertiary earners in their families. Economic hardship may be minimal for a briefly unemployed person who draws unemployment insurance and union-company layoff supplements and who is part of a family with other earnings and substantial net worth. In many cases, of course, unemployment of a household member is still a source of hardship.

The present conceptual and measurement weaknesses of unemployment have implications for both efficiency and equity. From the standpoint of the former, there must be a continued concern about the ability of the economy to generate appropriate employment opportunities for all potential labor force participants. In this efficiency framework, the accuracy of unemployment data is critical in order to help signal the availability of a work force for private investors.

Public efforts to promote a degree of equity among members of society may or may not be aided by unemployment data. The National Commission on Employment and Unemployment Statistics recognized the shortcoming of unemployment data used to target programs intended to alleviate economic hardship. Clearly, data needed for description and analysis of one issue (e.g., economic efficiency) may be quite different from the data needed for other, albeit related, purposes (e.g., alleviating economic hardship).

In recent years, only about 10 percent of poor Americans were unemployed (the incidence of poor people who were employed was much higher in rural than in urban areas) and less than half of the unemployed were economically disadvantaged (Ullman 1979). The degree of economic hardship engendered by unemployment is not known. Data relating employment status to income, earnings, and net worth would be valuable in gauging economic hardship and in developing appropriate policies for rural and for urban areas.

Specially commissioned studies of specific target groups or areas might prove adequate and less expensive than tinkering with present data collection procedures, particularly if the target group or area is only a small segment of the population that is sampled in present efforts. The population of migrant farm workers is an example of an important target group whose small numbers make it difficult or impossible to understand on the basis of the CPS and other samples of the total U.S. population. Likewise, certain areas might be targeted for special data collection efforts. There is a particular need to examine conditions in industries that are now hiring increasing numbers of migratory and imported laborers, such as the tobacco and apple industries of Virginia. Clearly, mere classification of the labor force on the land as employed or unemployed is not satisfactory; data are needed on earnings, income, and hours of work for the entire family unit in order to reveal the true employment and economic welfare picture.

High levels of unemployment are frequently acute, short-term phenomena more susceptible to amelioration by national monetary and fiscal policies than by the somewhat unwieldy long-term job development tools. Other federal efforts, including selected programs of the Economic Development Administration and Farmers Home Administration, are designed to alleviate chronic areawide underutilization of human resources through job development programs. At issue is the appropriate criterion to target such programs.

Possible candidates include poverty or median income, out-migration, unemployment, and underemployment.

Unemployment is not closely related to poverty or underutilized human resources as measured by underemployment. Persons can be poor because they have too few resources or because they are not using "adequate" resources fully. If inherent abilities are undeveloped, a cost-effective means to raise incomes is through programs of schooling in technical and general skills. Public assistance grants are a cost-effective means to raise incomes of the unemployable poor, such as the aged and totally disabled. The poor with adequate resources who are using them inefficiently or not at all may be helped by job development programs, but underemployment is a better indicator than poverty of the incidence of underutilized human resources. Income has many of the same disadvantages as poverty as a criterion for focusing job development programs.

High levels of out-migration imply that people are making adjustments to supply and demand conditions; it might be unwise to interfere with that process. Where there is marked out-migration, programs to provide more efficient labor markets through improved employment data on outlying areas may be required from the federal-state employment service. And local areas may need to be compensated for spillout of local investment in schooling of out-migrants.

Underemployment

Bringing jobs to people is likely to be most successful in raising earnings and living levels in places where people are unemployed or are working in jobs that do not utilize their potential--where workers will not be bid away from productive employment. Underemploymment is a useful measure of such a situation. Underemployment is measured as the difference between the output of individuals in a particular area and what they would produce if they were as productive as workers in the nation with similar age, education, and training. Underemployment includes, but is not confined to, unemployment.

Several procedures and formulas have been proposed to measure underemployment (Tweeten 1978), but some of the conceptually most promising alternatives are not available for rural counties and could be made available only at prohibitive cost. Some measures that hold promise have shown that underemployment is larger relative to unemployment in rural than in urban counties, but these measures have not been fully evaluated, let alone made operational. The National Commission on Employment and Unemployment Statistics wrestled with the issue but concluded that the current count of discouraged workers would not serve as an indicator of potential labor supply and thereby reflect the need for jobs. But a minority, including the chairman, Sar Levitan, stated (National Commission on Employment and Unemployment Statistics 1979:56):

> We believe that the objectivity of our labor force count would not be lessened if the discouraged workers were included in the

> total unemployment count. . . . Individuals who indicate that they are available and willing to work and who have sought work within the 6 months recommended by the commission should be counted among the unemployed. They are without jobs, they want work, are available for work, and should be included in the count of the nation's job deficit. Given the choice between continuing past questionable and arbitrary practices and improving the labor force count, even at the sacrifice of some continuity in the data, we opt for the latter.

Unemployment statistics, if accurate, are useful for measuring the need for short-run programs, such as public service employment, to cushion short-run economic setbacks. But a priority need for rural areas is an acceptable measure of underemployment, a measure that records long-term labor adjustment and job needs that could be used in allocating area development funds. Whether current data and concepts are adequate to construct a useful measure will not be known until the issue receives in-depth study.

> Recommendation: The panel recommends that the Statistical Policy Division in the Office of Management and Budget establish an interagency committee to guide the conceptual research for and the development of an underemployment index for counties on a periodic basis. The panel further recommends that the Bureau of Labor Statistics fund the research and assume the responsibility for implementing the procedures upon the completion of the methodological study.

CAPITAL AND EXPENDITURES

The previous section was devoted to the labor side of the economic development process; this section takes up the capital side. While some liberty is taken with the concept of capital, it seems reasonable to include in this section our discussion of data needs and limitations regarding business activity and federal grant and loan allocations. (Public taxes and revenues, which could also be discussed in this section, are discussed in Chapter 9.) In all cases these activities represent capital flows that generate an internal rate of return with significant development potential for rural America. At the same time, these activities represent the disposition and consequences of public and private allocations of funds and the interaction between the two.

Capital Flows

Data on financial and material capital movements as well as data on profits and rates of return on investment by firm and industry are especially deficient. The latter indicators are troubled by multiplant, multilocation firms (Janssen 1974). There are many difficulties associated with the measurement of both human and physical capital. Schultz (1979) has emphasized the critical need to observe inequalities in the form of capital and in the rate of return to capital ". . . because they are the mainspring of economic growth." Linking these inequalities to the growth potential and resulting income distribution in rural areas has not been explicitly dealt with by most research. One reason for this is the imprecise nature of most data on public and private capital flows. According to the participants in the panel's workshop for regional and state planners, data on public and private capital flows is the most serious data gap relating to rural development. The impression persists that private capital generally flows from rural to urban markets, thus hindering rural development efforts. Yet the necessary data to document these patterns for particular regions is inadequate or nonexistent, as in the case of the secondary mortgage market. For growing areas in desperate need of new and expanded infrastructure, such as the energy boom communities of the West, limited capital is an especially critical problem.

Ignorance of investment opportunities, social distance, and prospective rates of return are factors that limit capital mobility. These factors are more uncertain in remote rural areas and under depressed economic conditions. While interregional capital mobility and general equalization of returns have been enhanced by the national and international organization of capital markets, these sophisticated arrangements may be of little value to many rural communities. Knowledge of enterprise potential is always quite limited. Also, studies of substitution between capital and labor and of investment complementarity are generally lacking for most rural areas. One respondent suggests that lack of data, however, has not been the important factor hindering economic growth:

> In the state of Michigan, so many people and groups are encouraging economic development in rural areas that there is a very real danger that the greatest single economic boom will be only for economic development professionals. Historically, the problems in rural areas have not been identifying economic development potential but rather competing with more sophisticated and well-financed urban areas for development. The typical potential industry evaluating [our county] tends to be one interested in exploiting the lack of organized labor and unemployment problems of the area or in extracting natural resources until they are played out. Most of our communities, of course, prefer another type of economic development but do not have the resources to compete with the industrial development specialists hired by many of the communities in our market area [Livingston County, Michigan].

Small business enterprises generally cannot use national money markets and must depend heavily on local bank financial support. The extent to which local banks are willing to provide this support varies rather unsystematically, though limited evidence tends to suggest that rural areas may be ill-served (Shaffer 1977, Hooker 1970, Cecchi and Co. 1969). Published data of the Federal Deposit Insurance Corporation (FDIC) were combined with data from their unpublished Call Reports in a recent analysis of local bank support for municipal bonds. The FDIC data were not sufficiently specific to measure the degree of local bank support for local government bond issues. Intercounty branch banking makes it impossible to determine the relationship between bank assets and liabilities and county characteristics. More useful data will have to be obtained by direct survey. Attitudes toward local growth potential and risk-taking propensity may be the most important factors to analyze.

Business

Capital is generally transformed into a physical form in a local setting in generating jobs and income in rural areas. Business investments represent the private sector embodiment of this transformation. Therefore, data on business establishments provide important measures of the growth and development potential of rural areas and provide insight into the structural nature of the local economy.

Information on business in nonmetropolitan areas is available from numerous sources, including the survey of income and education, which provides data for as recently as 1975. The data permit a breakdown of employment and unemployment rates and of the income of wage and salary workers and self-employed workers by region and metropolitan-nonmetropolitan status. There are also some miscellaneous publications, many based on the current population survey or the decennial census (e.g., Bureau of the Census 1978c). The Directory of Federal Statistics for Local Areas, A Guide to Sources, 1976 (Bureau of the Census 1978a) is an excellent aid in locating data to meet specific needs. Another excellent source book is Guide to County Census Data for Economic Development (Bureau of the Census and Economic Development Administration 1979). The quinquennial economic censuses of industries, particularly the census of manufactures, and its supplement, the annual survey of manufactures, also provide helpful data.

The most timely and definitive source of detailed statistics on local areas is County Business Patterns, a series compiled and published annually by the Bureau of the Census, containing 54 reports: one for each state, the District of Columbia, Puerto Rico, a U.S. summary, and a report presenting data for all SMSAs. The reports are useful in analyzing market potential and the effectiveness of sales and advertising programs, setting sales quotas and budgets, analyzing the industrial structure of regions, making basic economic studies of small areas, and for other business activities.

In accordance with federal law, data that may disclose the operations of an individual employer are not published. However, the number of establishments in each type of business and their distribution by employment size class are not considered a disclosure, and these items may appear when other items of information, such as employment and payroll, are withheld. Data are not shown separately for any industry that does not have at least 50 employees in the area (county, state, or United States) covered by the tabulation. However, data for an unpublished industry are included in the total shown for the broader industry groupings of which it is a part.

The estimated employment for comparable industry groups, which are published monthly by BLS in *Employment and Earnings* and by the state employment agencies in their monthly news releases, may differ from the corresponding *County Business Patterns* figures for a number of reasons. There may be differences in level within national and state figures because BLS estimates are adjusted to levels (described above) that may differ from those in *County Business Patterns*. There are also other differences, such as: The two sets of data differ in overall scope (e.g., *County Business Patterns* excludes interstate railroads and government); the *County Business Patterns* establishment may differ from the BLS reporting unit; the industry classifications assigned to the same entity may differ; and statistics on employment from year to year in some 3-digit and 4-digit standard industrial classification (SIC) codes may not be comparable due to changes in the industrial classification manual, even though year-to-year comparisons are basically valid for major (i.e., 2-digit) SIC groups. SIC modifications have recently been reviewed by Hastings and Goode (1980).

Data on employment by occupation are collected in the decennial census, the current population survey, and BLS's occupational employment statistics (OES) survey, but there are serious problems of noncomparability among these series. In the past the OES did not use the standard occupational classification (SOC) categories although they are moving toward them. Occupational coding in both the census and the CPS is based primarily on job titles (plus information on industry and class of worker) rather than on occupational definition. The census and the CPS collect data from households; BLS surveys employers. *There should be better data on job holders cross-classified by industry and occupation, according to current Standard Industrial Classification (SIC) and Standard Occupational Classification (SOC) codes.* Data on industry and occupation frequently do not use the latest SIC and SOC codes. Except where retention of previous classification is required for continuity and comparison with past data, standard use of the latest SIC and SOC codes is desirable in order to facilitate use of the latter on jobs and industries from various sources.

Data on net job and industry movements can be calculated approximately from published data on numbers of employees and firms for successive years. Also, quinquennial data on migration patterns from the Census Bureau provide insight into movement of people. *Although data are available on the migration of people, data are needed on the migration, creation, and termination of individual businesses and attendant jobs.* Studies of these patterns have generally required either primary data (e.g., Barkley 1978) or careful modifications of data collected by state and regional agencies (e.g., Gunter 1977).

Another data set similar in many respects to County Business Patterns is the Dun and Bradstreet Dun's Market Identifiers (DMI) file. The complementarities, overlaps, and inconsistencies between DMI and other census-related data files are discussed in a recent conference report (Advisory Commission on Intergovernmental Relations 1979). The DMI file was viewed by participants as an alternative data set for community development analyses.

Much of the wealth of data from public and private sources is not useful for local development, however, as one respondent noted:

> The published state and federal statistics suffer from problems of incomplete reporting, insufficient geographic disaggregation and obsolescence by the time they become available. Because our study focused on the most rural part of our county, the published statistics were even more difficult to use as most reports do not disaggregate below the county level.

The same respondent also described unsuccessful efforts he has made to get local business data:

> The most difficult statistics for us to obtain and to have confidence in are economic. The volume and distribution of current economic activity are difficult to measure even in a small community. Often people are reluctant to provide officials with the kind of data that would be meaningful in assessing needs and in evaluating impacts of local rural development policy. We have used local certified public accountants, Chamber of Commerce officials, and other people as resources in giving us a general (and basically intuitive) understanding of the local economy. In addition we conducted a workshop for business and industry that helped explain our program and intentions but did not lead to the access to data about employment levels, payroll value added, or other data that would help us formulate policy [Livingston County, Michigan].

Allocating Federal Funds

The most readily available statistics about governmental activity involve public finances--data about revenues, expenditures, and debt. From a variety of federal and other sources, a great deal is known about the finances of individual governments at the national, state, and local levels. Finance data have a rich potential for the analysis of policies and programs. With both revenue and expenditure data, examinations of the total volume of public activities are possible.

Federal revenues and outlays represent a major flow of funds designed to achieve efficiency and equity goals in our society.

Data measuring these flows are major indicators of program emphases and scope for the nation as a whole and for particular areas or communities. Federal outlay statistics, obtained largely from administrative records, are reported annually by county for more than 70 agencies and 84 functions in Geographic Distribution of Federal Funds, published by the Community Services Administration. Outlay data have been used extensively for descriptive (Hendler and Reid 1980) and analytical (Nelson 1979) purposes, but limitations of the data undermine their credibility (Hines and Reid 1977). Hundreds of grant and other transfer programs distribute federal resources to state and local governments, private agencies, and individuals according to criteria that require the use of indicators of eligibility or need. The Catalog of Federal Domestic Assistance (Office of Management and Budget 1980) alone lists more than 1,000 federal aid programs, many of which directly or indirectly affect the development of rural communities and the welfare of their populations.

Intergovernmental grants and transfers from both the federal and state levels are important sources of public funds in rural communities. Groups that represent rural interests in national political circles generally maintain that their areas and communities receive less than their "fair" share of federal grants and other outlays (Deavers and Brown 1979). Determining who gets what in the federal system is, of course, primarily a policy-making or congressional-presidential matter. Questions relating to data are important in the design and implementation of programs because allocations require the use of indicators of need. Also, "good" data--data that are easily gathered, accurate, easily understood, and usable--can help clarify standards of efficiency and equity in deliberations about program goals.

Data requirements vary regarding the type of eligibility for these programs and methods of allocation of program funds. Many programs involving direct aid to local governments or other community agencies restrict their recipients as to population size or the relative urbanization of communities, with urban-metropolitan and rural-nonmetropolitan foci both represented. Once eligibility is determined, the process turns to the method of distributing the available amounts. The major distinction is between a more-or-less automatic allocation determined by an explicit formula that is made up of one or more indicators (population, poverty, unemployment, etc.) and discretionary grants determined by less specific criteria.

Entitlement programs such as general revenue sharing usually employ "hard" formulae, while the "softer" indicators are characteristic of such discretionary and highly competitive programs as the community facilities loans and grants of Farmers Home Administration. Some programs use both formula and discretionary methods; a notable example for rural communities is the nonmetropolitan portion of community development block grants, in which funds initially are allocated to state areas by formula (nonmetropolitan population, poverty, overcrowding) but then granted to individual communities after HUD's discretionary review of proposals.

For allocating federal funds, population is the most commonly used indicator, either as an absolute measure or as a control (per capita) for other measures such as income (U.S. House of Representatives 1978). Other indicators include unemployment, age, housing condition, and area.

Both functional and spatial "equity" are persistent concerns in the design and implementation of federal aid programs, particularly as communities, areas, and organized interests increasingly compete for portions of a stable or shrinking total pie. Often this is a matter of reconciling national policy objectives (i.e., the redistribution of resources and opportunities in favor of less advantaged populations) with local goals (i.e., subsidizing public works projects).

The allocation of federal funds to and within rural areas based on growth potential, fairness, or need is affected by two major matters of data availability and adequacy. First, standard definitions or indicators may not measure conditions uniformly between metropolitan and nonmetropolitan regions, or between big cities and rural localities. As we noted above, labor force statistics, in particular, vary by such geographic areas in how they reflect reality.

Second, it is generally more difficult to demonstrate or measure need in nonmetropolitan areas and small communities because data sets are relatively incomplete for less urbanized sections of the nation. In part this is a collection problem, especially for data sets that are derived from sample surveys. But it is also a compilation or publication gap in that relatively small chunks of existing data are presented for nonmetropolitan areas in the regular statistical series. The problem is especially acute for unincorporated communities or localities in nonmetropolitan areas and in the untracted (generally "nonurbanized") parts of metropolitan areas.

An underlying issue relates to the trade-offs between the use of narrowly defined variables that measure the needs of particular populations and the desire to increase the statistical relibility of allocators by restricting their number to a few series. Conflict arises between policy objectives and statistical purity, between the intent of different programs to target resources and the desirability of having a limited number of easily collected and accurate indicators with agreed-upon meanings. Perhaps it is too much to expect federal policy makers and program implementors to agree to confine their data uses to a small number of specific indicators given the varying objectives (i.e., water quality, improving rural communities, assisting low-income populations, etc.) of programs that deal with the economic development and social welfare of rural areas. But a minimal strategy would be to insist on continuing clarification of the meaning, limits, and improvement possibilities of whatever indicators are used.

Two federal programs of particular import to rural communities are the farm program and the business and industry program of the Farmers Home Administration. The farm program involves four types of loans: farm ownership loans for acquiring, enlarging, or improving family-sized farms or establishing nonfarm enterprises to supplement farm income; farm operating loans made to farmers and ranchers to reorganize the farming operation to make it more profitable, to purchase livestock, equipment, or supplies, to refinance or pay interest on debts, or to develop nonfarm enterprises to supplement farm income; farm emergency loans to farmers, ranchers, oyster planters, partnership, and private domestic corporations when a natural disaster has caused losses for which there would otherwise be no compensation; and emergency disaster loans made to farmers in areas affected by major disasters as designated by the FmHA state director. The factors considered in the formulas for allocating funds to the states for farm ownership loans are: number of small farms, number of farm tenants, and participation with other lenders; for farm operating loans, the factors are number of farms, number of small farms, farm population, farm tenants, and net farm income.

The goals of the business and industry program are to promote the improvement, development or financing of business, industry, and employment for the purpose of improving the economic or environmental climate in rural communities. The FmHA allocates funds to states in the business and industry program on the basis of two factors, rural population (weighted 66.7 percent) and rural income (weighted 33.3 percent). National allocations are based on both factors and use the 1970 census data. Although both factors are used to allocate funds within states, many states also consider unemployment, poverty, need, job creation potential, and the potential for involvement of outside capital. Program guidelines require that not more than $20,000 be used to create a job.

In some states, allocations are made on the basis of data generated from state unemployment compensation records or special surveys conducted by councils of governments (COGs) or area planning councils. In states with small rural or farm populations, the total state allocation may be small and allocations to districts or counties are often not made; instead, projects are selected by the state office from those proposed within the state. Targeting decisions in some states are made in terms of both FmHA national policy and established state policies, such as those requiring that agricultural and prime agricultural land be preserved. For example, in New York, targeting efforts focus on preserving land and encouraging agricultural enterprise by providing financing for marginal farm operators who have sound farm operation plans.

The effectiveness of the business and industry program in stimulating growth seems to be hampered by limited funds, administrative requirements, and insufficient data on the need for and expected outcomes of community economic development. The actual dollars allocated to a state may limit the manner in which program funds are managed as well as the number of programs funded. A second limitation is that of requirements for public services (e.g., for water and sewer facilities and utilities): higher utility costs and unavailability of industrial sites with adequate water and sewer facilities have hampered development. Difficulties in projecting outcomes of development and in identifying expected changes in the community are caused by a general paucity of data on these outcomes and by insufficient data about the economic condition of the area. Without such information, local decision making (and obtaining commitments for funds) is difficult.

Although the importance of the programs varies by state, the significance of the farm program can be demonstrated by the example of Virginia. In Virginia, 20 percent of the nonfarm jobs in the state are provided by the agricultural industry. The FmHA has provided 37 percent of the farm lending credit in the state (with banks providing 35 percent) and approximately 7 percent of Virginia's real estate credit (Virginia Farmers Home Administration 1980).

The Impact of Transfers and Grants

Many studies have estimated the impact of transfer payments on the quality of living, work behavior, and other dimensions of family life (Tweeten and Brinkman 1976). Some of the best of these studies have entailed carefully designed experiments to obtain definitive primary data for investigating labor supply and other responses of households to the negative income tax. Similar studies have investigated the impact on households of the food stamp and housing allowance programs. These studies have been limited in geographic, temporal, and program scope. The costs of obtaining primary data for each study are massive and ultimately prohibitive for comprehensive assessments of all programs. In general, however, people probably tend to underestimate the benefits derived from accurate data obtained in this expensive matter.

Conceptually, the most promising data to evaluate the impact of transfer payments as well as other federal programs are the comprehensive federal outlay statistics obtained largely from administrative records and compiled annually by the Community Services Administration. (These data were discussed above and also in Chapter 9.) The following recommendation is a reminder of the importance of this data set to broader economic development issues as well as to public service and community facilities issues.

Recommendation: The panel recommends that in reporting federal outlays data, the program agencies, in cooperation with the Office of Management and Budget and the Community Services Administration, make a greater effort to improve the quality and geographic detail of the data and to provide users with information on the quality and limitations of the various components.

REGIONAL ACCOUNTS

The construction of regional accounts goes back some decades and has several variants. The most common is one or another version of export base multiplier models of employment. These are easy to do in a rough-and-ready fashion, but are very inaccurate. More elaborate econometric models are sometimes used for regional planning, but in spite of their greater sophistication, they are unsatisfactory when examined closely. Their conceptual and data problems are severe. In view of the problems outlined above and the data limitations reported for a number of fundamental issues, the role of regional accounts should be fundamentally reexamined. What useful role can they play in the broad arena of rural development policy and how practical is their construction and utilization?

Hoover and Chinitz (1964) assert that regional accounts are useful tools of regional analysis to facilitate consistency-checking and impact evaluation. The "double-entry" balancing of regional transactions ensures the former, while the measurement of interrelated economic sectors facilitates the latter. The ability to use derived multipliers to measure the effects of one change on the balance of the system is the attractive general-equilibrium feature of most regional accounting frameworks. Thus, detailed accounts would be helpful primarily to understand economic structure, but they would not add significantly to policy analysis. They would illuminate structure rather than change. To be of value to planners and policy makers, regional analyses must be undertaken in a dynamic context. Hence if work on regional accounts is to be useful, it must be regarded as an ongoing rather than a sporadic activity.

Principles of "functional integration" and "homogeneity" were used by Nourse (1968:130) to justify "organizing the economic landscape of the United States into reasonable regions for meaningful presentation of greater statistical detail." These principles require reinterpretation in view of major interregional shifts in industrial activity. The small firms moving into rural America may be as likely to purchase inputs from abroad as from nearby factories, and their output may be as likely to enter international markets as local markets.

Therefore, the important question is whether regional accounts help deal with the current issues facing rural people. They may be too crude to assist in the highly localized impact assessments required by local communities and by state and federal agencies, yet they may be useful in understanding the interactions between, say, international capital markets and income distribution in rural areas. Our current inability to understand the dynamic linkages between national monetary and fiscal policy and regional economic affairs is partly due to the conceptual and measurement lags associated with regional accounting.

Overall, regional accounts have stressed goods production. They have been weak in such postindustrial features as transfers, service industries, and rent on resources. Proper regional accounting will have to come to terms with significant changes in the export orientation of many service industries (Smith 1979). The old classification systems need to be thoroughly overhauled.

Obviously, development of data will need to proceed hand in hand with conceptual improvements, as was the case in the development of national accounts. The fundamental difficulty is that regions are both more open and more variable as systems than the nation. At the same time, data are, for obvious reasons, more sparse.

For the reasons noted above, analytic efforts to develop state-level regional accounts deserve support as a continuing and evolving institutionalized activity. In view of the huge expense that would be associated with an attempt to replicate current national procedures for each of the 50 states, state-level effort should be regarded in large part as a research project in need of innovative thinking and procedures rather than as an extension of current methods to states. The panel endorses the current work of the Bureau of Economic Analysis on regional accounts by state.

The technical and institutional difficulties of constructing regional accounts at the substate level are even more imposing than the problems at the state level. Problems of disclosure, sample size, and larger relative changes in the variables are severe. Data on federal payments are readily available on a state basis and may be available on a substate basis. <u>State data on private transfers (e.g., private pensions, out-of-state student support) seem to be totally lacking.</u> These can be very important and more attention to this area is needed. Data on intergovernmental transfers, which are increasingly important, are generally available for states but not for substate areas. Tax, investment, and capital account data are generally inadequate. The panel does not recommend that the federal government mount a major effort to develop well-integrated, detailed regional economic accounts at the substate level. The cost is too high at this time relative to expected benefits. In addition, further progress at the state level is a logical precursor to a major investment in substate regional accounts.

The position of the panel should not be interpreted as one of discouraging individual efforts on substate accounts or of deemphasizing the importance of small-area economic data. Researchers who contribute to a better understanding of the structure and functioning of substate regions are making a valuable contribution to both local and national rural policy. In most, if not all, cases this research requires a careful examination and restructuring of existing data in acordance with the conceptual framework that is being used and tested. These frameworks often have many of the features of regional accounts.

Throughout the report, the panel emphasizes the importance of small-area data, including economic data. It would seem that much could be gained by treating nonmetropolitan areas on a regional basis for data gathering and reporting. This might be done, for instance, by more active use of BEA areas and by developing and using the standard statistical areas recommended in Chapter 2. (The issue of crossing state lines is beset with difficulties that must be considered carefully.)

Given such a set of regions, one possibility within reasonable cost is to have detailed and timely data from such administrative sources as the social security sample or the federal income tax sample for these areas. Similarly, survey data, such as that from the CPS or the annual housing survey, might be reported by these regions. Greater detail for a subset of the regions on a rotating periodic basis might be provided, analogous to the annual housing survey procedure for metropolitan areas. The most promising alternative may be to provide basic data for the state and substate multicounty districts that are now widely established over the nation.

DATA GAPS

1. Annual Internal Revenue Service data on adjusted gross income by county of residence.
2. The measurement of multiple job holding and the tabulation of the employment of all family members in family units.
3. Data relating employment status to income, earnings, and net worth.
4. Data on public and private capital flows.
5. Better data on job holders cross-classified by industry and occupation, according to current Standard Industrial Classification (SIC) and Standard Occupational Classification (SOC) codes.
6. Data on the migration, creation, and termination of individual businesses and attendant jobs.
7. State data on private transfers (e.g., private pensions, out-of-state student support).

NOTES

[1]Money income does not include wages received in kind (e.g., use of a business car, employer payments of medical expenses, or the rent-free housing of some hired farm workers), nonmoney transfers (e.g., food stamps, health benefits, and subsidized housing), the net value of home-produced goods and services (e.g., food grown and consumed by the household), and net rental value of owner-occupied homes. Money income is also defined as income received before payments for personal income taxes and deductions for items such as Social Security, Medicare premiums, and union dues.

[2]The Bureau of Labor Statistics publishes seven measures of unemployment (U1-U7); in the first quarter of 1979 they ranged from 1.2 percent for U1 (persons unemployed 15 weeks or longer as percent of civilian labor force) to 5.7 percent for the official rate to 7.9 percent for U7, a measure which includes discouraged workers (i.e., unemployed people who are not actively looking for work).

[3]The "handbook method" is a means of estimating unemployment in small areas in which the CPS sample is too small to provide reliable estimates. It is based on unemployment insurance records. Various steps are taken to extract employee place-of-residence data from these records, which contain employer-based place-of-work data. Other steps are taken to account for various categories of people not eligible for unemployment insurance.

REFERENCES

Advisory Commission on Intergovernmental Relations (1979) Dun's Market Identifiers File Data Users Conference. Washington, D.C.: Advisory Commission on Intergovernmental Relations.

Barkley, D.L. (1978) Plant ownership characteristics and the locational stability of rural Iowa manufacturers. Land Economics 54(1):92-99.

Bryant, C.D., Dudley, C.J., and Shoemaker, D.J. (1980) Occupational Diversity of Rural Residents in Virginia: A Research Study of Multiple Job Holding and Labor Exchange. Department of Sociology, Virginia Polytechnic Institute and State University, Blacksburg, Va.

Bureau of the Census (1978a) Directory of Federal Statistics for Local Areas, A Guide to Sources, 1976. Washington, D.C.: U.S. Department of Commerce.

Bureau of the Census (1978b) Money income in 1976 of families and persons in the United States. Current Population Reports, Series P-60, No. 114. Washington, D.C.: U.S. Department of Commerce.

Bureau of the Census (1978c) Social and economic characteristics of the metropolitan and nonmetropolitan population: 1977 and 1970. Current Population Reports, Special Studies P-23, No. 75. Washington, D.C.: U.S. Department of Commerce.

Bureau of the Census and Economic Development Administration (1979) Guide to County Census Data for Planning Economic Development. Washington, D.C.: U.S. Department of Commerce.

Cecchi and Co. (1969) Capital Resources in the Central Appalachian Region. Washington, D.C.: The Appalachian Regional Commission.

Deaton, B.J. (1979) Discussion. American Journal of Agricultural Economics 61(5):973-974.

Deaton, B.J., and Landes, M.R. (1978) Rural industrialization and the changing distribution of family incomes. American Journal of Agricultural Economics 60(5):950-954.

Deaton, B.J., Morgan, L.M., and Anschel, K.R. (1977) The Influence of Psychic Costs on Human Resource Allocation. Paper presented at the annual meeting of the American Agricultural Economics Association, San Diego, Calif.

Deavers, K.L., and Brown, D.L. (1979) Social and Economic Trends in Rural America. White House Rural Development Background Paper. Washington, D.C.

Economic Research Service (1974) Employment in Agricultural and Agribusiness Occupations: Region 3. ERS-573. Washingon, D.C.: U.S. Department of Agriculture.

Goldstein, H. (1979) State and local labor force statistics. Pp. 411-463 in Data Collection, Processing and Presentation: National and Local. Appendix, Vol. II of Counting the Labor Force. National Commission on Employment and Unemployment Statistics. Washington, D.C.: U.S. Government Printing Office.

Grinstead-Schneider, J.J., and Green, B.L. (July 1978) Adjustment stress on rural laborers in the Mississippi Delta and the Ozarks. Growth and Change 9(3):36-43.

Gunter, D.L. (1977) Factors Affecting Employment Patterns in Manufacturing Plants in Rural Tennessee, 1964-1973. Master's thesis. Department of Agricultural Economics, University of Kentucky, Lexington.

Hastings, S.E., and Goode, F.M. (1980) The Standard Industrial Classification of Establishments: 1957-1977. Bulletin No. 432. Agricultural Experiment Station, University of Delaware, Newark.

Hendler, C.I., and Reid, J.N. (1980) Federal Outlays in Fiscal 1978: A Comparison of Metropolitan and Nonmetropolitan Areas. Rural Development Research Report No. 25. Economics, Statistics, and Cooperatives Service. Washington, D.C.: U.S. Department of Agriculture.

Hines, F., and Reid, N. (1977) Using federal outlays data to measure program equity: opportunities and limitations. American Journal of Agricultural Economics 58(5):1013-1019.

Hoch, I. (1979) Settlement size, real income, and the rural turnaround. American Journal of Agricultural Economics 61(5):953-959.

Holden, R., Tobias, L., and Wertheimer, R. (1979) Differences in Living Cost Between Rural and Urban Areas, Final Report. Washington, D.C.: The Urban Institute.

Hooker, R.W. (1970) The Effects of the Financial Community's Structure on the Commercial Bank's Role as a Financier of Regional Growth. Discussion Paper No. 5. Center for Economic Development, University of Texas, Austin.

Hoover, E.M., and Chinitz, B. (1964) The role of accounts in the economic study of regions. Pp. 612-620 in J. Friedmann and W. Alonso, eds., Regional Development and Planning: A Reader. Cambridge, Mass.: MIT Press.

Internal Revenue Service (1977a) Statistics of Income, Small Area Data, 1972. Washington, D.C.: U.S. Department of the Treasury.

Internal Revenue Service (1977b) Statistics of Income, Small Area Data, 1974. Washington, D.C.: U.S. Department of the Treasury.

Janssen, L. (1974) Comparative Profit Rates of U.S. Manufacturing Firms by City Size. Master's thesis. Department of Agricultural Economics, Oklahoma State University, Stillwater.

Korsching, P., and Sapp, S. (1977) People and Jobs in Gadsden County. Special Report to Center for Rural Development. Institute of Food and Agricultural Sciences. Gainesville, Fla.: University of Florida.

Kuehn, J.A., Bender, L.D., Green, B.L., and Hoover, H. (1972) Impact of Job Development on Poverty in Four Developing Areas, 1970. Agricultural Economic Report No. 225. Economic Research Service. Washington, D.C.: U.S. Department of Agriculture.

Lazear, E.P., and Michael, R.T. (1980) Family size and the distribution of real per capita income. American Economic Review 70(1):91-93.

National Commission on Employment and Unemployment Statistics (1979) Counting the Labor Force. Washington, D.C.: U.S. Government Printing Office.

National Research Council (1980) Estimating Population and Income of Small Areas. Panel on Small-Area Estimates of Population and Income, Committee on National Statistics, Assembly of Behavioral and Social Sciences, Washington, D.C.: National Academy Press.

Nelson, M.K. (1979) Impacts of Federal Outlays on Community Development. Doctoral dissertation. Department of Agricultural Economics, Oklahoma State University, Stillwater.

Nilsen, S. (1979) Assessment of Employment and Unemployment Statistics for Nonmetropolitan Areas. Rural Development Research Report No. 18. Economics, Statistics, and Cooperatives Service, U.S. Department of Agriculture, Washington, D.C.

North Central Regional Center for Rural Development (1979) Proceedings of the Ex Ante Growth Impact Models Conference. Ames, Iowa: Iowa State University.

Norwood, J.L. (1977) Reshaping a statistical program to meet legislative priorities. Monthly Labor Review 100(11):6-11.

Nourse, H.O. (1968) Regional Economics. New York: McGraw-Hill.

Office of Management and Budget (1980) 1980 Catalog of Federal Domestic Assistance. Washington, D.C.: U.S. Government Printing Office.

Ross, P., and Green, B. (1979) Educational Impacts of Rapid Population Growth in Rural Communities. Economics, Statistics, and Cooperatives Service. Washington, D.C.: U.S. Department of Agriculture.

Schultz, T.W. (1979) The economics of being poor. Nobel Lecture. Stockholm, Sweden: Nobel Foundation.

Shaffer, R. (1977) Wisconsin commercial bank effects on community economic development. Economic Issues, No. 15. Department of Agricultural Economics, University of Wisconsin, Madison.

Shaffer, R., and Tweeten, L. (1974) Economic changes from industrial development in eastern Oklahoma. Oklahoma State University Bulletin B-715. Stillwater, Ok.: Agricultural Experiment Station, Oklahoma State University.

Smith, S. M. (1979) Export Orientation of Nonmanufacturing Businesses in Nonmetropolitan Communities. Paper presented at the annual meeting of the American Agricultural Economics Association, Pullman, Washington. University of Idaho. Research Series 224, Department of Agricultural Economics, University of Idaho.

Stolnitz, G.J. (1972) U.S. interindustry mobility, 1960-1968. Pp.109-119 in The Labor Force: Migration, Earnings and Growth. Proceedings of a conference held at Muscle Shoals, Alabama, sponsored by the Social Security Administration and the Tennessee Valley Authority.

Summers, G.F., Evans, S.D., Clemente, F., Beck, E.M., and Minkoff, J. (1976) Industrial Invasion of Nonmetropolitan America: A Quarter Century of Experience. New York: Praeger.

Tweeten, L. (1978) Rural Employment and Unemployment Statistics. Background Paper No. 4. National Commission on Employment and Unemployment Statistics, Washington, D.C.

Tweeten, L., and Brinkman, G. (1976) *Micropolitan Development*. Ames, Iowa: Iowa State University Press.

Ullman, J. (1979) Discussion of paper by Harold Goldstein. Pp. 470-472 in *Data Collection, Processing and Presentation: National and Local*. Appendix, Vol. II of *Counting the Labor Force*. National Commission on Employment and Unemployment Statistics. Washington, D.C.: U.S. Government Printing Office.

U.S. House of Representatives (1978) *The Use of Population Data in Federal Assistance Programs*. Subcommittee on Census and Population, Committee on Post Office and Civil Service. Washington, D.C.: U.S. Government Printing Office

Virginia Farmers Home Administration (1980) *1981 State Management Plan*. Richmond, Va.: Virginia Farmers Home Administration.

Youmans, E.G. (1977) The rural aged. *Annals* 429:81.

11

NATURAL RESOURCES AND ENERGY

Natural resource management has a direct impact on the quality of rural life and an indirect influence on the potential of rural areas for economic development. The relation of energy requirements and natural resource requirements to the satisfaction of human needs can best be defined in terms of such specific subjects as energy availability and use, water availability, air and water quality, and land use. This chapter discusses data and data needs in terms of those four subjects.

ENERGY AVAILABILITY AND USE

Changes in policy leading to changes in the cost and availability of energy affect both rural and urban life in three ways: the direct effect of energy policy on personal transportation and utility costs; the effect of energy policy on economic development potential; and the effect of local energy development (e.g., mining, deforestation) on neighboring communities. All three probably have a different and greater impact on rural people than on metropolitan people.

Impact on Individuals

The direct effect of energy policy on personal transportation and utility costs is of prime importance to rural America because of the greater distances rural people must travel to work, shop, and visit. The sparsely settled character of rural America makes extensive public transportation infeasible, and there are not as many opportunities for car pooling and other methods of reducing transportation costs. Thus, rural residents have fewer opportunities than urban residents to reduce the impact of rising energy prices (or even rationing) by changing transportation modes.

A need for data on personal travel in rural areas was raised during an interview with a Cooperative Extension Service district director and a regional and urban planning consultant in Wisconsin. The panel member conducting the interview reported:

An unmet data need which will become more critical in the future is information about the journey to work for rural areas. As the energy crunch tightens, this type of information is essential for assessing the differential impact of the energy crisis in rural areas. The changing composition of nonfarm employment for part-time farmers and the need for part-time farmers to find work in "nearby" places increases the importance of this type of information.

Changes in U.S. energy policy that affect the relative cost and availability of fuel sources are likely to have a greater impact on rural areas than on urban areas to the extent that urban areas have a greater range of alternative fuels. For example, rural households forced to depend on high-priced fuel oil may be adversely affected by the fuel oil crunch relative to metropolitan areas that have access to alternative fuels such as natural gas. As a respondent noted:

> . . . several communities in the region do not have access to natural gas. The result is many households heat with fuel oil which has doubled in price since last winter, putting an extreme burden on family budgets [Southwest Regional Development Commission, Minnesota].

This issue will intensify under the current federal synthetic fuels program, which will convert substantial quantities of coal to synthetic natural gas, with most of the gains going to urban centers.

Impact on Economic Development

Energy policy can have an especially significant impact on the economic development of rural areas because nonmetropolitan factories are typically farther from markets and inputs than metropolitan factories and because energy needs influence residential location decisions. Transportation costs are becoming an increasingly important location consideration for many types of industries, and areas remote from markets or materials will have increasing difficulty in maintaining or expanding their economic bases as energy prices rise.

Rising costs and shortages of fuel have already become an important problem for American farmers, and further increases will aggravate the problem. Most farmers rely heavily on gasoline or diesel power engines, and even the smallest farms now use mechanical assistance for many tasks--e.g., loading hay into lofts, filling silos, feeding livestock, and other chores. As some of our respondents noted:

> Farmers are being forced to greater and greater efficiency just to stay in business. The impact of increased fuel cost is going to be dramatic on farmers that are operating on marginal income. All this adds up to greater numbers of farm workers and families being displaced [Licking River Area, Kentucky].

> One policy issue . . . is energy. Being an agricultural area, petroleum products are in constant demand. The farmers are really impacted by the rising cost of fuel [Southwest Regional Development Commission, Minnesota].

> . . . the availability of motor fuel at affordable prices is becoming a critical concern, particularly to our agricultural enterprise which, contrary to most businesses, does not enjoy the luxury of being able to pass on to their customers these increased costs of production. Our farmers are faced . . . with the staggering question of whether they can even afford to plant their crop, knowing that market commodity prices may not return enough to them to even pay their fuel bills. I don't think I overrate this issue by saying that we face the real possibility of abandoning planting on thousands of acres of productive land, and putting farmers out of business [Bear River Association of Governments, Utah].

The economic vitality of small towns that have become "bedroom communities" may also suffer from rising energy costs. In recent years many urban people have moved to rural areas and commute to city jobs. These rural-to-urban commuters have been willing to pay higher transportation costs in order to enjoy the amenities of rural living, but they might elect to move back to urban centers and weaken the small town economic base if energy costs become too great. Some survey respondents noted this possibility:

> Caldwell . . . is (or was) feeling the effects of growth emanating from the Kansas City/St. Joseph urban complex prior to the advent of higher gasoline prices. I suspect that current gasoline prices have had a dramatic dampening effect on long-distance commuting from rural homesites into the metropolitan areas [Green Hills Regional Planning Commission, Missouri].

> Energy conservation is an . . . issue of current interest in Saginaw County. Energy is important for farm operations, and for those persons commuting from the rural areas to places of employment in the cities [Saginaw County, Michigan].

Current federal environmental programs have further discouraged rural-to-urban commuting by improving urban areas relative to rural areas. Commuting has been made even less attractive by energy cost increases, lower highway speed limits, and other programs designed to reduce energy demands. The formulation of energy policy and the planning of rural development require better understanding of the magnitude of rural-to-urban commuting and of the factors that influence it.

Impact on Energy Development Boom Areas

The energy resources of most communities are developed, but, rural communities in areas with substantial undeveloped energy sources are likely to face severe problems of managing rapid growth. Many types of energy development, most notably mining and power plant construction, have a substantial impact on rural areas, although the energy produced may be consumed in other regions. Both coal and shale oil, two prime candidates for accelerated development, are produced in sparsely settled rural areas, and the potential disassociation of the benefits from the local costs is of prime political importance.

Although properly managed development of energy resources can have a positive impact on the communities involved, such positive effects are not certain nor easy to achieve. At the very least, a great deal of rural development planning is necessary to handle effectively the boom town syndrome associated with energy development in sparsely settled areas.

Energy-Related Data Requirements

The first important energy-related data requirements are those associated with energy policy formulation. Public policy affecting energy resources is made primarily at the federal level, although some states levy taxes on mined coal. The data requirements can be viewed from the federal perspective, even though regional differences exist (e.g., issues of water and mineral development, important in the West, are not as important in the Southeast). As one respondent noted:

> Energy is the resource issue out here and national decisions on energy affect us more than anything we can do to or for ourselves at the local or state level [Hot Springs County, Wyoming].

Energy policy formulation involves decisions on many subjects, including foreign policy, energy development programs, and demand reduction or conservation programs. The data requirements for these activities are immense and include everything from routine energy consumption and price data to the latest information regarding potential exotic fuels. For this report, it is sufficient to focus on those data that relate to the impact of energy policy on rural regions.

Energy policy, which changes the cost and availability of energy, affects both individuals and communities. There are three important data requirements for measuring policy effects:

- Energy price and consumption data by purpose, fuel type, place of residence, and income class.
- Data on input substitution possibilities stemming from analysis of alternate modes of transportation available, the extent to which homes and businesses can be retrofitted to become more energy efficient, and alternate feasible modes of agricultural

production. These data need to be sufficiently detailed to permit assessing geographic, industrial, and income class differences.

- Data on the economic, environmental, social, and cultural status of the communities affected by energy development. The primary components would be demographic data, environmental quality data, the amounts and availability of local energy resources, and information on the capacity of local transportation, utility, and public service systems.

These data sets delineate the minimum information necessary for reasonable assessments of energy policy changes on human well-being, with emphasis on rural-urban differentials.

There are also energy-related data needs for rural development planning. Changes in energy cost and availability can have a substantial impact on the potential for rural development. The data base must be adequate for understanding or at least predicting the nature and magnitude of such impact. The principal data sets necessary for this purpose, in addition to those already mentioned, include:

- Data on the production and marketing cost structure of the types of business firms in rural areas.
- Data on the commuting patterns and residential preferences of rural residents.

This information, along with pertinent information from the energy policy data sets, would enable rural development planners to assess at least the broad impacts of energy cost and availability changes on given rural areas. Still more data would be needed to understand and predict more specific or less common effects, such as the effect of rising costs on the travel and recreation decisions of area residents. Although such data needs may be critical in selected areas, they are outside the scope of this report.

Currently Available and Needed Energy-Related Data

Substantial progress has been made in the collection of energy-related data since the energy crisis began in 1973. Although some of the data are not well integrated and may be hard to locate, much of the key information is available. At least two important periodical digests report energy statistics: Monthly Energy Review, published monthly by the Energy Information Administration (EIA) of the Department of Energy, and National Transportation Statistics, prepared and distributed annually by the Department of Transportation. (The data bases from which these publications are derived are not currently available for any other uses, and are thus not described in Appendix E.) The 1980 census also contains some data related to energy. With few exceptions, the statistics reported in the first two publications refer to the total United States, but occasionally they provide statistics for states and regions or census divisions. The census, however, has some small-area data.

The Monthly Energy Review contains information about energy consumption by sector, the consumption and disposition of natural gas and coal, generation of nuclear power, and the production of electricity by energy source. It also has energy prices, including average gasoline selling prices, residential heating oil prices by region, and average retail electricity prices. It frequently contains feature articles on timely subjects such as energy consumption, home heating conservation alternatives, motor gasoline supply and demand, and the solar collector industry.

National Transportation Statistics is a summary compilation of data gathered from a wide variety of government and private sources. It includes cost, inventory, and performance data describing the passenger and cargo operations of the following modes of transportation: air carrier, general (private) aviation, auto, bus, truck, local transit, rail, water, oil pipeline, and gas pipeline. The report includes basic descriptions of U.S. transportation such as operating revenues and expenses, number of vehicles and employees, and vehicle and passenger miles.

The 1980 census contains information at the county level about the costs and types of fuel used for domestic purposes (i.e., cooking, space and water heating, etc.) for rural and urban households. Ample data regarding available energy resources can be combined with census data to answer most of the key questions associated with the effects of coal mines, power plants, and other energy development activities. The Bureau of the Census (1980) publication, Energy Statistics Data Finder, provides a summary of census data on energy by title of publication, series report number, subject content, geographic detail, and report frequency.

From the perspective of rural development, the principal gaps in the energy-related data base are data on the possibilities of energy input substitition. Rural America must conserve energy and reduce the impact of rising energy prices, but little information is readily available about ways of achieving such reductions. Too few people are aware of the technologies available for this purpose. There has been inadequate dissemination of information on home insulation, home air conditioning, home and other building construction to cut heat losses and reduce air-conditioning requirements, generation of electricity by wind or water-powered generators, use of ground temperature for heating and air conditioning, use of plant materials to produce alcohol for fuel, use of manure and organic residues to produce methane gas, solar heating and cooking, and many other methods to reduce dependence on high-cost fossil fuels. Thus, too few data are available on the potential methods by which business firms and home owners might mitigate the effect of rising energy costs.

This lack of data is a national, not only a rural, problem. But the deficiency is particularly important in rural areas, where it is more difficult to offset negative effects through life-style changes and input substitutions. Several respondents noted their interest in substitution possibilities:

A coal-fired generation plant and possibly a gasohol plant is being considered in Comstock, Nebraska. If this project is completed, it would create sufficient power to adequately supply this portion of Central Nebraska for now and in the foreseeable future [Valley County, Nebraska].

[Conservation] is a high priority. More emphasis should be placed on energy use from biomass in the forest (i.e., demonstration grants). Chemical extraction and energy utilization will be the products [Superior California Development Council].

There is . . . much interest and concern over utilization of our natural resources and what alternatives we have. It appears there is a need for additional research to help us with our fuel problems, recycling of waste materials, and how to manage and conserve our resources [Lincoln Trail Extension Area, Kentucky].

Because of the dependence of rural economies on transportation and energy supplies, these have been expressed as concerns of local people. In meeting with local officials and citizens . . . issues such as alternate energy and hydropower have been expressed and there is the feeling that the negative feelings toward nuclear and coal should be moderated in some fashion. Energy has been expressed as the single most important issue for rural people [West Central Wisconsin Regional Planning Commission].

Decatur County has always been conservation-minded as our county is a leader in soil conservation in Kansas. This philosophy has carried on in energy conservation. Many of our farmers are very interested in the use of alcohol fuels [Decatur County, Kansas].

Data on how production costs are affected by change in energy costs are needed to assess the impact of rising energy costs on various types of business activity and on the location decisions of private industry. Such data are not generally available, mainly because of their proprietary character. The reluctance of private industry to release such information on costs is understandable, but this data gap precludes accurate predictions of the consequences of changes in energy policy and prevents rural communities from planning adequately for the provision of public facilities.

Urban workers who live in rural areas provide an economic base for many small towns. Little is known about the potential shifts in residence of rural-to-urban commuters that might result from rising energy costs. The effects of changes in energy policy cannot be assessed and careful community plans cannot be made until more is learned about the situations and attitudes of these rural-to-urban commuters.

WATER AVAILABILITY

Water is a major input in many types of economic activity; it is necessary for domestic needs, and it is a focal point for many recreational pursuits. Thus, water availability can influence the quality of life in rural areas and determine rural development potential.

Alternatives to current practice in water use are needed in some areas. Rapidly diminishing water tables and increasing populations in much of the Southwest portend serious problems of water availability. Research on replenishing underground water supplies with flood waters should be considered. Irrigation for agricultural needs can conserve more water, permitting the diversion of the water savings to satisfy urban water needs. Growth of low water-requiring crops such as guayule and jojoba may be needed if agriculture is to prosper (see National Research Council 1977).

Data Needs

Water availability is a potential constraint in rural development in many areas, particularly in the Southwest. Rural development officials in water-scarce areas must know the current and projected demand and supply situations for both surface and groundwater resources in order to determine community growth potential. As one respondent noted:

> Water resource management . . . [is a significant rural policy issue]. This involves federal, state and local agencies. It is exceedingly complicated. Basic data is needed with respect to water availability and education is needed with respect to water management policy and practice [Lincoln-Uinta Association of Governments, Wyoming].

Perhaps even more important than measures of water supply relative to projected demand is assessment of the potential for supply augmentation or demand reduction. The data needs for analyzing this potential include: data describing potential surface water storage sites; data that permit specifications of surface and groundwater linkage; data on the value of water in alternative uses, including price-quantity relationships; and data for assessing the economic feasibility of water development programs. These types of data would allow economic assessments of the possibilities for modifying water availability. Although preliminary information is probably sufficient for long-range rural development planning, more detailed and site specific data would be necessary for implementing water plans.

Good water resource planning requires a current and complete inventory of water resources. Data are needed on: pumping depths of wells by months, or at least by years; the lengths of streams with a specified fall in elevation per unit area; the volume of water during various seasons; the volumes of flood waters and ways of conserving them, at least in the West; and salt accumulations in the soil from irrigation (and methods needed to prevent such accumulation).

Current Data Availability and Gaps

An excellent data base exists on water availability. The U.S. Water Resources Council (1978) has completed the second national water assessment. The U.S. Geological Survey (USGS) has collected extensive data, especially for critical areas, and most states collect considerable supplementary data. The project files of the Army Corps of Engineers and the Water Power and Resources Service are also good sources of information. One or both of these agencies has investigated the needs and development potential of most critical water areas in the United States.

Relatively few general data gaps exist, although integration of existing data is often lacking. One weak research area is the linkage between surface and groundwater resources. This relationship is extremely important in irrigated regions where groundwater and surface water are hydrologically connected, but relatively little is known about it. Research is needed even to determine what data are germane. As one respondent noted:

> During the last two years I have been working with the West Central Minnesota Irrigation Association in trying to get the necessary local support and funding to do a deep water survey. In irrigation area development, the key information needed is the availability of water and once irrigation has begun, the effect of irrigation on water levels and quality [Pope County, Minnesota].

AIR AND WATER QUALITY

Rural development planners have relatively little direct involvement in formulating air and water quality policy. Nevertheless, such policy decisions can have substantial effects on rural areas, especially through their influence on the potential for rural development. Both state and federal regulations on air and water quality influence the relative attractiveness of different geographic locations for industrial development; they increase the cost of providing community services, and they may or may not improve the environmental quality of a given region. As one respondent complained:

> Improved natural resource management and conservation is viewed with much frustration by landowners and civic leaders. The views of the physically remote preservationists seemingly have more weight with bureaucratic decision-makers than those who suffer losses and must replace, repair, or at a minimum clean their property after seasonal flooding. The identified special interests, none of whom are personally affected in terms of

> losses or investments, exert abnormal pressures on those government agency representatives charged with the conduct of the programs to prevent floods and drain agricultural lands [Fayette County, Ohio].

A respondent (from Culpeper County, Virginia) noted that there is rural resistance to federal controls on air, water, and sedimentation. For example, auto emission standards have increased the cost of autos in many isolated rural areas where air quality was not a problem. On the other hand, water quality regulations have improved health and safety. Another respondent noted:

> The concern over degradation of rivers and lakes has been clearly shown . . . through the action of the towns and regional agencies. The towns in Northwestern Connecticut have established two river boards, one on the Housatonic and the other on the Shepaug-Bantam River. Lakes in the region . . . have received considerable study. These studies center on ways to prevent or correct water quality problems [Northwest Connecticut Regional Planning Agency].

Data Requirements

Data needs for policy on air and water quality should be examined to understand the differential effects of such policies on urban and rural areas. The data required for well-informed policy making on air and water qualtiy would: describe current environmental conditions in some geographic detail; assess the health, safety, and ecological implications of air and water pollution; and assess the costs or consequences of programs directed at reducing pollution. With the exception of descriptive data on the magnitude of air and water pollution, these data must be obtained from the scientific community and must be continually updated as new insights are gleaned from ongoing research. One respondent suggested such a research effort:

> Rural water systems are spreading at a very rapid rate and there is a need for higher quality water by a lot more residents. Do we come up with alternate ways of providing quality water at less costs? Why don't we research and find an individual home water system purifier that would probably cost much less than a rural water line and still provide adequate and quality water [Lincoln Trail Extension Area, Kentucky].

Data needed for rural development planning are similar, but in addition, rural development personnel must often prepare the environmental impact statements associated with proposed projects. Historically, government agencies have interpreted EPA guidelines and court decisions to require extremely detailed assessments of environmental consequences. Environmental impact statements have often included everything from very technical assessments of physical environmental effects to inventories of all flora and fauna in the vicinity of a project. These data needs are quite specific to a situation, but they have become better defined and less burdensome as the environmental impact statement process has matured.

Data Availability and Gaps

The key data associated with air and water quality are maintained by EPA and the USGS. These include a data service that reports the results of the environmental quality monitoring programs plus newsletters and bibliographies that are designed to keep affected parties abreast of the results of environmental quality analyses. (See Appendix D for descriptions of these data sets.)

With the exception of the area-specific data requirements of environmental impact statements, no existing data gaps are of particular significance to rural development objectives. There are ample data on most current environmental conditions. The deficiencies in any impact analysis are so specific to the situation or conceptually so complex that the need cannot be filled through a general data collection program.

LAND USE

Land use planning has become an increasingly sensitive issue in natural resource management as competing demands for natural resources have grown, in part because land use is closely identified with environmental concerns and with the preservation of rural America. The most important link between land use and rural development has been the dominant influence of land use planning as a method of guiding community growth. In many communities land use plans determine the location of utilities, the types of industries to be encouraged, the roads to be built, and the type of future the community will have.

Another major land use issue is the question of what, if anything, should be done to discourage urban development of prime agricultural land. One respondent noted the local support for such activity:

> Prior to our . . . opinion survey, most community leaders in eastern Livingston County perceived that the support for agricultural land retention came principally from recent urban immigrants who did not farm. Our opinion survey asked people in every community if they felt their local government should take positive steps to preserve agriculture. The results of the survey were cross-tabulated with income, household tenure, age, and length of residence. None of these variables explained the prevailing citizen opinion that agricultural lands should be retained by local action. It is our conclusion that these attitudes are shared throughout the general population and are not held by an urban elite. This information has given new

> credibility to agricultural retention activities [Livingston County, Michigan].

Nevertheless, protection of agricultural land is frequently a divisive issue. Some groups would like to see severe restrictions on the development of prime agricultural land because of aesthetic and potential food supply needs, while others believe that the market should be allowed to allocate land resources among competing uses, subject only to the protection of third parties. Several respondents noted the various pressures on this issue:

> Farmland preservation is a major issue. Farmers in the county wish to protect their lands from pressures to convert to urban uses for economic, aesthetic, and resource conservation reasons. They feel assistance must be provided to them if they are to continue agricultural practices, especially in areas adjacent to cities [Saginaw County, Michigan].

> . . . we can offer some perspective concerning rural existence and development in the shadow of an expanding metropolitan region. One issue that arises concerns the consumption of farmlands by residential development. This development is not accompanied by significant development in commercial and industrial activities. Thus, due to the lack of an expanding tax base, the rural counties and towns are having difficulty meeting the increasing demands for community facilities and services [Mid-America Regional Council, Missouri].

> There is considerable interest among local residents in preserving the agricultural land use in Teton County. There is growing recognition that the heirs of present ranchers will be forced to sell land for development in order to pay estate taxes [Teton County, Wyoming].

Other respondents described how the issue has been handled locally:

> Our land use ordinance reads that if a farmer desires to put more than one non-farm dwelling on his acreage, he must go through the procedures of a subdivision. We feel that at that point he must be interested in income . . . thus he should go through all the necessary subdivision requirements. Through the hearing process we will better know if there is some resistance to the plan [Dodge County, Minnesota].

> Our County Land Use Plan, adopted after considerable controversy, addresses quality of development, but not really the quantity. It does not designate any agricultural, wild life, or open space areas, although it does provide for open space. . . . Thus, even with a reasonably good Land Use Plan, growth and subdivision continue unabated. Most people here feel that, given the tremendous difference in land value for

agriculture and for development, government cannot fairly zone an area exclusively for open space or agriculture [Teton County, Wyoming].

A third key issue concerns public land use management. More than one-third of the nation's land resources are publicly owned and managed by either the Bureau of Land Management (BLM), the Forest Service or other federal agencies. In several western states, the proportion of the total land base in federal ownership exceeds 75 percent. Thus, public land use is of central importance to rural development in many areas, especially in the West. As one respondent noted:

> Natural resource management and conservation has been a strong, constant but not very dynamic concern of a core of responsible local citizens and public officials. There is an ongoing divergence of opinion, however, between the local citizens, who would maximize resource exploitation and federal agencies such as Forest Service and BLM which have tended to be more planning oriented, restrictive and conservationist in their approaches. Here again, practically all improvement measures have occurred only as a result of federal funding and federal management initiatives [Bear River Association of Governments, Utah].

Data Requirements

Data needs for private land use planning depend on how broadly the land use planning process is defined. The requirements are fairly straightforward if the definition is restricted to land use proper and excludes the many community planning functions that often are grouped under the rubric of land use. Data are needed that delineate the productive capability of the land and describe current land use patterns. Data on land use patterns should be detailed enough to permit mapping of specific types of land uses as well as general land use categories.

The data required for analyzing prime farmland include land capability data plus the analytical information needed to project future demands. One respondent noted data needs on this topic:

> Since there is a great concern about preserving prime agricultural land, it would be helpful to somehow be able to track the shift of land out of agriculture. These statistics are almost impossible to come by. Land owned by absentee landlords is difficult to classify. The Soil Conservation Service is in the process of completing a Land Inventory Monitoring Program. This will compare current land use and erosion status of about 800 locations within the county with status in 1963. The results of this survey will be sent to Ames, Iowa, for analysis. It would be extremely useful if some way could be found to expedite the analysis and return the

> information to the county because it is exactly the sort of information needed to begin the Agricultural Preservation Survey [Lebanon County, Pennsylvania].

The debate over preservation of prime farmland will remain confused until a standard set of defensible concepts and measurements of prime farmland is developed. Until then the available data are suspect and in some cases part of the problem. The panel has not discussed a recent comprehensive study of farmland preservation (U.S. Department of Agriculture and Council on Environmental Quality 1981) because it was not available while this report was being prepared. The study suggests that immediate federal, state, and local action be taken to protect farmland. We should note that their research and data recommendations concerning land use and preservation are similar to recommendations we are making more generally about rural data. Their recommendations include:

> The Office of Federal Statistical Policy and Standards [now the Statistical Policy Division], in consultation with other agencies, should develop a statistical protocol for federal agencies which collect and use natural resource data. Components of the protocol should cover standards for data collection techniques and requirements for appropriate statements of data limitations in connection with data publications or public release.
>
> USDA should develop a capacity for providing state or local governments with detailed statistical information on agricultural land use collected by federal agencies.
>
> A Data Advisory Group should be established in each state with membership of state and local officials. This group should advise agencies on how to make federal data collection programs more useful and accessible at the state and local level.

Many competing uses make the data requirements for public land management very broad. The sometimes simultaneous uses include timber production, mining and fossil fuel extraction, grazing, watershed protection, recreation, and wildlife protection. The greatest value of the public lands for many Americans is symbolic--their ownership in perpetual trust by the entire nation. Public land policy must recognize the competing demands of resource extractors, recreation seekers, homesteaders, and environmentalists. The demands of different groups for the same area often cannot be accommodated by the concept of multiple use, and there may be sharp conflicts even within major categories of users.

Often the contentious issues as well as the costs and benefits are specific to particular rural areas and communities. Nearby communities may be heavily affected by the types and intensity of uses on the public lands. As one respondent noted:

> Like much of Wyoming, Jackson Hole is experiencing tremendous growth pressures. Here, the pressures are not yet brought about by mineral exploration (although oil and gas development is increasingly likely); rather, it is the beauty of the area, the proximity to Grand Teton and Yellowstone National Parks, the recreation and tourist boom, and the desire for second homes and condominiums that impact us here [Teton County, Wyoming].

Communities must provide services to recreational users and other visitors--nonresidents who do not pay local taxes--but they benefit from the jobs and other activities generated from such federally provided goods as watersheds, roads, and recreation. Local desires often conflict with a federal agency's policy or practice, as in the designation of wilderness areas. Information based on research is needed on the costs and benefits of alternative uses of public land, including the impact of such uses on nearby communities.

Data Availabilitiy and Gaps

Most of the land use data that are relevant to rural development are compiled in the form of maps. The six most pertinent map resources cover soils, flood plains, wetlands, land uses, prime farmlands, and individual properties.

Soil maps Soil maps are available for much of the United States. Published surveys exist for 1,242 county or soil survey areas; 406 additional areas have been surveyed, with published maps expected soon. These maps vary in age from 1945 to the present, with a scale that ranges from 1:15,840 to 1:65,360.

Flood plain maps County and community floodplain maps are available from HUD or local units of government for all major cities and most rural areas with substantial flooding potential. Most of these maps are less than 10 years old and are at scales of from 1:7,920 to 1:126,720.

Wetland maps The U.S. Fish and Wildlife Service has mapped about 15 percent of the nation's wetland areas; the best information (less than 5 years old) is for the east and west coasts and the lower Mississippi. These maps are available at a scale of 1:244,000, but will be published at 1:100,000. As yet, very few have been published.

Land use maps Excellent land use maps are available from the USGS for all coastal areas, the Ozark region, the Northeast (except New York), and the Southeast. The mapping program for the entire nation will be completed by 1984. These maps are relatively current (within the last 6 years), and are available at a scale of 1:250,000 with some at 1:100,000. The status of the program is shown in Figure 1.

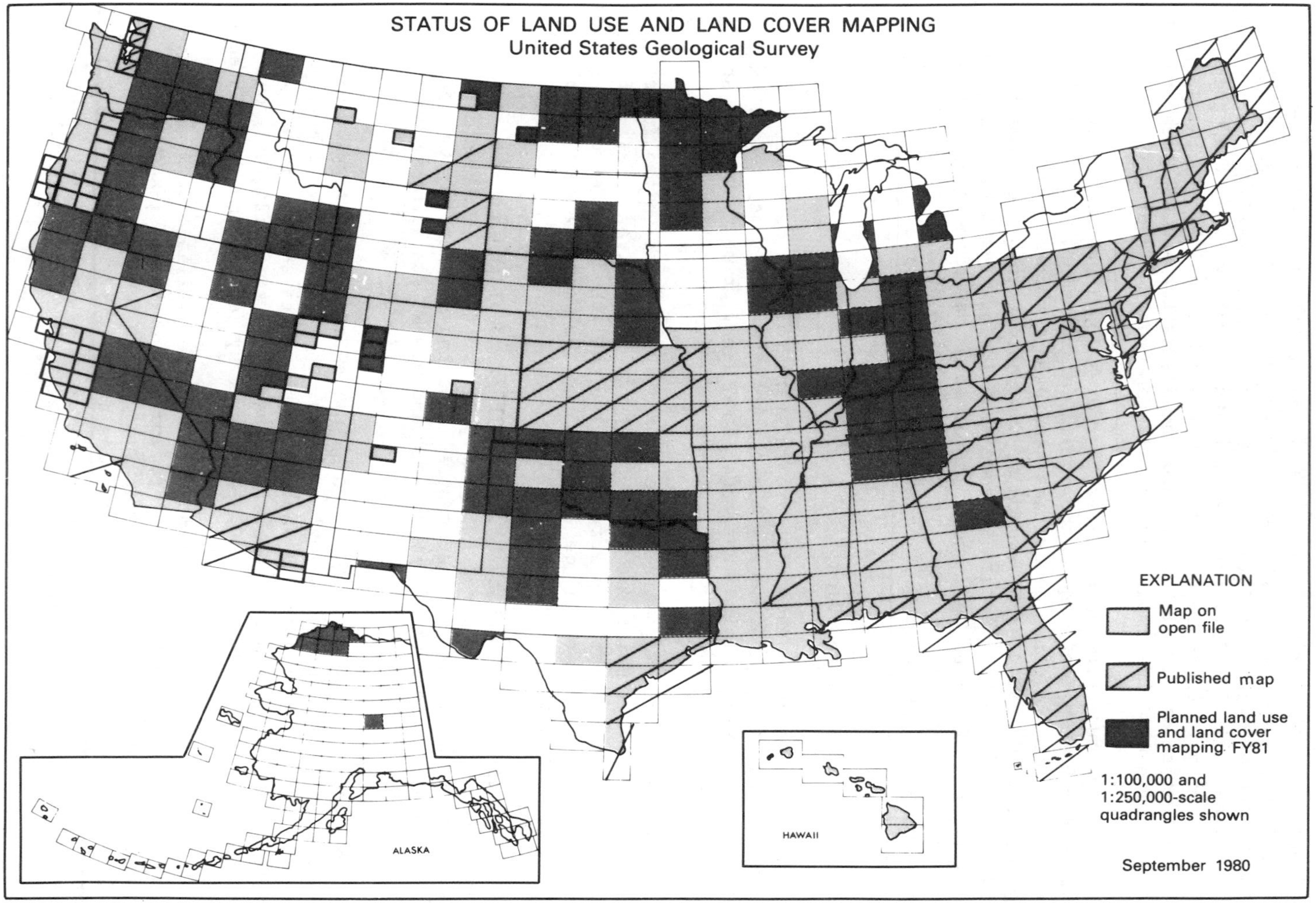

STATUS OF LAND USE AND LAND COVER MAPPING
United States Geological Survey
EXPLANATION
Map on open file
Published map
Planned land use and land cover mapping FY81
1:100,000 and 1:250,000-scale quadrangles shown
September 1980
ALASKA
HAWAII

FIGURE 1

Prime farmland maps The Soil Conservation Service (SCS) has published maps of "prime farmland" in 8 states at scales of 1:500,000 or 1:1,000,000 and in 262 counties at varying scales. Another 320 county maps are in progress. One drawback to these maps is that they use a definition of prime farmland that is not universally accepted; in fact, the concept of prime farmland still generates considerable debate.

Cadastral maps Cadastral maps, which show the boundaries of individual properties, are a useful source of information on land ownership units. Such maps may be found in county tax offices. In some counties, they have been compiled and bound in plat books that cover the entire county.

Summary Data for land use management are relatively abundant. The principal gaps are caused by the incomplete mapping activities of USGS, HUD, and SCS. Of particular significance are the uncompleted floodplain, wetlands, and land use maps. The agencies involved should be encouraged to complete the programs for the most important areas as soon as possible. One respondent noted that his county had filled this gap:

> The county staff has made great progress in identifying management techniques for the proper utilization of land and water resources. The varied landscape of western Livingston County has never been thoroughly classified and evaluated before this program. In 1979 a system of terrain classification was developed that is convenient to use and to understand and is scientifically reliable. This system groups together diverse landscape elements that have similar performance characteristics and it includes site specific detail to prevent the loss of wetlands, excessive erosion, or the pollution of groundwater supplies. More importantly, our classification scheme has been developed to be more understandable to citizens [Livingston County, Michigan].

DATA GAPS

1. Data on the potential methods by which business firms and home owners might mitigate the effect of rising energy costs.
2. Data on how production costs are affected by change in energy costs.
3. Data on potential shifts in residence of rural-to-urban commuters that might result from rising energy costs.
4. Standard set of defensible concepts and measurements of prime farmland.
5. Floodplain, wetlands, and land use maps.

REFERENCES

Bureau of the Census (1980) *Energy Statistics Data Finder*. Washington, D.C.: U.S. Department of Commerce.

National Research Council (1977) *Guayule: An Alternative Source of Natural Rubber*. Ad Hoc Panel, Board on Agriculture and Renewable Resources, Commission on Natural Resources. Washington, D.C.: National Academy of Sciences.

U.S. Department of Agriculture and Council on Environmental Quality (1981) *National Agricultural Lands Study: Final Report*. Washington, D.C.: U.S. Department of Agriculture and Council on Environmental Quality.

U.S. Water Resources Council (1978) *The Nation's Water Resources 1975-2000*. Second National Water Assessment. Washington, D.C.: U.S. Government Printing Office.

12

STRATEGIES FOR IMPROVING RURAL DEVELOPMENT INFORMATION

Methods of data collection and analysis must be varied and adaptive if the needs of rural development are to be met. While there is no substitute for high-quality data collected by a survey or census, data bases can be broadened by the informed use of statistical methods. Skillfully used, statistical techniques enable one to extract more information from existing data sources. Unfortunately, the skilled use of statistical techniques often requires a degree of technical training that is rare at the level of local rural planning and less widespread than desirable at the regional, state, and federal levels. We believe, however, that computer, satellite, photographic, and statistical technologies can be used to improve and expand the supply of local area data.

STATISTICAL METHODOLOGIES

In this section we briefly present some statistical methodologies that may have a role in the generation and analysis of data useful for rural development policy.

Direct Estimates for Small Areas

The panel recognizes that the demand for timely statistical data for small areas will forever outrun the capacity of statistical agencies. Pressure for information on the local level is mounting because of the use of such data in the allocation of funds to state, county, and municipal governments. As local agencies set up their own data collection operations, duplication of effort is inevitable.

Data collected in one way are satisfactory for one use, but frequently not for another. For example, a small rural area may be required by a federal granting agency to furnish estimates of certain kinds of housing. For the purposes of the grant application, an informal survey of housing conducted by local people may satisfy the granting agency. Such a survey may also play a useful role in increasing the knowledge of local planners about the local housing situation. In fact the granting agency could argue that requiring the local agency to conduct a survey to obtain the housing information provides a learning experience that justifies the effort. However, such local surveys will usually not meet the statistical requirements for a national data base. The fact that procedures differ from locality to locality will make it difficult to sum such local data sets into a meaningful national data set. The local data will be useful to the group collecting the data, the granting agency, and, perhaps, to other similar local groups, but not as input to regional or national estimates.

This is not to say that surveys conducted at less than national levels cannot be integrated into national data sets. But if local surveys are to be integrated into national data sets, then national procedures, standards, and definitions must be used. Because the introduction and supervision of federal standards increase costs and time requirements, it is not practicable or desirable that all local data collection should be so organized.

On the other hand, not all data collections designed to obtain data accurate at a national level for national planning purposes can be expected to furnish accurate data for small local areas. Costs often prohibit surveys of the size required to yield direct sample estimates for small areas. Federal agencies can, however, assist local agencies that wish to develop data bases consistent with the national statistics. The panel suggests that federal agencies, when it is practical and feasible, design surveys so that the basic survey design can be used to obtain national estimates, state estimates, county estimates, and metropolitan area estimates. The federal agency would use only the portion of the sample required for national estimates, but additional sample elements could be made available to local agencies that wish to conduct a survey for their area. The local agency could then obtain local estimates of the desired precision. In some cases, the local data might be integrated into the national data set. Experience would indicate the types of surveys for which augmented designs would be useful.

In addition to developing sample survey designs for local areas, federal and state agencies may be able to design standard questionnaires and tables so that the statistical summarizations and estimations for local surveys can be performed at a central office. This would ensure uniformity of estimates and analyses and will often be less expensive and require less time than would processing at the local or state level. The computing might be programmed so that local areas could obtain responses, analyses, and estimates via a telephone terminal.

A large proportion of the data needed for rural development policy will and should continue to be the product of decentralized data systems. The lack of consensus with regard to the problems and concepts underlying rural development policy, emphasized in Chapter 1, implies a need for varied and innovative approaches rather than standard practices. In addition, many of the uses of rural data occur at the local, regional, and state levels, and the particular needs in each situation are generally best satisfied by data gathered at the corresponding governmental level.

Recommendation: The panel recommends that the Farmers Home Administration encourage local efforts to generate rural development data for local purposes. To this end, the panel recommends that existing efforts at the local level be surveyed and that particularly innovative and useful examples be widely disseminated.

Estimates for Small Areas Based Upon Auxiliary Information

In many situations there exists a desire for estimates for small areas, but the cost of surveys of a sufficient size to provide reliable direct estimates would be prohibitive. In such situations it may be possible to use existing information to construct small-area estimates. Statistical techniques based on auxiliary variables attempt to identify relatively stable relationships between the variable of interest and observable explanatory variables. The relationships are estimated using data from an earlier census or from a sample in which the variable of interest is observed. The estimated relationships and currently observed values of the explanatory variables are then used to estimate the current value of an unobserved variable of interest (or a variable of interest observed with large error).

The report of the Panel on Small Area Estimates (National Research Council 1980) contains a description of methods of this type used by the Bureau of the Census to estimate the population of civil divisions of the country for intercensal years. There are a number of papers on these estimation techniques in the statistical literature (see the short bibliography at the end of this chapter); the paper by Purcell and Kish (1979) contains an excellent review of techniques, and the paper by Fay and Herriot (1979) contains a brief introduction to shrinkage-type procedures. We briefly outline one method of small-area estimation in Appendix G. We feel that the use of sample estimates in such procedures is very important as it permits the estimating equations to change as the basic relationships undergo structural change. We also recognize that it will not always be possible to use sample-based coefficients.

Recommendation: The panel recommends that state and federal agencies give high priority to upgrading the quality of small-area estimates and projections, particularly those used to allocate funds.

Administrative records (e.g., tax records, school records, and birth and death records) are often the observable variables used in small-area estimation. Modest modifications in administrative record-keeping practices could lead to sizable increases in the efficacy of administrative records for statistical estimation. For example, if each school district reported attendance by place of residence and if these data were tabulated, the data would be very useful for constructing estimates for small rural areas. The general need for place-of-residence data was noted in Chapter 2 in the discussion of the county as the basic building block of the data base. The panel commends the Internal Revenue Service (IRS) for its recent decision to include a place-of-residence question on the 1980 individual income tax returns, as recommended by the Panel on Small Area Estimates (National Research Council 1980). The IRS decision is an important step toward improved small-area estimates. The panel urges other agencies to follow suit in designing their administrative data collections.

The use of statistical techniques for small areas based on auxiliary information has had relatively limited trial in comparison with its potential. Exploration of possible refinements, extensions, and sources of auxiliary data should be conducted. One interesting and important statistical question is how the probabilistic structure of the sample of rural counties should be taken into account in applying the regression estimates to nonsampled counties. The types of benchmark information that may be useful as independent variables, and how these variables can be most effectively exploited, need to be investigated. Exploitation of geographic contiguity might be valuable in estimating characteristics of small rural areas. The possible methods of sampling rural areas for use in such analyses also need further study.

Possible innovations in the preparation of estimates include use of a system of special censuses or large-scale surveys for a selected sample of civil divisions or the use of the expanded current population survey as a means of calibrating a set of population estimates. The greatest demand for current data will come from those areas that are experiencing the fastest rate of change, and these are just the areas for which it is most difficult to make estimates. If rapidly growing areas can be crudely identified, greater research efforts or higher sampling rates can be assigned to such areas.

We believe that procedures based on auxiliary information have a definite and increasing role to play in providing estimates for small areas. However, the nature and shortcomings of such estimates must be understood. First, such estimates are not unbiased for each area (in the formal sampling definition of bias). That is, if the true value of the area is considered a fixed value, the expected value of the estimator is not that value. This means that there may be data uses for which the presence of this type of bias will need to be explicitly considered. The use of techniques based upon auxiliary data is relatively new, and the presentation of measures of reliability for the estimates is also in its infancy.

Techniques for Analysis of Experimental Data

This section briefly describes two techniques for analysis of experimental data that may prove useful in analyses for rural development policy. An example of data collected for policy purposes is the data collected by the Economic Development Administration (EDA) in the early 1970s for evaluation of special programs for reducing unemployment. The programs were used in only a fraction of the counties in the Midwest during 1967-71. Estimates of unemployment for all counties were available both before 1967 and after 1971. The usual political reasons prevented random selection of the "treated" counties, and the actual choice appears to have been a reflection both of the seriousness of unemployment in each county in 1967 and of the ability of counties to produce good proposals for using government funding. As a result funding did *tend* to go to counties with the more serious 1967 unemployment. Campbell's (1974) idea of a "regression-discontinuity" quasi-experiment has application in studies of this type. The regression-discontinuity design requires strong assumptions about linearity, or at least smoothness, of regression relationships in the absence of treatment effects.

Studies with application to rural development policy will almost always be multivariate studies. The regression and multivariate approaches frequently used in such studies are related to main-effect fractional replicate plans in factorial design theory. Often the factors or variables interact with each other, and such main-effect plans are not satisfactory. On the other hand, the procurement of data for all combinations of levels of many factors may be an insurmountable task. Therefore, the use of fractional replicate plans has a role to play in such studies. (These ideas are developed in Appendix H.)

ACCESS TO INFORMATION

Use of Existing and Planned Surveys

To meet data requirements for rural development, multiple data sources must be used. The collection of data by local agencies was discussed briefly in the section on small-area estimation. A primary data source is the decennial census. Other possible sources include large-scale surveys conducted by the federal government. There are two large-scale federal surveys that deserve special mention.

The survey of income and program participation (SIPP) is a new national longitudinal survey that, when fully operational, will collect data from about 40,000 households on income, wealth, eligibility for and participation in social programs, and related information. The fundamental objectives of the survey are to provide data on the impact, costs, and coverage of federal and state income transfer and service programs, and to assess the effects of possible changes in such programs or of alternative programs. The survey will provide estimates of participation for many programs, information on the joint receipt of benefits from several programs, and estimates of the number of people eligible for, but not participating in, specific programs.

The design of the survey is complex and reflects the type of compromises required in a multipurpose survey. While the primary purpose of SIPP is to provide national estimates, it may be expanded every 2-5 years to provide state data. Sample families will be followed if they move within or between the areas selected in the sample, and new households will be added to the sample. Interviews will be quarterly and staggered, with a flexible questionnaire design. Personal visits, mailbacks, and telephone interviews will be used. Administrative records of various programs will be used as frames to supplement the area sample.

SIPP is jointly sponsored by the Department of Health and Human Services and the Department of Commerce. The Bureau of the Census is responsible for data collection. After SIPP has been more fully developed, responsibility for it will be transferred to the Office of Research and Statistics in the Social Security Administration.

Current plans call for the survey to begin formally in 1982. Field tests, experiments, and some preliminary analyses have been conducted, and some results from pilot panel surveys in 1978 and 1979 are now available. A major redesign of the survey, incorporating data from the 1980 census, is planned for 1984. Because of the planned redesign, review of the purposes, design, concepts, methods of measurement, data collection, and analysis are still continuing.

The panel agrees with the general objectives of SIPP and supports the procedures being used in SIPP. Individual agencies collect data on their clients to meet legal requirements and for internal administration. They typically do not collect information on their clients' use of other programs nor do action agencies necessarily have good data on the number and type of potential clients who do not avail themselves of the services of the agency. Also, the data collected by a particular agency from its own clients is not necessarily the type required by planners charged with coordinating a number of agencies or developing new programs.

> Recommendation: The panel recommends that the Survey of Income and Program Participation be expanded to include samples of clients of rural development programs and rural clients of general programs. The panel recommends that agencies with rural development responsibilities provide the funding for the cost of the additional samples.

While we are not privy to the statistical sample design for SIPP, we assume that the general area sample will contain a sufficient number of rural residents to enable useful statements to be made at the national level about the rural portion of the population. The expansion of the survey to include coverage of the clients of public agencies concerned with rural development will also require some expansion in the questionnaire. This should result in little increase in the general respondent burden because the questions would be aimed at a specific group of respondents. The panel realizes that the expansion to include clients of rural development agencies will increase the sample size and, hence, the cost of the survey. The panel recommends the expansion of SIPP on the presumption that rural development agencies would contribute to the total cost of the survey.

The current population survey (CPS) provides monthly data by census region on total employment, both farm and nonfarm, and total unemployment. Using auxiliary samples and longer time periods, data are also given by state. Information on additional variables such as age, sex, race, family status, and education is also produced. The present sample is composed of 461 primary sampling units (PSUs), which are cities, counties, or groups of contiguous counties. About 55,000 households are interviewed each month in the national sample. There is also a state supplementary sample of about 30,000 interviews. Households are interviewed for four successive months, leave the sample for eight months, return for a final four months of interviews, and are then permanently replaced. Estimates are ratio estimates using external estimates of population in a number of age, sex, and race groups.

The CPS is currently under redesign and expansion to increase the reliability of data at the state and SMSA levels. The sample design is such that the fraction of the sample in rural areas is approximately equal to the fraction of the U.S. population in such areas.

The redesigned CPS sample will be large enough to provide direct sample estimates on the rural population only for regions composed of groups of states. We expect the expanded CPS sample to provide useful input for the construction of small area statistics, both urban and rural. (See the section above on estimates for small areas based on auxiliary information.)

Meeting the Need for Distributional Information

Progress toward meeting development goals often entails identifying a subgroup of the population, measuring the welfare of its members, and meeting their special needs. Thus, aggregate measures for the entire population of an area are often inadequate for supporting development policy. Choosing from numerous possible examples, we note that society is concerned with: the number of people living in poverty and the extent of their poverty, in addition to a concern for the per-capita income for all citizens; the number of people who are ill-housed, in addition to a concern for per-family or per-capita housing services among all citizens; and the number of people receiving inadequate public services, in addition to a concern for the average level of services provided to all people. Numerous programs targeted to specific subgroups of the population have been put into place in response to distributional goals and values.

The reporting of data has lagged behind the increasing commitment of society to distributional concerns and programs, although progress has occurred. Tabulations too often reflect the outdated view that aggregate or average measures for an entire population are sufficient measures of progress.

Recommendation: The panel recommends that government agencies include additional frequency distributions or measures of dispersion in presenting data, especially for income, wages, housing quality, health, and the adequacy of public services.

Computerized data bases should be structured so that distributional information can be easily extracted, subject to limitations of small sample size and requirements of confidentiality.

Statistical Assistance for Local Planners

A number of useful studies were received from the letter survey of rural planners (see Appendix D). Collection and dissemination of such successful case studies could aid other local planners. Some local planners have little statistical training. Agencies at the federal and state level could constructively provide statistical assistance to local agencies. A recommendation made in Chapter 9 warrants repeating here.

Recommendation: The panel recommends that the Statistical Policy Division initiate and coordinate the development of manuals to assist local officials and planners in the acquisition and analysis of data.

An attempt should be made to develop, in nontechnical language, the statistical tools most needed for exploitation of existing data bases. Sources of data could be identified and explained. In addition, it may be possible to develop manuals focused on sampling methods and questionnaire design for use in collection of certain kinds of local data.

Computerized Dissemination of Data

Retrieval systems for access to data bases will increasingly permit hands-on, terminal access to data bases of all kinds, and there is reason to believe that this development will extend to data bases relevant to rural development policy. There is need for coordination--probably by the federal government--of these rural data bases, existing and future. The development of data bases requires careful design to obtain data of high quality, a problem too easily ignored, even by professional statisticians. Careful design is also needed to keep from being overwhelmed by large amounts of data of little relevance or of limited comparability. For example, even excellent studies within counties or other small units should not ordinarily be placed into state, regional, or national data bases, unless it is possible to compare them directly with similar studies done elsewhere.

Access to data bases requires careful planning, as does the provision of common bases that can be shared with benefit by different classes of users. Common data structure and computer software, for example, allow transportability to other computer systems and greater ease for potential users. Although computer incompatibilities will always be to some degree an unpleasant fact of life, maximum compatibility should be sought. This area is one of the most important ones in which coordination by the federal government could be useful. There will also be problems of confidentiality and protection of data integrity as users at remote locations secure access via terminals and other output devices to central data bases.

There are many potential sources of useful data generated as a by-product of ongoing administrative activities of governmental units and of business and nonprofit organizations. Public utilities and telephone companies, for example, generate time-series data for small areas that are correlated with growth of population and employment. Tax receipts, building permits, and unemployment compensation are parallel examples from the public sector. However, there may be major difficulties in the integration of administrative data into data bases designed for rural development policy. For example, small administrative areas may not be comparable with the standard areas used for rural planning, or the definitions may not correspond sufficiently closely to the information needed for planning.

In the development of data bases, it may sometimes be desirable for governmental units to lease or purchase data bases developed by private firms, such as consulting firms specializing in information on industrial or commercial location. There is also need for comprehensive, up-to-date directories of available data bases, such as the base maintained by Montana State University (Gilchrist and Allard 1980).

It is important to recognize that computerized data banks cannot substitute for state statistical service centers that provide technical assistance concerning available data, data needed for a specific purpose, the limitations of the data, and advice on analysis and interpretation of the results of analysis.

REFERENCES

Campbell, D.T. (1974) Quasi-experimental designs. In H.W. Riecken and R.F. Boruch, eds., Social Experimentation: A Method for Planning and Evaluating Social Intervention. New York: Academic Press.

Fay, R.E., and Herriot, R. (1979) Estimates of income for small places: An application of James-Stein procedures to census data. Journal of the American Statistical Association 74:269-277.

Gilchrist, C.J., and Allard, C.A. (1980) New strategies for processing large data files in migration research. D.L. Brown and J.M. Wardwell, eds., New Directions in Urban-Rural Migration. New York: Academic Press.

National Research Council (1980) Estimating Population and Income of Small Areas. Panel on Small Area Estimates of Population and Income, Committee on National Statistics, Assembly of Behavioral and Social Sciences. Washington, D.C.: National Academy Press.

Purcell, N.J., and Kish, L. (1979) Estimation for small domains. Biometrics 35:365-384.

SELECTED BIBLIOGRAPHY ON STATISTICAL METHODOLOGY

Bryant, W.K. (1977) Rural economic and social statistics. Pp. 408-420 in G.G. Judge, R.H. Day, S.R. Johnson, G.C. Rausser, and L.R. Martin, eds., A Survey of Argicultural Economics Literature. Minneapolis, Minn.: University of Minnesota Press.

Carter, G.M., and Rolph, J.E. (1974) Empirical Bayes methods applied to estimating fire alarm probabilities. Journal of the American Statistical Association 69:880-885.

Cochran, W.G., and Cox, G.M. (1957) Experimental Designs. New York: Wiley.

Efron, B., and Morris, C. (1973) Stein's estimation rule and its competitors--an empirical Bayes approach. Journal of the American Statistical Association 68:117-130.

Ericksen, E.P. (1974) A regression method for estimating population changes of local areas. Journal of the American Statistical Association 69:867-875.

Federer, W.T. (1955) Experimental Design - Theory and Application. New York:Macmillan. (Republished by the Oxford and IBH Publishing Company, Calcutta, India, 1967, 1974, 1979.)

Gonzalez, M.E. (1973) Use and evaluation of synthetic estimates. Pp. 33-36 in 1973 Proceedings of the Social Statistics Section. Washington, D.C.: American Statistical Association.

Gonzalez, M.E., and Hoza, C. (1978) Small area estimation with application to unemployment and housing estimates. Journal of the American Statistical Association 73:7-15.

James, W., and Stein, C. (1961) Estimation with quadratic loss. Pp. 361-379 in Proceedings of the Fourth Berkeley Symposium of Mathematical Statistics and Probability, Vol. 1. Berkeley: University of California Press.

Kempthorne, O. (1952) Experimental Design and Analysis. New York: Wiley.

Searles, S.R. (1971) Linear Models. New York: Wiley.

13

SUMMARY AND RECOMMENDATIONS

INTRODUCTION

Background

Rural America is wondrously diverse. Some rural areas are changing rapidly; some are not. Some are bursting at the seams with new residents; some are quietly dying because they have been forsaken by succeeding generations of young people. Some rural areas are basking in prosperity, and their residents enjoy many of the amenities of urban life; some rural areas remain remote, isolated, and lonely places whose residents struggle to make ends meet in an oppressive atmosphere of grinding poverty. Some rural areas are becoming more and more like urban areas; others are becoming less so. One can have a hot argument about whether convergence or divergence is the more important trend for rural America, with compelling evidence on both sides: it all depends on the area and the traits that concern one most. Regions differ in culture and history. Communities range from a lobster port in Maine to a ski resort in Colorado, to a lumber town in Idaho. There are also similarities, however, in institutions and human aspirations and interactions. Few generalizations about rural America are valid, because any valid generalization would have to be so carefully hedged with qualifications that it could hardly be considered a generalization.

Rural areas will always be different from urban areas, to some degree, because of space and the cost of distance, which lead to many of the advantages and disadvantages of rural areas. Public and private institutions in rural areas must respond differently to the problems and potentials of open space and few people. Many rural people have job links with a natural resource base that demands extensive area for its effective use, and the rhythm and style of rural life are often tied closely to natural events. For many reasons, more rural than urban families are poor and live in substandard housing, and rural people suffer higher rates of chronic disease, infant mortality, and other measures of poor health (Deavers and Brown 1979).

We know a great deal about rural America, and the forces that are shaping it, but we know too little. "Where we are," "where we have been," and "how we got here" are all subject to dispute. The procedures used to collect and disseminate data about rural people and their problems have never been entirely satisfactory, and today they are increasingly obsolete. Current data practices emphasize a simple dichotomy between rural and urban, or between metropolitan and nonmetropolitan, but rural areas and people quite definitely are not a homogeneous and undifferentiated residual of urban or metropolitan America. Current data continue to be more available for farming than for other economic activities, but farming is only one of many economic activities in rural areas today. The census of population is taken only once a decade, and census data are soon out of date in rural communities, as elsewhere; but formulas for transferring federal and state funds to local governments, which have become an important source of revenue for rural governments, continue to use census data or crude estimates. Data on public and private economic activities in small areas are inadequate for evaluating the effects of governmental policies and programs on geographic patterns of development. Society's ability to alleviate the problems of the needy, who are still disproportionately concentrated in rural areas, is handicapped by the lack of data on target populations, program recipients, and program effects.

Discovering What Concerns Rural America

The panel and its staff undertook a variety of activities to obtain information for the study. Staff members interviewed officials at the national level and panel members interviewed people involved in rural development in their home states. A letter survey was mailed to more than 600 people, in a random sample of 465 counties, inquiring about rural development issues and data needs. Two workshops were convened to discuss the recommendations under consideration by the panel and to check the completeness of the list of data needs the panel had identified: the participants in the first workshop were regional (multistate) and state planners involved in rural development; the participants in the second workshop were representatives of rural interest groups.

Intended Audience

This report is intended primarily for policy makers and for decision makers who can initiate changes needed in information systems relevant to rural development. At the federal level, the Farmers Home Administration in the Department of Agriculture, the sponsor of the study, is a key agency because of its financial resources and network of personnel at county, substate, state, and federal levels. The Economic Development Administration in the Department of Commerce and the Department of Housing and Urban Development also have major financial resources and sizable staffs. Another key network of people and programs is the Department of Agriculture's Cooperative Extension

Service, which concentrates on information dissemination and collection and education (rather than on delivery of physical goods and services). These are the larger programs, but there are many others at federal and state levels. At the state level, there are state rural development coordinating committees with representation from key agencies. The panel urges the members of these committees to aid in the dissemination of this report and in the implementation of its recommendations.

Producers of data are another important part of the intended audience. Agencies at the federal level include, but are not limited to, Bureau of the Census (Department of Commerce), Bureau of Labor Statistics (Department of Labor), Economics and Statistics Service (Department of Agriculture), several agencies in the Department of Health and Human Services, and the National Center for Education Statistics (Department of Education). We hope the state rural development coordinating committees will also distribute this report to appropriate producers of data at the state level.

Another important set of readers are elected officials and their staffs at all levels of government. Providing timely and adequate resources is clearly crucial to improving the rural component of information systems.

Finally, some users of rural data will find our extensive documentation of sources of information useful. This documentation was an important and necessary part of our task, and we are pleased to share the results.

THE PROBLEM CALLED RURAL DEVELOPMENT

Improving the life of rural people is the major goal of rural development policy. Everyone agrees that society should strive to satisfy the basic physical needs of all people, which include enough food, clothing, and shelter for an active life and health care for preventable diseases and for curable illnesses. Other widely shared goals of development include better education, improved public services and community facilities, greater economic opportunity, and careful management of natural resources, especially nonrenewable resources. The pursuit of these specific development goals is influenced by two additional goals: an equitable distribution of opportunities, goods, and services, and self-determination at the community level.

Diverse philosophies characterize the debate about an appropriate national policy for rural development. For example, one view holds that the federal government should focus on human resource and job development programs for people who are poor or unemployed. Another view focuses on area development directly increasing the economic activity in a rural area through industrial, infrastructure, or other development programs. A third view holds that a unified national rural development policy is neither politically feasible nor socially desirable because rural areas are too heterogeneous and because people want local self-determination.

The panel takes no position on the appropriate public policy for rural development. The data concepts and procedures for collecting data that the panel recommends will be helpful to those who must select among policies and will also aid in the implementation of whatever national policy is chosen.

Two important principles emerge from an examination of current rural development policy: rural development is an ill-defined problem; and rural development must be part of total development.

Rural Development: An Ill-Defined Problem

The factual ("what is"), prescriptive ("what should be"), and operational ("how to get from here to there") dimensions of rural development are all ill-defined.

First, our knowledge of rural people and their environment is imperfect and incomplete. Regular collection of information about small, sparsely settled areas is expensive, and the data base for rural areas consists of annual statistics for large aggregations of areas with only occasional benchmark data for census years for small areas. The aggregated data are often misleading because rural areas are so heterogeneous. The panel believes, although it cannot be proved, that the diversity within rural society today exceeds that between rural and urban life.

Second, the prescriptive dimension of rural development is equally ill-defined because of the heterogeneity of rural areas, the political fragmentation of rural people, the disagreement among rural people about growth and planning, and the lack of coordination of governmental efforts on rural issues.

Third, the operational aspects of development policy are not well understood. Linkages between the tools available to government and their effects on the quality of life are well defined only when the chain of causation is short and direct. The indirect effects of programs probably are significant in the aggregate, but causal chains and magnitudes are largely a mystery.

The panel was charged to make recommendations, not about rural development policy and analysis, but rather about improving the statistical foundations for research, policy analysis, and program implementation. We would be remiss, however, if we failed to recognize current conditions and to anticipate future directions that are relevant to planning. Rural development will remain an ill-defined problem at the federal and state levels for the foreseeable future. Many individual rural communities will reach a consensus about their problems and needs, but those local decisions will be different from community to community, they will receive only casual and sporadic attention at state and federal levels, and they will not sum to a national policy in any conventional sense. Federal and state governments will continue to serve specific needs with specialized programs that are coordinated poorly if at all.

Information systems, if they are to be effective in such a policy environment, must be flexible and accessible at all levels of government. The heterogeneity of areas and changes of values and beliefs over time demand flexibility. Local decision makers must have access to data, and to producers of data, as they struggle to solve local problems while meeting the demands of state and federal requirements. Federal and state decision makers must have data that are comparable over many areas in order to make efficient and equitable allocations and to design appropriate programs. Although decisions must always be made in some degree of uncertainty, current information systems must be improved and augmented to meet those data needs.

Rural Development: Part of the Whole

The United States does not have, and should not attempt to develop, a comprehensive "rural data base" or a "rural data system" separate from the information systems for other sectors of the population. The growing interdependence of rural and urban people causes the problems of each group to affect the other, and policies designed to meet the needs of either group will affect the other. Rural areas do have unique features, however, as well as considerable diversity, and there are good reasons to ask whether rural residents are served adequately by current data systems and institutional arrangements.

These two related points indicate that the panel had a difficult task--a review of <u>all</u> data systems for accurate and equitable treatment of rural people and rural communities. The panel established priorities in attempting to make its task manageable, but it remained awesome even when it was restricted to subjects clearly and directly related to the quality of life of rural people.

RECOMMENDATIONS

The creation of information systems adequate for the needs of decision makers dealing with rural development requires a multidimensional strategy. Conventions and standards must be adopted in order to facilitate communication and mutual understanding, but these conventions should allow considerable flexibility. Improvements are needed in some of the basic procedures for generating and reporting data, which affect a number of data series. The institutions linking data producers and data users must be strengthened so that each group will understand the problems and potentials of the other. Finally, there are a few specific high priority needs for new data collection instruments and improvement of existing procedures. Our strategy and recommendations emphasize the development of the essential institutions, standards, and methodology rather than new, large-scale data collections. The panel was mindful of the cost implications of the recommendations and was parsimonious in recommending the collection of new data. Most of the recommendations can be implemented at a relatively low cost. (The chapter designation following each recommendation indicates where the detailed disucssion of the recommendation and underlying rationale can be found.)

Conventions and Standards

County building blocks Rurality is a multidimensional phenomenon and no single definition of rural is satisfactory for all purposes. There are obvious polar extremes of urban and rural, but in the fuzzy middle ground, a value that is critical in terms of one criterion may have little or no significance in terms of others. There is no clear, unique, and unambiguous concept of "rural"; it is a concept evolving out of experience that, by consensus, is accepted as having meaning but one that cannot be defined precisely.

Current reporting practices for rural data are highly variable and often frustrate rather than facilitate aggregation and comparisons. Since no single definition of rural is feasible or desirable, data should be organized in a building-block approach. The basic building blocks of the data base should facilitate aggregation regardless of how rural is defined. The county is the most commonly used geographic unit for reporting small-area data.

> Recommendation: County Coding. The panel recommends that federal and state data be recorded with a county code to permit tabulations for individual counties and groups of counties (Chapter 2).

The multiple programmatic definitions of rural have discouraged evaluations of the effects of governmental activities on the geographic distribution of growth. The difficulties of aggregating data and making comparisons between programs have frustrated the coordination and assessment of overall economic development policy. Although no single definition of rural would be appropriate for all purposes, varying legislative requirements and agency interpretations have created a great deal of confusion within the federal government. Of course each agency must administer its programs in compliance with the law, but at the very least its projects should be identified by a county code. It is especially important for federal agencies awarding grants or contracts to include the county code in their records.

County classification To make comparisons and assessments of the geographic impacts of programs, a common aggregation scheme for counties is needed. A further distinction between urban and rural areas within counties would be desirable. The Statistical Policy Division in the Office of Management and Budget should take the lead at the national level in initiating and coordinating development and in overseeing implementation.

> Recommendation: Classification Scheme for Nonmetropolitan Counties. The panel recommends that a standard classification of nonmetropolitan counties relating to level of urbanization (in the spirit of the Hines et al. (1975) classification) be developed for use in program analysis and evaluation at each level of government. If possible, the county classification

should be suppplemented by a distinction between urban and rural areas within counties (Chapter 4).

Federal role Although many programs and data systems are appropriately left to state and local governments, the use of standardized definitions and procedures at state and national levels has distinct advantages. The function of making comparisons and aggregating state data, which is necessary for improved understanding, can be performed effectively only at the federal level in a broad and continuing dialogue between users and producers of data at the local, state, and federal levels. The responsibility for coordination and standards at the federal level should be in the Statistical Policy Division.

Recommendation: Federal Role in Coordination and in Setting Standards. The panel recommends that the federal government take a more active role in the coordination of statistical activities and in developing and promulgating common definitions and other statistical standards that are appropriate for implementation at the federal, state, and local levels (Chapter 4).

State role Statistical activities and standards must also be managed at the state level. States are solely responsible for many statistical programs, and state officials have a major interest in many other statistical activities in which the state shares responsibility for producing data with other levels of government or for which the state is a major user of data produced by other governmental levels. The panel believes that each state should have a program-neutral statistical coordinating agency with statewide responsibilities. Developing statistical standards is a consensus-building process that needs to be very open and to be managed in a way that recognizes the many difficult decisions on use and production of data that must be made at each level of govenment.

Recommendation: State Role in Coordination and in Setting Standards. The panel recommends that each state designate or develop an organization for managing the state's role in statistical coordination and in establishing and implementing standards, if such an organization does not now exist (Chapter 4).

Basic Procedures for Generating and Reporting Data

Standard statistical areas The difficulties of defining rural should not be allowed to result in inequitable treatment for rural people, as may occur when rural is defined as the residual that remains after the delineation of urban. The quantity and quality of statistical measures for the general population and for specific target groups should be comparable over rural and urban areas.

A specific concern of the panel is that the "balance of state" statistics often reported for nonmetropolitan areas are inadequate. Standard metropolitan statistical areas (SMSAs) are used extensively for statistical purposes, leaving other areas in a residual non-SMSA, or nonmetropolitan, category. Urban centers are designated as SMSAs when they exceed a population of 50,000, and additions occur frequently. A common practice is to compile and report data for states, SMSAs, and a residual "balance of state." Longitudinal comparisons are hindered by the frequent changes in the "balance of state" category that result from the proliferation of SMSA designations. In addition, the statistics generated and reported for non-SMSA areas often apply to very large aggregations of people.

Procedures for obtaining, analyzing, and reporting data should be developed to provide data for rural people and problems that are comparable in scope and reliability to those for SMSAs. Designation of standard statistical areas (SSAs) encompassing the entire geographic area of the nation would provide continuous, inclusive, and systematic data based on boundaries that would be changed less frequently than the presently relaxed SMSA criteria. The SSAs would be delineated in cooperation with states, conforming where possible to substate planning and development districts, but encompassing more than one such district when necessary to meet the statistical reliability standards now used for SMSAs. Delineations would consider nodal and homogeneous areas as used in designation of substate districts. The procedure would preserve the building-block approach for county data with appropriate urban orientation codes to facilitate analysis of county differences within rural SSAs as well as among rural and urban SSAs. If continued use of the label "SMSA" is deemed useful for an urban subset of the SSAs, the rural SSAs could be labelled standard rural statistical areas (SRSAs).

> Recommendation: Standard Statistical Areas. The panel recommends that the Statistical Policy Division in the Office of Management and Budget develop and implement a system of standard statistical areas (an extension of the present set of SMSAs) to encompass the entire geographic area of the nation (Chapter 2).

Small-area data The cost of surveys large enough to provide reliable direct estimates of desired measures for small local areas is prohibitive in many situations. In such situations it may be possible to use existing information to construct local area estimates. Some of the more promising statistical techniques are described in the panel's report (see Chapter 12 and Appendixes G and H). The 1980 census data provide a timely benchmark for evaluating and refining the methodology for making estimates and projections for small areas. The need for improved estimates is especially great for statistics that are used to allocate intergovernmental grants because the quality of those data is vital to program equity.

> Recommendation: Small-Area Estimates and Projections. The panel recommends that state and federal agencies give high priority to upgrading the quality of small-area estimates and projections, particularly those used to allocate funds (Chapter 12).

Health One of the most important components of federal health programs aimed at alleviating geographic maldistribution of resources is the identification and designation of those specific areas that are most in need. While several shortage or medical "underservice" indexes have been developed in order to allocate resources, the degree to which any of these indexes contain the appropriate indicators to specify those areas with the most health problems or the least medical care is not clear. The indexes used now depend heavily on the physician/population ratio, a measure that has been found to be misleading in several respects as an indicator of medical need. More work is required to reach consensus on an acceptable definition of health service scarcity and to isolate and combine the various indicators of this important rural problem.

> Recommendation: Measures of Health Service Scarcity. The panel recommends that such Public Health Service agencies as the Health Resources Administration and the Health Services Administration devote further effort to the development of a definition of health service scarcity and to research on measures of this concept (Chapter 7).

Education Education is an important factor in individual and community development. The financing and organization of schools are major concerns of state and local governments. The low density of students in rural areas affects school organization. Despite these compelling and well-known facts, the National Center for Education Statistics does not tabulate data on a rural-urban spectrum. A first step to improving data on education would be to code school districts using the county classification scheme for nonmetropolitan counties recommended above. A more refined alternative would be based on the size of the largest place in the school district. Ultimately classification of schools on a rural-urban spectrum would be desirable.

> Recommendation: Rural-Urban Codes for School Districts. The panel recommends that codes for rural-urban location of school districts be recorded with all school district data (pupil, personnel, curriculum, finance, and facilities) to facilitate comparison of resources available to rural and urban school districts. The National Center for Education Statistics is the appropriate organization to implement this recommendation (Chapter 8).

Local data The panel has emphasized the limitations of federal and state data sets in applications to problem definition and solution at the local level. A desirable information network for rural development could not be complete and adequate without primary data collected at the local level to meet local objectives. At that level, expressions of goals, aspirations, attitudes, and perceived problems can be generated. Many states and communities have been experimenting with practical and inexpensive methods for generating such data.

Recommendation: Local Data Gathering. The panel recommends that the Farmers Home Administration encourage local efforts to generate rural development data for local purposes. To this end, the panel recommends that existing efforts at the local level be surveyed and that particularly innovative and useful examples be widely disseminated (Chapter 12).

Distributional statistics Progress toward meeting development goals often entails identifying particular groups of the population, measuring their welfare, and meeting their special needs. Public opinion has shifted from a general faith in the goodness of aggregate growth to more sophisticated concerns for the quality of growth, including the question of who gains and who loses. Numerous action programs targeted for specific groups of the population have been a response to distributional goals and values.

The reporting of data has not kept pace with the increasing commitment of society to distributional concerns and programs. Tabulations too often reflect the outdated view that aggregate or average measures for an entire population are sufficient measures of progress. There is potential for improved practices because computerized data bases can be structured so that distributional information may be easily extracted, subject to limitations of small sample size and requirements of confidentiality.

Recommendation: Distributional Measures. The panel recommends that government agencies include additional frequency distributions or measures of dispersion in presenting data, especially for income, wages, housing quality, health, and the adequacy of public services (Chapter 12).

Institutional Linkages

The panel's review of the current statistical activities for rural development reveals a pressing need for better communication linkages among the parts. In fact, the linkages and coordinating institutions are either missing or so poorly developed that the term "information system" is not even appropriate. The recent conclusion of the Advisory Commission on Intergovernmental Relations that "contemporary federalism is in serious disarray" (Beam 1980:6) applies to rural development with particular force. Some settled order of compatible roles and of linking decision institutions must prevail from local through federal levels of government before one can specify a coherent rural development policy data base.

State statistical service centers The ideal information system for development policy, rural and urban, should recognize the complementary roles of local, substate, state, and federal governments. The system should facilitate communication of data needs from users to producers of data and of information on potential effective uses of existing data from producers to users. At the local and state level the system should facilitate comparisons and linkages among data sets. The system should not be designed and administered solely as a means of disseminating data from producers to users of data. Without an effective two-way linkage of users and producers of data, maintaining policy relevance in information systems is impossible, and statistical resources will not be used efficiently.

> Recommendation: State Statistical Service Centers. The panel recommends that each state develop or designate a lead institution (or institutions) in the state to facilitate local government access to state and federal statistical information, if no such institution currently exists. The panel further recommends that the federal government encourage use of the statistical service centers by providing general financial assistance and, in addition, that federal program agencies fund the centers to maintain the local and state data bases necessary for application to their programs (Chapter 4).

No confidential information, only publicly available statistical aggregates, would be maintained by these centers. The centers should provide information on statistical data sources, prepare tabulations on request, and provide other appropriate services. Some states may wish to place in the center the responsibilities for statistical coordination and standardization that we recommended above. The center itself should not produce statistics, because doing so might generate bureaucratic conflicts in the statistical system. We note that some states have already established statistical service centers.

State statistical service centers would focus the demand for new data and together would have the political leverage necessary to ensure a response from the federal statistical system. The necessity for such institutions to communicate state and local data needs is underlined by the administration's failure to provide planning money for the mid-decade census authorized by Congress. A mid-decade census is critical for major improvements in state and local data. During a workshop at the National Rural Center, a member of President Carter's White House staff indicated that they were surprised by the lack of support for the mid-decade census. He added that the administration probably would not have withheld planning funds for a mid-decade census in fiscal year 1981 if, for example, the National Governors' Association had supported the idea of such a census.

Representation and data for users One way to ensure that the interests of local and regional users are considered in planning federal statistical programs is to invite them to serve on the various advisory committees. The federal government should provide supporting services to the information network and should serve as a central contact point and guide for those seeking information.

Recommendation: Representation on Advisory Committees. The panel recommends increased representation of local and regional users of information on federal statistical advisory committees (Chapter 4).

Recommendation: Federal Information Locator System. The panel recommends that the Federal Information Locator System (FILS) be developed as rapidly as possible with an expanded mission to provide public access to federal data sources (Chapter 4).

The FILS is presently designed to serve the process of internal federal government forms clearance, not user needs, so additional information on data characteristics would have to be added to FILS. Before FILS could be of substantial value to users, several user services would also have to be developed. These user services should include, but not be limited to, serving as a central contact point for information on data availability and sources, preparing annual guides to federal statistical sources, and maintaining a computerized bibliography of major regional and local data collection efforts. If the Office of Management and Budget, which operates FILS, is not considered the appropriate location for such a data user service, it could be located elsewhere as long as an interactive computer link to FILS is provided; to do otherwise would lead to major duplication of partially identical files.

Statistical training There is generally a low level of statistical training at the local level, although there are notable exceptions. A constructive activity for agencies at the federal and state level would be provision of statistical assistance to local agencies. An attempt should be made to develop in nontechnical language the statistical tools most needed for exploitation of existing data bases. Sources of data could be identified and explained. In addition, it may be possible to develop manuals focused on sampling methods and questionnaire design for use in collection of certain kinds of local data.

Recommendation: Manuals on Acquisition and Analysis of Data. The panel recommends that the Statistical Policy Division initiate and coordinate the development of manuals to assist local officials and planners in the acquisition and analysis of data (Chapters 9 and 12).

Data for grant applications Documenting need in grant applications is one of the major uses of data at the local level. Local governments rely heavily on generalists and have limited capacity to handle the myriad requirements and expectations of state and federal agencies. The burden on local units could be lightened by better coordination at state and federal levels. This could be effected by leadership from the Statistical Policy Division.

> Recommendation: Standardized Data Requests. The panel recommends that application and reporting forms required by federal and state agencies be standardized to the extent possible and that the instruction sheet provide references to data sources when the form requires data from federal statistical publications (Chapter 4).

High-Priority, Specific Data Bases

Mid-decade census The 1980 census data, which will become available during 1981, will meet many data needs. The 1980 census, however, will show how quickly such data become obsolete and may well also show how estimates based on the 1970 census in many instances were not serviceable during the last years of the 1970s. There is every reason to believe that changes in the 1980s will be rapid and that reliance on the 1980 census in the latter part of the 1980s will be very misleading. One solution is to be found in the proposal for a mid-decade census, as provided by law. The panel recognizes that it is unlikely that a mid-decade census could be conducted in 1985 because of the lack of planning appropriations in the budgets for fiscal 1981 and fiscal 1982. The success of all major statistical collections requires careful advance planning, but especially in this case, since the activity will either be the first mid-decade census or the largest sample survey attempted in this country.

> Recommendation: Mid-Decade Census. The panel recommends that the mid-decade census of population and housing be implemented at the earliest possible date--in 1985 if possible--as required by the 1976 legislation. If the mid-decade effort takes the form of a large sample survey rather than a complete count, the panel further recommends that the sample be large enough to permit direct estimates or good regression estimates for all counties, the basic building blocks of the data system (Chapter 5).

Federal outlays The annual reports by the Community Services Administration (CSA) about federal outlays by program and county are a valuable source of information about federal influences on the geographic distribution of development. The federal outlays data can sometimes be used in combination with other data to evaluate specific programs. The principal problem with these data is their uneven quality. Some agencies give low priority to producing high-quality estimates for CSA. Major problems are the failure to report subcontracts let by private firms with prime contracts and grants and the failure to report transfers by states to local governmental units. Some of the proration procedures used in the absence of direct estimates are very crude.

Recommendation: Federal Outlays. The panel recommends that in reporting federal outlays data, the program agencies, in cooperation with the Office of Management and Budget and the Community Services Administration, make a greater effort to improve the quality and geographic detail of the data and to provide users with information on the quality and limitations of the various components of the report (Chapter 10).

Survey of income and program participation The survey of income and program participation (SIPP) is a promising endeavor. Individual agencies collect data on their clients to meet legal requirements and for internal administration. They typically do not collect information on their clients' use of other programs, nor do action agencies necessarily have good data on the number and type of potential clients that do not avail themselves of the services of the agency. Also, the data collected by a particular agency from its own clients are not necessarily of the type required by planners charged with coordinating a number of agencies or developing new programs.

Recommendation: Survey of Income and Program Participation. The panel recommends that the survey of income and program participation be expanded to include samples of clients of rural development programs and rural clients of general programs. The panel recommends that agencies with rural development responsibilities provide the funding for the cost of the additional samples (Chapter 12).

Underemployment index Unemployment rates reported for rural areas, especially those that are economically depressed, are an inadequate measure of the underuse of human resources (Nilsen 1979, Tweeten 1978) because: potential workers who are relatively immobile become discouraged and do not seek work when local job opportunities are chronically lacking; the costs of additional active search for jobs exceed gains more quickly in rural areas with few employers than in urban areas with many employers; underemployed seasonal workers and self-employed workers are often classified as employed when urban criteria are applied in rural areas; and relatively few jobs in rural areas are covered by unemployment compensation.

The failure of unemployment rates to measure the underuse of human resources can be costly for rural areas because government allocations to areas are increasingly tied to statistical formulas. In 1976, for example, some $16 billion in federal funds was allocated according to criteria of employment or unemployment (Norwood 1977).

A preferable measure of underutilized labor in rural areas is underemployment. Underemployment is measured as the difference between the output of individuals in a given area and what they would produce if they were as productive as workers in the nation with similar age, education, and training; it includes, but is not confined to, unemployment. Although several procedures and formulas have been proposed to measure underemployment (for a review see Tweeten 1978), an in-depth study is needed to ascertain whether current data and concepts are adequate to construct a useful measure.

> Recommendation: Underemployment Index. The panel recommends that the Statistical Policy Division of the Office of Management and Budget establish an interagency committee to guide the conceptual research for and the development of an underemployment index for counties on a periodic basis. The panel further recommends that the Bureau of Labor Statistics fund the research and assume the responsibility for implementing the procedures upon the completion of the methodological study (Chapter 10).

Rural cost-of-living index Meaningful comparisons of the economic well-being of communities, regions, and program target groups require that wages, salaries, income, net worth, transfers, outlays, taxes, and other dollar indicators be expressed in comparable units. Data series often are deflated for the cost-of-living differences of regions and sectors, but they cannot be adjusted for urban-rural differences because we have no good measure of these differences.

Rural cost-of-living data should identify differences between rural areas in different parts of the nation and between urban and rural areas in each region. These differences probably would change only slowly, and an annual updating for benchmark purposes would be adequate. Month-to-month adjustments could be based on changes in the urban consumer price index. A recent study by the Urban Institute (Holden et al. 1979) is a useful starting point for developing a measure of regional cost-of-living differentials.

> Recommendation: Rural Cost-of-Living Index. The panel recommends that the Bureau of Labor Statistics provide an annual index of cost-of-living differentials between each of eight to ten rural areas and selected urban areas (Chapter 10).

A Word on Costs

The panel considered estimating the financial and staff resources that would be required to implement its recommendations. Such estimates would force the panel to be fiscally responsible in its recommendations; in addition, since many of the recommendations entail relatively low costs, making this fact known to decision makers might hasten implementation of the recommendations. However, there are several arguments against providing cost estimates. First, an estimate made today might be unrealistic at a future date when an agency considers implementation of a recommendation and thus might be a barrier to implementation. Second, the panel was composed largely of university faculty members who are inexperienced in estimating the costs of federal and state statistical activities. The panel might have requested the federal agencies designated to implement some of the recommendations to make cost estimates, but it was considered unlikely that they would be willing to devote the staff time unless the recommended activity were already on the planning horizon. Also, cost estimates for recommendations for changing organizational structures in the states could be expected to vary widely among states. Finally, the contract for the study did not call for cost estimates. On the basis of these arguments, the panel decided against making estimates of the resources required to implement the recommendations.

DATA GAPS

The panel has made recommendations above to fill the five data gaps identified as most important for rural development policy. Chapter 2 and each chapter devoted to a specific substantive topic (Chapters 5-11) have a detailed list of additional data gaps. The breadth of rural development policy and the heterogeneity of rural communities are mirrored in the wide array of specific data gaps compiled by the panel in its work. If our recommendations concerning general procedures and other institutional matters are implemented, many of the specific data listed in the chapters would become available, some through new surveys and others because data collection and tabulation would be facilitated by the new standard definitions and codes. Some data would also be collected and published because new organizational structures, such as state statistical service centers, would focus the demand for new data and would have the political leverage necessary to ensure a response from the federal statistical system.

Although the panel has recommended only a few new data bases, we consider the following data gaps, selected from the more inclusive lists in each chapter, to be high-priority items for statistical agencies to consider:

> Data Gap: Direct measurement and indirect estimation of migration flows into and out of small areas.

The inadequacy of migration data is probably the weakest link in making population estimates and projections for local areas. While births and deaths are known from registration data, data are lacking about the people who have moved into or out of an area. Migration affects both the number of people and their characteristics and is a major factor in population change in most areas. For example, migration of the elderly is thought to have contributed to recent population growth in several rural counties.

> Data Gap: Data on schooling for the appropriate jurisdictional level, especially data on outputs, e.g., retention (or dropout) rates, age-grade retardation, incidence of post-secondary schooling, and educational attainment.

Public schools usually represent the largest category of public investment in rural communities, and schools are an important agency of social and economic development. There is little evidence, however, that education planners have much information about public education and its effects.

<u>Data Gap</u>: Measurement of multiple job holding and the tabulation of the employment of all family members in family units.

There is a complex relationship between families and employment activities, which may have important implications for rural labor markets. For example, a study of one rural area found that labor force entry and exit of household members was an important determinant of the distribution of family incomes. Available data have only limited information on employment by family composition and on multiple job holding by individuals. Designing the necessary data tabulations would be a difficult but valuable activity.

<u>Data Gap</u>: Annual Internal Revenue Service data on adjusted gross income by county of residence.

Although the Bureau of Economic Analysis constructs annual estimates of personal income by county, its definition of personal income differs from the IRS's definition of adjusted gross income. Information on adjusted gross income is especially useful for analyzing the effects of federal fiscal decisions on small areas. The data would be more valuable if it were available on an annual basis rather than only in selected years.

<u>Data Gap</u>: County data on access to health care variables, including ability to pay.

Access is an important but complex topic in any discussion of rural health care. Access to health care can be measured by assessing various deterrents to access such as lack of knowledge, finances, geography, timeliness, and sociocultural acceptability. Some studies using national data sets have found that rural people are disadvantaged with regard to access to health care. However, more refined data, such as those at the county level, are needed in order to analyze, compare, and combine the various indicators of access.

<u>Data Gap</u>: Use and impact of housing subsidy programs for low-income and other groups.

Rural areas have a disproportionate share of housing that fails to meet accepted standards of quality, but they have fewer savings and loan institutions for financing new construction. Therefore, federal housing subsidy programs, especially those of FmHA, are particularly important. The targeting of those programs to low-income and minority people is a priority, and data are needed in order to determine whether this is happening.

Data Gap: National data on perceptions of both factual and value issues.

Rural development goals include such various things as meeting basic human needs, economic security, education, natural resource protection, and equity. Information on the disparity between these goals and reality, as perceived by rural people, is useful to policy makers. While local community surveys about values and perceptions of issues have been used in setting local priorities, such surveys at the national level would be able to clarify broad trade-offs, establish targets and measure progress.

These data gaps deserve the serious attention of appropriate agencies. In some cases modification of existing collections might meet the need. In others more effort would be required. In the absence of a coordinated set of policy institutions, the panel finds it difficult to establish priorities for filling these data gaps. Each item on the list, however, is directed at an important facet of improving the quality of life of rural people.

CONCLUSION

Rural development policy and the data needs for it are ill-defined. Today only pieces are known or even knowable. The precondition for greater coherence is a more integrated and coordinated set of institutions to support policy making and its data base. The panel has addressed this problem within the scope of its mandate and knowledge. It is not the province of the panel to say what rural policies and policy-making institutions should exist. Rather, we have considered the statistical institutions and linkages needed to support coherent policy making. We have identified new and modified statistical conventions and standards that are needed, and we have also recommended new or changed procedures for producing and reporting data on rural America. We have also recommended high-priority, specific data bases.

Rural America is in passage. Its future is unknown. Its people are growing in numbers and diversity. A more complex economic and social fabric creates many opportunities and dangers about which decisions must be made. Many of these decisions are of immense significance not only for rural areas and rural life but for all America. Improving the data base for such decisions is imperative.

REFERENCES

Beam, D.R. (1980) Forecasting the future of federalism. Intergovernmental Perspective 6(3):6-9.

Deavers, K.L., and Brown, D.L. (1979) Social and Economic Trends in Rural America. White House Rural Development Background Paper. Washington, D.C.: U.S. Government Printing Office.

Hines, F.K., Brown, D.L., and Zimmer, J.M. (1975) Social and Economic Characteristics of the Population in Metro and Nonmetro Counties, 1970. Agricultural Economic Report No. 272. Washington, D.C.: U.S. Department of Agriculture.

Holden, R., Tobias, L., and Wertheimer, R., II (1979) Differences in Living Cost Between Rural and Urban Areas, Final Report. Washington, D.C.: The Urban Institute.

Nilsen, S.R. (1979) Employment and Unemployment Statistics for Nonmetroplitan Areas. Background Paper No. 33. National Commission on Employment and Unemployment Statistics, Washington, D.C.

Norwood, J.L. (1977) Reshaping a statistical program to meet legislative priorities. Monthly Labor Review 100(11):6-11.

Tweeten, L. (1978) Rural Employment and Unemployment Statistics. Background Paper No. 4. National Commission on Employment and Unemployment Statistics, Washington, D.C.

APPENDIX A

ANALYTIC DEFINITIONS OF "RURAL"

This appendix provides detailed definitions of the rural or complementary urban concepts discussed in Chapter 2.

URBAN POPULATION

The definition of the groups that are included in the urban population in the 1980 census remains the same as in the 1970 census (communication to the panel from Joel Miller of the Bureau of the Census, January, 1981). However, the new definition of urbanized areas, which is presented below, has a slight impact on the size of this population group. By definition (Bureau of the Census 1978:xxix):

> The urban population comprises all persons living in (a) places of 2,500 inhabitants or more incorporated as cities, boroughs (except in Alaska), villages, and towns (except in the New England States, New York, and Wisconsin), but excludes persons living in rural portions of <u>extended</u> cities (i.e., cities whose boundaries have been extended, such as city/county consolidation to include sizable portions of territory that is rural in character); (b) unincorporated places of 2,500 inhabitants or more; and (c) other territory, incorporated or unincorporated, included in urbanized areas (a central city or cities and surrounding closely settled territory) at the time of the . . . census.

RURAL POPULATION

The rural population as defined by the Bureau of the Census (1972: App-2) includes all people not classified as part of the urban population.

URBANIZED AREA

Urbanized areas are defined by Bureau of the Census (1980):

An urbanized area comprises an incorporated place[1] and adjacent densely settled surrounding area that together has a minimum population of 50,000.[2]

The densely settled surrounding area consists of:

1. Contiguous incorporated or census designated places having:
   a. A population of 2,500 or more; or,
   b. A population of less than 2,500 but having either a population density of 1,000 persons per square mile, closely settled area containing a minimum of 50 percent of the population, or a cluster of at least 100 housing units.
2. Contiguous unincorporated area which is connected by road and has a population density of at least 1,000 persons per square mile.
3. Other contiguous unincorporated area with a density of less than 1,000 persons per square mile, provided that it:
   a. Eliminates an enclave of less than 5 square miles which is surrounded by built-up area.
   b. Closes an indentation in the boundary of the densely settled area that is no more than 1 mile across the open end and encompasses no more than 5 square miles.
   c. Links an outlying area of qualifying density, provided that the outlying area is:
   (1) Connected by road to, and is not more than 1- 1/2 miles from, the main body of the urbanized area.
   (2) Separated from the main body of the urbanized area by water or other undevelopable area; is connected by road to the main body of the urbanized area; and, is not more than 5 miles from the main body of the urbanized area.
4. Large concentrations of nonresidential urban area (such as, industrial parks, office areas, and major airports) which have at least one-quarter of their boundary contiguous area.

---

[1]In Hawaii and Puerto Rico, incorporated places do not exist in the sense of functioning local governmental units. In Hawaii, census designated places are used in defining a central place and for applying urbanized area criteria; in Puerto Rico, zonas urbanas and aldeas are used.

[2]The rural portions of extended cities, as defined in the Census Bureau's extended city criteria, are excluded from the urbanized area. In addition, in order for an urbanized area to be recognized, it must include a population of at least 25,000 that does not reside on a military base.

METROPOLITAN STATISTICAL AREA

The following standards will be followed by the Bureau of the Census in establishing metropolitan statistical areas based on the 1980 census (Federal Committee on Standard Metropolitan Statistical Areas 1979:38-43). Sections 8, 11.B, 16.B, and part of 16.C of the standards deal only with the selection of titles and are not presented here.

Basic Standards

Sections 1 through 8 apply to all States except the six New England States. They also apply to Puerto Rico.[3]

Section 1. Population Size Requirements for Qualification

A. Each metropolitan statistical area must include a city which, with contiguous, densely settled territory, constitutes a Census Bureau-defined urbanized area with at least 50,000 population.[4]

B. If a metropolitan statistical area's largest city has less than 50,000 population, the area must have a total population of at least 100,000.[5]

Section 2. Central Counties

A county is designated as a central county of the metropolitan statistical area if:

A. At least 50 percent of its population lives in the urbanized area that resulted in qualification under Section 1A; or

B. At least 2,500 of its population lives in a central city of the metropolitan statistical area.[6]

---

[3]Those provisions of Sections 1 through 8 which are applicable to New England are specified in the standards relating to New England (Sections 12 through 16).

[4]A metropolitan statistical area designated according to standards in effect at the time of designation will not be disqualified on the basis of lacking an urbanized area of at least 50,000 population.

[5]A metropolitan statistical area designated on the basis of census data according to standards in effect at the time of designation will not be disqualified on the basis of lacking a total population of at least 100,000.

[6]See Section 4 for the standards for identifying central cities.

Section 3. Outlying Counties

A. An outlying county is included in a metropolitan statistical area if any one of the four following conditions is met:

(1) At least 50 percent of the employed workers residing in the county commute to the central county(ies) and the population density of the county is at least 25 persons per square mile.

(2) From 40 to 50 percent of the employed workers commute to the central county(ies), and the population density is at least 35 persons per square mile.

(3) From 25 to 40 percent of the employed workers commute to the central county(ies), the population density is at least 35 persons per square mile, and any one of the following conditions also exists:

  (a) Population density is at least 50 persons per square mile.

  (b) At least 35 percent of the population is urban.

  (c) At least 10 percent, or at least 5,000, of the population lives in the urbanized area that resulted in qualification under Section 1A.

(4) From 15 to 25 percent of the employed workers commute to the central county(ies),[7] the population density is at least 50 persons per square mile, and any two of the following conditions also exist:

  (a) Population density is at least 60 persons per square mile.

  (b) At least 35 percent of the population is urban.

  (c) Population growth between the last two decennial censuses is at least 20 percent.

  (d) At least 10 percent, or at least 5,000, or the population lives in the urbanized area that resulted in qualification under Section 1A.

B. If a county qualifies on the basis of commuting to the central county(ies) of two different metropolitan statistical area, it is assigned to the area to which commuting is greatest, unless the relevant commuting percentages are within 5 points of each other, in which case local opinion about the most appropriate assignment will be considered.

---

[7]Also accepted as meeting this commuting requirement are:

(a) The number of persons working in the county who live in the central county(ies) is equal to at least 15 percent of the number of employed workers living in the county; or

(b) The sum of the number of workers commuting to and from the central county(ies) is equal to at least 20 percent of the number of employed workers living in the county.

Section 4. Central Cities

Recognized as the central city(ies) of the metropolitan statistical area are:

A. The city with the largest population in the metropolitan statistical area.

B. Each additional city with a population of at least 250,000 or with at least 100,000 persons working within its limits.

C. Each additional city with a population of at least 25,000, an employment/residence ratio of at least 0.75, and outcommuting of less than 60 percent of its resident employed workers.

D. Each city of 15,000 to 25,000 population which is at least one-third as large as the largest central city, has an employment/residence ratio of at least 0.75, and has outcommuting of less than 60 percent of its resident employed workers.

Section 5. Consolidating Adjacent Metropolitan Statistical Areas

Two adjacent metropolitan statistical areas defined by Sections 1 through 4 are consolidated as a single metropolitan statistical area provided all of the following conditions are met:

A. The commuting interchange between the two metropolitan statistical areas is equal to:

(1) At least 15 percent of the employed workers residing in the smaller metropolitan statistical area, or:

(2) At least 10 percent of the employer workers residing in the smaller metropolitan statistical area, and

(a) The urbanized area of a central city of one metropolitan statistical area is contiguous with the urbanized area of a central city of the other metropolitan statistical area, or

(b) A central city in one metropolitan statistical area is included in the same urbanized area as a central city in the other metropolitan statistical area.

B. At least 60 percent of the population of each metropolitan statistical area is urban.

C. The total population is at least 1 million.

Section 6. Combining Adjacent Metropolitan Statistical Areas

Two adjacent metropolitan statistical areas defined by Sections 1 through 4 and not included in a consolidation by Section 5 will be combined as a single metropolitan statistical area if:

A. Their largest central cities are within 25 miles of each other, or their urbanized areas are contiguous; and

B. There is definite evidence that the two areas are closely integrated with each other economically and socially; and

C. Local opinion in both areas supports the combination.

Section 7. Levels

A. Each metropolitan statistical area defined by Sections 1 through 6 is categorized in one of the following levels based on total population.

Level A--Metropolitan statistical areas of 1 million or more.

Level B--Metropolitan statistical areas of 250,000 to 1 million.

Level C--Metropolitan statistical areas of 100,000 to 250,000.

Level D--Metropolitan statistical areas of less than 100,000.

B. Areas assigned to Levels B, C, or D are designated as metropolitan statistical areas. Areas assigned to Level A are not finally designated or titled until they have been reviewed under Sections 9 and 10.

Standards for Primary and Consolidated Metropolitan Statistical Areas

Sections 9 through 11 apply to Level A metropolitan statistical areas outside New England.

Section 9. Qualifications as a Primary Metropolitan Statistical Area

Within a Level A metropolitan statistical area:

A. Any county or group of counties that was recognized as a separate metropolitan statistical area on January 1, 1980, will be recognized as a primary metropolitan statistical area, unless local opinion does not support its continued separate recognition for statistical purposes.

B. Any additional county or group of counties for which local opinion strongly supports separate recognition will be considered for identification as a primary metropolitan statistical area, provided a county is included which has:

(1) At least 100,000 population;
(2) At least 60 percent of its population urban; and
(3) Less than 50 percent of its resident workers commuting to jobs outside the county.

C. The geographic definition of any area recognized by Section 9A, and the identification and definition of any area under Section 9B, are subject to the specific statistical guidelines detailed in the Procedures supplement to these standards.

D. If any primary metropolitan statistical area or areas have been recognized under Sections 9A through C, the balance of the Level A metropolitan statistical area is also recognized as a primary metropolitan statistical area.[8]

Section 10. Levels and Titles of Primary Metropolitan Statistical Areas

A. Primary metropolitan statistical areas are categorized in one of four levels according to total population, following the standards of Section 7A.

B. Primary metropolitan statistical areas are titled in either of two ways:

(1) Using the names of up to three cities in the primary metropolitan statistical area that have qualified as central cities of the Level A metropolitan statistical area under Section 4, following the standards of Section 8 for selection and sequencing; or

(2) Using the names of up to three counties in the primary metropolitan statistical area, sequenced in order from largest to smallest population.

C. Local opinion on the most appropriate title will be considered.

Section 11. Designation . . . of Consolidated Metropolitan Statistical Areas

A. Each Level A metropolitan statistical area in which primary metropolitan statistical areas have been defined by Section 9 is designated a consolidated metropolitan statistical area. A Level A metropolitan statistical area in which no primary metropolitan statistical areas have been defined is designated a metropolitan statistical area, and is titled according to Section 8.

Standards for New England

In the six New England States, the cities and towns are administratively more important than the counties, and a wide range of data is compiled locally for these entities. Therefore, the cities and towns are the units used to define metropolitan statistical areas in these States. The New England standards are based primarily on population density and commuting. Sections 12

---

[8]If Section 9D would result in the balance of Level A metropolitan statistical area including a noncontiguous county, this county will be added to the contiguous primary metropolitan statistical area to which it has the greatest commuting.

and 13 constitute the basic standards for New England metropolitan statistical areas. As a basis for measuring commuting, a central core is first defined for each New England urbanized area, corresponding to the central counties that are identified in the States outside New England.

Section 12. New England Central Cores

A central core is determined in each New England urbanized area through the definition of two zones.

A. Zone A comprises:

(1) The largest city in the urbanized area.

(2) Each other place in the urbanized area or in a contiguous urbanized area that qualifies as a central city under Section 4, provided at least 15 percent of its resident employed workers work in the largest city in the urbanized area.

(3) Each other city or town at least 50 percent of whose population lives in the urbanized area or a contiguous urbanized area, provided at least 15 percent of its resident employed workes work in the largest city in the urbanized area plus any additional central cities qualified by Section 12A(2).

B. Zone B comprises each city or town which:

(1) Has at least 50 percent of its population living in the urbanized area or in a contiguous urbanized area; and

(2) Has at least 15 percent of its resident employed workers working in Zone A.[9]

C. The central core comprises Zone A, Zone B, and any city or town that is physically surrounded by Zones A or B, except that cities or towns that are not contiguous with the main portion of the central core are not included.

D. If a city or town qualifies under Sections 12A through C for more than one central core, it is assigned to the core to which commuting is greatest, unless the relevant commuting percentages are within 5 points of each other, in which case local opinion as to the most appropriate assignment will also be considered.

---

[9]Also accepted as meeting this commuting requirement are:

(a) The number of persons working in the subject city or town who live in the specified city or area is equal to at least 15 percent of the employed workers living in the subject city or town; or

(b) The sum of the number of workers commuting to and from the specified city or area is equal to at least 20 percent of the employed workers living in the subject city or town.

Section 13. Outlying Cities and Towns

A. A city or town contiguous to a central core as defined by Section 12 is included in its metropolitan statistical area if:

(1) It has a population density of at least 60 persons per square mile and at least 30 percent of its resident employed workers work in the central core; or

(2) It has a population density of at least 100 persons per square mile and at least 15 percent of the employed workers living in the city or town work in the central core.[10]

B. If a city or town has the qualifying amount of commuting to two different central cores, it is assigned to the metropolitan statistical area to which commuting is greatest, unless the relevant commuting percentages are within 5 points of each other, in which case local opinion as to the most appropriate assignment will also be considered.

C. If a city or town has the qualifying level of commuting to a central core, but has greater commuting to a nonmetropolitan city or town, it will not be assigned to any metropolitan statistical area unless the relevant commuting percentages are within 5 points of each other, in which case local opinion as to the most appropriate assignment will also be considered.

Section 14. Applicability of Basic Standards to New England Metropolitan Statistical Areas

A. An area defined by Sections 12 and 13 qualifies as a metropolitan statistical area provided it contains a city of at least 50,000 population or has a total population of at least 75,000.[11]

B. The area's central cities are determined according to the standards of Section 4.

---

[10]Also accepted as meeting this commuting requirement are:

(a) The number of persons working in the city or town who live in the central core is equal to at least 15 percent of the employed workers living in the city or town; or

(b) The sum of the number of workers commuting to and from the central core is equal to at least 20 percent of the employed workers living in the city or town.

[11]A New England metropolitan statistical area designated on the basis of census data according to standards in effect at the time of designation will not be disqualified on the basis of lacking a total population of at least 75,000.

C. Two adjacent New England metropolitan statistical areas are consolidated as a single metropolitan statistical area provided the conditions of Section 5 are met. Section 6 is not applied in New England.

D. Each New England metropolitan statistical area defined by Sections 14A through C is categorized in one of the four levels specified in Section 7A. Areas assigned to Levels B, C, or D are designated as metropolitan statistical areas. Areas assigned to Level A are not finally designated until they have been reviewed under Sections 15 and 16.

E. New England metropolitan statistical areas are titled according to the standards of Section 8.

Section 15. Qualification as a Primary Metropolitan Statistical Area

Within a Level A metropolitan statistical area in New England:

A. Any group of cities and towns that was recognized as a separate metropolitan statistical area on January 1, 1980, will be recognized as a primary metropolitan statistical area, unless local opinion does not support its continued separate recognition for statistical purposes.

B. Any additional group of cities and/or towns for which local opinion strongly supports separate recognition will be considered for identification as a primary metropolitan statistical area, provided:

(1) The total population of the group is at least 75,000;

(2) It includes at least one city with a population of 15,000 or more, an employment/residence ratio of at least 0.75, and outcommuting of less than 60 percent of its resident employed workers; and

(3) It contains a core of communities, each of which has at least 50 percent of its population living in the urbanized area, and which together have less than 60 percent of their resident workers commuting to jobs outside the core.

C. The geographic definition of any area recognized by Section 15A, and the identification and definition of any area under Section 15b are subject to the specific statistical guidelines detailed in the Procedures supplement to these standards.

D. If any primary metropolitan statistical area or areas have been recognized under Section 15A through C, the balance of the Level A metropolitan statistical area is also recognized as a primary metropolitan statistical area.[12]

[12]If Section 15D results in the balance of the Level A metropolitan statistical area including a noncontiguous city or town, this place will be added to the contiguous primary metropolitan statistical area to which it has the greatest commuting.

Section 16. Levels . . . of New England Primary and Consolidated Areas

A. New England primary metropolitan statistical areas are categorized in one of four levels according to total population, following Section 7A.

C. Each Level A metropolitan statistical area in New England in which primary metropolitan statistical areas have been defined by Section 15 is designated a consolidated metropolitan statistical area.

REFERENCES

Bureau of the Census (1972) _1970 Census of Population: General Social and Economic Characteristics, United States Summary_. PC(1)-C1. Washington, D.C.: U.S. Department of Commerce.

Bureau of the Census (1978) _County and City Data Book, 1977: A Statistical Abstract Supplement_. Washington, D.C.: U.S. Department of Commerce.

Bureau of the Census (1980) Urbanized area criteria. _Federal Register_ 45(195):66185.

Federal Committee on Standard Metropolitan Statistical Areas (1979) The metropolitan statistical area classification. _Statistical Reporter_ 80-3(December):33-45.

APPENDIX B

LETTER SURVEY OF STATE AND LOCAL RURAL DEVELOPMENT ISSUES

LIST OF TABLES

LIST OF FIGURES

The sample design used for the letter survey of local rural development people was a random sample of 465 counties, stratified by state, by degree of urbanization, and by socioeconomic status. The urbanization strata used were the nine categories of metropolitan status and urban orientation (size/adjacency) described below. County socioeconomic status was obtained from a publication on *Indicators of Social Well-Being for U.S. Counties* (Ross et al. 1979).

The classification of counties used is that developed by Hines et al. (1975); the number of counties in each group is based on SMSA designations as of 1973 using 1970 county population (Ross et al. 1979):

I. Metropolitan (SMSA) counties:
   1. Greater metropolitan--counties of SMSAs having at least 1 million population in 1970 (175 counties).
   2. Medium metropolitan--counties made up SMSAs of 250,000 to 999,999 population (258 counties).
   3. Small metropolitan--counties made up SMSAs of less than 250,000 population (179 counties).

II. Nonmetropolitan (non-SMSA) counties:
   4. Urbanized adjacent--counties contiguous to SMSAs and having an aggregate urban population of at least 20,000 residents (191 counties).
   5. Urbanized not adjacent--counties not contiguous to SMSAs and having an aggregate urban population of at least 20,000 inhabitants (137 counties).
   6. Less urbanized adjacent--counties contiguous to SMSAs and having an aggregate urban population of 2,500 to 19,999 inhabitants (564 counties).
   7. Less urbanized not adjacent--counties not contiguous to SMSAs and having an aggregate urban population of 2,500 to 19,999 inhabitants (721 counties).
   8. Totally rural adjacent--counties contiguous to SMSAs and having no urban population (246 counties).
   9. Totally rural not adjacent--counties not contiguous to SMSAs and having no urban population (626 counties).

For the selection of counties, the counties were arranged by metropolitan status/urban orientation code, and within each code, by states in alphabetical order, and within state by socioeconomic status. Beginning at a random starting point, every sixth county was then selected from the six nonmetropolitan size/adjacency categories, while every twelfth county was selected from the three metropolitan size/adjacency categories. This selection process resulted in a sample of counties distributed by state and size/adjacency strata as shown in Tables 1 and 2.

The distribution of sample counties by region is displayed in maps in Figures 1-8. The regional divisions used in the maps are those of the Bureau of the Census, as follows:

New England: Maine, New Hampshire, Vermont, Massachusetts, Rhode Island, Connecticut

Middle Atlantic: New York, New Jersey, Pennsylvania
South Atlantic: Delaware, Maryland, Virginia, West Virginia, North Carolina, South Carolina, Georgia, Florida (also, District of Columbia)
East South Central: Kentucky, Tennessee, Alabama, Mississippi
West South Central: Arkansas, Louisiana, Oklahoma, Texas
East North Central: Ohio, Indiana, Illinois, Michigan, Wisconsin
West North Central: Minnesota, Iowa, Missouri, North Dakota, South Dakota, Nebraska, Kansas
Mountain: Montana, Idaho, Wyoming, Colorado, New Mexico, Arizona, Utah, Nevada
Pacific: Washington, Oregon, California, Alaska, Hawaii

TABLE 1 Distribution of Sample of Nonmetropolitan Counties, by State and Metropolitan Status/Urban Orientation Category

State	Metropolitan Status/Urban Orientation					
	Urbanized Adjacent	Urbanized Not Adjacent	Less Urbanized Adjacent	Less Urbanized Not Adjacent	Totally Rural Adjacent	Totally Rural Not Adjacent
Alabama	1	0	4	1	2	0
Alaska	0	0	1	0	1	2
Arizona	0	1	0	1	0	0
Arkansas	0	1	2	5	1	2
California	1	1	1	1	1	1
Colorado	0	0	1	2	1	4
Connecticut	1	0	0	0	0	0
Delaware	0	0	0	1[a]	0	0
Florida	1	1	1	2	1	1
Georgia	1	1	5	7	3	5
Hawaii	0	0	0	1[a]	0	0
Idaho	0	1	1	3	0	2
Illinois	2	0	5	4	1	2
Indiana	1	0	5	2	2	0
Iowa	1	1	4	6	1	2
Kansas	1	1	1	6	1	6
Kentucky	1	0	3	5	3	6
Louisiana	1	0	4	1	1	1
Maine	0	0	1	1	0	0
Maryland	0	0	1	0	1	0
Massachusetts	0	0	0	0	0	1
Michigan	0	1	2	3	1	2
Minnesota	1	0	3	5	1	2
Mississippi	1	1	2	5	1	3
Missouri	0	1	4	5	1	6

Montana	0	0	0	3	2	4
Nebraska	0	0	2	4	0	9
Nevada	0	0	0	1	0	1
New Hampshire	1	0	0	0	0	0
New Jersey	1	0	0	0	0	0
New Mexico	0	1	1	2	0	1
New York	2	0	2	1	0	0
No. Carolina	1	2	3	3	1	4
No. Dakota	0	0	1	1	0	6
Ohio	3	0	4	1	0	1
Oklahoma	0	1	3	4	0	2
Oregon	1	0	1	2	0	1
Pennsylvania	2	1	1	2	0	1
Rhode Island	0	0	0	0	0	0
So. Carolina	0	1	3	1	1	0
So. Dakota	0	0	1	3	0	7
Tennessee	1	0	4	3	3	1
Texas	1	2	11	10	5	5
Utah	1	0	0	1	1	1
Vermont	0	1	0	1	0	1
Virginia	0	1	2	2	3	4
Washington	1	0	1	1	1	1
W. Virginia	0	0	2	2	1	2
Wisconson	1	1	3	2	1	2
Wyoming	0	0	0	2	0	2
TOTAL	30	22	96	117	43	104

[a]Not in original sample, added to have all states represented.

TABLE 2 Distribution of Sample of Metropolitan Counties by State and Metropolitan Code

State	Metropolitan Code		
	Large Metro	Medium Metro	Lesser Metro
Alabama	0	1	1
Alaska	0	0	0
Arizona	0	0	0
Arkansas	0	0	1
California	1	1	1
Colorado	0	0	0
Connecticut	0	0	0
Delaware	0	0	0
Florida	0	1	1
Georgia	1	1	1
Hawaii	0	0	0
Idaho	0	0	0
Illinois	1	0	1
Indiana	1	2	1
Iowa	0	0	0
Kansas	0	0	1
Kentucky	0	1	0
Louisiana	0	1	0
Maine	0	0	1
Maryland	1	0	0
Massachusetts	0	0	0
Michigan	1	1	1
Minnesota	0	0	0
Mississippi	0	0	1
Missouri	1	0	0

Montana	0	0	0
Nebraska	0	1	1
Nevada	0	0	0
New Hampshire	0	0	0
New Jersey	0	0	0
New Mexico	0	0	0
New York	1	2	0
North Carolina	0	1	1
North Dakota	0	0	0
Ohio	1	1	2
Oklahoma	0	1	0
Oregon	0	0	0
Pennsylvania	0	1	0
Rhode Island	0	1	0
South Carolina	0	1	0
South Dakota	0	0	1
Tennessee	0	1	0
Texas	1	1	2
Utah	0	0	0
Vermont	0	0	0
Virginia	0	1	2
Washington	0	0	0
West Virginia	0	1	1
Wisconsin	0	0	0
Wyoming	0	0	0
TOTAL	10	22	21

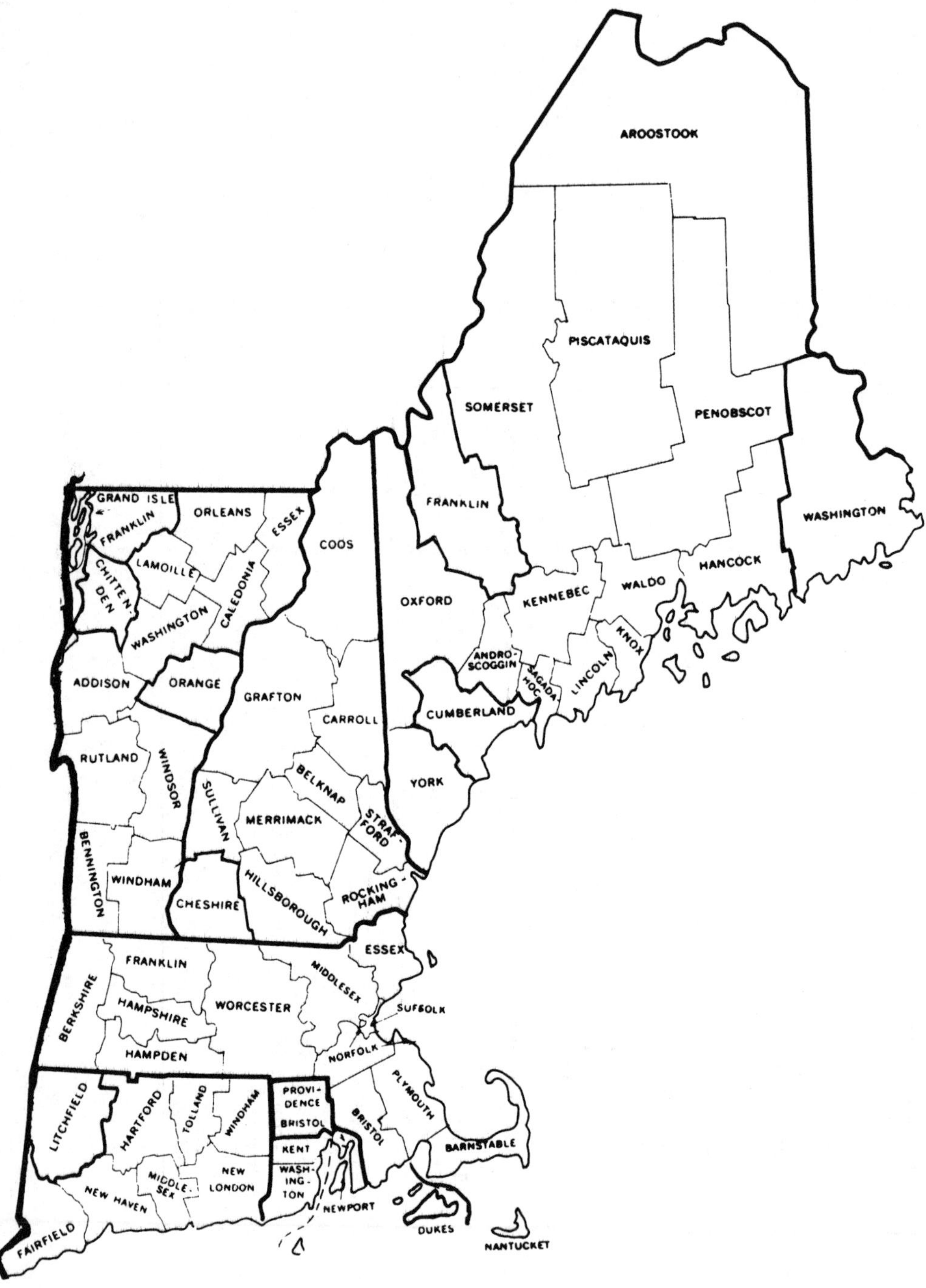

FIGURE 1 New England region: sample counties.

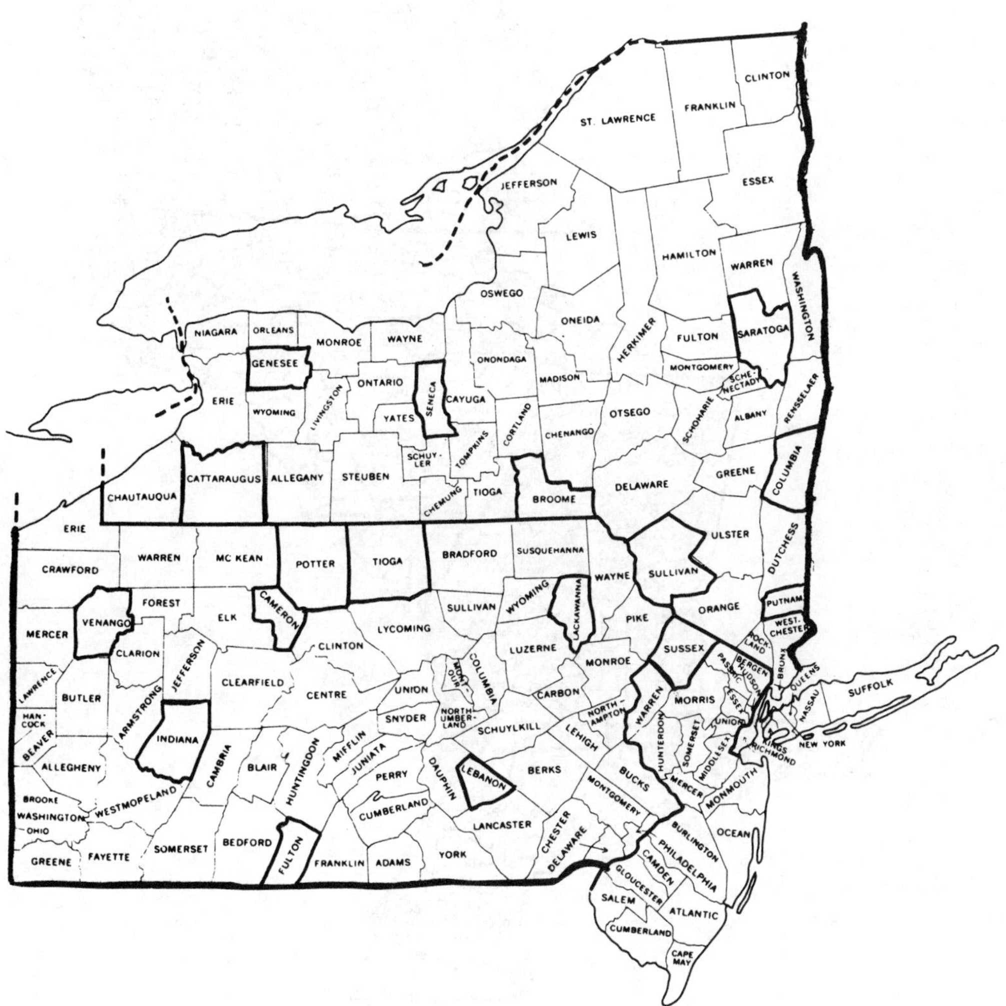

FIGURE 2 Middle Atlantic region: sample counties.

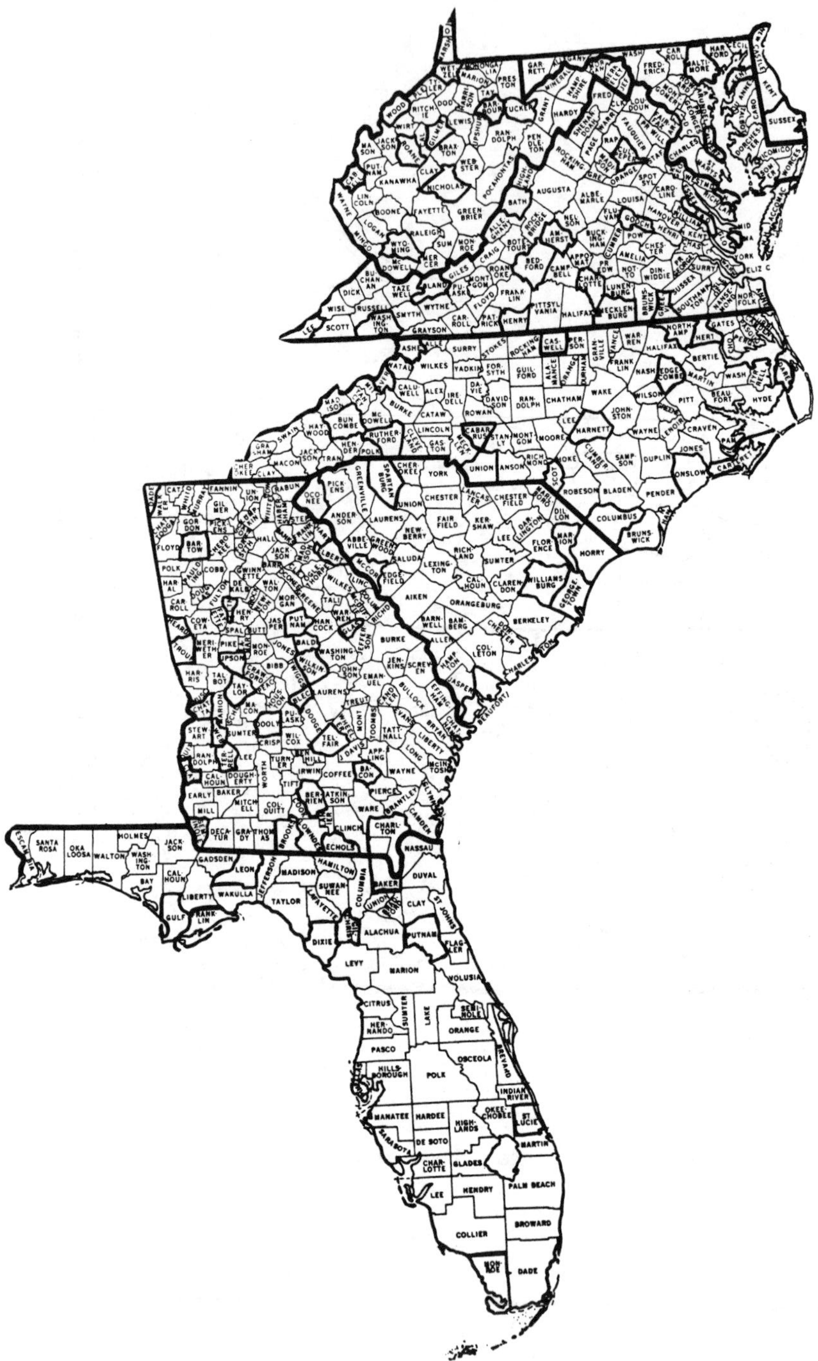

FIGURE 3 South Atlantic region: sample counties.

FIGURE 4 East South Central region: sample counties.

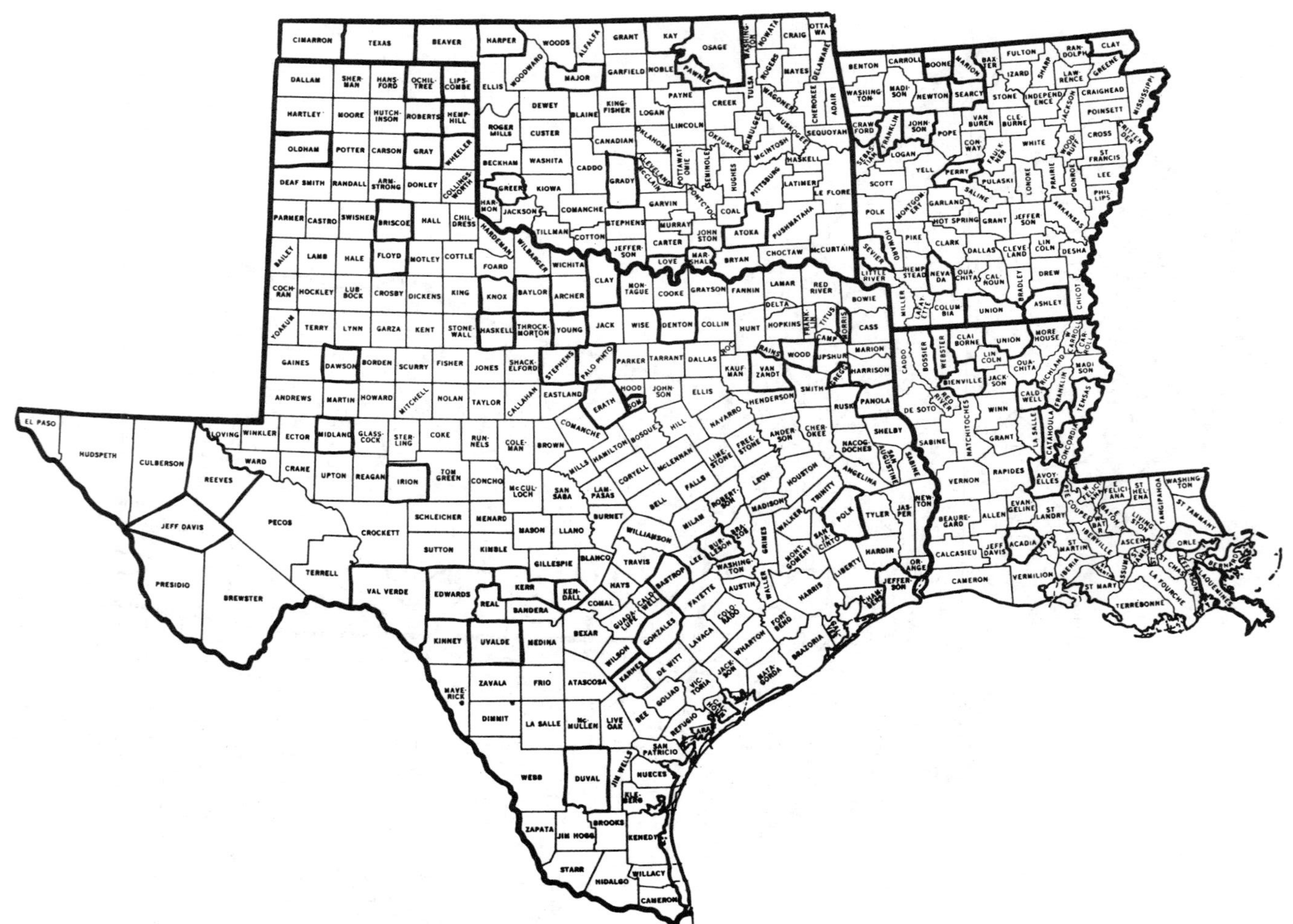

FIGURE 5 West South Central region: sample counties.

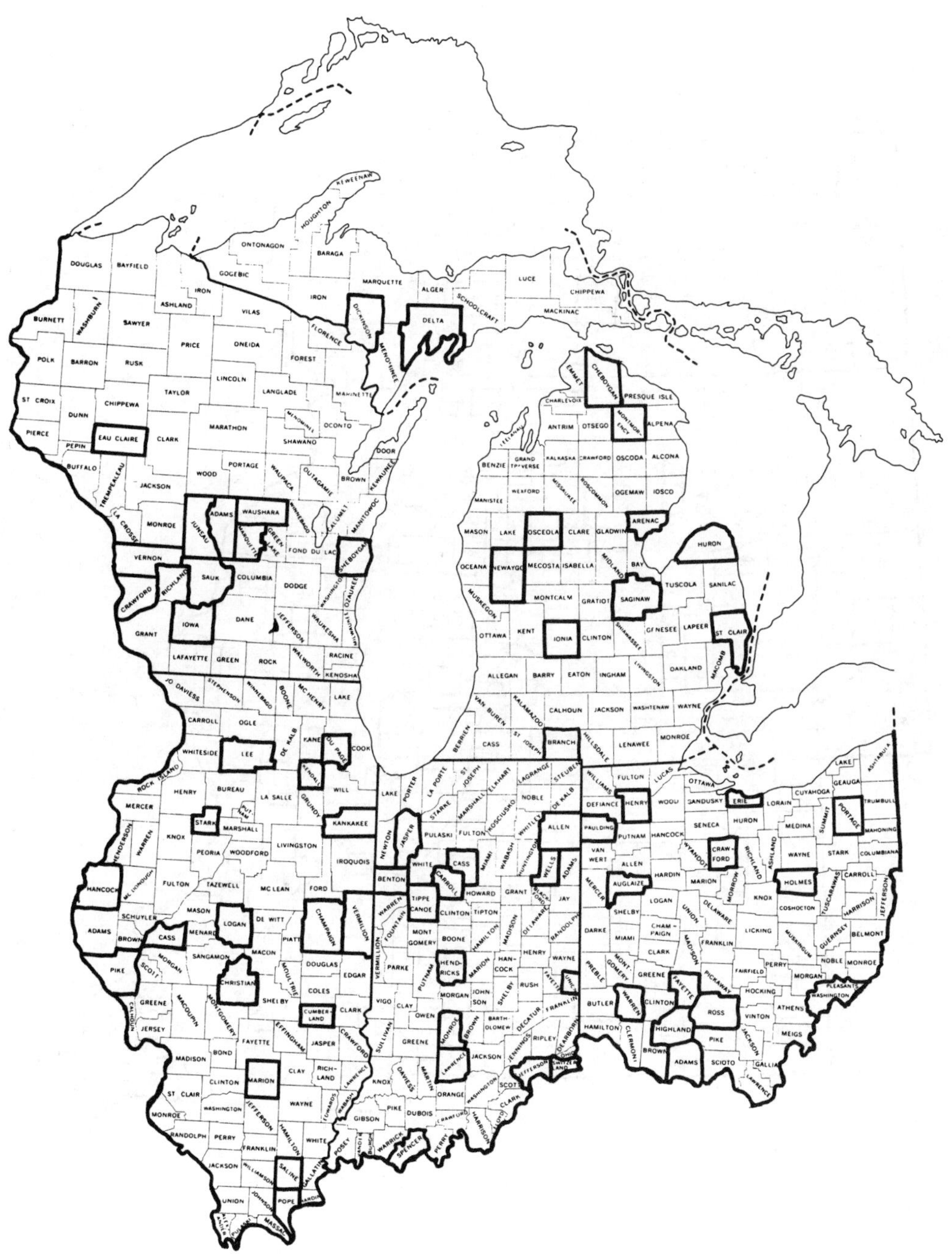

FIGURE 6 East North Central region: sample counties.

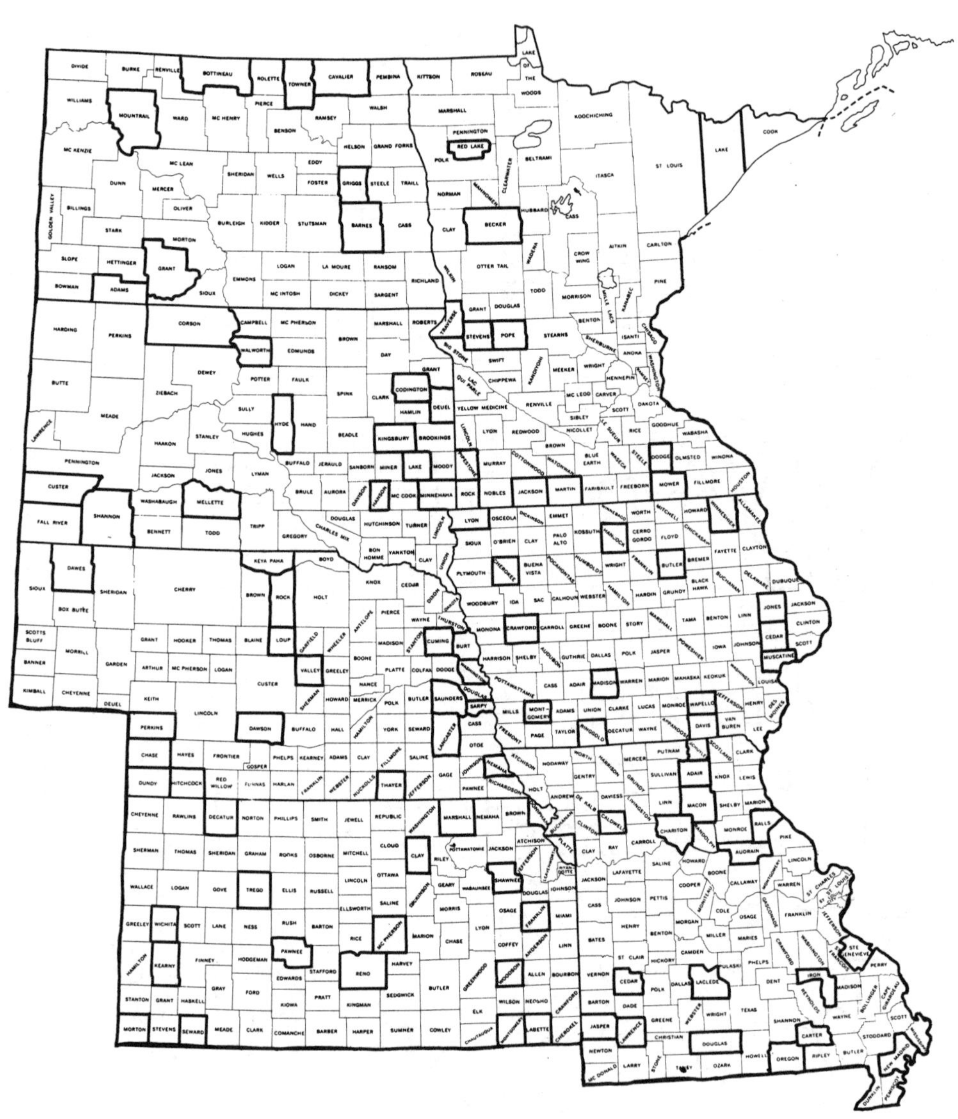

FIGURE 7 West North Central region: sample counties.

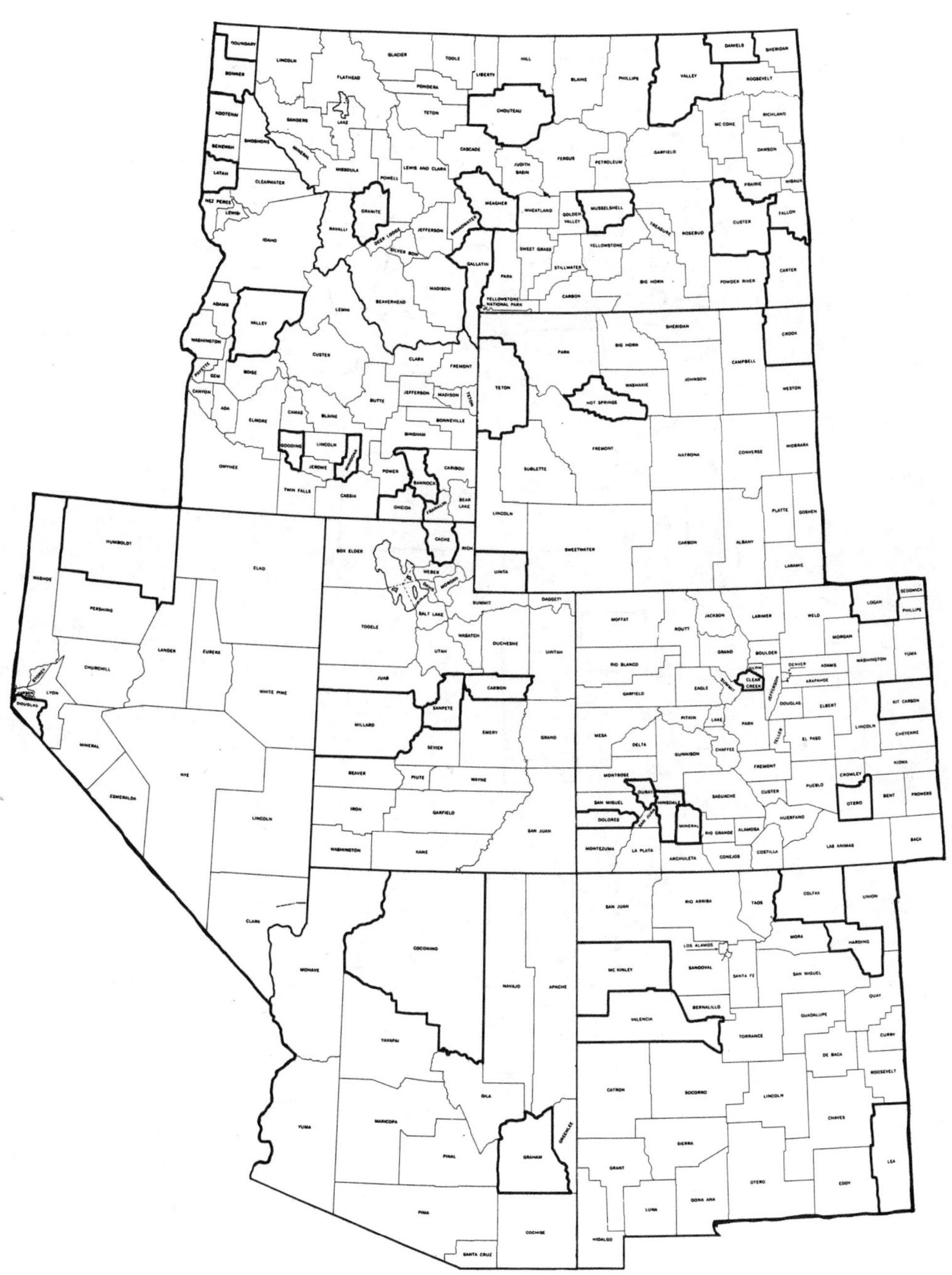

FIGURE 8 Mountain region: sample counties.

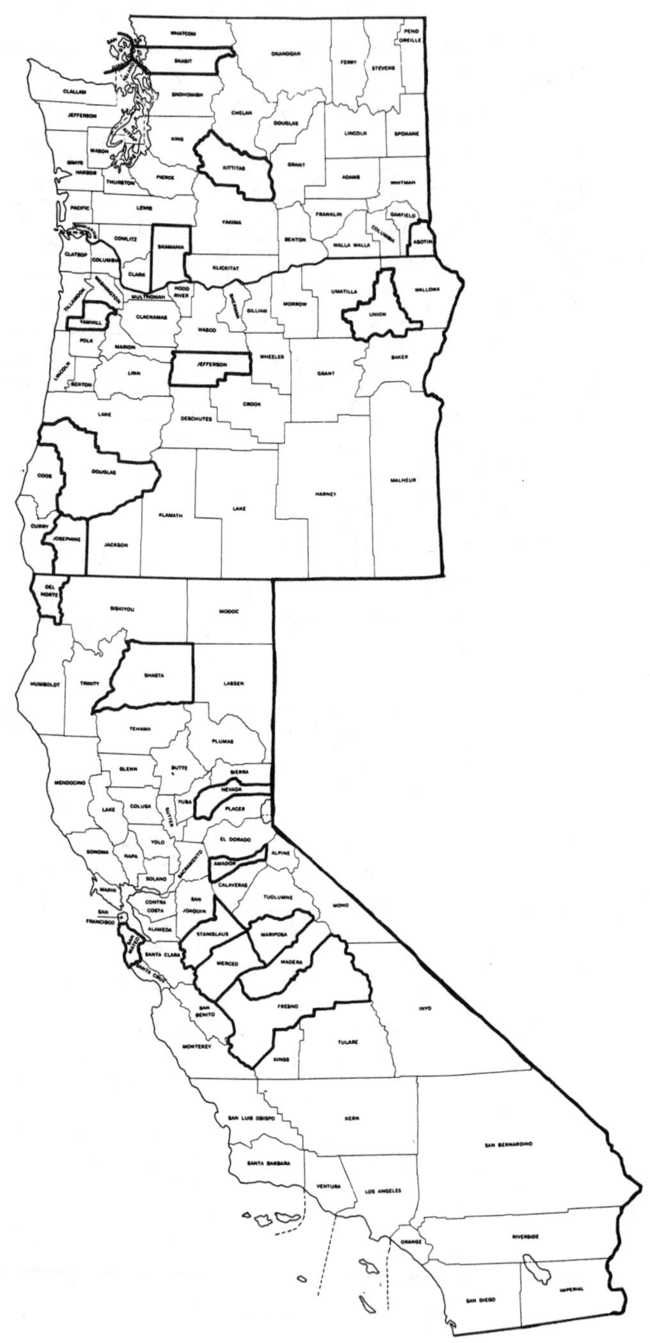

FIGURE 9 Pacific region: sample counties.

November 9, 1979

Dr. J. Michael Sprott
Auburn University
Auburn, Alabama 36830

Dear Dr. Sprout:

The Farmers Home Administration has asked the National Academy of Sciences to undertake a study on Statistics for Rural Development Policy. The Academy has appointed a special Advisory Panel to guide the study. A list of the members of the panel is enclosed. The study plan calls for interviewing policy makers and corresponding with directors of rural development plans in order to identify current and near future policy issues, statistics required for clarification of these issues, and data needed for policies and plans for developing rural areas. I am writing to seek your assistance in identifying directors of rural development plans in your State.

More specifically, we are interested in rural development plans that were completed in 1978 or 1979, or are still in process, that pertain to any of the counties listed in Enclosure B. The method used to select counties within States was designed to give us a good national cross-section of non-metropolitan counties and a small sample of metropolitan counties.

We are interested in rural development plans for the county or a part of the county, in plans for a region which includes all or part of the county, and in State plans which affect the county. For the metropolitan counties, our interest is limited to the county's rural areas and the special development problems which occur because of proximity to a large city.

It would be extremely helpful if you could send a list of names and addresses of directors for rural development plans relating to these counties. We are using the broad definition of rural development issued by the Secretary of Agriculture, Bob Bergland, on March 21, 1979: "Rural development is the deliberate actions of communities, groups, and individuals to improve income levels, to provide adequate housing and a variety of essential community facilities and services, and to enhance economic and social opportunities for rural people."

In conversations with people at the State level, I have learned of special rural development efforts in some counties. If there is an exceptional program in your State that you think we should consider in our study, even though it is

FIGURE 10 Letter mailed to state contacts.

not in a listed county, please include it in your response. We would need the name and address of a person knowledgeable about the program and the county involved.

After talking with some people at the State level about our request, we are convinced that it can be difficult to keep abreast of all plans for rural development in a State. For this reason, I am sending a similar letter to the Chairperson of the Rural Development Coordinating Committee for your State. The name, address, and telephone number of the Chairperson are shown below for your convenience should you wish to prepare a coordinated reply.

Your help in identifying directors of rural development planning studies will be deeply appreciated. As you well know, the highly diverse character of the programs and the funding sources make it impossible to compile a representative list here in Washington. There has never been a systematic assessment of the data required for rural development. This study could have a profound effect on the ability of rural communities to take advantage of programs and opportunities at other levels of government. It would be useful to have your response by mid December as we plan to mail letters to the directors of the rural development plans early in January. Should you have any questions, you may call Dorothy Gilford, Study Director for the project, at 202-389-6997.

We would value any suggestions you might have that would help us with this study. It would be particularly helpful to have comments from you on what you consider to be the two or three most important issues for rural development in your State.

Sincerely yours,

James T. Bonnen, Chairman
Panel on Statistics for
Rural Development Policy

Enclosures

Similar letter sent to:

Mr. Wallace Steele
Agricultural Stabilization
& Conservation Service
P. O. Box 891
Montgomery AL 36102
(Tel: 202-832-7230)

FIGURE 10 (Continued)

March 18, 1980

Mr. James Svoboda
Executive Director
Agricultural Stabilization and
Conservation Service
Box 99
Burwell, NE 68823

Dear Mr. Svoboda:

The Farmers Home Administration has asked the National Academy of Sciences to undertake a study on Statistics for Rural Development Policy. The Academy has appointed a special Advisory Panel to guide the study. The Chairman of the Panel is Dr. James T. Bonnen of Michigan State University. The study plan calls for corresponding with administrators of rural development programs and planning activities in order to identify current and near future policy issues, statistics required for clarification of these issues, and data needed for programs and plans for developing rural areas.

Mr. R. Douglas Horrocks of the Farmers Home Administration in Lincoln gave me your name as an individual who would be knowledgeable about rural development programs for Loup County. We seek your assistance in three aspects of our study:

1. We would appreciate your sending us copies of documents prepared during the past two years pertaining to rural development programs or plans for Loup County that illustrate the types of data used in rural development programs. We are interested in documents or plans for the entire County or part of the County, for a region that includes all or part of the County, and in State programs or plans that affect the County. If no programs exist, it would be helpful to know that. (Illustrative examples of documents are a county plan for preservation of agricultural land, a proposal to a federal or state agency for funds for a rural development project or a study of health care delivery needs for a region. Obviously, there are many other types of documents.)

2. If you had difficulty finding certain kinds of statistics for use in your rural development programs or plans, it would be helpful to have a list of the specific kinds of data that would have been useful. (As an example, a recent letter from the Texoma Regional Planning Commission expressed need for accurate estimates of populations for rural areas in the region.)

FIGURE 11 Letter mailed to local contacts.

3. In the course of interviewing federal policy analysts for rural development, we have identified a number of issues. We believe you can help us put these issues in perspective. A list of the broad issues that we have identified is enclosed. We would be grateful for your comments on two or three of the issues in this list that you consider to be the most important rural development issues in your County. We are wary of our own preconceptions; your views, with those of others, will be important to us in shaping the study. If there are other current or prospective issues you think we should consider, we would appreciate your suggestions. Individual comments will not be identified in the Panel report.

For your information, a list of the members of the Advisory Panel for the study is enclosed. A limited number of copies of the report of the study will be available for free distribution, on request.

Should you have any questions, you may call me at 202-389-6997. We will greatly appreciate receiving a reply from you by April 15, 1980.

Sincerely yours,

Dorothy M. Gilford
Study Director

Enclosure

FIGURE 11 (Continued)

RURAL DEVELOPMENT POLICY ISSUES

I. Improved education and job training

II. Enhanced awareness of the political and social environment

III. Provision of adequate human maintenance services

IV. Provision of adequate community facilities and services

V. Equity and improved access for local communities seeking state or Federal funds

VI. Improved natural resource management and conservation

VII. Encouraging economic development

FIGURE 11 (Continued)

TABLE 3 Issues Identified by State-Level People: Summary Table[a]

	Total	New England	Middle Atlantic	East North Central	West North Central	South Atlantic	East South Central	West South Central	Mountain	Pacific
Number of States	50	6	3	5	7	8	4	4	8	5
Issues										
I. Improved education and job training	14	1	4	1	3	0	2	1	0	2
II. Improved political and social environment	24	1	1	6	4	6	0	0	5	1
III. Provision of adequate human services maintenance	43	3	6	1	6	5	7	7	8	0
IV. Provision of adequate community facilities and services	42	1	3	3	7	4	4	2	13	5
V. Resolving Financial problems	17	0	0	2	3	2	0	1	6	3
VI. Improved natural resource management and conservation	65	4	7	6	13	13	4	2	12	4
VII. Encouraging economic development	49	7	9	4	11	7	2	2	5	2

[a]All numbers represent number of times issue or sub-issue was mentioned by state officials in that region.

TABLE 4 Issues Identified by State-Level People: Detailed Table

Issues	Region									
	Total	New England	Middle Atlantic	East North Central	West North Central	South Atlantic	East South Central	West South Central	Mountain	Pacific
I. Improved education & job training	5		1		1		2	1		
A. Primary & secondary education	1									1
1. Adjusting to declining enrollments										
B. Post-secondary technical and vocational training	1	1								
1. Young adults entering labor force for first time										
a. Low income	1		1							
b. Minority	2		2							
c. Developmentally disabled	1				1					
2. Adults seeking to re-enter or retool										
3. Training programs designed to fulfill manpower requirements of prospective employers										
C. Better secondary education for improved access to college degree programs										
D. Leadership training for adults who desire to play a larger and more effective role in local institutions	3			1	1					1
II. Improved political and social environment										
A. Political										
1. Understanding of how to impact representative government at the local, state, and federal level	1				1					
2. Understanding of how citizens in a community are impacted by programs administered at the local, state, and federal level (public policy education)	3			2	1					
3. Modifications of political institutions and the consequences, including the										

TABLE 4 (Continued)

Issues	Region: Total	New England	Middle Atlantic	East North Central	West North Central	South Atlantic	East South Central	West South Central	Mountain	Pacific
implementation of more comprehensive planning										
a. Home rule hurts state planning	1					1				
4. Nature of regulations (environment, safety, health, etc.) and their impacts	2					1			1	
5. Strengthen local governments	3			1		1				1
a. Administration	2			1		1				
b. Human relations training for local officials	1			1						
c. Aid local planning	2				1				1	
6. Better federal/state/local relations	4				1	1			2	
7. More public involvement in rural development	4	1	1	1		1				
B. Social										
1. Preservation of items & sites of historical importance										
2. Understanding of the forces which led to today's society - locally, regionally, and nationally										
3. Understanding of the inter-dependencies between a local community and the rest of society which imply both opportunities and constraints for local initiatives										
4. Understanding of how citizens and groups in a community are impacted by change and how their differing values and backgrounds cause them to react differently (new migrants have different values)	1								1	

III. Provision of adequate human maintenance services	3							2	1	
A. General support	1		1							
1. Improvements in the level of general income support	1				1					
a. Loans to poor and minorities	1					1				
2. Improvements in local delivery systems	1								1	
a. Food stamps	1				1					
B. Categorical programs										
1. Food										
2. Housing	9	3	1		2	1			2	
a. Elderly	3		1				1	1		
b. Low income	2					1	1			
c. Minority	2						1	1		
d. Young couples	1							1		
3. Medical	6		1	1		1		1	2	
a. Elderly	2		1				1			
b. Low income	2		1				1			
c. Need emergency services	2				1		1			
d. Need doctors	4				1		1	1	1	
C. Reduction of human deprivation										
1. Elderly services										
D. Need resources	1					1				
E. Problems of increased population	1								1	
IV. Provision of adequate community facilities and services	15		2	2	1	2	2	2	3	1
A. Water	3				1				2	
B. Sewer	3				1				2	
C. Solid waste disposal										
D. Fire protection										
E. Transportation	5	1			1				2	1
1. People	3		1		1					1
a. Roads										
(1) Innovative systems	1						1			
b. Rail	2				1		1			
c. Air	1								1	
2. Commodities	1									1
a. Roads										
b. Rail										
c. Air										
F. Public residential housing										
G. Community buildings										
1. Senior citizens centers	1								1	

TABLE 4 (Continued)

Issues	Region: Total	New England	Middle Atlantic	East North Central	West North Central	South Atlantic	East South Central	West South Central	Mountain	Pacific
H. Recreation	3				1	1			1	
1. Parks										
I. Programs responding to asocial behavior among young adults, such as delinquency, drug addiction and unwed pregnancies										
J. Law enforcement	2			1		1				
K. Improved understanding of the financing of community facilities and services										
L. Different service management alternatives	1									1
M. Problems with increased population	1								1	
V. Resolving financial problems	3							1	2	
A. Intergovernmental										
1. Improved awareness of grant opportunities	2					1			1	
a. Need grant specialist	1								1	
2. Improved ability to respond quickly and adequately to opportunities										
3. More equitable treatment by agencies of local community proposals	1				1					
a. Allocation criteria favor urban areas	1								1	
B. Intragovernmental	1									1
1. Inflation	2				1					1
2. Lack of resources	4			2		1				1
3. Declining tax base	1				1					
4. Low tax base (do not own land)	1								1	
VI. Improved natural resource management and conservation	5	1				1		1	1	1
A. Land	2				1	1				
1. Planning to accommodate competing needs (e.g., residential, industrial, agricultural, recreational, natural)	3					3				

a. Preservation of agricultural land	11	3	3	1	1	2	1			
b. Faulty land titles	1								1	
c. Deciding what level of government should control land	4			1			1		1	1
d. Transfer of development rights	1		1							
2. Conservation, including prevention of erosion	3		2	1						
B. Water	6				1	1			2	2
1. Quality, including efforts to restrict pollution from sediment, human waste, animal waste, industrial waste, and agricultural chemicals	3			1			1	1		
2. Flood control	1						1			
3. Drainage										
4. Irrigation	1								1	
5. Scarcity	2				1				1	
a. Import system	1								1	
b. Prior rights of Indians	1								1	
c. Domestic vs. agricultural vs. industrial use	1								1	
C. Air quality										
D. Woodland management										
E. Energy	4				2	2				
1. Conservation	4		1	1	1	1				
a. By means of land use patterns	1				1					
b. By means of tillage methods	1				1					
2. Understanding and adjusting to changes brought about by higher costs of energy	1				1					
3. Alternate sources	3			1	2					
4. Dealing with impact of energy development	4				1	1			2	
F. Coastal resource management	1					1				
VII. Encouraging economic development	13	1	4	1	1	1	1	2	2	
A. Programs applicable to businesses in any sector	1					1				
1. Aid existing businesses in the local community to continue and to expand	3		1	1	1					

TABLE 4 (Continued)

Issues	Region									
	Total	New England	Middle Atlantic	East North Central	West North Central	South Atlantic	East South Central	West South Central	Mountain	Pacific
2. Attract new businesses to the community	1				1					
a. Provision of industrial park or other facility										
b. Community promotion										
3. Manage economic growth through appropriate planning and institutional change	2								1	1
4. Manage economic decline through appropriate planning and institutional change	1		1							
5. Facilitate economic growth by encouraging development of innovative enterprises										
a. Food-sharing cooperatives	1			1						
6. Encourage in-state processing of in-state products	1				1					
B. Programs applicable to a specific sector										
1. Agriculture										
a. Small farm aid and development	8	2	1		2	2			1	

b. Improved productivity on existing commercial farms	1				1					
2. Health										
a. Attract medical staff										
b. Improve facilities										
3. Tourist trade and recreation development										
4. Manufacturing										
5. Development of craft skills and merchandising										
6. Retail trade facilities	1				1					
C. Improve tax structure	1	1								
D. Need jobs	11	2	1		3	2	1		1	1
1. Need employment diversification	1					1				
E. Need credit policies	1			1						
F. Need adequate technical staff to carry out rural development projects	1		1							
G. Must be nonexploitative (of resources)	1	1								

TABLE 5 Individuals in Sample, by Region and Type: Summary Table

	Region									
	New England	Middle Atlantic	East North Central	West North Central	East South Central	South Atlantic	West South Central	Mountain	Pacific	Total
States	6	3	5	7	4	8	4	8	5	50
Counties	10	17	65	99	56	85	70	41	24	465
Letters Mailed	22	33	87	122	66	143	104	71	43	691
Type of Recipient										
State Level	2	3	3	1	0	24	4	5	0	42
Regional Planning Agencies	6	1	18	50	33	52	26	25	2	213
County Planning Departments	3	9	23	0	0	8	0	18	11	72
Federal Agencies	5	19	16	62	17	42	20	6	9	196
Other	6	1	27	9	16	17	54	17	21	168

TABLE 6 Individuals in Sample, by Region, Type, and Official Position

	New England					
	Maine	New Hampshire	Vermont	Massachusetts	Rhode Island	Connecticut
Number of Counties	3	1	3	1	1	1
State Level						
FmHA			(1)*			
Planning Office		1	1			
Local Level						
Regional Planning & Development Agency (COG)		1	1(2)			3(1)
Regional Economic Development Agency			1			
Regional Resource Conservation Agency			1(1)			
County Planning Agency		1	1		1	
Local Government					1(5)	
County Health Service	1					
Private Business						(1)
Educator						(1)
Not Identified				1		
Federal Agency						
FmHA	2					
County Extension					1	1
Soil Conservation						(1)
Farm Credit						1
Exemplary County (not in sample)				1 Hampshire		

TABLE 6 (Continued)

	Middle Atlantic		
	New York	New Jersey	Pennsylvania
Number of Counties	8	1	8
State Level			
Department of Community Affairs		1	
Department of Environmental Resources		1	
Department of Agriculture		(1)	
Bureau of Forests			1
FmHA		(1)	
Local Level			
Regional Planning & Development Agency (COG)			1
County Planning Agency	8(2)		1
Rural Development Committee			1
Federal Agency			
FmHA	8		
County Extension		1(1)	8
Soil Conservation			1
ASCS			1

TABLE 6 (Continued)

	South Atlantic							
	Dela-ware	Mary-land	Vir-gin-ia	West Vir-ginia	North Caro-lina	South Caro-lina	Geor-gia	Flor-ida
Number of Counties	1	3	15	9	16	7	25	9
Multi-State Level								
Appalachian Regional Commission					1			
Coastal Plains Regional Commission						(1)		1
Bel-o-Mar Regional Council and Inter-state Planning Commission				1				
State Level								
State University								
Vice-President for Services							1	
Agricultural Experiment Station							1	
Agricultural Research Service					(1)			
Center for Rural Resource Development					1			
Academic					(1)			
FFA					(1)			
4-H					(1)			
ASCS					(1)		1	
Soil Conservation Service					(1)	1	1	
Farmers Home Administration					(1)	1		
Department of Agriculture					1		(1)	
Department of Community Affairs							(1)	
Department of Nat'l Resources and Community Development					1(1)			
Department of Commerce					1(1)			
Department of Administration					1(2)			
Department of Parks, Recreation and Tourism						1		
Water Resources Commission						1		
Land Resources Commission						1		
Development Board	1					1		

TABLE 6 (Continued)

	South Atlantic							
	Dela-ware	Mary-land	Vir-gin-ia	West Vir-ginia	North Caro-lina	South Caro-lina	Geor-gia	Flor-ida
Governor's Office								
Planning and Budgeting								1
Economic and Community Development				1				
Energy Resources						1		
Economic Development & Transportation						1		
State Health Project	1							
Rural Electrification Administration					1			
Institute for Res. on Human Resources					1			
National Forests in North Carolina					1			
Local Level								
Regional Planning and Development Organization (COG)			12	5	12	5	13	5
Multi-county Development Association					4(2)			
County Planning Agency		1(5)				2(6)		5
County Commissioners					8(8)			1
County Economic Development Commission	1	2(2)						
Federal Agency								
Farmers Home Administration		1(2)					8	
County Extension	2	(1)	15		4(12)			9
Soil Conservation		3(4)						
Exemplary County (not in sample)								1 Gadsden

*Indicates number of people in this category who did not receive letters.

TABLE 6 (Continued)

	East South Central			
	Kentucky	Tennessee	Alabama	Mississippi
Number of Counties	19	13	10	14
Local Level				
Regional Planning & Development Agency (COG)				
Staff		6	6	8
Board				13(27)
County Development Agency		5	10	
County Government		1		
Chamber of Commerce		1		
Federal Agency				
County Extension	17			

	West South Central			
	Arkansas	Louisiana	Oklahoma	Texas
Number of Counties	12	9	11	38
State Level				
State University				
Cooperative Extension	1(1)			
Academic	1			
FmHA	1			
ASCS	1			
Local Level				
Regional Planning & Development Agency (COG)	7	1(1)		18
Rural Development Committee		9	6(1)	
Local Government		5		38
Federal Agency				
FmHA	7		5	
County Extension	2		2	
Soil Conservation			1	
ASCS			3	
Exemplary County (not in sample)	1 Mississippi			

TABLE 6 (Continued)

	East North Central				
	Ohio	Indiana	Illinois	Michigan	Wisconsin
Number of Counties	13	14	16	12	10
State Level					
Department of Commerce & Community Affairs			1		
Department of Management & Budget				1	
Governor's Office					
Regional Task Force				1	
Local Level					
Regional Planning & Development Agency (COG)			7	6	5
County Planning Agency	3	1	5	10	4
County Government				1	
County Economic Development Organization		1			2(28)
Community Action Council					1
County Housing Authority					1
Educator	1				
Clergyman		1			
Not Identified	2(4)	13(4)			
Federal Agency					
County Extension	11(1)	2		1	2
Exemplary County (not in sample)			2 Rock Island Macoupin	Livingston Washtenaw	

TABLE 6 (Continued)

	West North Central						
	Minnesota	Iowa	Missouri	No. Dakota	So. Dakota	Nebraska	Kansas
Number of Counties	12	15	18	8	12	17	17
State Level							
Planning Bureau					1		
Local Level							
Regional Planning & Development Agency (COG)	6	11	14	5	5	9	
Regional Concerted Services	1						
County Government						1	
Community Betterment Program							7(11)
Federal Agency							
FmHA					5		
County Extension	11		14			9	18
Soil Conservation						2	
ASCS						3	

TABLE 6 (Continued)

	Mountain							
	Montana	Idaho	Wyoming	Colorado	New Mexico	Arizona	Utah	Nevada
Number of Counties	9	7	4	8	5	2	4	2
Multi-State Level								
Four Corners Regional Commission							1	
Bear River Resource Conservation and Development							1	
State Level								
State University								
Academic					1			
FmHA			(1)					
Rural Development Committee			1					
Department of Planning		1			1			
Department of Economic Planning & Development			(1)					
Governor's Office								
Planning Coordinator			1					
Local Level								
Regional Planning & Development Agency (COG)	4	5		6	5	2	3	
Regional Human Resource Development Council	5							
County Planning Agency	7(3)		4	5		1		1
County Government				4(4)		2		1
County Development Agency	1							
County Community Development Agency	1					1		
Rural Development Committee						1		
Federal Agency								
FmHA			3			1		
County Extension						1		

TABLE 6 (Continued)

	Pacific				
	Washington	Oregon	California	Hawaii	Alaska
Number of Counties	5	5	9	1	4
Local Level					
Regional Planning & Development Agency (COG)	(2)		2		
County Economic Development Agency			8(2)	1	
County Planning Agency	5(2)		5(2)	1(1)	
Community Action Committee	1(1)				
Indian Tribe	1				
Local Government				(1)	4
Port Manager	1(1)				
Private Company	1			1	
Academic		1			
Not Identified	1(4)				
Federal Agency					
FmHA	(2)			(1)	
County Extension	1(1)	4		(1)	
Soil Conservation	1(2)				
ASCS	1				
Corps of Engineers	1(1)				
National Park Service	1(2)				
State Agency					
Natural Resources	(1)				
Employment Security	(1)				

TABLE 7 Response Rates in Local Survey, by Region

Variable	Region: New England	Middle Atlantic	East North Central	West North Central	East South Central	South Atlantic	West South Central	Mountain	Pacific	Total
States	6	3	5	7	4	8	4	8	5	50
Counties in Sample	10	17	65	99	56	85	70	41	24	465
Letters Mailed	22	33	87	122	66	143	104	71	43	691
Responses Received	3	16	39	58	26	52	27	25	11	257[a]
Counties Represented in Responses	3	11	39	57	29	56	30	22	10	257[a]
Percentage of Counties Represented in Responses	30%	65%	60%	58%	52%	66%	43%	54%	42%	55%

[a] "Responses received" and "counties represented" do not have the one-to-one relationship that these coincidental figures suggest. Two or three responses were received from various officials in some sample counties while some responses (from, e.g., a regional organization official) covered two or three sample counties.

TABLE 8 Response Rates in Local Survey by Metro Status/Urban Orientation

	SMSA			Adjacent to SMSA			Nonadjacent to SMSA		
	Large	Medium	Small	Urban	Less Urban	Totally Rural	Urban	Less Urban	Totally Rural
Sample Counties[a]	10	22	21	30	95	42	22	119	102
Responding Counties[a]	6	11	11	21	49	28	11	66	55
Percent	60	50	52	70	52	67	50	56	54

[a]Refers to local letters only.

TABLE 9 Response Rates in Local Survey by Official Position of Local Contact

	Regional Planning Organizations (COG's)	County and Local Planning Departments	Cooperative Extension, Farmers Home Admin. Rural Development Committee	Other Local Representatives of Federal Agencies (mostly ASCS)	Other Local Government and Business Organizations	Misc.	Total
Letters Mailed	199	70	208	22	122	33	654
Responses Received	93	31	94	12	22	6	258
Percent	46	43	45	50	17	18	

TABLE 10 Number of Times Issues were Mentioned in Local Letters, by Metropolitan Status/Urban Orientation of County: Summary Table

	Total	Metropolitan			Nonmetropolitan					
					Adjacent to SMSA			Not Adjacent to SMSA		
		Large	Medium	Small	Urban	Less Urban	Totally Rural	Urban	Less Urban	Totally Rural
Number of counties in sample	467	10	22	21	30	95	42	22	119	102
Number of counties with responses	216	5	11	8	19	37	22	10	55	49
ISSUES										
I. Provision of adequate	61[a]	0	3	1	1	11	5	4	16	20
human maintenance services	0.28[b]	-	0.27	0.12	0.05	0.29	0.22	0.40	0.29	0.41
II. Improved education and	71	1	3	4	4	12	9	8	11	19
job training	0.33	0.20	0.27	0.50	0.21	0.32	0.41	0.80	0.20	0.39
III. Provision of adequate	305	8	12	16	26	36	32	13	80	82
community facilities and services	1.41	1.60	1.09	2.00	1.36	0.97	1.45	1.30	1.46	1.67
IV. Encouraging economic development	224	1	10	10	10	31	27	16	55	64
	1.04	0.20	0.91	1.25	0.53	0.83	1.23	1.60	1.00	1.31
V. Improved natural resources	192	7	17	11	20	30	12	8	47	40
management and conservation	0.89	1.40	1.54	1.38	1.05	0.81	0.54	0.80	0.86	0.82
VI. Equity										
VII. Improved political and social	64	5	6	4	1	10	7	1	17	13
environment	0.30	1.00	0.54	0.50	0.05	0.28	0.32	0.10	0.31	0.26
VIII. Resolving financial problems	254	4	7	11	30	37	22	12	72	56
	1.18	.80	0.64	1.38	1.58	1.00	1.32	1.20	1.31	1.14

[a]Number of times issue or subissue was mentioned.

[b]Average number of times issue or subissue was mentioned, by counties with responses.

TABLE 11 Number of Times Issues Were Mentioned in Local Letters, by Metropolitan Status/Urban Orientation of County: Detailed Table (Percentages are Based on Number of Responding Counties in the Type[a])

		Metropolitan			Nonmetropolitan					
					Adjacent to SMSA			Not Adjacent to SMSA		
	Total	Large	Medium	Small	Urban	Less Urban	Totally Rural	Urban	Less Urban	Totally Rural
Number of Counties in sample	467	10	22	21	30	95	42	22	119	102
Number of Counties with responses	216	5	11	8	19	37	22	10	55	49
ISSUES										
I. Provision of Adequate Human Maintenance Services	61	0	3	1	1	11	5	4	15	20
A. Housing	6%[b] (13)		9% (1)		5% (1)	5% (2)		20% (2)	7% (4)	6% (3)
1. Elderly	1% (2)									4% (2)
2. Low income	1% (3)									6% (3)
3. Siting problems	0% (1)							10% (1)		
B. Medical	6% (12)					8% (3)	5% (1)		4% (2)	12% (6)
1. Elderly	1% (3)					3% (1)			4% (2)	
2. Need emergency services	2% (5)					3% (1)			5% (3)	2% (1)
3. Need doctors	1% (3)					3% (1)			2% (1)	2% (1)
C. Elderly	3% (7)					3% (1)	5% (1)		4% (2)	6% (3)
D. Handicapped	0% (1)					3% (1)				
E. Unspecified	5% (11)		18% (2)	13% (1)		3% (1)	14% (3)	10% (1)	4% (2)	2% (1)
II. Improved Education and Job Training	71	1	3	4	4	12	9	8	11	19
A. Primary and Secondary Education	4% (8)				11% (2)	5% (2)	9% (2)			4% (2)
1. Adjusting to declining enrollments	1% (2)									4% (2)
2. Failure of school administration	0% (1)							10% (1)		

TABLE 11 (Continued)

	Total	Metropolitan Large	Metropolitan Medium	Metropolitan Small	Nonmetropolitan Adjacent to SMSA Urban	Nonmetropolitan Adjacent to SMSA Less Urban	Nonmetropolitan Adjacent to SMSA Totally Rural	Nonmetropolitan Not Adjacent to SMSA Urban	Nonmetropolitan Not Adjacent to SMSA Less Urban	Nonmetropolitan Not Adjacent to SMSA Totally Rural
3. Dropout rate	0%							10%		
	(1)							(1)		
4. Juvenile delinquency	0%							10%		
	(1)							(1)		
5. Drugs	0%							10%		
	(1)							(1)		
6. Overcrowded classrooms	0%									2%
	(1)									(1)
B. Post-Secondary Vocational and Technical Training	12%		18%		11%	11%	23%	20%	7%	12%
	(25)		(2)		(2)	(4)	(5)	(2)	(4)	(6)
C. Leadership Training for Adults	1%					5%			2%	
	(3)					(2)			(1)	
D. Unspecified	13%	20%	9%	50%		11%	9%	20%	11%	16%
	(28)	(1)	(1)	(4)		(4)	(2)	(2)	(6)	(8)
III. Provision of Adequate Community Facilities and Services	305	8	12	16	26	36	32	13	80	82
A. Water	18%	40%	18%		26%	8%	27%	10%	20%	16%
	(38)	(2)	(2)		(5)	(3)	(6)	(1)	(11)	(8)
B. Sewer	17%	20%	18%		32%	3%	27%	10%	22%	15%
	(37)	(1)	(2)		(6)	(1)	(6)	(1)	(12)	(8)
C. Solid waste disposal	5%					5%		20%	5%	6%
	(10)					(2)		(2)	(3)	(3)
D. Fire protection	6%					5%			11%	12%
	(14)					(2)			(6)	(6)
E. Transportation	3%			13%			14%	10%		4%
	(7)			(1)			(3)	(1)		(2)
1. People	2%					3%			4%	2%
	(4)					(1)			(2)	(1)
a. Roads	6%				11%	8%			7%	6%
	(12)				(2)	(3)			(4)	(3)
b. Innovative systems	1%				5%	3%				
	(2)				(1)	(1)				
c. Rail	1%					3%				2%
	(2)					(1)				(1)

d. Air	0% (1)								2% (1)	
e. Hard to cut gas use	0% (1)					3% (1)				
2. Commodities	1% (2)								4% (2)	
a. Roads	1% (2)				5% (1)				2% (1)	
b. Rail	2% (4)			13% (1)					2% (1)	4% (2)
F. Community buildings	1% (3)		9% (1)							4% (2)
1. Senior citizens centers	2% (4)			13% (1)	5% (1)	3% (1)				2% (1)
2. Youth	1% (3)			13% (1)		3% (1)				2% (1)
3. Day care center	0% (1)			13% (1)						
4. Migrant workers	0% (1)					3% (1)				
G. Recreation	6% (14)			13% (1)		5% (2)	5% (1)		7% (4)	12% (6)
H. Law enforcement	4% (9)								7% (4)	10% (5)
I. Bridge repair	1% (2)				5% (1)					2% (1)
J. Repair, renovation, or replacement of facilities	5% (10)					3% (1)			9% (5)	8% (4)
K. Different service management alternatives	1% (3)		9% (1)			3% (1)			2% (1)	
L. Improved understanding of the financing of services where population is dispersed	5% (10)	20% (1)	9% (1)	25% (2)			5% (1)	10% (1)	2% (1)	6% (3)
M. Problems because of increased population	1% (2)					3% (1)				2% (1)
N. Problems because of dispersed development	3% (6)			13% (1)	11% (2)	5% (2)	5% (1)			

TABLE 11 (Continued)

		Metropolitan			Nonmetropolitan					
					Adjacent to SMSA			Not Adjacent to SMSA		
	Total	Large	Medium	Small	Urban	Less Urban	Totally Rural	Urban	Less Urban	Totally Rural
O. Growth of single issue constituencies has raised threshold of "adequate"	0%	20%								
	(1)	(1)								
P. Unspecified	46%	60%	45%	88%	37%	30%	64%	70%	40%	49%
	(100)	(3)	(5)	(7)	(7)	(11)	(14)	(7)	(22)	(24)
IV. Encouraging economic development	224	1	10	10	10	31	27	16	55	64
A. Aid existing businesses in the local community to continue and expand	4%				5%	3%			9%	4%
	(9)				(1)	(1)			(5)	(2)
B. Stop regulating business	1%				5%	3%			2%	
	(3)				(1)	(1)			(1)	
C. Attract new business to the community	6%					3%	18%	10%	4%	8%
	(12)					(1)	(4)	(1)	(2)	(4)
1. Provision of industrial park or other facility	1%		9%				5%			2%
	(3)		(1)				(1)			(1)
2. Recover investment in industrial park	0%			13%						
	(1)			(1)						
3. Community promotion	1%	20%								4%
	(3)	(1)								(2)
4. Agriculture-related	0%									2%
	(1)									(1)
D. Manage economic growth through appropriate planning and institutional change	1%						5%			2%
	(2)						(1)			(1)
E. Manage economic (and population) decline through appropriate planning and institutional change	0%								2%	
	(1)								(1)	
F. Encourage in-state processing of in-state products	5%			13%			14%		5%	8%
	(11)			(1)			(3)		(3)	(4)

G. Small farm aid and development	2% (5)		9% (1)				5% (1)		2% (1)	4% (2)
1. Improved productivity on existing commercial farms	1% (3)						5% (1)			4% (2)
2. Farm credit (interest rates too high)	1% (2)								2% (1)	2% (1)
H. Tourist trade and recreation development	2% (4)					5% (2)			4% (2)	
I. Develop existing retail and service sectors	1% (3)						5% (1)			4% (2)
J. Protect existing retail and service sectors from competition of nearby metro areas	0% (1)								2% (1)	
K. Improve tax structure	0% (1)	9% (1)								
L. Get rid of unfair competition of tax loss farmers	0% (1)									2% (1)
M. Need jobs	13% (27)		9% (1)	25% (2)	5% (1)	14% (5)	23% (5)	20% (2)	13% (7)	8% (4)
1. Need employment diversification	7% (15)			13% (1)		3% (1)	5% (1)	30% (3)	9% (5)	8% (4)
2. Need jobs using appropriate technology	0% (1)				3% (1)					
3. Young people are leaving	5% (11)			13% (1)		3% (1)	5% (1)	10% (1)	7% (4)	6% (3)
4. Youth unemployment	1% (2)							10% (1)		2% (1)
5. Underemployment	0% (1)									2% (1)
N. Need adequate technical staff or T.A. to carry out rural development projects	1% (2)								4% (2)	
O. Must be nonexploitative (of resources)	3% (6)			13% (1)	11% (2)	3% (1)	5% (1)	10% (1)		

TABLE 11 (Continued)

		Metropolitan			Nonmetropolitan					
					Adjacent to SMSA			Not Adjacent to SMSA		
	Total	Large	Medium	Small	Urban	Less Urban	Totally Rural	Urban	Less Urban	Totally Rural
P. Unspecified	43% (93)		55% (6)	38% (3)	26% (5)	46% (17)	32% (7)	70% (7)	36% (20)	57% (28)
V. Improved Natural Resource Management and Conservation	192	7	17	11	20	30	12	8	47	40
A. Land	0% (1)									2% (1)
1. Planning to accommodate competing needs (e.g., residential, industrial, agricultural, recreational, natural)	6% (12)		18% (2)	13% (1)	16% (3)		5% (1)		4% (2)	6% (3)
a. Preservation of agricultural land	17% (36)	60% (3)	55% (6)	25% (2)	26% (5)	27% (10)	9% (2)		13% (7)	2% (1)
b. Deciding what level of government should control land	3% (6)			13% (1)				10% (1)	5% (3)	2% (1)
c. Need zoning	3% (6)	20% (1)	9% (1)			5% (2)	5% (1)			2% (1)
d. Payments to land owners to provide incentives for desirable land treatment practices	2% (4)				5% (1)	3% (1)				4% (2)
e. Distant preservationists force local inhabitants to bear financial losses (for replacement and repairs)	0% (1)			13% (1)						
2. Conservation, including prevention of erosion	11% (24)		9% (1)	13% (1)	5% (1)	11% (4)	9% (2)	10% (1)	13% (7)	14% (7)

B. Water	1% (3)								2% (1)	4% (2)
1. Quality, including efforts to restrict pollution from sediment, human waste, animal waste, industrial waste, and agricultural chemicals	6% (13)	20% (1)	18% (2)		25% (2)	5% (2)			7% (4)	4% (2)
2. Flood control	1% (2)		9% (1)						2% (1)	
3. Irrigation	2% (5)								5% (3)	4% (2)
4. Scarcity	1% (3)									6% (3)
C. Air quality	0% (1)		9% (1)							
D. Woodland management	2% (5)		9% (1)					10% (1)	5% (3)	
E. Coastal resource management	0% (1)								2% (1)	
F. Energy	0% (1)								2% (1)	
1. Conservation	4% (9)			38% (3)		5% (2)	5% (1)			6% (3)
2. Understanding and adjusting to changes brought about by higher costs of energy	2% (5)				25% (2)	5% (2)			2% (1)	
3. Alter negative feelings toward nuclear and coal	0% (1)							10% (1)		
4. Alternate sources	2% (5)				13% (1)			20% (2)		4% (2)
5. Dealing with impact of energy development	3% (6)					3% (1)			7% (4)	2% (1)
6. Unspecified	20% (42)	40% (2)	18% (2)	25% (2)	26% (5)	16% (6)	23% (5)	20% (2)	16% (9)	18% (9)
VI. <u>Equity of sharing services and benefits, and equal access to the channels of occupational and geographic mobility</u>										

TABLE 11 (Continued)

	Total	Metropolitan			Nonmetropolitan					
					Adjacent to SMSA			Not Adjacent to SMSA		
	Total	Large	Medium	Small	Urban	Less Urban	Totally Rural	Urban	Less Urban	Totally Rural
VII. Improved political and social environment	64	5	6	4	1	10	7	1	17	13
A. Understanding of how to impact representative government at the local, state, and federal level	3% (7)	20% (1)	9% (1)			5% (2)			5% (3)	
B. Understanding of how citizens in a community are impacted by programs administered at the local, state, and federal level (public policy education)	1% (2)	20% (1)							2% (1)	
C. Modifications of political institutions and the consequences, including the implementation of more comprehensive planning	1% (3)	20% (1)							4% (2)	
D. Nature of regulations (environmental, safety, health, etc.) and their impacts	7% (15)		9% (1)	13% (1)	5% (1)	9% (2)		11% (6)	4% (2)	
E. Strengthen local governments	1% (2)					3% (1)				2% (1)
1. Administration	2% (5)			25% (2)		3% (1)	9% (2)			
2. Aid local planning	0% (1)								2% (1)	
F. Better federal/state/local relations	0% (1)							10% (1)		
1. Reduce government interference in local affairs	2% (5)					5% (2)				6% (3)
2. Better understanding of federal and state tax structure	0% (1)									2% (1)

	G. More public involvement in rural development	2% (4)			13% (1)		3% (1)	5% (1)		2% (1)	
	H. Preservation of items and sites of historical importance	1% (2)	20% (1)	9% (1)							
	I. Understanding of the forces which led to today's society--locally, regionally, nationally	1% (3)		9% (1)						2% (1)	2% (1)
	J. Understanding of the interdependencies between a local community and the rest of society which imply both opportunities and constraints for local initiatives	2% (4)		9% (1)				5% (1)			4% (2)
	K. Understanding of how citizens and groups in a community are impacted by change and how their differing values and backgrounds cause them to react differently (new migrants have different values)	0% (1)		9% (1)							
	L. Too much of both	0% (1)					3% (1)				
	M. Unspecified	3% (7)	20% (1)					5% (1)		4% (2)	6% (3)
VIII.	<u>Resolving Financial Problems</u>	254	4	7	11	30	37	25	12	72	56
	A. Improved awareness of grant opportunities	3%	20%			5%	3%	5%		2%	2%
	1. Need grant specialist	8% (17)			13% (1)	11% (2)	11% (4)	9% (2)	10% (1)	5% (3)	8% (4)
	2. Need to encourage assistance of state and federal legislators	0% (1)								2% (1)	

TABLE 11 (Continued)

	Total	Metropolitan Large	Metropolitan Medium	Metropolitan Small	Nonmetropolitan Adjacent to SMSA Urban	Adjacent to SMSA Less Urban	Adjacent to SMSA Totally Rural	Not Adjacent to SMSA Urban	Not Adjacent to SMSA Less Urban	Not Adjacent to SMSA Totally Rural
VIII. Resolving Financial Problems (cont'd)										
B. Improved ability to respond quickly and adequately to opportunities	2% (5)			13% (1)		3% (1)			2% (1)	4% (2)
1. Grants cost too much	6% (12)				11% (2)		9% (2)		7% (4)	8% (4)
2. Grants are not appropriate to needs	6% (12)				11% (2)	3% (1)		10% (1)	11% (6)	4% (2)
3. Federal grant requirements and mandates are oppressive (too bureaucratic)	10% (22)	20% (1)	9% (1)	13% (1)	11% (2)	5% (2)	18% (4)		13% (7)	8% (4)
a. Professional services	2% (5)		9% (1)			3% (1)			5% (3)	
b. Davis-Bacon	1% (2)								4% (2)	
c. Environmental Impact Statements	1% (2)								4% (2)	
4. Federal grant requirements cause local structure changes (e.g., special districts)	0% (1)		9% (1)							
C. More equitable treatment by agencies of local community proposals	17% (37)		27% (3)		11% (2)	14% (5)	23% (5)	50% (5)	18% (10)	14% (7)
1. Allocation criteria favor urban areas	16% (35)		9% (1)	25% (2)	21% (4)	16% (6)	14% (3)	30% (3)	20% (11)	10% (5)
2. Federal and state governments are undependable	0% (1)					3% (1)				

3. Not enough funding for all projects - government should target funds better	5% (10)	20% (1)	13% (1)	5% (1)	3% (1)	9% (2)		5% (3)	2% (1)
D. Prefer to keep money locally	2% (4)				5% (2)				4% (2)
E. All grant money should be without requirements	0% (1)			5% (1)					
F. Self-sufficiency is a virtue	3% (6)				3% (1)			2% (1)	8% (4)
G. Need federal funds	7% (15)		13% (1)	16% (3)	8% (3)		10% (1)	7% (4)	6% (3)
H. Coordination of federal funds	0% (1)							2% (1)	
I. Inflation	4% (8)		25% (2)	5% (1)	3% (1)	9% (2)		2% (1)	2% (1)
J. Lack of resources	13% (28)		13% (1)	26% (5)	16% (6)		10% (1)	9% (5)	20% (10)
K. Low or declining tax base	6% (12)	20% (1)	13% (1)			14% (3)		7% (4)	6% (3)
1. Do not own land	0% (1)								2% (1)
2. No commercial industry	0% (1)			5% (1)					
L. Reduce taxes	1% (2)				3% (1)			2% (1)	
M. Interest rate ceilings on municipal bonds are too low	0% (1)					5% (1)			
N. Bond issues put burden on fixed income people	2% (4)			5% (1)				2% (1)	4% (2)

TABLE 11 (Continued)

		Metropolitan			Nonmetropolitan					
					Adjacent to SMSA			Not Adjacent to SMSA		
	Total	Large	Medium	Small	Urban	Less Urban	Totally Rural	Urban	Less Urban	Totally Rural
O. Special districts are in debt	0%				5%					
	(1)				(1)					
P. User charges are too high	0%				5%					
	(1)				(1)					

[a]A county may be represented more than once in any column total, therefore these totals cannot be presented as % of responses, and therefore cannot be compared across columns.

[b]Vertical percent of responding counties.

TABLE 12 Number of Times Issues Were Mentioned in Local Letters, by Region: Summary Table

	Total	New England	Middle Atlantic	East North Central	West North Central	South Atlantic	East South Central	West South Central	Mountain	Pacific
Number of counties in sample	467	10	17	65	99	85	56	70	41	24
Number of counties with responses	216	3	9	30	53	51	22	19	20	9
ISSUES										
I. Provision of adequate human	61[a]	0	2	7	18	13	12	6	3	0
maintenance services	0.28[b]	-	0.22	0.23	0.34	0.26	0.54	0.32	0.15	-
II. Improved education and	71	0	0	7	17	28	5	10	4	0
job training	0.33	-	-	0.23	0.32	0.55	0.23	0.53	0.20	-
III. Provision of adequate										
community facilities	305	2	17	35	74	87	42	20	19	9
and services	1.41	0.67	1.89	1.17	1.40	1.71	1.91	1.05	0.95	1.00
IV. Encouraging economic	224	2	13	28	57	63	25	16	11	9
development	1.04	0.67	1.44	0.93	1.08	1.24	1.14	0.84	0.55	1.00
V. Improved natural resource	192	9	8	36	34	44	26	5	19	11
management and conservation	0.89	3.00	0.89	1.20	0.64	0.86	1.18	0.26	0.95	1.22
VI. Equity										
VII. Improved political and	64	0	2	12	11	16	9	6	6	2
social environment	0.30	-	0.22	0.40	0.21	0.31	0.41	0.32	0.30	0.22
VIII. Resolving financial problems	254	1	4	32	79	48	31	16	35	8
	1.18	0.33	0.44	1.07	1.49	0.94	1.41	0.84	1.75	0.89

[a] Number of times issue or subissue was mentioned.

[b] Average number of times issue or subissue was mentioned by counties with responses.

TABLE 13 Number of Times Issues Were Mentioned in Letters, by 1970-75 Population Change: Summary Table

	Total	Population Decline	Population Growth	
			Less than U.S. (4.8%)	More than U.S.
Number of counties in sample	467	-	-	-
Number of counties with responses	216	59	60	97
I. Provision of adequate human	61[a]	16	18	27
maintenance services	0.28[b]	0.27	0.30	0.27
II. Improved education and	71	18	27	26
job training	0.32	0.30	0.45	0.26
III. Provision of adequate				
community facilities	305	73	90	142
and services	1.41	1.23	1.50	1.46
IV. Encouraging economic	224	76	74	74
development	1.03	1.28	1.23	0.76
V. Improved natural resource	192	62	56	74
management and conservation	0.89	1.05	0.93	0.76
VI. Equity	-	-	-	-
VII. Improved political and	64	11	17	36
social environment	0.29	0.19	0.28	0.37
VIII. Resolving financial	254	67	70	117
problems	1.18	1.14	1.17	1.21

[a]Number of times issue or subissue was mentioned.

[b]Average number of times issue or subissue was mentioned by counties with responses.

TABLE 14 Types of Data Needs Mentioned by Local Respondents[a]

	"Better" "More" (Not Specified)	More Disaggregated[b]	More Frequent	Need This for Grants
Type of Data				
Population	*25*	*79*	*57*	*10*
Social	1	12	4	
Social service need	2	2		
Economic		3	1	
Income	4	16	14	4
Family		1		
Per capita	2	2		
Poverty level	5	4		2
Farm/nonfarm	2	1		1
Age groups	2	8	2	
Migration	1		2	
No. illegal aliens	1			
Density	1			
Unspecified	4	30	34	3
Housing	*20*	*15*	*9*	*3*
Condition	4	4	3	
Substandard	2	2		
Black/White	1			
Occupancy		1		
Own/rent	2			
Rent as percent of income		1		
Demand	2	1		
New purchasers	1			
School-age children	1			
Speculation/live year round	1			
Location	1			
Construction starts	1	1		
Federally subsidized	1			
Unspecified	3	5	6	3

TABLE 14 (Continued)

	"Better" "More" (Not Specified)	More Disaggregated[b]	More Frequent	Need This for Grants
Employment	*19*	*21*	*11*	*3*
Types of employment (e.g., SIC)	1	1		
Projected trends	1			
Agricultural	2	2	2	1
Salaried/unsalaried	2			
Full-time/part-time	2			1
Seasonal changes	1			
Payroll	1			
Wage rates	1	1		
Place of work (employment by firm)		2		
Labor force potential (population by age & race)	3	2	1	
Job vacancies	2			
Job turnover	1			
Unemployment	2	7	3	
Unspecified	1	6	5	1
Education	*6*	*2*	*0*	*0*
Vocational				
Where provided		1		
Kinds provided		1		
Percent high school graduates enter	1			
High school completions	1			
By work skill	1			
Percent high school graduates enter college	1			
High school dropouts	1			
Unspecified	1			

Transportation	*9*	*0*	*0*	*0*
Availability	2			
Demand	1			
Frequency	2			
Destination	1			
Traffic counts	1			
Worker commuting patterns	2			
Unspecified				
Crime	*0*	*1*	*0*	*0*
Unspecified		1		
Natural resources	*20*	*7*	*1*	*0*
Land				
Land use	3	1	1	
Land cover	1			
Public land	1			
Agricultural land availability	3			
Irrigated acreage	1			
Rate of farm abandonment	1			
Land ownership, absentee/local	1			
Land ownership by farm operating unit/other	1			
Landstat data	1			
Geocoded data	1	1		
Water				
Consumption trends		1		
Availability	2			
Lake crowding potential	1			
Waste water treatment demand		1		
Energy				
Availability		1		
Use	1	1		
By fuel type		1		
Urban/rural	1			
Noncommuter gas use by urban/rural	1			
Unspecified				

TABLE 14 (Continued)

	"Better" "More" (Not Specified)	More Disaggregated[b]	More Frequent	Need This for Grants
Local government facilities/cost	*12*	*1*		
Inventory of facilities (e.g., buildings, roads, bridges)	1	1		
Need for facilities	1			
Need for rural utilities	2			
Use of health facilities and services	1			
Recreation inventory	1			
Government costs (operations, maintenance, debt service)	3			
Government revenues	2			
Unspecified	1			
Economic development	*14*	*1*		
Agriculture	2			
Capital investment	1			
Revenue generated	1	1		
Effects of energy crisis on agriculture	1			
Effects of minimum tillage on agriculture	1			
Livestock type and quality	1			
Manufacturing	1			
Raw materials needs of potential locators	1			
Value added	1			
Tourism	1			
Expenditures by local/out-of-state travelers	1			
Energy boom	1			
Economic impact of a particular industry	1			
Unspecified				

Business	*5*	*1*		
Retail sales	1	1		
Community categories	1			
Service sector	1			
Buying trends	1			
Money turnover rates	1			
Unspecified ("all data")	*3*	*11*	*5*	*2*

[a] Data in this table and the accompanying list were taken from the letters of 86 local respondents in counties and multicounty regions, representing 111 counties. There was no limit to the number of data needs each respondent could list.

[b] Disaggregation suggestions include township, rural government units, rural areas, villages, unincorporated areas, small communities, minor civil divisions under 10,000 population, sub-county, sub-township, communities under 2500, block face, and small municipalities.

REFERENCES

Hines, F.K., Brown, D.L., and Zimmer, J.M. (1975) *Social and Economic Characteristics of the Population in Metro and Nonmetro Counties, 1970*. Agricultural Economic Report No. 272. Washington, D.C.: U.S. Department of Agriculture.

Ross, P.J., Bluestone, H., and Hines, F.K. (1979) *Indicators of Social Well-Being for U.S. Counties*. Rural Development Research Report No. 10. Washington, D.C.: U.S. Department of Agriculture

APPENDIX C

PARTICIPANTS, WORKSHOP OF STATE AND REGIONAL OFFICIALS AND WORKSHOP OF RURAL INTEREST GROUPS

WORKSHOP OF STATE AND REGIONAL OFFICIALS

Invitees

ALVIN SOKOLOW *(Workshop Chairman), Member,* Panel
WILLIAM BECHTEL,* Federal Co-Chairman, Upper Great Lakes Regional Commission, Washington, D.C.
JAMES BONNEN, *Chairman,* Panel
FRED BURKE, Senior Planning Advisor, Appalachian Regional Commission, Washington, D.C.
CAROLYN CARROLL, Consultant, Panel
KENNETH L. DEAVERS, Director, Economic Development Division, Economics, Statistics, and Cooperative Services, U.S. Department of Agriculture
VIJAY DESHPANDE, Research Director, Upper Great Lakes Regional Commision, Washington, D.C.
PETER DETWILLER, Director, Local Government Unit, Office of Planning and Research, State of California, Sacramento, California
DOROTHY GILFORD, Study Director, Panel
WILLIAM GLENNON, Economist, Old West Regional Commission, Rapid City, South Dakota
EDWIN GOLDFIELD, Executive Director, Committee on National Statistics
JOE HARRIS, Resource Economist, Camp, Dresser and McKee, Austin, Texas
PHILLIP HARRIS,* Assistant Area Director, Federal Regional Council of New England, Boston, Massachusetts
LOUIS HIGGS, Executive Director, Four Corners Regional Commission, Albuquerque, New Mexico
LINDA INGRAM, Research Associate, Panel
MICHAEL MARKOWSKI, Rural Development Specialist, Farmers Home Administration, Harrisburg, Pennsylvania
SARA MAZIE, Policy and Research Analyst, Office of Policy Development, Farmers Home Administration, U.S. Department of Agriculture
ERNEST METIVIER, Director, Economic Development, Office of Planning and Budget, Atlanta, Georgia
THELMA NEAL, Secretary, Panel
RAYMOND RIGGS,* Program Officer, Ozarks Regional Commission, Little Rock, Arkansas
HARRY ROBERTS, *Member,* Panel

JEFFREY SOULE, Policy Development Staff, Farmers Home Administration,
U.S. Department of Agriculture
MARTA TIENDA, *Member,* Panel

*Did not attend.

WORKSHOP OF RURAL INTEREST GROUPS

Attendees

JIM BONNEN, *Chair,* Panel
BOB ALEXANDER, National Governors Association
JACK CORNMAN, National Rural Center
IRMA ELO, National Rural Center
DAVID GALLAGHER, National Association of Towns and Townships
DOROTHY GILFORD, *Study Director,* Panel
BILL MURRAY, National Rural Electric Cooperatives Association
GAIL PARKS, National Rural Center
GEORGE RUCKER, Rural America
MIKE SCIACCA, National Demonstration Water Project
AL SOKOLOW, *Member,* Panel
LEO TRICE, Housing Assistance Council
MIKE WELCHE, National Rural Center

APPENDIX D

LOCAL PLANNING DOCUMENTS: BIBLIOGRAPHY AND EXCERPTS

This appendix contains excerpts from some of the documents received from the local survey and a bibliography of all of them. They have been grouped into ten functional areas: general development, economic development, housing, land use, community facilities, natural resources, health, transportation, social services, and recreation. Each of the ten sections of the appendix, corresponding to the functional areas, contains a brief introduction, followed by the excerpts, and concludes with the bibliography.

The excerpts were selected to represent a range of functional and geographical areas and to illustrate techniques for data generation or production. In every case they are either condensed versions of sections of the documents or exact quotes with occasional editing for clarity.

GENERAL DEVELOPMENT

General development plans are financed primarily by HUD, but also by EDA and FmHA. They generally have sections on population, land use, the economy, utilities, transportation, community facilities and services, and capital improvements. The data examples presented here show population figures because examples of the other types of data may be found in later sections on more specialized plans.

The first example compares the population trends for Chouteau County and Montana from 1920 to 1970 and describes some of the reasons for Chouteau's decline.

The second example, from Fairbanks, Alaska, describes the geographic and economic factors that have affected popuE

The third example examines long-term population trends in central Georgia and presents tables on recent out-migration by race.

The next example, from Carson Valley, Nevada, compares various population projections made for the area and briefly discusses the problems of estimating future populations.

The last example examines population change in Yamhill County, Oregon, and describes the economic growth underlying these changes.

CHOUTEAU, MONTANA

Chouteau County Comprehensive Plan, n.d., pp. 36-37.

Chart 1 compares the population trends for Chouteau County and Montana from 1920 to 1970. As the population in Montana steadily

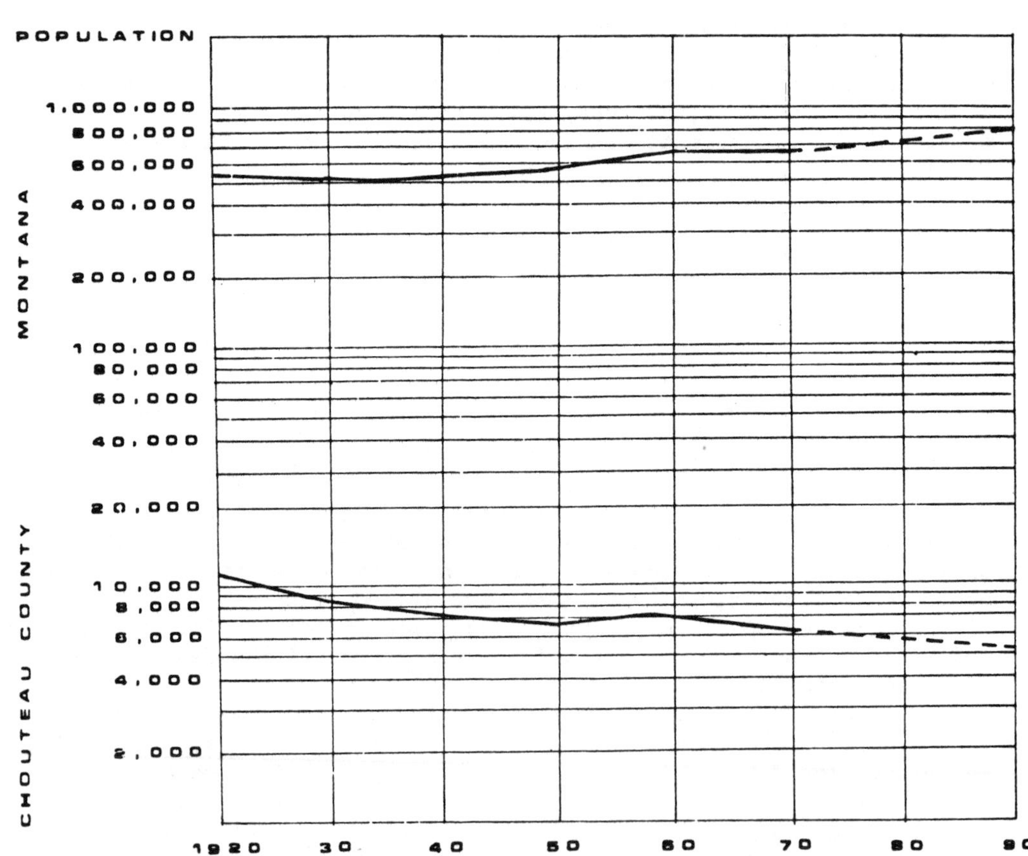

increases, the Chouteau County population decreases. It is predicted that this trend will continue, especially if the county maintains its one-industry standing. Agriculture does not provide more and varied jobs in the county (there are no major agriculture-related industries in the county); therefore, the labor force (18-64) is not encouraged to stay within the county. The only industries that may cause a population rise in the future would be mineral exploration and the newly designated Wild and Scenic River Route on the Missouri. The latter would bring in Federal employees, as well as new business owners (motels, eating and drinking establishments and curio shops) to accommodate the tourists.

As mentioned previously, out-migration rates are very high in Chouteau County. Figure 1 exemplifies this condition by counties in the state. Chouteau County lost 19 of every 100 people to out-migration in the year 1960 and 1970. There has been almost a 50 percent increase in the number of people migrating from the county since 1960, as compared to the migration rate of 1950-1960. This is a tremendous increase of people leaving the county (see Table 5).

Table 5 Net Migration, 1950 to 1960, and 1960 to 1970

Net Migration 1950 to 1960	Net Migration 1960 to 1970	Percent Change Between Decennia
-923	-1380	-49.5%

U.S. Bureau of the Census

It is predicted that with continued 1960-1970 migration trends, Chouteau County will have a population of 5,568 by 1980. The migration rate for the years 1970-1973 has been even higher than the 1960-1970 period, resulting in a projected estimate of 4,884 people in 1980 with the continued 1970-1973 migration trends. If there was no net migration in the 1970-1980 period, the population of 1980 is estimated to be 7,040.

FAIRBANKS, ALASKA

Tryck, Nyman, and Hayes (for the State of Alaska), Fairbanks North Star Borough Comprehensive Development Plan: Resources for Planning, n.d., pp. 78-87.

Population

The information used in compiling this report was obtained from the various publications, reports, and computer tapes distributed by the Bureau of the Census resulting from the 1970 decennial census.

Information was also obtained from various State of Alaska, Department of Labor publications concerning the census information and from documents published by the University of Alaska Institute for Social, Economic and Government Research (ISEGR).

Because of changes that have occurred in the size, number, and configurations of the geographic units utilized in Fairbanks while collecting data for the various censuses, it is difficult to draw accurate comparisons or conclusions as to changes in population characteristics within the area of the Fairbanks North Star Borough. For instance, in the 1960 Census, enumeration districts were developed on the basis of an estimated population of 700 persons per district. This was also done in the 1950 decennial census. However, in 1970, there appeared to be no such criteria used in developing the districts. Their size and configuration indicate that they were instead drawn at random. The 1970 census utilized 47 enumeration districts. They ranged in population from zero population (three districts) to 5,584 inhabitants. There were also no geographic criteria used in determining the size, configuration, and location of the districts. This is evident in the fact that enumeration district Number 8 consists of three city blocks, while enumeration district Number 29 comprises nearly eighty percent of the entire Borough land area. Because of this, comparison of population in any relatively small area over an extended period of time is extremely difficult and in some cases, impossible. Thus, it is often necessary to speak only of changes in the total population over a given period and given characteristics for the entire area at some given point in time. Some rough comparisons are possible, but they should be approached with caution.

These problems in utilizing the census information associated with the poor comparability of the data point out the need for a uniform system of enumeration districts that can be used as a basis for data collection and community analysis. This is true not only in terms of the federal census but for all other types of information that might be used in community studies by both the private and public sectors.

B. Population Determinants in the Fairbanks Area.

Demographic characteristics in most population centers are determined by a common set of influences. These influences include such things as the physical location of the area, transportation routes to and from the area, the economic base of the area, and the availability of land for development and expansion. In view of these determinants, the location of Fairbanks is good in terms of potential economic and population growth. It is located at the confluence of several transportation routes, both land and air. The Alaska Railroad, which begins in Seward, goes through Anchorage to Fairbanks. The Alaska Highway, the Richardson Highway, and the recently constructed Anchorage-Fairbanks Highway, have their termini in the Fairbanks area. The community also has an International Airport located within metropolitan Fairbanks.

All of the transportation routes are especially important in this case because of the location of Fairbanks within the state. Fairbanks is the northernmost major population center within the state and is located near the geographic center of the State of Alaska. For these reasons and because of its transportation characteristics, Fairbanks has and will continue to serve as the "jumping off place" for men and materials going further north into the bush areas and to the North Slope of Alaska. In short, development of almost all lands in the northern half of the state will undoubtedly be accomplished utilizing Fairbanks as an economic and transportation center.

Fairbanks is fortunate in that it is not "land locked" as is Anchorage. There is ample undeveloped land in the surrounding area that can be utilized for expansion. To the immediate west of the Fairbanks metropolitan area is Ft. Wainwright which will preclude development in that direction, although the possible release of some of that land in the future may remove that barrier to some extent. Most of the remaining surrounding properties are available for expansion and growth of the metropolitan area.

There are, however, a variety of conditions within the Fairbanks area which will affect land to the extent that it either has not or should not be developed for certain uses. These conditions are physical in nature and, where found, are inherent properties of the land. For instance, in many areas, especially to the north and west of Fairbanks, there are large peat and muskeg deposits. The drainage characteristics of these areas are very poor and because of the soil conditions, they are very susceptible to frost heave. Thus, development of these swamp areas is not likely to occur in the foreseeable future. Another problem, especially to the north of Fairbanks, is the presence of steep slopes. Some of these lands would be subject to landslides and in many cases bedrock is near enough to the surface of the ground to preclude the utilization of on-site sewage disposal systems. One development problem unique to the Fairbanks area as opposed to other population centers in the state is the fact that north-facing slopes within the area are often subject to permafrost. This makes development of those properties next to impossible under conventional construction methods.

Even considering these factors, however, at the present time there is no real land shortage in the Fairbanks area. If proper care is taken in developing what land is still available, there should not be a land shortage in the foreseeable future. Thus, land availability should not be a factor in determining population growth of the Fairbanks area.

C. Population Trends 1910-1970.

Population growth and the characteristics of a community can be affected by a wide variety of factors. These factors vary from location to location and their net effect will depend on the specific situation and the locality involved The major influences on the Fairbanks population have been natural resource development and the providing of transportation and services to interior Alaska. What is now known as Fairbanks was first established in 1901 as a trading post along the Nenana River to serve the gold prospectors that were then combing the Tanana Valley. Easily accessible gold was found in relatively large quantities and there was a rapid growth in the population. By the first census taken for Fairbanks in 1910 there were approximately 11,000 people living in the surrounding areas.

In the second decade of the century, however, the easiy accessible gold became exhausted and the population declined quite rapidly. The cost of mining the remaining gold by the methods known then was too great to justify that type of operation in the Fairbanks area; thus by 1920, the population of the district had dwindled to 2,182.

The 1920s was a decade of rebuilding Fairbanks on a more solid base. The Alaska Railroad from Seward to Fairbanks was completed during that decade and the Alaska Agricultural College and School of Mines opened in 1922. The railroad provided a year-round transportation route to and from Fairbanks and the college helped develop new methods of large scale gold extraction that made the mining of the less accessible gold in the area more economical. By 1929 the population of the area had grown to 3,446. The 1930s were a period of depression for the rest of the nation, but the economy of Fairbanks had received a shot in the arm by the gold mining industry and the town continued to thrive. Gold and gold-related commerce allowed the village to increase in size and prosper. By 1939 the population was 5,692.

The next decade brought a period of unprecedented growth for the Fairbanks area. World War II brought much government and military money into the area. Ft. Wainwright and Eielson Air Force Base were both constructed during that period, resulting in a large influx of laborers and military personnel. The Alaska Highway was also completed during this period, adding another transportation link to the Fairbanks economy. By 1950 the population had grown to 19,409 people, an increase of 241 percent in just 10 years.

During the 1950s, the rate of population growth slowed somewhat but the Fairbanks economy continued to boom. The Korean War and the ensuing Cold War stimulated the economy. There were expanding military establishments and increasing governmental influence in the area. Fairbanks continued to establish itself as a transportation and service hub for the interior portions of Alaska. The University of Alaska continued to grow and exert a positive influence on the Fairbanks area. By 1960 the population of the district had grown to 43,412. In the 1960s the military influence in the Fairbanks area leveled off. There was very little increase in the military community and military-related construction slowed down. At the same time, however, oil exploration picked up and accounted for the 15 percent increase in population that occurred during this decade. Although the rate of population or economic growth had slowed a great deal, the growth that did occur during that decade was based on a continuing local economy that was not being artificially pumped up by an influx of government dollars. In 1970 the population of the Fairbanks district had increased to 50,043 people.

In the year 1970 approximately the same percentage of the total Alaskan population lived in Fairbanks as lived there in the year 1910. During that 60 year period, however, that percentage of population fluctuated by over 50 percent. Much of this fluctuation is directly related to the growth of Anchorage. The growth of the total population in the Fairbanks area and the state are graphically portrayed by Table 6-A.

Table 6-A Population Growth, 1910-1970, City of Fairbanks, ED19 and Alaska

Year	Election Dist. 19	Change (Percentage)	City of Fairbanks	Change (Percentage)	Alaska	Change (Percentage)	Fairbanks Area as a Percentage of Alaska
1910	11,000[a]		3,541		69,000		15.9
1920	2,182	- 80	1,155	- 67	55,000	- 14	4.0
1929	3,466	+ 58	2,101	+ 82	59,278	+ 8	5.8
1939	5,692	+ 65	3,455	+ 64	72,524	+ 22	7.8
1950	19,409	+241	5,771	+ 67	128,643	+ 77	15.1
1960	43,412	+124	13,311[c]	+131	226,167	+ 76	19.2
1970	50,043[b]	+ 15	14,771[d]	+ 11	302,173	+ 34	16.6

[a]Approximate.
[b]Estimate based on combination of Fairbanks and SE Fairbanks Census Division.
[c]Annexation to City accounted for 4,995 of this increase.
[d]Does not include annexation after January 1, 1970.

Source: U.S. Census Population and Fairbanks Metropolitan Area Transportation Study, Vol. 2, p. 9.

Age Characteristics. The distribution of the age characteristics of the Fairbanks population has remained relatively static over the last decade as can be seen in Table 6-D. There has been relatively little change in the percentage of the population in each age group between the 1960 and the 1970 census. Possibly the only significant trends that should be pointed out are the fact that the 0-17 year-old age group dropped 1 percent as a proportion of the total population. The 45-64 year-old age group gained 1 percent in proportion to the total population. This would indicate that, as young people mature in the Fairbanks area, fewer of them are leaving the Fairbanks area and are thus increasing the size of the next higher age group. The same would be true of the increase in the 45-64 year-old age group. It is becoming easier for the middle-aged person with a family to make a living and support a comfortable life-style in the Fairbanks area.

Table 6-D Fairbanks Area Percent Population Change by Age Group, 1960-1970

Age Group	1960	1970	Percentage of Change
0-17	36.4%	35.4%	-1.0
18-44	52.4%	52.5%	+ .1
45-64	9.8%	10.8%	+1.0
65+	1.4%	1.3%	- .1

Of obvious significance is the fact that when compared to Anchorage, the remainder of Alaska, and the United States as a whole, the Fairbanks area has an extremely high proportion of people in the 18-44 year-old age group and a very low proportion of people in the 65 and over age group (Table 6-E). This lop-sided distribution is caused in part by many of the same factors that affect the sex ratios. First is the military, which includes large numbers of people in the 18-44 year-old bracket and second is the relatively large number of people who come to Alaska, and subsequently, Fairbanks, after they are out of high school and ready to "make their fortune." These people tend to live and work in the Fairbanks area while they are younger and then to migrate out of the state as they get older. This also explains the low proportion of older people who live in the Fairbanks area. Because of the high cost of living in Fairbanks and the fixed income on which many retired people must live, it is very difficult for them to maintain a comfortable standard of living in the Fairbanks area.

Table 6-E Percent Population Distribution by Age Group for Fairbanks, Anchorage, Alaska, and the U.S.

Age Group	Fairbanks	Anchorage	Alaska	U.S.
0-17	35.3%	39.7%	39.9%	35.0%
18-44	52.5%	46.0%	44.2%	34.8%
45-64	10.8%	13.0%	13.6%	20.5%
65+	1.3%	1.4%	2.3%	9.6%

Race Characteristics. Much of the racial information published by the United States census is broken down into only three categories: white, black, and other. Thus, this is sometimes what must be used in terms of comparison. Throughout Alaska, however, the other category is more important than in other states because of the large number of Alaska native people residing in the state (see Table 6-G). As shown in Table 6-F, between 1960 and 1970, the relative number of white residents of the Fairbanks area decreased while the number of black residents increased only slightly and the number in the "others" category remained the same. At the same time, the number of Indians, Eskimos, and Aleuts increased by a substantial amount. This is indicative of the fact that over the past ten years there has been a marked migration of Alaska natives from the village and bush areas of Alaska into the larger metropolitan areas.

On the other hand, when compared to the remainder of Alaska, Fairbanks has a relatively high percentage of white population and a low percentage in the "other" category. It should be pointed out also that the black population of both Alaska and Fairbanks is substantially lower than that of the United States as a whole.

Table 6-F Race Distribution-Fairbanks Area, 1960-1970

Year	White	Black	Indian	Eskimo and Aleut	Other	Total
1960 Number	39,345	2,348	831	306	528	43,412
Percentage	90.6	5.4	1.9	.8	1.2	100
1970 Number	44,351	2,788	1,499	809	596	50,043
Percentage	88.6	5.6	3.0	1.6	1.2	100

Table 6-G Race Distribution--1970, Fairbanks - Alaska - U.S.

Race	Fairbanks	Alaska	U.S.
White	88.6%	78.8%	87.7%
Black	5.6%	3.0%	11.2%
Other	5.8%	18.2%	1.1%

Source for tables in this section:
Alaska's Population and School Enrollments, compiled by Peter C. Lin, Review of Business & Economic Conditions, University of Alaska, Vol. VIII, No. 5, Dec. 1971.

BLECKLEY AND TELFAIR, GEORGIA

Heart of Georgia Area Planning and Development Commission, Area Development Plan, 1979, pp. 9, 11, 21-22, 24-25.

Population Analysis

The purpose of this portion is to define those aspects of the regional population which will assist in the planning process for the future development of the Heart of Georgia Planning Area. To accomplish this an analysis must be made of such population aspects as growth trends, density, and composition.

Population Growth. Table 3 presents a half century of population growth (1920-1970) and illustrates the need for stabilizing factors to influence the area. Between 1920 and 1970 the state grew by almost 60 percent, but during the same time period the Heart of Georgia area lost over one-fourth of its population (28.4 percent) with over 40,000 people leaving the area, probably in search of better opportunities. This trend slackened in the past two decades, with a 8.6 percent decline in population occurring between 1950 and 1960, and a 2.1 percent decline in population between 1960 and 1970.

Table 4 gives the 1920 to 1970 population for the 10 largest cities within the study area. In contrast to the counties, none of these cities lost population during this same 50-year period.

Net Migration. Net migration is the net difference between the number of people moving into an area (in-migration) and the number of persons moving out of an area (out-migration) within a given period of time.

If the number of in-migrants exceeds the number of out-migrants, the net difference is in-migration and adds to the population of an area. On the other hand, if the number of out-migrants exceeds the number of in-migrants, the net difference is out-migration and it subtracts from the population of the area. The causes of migration are too numerous to attempt to list. For the Heart of Georgia Planning Area the principal reason would be the agricultural revolution which completely altered the economic makeup of the county.

Out-migration has been a severe handicap to the Heart of Georgia Area's population. In the past decade (1960-1970) the area lost 13,000 people to out-migration (refer to Table 6 and Illustration 4). Of this number, 77.7 percent were blacks. Every county in the area lost a portion of its black population but three counties have experienced a slight in-migration of whites.

Table 3 Population Trends, Counties, 1920-1970

County	Population						Population Change					
							1950 - 1960		1960 - 1970		1920 - 1970	
	1920	1930	1940	1950	1960	1970	#	%	#	%	#	%
Bleckley	10,532	9,133	9,655	9,218	9,642	10,291	424	4.6	649	6.7	-241	-2.3
Dodge	22,540	21,599	21,022	17,865	16,483	15,658	-1,382	-7.7	-825	-5.0	-6,882	-30.5
Laurens	39,605	32,693	33,606	33,123	32,313	32,738	-810	-2.4	425	1.3	-6,867	-17.3
Montgomery	9,167	10,020	9,668	7,901	6,284	6,099	-1,617	-20.5	-185	-2.9	-3,068	-33.5
Pulaski	11,587	9,005	9,829	8,808	8,204	8,066	-604	-6.9	-138	-1.7	-3,521	-30.4
Telfair	15,291	14,997	15,145	13,221	11,715	11,394	-1,506	-11.4	-321	-2.7	-3,897	-25.5
Treutlen	7,664	7,488	7,632	6,522	5,874	5,647	-648	-9.9	-227	-3.9	-2,017	-26.3
Wheeler	9,817	9,149	8,535	6,712	5,342	4,596	-1,370	-20.4	-746	-14.0	-5,221	-53.2
Wilcox	15,551	13,439	12,755	10,167	7,905	6,998	-2,262	-22.2	-907	-11.5	-8,513	-54.9
Heart of Georgia Area* Total	141,754	127,523	127,847	113,537	103,762	101,474	-9,775	-8.6	-2,275	-2.1	-40,227	-28.4

* These numbers were compiled and applied by the Heart of Georgia Planning and Development Commission.

Georgia	2,895,832	2,908,506	3,123,723	3,444,578	3,943,116	4,589,575	498,538	14.5	646,459	16.4	1,693,743	58.5

Source: Population Trends of Georgia Cities and Towns:
A Half Century of Population Growth
University of Georgia
Appendix Table 1 pp. 41-67

Table 4 Population Trends, Cities, 1920-1970

		POPULATION						POPULATION CHANGE					
								1950-1960		1960-1970		1920-1970	
		1920	1930	1940	1950	1960	1970	#	%	#	%	#	%
1.	Dublin	7,707	6,681	7,814	10,232	13,814	15,143	3,582	35.0	1,329	9.6	7,436	96.5
2.	Eastman	2,707	3,022	3,311	3,597	5,118	5,416	1,521	42.3	298	5.8	2,709	100.1
3.	Cochran	2,021	2,267	2,464	3,357	4,714	5,161	1,357	40.4	447	9.5	3,140	155.4
4.	Hawkinsville	3,070	2,484	3,000	3,342	3,967	4,077	625	18.7	110	2.8	1,007	32.8
5.	McRae	1,273	1,314	1,595	1,904	2,738	3,151	834	43.8	413	15.1	1,878	147.5
6.	Soperton	1,033	1,081	1,339	1,667	2,317	2,596	650	39.0	279	12.0	1,563	151.3
7.	East Dublin	-	-	-	-	1,677	1,986	1,677	-	309	18.4	1,986	-
8.	Mount Vernon	722	779	900	990	1,166	1,579	176	17.8	413	35.4	857	118.7
9.	Rochelle	1,046	1,053	1,175	1,097	1,235	1,380	138	12.6	145	11.7	334	31.9
10.	Lumber City	978	1,043	1,044	1,232	1,360	1,377	128	10.4	17	1.2	339	40.8

SOURCE: Population Trends of Georgia Cities and Towns: A Half Century of Population Growth University of Georgia, Appendix, Table 1, pp. 41-67.

Table 6 Net Migration, 1960-1970

County	White	Black	Total
Bleckley	556	-910	-354
Dodge	-879	-1,416	-2,290
Laurens	-477	-2,943	-3,920
Montgomery	104	-1,021	-917
Pulaski	131	-1,104	-973
Telfair	-806	-848	-1,654
Treutlen	-365	-543	-908
Wheeler	-563	-574	-1,137
Wilcox	-593	-750	-1,343
Heart of Georgia Area	-2,892	-10,109	-13,001
Percentage of Total Population	3.1	10.9	14.0

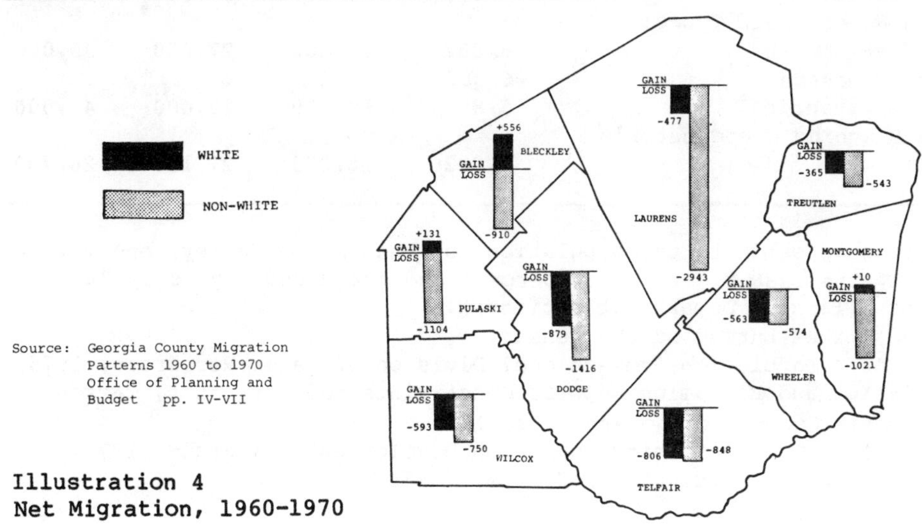

Illustration 4
Net Migration, 1960-1970

DOUGLAS, NEVADA

Douglas County Planning Department, Carson Valley General Plan, 1980, pp. 84-86.

Future Population

Estimating future population growth is an extremely uncertain occupation. Some of the problems encountered when trying to estimate future populations are:

Extrapolating of past growth trends into the future.
An inability to control occurrences in areas outside the study area which directly affect population growth within the study area.
A difficulty in incorporating all relevant elements into a population growth model.
An inability to predict future events that may directly affect population growth.

Despite the difficulty in predicting future populations, many state and federal regulating agencies mandate that these estimates be made. Due to these requirements, many various predictions for Douglas County as a whole have been made and are listed in the following table:

Population Projections for Douglas County[a]

Organization	1970[b]	1980	1990	2000
Bureau of Business and Economic Research	6,882	15,262	22,591	27,538
Division of Water Resources[c]	6,882	13,000	17,000	20,000
Carson River Basin Council of Governments[d]	6,882	18,000	27,000	35,000
State of Nevada	6,882			
Vasey Engineering[e]	6,882	19,500	29,000	42,000
State Planning Coordinator's Office[f]	6,882	16,035	21,130	28,700

[a]In order to estimate the population for the Carson Valley, one may multiply the 1980 figure by 60 percent and the 2,000 figure by 70 percent (Planning Department estimate).
[b]United States Bureau of the Census.
[c]Small Area Population Projections, Division of Water Resources, 1976.
[d]Population and Economics Report, Constraints and Forecasts, Carson River Basin Council of Governments, 1973.
[e]Carson River Basin Housing and Urban Development 701 Study, 1977.
[f]State Planning Coordinator's Office, 1978.

It is important to know upon what basis the population estimates are made. This information is important for future determinations as to the validity of past population projections. For example, the most recent Douglas County staff population estimate was based upon current buildout patterns in certain parts of the Carson Valley and the future real estate market in those areas. If these estimates are found to be faulty in the future, then the assumptions upon which they are based may be examined to find the flaw in the logic.

YAMHILL, OREGON

Yamhill County Department of Planning and Development, Yamhill County Comprehensive Plan, 1974 (Addendum 1978), pp. 15-18.

Population and Economic Trends and Projections

Since the early 1960s, the population trends of Yamhill County have paralleled the steady growth rate of the Willamette Valley, showing a 24 percent increase between 1960 and 1970[5], and an estimated eight percent increase between 1970 and 1973[6]. Increases in the County's population are largely caused by net in-migration. Between 1960 and 1970 the average annual share of population increase due to net in-migration was three times that due to natural increase, while for the state as a whole these two factors had nearly equal influence.

Table 1 Components of Population Change, Natural Increase and Net In-Migration, Yamhill County and Oregon, 1960-1970[a]

	Population Change 1960-1970			Average Annual Share of Population Change Due to:	
	Number	Natural Increase	Net In-Migration	Natural Increase	Net In-Migration
Yamhill County	7,735	1,940	5,795	0.5	1.6
Oregon	322,689	164,043	158,655	0.8	0.8

[a]U.S. Census, 1970 Number of Inhabitants.

[5]U.S. Bureau of the Census, Number of Inhabitants, Oregon (Washington: U.S. Government Printing Office, July, 1971). All population figures for decennial years used throughout the report taken from Number of Inhabitants publications.
[6]Population Estimates of Counties and Incorporated Cities of Oregon (Portland: Portland State University Center for Population Research and Census, 1971, 1972, 1973). All population figures for years other than decennial years used throughout the report taken from this source.

Growth in the Incorporated Areas. The greatest influence on the County's renewed growth since the 1960s has been the expanding Portland metropolitan area which is spilling over into the northeast part of the County. The four cities in that sector, Newberg, Dundee, Dayton, and

Lafayette, have shown very high growth rates in recent years. Their population increase totaled 54 percent between 1960 and 1970 and an estimated 25 percent betweeen 1970 and 1973. These figures are somewhat influenced by annexations to the City of Newberg (see Table 2), but the bulk of the growth has been caused by migration. This increase in primarily residential growth has meant, too, that between 25 and 50 percent of the County's total work force is currently employed outside its boundaries. However, it has also meant a stimulation of retail trade and of the service industries within the County, making the service industries now the largest employer in Yamhill County.

The City of McMinnville, the largest incorporated area in the County, has shown marked population increases, although its growth rate (32 percent) did not approach that of the northeast sector in the 1960-1970 decade. In recent years McMinnville's growth rate has averaged nearly 7 percent a year, a figure sharply influenced by annexations in 1971. McMinnville has now annexed virtually all fringe area development which might add appreciably to its population. A vigorous policy of industrial attraction in the late 1960s has made McMinnville the place of greatest employment opportunity in the County, and has resulted in manufacturing employment maintaining about a one-quarter share of the County's total work force.

Yamhill, Carlton, and Amity have retained their rural character and continue to show steady but moderate growth. They are off the main Highway 99W-18 arterial and consequently hae experienced little impact from Portland area growth. Having little economic diversification, they attract few people for employment. Retail and service enterprises, along with a little light industry, form the basis of their economies. The relatively high percentage of persons aged 65 and over living in these towns (16 percent in 1970) suggests that they are popular as retirement settlements.

Although Sheridan and Willamina showed rapid rates of growth earlier in the century when forest products were a booming industry, the decline of that industry has brought a slowdown in the growth of both cities. Highway 18 passes by both cities, however, their distance from urban areas has thus far minimized commuter residential growth. These towns, too, show a high percentage of persons in the 65-and-over age group (17 percent in 1970), indicating that growth in these areas can be at least partially attributed to a large retired population. Moderate diversification in the economy has also taken place with the attraction of a new mobile-home plant to Sheridan.

Rural-Urban Shifts. The national trend toward fewer, larger farms brought about by mechanization has been paralled in this County. This trend, coupled with the desire for urban conveniences, has meant that an increasingly large share of the population is moving off the farm and into the city. Indeed, census data indicate that in 1970 only nine percent of the work force was engaged in agriculture and forestry, down from 34 percent in 1940. The smaller percentage of Yamhill County residents in the 20-64 age group (48 percent in 1970, compared to a state average of 52 percent) would indicate that this move away from

Table 2 Population of Incorporated and Unincorporated Areas of Yamhill County, 1940-1970 and 1973, with Percentage Changes[a]

Areas	1940	1950		1960		1970		1973	
Amity	545	672	+23%	620	- 8%	708	+14%	840	+19%
Carlton	864	1,081	+25%	959	-11%	1,126	+17%	1,270	+13%
Dayton	506	719	+42%	673	- 6%	949	+41%	1,110	+17%
Dundee	209	308	+47%	318	+ 3%	588	+85%	880	+50%
Lafayette	409	662	+62%	553	-16%	786	+42%	1,000	+27%
McMinnville	3,706	6,635	+79%	7,656[b]	+15%	10,125[c]	+32%	12,250	+21%
Newberg	2,960	3,946	+33%	4,204[d]	+ 7%	6,507[e]	+55%	8,020	+23%
Sheridan	1,293	1,922	+48%	1,763	- 8%	1,881	+ 6%	2,035	+ 8%
Willamina	1,255	1,614	+29%	960	-11%	1,193	+24%	1,280	+ 7%
Yamhill	418	539	+29%	407	-24%	516	+27%	555	+ 8%
Total Incorporated	12,166	18,098	+49%	18,113	0%	24,379	+35%	29,240	+20%
Total Unincorporated	14,169	15,386	+ 9%	14,365	- 7%	15,834	+10%	14,160	-12%
County Total	26,335	33,484	+27%	32,478	- 3%	40,213	+24%	43,400	+ 8%

[a]U.S. Census, Number of Inhabitants, and Center for Population Research.
[b]Includes 200 persons added by annexation 1950-1960 (21% of net increase).
[c]Includes 326 persons added by annexation 1960-1970 (33.5% of net increase).
[d]Includes 338 persons added by annexation 1950-1960 (more than total overall increase).
[e]Includes 541 persons added by annexation 1960-1970 (28% of net increase).

the farm has meant that many persons leave the County to seek employment opportunities.

The trend toward movement into the metropolitan areas and into the incorporated centers of the County is being offset by other population shifts. While Portland continues its desirability as a place of employment opportunity, many former urbanites are choosing to pay the price of long commuting distances in order to acquire greater privacy and open space in which to live. This has meant an increase in non-farm rural development in the County, occurring usually at the edges of urban areas. The result is a pattern of large-acreage residential ownerships spreading beyond the urban service area.

Bibliography: General Development

Calhoun, Cherokee, Cleburne, and Talladega, Alabama. East Alabama Regional Planning and Development Commission, Region IV Areawide Action Program, 1979 (134 pgs.).

Greene, Alabama. Alabama Cooperative Extension Service, "Facts for Programming Community Resource Development in Greene County," 1979 (2 pgs.).

_________, "Impact 80 - Greene" (9 pgs.).

Greene County Rural Development Committee, "Greene County Rural Development Committee Progress Report for 1979 and Plan of Action-1980" (3 pgs.).

West Alabama Planning and Development Council, "Greene County, Alabama" (14 pgs.).

Greene and Pickens, Alabama. West Alabama Planning and Development Council, Areawide Action Plan (214 pgs.).

Lowndes, Alabama. South Central Alabama Development Commission, Comprehensive Plan Evaluation, Fort Deposit, Alabama, 1979 (92 pgs.).

Limestone, Alabama. Limestone County Commission, "Comprehensive Plan Summary-Limestone County, Alabama" (brochure).

Fairbanks, Alaska. Agricultural Experiment Station-School of Agriculture and Land Resources Management and the Institute of Social and Economic Research, University of Alaska, Yukon-Porcupine Regional Planning Study, 1978 (280 pgs.).

Tryck, Nyman, and Hayes (for the State of Alaska), Fairbanks North Star Borough Comprehensive Development Plan: Resources for Planning (189 pgs.).

Coconino, Arizona. Coconino County Planning Department, "South Grand Canyon Specific Area Study," 1978 (18 pgs.). Coconino County, Sedona Community Plan (27 pgs.).

Graham, Arizona. Citizens Advisory Planning Committee, "Results of the Safford Community Opinion Survey," 1978 (4 pgs.).

"Citizens Task Force on Government: A Report to the City Council of Safford," 1978 (7 pgs.).

Cooperative Extension Service, University of Arizona, "Ideas for Arizona Communities: Safford Planning Program," 1978 (3 pgs.).

Arkansas. Arkansas Cooperative Extension Service, "Community Development Program Components, FY 80 Narrative" (17 pgs.).

_______, "FY 80 Community Development Program Planning Materials Developed by State and District CRD Staffs" (24 pgs.).

Mississippi, Arkansas. Arkansas Extension Service, "Proposal for Rural Development" (to USDA under Title V), 1977 (13 pgs.).

Searcy, Arkansas. Northwest Arkansas Economic Development District, Inc., Searcy County Area Household Survey Report (23 pgs.).

Searcy County Action Program Committee, Socio-Economic Study of Searcy County (46 pgs.).

Merced, California. Merced County Planning Department, "Planada Community Development Plan," 1978 (13 pgs.).

Shasta, California. Economic Development Corporation of Shasta County, Shasta County Statistics, 1978 (30 pgs.).

Colorado. Colorado Department of Local Affairs, Division of Commerce and Development, "Growth and Human Settlement Policies and Regional and Local Targeting Strategies," 1979 (33 pgs.).

Kit Carson, Colorado. Colorado Division of Planning, "Human Settlement Policies," 1979 (18 pgs.).

Colorado East Central Council of Governments, "Processes" (for utilizing federal and/or state programs), 1977 (9 pgs.).

_______, "Seeking Grant Assistance" (8 pgs.).

New Castle, Delaware. New Castle County Department of Community Development and Housing and Department of Planning, "Area Problems Tabulation: Lower New Castle County Area Development Project" (11 pgs.).

Sussex, Delaware. Town of Delmar, Application to HUD (CDBG-Small Cities) for funds for comprehensive community development program, 1978 (36 pgs.).

Baker, Florida. Kellum, Patterson, and Bell, Inc. for Baker County Commission, Comprehensive Plan: Baker County and City of Macclenny: Vol. I: Research Findings and Analysis Phase (103 pgs.); Vol. II: Plan Phase (154 pgs.); Vol. III: Implementation Phase (39 pgs.).

St. Lucie, Florida. Planning Design Group, Plan for St. Lucie/West Area, 1978 (44 pgs.).

Georgia. Georgia Cooperative Extension Service, "Population Figures and Per Capita Personal Income for Georgia Counties," 1979 (5 pgs.).

Baldwin, Putnam, and Wilkinson, Georgia. Oconee Area Planning and Development Commission, Area Development Plan, 1980-1984 (171 pgs.).

Bleckley and Telfair, Georgia. Heart of Georgia Area Planning and Development Commission, Area Development Plan, 1980 (162 pgs.)

_______, Area Development Plan, 1979 (108 pgs.).

Clayton, Georgia. Atlanta Regional Commission, Regional Development Plan, 1976 (84 pgs.).

Dade, Georgia. Coosa Valley Area Planning and Development Commission, Trenton, Georgia Community Development Plan, 1977 (81 pgs.).

Elbert, Georgia. County Extension, "Governor's All-Star Program: City of Elberton Survey Report," Sept. 1977 (5 pgs.).

Northeast Georgia Area Planning and Development Commission, Northeast Georgia Area Development Plan 1980 (231 pgs.).

_______, Elberton Comprehensive Plan, Vol. I: Planning Plan, 1976 (135 pgs.).

Glascock, Georgia. Central Savannah River Area Planning and Development Commission, The Central Savannah River Area: A Plan for Its Development FY 1979-FY 1981: Vol. II Progress Report: Glascock County (13 pgs.).

_______, Sketch Plan, Glascock County, 1973 (126 pgs.).

Heard and Troup, Georgia. Chattahoochee-Flint Area Planning and Development Commission, Chattahoochee-Flint Areawide General Development Plan, 1975 (213 pgs.).

Upson, Georgia. McIntosh Trail Area Planning and Development Commission, Upson County, Georgia Comprehensive Plan, 1976 (216 pgs.).

Terrell, Georgia. Southwest Georgia Planning and Development Commission, Community Development Concept Plan: City of Dawson, 1979 (113 pgs.).

Maui, Hawaii. Maui County, "The General Plan of the County of Maui" (47 pgs.).

_______, "Ordinance Adopting the General Plan and Providing for Community Plans for the County of Maui," 1980 (7 pgs.).

Idaho. Idaho Division of Budget, Policy Planning and Coordination, Idaho's Tomorrow, 1976 (47 pgs.).

"Goals for Idaho's Tomorrow," 1976 (21 pgs.).

Bannock, Idaho. Idaho Division of Budget, Policy Planning, and Coordination, "County Profiles of Idaho: Indicators for a Development Strategy," approx. 1976 (6 pgs.--excerpt on Bannock).

Illinois. Governor's Office, Illinois Rural Planning Council, The Revitalization of Rural Illinois, approx. 1979 (161 pgs.).

_______, The Revitalization of Rural Illinois: Summary, approx. 1979 (60 pgs.).

Christian, Illinois. West Central Illinois Valley Regional Planning Commission, Technical Assistance Report and Planning Information Base Report, 1979 (60 pgs.).

Hancock, Illinois. Western Illinois Regional Council, Western Illinois Data Book, 1975 (82 pgs.).

_______, Policy Framework for Community Development in Western Illinois (30 pgs.).

Logan, Illinois. Logan County Regional Planning Commission, Logan County: Directives for Growth, 1978 update (250 pgs.).

Marion, Illinois. South Central Illinois Regional Planning and Development Region, Regional Development Policies: South Central Region, 1978 (252 pgs.).

Allen, Indiana. Allen County Plan Commission, The Comprehensive Plan of Allen County Indiana, 1976 (130 pgs.).

Benton, Indiana. Cooperative Extension Service, Purdue University, "Benton County Examines Itself: A Summary of Findings from a Recent County-Wide Survey" (8 pgs.).

Cass, Indiana. Cass County Commissioners Ad Hoc Committee on Population, "Ad Hoc Committee Report on Population Decline," 1979 (27 pgs.).

Jefferson, Indiana. Board of County Commissioners, Development Plan for Jefferson County, Indiana, 1976 (86 pgs.).

Indiana Department of Commerce, "Indiana County Profiles: Jefferson," 1980 (11 pgs.).

Madison Special Projects Office, "Report to Common Council (on federal/state grants), 1980 (9 pgs.).

Martin, Indiana. Cooperative Extension Service, Purdue University," Martin County, U.S.A.," 1979 (9 pgs.).

Spencer, Indiana. Cooperative Extension Service, Purdue University, An Assessment of the Greater Grandview Community and Its Opportunities for Improvement, 1977 (39 pgs.).

Hancock, Iowa. Iowa Development Commission, 1980 Statistical Profile of Iowa (15 pgs.--excerpts).

Lyon and Dickinson, Iowa. Northwest Iowa Regional Council of Governments, Application to FmHA for funds for development of a comprehensive strategy for rural development which will principally benefit unemployed, underemployed, low income, elderly, and minority residents, 1980 (17 pgs.).

Muscatine, Iowa. Bi-State Metropolitan Planning Commission, Muscatine County Development Guide, 1979 (92 pgs.).

Barton, Kansas. Cooperative Extension Service, Kansas State University, "Arkansas Town on the Move through Total Community Development: Hoisington: A Community with Pride," 1976 (23 pgs.).

Decatur, Kansas. Decatur County Area Chamber of Commerce, "Decatur County Community Profile" (4 pgs.).

Kansas Department of Economic Development, "Community Profile: Oberlin, Kansas," 1980 (4 pgs.).

Northern Natural Gas Company, "Small Town Business Area Physical Redevelopment: Science or Serendipity" (29 pgs.).

Northwest Kansas Planning and Development Commission, Decatur County Planning Study 1979 (135 pgs.).

Franklin, Kansas. Franklin City-County Planning Commission, Comprehensive Plan for the Unincorporated Area of Franklin County, Kansas, 1980-2000 (6 pgs.--excerpt).

Pawnee, Kansas. Cooperative Extension Service, Kansas State University, "Activities and Action Stir Community Pride: Westmoreland," 1977 (31 pgs.).

Reno, Kansas. Reno County Rural Development Committee, "1980 Reno County Plan of Work" (4 pgs.).

Rush, Kansas. Cooperative Extension Service, Kansas State University, "Steps to Success: A Kansas Town on the Move: The LaCross Model," 1978 (19 pgs.).

Kentucky. Christenson, James A., Paul D. Warner, and L. Sue Greer, "Quality of Life in Kentucky Counties," Community Development Issues, Vol. 1, July 1979 (8 pgs.).

____________, "Policy Issues in Kentucky," Community Development Issues, Vol. 2, January 1980 (4 pgs.).

Christenson, James A., Paul D. Warner, and Verna Keith, "Citizens Set Priorities for Spending Tax Dollars," Community Development Issues, Vol. 1, September 1979 (12 pgs.).

Cooperative Extension Service, University of Kentucky, "Building Better Communities: A Statewide Survey" (11 pgs.).

Warner, Paul D., James A. Christenson, and Verna Keith, "Changes in Spending Priorities, 1975 to 1979," Community Development Issues, Vol. 1, November 1979 (6 pgs.).

Bath, Menifee, and Morgan, Kentucky. Gateway District Rural Development Committee, "Plan of Action, FY 1980" (5 pgs.).

Livingston, Kentucky. Pennyrile District (9 counties) Rural Development Committee, "Rural Development Program Plans of Action," 1980 (12 pgs.).

Menifee, Kentucky. Menifee County Rural Development Committee, "Rural Development Program Plan of Action, 1980" (6 pgs.).

Union, Louisiana. Union Parish Rural Development Committee, "Union Parish Problem Identification Survey" (15 pgs.).

Baltimore, Maryland. Baltimore County Council, Growth Management Bill, 1979 (23 pgs.).

Delta and Dickinson, Michigan. Central Upper Peninsula Planning and Development Regional Commission, Regional Development Guide, Vol. 1, Executive Summary, 1980 (134 pgs.).

Dickinson, Michigan. Central Upper Peninsula Planning and Development Regional Commission, "Dickinson County Population Study," 1977 (9 pgs.).

Ionia, Newaygo, and Osceola, Michigan. Cooperative Extension Service, Michigan State University, Revised County and Regional Factbook Region VIII, 1979 (45 pgs.).

Livingston, Michigan. Office of County Planning, "Overview of Rural Development Planning Activities," 1980 (3 pgs.).

_____________. Rural Development Planning Program for Western Livingston County, Open File Report: Physical Resources (45 pgs.).

_______, Open File Report: Preparation for Community Decision Making (25 pgs.).

_______, Strategies for Future Development: Issues for Discussion (53 pgs.).

________, Western Livingston County Planning Opinion Survey (68 pgs.).

Montmorency, Michigan. Northeast Michigan Council of Governments, Montmorency County Comprehensive Plan, 1979 (108 pgs.).

Minnesota. Minnesota Analysis and Planning System, University of Minnesota, Agricultural Extension Service, Data File Inventory, 1978 (37 pgs.).

Mower, Minnesota. Austin-Mower County Planning Department, Austin-Mower County Comprehensive Plan, 1974 Update (138 pgs.).

Pipestone, Minnesota. Community Resource Development Agent, "Pipestone County Community Resource Development Activity, 1980" (3 pgs.).

Jackson, Mississippi. HUD, Federal Insurance Administration, "Flood Insurance Study: Jackson County, Mississippi" (13 pgs.).

Jackson County Planning Commission, Statistical Data: Jackson County, Mississippi (87 pgs.).

Carter, Missouri. Ozark Foothills Regional Planning Commission, "Local Community Development Plan for the City of Ellsinore, June 1976" (12 pgs.).

_______, "Local Community Development Plan for the City of Grandin, June 1976" (13 pgs.).

_______, "Van Buren, Missouri Community Profile" (18 pgs.).

Iron and Ste. Genevieve, Missouri. Extension Division, University of Missouri-Columbia, Southeast Missouri Regional Profile 1975 (106 pgs.).

Macon and Ralls, Missouri. Extension Division, University of Missouri-Columbia, Mark Twain Regional Profile 1975 (111 pgs.).

New Madrid, Missouri. Bootheel Regional Planning Commission, "Bootheel Regional Goals," 1980 (12 pgs.).

Montana. Montana Department of Community Affairs, Community Development Division, "Inventory of Local Planning Efforts," 1980 (10 pgs.).

Chouteau, Montana. Chouteau County Comprehensive Plan. n.d. (85 pgs.)

Meagher, Montana. Meagher County Planning Board, Meagher County Comprehensive Plan, 1977 (96 pgs.).

Hitchcock, Nebraska. Culbertson Planning Commission (by Oblinger-Smith Corporation), Comprehensive Plan, Culbertson, Nebraska, 1978 (122 pgs.).

Southwest Nebraska Council of Governments, Regional Background Report for Dundy, Frontier, Furnas, Hayes, Hitchcock and Red Willow Counties, 1978 (84 pgs.).

_______, Regional Development Plan, 1978-1979 (118 pgs.).

Trenton Planning Commission (by Oblinger-Smith Corporation), Comprehensive Plan - Trenton Nebraska, 1978 (127 pgs.).

Douglas, Nevada. Douglas County Planning Department, Carson Valley General Plan, 1980 (184 pgs.).

Humboldt, Nevada. Humboldt Regional Planning Commission, General Plan, 1979 (32 pgs.).

New Jersey. New Jersey Department of Community Affairs, Division of Planning, Preface to Rural Planning in New Jersey: A Summary of Monographs (48 pgs.).

New Mexico. New Mexico State Rural Development Committee, "Rural Development Primer" (brochure).

Harding, New Mexico. Eastern Plains Council of Governments, "Comprehensive Rural Area Development Program Phase II" (15 pgs.).

_______, Resource Directory for Planning District IV (77 pgs.).

Lea, New Mexico. City of Hobbs, Community Development Department, Application to HUD (CDBG) for funds for comprehensive neighborhood community development plan, 1979 (34 pgs.).

Southeastern New Mexico Economic Development District, "Jal, New Mexico, Community Development Profile and Plan," 1974 (23 pgs.).

Putnam, New York. Putnam County Planning Board, Putnam County Data Book, 1977 (117 pgs.).

Seneca, New York. Seneca County Planning Board, Seneca County Development Plan, 1977 (41 pgs.).

Seneca County Planning Department, Seneca County Community Data Sheets, 1979 (91 pgs.).

North Carolina. North Carolina Agricultural Extension Service, Western Carolina University, Center for Improving Mountain Living/Division of Economic Development, "The Community Resource Inventory: A Tool for Achieving Rural Area Development," 1976 (7 pgs.).

North Carolina Agricultural Extension Service and Center for Rural Resource Development, Proceedings of Symposium of Rural Development

Policies and Issues, Report No. 7, 1977 (64 pgs.).
North Carolina Department of Administration, Division of Policy Development, Balanced Growth in North Carolina: A Technical Report, 1979 (331 pgs.).

Columbus, North Carolina. Cape Fear Council of Governments, Growth of the Cape Fear Region, 1977 (25 pgs.).

Cavalier and Towner, North Dakota. North Central Planning Council, Comprehensive Plan, Vol. I: History, Inventory, and Analysis, 1977 (191 pgs.).

Warren, Ohio. Warren County Regional Planning Commission, Little Miami River Corridor Plan, Warren County, Ohio, 1979 (269 pgs.).

Yamhill, Oregon. Yamhill County Department of Planning and Development, Yamhill County Comprehensive Plan, 1974 (Addendum 1978) (216 pgs.).

South Carolina. Office of the Governor, Division of Administration, South Carolina--Growth and Development, 1978 (172 pgs.).

McCormick, South Carolina. Upper Savannah Council of Governments, Statistical Reference: McCormick County (25 pgs.).

Oconee and Spartanburg, South Carolina. South Carolina Appalachian Council of Governments, Appalachian Statistics, 1978 (62 pgs.).
_______, Areawide Action Plan for the South Carolina Appalachian Region, 1979 (84 pgs.).

South Dakota. South Dakota State Planning Bureau, Public Investment Planning, 1978 (554 pgs.)
_______, South Dakota Public Investment Plan, 1979 (199 pgs.).

Custer and Shannon, South Dakota. Sixth District Council of Local Governments, Guide to Data Resources (248 pgs.).
_______, Public Investment Plan, Fifth Stage, 1979 (204 pgs.).

Hanson, South Dakota. Hanson County Planning Commission, "Hanson County Comprehensive Plan," 1977 (41 pgs.).

Minnehaha, South Dakota. Southeastern Council of Governments, Public Investment Plan, 1979 Update (56 pgs.).

Bedford, Tennessee. Tenco Developments, Inc., "Pre-Application to Farmers Home Administration, Rural Development Plan for Bedford County" (for Area Development Assistance Planning Grant), 1979 (32 pgs.).

Benton, Tennessee. Northwest Tennessee Development District, Needs and goals survey and analysis of results (13 pgs.--excerpt).

Grundy, Tennessee. Tenco Developments, Inc., Proposal to Farmer's Home Administration Rural Development Plan for Grundy County (for Area Development Assistance Planning Grant), 1980 (24 pgs.).

Shelby, Tennessee. Memphis and Shelby County Office of Planning and Development, Memphis Population 2000, 1979 (25 pgs.).

Bastrop, Texas. Capital Area Planning Council, "Capco Draft Rural Development Policy Document," 1979 (18 pgs.).
Southwest Texas State University Community Development Institute, Bastrop County Plan, 1978 (144 pgs.).

Baylor, Clay, and Young, Texas. Nortex Regional Planning Commission, 1979 Twelve-County Regional Development Plan for the North Texas Planning Region (333 pgs.).

Karnes, Texas. Alamo Area Council of Governments, City of Kenedy Community Improvement Program, 1979 (91 pgs.).

Kendall, Texas. Alamo Area Council of Governments, "Kendall County Profile," 1979 (10 pgs.).

Kerr, Texas. Alamo Area Council of Governments, "Kerr County Profile," 1979 (11 pgs.).

Millard and Sanpete, Utah. Six-County Commissioners Organization, Six County Development Plan 1979 (193 pgs.).

Bland, Virginia. Bland County Planning Commission, Comprehensive Plan, Bland County, Virginia, 1980-amended (112 pgs.).

Charlotte, Virginia. Keysville Town Council, Keysville Downtown Update Plan, 1978 (38 pgs.).

King and Queen, Virginia. County Planning Commission, King and Queen County Comprehensive Plan - 1979 (96 pgs.).

King and Queen County Needs Assessment Committee, "King and Queen County Needs Assessment Survey," (14 pgs.).

Virginia Department of Planning and Budget, Data Summary - King and Queen County, 1978 (37 pgs.).

Lee, Virginia. Lee County Planning Commission, Lee County Comprehensive Plan, 1979 (129 pgs.).

Mathews, Virginia. Mathews County Planning Commission, Mathews County Comprehensive Plan, 1976 (74 pgs.).

Mecklenburg, Virginia. Mecklenburg County Planning Commission, Mecklenburg County Plan, 1975 (85 pgs.).

Southside Planning District Commission, Management Plan FY 1980 (32 pgs.).

Washington, Virginia. Washington County Planning Commission, Vol. 1, Comprehensive Development Plan, Washington County Virginia 1978 (97 pgs.).

West Virginia. Governor's Office of Economic and Community Development, West Virginia State Development Plan, 1980 (331 pgs.).

Roane and Wood, West Virginia. Mid-Ohio Valley Regional Planning and Development Council, Regional Development Program 1979-1980 (246 pgs.).

Crawford and Vernon, Wisconsin. Mississippi River Regional Planning Commission, Rural Investment Strategy Final Report: Area Development Assistance Planning Grant, 1979 (64 pgs.).

Eau Claire, Wisconsin. West Central Wisconsin Regional Planning Commission, Development Assistance Manual, 1979 (79 pgs.).

______, Rural Community Development Project: Final Report, 1980 (34 pgs.).

Marquette and Waushara, Wisconsin. East Central Wisconsin Regional Planning Commission, The Population of East Central Wisconsin, 1977 (103 pgs.).

Teton, Wyoming. Teton County, Teton County Comprehensive Plan and Implementation Program, 1977 (146 pgs.).

______, Amendment to the Comprehensive Plan, Teton County, Wyoming, 1980 (146 pgs.).

Teton County Growth Study Committee (for Teton County Commissioners), "Growth in Teton County, 1967-1978," 1978 (pgs. 34).

Uinta, Wyoming. Lincoln-Uinta Association of Governments, Uinta County Comprehensive Plan, 1977 (89 pgs.).
"Population Growth Projections," 1980 (8 pgs.).
"1979 Year-End Population Estimates," 1980 (9 pgs.).

ECONOMIC DEVELOPMENT

Economic development plans are financed by EDA. They usually have sections on demographic characteristics, the labor force and employment, economic structure, geography and physical infrastructure, and potentials and constraints.

The first example of plan data is from a Texas plan. It breaks down the factors of military spending in Corpus Christi in order to suggest the effect of any base closings.

The second example, from souteastern Utah, lists the sources of financial resources available for economic development in an energy boom area. These are broken down by county and by private bank/government agency.

The third example, from Ionia County, Michigan, is a demographic and occupational profile of the unemployed. The data were obtained from the Michigan Employment Security Commission.

The next example reports on an Idaho survey of attitudes toward growth and development. Respondents were asked how important several possible impacts of new industrial location would be to them. Responses were then correlated with respondents' background.

The fifth example, from Virginia, is a local social indicator analysis. Indicators for economic well-being, housing, employment, population, education, and health are selected, measured, and compared across several counties. Relations among indicators are also examined.

The sixth example is from a study of new manufacturing plants in the nonmetropolitan Ozark region. After discussing their data sources and limitations, the authors conclude that more new operating plants were located in nonmetropolitan than metropolitan Ozark areas during the period 1967-1974. There is a detailed breakdown of plant locations by county size and adjacency to metropolitan areas.

The next example, from the University of Arizona's Cooperative Extension Service, suggests procedures for estimating personal income in a local area. It specifies the data sources to use, the transformation to be performed, and several practical applications.

The last example, from the Michigan Office of Intergovernmental Relations, describes a method of developing a community distress index. The index uses measures of wealth, employment, housing, tax effort, and state equalized value and can be applied to both cities and counties.

DUVALL, TEXAS

Coastal Bend Council of Governments, Overall Economic Development Program: Final Report, 1977, pp. 121-123.

Coastal Bend Military Installations

Military bases have been traditional major employers. Events of the past year indicate that there is a definite possibility that the naval bases in the region might be closing in the near future. Table 14 dramatically presents the impact that military spending has on the area. The civilian personnel at the Corpus Christi Naval Air Station number 1,327 with a direct payroll in excess of $16 million. There are 2,478 military personnel reported working at the Naval Air Station. The total number of military personnel for the Corpus Christi installations number 3,157; this represents 815 less personnel than in August 1974. The total direct pay for all personnel was $91.8 million. When the indirect employment and total dollar impact loss is calculated the impact is very significant. Over 13,138 jobs would be affected (7 percent of local employment) with a dollar loss of $212.1 million.

Beeville and Kingsville also have naval air stations. While the number employed at these naval air stations doesn't approach the number at Corpus Christi, their impact on the local economy is even more significant. If these installations were to close, the total personnel impact loss would be 7,207 jobs; 3,556 in Beeville (28 percent of local employment), and 3,651 in Kingsville (21 percent of local employment). The total dollar loss is equally disconcerting; $45.4 million in Beeville, and $43.0 million in Kingsville.

In the Coastal Bend Region, this represents a potential disaster. The total military complement of 6,784 spend $42.9 million in the regions. The direct civilian employment affected by these closings is 6,029 jobs. The loss in direct pay would almost be $79.2 million. This represents a total direct loss of $123.1 million for the district's economy. When the indirect costs are included, there are 20,345 jobs affected with a total dollar loss of $300.5 million.

While the naval air stations in the region have not completely shut down, the Department of Defense has indicated that there is a real possibility that it will happen in the near future. If a shutdown or even a major cutback does occur, the total impact on the regional economy will be of major proportions.

CARBON, UTAH

Southeastern Utah Economic Development District, Overall Economic Development Program 1979, pp. 33-36.

It is abundantly evident that changes have occurred in the four counties during the 1970s. It is clear that the changes have been generated by the development of energy-related industries including

Table 14 Factors of Military Spending in Corpus Christi, Texas, 1975-1976

Organization	Military Personnel	Military Pay	Civilian Personnel	Civilian Pay	Total Personnel	Total Pay	Total Personnel Impact Loss	Total Dollar Impact Loss	Percent of Local Employment
CORPUS CHRISTI									7
Naval Air Sta.	2,478	$17,780,000	1,327	$16,044,700	3,805	$33,824,700	6,119	$ 98,429,877	
Naval Regional Medical Ctr.	342	1,150,000	137	285,000	479	1,435,000	774	4,175,850	
Army Depot	44	1,360,000	3,766	53,000,000	3,810	54,360,000	5,762	103,284,000	
Coast Guard Air Station	113	1,311,400	-	-	113	1,311,400	186	3,816,174	
Marine Corps Detachment	180	828,000	-	-	180	828,000	297	2,409,480	
Sub-Total:	3,175	22,429,400	4,230	$69,329,700	8,387	$91,759,100	13,138	$212,115,381	7
BEEVILLE Naval Air Sta.	1,734	9,983,700	454	5,602,800	2,188	15,586,500	3,556	45,356,715	28
KINGSVILLE Naval Air Sta.	1,893	10,525,300	345	4,252,800	2,238	14,778,100	3,651	43,004,271	21
SO. TEX. REGION TOTAL	6,784	$42,938,400	6,029	$79,185,300	12,813	$122,123,700	20,345	$300,476,367	

coal, uranium, and oil and gas mining activities. The effects of these basic industry developments have spread into all other major industrial sectors, particularly construction--both nonresidential in the power plants in Emery County, and residential throughout the district. The trade sector has been significantly impacted by the developments both in terms of new jobs created and in new and larger volumes of retail sales. Expanded population, new births, school enrollments, and registration of vehicles have occurred. All of these changes have brought new opportunities and challenges to the district's residents. A continuing problem which may dampen a portion of the potential economic development in Southeastern Utah is financial. While major Utah financial institutions are well represented in the district, the financing of certain types of projects is scarce for local entrepreneurs. Many observers of the financial scene in the area are of the opinion that Utah's banks and financial institutions could and should be more aggressive in lending to commercial and industrial prospects. For example, it is extremely difficult to obtain a small business loan for a period exceeding 90 days. The only long-term financing generally available involves real estate or loans guaranteed by an agency such as the Small Business Administration.

If more "start-up" money was available on easier terms, it is probable that more small businesses, particularly in Emery County, would be in existence, supplying the needs of the population influx.

The tabulation on the following page shows all financial resources available in the district, including governmental agencies.

IONIA, MICHIGAN

Ionia County Planning Commission, Ionia County Overall Economic Development Program, Spring 1977, pp. 29-30, 74-75.

The occupational profile of the unemployed (Table 10) presents both a flow of Michigan Employment Security Commission (MESC) registrants from October 1976 through February 1977 and a cross section of the active file as of the end of February. The active file list contains a broad distribution of occupational skills. A rather large number of professional/administrative workers is present, consistent with the suggestion that there may be a slackness in local opportunities of this type. Machine trades and bench work are well represented, as is a variety of structural work. These may be in part the consequence of the cyclical slump of the economy referred to earlier. Clerical, sales, and service workers are also present in large numbers.

This array appears to suggest that a wide variety of work skills are available to be tapped in any development effort. It also indicates a present waste of human resources through lack of opportunity. The table also reveals that women, though predictably concentrated in clerical, sales, and service categories, also constituted almost one-half of the benchwork roster, and more than a third of the professional/administrative applicant file. Minorities, consistent with their small share of population, comprised 1 to 3 percent of the active applicants in most categories.

Financial Resources Available in Southeastern Utah Communities

	Banks-Savings and Loans	SBA	FmHA	EDA	EPA	HUD	FCRC	State	Special Districts
		(Guarantee)	(Grants and Loans)	(Grants and Loans)	(Grants and Loans)	(Grants)	(Grants)	(Grants and Loans)	
Carbon County									
East Carbon	Zion's First National			X		X		X	
Helper	First Security Commercial Security[a]				X		X		Price River Water Improvement Dist.
Hiawatha				X			X		
Price	American Savings & Loan Capitol Financial Services Commercial Security[a] First Federal Savings & Loan First Security The Lockhart Company Pacific Finance Walker Bank & Trust Zion's First National		X	X	X		X	X	Price River Water Improvement Dist.
Scofield							X	X	
Sunnyside				X			X	X	
Wellington			X		X		X	X	
Emery County									
Castle Dale	First Security Zion's First National		X		X		X	X	Castle Valley Special Service District
Cleveland			X		X		X	X	Castle Valley Special Service District
Elmo					X		X	X	Castle Valley Special Service District
Emery			X		X		X	X	Castle Valley Special Service District
Ferron	Zion's First National		X		X	X	X	X	Castle Valley Special Service District

Green River	Commercial Security	X	X	X	X	X	Castle Valley Special Service District
Huntington	First Security	X		X	X	X	Castle Valley Special Service District
Orangeville						X	Castle Valley Special Service District
<u>Grand County</u>							
Moab	First Security First Western National	X		X	X	X	
Spanish Valley[b]		X			X		Spanish Valley Water & Sewer Improvement District
Thompson[b]						X	Thompson Water Improvement District
<u>San Juan County</u>							
Blanding	First Security	X					
Bluff						X	
Monticello	First Security First Western National	X				X	
Mexican Hat[b]							

[a] Formerly Helper State Bank
[b] Unincorporated

Table 10 Profile of the Unemployed (Employment Service Applicants, 1 Oct.-28 Feb. 77, Ionia Office, MESC)

Occupation	Total Registrants During Period		Active File, end of period: Number	Percent Fem.	Percent Min.
TOTAL	4,542		1,989		
Professional, etc.,	384		120	36	3
Medicine and health		41			
Education		68			
Administrative		58			
Managers and officials		116			
Clerical and Sales,	637		217	68	1
Stenographers, etc.		74			
Computing, acct. recording		196			
Material/prod. recording		74			
Sales, commods.		70			
Merchandising, ex. sales		124			
Service,	754		322	59	4
Food and beverage		375			
Misc. personal		121			
Building, etc.		144			
Farming, etc.	268		116	12	22
Processing,	134		71	25	7
Food		48			
Machine Trades,	440		257	14	3
Metal machining		79			
Metal working		130			
Mechanics and machine repair		158			
Bench Work	483		219	48	3
Metal products		372			
Fabric		53			
Structural Work,	628		288	6	3
Metal fabricating		88			
Welders, etc.		90			
Electrical		50			
Excavating, etc.		79			
Construction		240			
Miscellaneous,	814		379	14	3
Motor freight		152			
Transportation		93			
Packaging		530			

Source: Michigan Employment Security Commission, Employment Security Automated Reporting System

The demographic traits of 2,283 active applicants (Table 11) reveals patterns consistent with other data. Two-thirds of the list were male, 2 percent were non-white (but 3.2 percent were Spanish American). By education, 43 percent had completed twelfth grade, 42 percent had completed grades 8-11. Only 4 percent had less than eighth-grade education, but almost 12 percent had more than twelfth-grade training. By age, 26 percent were under 22, 55 percent were in the age range 22-39 years, while 18 percent were age 40 or over. Seven percent suffer some handicap.

Data to provide wage and salary comparisons unfortunately are not available. MESC information is available on average weekly earnings in covered employment. Variances in these, of course, are affected by relative wages for comparable work, average weekly hours, and variations in the mix of jobs held. As an indication of relative income, however, it is worth noting that in 1975 the value was $222 for all of Michigan, and $201 for the Lansing-East Lansing SMSA. Within the SMSA, Ionia County realized $160, substantially less. The Ionia figure was about equal to the Clinton County figure, lower than the $176 of Eaton County and the $209 of Ingham County. This relative Ionia position is comparable to the personal income data.

IDAHO

Idaho Division of Budget, Policy Planning, and Cordination, Attitudes Toward Population Growth and Economic Development in Idaho, 1978, pp. 2, 6, 12, 14-16.

The Survey

A questionnaire designed to measure attitudes toward growth and development was mailed to a randomly selected sample of 3,000 Idaho residents. The sample was selected randomly from telephone directories covering the entire state. From the initial sample of 3,000, 765 were eliminated due to incorrect mailing addresses and respondents in failing health or deceased. Thus, the eligible sample consisted of 2,235 respondents.

The initial questionnaire was mailed in late November 1977 with a follow-up postcard and two follow-up letters containing new questionnaires. The mailings were completed in January 1978 with 1,453 useable questionnaires. This represents a response rate of 65 percent.

To obtain an equal number of males and females, half of the questionnaires were sent to females and half to males. The sex of the respondent was requested in the cover letters. As a result, 51 percent of the respondents are male and 49 percent are female.

Respondents were asked how important a number of community impacts would be to them if an industry desired to locate in their community. Table 5 shows that environmental pollution and the impact on community services were of major concern, with other factors grouped as slightly less important.

Table 11 Demographic Traits of the Unemployed

	New Applicants Inc. Partial	Total Applicants Available This Period	Active File End of Period	
TOTAL	1,913	5,290	%	2,283
Age				
under 20	391	744	12.1	277
20-21	298	717	14.1	321
22-24	294	830	16.2	370
25-29	276	945	19.2	438
30-39	357	972	20.1	459
40-44	77	278	5.7	129
45-54	111	373	6.8	155
55-64	102	334	4.8	109
65+	27	97	1.1	25
Sex				
Male	1,206	3,325	66.3	1,514
Female	707	1,965	33.7	769
Highest School Grade				
0-7	89	203	3.7	84
8-11	694	1,966	41.7	952
12	888	2,421	43.0	982
12+	242	700	11.6	265
Ethnic Group				
White	1,875	5,187	98.0	2,238
Black	28	77	1.4	33
Am. Ind.	5	9	.2	5
Other	5	17	.3	7
INA	0	0	0.0	0
Sp. American	104	243	3.2	75
Handicapped	126	359	7.4	170

Source: Michigan Employment Security Commission, Employment Security Automated Reporting System.

Table 5 Importance of Consideration if a New Industry were to Locate in a Community

	Not Important Percent	Slightly Important Percent	Moderately Important Percent	Very Important Percent
Amount of pollution	2	8	21	69
Amount of energy needed	3	12	33	52
Impact on community services (schools, police, fire, etc.)	1	9	26	64
Number of new people it would bring to the community	4	12	32	51
Number of jobs it would create	5	10	31	54
Impact of housing	3	11	32	54
Variety of jobs it would create	6	13	35	46

Table 7 shows the influence of background variables on the importance of several areas impacted by growth.

Those variables showing the strongest relationships are growth and the preservation orientation. Those favoring a high growth rate tended to view the number and variety of jobs as most important with pollution, energy needs, increased demand for community services, and number of new people as being less important. Those with a high preservation orientation felt just the opposite; pollution, energy requirements, increased demand for community services, and number of new residents were the most important impacts, while the number and variety of new jobs were of little importance. Older people viewed pollution and number of new people of lesser importance than did the younger. Those with higher education are less likely to view the number and variety of jobs and housing as important impacts of growth.

HENRY, VIRGINIA

West Piedmont Planning District Commission, An Economic Analysis for Development of the Counties, Cities, and Towns of the West Piedmont Planning District, 1975, pp. 30-32, 34-37.

Indicators of Social Well Being

At the outset of this study, the West Piedmont Planning District Commission indicated a need for some measures of the social and

Table 7 Impacts of New Industry by Background Variable

	Pollution	Energy Needed	Community Services	Number of New People	Number of Jobs	Housing	Variety of Jobs
Time in State	-.08	.08*	.13**	-.01	.06	.10	.11*
Education	.08*	-.09*	-.06**	.03	-.10*	-.10**	-.14**
Age	-.17**	.02	.08	-.13**	-.03	.03	.03
Income	.02	-.02	.03	.04	-.08	-.04	-.12*
Preservation Orientation[a]	.44**	.22**	.09*	.19**	-.17	.00	-.15**
Growth	-.19**	-.11*	-.12*	-.17**	.21**	-.04**	.22**

*Significant at 0.05 level using chi square.
**Significant at 0.01 level using chi square.

[a]The items used by the preservation scale are:

1. We have enough state parks in Idaho;
2. The use of rivers to provide electricity, irrigation, and water for domestic use should be given high priority in Idaho;
3. We have enough irrigated farm land in southern Idaho;
4. We have enough legally designated wild and scenic rivers in Idaho;
5. We have enough industrial development in Idaho;
6. Enough land has been set aside for wildlife protection and recreation;
7. The best use of mountainous forested land in Idaho is to provide timber products and jobs for Idahoans;
8. We have enough area legally designated as wilderness in Idaho;
9. A growing population is necessary for a vital economy in Idaho; and
10. We have enough roadless areas.

economic conditions of the people in the area. Such measures could serve as a basis for evaluating the status of the area and working and planning for future development. Hopefully, they would help identify various aspects of living conditions in which the area is either comparativly high or low. Furthermore, they should serve as benchmarks for gauging changes in these conditions as growth and development take place.

A list of indicators of social well being is virtually unending. It includes indicators such as income, health, education, housing, population, public safety, and leisure and recreation. After careful consideration of several indicators, the following six were chosen for examination mainly because of availability of sufficient and complete data: economic well being, housing, employment, education, health, and population. Both education and health indicators were further divided into subgroups of inputs and outputs. The measurements used for the development of each of these social indicators are identified in Table 4.

The rankings of the counties and cities of the WPPD based upon the index for each social indicator are summarized in Table 5. The results shown in this table give the rank of each WPPD jurisdiction among the total number of cities and counties in Virginia considered. For example, Table 5 shows that of the 102 counties and cities considered, Franklin County ranked 24th in housing, 48th in employment, 51st in economic well being, 65th in health inputs, and 70th in health outputs.

Economic Well Being and Employment. It appears that the counties of WPPD, with the exception of Pittsylvania (excluding Danville) have satisfactory rankings near the middle of the state. A significant gap exists between Henry County and the rest of the WPPD. However, Pittsylvania County's rank for economic well being is somewhat misleading since Danville is included and contributes significantly to Pittsylvania's relatively high standing. Large numbers of poor families, low levels of their educational achievements, and low wages per employed worker can be cited as a few factors behind Pittsylvania's relatively low rank for "employment' indicator.

Housing. Henry County ranks 79th in 102 cities and counties of Virginia. Ranks of other counties were as follows: Pittsylvania - 30th, Franklin - 24th, and Patrick - 20th. The lower rank for Henry County can be explained by the fact that, while quality and availability of housing is high in Henry County, the cost of housing is also high. This observation further suggests that low and middle-income families will have difficulty affording a house in Henry County.

Education. The Education Outputs (quality of student performance in the public school system) show a fairly large gap between the cities and the counties. For example, in terms of education outputs, Martinsville ranked 24th and Danville 27th in 128 counties and cities of Virginia. Pittsylvania County ranked 115th. Henry County ranked 68th, Franklin County 67th, and Patrick County 61st. The WPPD

Table 4 Measurements Used for Social Indicator Analysis

Social Indicator	Measurement
Economic Well Being	—mean family income —percent of famiiles within 125% of defined poverty level —percent of families earning top 60% of income —income per employed worker —wealth related income per family —percent of males 25 years or older with college degree
Housing Indicator	—number of available housing units per person —percent of housing units without plumbing —percent of families not able to afford median value house
Employment	—percent of labor force employed —average weekly wage of construction workers —average weekly wage of manufacturing workers —average weekly wage of service workers
Population	—net migration, 1960-1970 —change in percent of total population less than 18 and greater than 65 years old —change in percent of population with high school diplomas.
Education Inputs	—percent of instructional personnel holding advanced degrees —pupil/teacher ratio for classroom teaching positions —total cost per pupil in average daily membership, regular day school
Education Outputs	—percent of high school students who don't drop out of school —percentile rank in reading achievement test, grade 11, 1973-74 —percentile rank in composite achievement, grade 6, 1973-74
Health Inputs	—total dentists per 1,000 population —general practitioners per 10,000 population —total office based doctors per 10,000 population
Health Outputs	—age of population to adjust death rate —infant mortality rate —preventable disease deaths as proportion of total deaths

communities generally rank much higher on Educational Output than on Educational Inputs. The extremely low ranks for Educational Inputs in WPPD, when compared to the Economic Well Being ranks, suggest some unwillingness to devote more resources to the public school system.

Population. The Population Indicator measures primarily net migration rates from 1960 to 1970. Henry County ranks quite high in the state and was only one of 47 jurisdictions that had a net in-migration in the state. The other WPPD communities had net

Table 5 Summary of Rankings within Virginia of Counties and Cities of the West Piedmont Planning District Based Upon Selected Social Indicators

Indicator	No. of areas in ranking[a]	Rankings					
		Franklin	Henry	Patrick	Pittsylvania	Danville	Martinsville
Economic Well Being	102	51	26	64	49	b/	c/
Employment	102	46	20	55	44	b/	c/
Housing	102	24	79	20	30	b/	c/
Education Outputs	128	67	68	61	115	27	24
Education Inputs	128	119	127	124	102	42	19
Population	125	45	15	60	69	51	41
Health Inputs	102	65	45	71	47	b/	c/
Health Outputs	102	70	76	60	65	b/	c/

a/Data for some indicators were available for counties and cities separately, for others only combined county-city were available.

b/Included in Pittsylvania County for these measures.

c/Included in Henry County for these measures.

out-migration, however, they rank relatively high since the educational achievement level of the adult population increased substantially during the decade of the sixties.

Health. The Health Indicators show WPPD communities are just below the top 50 percent of the state's counties and cities. The rank of Health Inputs for both Henry and Pittsylvania counties are enhanced by the concentration of professional medical people in Danville and Martinville.

Overall Status. It is difficult to draw definite conclusions from the six social indicators. However, as a general note it can be said that the WPPD ranks at about the state "average" on the social indicators.

Relationships Between Indicators. To gain insights into overall community achievement, the relationship between the community's level of Economic Well Being (EWB) and other social indicators was investigated. Correlation analysis was employed to estimate the strength of the relations. The results of the correlation analysis are presented in Table 6.

The results of Table 6 are quite illuminating. The EWB indicator is strongly related to Employment, Housing, Population, and Educational Outputs. Thus, communities that rank high on EWB appear to also rank high on these other indicators. This is not, of course, surprising, but it does suggest that the quantity and quality of employment, desirable migration trends, and the products of the school systems do relate to the level of Economic Well Being.

This relationship of EWB with Educational Outputs is even more interesting when it is realized that there is only a weak relationship between Educational Inputs and Outputs. This correlation was found to be only .31. Again, this does not necessarily suggest a causation, but it is worth noting that Educational Outputs do vary more closely with EWB than the Educational Inputs. In fact, the .31 correlation between outputs and inputs is low enough to cast some doubt upon the role the school system plays in the performance of the student. While this study is not designed to pursue this point, the results are thought-provoking. More specifically, these results suggest that a student's background may play a role in determining his performance, regardless of the qualities of the school system. On this same general subject, it is also of interest to note that the EWB does not correlate well with Educational Inputs. Thus, school "quality" (as measured here) cannot be expected to vary with EWB, nor does it vary with Educational Outputs.

The relationship between EWB and Housing is a strong one; however, it is most unique. Reference to Figure 13 below will make this point clearer. In Figure 13, the line ab represents what happens to the Housing index as EWB improves. At first, improvements in EWB suggest improvements in the Housing index. However, beyond a certain point improvements in EWB are related to a decline in the Housing indicator. This seemingly strange result was explained by more careful examination

Table 6 Correlation of Social Indicators with the Economic Well Being Indicator (EWB)

Indicator	Measure of Correlation
Economic Well Being	1.0
Employment	.74
Housing	.76
Population	.66
Educational Inputs	.33
Educational Outputs	.72
Health Inputs	.33
Health Outputs	—.08

of the Housing index itself. As EWB increases from a low level, housing quality improves and the number of houses available increases as people are able to afford more and better homes. However, beyond a certain point, as the level of economic welfare increases, in most cases the costs of housing does also. This result is such that community economic growth appears to mean that the residents of that community will be forced to purchase housing that they are less able to afford. This result confirms a commonly stated concern: in communities that are "richer," low and middle income families are going to be hard pressed to find housing they can afford.

The correlation analysis shows that little relationship exists between EWB and the Health indicator. Also of note is that the correlation between the Health Input and Output indicators in .08. Hence, it does not appear that the indicators of health, as measured in this study, are closely related to economic status or each other. The Health Input indicators as measured, however, include only doctors and dentists. One might expect these professionals to be located near urban areas and hospital facilities. Since we have no measure of "urbanness" or availability of hospital facilities, it is unlikely that any of the indicators used here would be correlated with Health Inputs. Nonetheless, it seems that the relatively low rank of WPPD counties is indicative of the general problem of providing adequate health care in more rural areas.

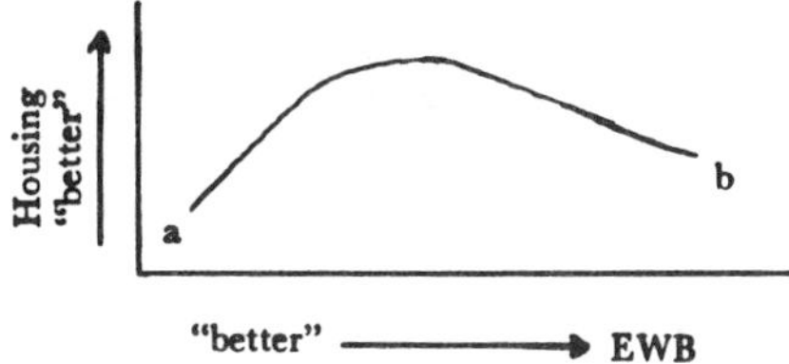

Figure 13 General Relationship of EWB to Housing.

In summary, it appears that movements of the EWB indicator will be correlated with movements of four indicators: Employment, Housing, Population, and Education Outputs. Although Health Input and Education Input do not move with EWB, they are variables that are under the control of local authorities. The community therefore may choose to put more funds and effort into hospital and educational facilities. However, they should be cautioned that the evidence here suggests little connection between the inputs into the health and education processes and their outputs.

MISSOURI

Economic Research Service, USDA, and University of Missouri Agricultural Experiment Station. New Manufacturing Plants in the Nonmetro Ozarks Region, Agricultural Economic Report No. 384, 1977, pp. 1-4, 6-8.

Introduction

This report describes the distribution of new plants locating in five Ozarks states from 1967 to 1974. The description uses two variables: plant employment size and town population size. The study finds that new plants within the Ozarks region are locating more in nonmetropolitan towns than in metropolitan areas. These new nonmetropolitan plants represent diverse industries and are dispersed among many nonmetropolitan towns of varying sizes.

Study Area. The study area included Arkansas, Kansas, Louisiana, Missouri, and Oklahoma, which comprise the Ozarks Economic Development Region as specified under P.L. 89-136, the Public Works and Economic Development Act of 1965. Counties in these states were classified by metropolitan status; namely, metropolitan core, other metropolitan, nonmetropolitan adjacent to a metropolitan core county, and nonmetropolitan not adjacent to a metropolitan core county. The classification of Standard Metropolitan Statistical Areas (SMSA) in this report conforms to that of the Office of Management and Budget as announced on February 8, 1974.[1] Metropolitan core counties were defined as those counties with 20 percent or more of their population residing inside urbanized areas as delineated in the 1970 Census of Population and/or the counties containing the central city of a metropolitan area. Legally defined towns within urbanized areas were combined with the central city's urbanized area. Alexandria, Louisiana, and Fayetteville-Springdale, Arkansas, were placed in the category of towns with 50,000 to 99,999 persons even though their central cities had fewer than 50,000 people in 1970. Towns within each

[1]SMSAs are defined as a county or group of contiguous counties which contain at least one city of 50,000 inhabitants or more, or "twin cities" with a combined population of at least 50,000.

Table 4 Distribution of new operating plants by 1970 town size, five-State regions, 1967-74

Area 1/	Total plants	Plants with employment of					
		1 to 9 2/	10 to 49	50 to 99	100 to 249	250 to 499	500 or more
				Number			
All places	2,617	885	963	302	309	114	44
				Percent 3/			
All places	100.0	100.0	100.0	100.0	100.0	100.0	100.0
Metro counties with urbanized area of:	40.4	38.0	44.9	36.4	40.5	33.3	38.6
100,000 or more	34.9	36.2	38.8	27.8	30.7	23.7	31.8
50,000 to 99,999	5.5	1.8	6.0	8.6	9.7	9.6	6.8
All nonmetro counties	59.6	62.0	55.1	63.6	59.5	66.7	61.4
Nonmetro counties adjacent to metro core:	15.1	12.9	14.3	20.9	17.2	16.7	20.5
25,000 to 49,999 city	1.8	2.6	1.5	1.7	1.0	0.9	2.3
10,000 to 24,999 city	2.7	2.3	2.6	3.0	3.6	2.6	4.5
5,000 to 9,999 city	1.9	0.9	1.6	3.6	2.9	2.6	6.8
2,500 to 4,999 city	3.1	2.3	3.3	5.6	2.6	1.8	2.3
1 to 2,499 city	5.7	4.9	5.4	7.0	7.1	8.8	4.5
Nonmetro counties not adjacent to metro core:	44.4	49.2	40.8	42.7	42.4	50.0	40.9
25,000 to 49,999 city	3.2	2.9	3.1	2.0	3.9	7.0	6.8
10,000 to 24,999 city	8.6	5.8	9.1	10.3	10.0	13.2	18.2
5,000 to 9,999 city	7.3	3.8	7.4	10.3	13.3	9.6	4.5
2,500 to 4,999 city	8.2	9.3	7.7	8.9	6.5	6.1	9.1
1 to 2,499 city	17.2	27.3	13.5	11.3	8.7	14.0	2.3

1/ The classification of SMSA's in this report conforms to that of the Office of Management and Budget as announced on Feb. 8, 1974. City population is that given in the 1970 Census of Population. Metro core counties are listed in text footnote 5.

2/ For Arkansas, this group includes plants with 1 to 10 employees; for Louisiana, this group includes plants with 1 to 7 employees.

3/ Percentages may not add to totals because of rounding.

county classification were subdivided into subgroups based on city sizes in 1970, as shown in Table 4 and most subsequent tables.

Data Sources. Primary data sources were state directories of manufacturers and also annual reports of new, announced, and expanded plants. These directories and annual reports were prepared by or published from data furnished by each state's Department of Industrial Development.[2] Annual reports included both newly operating plants and also announcements of intended new plants compiled from various sources including newspaper clippings and chambers of commerce. Directories of manufacturers, not necessarily published annually, catalogued all plants in operation at the time of publication, no matter when they were established. Annual reports of new and announced plants were not available for Louisiana; however, the state's 1975 directory of manufacturers did contain the year of establishment for plants. For all five states, SIC codes were determined according to the 1972 Standard Industrial Classification Manual.[3]

New plants in each state included not only newly organized plants but also plants relocating from another state or from another town within the same state. Annual reports of new and announced plants were cross-checked with each state's directory of manufacturers to determine if the plants were actually operational and if they had survived at their chosen locations. Some new plants could cease operations because of poor location choices or management problems. Survival suggested that the chosen town was at least a viable location (but not necessarily an optimal location).[4] In cross-checking annual reports and the directors of manufacturers, changes in plant names or affilitations were identified insofar as possible. Table 2 outlines the process used to define 1967-74 new operating plants in the five Ozarks states and 1967-69 new plants ceasing operation in Arkansas, Kansas, Missouri, and Oklahoma.

Manufacturing plants were classified by employment size into six categories. Actual employment was available only for Missouri and Oklahoma; the remaining states reported only employment size classes. In this report, the employment size class associated with each new operating plant was that reported in the states' latest directories of manufacturers. The employment size class for 1967-69 new plants which ceased operation was that reported in the state's 1970 or 1971 directories, if available, or, if not available, that reported in the annual reports.

---

[2]Arkansas Industrial Development Commission, Kansas Department of Economic Development, Louisiana Department of Commerce and Industry, Missouri Division of Commerce and Industrial Development, and Oklahoma Department of Industrial Development. We appreciate the assistance of these organizations in furnishing data.

[3]Office of Management and Budget, Standard Industrial Classification Manual, 1972. Washington: U.S. Government Printing Office, 1972

[4]This is similar to the survival argument proposed by Edgar M. Hoover, The Location of Economic Activity. New York: McGraw-Hill Book Co., 1948, pp. 9-10.

Table 2--Outline of data sources used to define new plants

New operating plants, 1967-74			New plants ceasing operation, 1967-69		
State	Initial plants considered	Selection of plants	State	Initial plants considered	Selection of plants
Arkansas Oklahoma Missouri	Plants listed in 1967-74 annual reports of new and announced plants	Plants also listed in State's 1976 Directory of Manufacturers	Arkansas Oklahoma	Plants listed in 1967-69 annual reports of new and announced plants	Plants also listed in 1970 Directory but not in 1976 Directory of Manufacturers
Kansas	Plants listed in 1967-74 annual reports of new and announced plants	Plants also listed in State's 1974 Directory of Manufacturers or in "New Plants in Production" section of 1973 or 1974 annual reports of new and announced plants	Missouri	Plants listed in 1967-69 annual reports of new and announced plants	Plants also listed in 1971 Directory but not in 1976 Directory of Manufacturers
			Kansas	Plants listed in 1967-69 annual reports of new and announced plants	Plants also listed in 1970 Directory but not in 1974 Directory of Manufacturers
Louisiana	Plants listed in 1975 Directory of Manufacturers	Year of establishment stated to be 1967 through 1974 in 1975 Directory of Manufacturers	Louisiana	Not determined	Not determined

Data Limitations. Differences in the state's reporting of new plants prevented some interstate comparisons. In the five-state area, 2,617 operating manufacturing plants, new during 1967 through 1974, were identified. Of these, 885 had fewer than 10 employees.[5] Most of these small plants, 88 percent, were reported in Kansas and Missouri. The apparent omission of small plants in the other state's annual reports was either intentional because of their size or was associated with the exclusion of certain industry types, for example, bakeries and printing shops.

More New Operating Plants Located in Nonmetropolitan than Metropolitan Ozarks Areas

The largest percentage of new plants for a specified county grouping went to the nonmetropolitan counties not adjacent to metropolitan cores (44 percent compared to 40 percent for metropolitan counties and 15 percent for nonmetropolitan counties adjacent to metropolitan cores, according to Table 4). Within the metropolitan grouping, areas with cities of 100,000 or more people obtained most of the plants, while within the nonmetropolitan grouping, towns of fewer than 25,000 persons not near a metropolitan core had most of the new operating plants (Table 4). Towns of fewer than 2,500 persons not near a metropolitan core had a substantial share of these new plants. Considering both nonmetropolitan town sizes and location relative to metropolitan cores, over 64 percent of the plants locating in nonmetropolitan towns of 25,000 or more people were in counties not adjacent to metropolitan cores. Over 72 percent of the plants locating in each nonmetropolitan town category of less than 25,000 population were in counties not adjacent to metropolitan cores.

GRAHAM, ARIZONA

Douglas Dunn and Douglas Cox, Cooperative Extension Service, University of Arizona, Socio-Economic Indicators for Small Towns, 1979, pp. 3-38.

Personal Income

Estimates of personal income can provide an indication of the "potential" purchasing power of people living within your town's "trade area." Trade area population and personal income levels are the first two figures a prospective businessman will want in undertaking a market feasibility study on your community.

Data Gathering. Personal family income is another of the statistics available from the U.S. Census. Average family income within your town

[5]For Arkansas, the employment size class was 1 to 10 employees; for Louisiana, the employment size class was 1 to 7 employees. For the remainder of this report, these size classes will be considered as equivalent to 1 to 9 employees.

and county can be found in the Bureau of the Census publication," 19__ Census of Population: General Social and Economic Characteristics: Arizona." Tables 41, 42, and 44, Summary of Social and Economic Characteristics. (See the next page for example. The desired information is starred.)

The Bureau of the Census also publishes per capita income estimates for counties and incorporated towns--at two year intervals following the Census. These estimates are obtained by subscribing to the earlier mentioned publication, "Population Estimates and Projections Reports Series P-25." These per capita updates, calculated in April, represent the estimated average money income received per person in your community (county) during the prior calendar year. This estimate is based on family income data from the last Census, income tax data from the Internal Revenue Service, and aggregate money income data from the Bureau of Economic Analysis. The per capita income estimate includes wage and salary income, net farm and non farm self-employment income, social security and other retirement income, public assistance, and income from interest, dividends, alimony, etc.--before deductions have been made for personal income taxes, social security, etc.

Estimating Personal Income. Although the Census Bureau provides per capita income estimates at two-year intervals, you may on your own wish to compute yearly estimates. Table 8 illustrates a method for deriving such income estimates based on (a) your town's current "trade area" population, (b) the most recent Bureau of the Census "Per Capita Income" figure for your town, and (c) the "Gross National Product Deflator," to adjust for inflation.

Step 1. Estimate your town's "trade area" population by multiplying (a) December residential electric hook-ups by (b) "average number of persons per household."

Step 2. Obtain the most recent Bureau of the Census per capita income figure for your town. Use it as your base year. (In Table 8, the most recent per capita income figure available was for 1974, $3,904.)

Step 3. Multiply (a) your "trade area" population figure as derived in Step 1 by (b) the base year per capita income figure from Step 2.

Step 4. Obtain the "Gross National Product Deflator" for the base year and each year up to the current year. Call the Documents Section of the University of Arizona Library, 626-4871, or the Economic Research Department of the Valley National Bank, 261-2694, and request the GNP Implicit Price Deflator for the desired year(s), as found in the Survey of Current Business, Bureau of Labor Statistics. The GNP Deflators for 1974 through 1978 are listed in Table 8.

Step 5. Divide (a) the GNP Deflator for the year under study by (b) the base year's GNP Deflator. The resulting ratio indicates the impact of inflation on income between the two years being compared. For example, in Table 8, the 1978 GNP Deflator (152.09) is divided by the base year 1974 GNP Deflator (116.2) to arrive at an inflation ratio of 1.31.

Table 42 Summary of Social and Economic Characteristics: 1970

[Data based on sample, see text. For minimum base for derived figures (percent, median, etc.) and meaning of symbols, see text]

Places of 2,500 to 10,000	Total population		Native population – Percent residing in State of birth	Persons 25 years old and over		Nonworker-worker ratio	Female, 16 years and over – Percent in labor force	Civilian labor force – Percent unemployed	Employed persons – Percent in manufacturing industries	Families		
											Percent with income of –	
	Number	Percent foreign born		Median school years completed	Percent who completed 4 years of high school or more					Median income (dollars)	Less than poverty level	$15,000 or more
Ajo (U)	5 871	8.6	64.7	11.9	49.5	1.88	26.7	3.3	5.3	9 884	8.9	12.5
Avondale	6 303	6.2	41.5	8.7	29.1	2.27	35.2	8.3	22.8	6 086	28.0	6.0
Benson	2 839	3.4	38.8	12.1	51.7	2.01	28.9	5.5	17.8	7 868	15.1	12.3
Bisbee	8 328	5.8	53.4	12.0	50.3	1.81	29.0	4.0	9.6	9 948	8.1	14.0
Buckeye	2 599	1.8	38.2	11.7	48.5	1.54	47.9	5.9	17.5	8 737	18.8	14.0
Cashion (U)	2 583	7.2	49.6	7.5	14.4	2.18	28.4	1.8	17.1	5 681	36.6	4.5
Clifton	5 087	4.8	63.1	11.7	48.0	1.77	27.0	4.3	3.4	10 542	6.4	14.5
Coolidge	4 651	2.4	47.0	11.5	47.5	1.76	41.9	4.2	8.1	7 942	17.1	14.7
Cottonwood	2 715	1.1	41.1	11.8	48.7	1.92	33.1	3.5	23.5	6 975	18.3	6.5
El Mirage	3 227	6.4	45.0	7.4	13.8	2.32	31.1	8.7	12.0	5 131	36.9	2.4
Eloy	5 262	5.7	53.5	8.5	27.6	1.96	43.2	8.2	13.5	6 039	33.8	8.0
Fort Huachuca (U)	6 520	6.1	7.4	12.6	78.8	1.94	25.1	14.1	8.0	6 765	10.0	6.5
Globe	7 381	3.0	56.7	12.0	50.6	1.75	29.2	2.7	19.6	8 558	8.7	11.3
Holbrook	4 759	1.8	57.4	12.2	58.2	1.69	47.9	1.7	2.5	8 810	11.0	13.4
Kearny	2 829	2.4	52.2	12.4	65.6	1.62	34.3	-	4.6	11 579	-	25.3
Kingman	7 338	2.5	31.3	12.3	61.3	1.51	39.7	4.1	7.3	10 183	7.5	16.7
Luke (U)	5 047	2.8	5.3	12.7	86.5	0.84	29.3	2.7	16.6	9 198	1.2	12.5
Miami	3 462	7.0	65.5	11.0	41.8	1.87	26.9	3.2	24.4	7 687	10.9	10.0
Nogales	8 950	30.2	67.8	8.7	33.6	2.20	33.5	4.6	5.0	6 593	26.5	11.4
Paradise Valley	7 178	3.2	18.9	14.7	90.4	1.84	28.9	1.3	18.7	24 854	3.2	75.5
Peoria	4 673	7.4	45.5	9.0	29.3	1.83	35.8	3.9	14.2	6 832	20.9	7.8
Safford	5 333	2.3	55.7	12.1	52.1	1.78	36.4	3.3	8.5	7 844	13.7	7.9
San Carlos (U)	1 926	-	82.4	9.6	30.0	3.22	24.5	4.5	3.8	4 950	47.2	3.9
San Manuel (U)	4 333	2.6	46.6	12.3	63.2	2.01	27.3	4.8	28.9	10 063	4.5	15.5
Sierra Vista	6 689	6.1	17.7	12.6	77.1	1.36	39.7	5.1	3.1	11 811	7.6	35.0
South Tucson	6 220	17.1	75.4	8.3	23.6	2.30	27.9	8.4	9.3	5 284	33.2	6.0
Superior (U)	4 976	6.7	70.2	10.1	37.0	2.08	24.2	7.0	4.8	8 910	11.0	12.8
Tolleson	3 881	11.2	54.3	7.9	21.3	2.03	36.1	4.6	16.9	6 260	26.1	4.8
West Yuma (U)	5 457	3.1	35.2	12.0	50.4	1.59	38.5	5.3	6.4	7 971	16.0	15.8
Wickenburg	2 698	4.9	24.8	12.2	55.8	1.70	39.0	1.1	1.9	7 179	9.8	5.1
Willcox	2 939	0.4	43.2	12.2	56.1	1.47	45.2	4.0	3.8	9 069	17.1	14.4
Williams (U)	3 443	4.1	7.9	12.6	79.4	0.91	29.4	6.9	16.7	7 567	6.7	6.7
Winslow	8 056	2.7	51.1	12.0	50.7	1.75	38.1	4.5	7.6	8 825	12.6	16.0
Yuma Station (U)	3 460	2.3	7.8	12.5	69.0	0.68	24.0	10.1	10.6	7 791	10.3	10.5

Table 44 Summary of Economic Characteristics by Counties: 1970

[Data based on sample, see text. For minimum base for derived figures (percent, median, etc.) and meaning of symbols, see text]

Counties	Nonworker-worker ratio	Percent in labor force					Civilian labor force—Percent unemployed	Employed persons			Worked during census week—Percent working outside county of residence	Persons who worked in 1969—Percent worked 50 to 52 weeks	Families		
		Female, 16 years and over	Married women, husband present		Male			Percent in manufacturing industries	Percent in white-collar occupations	Percent government workers			Median income (dollars)	Percent with income of—	
			Total	With own children under 6 years	18 to 24 years	65 years and over								Less than poverty level	$15,000 or more
The State	**1.62**	**39.0**	**36.3**	**27.8**	**73.9**	**19.1**	**4.2**	**15.6**	**51.2**	**18.9**	**2.9**	**54.1**	**9 187**	**11.5**	**18.6**
Apache	3.63	27.4	30.4	29.7	42.2	13.9	8.8	8.1	49.3	55.6	5.6	48.9	5 007	46.2	6.1
Cochise	1.61	33.5	30.5	22.6	85.7	20.2	5.1	11.0	48.0	31.1	3.0	59.9	8 333	13.4	14.7
Coconino	1.82	40.3	40.8	30.1	51.3	20.4	4.8	7.3	55.8	36.5	3.5	44.9	8 715	17.0	16.1
Gila	1.97	28.6	26.4	19.6	75.1	18.1	3.8	17.9	36.5	16.6	5.0	61.6	7 886	14.9	10.3
Graham	2.21	30.3	29.8	17.9	49.5	27.3	3.7	5.9	40.0	22.6	19.3	50.0	7 262	19.1	8.5
Greenlee	1.75	26.0	24.0	14.2	73.8	43.9	3.7	3.6	27.3	10.3	2.0	62.3	10 044	8.1	12.0
Maricopa	1.47	42.3	39.2	30.6	79.1	19.5	3.9	20.3	53.4	15.3	1.5	53.5	9 856	8.9	21.3
Mohave	1.67	34.7	32.8	27.3	84.3	17.1	6.3	8.7	40.7	16.4	12.5	51.6	9 241	9.7	15.6
Navajo	2.67	32.3	32.7	25.7	50.7	22.5	6.6	13.8	43.7	31.5	6.7	51.9	6 849	31.7	9.5
Pima	1.67	35.9	32.8	23.5	69.3	17.6	4.0	8.5	53.0	21.7	3.0	54.7	8 943	10.8	18.2
Pinal	2.14	32.3	30.8	25.4	57.4	21.1	5.0	10.2	32.3	19.1	10.7	55.9	7 935	17.4	11.6
Santa Cruz	1.99	34.5	28.5	23.4	71.1	28.4	3.7	5.4	54.4	20.4	6.4	62.8	7 948	20.0	17.1
Yavapai	1.92	32.4	31.6	25.3	69.8	14.5	4.3	9.4	44.2	19.9	6.1	55.0	7 405	14.6	10.6
Yuma	1.47	38.7	36.0	26.4	86.5	19.9	4.8	4.7	44.3	26.0	4.3	58.8	8 188	13.4	14.4

Table 8 Technique for Estimating Total and Per Capita Income Within the Willcox "Trade Area"

	Step 1						Step 2		Step 3
Year	December Electric Hook-ups For Trade Area				Willcox Trade Area Population		1974 Per Capita Income		Trade Area Income before Adjustment for Inflation
1974	3,145	X	3.37	=	10,599	X	$3,904	=	$41,378,500
1975	3,318	X	3.37	=	11,182	X	3,904	=	43,654,500
1976	3,340	X	3.37	=	11,256	X	3,904	=	43,943,400
1977	3,453	X	3.37	=	11,637	X	3,904	=	45,430,800
1978	3,569	X	3.37	=	12,028	X	3,904	=	46,957,300

Step 4				Step 5	Step 6		
GNP Deflator (1972 = 100)				Inflation Ratio	Trade Area Income Adjusted for Inflation	Per Capita Income	Year
116.20	÷	116.2	=	1.00	$41,378,500	$3,904	1974
126.37	÷	116.2	=	1.09	47,583,400	4,255	1975
133.76	÷	116.2	=	1.15	50,534,900	4,490	1976
141.61	÷	116.2	=	1.22	55,425,600	4,763	1977
152.09	÷	116.2	=	1.31	61,514,100	5,142	1978

Step 6. Multiply (a) the base year income figure derived in Step 3 by (b) the inflation ratio derived in Step 5. The resulting figure is an estimate of the combined personal income of all families residing within your town's "trade area." Per capita income can be derived by dividing this aggregate figure by your trade area population.

Your local Extension Community Development Specialist can assist you in making these calculations.

Practical Application of Data. Personal income figures can be used to describe the "potential" purchasing power of your town's "trade area." When the current "trade area" population is multiplied by current per capita income, the result is a figure that represents a dollar flow potential for the area. Of course, a portion of this total income estimate will go into savings, taxes, and social security and retirement programs. The portion of total personal income which is in turn available for consumption will vary widely between families. Research would indicate that the average family spends 65 to 80 percent of their total personal income on personal consumption, approximately 25 percent of which goes for housing.[1] Thus for the case community of Willcox, it can be estimated for 1978 that 70 percent of the "trade area's" $61,514,100 personal income, or $43,059,900 is spent on consumption. When this figure is compared with the $20,028,900, Wilcox's total taxable sales in 1978 as derived from sales tax collections, it can be estimated that less than half of the purchases made by "trade area" residents are purchased in Willcox. While the above comparisons are very rough approximations, they do provide some indication of the potential purchasing power of your town's trade area.

Another important indicator derived from personal income is the number of families within your town with incomes below the poverty level. If your town has a higher percentage of low income families than the state average, you will have a better chance of qualifying for state and federal economic development assistance. This statistic is obtained from the Bureau of the Census publication "19__ Census of Population: General Social and Economic Characteristics," Tables 41, 42, and 44, Summary of Social and Economic Characteristics, under the column titled Families, Percent with Income of Less than Poverty Level. (See Table 42 for example.)

[1]Source: Typical family budgets for towns of 2,500 to 50,000 in the western states, "Autumn 1977 Family Budgets and Comparative Indexes for Selected Areas," News, April 26, 1978, United States Department of Labor, Bureau of Labor Statistics.

MICHIGAN

Michigan Office of Intergovernmental Relations and Department of Management and Budget, _Michigan Community Indicators, Volume A; Composite,_ 1980, pp. 1, 3-8, 12.

The Method and Use of _Michigan Community Indicators_

The present collection of _Michigan Community Indicators_ encompasses all of Michigan's counties, cities, and townships. The specific data selected for inclusion have been chosen for their value--and common use--in comparing socioeconomic conditions of communities. Availability of pertinent data on a uniform basis is also an important consideration. The data selected are of a type that lend themselves to annual revision; therefore, maintenance of these indicators is an ongoing process in an effort to keep them as current and meaningful as possible.

The seven principal indicators used by the Office of Intergovernmental Relations (OIR) are together a combination of rather different factors that yield a generalized measure of "distress." These seven factors, or indicators, are mathematically combined in a formula which, generally speaking, compares need with ability to meet that need. The nature of the distress indicated is not very precise, though it may be justified as pointing to a financial problem.

For every set of governmental units, correlations were performed for each indicator and the need index. In a majority of the cases, strongest correlations were found among cities, followed by counties and townships respectively. Although none of the correlations approached +1 or -1, it can be said in general that correlative directions were established. For instance, per capita income, State Equalized Value (SEV) per capita, and SEV trend all follow a negative relationship with the need index. In other words, smaller values of these indicators are mutually related with larger values of need.

Positive correlation values were established between need and percent unemployment, percent in poverty, and pre-1940 housing, confirming what could be logically assumed: that higher values of these indicators are closely related with higher need index values.

The most significant correlations occurred between the need index and the "income" indicators, namely unemployment, per capita income, and percent in poverty. When these three indicators were cross-correlated, it was discovered that the strongest correlative relationships occurred in counties. Weaker relationships found in cities and townships could be explained by the nature of data collection at sub-county levels.

One should also be aware that absolute need indicators formula values have been suppressed in order to maintain an arbitrary range of values. This arbitrary suppression known as "normalization" yields values between 0.500 and 2.00. While the real rank order by need index is not altered, it should be kept in mind that these values have been "squeezed" together.

NOTES ON NEED INDEX OIR, 25 October 79

Formula employed is as follows:

$$\frac{(P_i/P) \times (U_i/U) \times (RTE_i/RTE) \times (H_i/H)}{(Y_i/Y) \times (SEV_{ci}/SEV_c) \times (SEV_{ti}/SEV_t)}$$

where: subscript "i" indicates a given unit's value which in turn is divided by the comparable state average value.

P = % families in poverty (1970, U.S. Census of Population)

U = % unemployed (1978 annual average, MESC)

RTE = relative tax effort (1978, derived from Michigan Tax Commission data)

H = housing structures built before 1940 (1970, U.S. Census)

Note: this element not used in county formula.

Y = per capita income (1975, U.S. Bureau of Census

SEV_c = SEV per capita (1976, OIR calculations from U.S. Bureau of Census and Michigan Tax Commission data)

SEV_t = SEV trend (% change, 1973-78, OIR calculation)

1. A larger need index value indicates greater need.
2. Rank order based on "worst first," i.e., a prior position (or a smaller rank order number) indicates greater need. This applies to both the need index and the individual distress indicators.
3. Need Index #1: includes Housing Indicator applied to cities
   Need Index #4: excludes Housing Indicator applied to counties

Selected Distress Indicators: Michigan Counties and Cities, October 1979

Notes on Calculations and Data Sources

Col. 1: Population

Source: United States Department of Commerce, Bureau of the Census, Current Population Reports, Michigan. Population Estimates and Projections. Series P-25, No. 761, January, 1979.

Data supplied by same source for the column on county report labeled 1970-1976 percent change in population.

Col. 2: Percent Unemployed

Source: Michigan Employment Security Commission, Civilian Labor Force and Wage and Salary Employment Estimates, Michigan: County, Multi-County, and Selected City and Townships.

Data shown for cities are annual average, 1978. Data shown for counties are annual average, 1978. Benchmark CPS 1977.

Data for labor market areas apportioned to individual counties by standard MESC methodology.

Col 3: Per Capita Income

Source: Current Population Reports. 1976 Population Estmates and 1975 Per Capita Income Estimates for Counties, Incorporated Places, and Selected Minor Civil Divisions in Michigan. Series P-25, No. 761, January, 1979.

Col. 4: Percent Families in Poverty

Source: U.S. Census of Population, 1970, General Social and Economic Characteristics: Michigan. PC(1)-C24. U.S. Department of Commerce, Bureau of Census.

Data show percent of families with family income less than poverty level in 1969.

Col. 5: SEV Per Capita

Source: SEV (State Equalized Value): Michigan State Tax Commission, Average Tax Rate Data. Population: Current Population Reports. U.S. Department of Commerce, Bureau of Census. Series P-25, No. 761, January, 1979.

Data shown are 1976 total SEV by county/city divided by estimated population as of 1 July 1976.

Col. 6: SEV Trend
Source: Michigan State Tax Commission, Average Tax Rate Data.
Data depict the percent increase in total SEV by county/city from 1973 to 1978. After 1975, business inventory values were removed from the SEV base. To make 1973 and 1978 SEV data reasonably comparable, the 1975 inventory SEV was added to the total SEV for 1978.

Col. 7: Relative Tax Effort
Source: Michigan State Tax Commission.
Data for 1976 show the dollar sum of county and local government property tax collections per $1,000 of State Equalized Value of taxable property.

Col. 8: Housing: Percent pre-1940.
Source: U.S. Census of Housing, 1970, Detailed Housing Characteristics: Michigan. HC(1)-B24. U.S. Department of Commerce, Bureau of Census.
Data show the percent share of total housing stock constructed prior to 1940.

Caution should be exercised when evaluating any given community solely on the basis of its rank order position. This is mentioned because in every case (counties, cities, and especially townships) when two units have the same indicator value, their rank in that instance is determined on a code number basis.

Michigan Community Indicators is not intended to be the sole determining factor in targeting assistance. Rather, this collection is intended to help determine which communities are in a state of relative distress. This collection should be used with a clear understanding of their limitations and an understanding of the purpose for which they are used. As mentioned above, this collection would be most pertinent when determining a generalized measure of financially oriented distress. It is entirely possible that a completely different set of indicators would be more appropriate for determining levels of distress in other areas, e.g, social conditions. Perhaps more important than the specific data found in this collection is the concept which has been developed. A "need index" is developed by combining a selected group of variables into a formula, into which data are inserted to produce an index score expressing distress level for the area being evaluated. Need indexes have the potential to be an effective method of evaluating distress since any existing difference in data value is incorporated into the index and since multiple dimensions of distress are taken into account.

Michigan Counties: Distress Indicators by Individual Indicator

			NEED INDEX #4				NEED INDEX #4
1	17000	CHIPPEWA	1.769	46	74000	ST CLAIR	0.963
2	31000	HOUGHTON	1.758	47	11000	BERRIEN	0.963
3	16000	CHEBOYGAN	1.605	48	10000	BENZIE	0.962
4	42000	KEWEENAW	1.480	49	78000	SHIAWASSEE	0.962
5	48000	LUCE	1.389	50	06000	ARENAC	0.958
6	66000	ONTONAGON	1.350	51	38000	JACKSON	0.950
7	27000	GOGEBIC	1.349	52	60000	MONTMORENCY	0.949
8	77000	SCHOOLCRAFT	1.332	53	54000	MECOSTA	0.944
9	07000	BARAGA	1.312	54	43000	LAKE	0.936
10	64000	OCEANA	1.272	55	12000	BRANCH	0.928
11	82000	WAYNE	1.243	56	39000	KALAMAZOO	0.906
12	68000	OSCODA	1.241	57	41000	KENT	0.896
13	21000	DELTA	1.241	58	46000	LENAWEE	0.895
14	59000	MONTCALM	1.221	59	20000	CRAWFORD	0.889
15	04000	ALPENA	1.197	60	75000	ST JOSEPH	0.888
16	65000	OGEMAW	1.147	61	79000	TUSCOLA	0.874
17	18000	CLARE	1.145	62	14000	CASS	0.873
18	62000	NEWAYGO	1.131	63	30000	HILLSDALE	0.862
19	71000	PRESQUE ISLE	1.129	64	81000	WASHTENAW	0.849
20	29000	GRATIOT	1.128	65	44000	LAPEER	0.837
21	61000	MUSKEGON	1.126	66	52000	MARQUETTE	0.819
22	83000	WEXFORD	1.125	67	05000	ANTRIM	0.800
23	02000	ALGER	1.119	68	67000	OSCEOLA	0.798
24	36000	IRON	1.110	69	23000	EATON	0.796
25	35000	IOSCO	1.099	70	32000	HURON	0.795
26	40000	KALKASKA	1.092	71	19000	CLINTON	0.794
27	22000	DICKINSON	1.060	72	09000	BAY	0.786
28	57000	MISSAUKEE	1.053	73	70000	OTTAWA	0.775
29	25000	GENESEE	1.046	74	50000	MACOMB	0.769
30	72000	ROSCOMMON	1.040	75	24000	EMMET	0.755
31	80000	VAN BUREN	1.033	76	58000	MONROE	0.746
32	33000	INGHAM	1.030	77	63000	OAKLAND	0.719
33	55000	MENOMINEE	1.026	78	28000	GD TRAVERSE	0.689
34	26000	GLADWIN	1.026	79	47000	LIVINGSTON	0.685
35	37000	ISABELLA	1.024	80	69000	OTSEGO	0.645
36	49000	MACKINAC	1.022	81	53000	MASON	0.638
37	34000	IONIA	1.020	82	45000	LEELANAU	0.576
38	13000	CALHOUN	1.011	83	56000	MIDLAND	0.572
39	51000	MANISTEE	1.007				
40	76000	SANILAC	0.992				
41	03000	ALLEGAN	0.988				
42	15000	CHARLEVOIX	0.975				
43	73000	SAGINAW	0.975				
44	08000	BARRY	0.970				
45	01000	ALCONA	0.969				

*The Need Index employed for all three sets of governmental units was exactly the same, with one exception. The indicator of housing age is most applicable in urban areas or at least in units having more or less similar urban or rural conditions. Due to the variance of urban vs. rural conditions in counties across the board, it was decided that pre-1940 housing may be misleading.

Bibliography: Economic Development

Greene, Alabama. Greene County Rural Resource Development Committee, "Greene County, Alabama, Overall Economic Development Program, Progress Report 1979" (10 pgs.).

Henry, Alabama. Southeast Alabama Regional Planning and Development Commission, Overall Economic Development Program: Southeast Alabama Economic Development District, 1977 (253 pgs.).

Limestone, Alabama. Athens-Limestone County Chamber of Commerce, Inc., "Information for Industrial Development" (brochure).

Top of Alabama Regional Council of Governments, Economic Atlas-1979, 1978 (231 pgs.).

Tallapoosa, Alabama. East Alabama Regional Planning and Development Commission, Tallapoosa County Overall Economic Development Program, 1977 (38 pgs.).

Fairbanks, Alaska. Fairbanks Town and Village Association for Development, Inc.: The Overall Economic Development Program for Fairbanks and the Interior of Alaska, 1979 (68 pgs.).

_______, A Report of the Upper Tanana Regional Forum on the Impact of Construction and Operation of the Alcan Gas Pipeline, 1979 (64 pgs.).

Coconino, Arizona. Coconino County Community Development Department, Coconino County Overall Economic Development Plan, 1979 (241 pgs.).

Graham, Arizona. Dunn, Douglas and Cox, Douglas. Cooperative Extension Service, University of Arizona, Socio-Economic Indicators for Small Towns, 1979 (43 pgs.).

_______, Marketing the Small Town, 1979 (31 pgs.).

_______, "Discussion Paper on the Need for Community-Oriented Economic Planning Assistance to Arizona's Non-Metropolitan Communities" (9 pgs.).

Citizens Advisory Planning Committee, "Citizens Task Force on Industry/Employment: A Report to the City Council of Safford," 1978 (8 pgs.).

Cooperative Extension Service, University of Arizona, "Title V Proposal: Impact of Agriculture on the Graham County Economy" (1 pg.).

_______, "Market Analysis of the Safford Trade Area" (5 pgs.).

Ashley, Arkansas. County Extension Service, "Labor Survey of High School Students," 1977 (1 pg.).

Amador, California. Merced County Overall Economic Development Commission, Overall Economic Development Program--Merced County, 1979 (71 pgs.).

Shasta, California. Economic Development Corporation of Shasta County, Business and Industrial Directory for Shasta County, 1979 (77 pgs.).

_______, "Community Economic Profile for Shasta County, California" (4 pgs.).

Overall Economic Development Program Committee, Shasta County Overall Economic Development Program, 1979 (79 pgs.).

Kit Carson, Colorado. Colorado Division of Planning: "Eastern Plains material to be included in Vol. 2 of From Bonanza to Last Chance: Changing Economic Expectations in Colorado," 1978 (20 pgs.).

_______, "Colorado Economic Development Issues Regional Analysis: East Central," 1977 (21 pgs.).

Colorado East Central Council of Governments: Tourism Feasibility Study, 1980 (169 pgs.).

Delaware. State of Delaware, "Delaware Rural Economic Development Strategy: Objectives and Need for This Assistance" (9 pgs.).

Georgia. Georgia Department of Labor, "Civilian Labor Force Estimates," 1980 (12 pgs.).

Berrien, Brooks, Clay, Dooly, Echols, Seminole, Taylor, Terrell, and Webster, Georgia. Coastal Plain Area Planning and Development Commission, "Vegetable Processing Opportunities in Southwest Georgia," 1978 (25 pgs.).

Clay, Georgia. Glover, Robert S. (University of Georgia Extension), "Economic and Marketing Considerations for a Grain Elevator Export Facility at Fort Gaines, Georgia," approx. 1979 (30 pgs.).

Dade, Georgia. Dade County, "Dade County Industrial Park Feasibility Study" (application to Appalachian Regional Commission) 1978 (24 pgs.).

Community Economics Projects Group, "Dade County, Georgia, Labor Market Area," 1979 (17 pgs.).

Georgia Department of Industry and Trade, "Economic Development Profile: Dade County, Georgia," approx. 1978 (6 pgs.).

Elbert, Georgia. Northeast Georgia Area Planning and Development Commission, Northeast Georgia Regional Public Investment Program, 1979 (40 pgs.).

Glascock, Georgia. Glascock County, application to the Association of County Commissioners of Georgia to be selected as one of the pilot counties for the Task Force for Economic Development, 1979 (2 pgs.).

Telfair, Georgia. Georgia Department of Industry and Trade, "Economic Development Profile: Telfair County, Georgia," approx. 1979 (6 pgs.).

Seminole and Terrell, Georgia. Southeast Georgia Planning and Development Commission, Overall Economic Development Program (2 vols.), 1980 (358 pgs.).

Idaho. Idaho Division of Budget, Policy Planning, and Coordination, Attitudes Toward Population Growth and Economic Development in Idaho, 1978 (37 pgs.).

_______, Economic Development Activities on Indian Reservations in Idaho, 1979 (25 pgs.).

Idaho Division of Economic and Community Affairs, Bureau of Economic Resources and Community Affairs, Growth Strategies for Idaho: Goals and Objectives, 1980 (28 pgs.).

Idaho Division of Tourism and Industrial Development, Incredible Idaho, A Land for All Seasons, Vol. 7, No. 4 (Spring 1976). Special Issue, "Idaho's Tomorrow" (36 pgs.).

Latah, Idaho. Clearwater Economic Development Association, Overall Economic Development Plan, 1979 (136 pgs.).

Christian, Illinois. West Central Illinois Valley Regional Planning Commission, Population and Economic Analysis, 1978 (124 pgs.).

Benton, Indiana. Cooperative Extension Service, Purdue University, "Attitudes toward Jobs and Industry" (10 pgs.).

_______, "Population and Economic Statistics for Benton County" (5 pgs.).

Cass, Indiana. Industrial Park Study Committee, "Final Report" (to County Commissioners), 1980 (13 pgs.).
Indiana Department of Commerce, "Handbook for Local Industrial Development" (18 pgs.).

Jasper, Indiana. Kankakee-Iroquois Regional Planning Commission, Overall Economic Development, 1979 (85 pgs.).

Lawrence, Indiana. City of Mitchell, Indiana, "Proposal to HUD (UDAG) for development of industrial park for joint venture sawmill and process timber industry and metal manufacturing firm," 1978 (67 pgs.).

Spencer, Indiana. Pond, Martin T., and R. Rodman Ludlow, "An Employer Program to Improve Career Orientations of High School Students," approx. 1975 (15 pgs.).
Cooperative Extension Service, Purdue University, "Report on Impact on Study" (results of a survey about impact of new employer), 1979 (9 pgs.).

Butler, Iowa. Northland Regional Council of Governments, Overall Economic Development Program, 1980 (106 pgs.).

Winneshiek, Iowa. Upper Explorerland Regional Planning Commission, "Winneshiek County: The Area and its Economy" (23 pgs.).

Pawnee, Kansas. Pawnee County Extension Office, "Market Swine Survey," 1980 (4 pgs.).

Bath, Kentucky. Kentucky Department of Commerce, Industrial Resources: Owingsville (33 pgs.).

Fulton and Marshall, Kentucky. Sears, Gilbert (Area Extension Specialist in Community Resource Development, University of Kentucky College of Agriculture), "Purchase Area Agriculture 1978 - Estimated Production Data and Estimated Product Value Data" (36 pgs.).

Marshall, Kentucky. Sears, Gilbert (Rural Development Specialist, University of Kentucky College of Agriculture), "A Partial Analysis to Determine the Economic Impact of Abandoning the Louisville and Nashville Rail Line from Paducah, Kentucky to a Point North of Murray, Kentucky" (14 pgs.).

Tensas, Louisiana. North Delta Regional Planning and Development District, Inc., Overall Economic Development Plan Update FY 79 (70 pgs.).

Dickinson, Michigan. Central Upper Peninsula Planning and Development Regional Commission, "Dickinson County Economy" (16 pgs.).

Michigan. Michigan Office of Intergovernmental Relations and Department of Management and Budget, Michigan Community Indicators, Volume A: Composite, 1980.

Huron, Michigan. Huron County Board of Commissioners, Huron County Overall Economic Development Plan, 1978 (134 pgs.).
East Central Michigan Planning and Development Region, Overall Economic Development Program, Huron County, 1979 (30 pgs.).

Ionia, Michigan. Ionia County Planning Commission, Ionia County Overall Economic Development Program, Spring 1977 (81 pgs.).

Ionia, Newaygo, and Osceola, Michigan. West Michigan Regional Planning Commission, Overall Economic Development Program, 1977 (242 pgs.).

Montmorency, Michigan. Montmorency County Board of Commissioners, "Addendum to 1976 Montmorency County Overall Economic Development Plan," 1977 (10 pgs.).

Saginaw, Michigan. Overall Economic Development Committee, Overall Economic Development Program for Saginaw County, 1976 (86 pgs.).

Saginaw County Planning Commission, "Annual Update, Overall Economic Development Program for Saginaw County, June 1979" (4 pgs.).

Minnesota. Dorf, Ronald J., Thomas P. Jorgens, and Gordon D. Rose (Agricultural Extension Service, University of Minnesota), "The Fiscal Impact of Federal and State Waterfowl Production Areas on Local Units of Government in West Central Minnesota," 1979 (10 pgs.).

Becker, Pope, Stevens, and Traverse, Minnesota. Minnesota Agricultural Extension Service, Proposal to Upper Great Lakes Regional Commission for a sawmill technician, 1979 (8 pgs.).

_______, "Sawmill Owner/Operators Increase Your Profits: Become a Cooperator in the New Sawmill Assistance Program" (brochure).

North Central Minnesota Forestry Development Committee, Proposal to Minnesota Rural Development Council for sawmill technician and forest industry coordinator representative, 1979 (7 pgs.).

West Central Regional Development Commission, Annual Overall Economic Development Program Report, 1979 (174 pgs.).

_______, Manpower Data File 1979 (142 pgs.).

Jackson, Pipestone, and Rock, Minnesota. Southwest Regional Development Commission, Region 8 Employment and Training Plan, 1980 (57 pgs.).

Lake, Minnesota. Agricultural Extension Service, University of Minnesota, A Needs Assessment of Tourism Firms Serving the Boundary Waters Canoe Area Wilderness Vicinity, Oct. 1979 (44 pgs.).

Arrowhead Regional Development Commission, Overall Economic Development Guide for the Arrowhead Region, 1975 (235 pgs.).

Red Lake, Minnesota. Red Lake County, "Red Lake County OEDP Annual Report and Update," 1979 (16 pgs.).

Jackson, Mississippi. DOD, President's Economic Adjustment Committee, Economic Adjustment Program: Federal Team Visit Report: Jackson County, Mississippi, 1979 (157 pgs.).

Southern Mississippi Planning and Development District, "Agri-Business Development Assistance Program" (1 pg.).

Missouri. Economic Research Service, USDA, and University of Missouri Agricultural Experiment Station, New Manufacturing Plants in the Nonmetro Ozarks Region, 1977 (33 pgs.).

Kuehn, John A., Curtis Braschler, and J. Scott Shonkwiler, "Rural Industrialization and Community Action: New Plant Locations Among Missouri's Small Towns," Journal of the Community Development Society, Vol. 10, No. 1 (Spring 1979) (13 pgs.).

Caldwell, Missouri. Green Hills Regional Planning Commission, Overall Economic Development Program, 1980 (18-pg. excerpt).

Carter, Missouri. Ozark Foothills Regional Planning Commission, Overall Economic Development Program, Phase III, 1976 (66 pgs.).

Jasper, Missouri. Ozark Gateway Council of Governments, Jasper County, Missouri Overall Economic Development Plan, 1977 (56 pgs.).

_______, "Jasper County Missouri Overall Economic Development Plan Annual Update," 1979 (8 pgs.).

Lawrence, Missouri. Lawrence County Court, Lawrence County Overall Economic Development Program, 1977 (27 pgs.).

New Madrid, Missouri. Bootheel Regional Planning Commission, Revised Overall Economic Development Program 1979 (138 pgs.).

Colfax, New Mexico. North Central New Mexico Economic Development District, Regional Development Plan for the North Central New Mexico Economic Development District, 1977 (312 pgs.).

______, Regional Development Plan for the North Central New Mexico Economic Development District, revised 1978 (345 pgs.).

Harding, New Mexico. Eastern Plains Council of Governments, Initial Overall Economic Development Program 1977 (71-pg. excerpt).

______, Carbon Dioxide Development in Northeastern New Mexico: An Interim Report (33 pgs.).

Broome, New York. Broome County Planning Department, Broome County Overall Economic Development Program, 1978 (194 pgs.).

Southern Tier East Regional Planning and Development Board, Economic Viability of the Farming Industry in the Southern Tier East Region, 1979 (67 pgs.).

North Carolina. Fearn, Robert M., Paul S. Stone, and Steven G. Allen, Department of Economics and Business, North Carolina State University, Employment and Wage Changes in North Carolina, Economics Information Report No. 60, 1980 (38 pgs.).

Governor's Advisory Task Force on Wood Lot Management, "Recommendations to Increase the Productivity of Small Wood Lots in North Carolina," 1978 (10 pgs.).

North Carolina Agricultural Extension Service, "Employment and Wage Changes in North Carolina," Tar Heel Economist, November 1979 (4 pgs.).

______, State Task Force on Rural Energy and North Carolina Rural Development Committee, North Carolina Energy Handbook, 1979 (30 pgs.).

North Carolina Agricultural Extension Service and Center for Rural Resource Development, Exploratory Analysis of the Market Potential for Native Woody Ornamentals, Report No. 12, 1978 (81 pgs.).

Cavalier and Towner, North Dakota. North Central Planning Council, Comprehensive Plan, Vol. II: Overall Economic Development Program, 1977 (195 pgs.).

Greer, Oklahoma. Greer County Commissioners, An Overall Economic Development Program for Greer County, 1972 (51 pgs.).

Indiana, Pennsylvania. Pennsylvania State Extension Service, "FY 77 Plan of Work, Title V, Rural Development Act of 1972, Socioeconomic Development in Rural Pennsylvania FY 77-79: Phase II" (9 pgs.).

Oconee and Spartanburg, South Carolina. South Carolina Appalachian Council of Governments, Appalachian Regional Investment Strategies, 1980 (61 pgs.).

Bedford, Tennessee. "Charter of Incorporation of Tennessee Trails "(a non-profit corporation to promote economic development in south central Tennessee) (3 pgs.).

Tenco Developments, Inc. "Bedford County Industrial Development Expansion Program (Application to FmHA for Community Economic Development Grant), 1979 (46 pgs.).

Shelby, Tennessee. Memphis and Shelby County Office of Planning and Development, Memphis Economy 2000, 1979 (28 pgs.).

Bastrop, Texas. Bastrop County OEDP Committee, Bastrop County Overall Economic Development Program, 1976 (50 pgs.).

Duval, Texas. Coastal Bend Council of Governments, Overall Economic Development Program, Final Report, 1977 (228 pgs.).

______, 1979-80 Annual Overall Economic Program Update (30 pgs.).

Floyd, Texas. South Plains Association of Governments, Overall Economic Development Program: Floyd County, 1973, revised 1977 (103 pgs.).

Cache, Utah. Bear River Association of Governments, Bear River District Overall Economic Development Plan, 1979 (98 pgs.).

Carbon, Utah. Southeastern Utah Association of Governments, "Socio-Economic Impacts of Energy Development in Southeastern Utah" (9 pgs.).

Southeastern Utah Association of Governments and Economic Development District, Four Corners Regional Commission, Southeastern Utah Regional Report and Investment Strategy 1979 (129 pgs.).

Southeastern Utah Economic Development District, Overall Economic Program 1979 (93 pgs.).

Vermont. State Planning Office, Economic Development Policies and Strategies for Vermont, 1979 (23 pgs.).

Henry, Virginia. West Piedmont Planning District Commission, An Economic Analysis for Development of the Counties, Cities and Towns of the West Piedmont Planning District, 1975 (70 pgs.).

Henry County and the City of Martinsville, Overall Economic Development Program, 1977 (34-pg. excerpt).

Lee, Virginia. Lenowisco Planning District Commission, Areawide Action Program-Overall Economic Development Program (Revised), 1979 (141 pgs.).

Mecklenburg, Virginia. Southside Planning District Commission, Economic Development in the Lake Gaston Area, 1979 (83 pgs.).

______, District Trends, Vol. 2, No. 1, February 1980: Quarterly Report on Economic and Social Trends (10 pgs.).

Kittitas, Washington. Kittitas-Yakima Resource Conservation and Economic Development District, Overall Economic Development Program 1980 (256 pgs.).

Eau Claire, Wisconsin. West Central Wisconsin Regional Planning Commission, District Overall Economic Development Program for the West Central Wisconsin Region: Initial Stage, 1978 (230 pgs.).

Iowa, Wisconsin. Iowa County Overall Economic Development Committee and Southwestern Wisconsin Regional Planning Commission, Iowa County Overall Economic Development Program, 1977 (109 pgs.).

Marquette and Waushara, Wisconsin. East Central Wisconsin Regional Planning Commission, A Strategy for Economic Development, 1979 (25 pgs.).

HOUSING

Most housing plans are financed by HUD. They generally include information on these topics: housing conditions and status; recent housing trends; housing starts; mobile homes; calculations of future housing demand and housing assistance needs; identification of low-income, minority, and elderly households; local housing regulations; and federal housing programs.

The first example of housing plan data, from west central Illinois, illustrates the types of housing data that can be used to make population estimates, e.g., building permits and water meter hookups.

The second example describes and presents some results from a housing survey done in Teton County, Wyoming. Apartment, condominium, and mobile home dwellers are compared.

The third example, from Iowa, explains a procedure used to compute and update a housing needs index. The index takes into account both poor housing and low-income population.

The next example, also from Iowa, presents in graphic form the results of a local housing condition survey.

The last example, from Lowndes County, Alabama, is also a calculation of the demand for assisted housing. The demand is broken down by minority, elderly, and household size.

CHRISTIAN, ILLINOIS

West Central Illinois Valley Regional Planning Commission, Summary Housing Assistance Plan, 1979, pp. 17-20.

Housing Construction Since 1970

A survey of available building permit data has been compiled and appears on Table 11. Information was available for Christian and Calhoun counties, Jerseyville, Pana, Taylorville, and Brighton, with the best information received from Christian County and Jerseyville. Information regarding new water hookups had also been obtained from several municipalities and appears on Table 12. Other information concerning population growth and new housing construction was obtained by visual survey. In addition, public housing construction since 1970 has also been surveyed, with tabulation for each county appearing in Table 13.

The above referenced data were then used to prepare the Regional Planning Commission (RPC) population estimates for the six-county area. Since the building permit data were minimal for large areas of the region, these estimates may not be too accurate. To contrast, however, this is the best method available due to time and financial constraints.

Table 11 Building Permit Data for Housing Constructions or Improvements, 1970-1978

City or County	Years Covered	Single Family Homes	Multi-Family Homes	Demolitions (estimated)	New Mobile Homes	Rehabilitations	Total New Housing Units
Calhoun County	75-78	85	0	15 per year	80	0	160
Taylorville	75-78	150	133	10 per year	0	18	283
Pana	70-78	90	51	13	32	23	173
Christian County balance*	70-78	668	49	140	342	38	1,059
Jerseyville	70-78	160	82	30	32	63	274
Brighton Township and areas within 1/2 mile in Macoupin County	72-78	90	41	30	25	0	156

*Includes all rural areas of the County and all municipalities except Bulpitt, Edinburg, Kincaid, Mt. Auburn, Pana, Palmer, Stonington, Taylorville and Tovey.

Table 12 Municipal Water Meter Information

Area	New Residential Hookups Since 1970	Estimated Population Increase
Carlinville[1]	300	815
Hillsboro[2]	215	574
Litchfield[3]	200	503
Girard[4]	135	358
Stauton[5]	10	4
Carrollton[6]	48	119

Notes:

[1]Approximately 90 percent of the new water connections to the Carlinville system were in Carlinville Township, with the remaining 10 percent being in Brushy Mound Township. In addition, there were approximately 10 new homes built in the Township.

[2]These hookups were all within the city limits of Hillsboro and do not include growth which has occurred in Taylor Springs, Schramm City, or in outlying areas of Hillsboro Township. Twelve of the hookups were multi-family units.

[3]Of the 200 new hookups, all were within the city limits of Litchfield, with 60 percent being in North Litchfield Township and 40 percent in South Litchfield Township. Eight of these hookups were to new multi-family units.

[4]Almost all of the new hookups for Girard were within the city limits.

[5]Staunton has had relatively little growth in the number of water customers since 1970. However, there have been approximately 26 new homes built near the city limits in the last two years.

[6]Carrollton has had 48 new water customers since 1970, with 27 being single-family home and 21 being mobile homes. There have also been six demolitions.

Table 13 Public Housing Construction, 1970-1978

County	Elderly	Regular	Large	Total
Calhoun	0	0	0	0
Christian	124	8	0	132
Greene	50	0	0	50
Jersey	12	0	0	12
Macoupin	38	22	0	60
Montgomery	0	0	0	0
Region Total	224	30	0	254

TETON, WYOMING

Teton County Housing Committee, A Housing Study of Teton County, 1979, pp. 12-13, 28-29, 36-37.

As the Housing Committee began its work, it soon discovered that, although everyone was certain there was a housing "problem" and could point to some evidence of it, there were few reliable data to work with. Committee members reviewed available statistics from the State Department of Planning and Economic Development, the Census Bureau, county and town offices, the Federal Housing Administration and Farmers' Home Administration, local lending institutions and real estate offices. The information was either too specialized, or sketchy and inconsistent.

The committee thus recommended that a housing survey be undertaken. With assistance from the County Planning Office, a two-part study was designed. In June, the County Commission agreed to fund the survey, and work began almost immediately.

Methodology

Modeled after similar studies done in Texas and Oregon, the Teton County Housing Study inventories existing housing units, evaluated housing conditions, and obtained opinions of a sample of county residents about their housing situation. Under the direction of Sue Enger of the County Planning Office, a Condition Survey form and Personal Interview questionnaire were designed, with assistance and review by Dr. Clynn Phillips of the University of Wyoming and John Cummings, Housing Specialist with the State Department of Planning and Economic Development. Three interns were selected (one provided by the internship program at the University of Wyoming) and trained in surveying and interviewing techniques. The Housing Study itself was conducted from June through early September of 1978.

Housing Condition Survey. The survey team set out to inventory every identifiable housing unit in Teton County, to determine numbers and types of units, and to evaluate their conditions, based on external indicators. The surveyors rated six characteristics for each unit on a scale of one to seven, by comparing them with pictures which had already been rated by experts. Condition rated were roof, foundation, windows and trim, exterior walls, doors and trim, and porch and front entry way. Ratings were then combined for each unit to arrive at a composite rating for overall condition. A rating of 1-3.5 was considered sound; 3.6-4.9 was marginal; 5-7 was inadequate.

Personal Interviews. At approximately every twelfth unit, a personal interview was conducted to obtain information about the occupants, their housing situation, their housing preferences, and other data.

Comparisons

Apartment Dwellers. Apartment dwellers are young (83 percent of household heads under 34); have recently come to Teton County (75 percent within the last five years); pay excessive housing costs (47 percent pay more than 25 percent of income or are on the borderline); and tend to be in the middle income range (53 percent have annual incomes between $10,000 and $19,999, although another 16 percent have incomes below $5,000 annually). They are not as satisfied with their housing as others (only 57 percent say they are satisfied, and 59 percent are actively looking for new housing.

Comments. When asked for comments people talked about all phases of the housing situation: needs and problems, causes of problems, and possible solutions. The most frequently-made comments related to the high cost of housing and the need for lower prices, with many people citing especially the expensive rental housing. Many spoke of poor quality in the lower price ranges. Mobile homes were often mentioned as a solution to housing problems, but many people added that mobile home parks should be spacious, well-landscaped, and well-planned. Some said that the master plan densities caused high-priced housing; an equal number said the plan should be followed, while others said growth should be slowed and construction limited.

A summary of comments follows.

A Summary of Comments or Suggestions

Type of Comment	# of People Mentioning
General comments on housing:	
Housing (including rentals) too expensive	51
Land too expensive	16
Need low cost housing	22
Hard for young people	11
Shortage of housing	11
Low cost housing promised, but it turns into more expensive housing	11
Need more rental housing	5
Rental situation has improved	2
Jackson is becoming a typical resort (like Aspen)	2
Not much can be done; it can't get better	8
Need more housing for middle income people	5
Low-income people must live in Victor, camp out, etc.	5
Too much housing is for wealthy people	4
Not everyone can own a house	2

Type of Comment	# of People Mentioning
Sources of housing problems:	
Too much greed, slumlords taking advantage	10
Realtors inflate prices	2
Park Service is buying up housing units	3
Land costs are too high	16
Outsiders increase land costs	2
Property taxes are too high	2
Not much private land available	6
Solutions:	
May need federal subsidy	2
Keep government out, let private sector provide housing	4
County Commission should get involved	2
(See also comments on mobile homes, employee housing, planning and zoning)	
Quality of housing:	
Low cost housing too often low quality, more quality housing needed, building codes, some need renovation, etc.	18
Employee housing:	
Need cheaper housing for employees and working people	38
Need specified dorms for employees (hostels)	6
Employers should provide housing or pay toward housing	6
Wages and rents are out of balance	9
Mobile Homes:	
Mobile homes (or mobile home parks) are needed	17
Mobile home parks are needed, but must be landscaped, spacious, planned, etc.	22
Mobile homes should be allowed on individual lots	3
Mobile homes should be looked on more favorably, better than shacks, etc.	4
Mobile homes should be in mobile home parks	2
Make restrictions on mobile homes more lenient	3
Should be fewer mobile homes	5
Zoning and Planning:	
Need zoning and planning, follow the plan, don't allow haphazard building, consider environment, etc.	11
Master plan densities too restrictive, hurt housing	11
Stop or slow building, slow down growth, keep low densities	17
Dislike Horn Addition-type housing, lots too small, crowded together	8
Don't tell a person what he can do with his land	5

COMPARISONS: Apartment, Condominium, and Mobile Home Dwellers

	All Housing (294)	Apartments (36)	Condo-miniums (27)	Mobile Homes (44)
Age of Head of Household				
Under 34	47%	83%	59%	57%
35 - 50	27%	11%	26%	25%
51 - 64	14%	3%	11%	9%
65+	12%	3%	4%	9%
Length of Residence in County				
Under 1 year	12%	36%	31%	21%
1 - 4 years	28%	39%	42%	44%
5 - 9 years	23%	15%	12%	24%
10+ years	37%	9%	15%	12%
Income				
Under $5,000	8%	17%	--	15%
$ 5,000 - 9,000	19.5%	10%	20%	30%
$10,000 - 14,999	19.5%	23%	32%	27.5%
$15,000 - 19,999	17%	30%	8%	15%
$20,000 - 24,999	13%	10%	12%	10%
$25,000+	23%	10%	28%	2.5%
Own or Rent				
Rent	35%	100%	44%	32%
Own	65%	--	56%	68%
Average Monthly Housing Costs Including Utilities (for those reporting all costs)		$245	$370	$199
Renters		$245	$358	$233
Owners		N/A	$375	$187
Town		$238	$361	$186
County		$269	$377	$213
Paying Excessive Housing Costs (more than 25% of gross income)				
Yes	22%	40%	42%	19%
Borderline	9%	7%	8%	11%
Opinion on Costs				
Too High	30%	44%	52%	32%
Not too High	70%	56%	48%	68%
Satisfied with Present Housing				
Yes	77.5%	57%	73%	66%
No	22.5%	43%	27%	34%
Type of Housing Preferred				
House	94%	93%	92%	84%
Apartment	2%	7%	--	--
Mobile Home	3%	--	4%	16%
Condominium	1%	--	4%	--
Actively Looking for New Housing	28%	59%	38%	36%

Notes

1. Percentages are based on the number of actual responses received for each question. Since some of the base numbers are fairly small (e.g., condominium residents), some caution should be exercised in making broad generalizations.
2. Figures are rounded to the nearest percent or dollar.

BUTLER, IOWA

Iowa Northland Regional Council of Governments, Rural Housing Implementation Strategy, 1979, pp 30-36.

Element 1: 1970 Housing Needs Index

In assessing housing needs, it is necessary to begin with an estimate of inadequate housing units in 1970, the latest year for which accurate and reliable basic census data are available. In the 1970 census, the specific condition of a unit, i.e., sound, deteriorated, or dilapidated, was absorbed under plumbing data and used in this manner as a definition of a "substandard" unit. In the Waterloo metropolitan area, a windshield survey was also conducted in early 1970 and the number of units lacking plumbing as defined in the 1970 census was found extremely close to the total number of units not sound (i.e., sum of deteriorated and dilapidated units) as found by the windshield survey.

However, using only the substandard units proved to be too narrow a focus of housing need. In 1973, using original 1970 census data (15 percent to 20 percent samples), the Bureau of the Census prepared for HUD new measures of inadequate housing units, reflecting household characteristics as well as physical attributes of the unit. These special unpublished printouts provided cross tabulations (thus not counting a unit twice) of household size, race, income, tenure, and condition of housing for counties in Iowa. These indicators for housing deficiency are believed to correlate more closely with "inadequate" housing than any other data source available. The four variables used in cross tabulations to define "inadequate" housing are:

1. Units built prior to 1939 and valued at less than $7,500, except in a metropolitan area where a $10,000 value was used (the assumption here is that the older a unit the more likely it is to be physically deficient; however, since many 30-year old homes are adequate, value was cross tabulated with age to classify it as physically inadequate); and/or

2. Units lacking some or all plumbing facilities (those lacking hot piped water, a flush toilet, or a bath or a shower are viewed as physically inadequate); and/or

3. Units with more than 1.25 persons per room (overcrowding does not indicate physical inadequacy, but it does show that the spatial needs of a household are not being met); and/or

4. Households paying more than 25 percent of their gross income for rent (it is felt that households paying more than 25 percent of their gross income for rent are experiencing excessive housing costs). Although this variable does not directly relate to the physical aspects of housing need, it does pose a welfare problem and is used herewith to quantify housing needs. This variable is discussed later in the report in further detail.

A cross tabulation of these variables was done through state computer systems and was found that the INRCOG region has 7,622 inadequate owner-occupied houses or households in need and 6,361 inadequate renter-occupied units in 1970. This need is calculated on the assumption that all families below 80 percent of median income* are housed in inadequate quarters and need help. Others with over 80 percent of the median income live in inadequate units by choice.

The 80 percent figure corresponds with the income limits for the Section 8 Housing Assistance payment program administered by the Department of Housing and Urban Development and the programs of the Iowa Housing Finance Authority.

A further refinement of these criteria is made to include one person, nonelderly households which normally do not qualify for the housing programs currently in operation.

The cross tabulation of the four indicators of indequate housing units show breakdowns by household size and by income level. Thus, by cross-tabulating the indicators of inadequate housing with the income criteria above, it was found that the INRCOG region has 4,054** inadequate owner-occupied houses or households in need and 4,709** inadequate renter-occupied housing units in need of assistance. This is a total of 8,763 units or 12.97 percent of the total occupied housing stock in INRCOG's region in 1970.

Vacancy Rate Adjustment

The vacancy rates indicate the potential tightness in the housing market in a particular area. This is an important factor in establishing the exact housing need index for the area. An adequate reserve of vacant units is an element in providing additional choice and flexibility in the normal working of the housing market. An adequate vacancy rate was seen as 1 percent for owner units and 5 percent for rental units, as per the recommendation of HUD. With the recent cost of housing, rising interest rates, and tight mortgage funds, it would be prudent to assume that the above recommended adequate levels should be considered much more than adequate. An area with few vacant units does promote artificially inflated housing costs. On the other hand, high vacancy rates indicate that the housing is overbuilt and any additional housing and building activity will result in serious negative effects on the local housing market. Thus, a balance is extremely important in order to maintain a healthy housing market.

The 1970 census accounted for vacant units by county. These figures include units vacant for sale or units vacant for rent, specifically excluding vacant units that are uninhabitable, condemned, or about to be demolished.

---

*HUD guidelines and requirements for family eligibility for Section 8 housing assistance.

**These figures are developed by each county by county computer tabulations from the Iowa Office for Planning and Programming.

The vacancy rates vary by county in the INRCOG region, but by applying the overall adjustment for vacancy rates to the region's 1970 housing needs, need increases to 4,057 owner-occupied households, and the need decreases to 4,611 renter-occupied households, for a total housing needs index in 1970 of 8,668 households (refer to Table 11).

Element 2: Update Housing Needs Through 1982

Updating the 1970 housing needs index through 1982 requires two fundamental adjustments: (1) the increase in substandard housing units 1970-1982, and (2) the increase in low- and moderate-income households during the period of 1970-1982.

An estimate for substandard units in the 1970s was derived, based upon the data published in a report entitled "Plumbing Facilities and Estimates of Dilapidated Housing" by the Bureau of the Census in November 1973, which provides an inventory change on the structural condition of the units during 1960. It is assumed for purposes of this report that the changes in the housing stock of the 1970s will follow the pattern set in the 1960s.

The second element of updating the housing needs assessment through 1982 is the increase in low- and moderate-income households resulting from population growth or formation of extra households due to a decrease in the size of households. County population forecasts were made for the years 1980, 1990, and 2000 in the Land Use and Growth Policy Plan adopted by INRCOG and later approved by the Department of Housing and Urban Development on May 15, 1978. These figures are included in Appendix B of the A-HOP, and 1982 calculations for the total number of households are adopted from these figures for each one of the six counties in the INRCOG region, i.e., Black Hawk, Bremer, Butler, Buchanan, Chickasaw, and Grundy.

In converting the population forecasts into household estimates, consideration was given to the changing trends of household size, relationships of people housed in group quarters, current death and birth rates, and current figures on in- and out-migration. Also, any local policy in regard to aggressive or passive desire to grow on the part of local business leaders and county officials was duly considered. These projections were also coordinated with the land use policy committees in each of the six counties working on future land use policies for the state of Iowa.

To estimate the number of these new households that will likely be in need of housing assistance, it is assumed that households in need will represent the same proportion of total housing in 1982 as they did in 1970. The reason for making such an assumption is that while

---

Note: As a general state-wide and nation-wide trend, the percent of dilapidated units with all plumbing is increasing, while the percent of units lacking plumbing facilities is decreasing. At the "update housing needs" stage, data on the units receiving housing assistance are not considered yet. They will be considered later in the allocation plan.

Table 10 Increase of Households in Need*

County	Total Households 1980	Increase in Households 1970-1980	Percent of Households in Need 1970	Increase in Households in Need 1970-80
Black Hawk	49,385	7,872	15.3	1,204
Bremer	9,559	2,339	9.3	217
Buchanan	7,894	845	15.2	128
Butler	6,587	737	11.2	82
Chickasaw	5,419	627	12.9	81
Grundy	5,353	485	8.0	39

NOTE: Additional household need for 1970 through 1982 comes to a total of 2,101 households for INRCOG's region: Black Hawk, 1,445; Bremer, 260; Buchanan, 154; Butler, 98; Chickasa, 97; and Grundy, 47.

*This need factor was developed by the Office for Planning and Programming computer printouts.

Source: INRCOG Projections.

certain indicators of "inadequate" housing show a decrease in the incidence of inadequate housing (i.e., dilapidated units, units lacking plumbing, overcrowded units), other indicators show an increase (i.e., the number of households paying more than 25 percent of their income for rent). The following illustration from the Bureau of National Affairs indicates the above point as it was published in the May 31, 1976, issue of the Housing and Development Reporter.

Table 12 Incidence of Inadequate Housing

Characteristics	1950	1960	1970	1973	1974
Dilapidated	9.1%	4.3%	3.7%	NA	NA
Lacking Plumbing	34.0%	11.7%	5.1%	3.6%	3.2%
Overcrowded	15.8%	11.5%	8.0%	5.6%	5.3%
Rent-Income Ratio Over 25%	30.8%	35.3%	39.4%	40.9%	42.0%

Source: Bureau of National Affairs 1976 Report.

Table 11 Estimate of Housing Needs in Region 7 (INRCOG)

County	Inadequate Owner-Occupied Units in Need 1970	Owner Vacancy Adjustment	Inadequate Renter-Occupied Units in Need 1970	Rental Vacancy Adjustment	Units Becoming Inadequate 1970-1982	Increase in Households in Need 1970-1982*	Total Need in 1982
Black Hawk	2,149	2	3,443	(75)	192	1,445	7,156
Bremer	273	(1)	363	(6)	47	260	936
Buchanan	606	(1)	357	(8)	44	154	1,152
Butler	435	1	185	(5)	38	98	752
Chickasaw	386	3	196	(7)	34	97	709
Grundy	205	(1)	165	3	34	47	453

*INRCOG's Year 2000 Land Use Policies and Projections.

With the recent rapid increases in home values relative to incomes, this factor of ability of households to afford decent housing becomes a very crucial element. In fact, top economists of HUD have predicted that, "As we run out of dilapidated units to replace or repair, the rent-income standard is likely to emerge as the most significant indicator of housing deficiency for the U.S." And while the above table only reflects rental households paying more than 25 percent for housing costs, the data published on homeowners reflects similar trends and difficulty in obtaining decent housing at a reasonable cost.

Thus, the percentage of households in need of the total occupied housing stock in 1970 is multiplied by the increase in households from 1970-1982 (Table 11) to estimate the households in need of housing assistance from 1970-1982. This results in an additional 2,101 households in need of housing assistance by 1982 (see Table 11).

Using the components described in elements 1 and 2, the housing needs assessment can be summarized by the following equation:

Step 1: Inadequate units of low and moderate income people in 1970
± Vacancy adjustment
= Housing Need Index 1970

Step 2: Housing Need Index 1970
+ Increase in inadequate units 1970-1982
+ Increase in low and moderate income households
= Housing needs through 1982

Table 11 estimates housing needs by county for Region 7 through 1982.

BUTLER, IOWA

Iowa Northland Regional Council of Governments, Rural Housing Implementation Strategy, 1979, pp. D-1, D-2.

Region's Housing Condition

Based upon a Housing Condition Survey conducted throughout the region in 1975-1976, it was found that 90 to 95 percent of the non-SMSA counties' housing stock was in sound condition.

In the non-SMSA area the highest percent of substandard units was found in Chickasaw County, i.e., 9.9 percent of all units, and the lowest percent of substandard units was found in Grundy County, i.e., 4.4 percent of the housing stock.

Staff personnel from INRCOG, while conducting the housing survey, considered various building elements such as doors and windows, roofs, roof lines, chimneys, guttering, foundations, porches and exterior walls. These elements were recorded, mapped, and classified by housing condition. These housing conditions are: (1) sound, (2) deteriorating, and (3) dilapidated.

HOUSING CONDITIONS

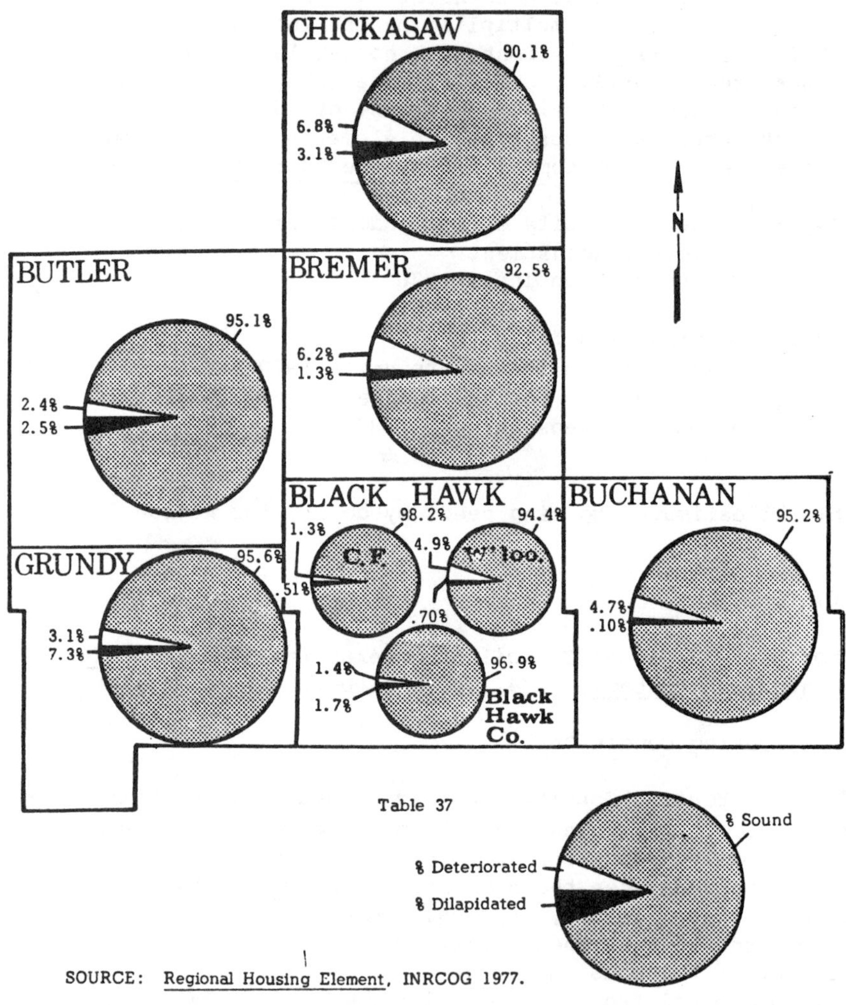

Table 37

SOURCE: Regional Housing Element, INRCOG 1977.

(1) Sound Housing - has no defects or only those which normally are corrected by regular maintenance. Examples include: lack of paint, slight damage to porch or steps, and chipping of mortar between bricks on walls and chimney;

(2) Deteriorating Housing - needs more repair than that provided by regular maintenance. The defects are of a nature that must be corrected soon if the unit is to continue providing a safe and adequate shelter. Examples include cracks and holes in foundations, missing or broken siding covering, broken and deteriorating doors and window casings, unsafe steps and porches, and damaged or missing roof covering;

(3) Dilapidated Housing - does not provide, in its present condition, safe and adequate shelter, and it endangers the health, safety, and well-being of occupants.

LOWNDES, ALABAMA

Consolidated Planning Services, Inc., Housing Plan, Lowndes, County, Alabama, April 1977, pp. 45-48.

Assisted Housing Demand

The demand for assisted housing is based on the estimated number of households whose incomes are less than 80 percent of the median county income adjusted to household size, the cutoff point for assistance under the U.S. Department of Housing and Urban Development's current major subsidy program, Section 8 Housing Assistance Payments Program. Calculations for assisted housing demand are based upon information compiled by HUD's Economic Market Analysis Division (EMAD) which cross-tabulated 1970 Census information to obtain housing unit occupancy characteristics. The information was tabulated separately for owner- and renter-occupied units. Cross-tabulations included tenure, household size, household income, age (elderly/non-elderly), and race of the head of household. This information was used to determine the proportion of households with incomes below 80 percent of the county median income as identifed in the 1970 Census (as adjusted for household size). These proportions were then applied to estimates of the number of 1977 households in Lowndes County fitting the chosen categories. The categories of assistance needs are elderly households, small households, and large households. In the incorporated areas, assistance needs were based on information on income groups obtained directly from the 1970 Census. The proportion calculated was applied to the estimated number of 1977 households and the number of households with incomes below 80 percent of the county median.

Calculations indicate that Lowndes County has approximately 1,484 households requiring assistance in the form of housing subsidies. Needed assistance occurs more in renter-occupied households, approximately 63 percent, as opposed to 37 percent for owner-occupied households. Just over half (806) of the households requiring assistance are elderly. Small households (four or fewer persons) comprise 22.9 percent of those needing assistance. These households

Table 19 Lowndes County Households Requiring Assistance, 1977

		Total Households			Minority Households		
		Total	Owner	Renter	Total	Owner	Renter
All Households Requiring Assistance	Total =	1,484	552	932	1,295	411	884
	% of all =	100%	37.2%	62.8%	100%	37.1%	68.4%
Elderly Households Requiring Assistance	Total =	806	341	465	678	241	437
	% of all =	54.3%	23.0%	31.3%	52.4%	18.6%	33.8%
Small Households Requiring Assistance[1]	Total =	340	131	209	280	91	189
	% of all =	22.9%	8.8%	14.1%	21.6%	7.0%	14.6%
Large Households Requiring Assistance[2]	Total =	338	80	258	337	79	258
	% of all	22.8%	5.4%	17.4%	26.0%	6.1%	19.9%
Percent of Countywide Households		43.2%	32.9%	62.8%	37.7%	24.4%	59.5%

[1]Small households are defined as those with four or fewer persons, not including elderly households.
[2]Large Households are defined as those with five or more persons, not including elderly households.

Source: Consolidated Planning Services, Inc., 1970 Census, and U.S. Dept. of HUD, EMAD Division.

Table 20 Total Households of Incorporated Areas Requiring Assistance, 1977

	Haynesville	Lowndesboro	Benton	Fort Deposit	Rural Balance
Total Households Requiring Assistance	59	28	33	179	1185
Percent of All Households Countywide Requiring Assistance	4.0	1.9	2.2	12.1	79.8
Percent of Total Households to Countywide	5.3	2.9	1.3	14.5	35.2

Source: Consolidated Planning Services, Inc., 1970 Census.

are in need of units with one to three bedrooms. Large households are those with more than four persons requiring more than three bedrooms. Approximately 338 large households are in need of assistance in the form of housing subsidies. County-wide, nearly half of all households appear to require housing assistance. More than 62 percent of all renter households and over 32 percent of all owner households are in need of assistance. The greatest single need for assistance is by Lowndes County's elderly households. Calculations are based on the 1970 median income of $3,823, 80 percent of which is $3,058 (with adjustments up or down by household size), as published by DHUD/EMAD, April 9, 1976. Lowndes County median income for 1976 was published at $5,700 by the same agency. However, the consultant is of the opinion that the higher median income reflects an upward shift of all incomes, and the category distributions remain the same as for 1970 census data.

Lowndes County's only low rent public housing is located in Fort Deposit and managed by the South Central Regional Housing Authority. While the needs of a small segment of the community's households requiring assistance are being met, there still remains a large number of households in need of but not receiving assistance.

Proportionally, housing assistance needs, while extensive countywide, are more extensive in rural areas of the county. Just under 80 percent of county households requiring assistance are located in rural areas. This comes as no surprise considering the fact that rural areas of the county have by far the highest proportion of substandard housing and lowest incomes. Throughout the county, elderly households are the segment of the county total most in need of immediate attention. Lowndes County households requiring assistance are indicated in Table 19. Incorporated area households requiring assistance are indicated in Table 20.

Bibliography: Housing

Alabama. Alabama Cooperative Extension Service, "Community Housing," 1980 (4 pgs.).

Limestone, Alabama. Top of Alabama Regional Council of Governments, TARCOG Regional Housing Plan, 1977 (157 pgs.).

Lowndes, Alabama. South Central Alabama Development Commission, Housing Market Analysis, Fort Deposit, Alabama, 1979 (60 pgs.).

_______, Housing Plan, Lowndes County, Alabama, 1977 (97 pgs.).

Litchfield, Connecticut. Northwestern Connecticut Regional Planning Agency, NWCRPA Regional Housing Policies Plan, 1977 (3 pgs.).

Sussex, Delaware. Delaware Cooperative Extension Service, "Single Purpose Small Cities CDBG Housing Assistance Plan Household Needs Field Survey" (7 pgs.).

Town of Bridgeville, Application to HUD (CDBG, Small Cities) for funds for community development project, housing code enforcement program, housing rehabilitation program, and recreational park for low-to-moderate income neighborhood, 1979 (43 pgs.).

Sussex, Delaware. Town of Milton, Delaware, Proposal to HUD, CDBG, Small Cities Program for money for rural rental housing and replacement of water valves, 1980 (30 pgs.).

Monroe, Florida. Monroe County Planning Department, Monroe County Housing Element, 1977 (104 pgs.).

Bacon, Georgia. Alma-Bacon County Community Development Agency, Application to HUD (CDBG) for funds for neighborhood revitalization, community-wide housing and community-wide public facilities and improvements, 1979 (62 pgs.).

_______, Application to HUD (CDBG) for funds for neighborhood revitalization, housing, community facilities and public improvements, and economic development, 1978 (42 pgs.).

City of Alma, Application to HUD (Small Cities Program) for funds for comprehensive three year program to provide housing and public facility improvements in a defined low income neighborhood, 1979 (49 pgs.).

_______, Application to HUD (CDBG-Small Cities) for funds for housing rehabilitation, 1980 (34 pgs.).

Elbert, Georgia. Northeast Georgia Area Planning and Development Commission, Northeast Georgia Areawide Housing Opportunity Plan, 1979 (110 pgs.).

_______, Northeast Georgia Areawide Housing Element, 1977 (pp. 137).

Taylor, Georgia. Taylor County, application to HUD (CDBG, small cities program) for housing assistance, 1978 (14 pgs.).

Illinois. Illinois Department of Local Government Affairs, County Household and Housing Profiles, 1979 (109 pgs.).

Christian, Illinois. West Central Illinois Valley Regional Planning Commission, Regional Policies Guide: Land Use Element and Housing Element, 1978 (189 pgs.).

_______, Summary Housing Assistance Plan, 1979 (94 pgs.).

Hancock, Illinois. Western Illinois Regional Council, Western Illinois Regional Housing Opportunity Plan, 1979 (139 pgs.).

Butler, Iowa. Iowa Northland Regional Council of Governments, Rural Housing Implementation Strategy, 1979 (114 pgs.).

_______, A Housing Opportunity Plan, 1979 (63 pgs.).

_______, Regional Housing Element, 1977 (107 pgs.).

Winneshiek, Iowa. Winneshiek County Board of Supervisors, "Proposal to HUD (Community Development Block Grants-Discretionary) for a housing rehabilitation program to serve low-income and handicapped persons and senior citizens" (4 pgs.).

Henry, Kentucky. Eminence, Kentucky, Housing Authority, "Proposal to HUD for low-income public housing project" (12 pgs.).

Washington, Maine. Washington County Regional Planning Commission, Housing Element of the Regional Comprehensive Plan, 1979 (68 pgs.).

Calvert, Maryland. Calvert County Planning Department, Calvert County Housing Survey: A Visual Survey of Housing and an Overview of Growth in Calvert County, Maryland, 1977 (58 pgs.).

Dickinson, Michigan. "Issues and Problems in Housing - Dickinson County," 1979 (3 pgs.).

Ionia, Newaygo, and Osceola, Michigan. West Michigan Regional Planning Commission, Regional Housing Plan, 1977 (77 pgs.).

Mower, Minnesota. Franklin, Daryl W., "Minnesota County Develops Subsidized Housing for Smaller Communities," Small Town, January 1979 (4 pgs.).

Caldwell, Missouri. Green Hills Regional Planning Commission, Green Hills Areawide Housing Opportunity Plan, 1979 (110 pgs.).

Carter, Missouri. Foothills Regional Planning Commission, Regional Housing Assistance Plan, Ozark Foothills Region, July 1978 (25 pgs.).

Schuyler, Missouri. Northeast Missouri Regional Planning Commission, Northeast Missouri Areawide Housing Opportunity Plan, 1979 (5 pgs.).

Cattaraugus, New York. Cattaraugus County Planning Board, Housing in Cattaraugus County: A Preliminary Overview, 1974 (55 pgs.).

_______, Housing in Cattaraugus County: Objectives and Activities, 1976 (68 pgs.).

North Carolina. Brooks, William J., Jr., et al. (North Carolina Agricultural Extension Service), Developing a Mobile Home Park or Subdivision, 1978 (32 pgs.).

Phillips, Joseph A., Daphne Webster, William J. Brooks, Jr.(North Carolina Agricultural Extension Service), Selecting and Developing a Lot for Your Mobile Home, 1978 (24 pgs.).

Stone, Paul S., William J. Brooks, Jr., and Hugh L. Liner, North Carolina Agricultural Extension Service, Comparative Costs of Mobile and Conventional Home Ownership, 1979 (31 pgs.).

Carteret, North Carolina. Collins, John N., and C. Paul Marsh, North Carolina Agricultural Extension Service, "Mobile Home Residents in North Carolina: A Socio-demographic Profile," 1979 (22 pgs.).

Harnett, North Carolina. Region "M" Council of Governments, Areawide Housing Opportunity Plan, 1979-1980 (90 pgs.).

Rutherford, North Carolina. Isothermal Planning and Development Commission, Regional Land Use and Housing Element 1978 (122 pgs.).

Ross, Ohio. Ross County-Chillicothe Planning Commission, Neighborhood Redevelopment and Conservation Plans, 1979 (96 pgs.).

_______, Housing Assistance Programs for Low and Moderate Income Persons in Ross County, 1980 (86 pgs.).

South Carolina. Office of the Governor, Division of Administration, South Carolina Housing Element, 1978 (130 pgs.).

McCormick, South Carolina. Upper Savannah Council of Governments Housing Implementation Plan: Strategies for Government: Part 6--McCormick County, 1978 (57 pgs.).

Custer, South Dakota. City of Custer, Application to HUD (CDBG) for funds for a comprehensive program aimed at conserving the housing stock, eliminating a public health threat, and renovating the infrastructure of an isolated low income neighborhood, 1979 (23 pgs.).

Benton, Tennessee. Northwest Tennessee Development District, Areawide Housing Opportunity Plan, 1979-1981 (140 pgs.).

Shelby, Tennessee. Memphis and Shelby County Office of Planning and Development, Memphis Housing 2000, 1979 (27 pgs.).

Cache, Utah. Bear River Association of Governments, Housing in Utah's Bear River District: Box Elder, Cache, and Rich County, 1978 (143 pgs.).

Charlotte, Virginia. Piedmont Planning District Commission, Housing Study District Housing Plan for Piedmont Planning District, 1977 (43 pgs.).

Henry, Virginia. West Piedmont Planning District Commission, Housing Needs and Opportunities in the West Piedmont Planning District, 1979 (225 pgs.).

King and Queen, Virginia. Middle Peninsula Planning District Commission, Housing Issues: Problems, Obstacles, Programs, 1977 (189 pgs.).

Mathews, Virginia. Middle Peninsula Planning District Commission, Housing Issues: Problems, Obstacles, Programs, 1977 (189 pgs.).

Mecklenburg, Virginia. Southside Planning District Commission, Regional Housing Element, 1978 (98 pgs.).

Marquette and Waushara, Wisconsin. East Central Wisconsin Regional Planning Commission, Government Assisted Housing, 1977 (57 pgs.).

_______, Housing Conservation, 1977 (67 pgs.).

_______, New Housing, 1978 (55 pgs.).

Crook, Wyoming. Town of Moorcroft, "Summary Sheet for FmHA '601' Project" (applications for acquisition and development of 35 acres of land for housing and park), 1979 (2 pgs.).

_______, "Summary Sheet for FmHA '601' Project" (application for acquisition and development of 22 acres of land for housing and park), 1979 (1 pg.).

Teton, Wyoming. Teton County Housing Committee (for Teton County Commissioners), "A Housing Study of Teton County," 1979 (38 pgs.).

LAND USE

Land use plans are financed by HUD. They include information on existing land conditions such as physical characteristics (e.g., geology, hydrology, topography, soils, and vegetation), the location and characteristics of existing development, community facilities, ownership patterns and land use categories. They also contain growth trends and projections, present alternative future patterns, and suggest the policies needed to implement them.

The first example is from a survey of farmers about farmland in Rhode Island. The survey looked at such questions as the age of the farmer, size of farm, past growth of farm, and future plans for the farm in order to evaluate the status of prime farmland in one local area.

The second example contains land use projections for Memphis and Shelby County, Tennessee. Several categories of residential, industrial, and commercial uses are projected for 1990 and 2000.

The next example concerns groundwater quality in Ross County, Ohio. Much attention is given in land use plans to cataloging the natural features and resources of an area in order to have full knowledge of what the development ramifications would be. In this case, available information from the Ohio EPA on groundwater characteristics at several well sites is presented.

The last example presents a survey of several local elected officials in Idaho about the protection of agricultural land. They were asked about their reasons for wanting to protect agricultural land and about various protection methods that might be used.

PROVIDENCE, RHODE ISLAND

League of Women Voters of Cranston and Cranston Conservation Commission, West Cranston Farmland Survey and Report, 1979, pp. 2-14, 18.

The West Cranston Farmland Survey was conducted by the Cranston League of Women Voters and the Cranston Conservation Commission.

Survey Objectives and Methods

When this project first started in May 1977 the purpose was to inventory and evaluate the status of agricultural land in West Cranston, all of which is considered to be "prime" farmland. Active farmers were personally interviewed. Those who owned prime farmland, but did not farm it, were interviewed by telephone. Thirty-five farmers were personally interviewed in West Cranston.

Some of the farmlands in West Cranston have been in the same families for many years. The average years of ownership is 37 years, with some as long as 75 to 100 years. However, 25 percent of the farms have been owned for less than 20 years (see Table 2).

The survey showed that the average age of the farm operators is 46 years. About 34 percent of the farmers are 39 years of age or younger (Table 3). By way of comparison, the national average age of farmers was 51.7 years in 1974 and for the same year in all of Rhode Island, the average was 53.2 years.

The total number of acres being farmed by the respondents of the survey, including those rented both to and from other owners, is 1,514.5 acres. Of the farm owners surveyed, four have agricultural holdings in other towns in Rhode Island.

Table 2 Number of Years Farm Has Been in Family

Number of Years Farm Has Been in Family

Years	No. of Farms	% of Total
70 and more	3	9%
60 - 69	2	6%
50 - 59	6	17%
40 - 49	6	17%
30 - 39	4	11%
20 - 29	5	14%
10 - 19	5	14%
Less than 10	4	11%

Average 37 years, mean 30-39 years.

Table 3 Age for Farm Operators

Age of Farm Operators	
Age	% of Total
60 or more	26%
50 - 59	26%
40 - 49	14%
30 - 39	23%
20 - 29	11%

The average acres per farm is 41. Table 5 shows high variation from farm to farm. Almost 30 percent of farms are on less than 10 acres, 20 percent are less than 20 acres; however, 20 percent of the farms are 60 or more acres.

Figure 2 shows the current use of farmlands on the surveyed farms; 57 percent of the land is used for permanent pasture, hayland, cropland, and orchard.

There has been a total of 245 acres bought and sold over the last ten years among those surveyed. A total of 132 acres were sold or deeded for a riding school, for housing, for open space, for truck farming, etc. A total of 113 acres were bought.

It is interesting to note that 95 percent of the respondents have been approached to sell their land to developers. This shows the pressure on the farmers in West Cranston to sell the remaining agricultural lands in that area.

According to the data, 64 percent of those surveyed are relying on farming for 90 to 100 percent of their income. Only 27 percent of the

Table 5 Acres Owned in West Cranston

Acres Owned in West Cranston		
No. of Acres	No. of Farms	% of Total
Less than 10	10	29%
10 - 19	7	20%
20 - 29	2	6%
30 - 39	2	6%
40 - 49	3	8%
50 - 50	4	11%
60 or more	7	20%
	35	100%

High 250 Low 3 Median 20 - 29

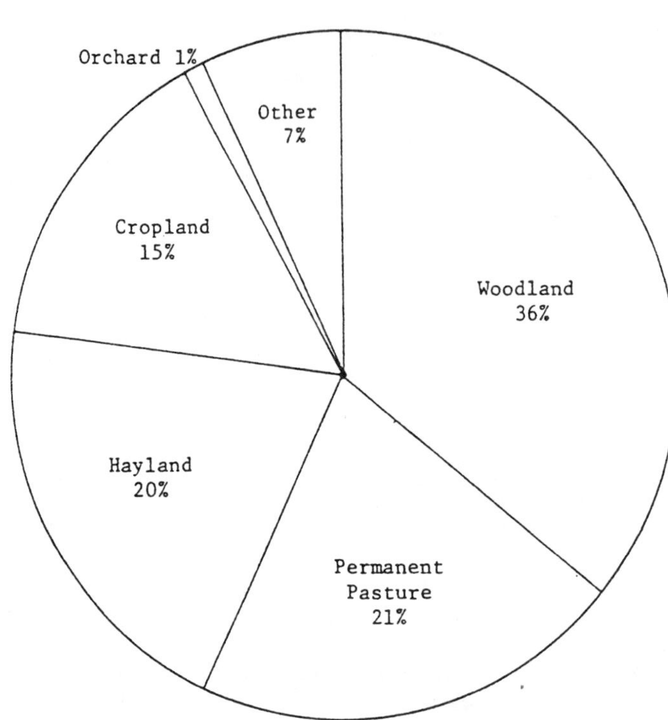

Figure 2 Present Use of Land on Farms Surveyed

Table 7 Percentage of Income Derived from Farming

Percentage of Income Derived from Farming

% of Income	% of Total
100%	50%
90 - 99%	14%
50 - 70%	9%
20 - 30%	9%
10 - 19%	9%
Less than 10%	9%

This table is based on estimates of 22 farms which are commercial-agricultural enterprises and which responded to income questions.

families receive what would be considered a minor portion of their income (0-30 percent) from farming (Table 7). This suggests that many of the farmers in West Cranston are committed to farming as an occupation and way of life, a commitment necessary to maintain a viable agricultural industry.

An attempt was made to determine what most felt were the major problems farm owners in Cranston faced. Table 10 is an overall summary of the responses that were received. The problems singled out most often are:

1. High production costs, with 24 out of 26 respondents citing it as either a major or minor problem.
2. Taxes.
3. Low prices for farm products.
4. Labor availability
5. Development pressures.

It was also determined that for the most part the farm owners in Cranston would like to keep their farms for at least the next five to ten years. Out of the 34 responses received, 29 or 85 percent plan, despite obvious development pressures, to keep their land (see Table 11).

In an effort to get an idea of what the long-range use for the farmland is, the survey asked what farm owners plan for the land once they step down. Of the 35 surveyed, 22 indicated that they would deed their land to heirs, 5 are planning to sell, and 8 had other plans. Assuming a tradition of farming within families, this would imply that for much of the land an attempt will be made to retain it in farming.

Table 12 shows that, in general, the support for keeping land in agriculture, for agricultural zoning, and for a development rights program is very strong.

Table 10 Problems Faced by Farm Owners in Cranston

Problems Faced by Farm Owners in Cranston

	Major	Minor	No Problem
1. Labor Availability	7	8	11
2. Market Availability	2	4	19
3. Machinery Availability	-	6	20
4. Parts for Repair	3	8	14
5. Feed Availability	-	3	19
6. Fertilizer Availability	-	-	25
7. Veterinary Services	4	2	16
8. High Production Costs	19	5	2
9. Low Prices for Products	10	6	8
10. Taxes	11	6	9
11. Development Pressure	4	10	10
12. Federal Regulations	3	7	16
13. State Regulations	3	5	18
14. Local Regulations	1	6	18

Table 11 Plans for Farms Over the Next Five to Ten Years

Plans for Farms Over the Next Five to Ten Years

Plans	No. of Farms	% of Total
Keep	29	85%
Develop	1	3%
Other	4	12%

Table 12 Attitude on Keeping Land in Agriculture

Attitude on Keeping Land in Agriculture
Agricultural Zoning* and Development Rights Plan**

Issue	Yes	No	Uncertain/ No Answer
Keep Land in Agriculture	91%	3%	6%
Agricultural Zoning	74%	14%	12%
Development Rights	63%	11.5%	25.5%

*Zoning for the purpose of retaining land as farm land.

**A plan for owners of property to receive the difference between the value of property assessed as farmland and its much higher value for development. In return for this the farmer would agree not to sell the land for development. The farmer still would own the land, work it or sell it for any purpose other than development as he pleases; the deed would be rewritten accordingly.

The result of this study shows that:

1. Some farmland has been in the same family for generations, but 25 percent of the farms have been owned less than 20 years. This indicates that there is still an interest in farming the land.

2. One-third of the farmers interviewed were 39 years of age or younger.

3. The newer farms are smaller, reflecting the rising cost of land.

4. Seventy-five percent of the farmers depend on farming for most of their income. This suggests that the majority are committed to farming as an occupation and as a way of life, a commitment necessary to maintain a viable agricultural industry.

Conclusions and Recommendations

While this survey clearly indicates pressure on these landowners to sell their land for other uses, the majority of them would like to hold on to their land and continue farming.

The necessity to preserve prime farmland may be important for several reasons. It is ideal land to produce food most efficiently in this state. Local production can eliminate expensive trucking and ensure freshness. Increasing energy costs and conversion of farmland in other states to uses other than farming may make local production more desirable in the future.

Developing prime farmland changes irreversibly the potential of the land for food production, since we cannot manufacture any new farmland. Farmland is valuable open space and it is an aesthetic asset to the city.

SHELBY, TENNESSEE

Memphis and Shelby County Office of Planning and Development, Memphis 2000: Land Use, 1979, pp. 25-28.

Projected Land Use: 1990 and 2000

Two land use projections were prepared: A short-range forecast for 1990 and a long-range forecast for 2000. The two projections were calculated for distinct purposes. In the Memphis 2000 Plan the long-rang projection will provide the basis for a general concept or pattern of land use. The short-range projection is to be used for monitoring progress on the plan and for interim implementation strategies to achieve the 2000 goal. Furthermore, the short-range projection provides direction for evaluating both private development proposals and priorities for public expenditures represented in the Capital Improvement Program processes.

The projections indicate that approximately 170,000 acres will be in urban uses by 1990, an addition of some 30,000 acres over 1975. By 2000, roughly 23,000 more acres will be urbanized, increasing the total developed area in the county to 193,000 acres. By then Shelby County will be approximately 40 percent developed for urban uses.

Residential

Housing need for 1990 and 2000 was presented in the Memphis 2000 Housing Background Report. The projections of land to be required for residential use as well as the density standards and the demand are shown in Table 6. The projections indicate that residential land in 2000 will increase by 56 percent over 1975. Like previous land use distributions, the year 2000 space requirements indicate that residences will consume the largest portion of the developed area.

Table 6 Residential Land Use Projections, 1990 and 2000

Land Use Category	1975 Land Use (Acres)	Density Standard Units/Acre	Determinant-Change In Number of Dwelling Units		Additional Acres		Total Acres	
			1975-1990	1990-2000	1990	2000	1990	2000
Total	54,168	4.65	80,439	58,417	18,082	12,299	72,254	84,553
Low-Medium Density	49,897	3.92	67,088	44,135	17,114	11,259	67,011	78,270
Medium-High Density	4,271	13.73	13,351	14,282	972	1,040	5,243	6,283

Source: MATCOG/MDDD, Areawide Waste Treatment Management Plan, 1976; Memphis and Shelby County Office of Planning and Development, 1979.

Table 7 Industrial Land Use Projections, 1990 and 2000

Land Use Category	1975 Land Use (Acres)	Density Standard Employees/Acre	Determinant-Change In Number of Employees		Additional Acres		Total Acres	
			1975-1990	1990-2000	1990	2000	1990	2000
Total	17,067	19.89	21,225	15,759	2,747	2,144	19,814	21,958
Wholesale-Warehousing	3,482	8.25	9,265	7,241	1,123	878	4,605	5,483
Manufacturing	4,058	15.70	8,235	6,338	525	407	4,583	4,990
Transportation, Communication-Public Utilities	9,527	2.48	2,725	2,130	1,099	859	10,626	11,485

Source: MATCOG/MDDD, Areawide Waste Treatment Management Plan, 1976; Memphis and Shelby County Office of Planning and Development, 1979.

Industrial

Demand for industrial land use changed in accordance with employment levels. Employment in industry was projected by sector, based on the total employment figures appearing in the Memphis 2000 Economic Background Report. The change in employment for each of the industrial subcategories as well as the density standards and projections are shown in Table 7.

Being the regional distribution center for the mid-south, employment levels in the transportation-communication-public utilities subcategory were projected to continue to expand rapidly. This subcategory accounted for the majority of industrial land in 1975 and was projected to remain the largest industrial user in 1990 and 2000.

Manufacturing was the second largest industrial user of land in 1975. However, due to trends in manufacturing employment, it has been projected to require only small increases in acreage, less than for either of the other subcategories. With a modest expansion, manufacturing in 1990 and 2000 will be the smallest user of industrial land.

Wholesale-warehousing was projected to demand more additional acres than either the transportation or manufacturing subcategories, due to large anticipated increases in employment. With the expansion of employment and the corresponding requisite increase in land for this use, by 2000, wholesale-warehousing will use the second largest amount of industrial land.

Commercial and Public Facilities

Growth in the remaining categories of commercial, streets, and public/quasi-public buildings and open space rely on consumers or users of the property, which are generally the resident population. The total population of Shelby County for 1990 and 2000 was presented in the Memphis 2000 Population Background Report. The report indicates that population will increase by approximately 208,000 persons. Based on that increase, land requirements in 1990 and 2000 were calculated for these uses and are shown in Table 8.

Both commercial uses and public buildings need relatively small amounts of land to serve the population. In contrast, public open space and streets require a great deal of additional land to serve the same increase. Streets were projected to consume slightly more than 44,000 acres by 2000, an amount of land second only to residential land uses. The land use figures presented in Tables 6-8 reflect total acres of each land use for the year 2000 as well as the area that needs to be added for the periods 1975 to 1990 and 1990 to 2000.

Table 8 Commercial and Public Facility Land Use Projections, 1990 and 2000

Land Use Category	1975 Land Use (Acres)	Density Standards Population/Acre	Determinant-Change In Number of Persons		Additional Acres		Total Acres	
			1975-1990	1990-2000	1990	2000	1990	2000
Commercial	5,180	151.10	121,000	87,200	801	577	5,981	6,558
Public/Quasi-Public Buildings	5,956	131.40	121,000	87,200	921	664	6,877	7,541
Public/Quasi-Public Open Space	21,899	35.73	121,000	87,200	3,387	2,441	24,186	27,727
Streets	35,008	22.35	121,000	87,200	5,414	3,902	40,422	44,329

Source: MATCOG/MDDD, Areawide Waste Treatment Management Plan, 1976; Memphis and Shelby County Office of Planning and Development, 1979.

ROSS, OHIO

Ross County-Chillicothe Planning Commission, Optimum Land Use Policy and Plan: Ross County and Chillicothe, Ohio, 1978, pp. 46-49.

Groundwater Quality

All natural waters above and below the ground carry dissolved substances in varying concentrations which in turn govern water quality. Climate, soils, geology, the influence of plants and animals, and the artificial effects of human activities all play a part in determining the chemical character of water.

Most groundwater resources are clear and virtually free of suspended matter and micro-organisms due to the filtering action of granular rocks and oils. However, groundwater usually has a higher concentration of dissolved minerals than surface water since it is in constant contact with soluble minerals in rocks and soils.

Groundwater quality is largely controlled by the mineral composition of the surrounding aquifer. Because of its isolation from the atmosphere and growing vegetation, groundwater contains little or no dissolved oxygen, but it may have other gases, particularly carbon dioxide and occasionally hydrogen sulfide. The temperature of groundwater is not influenced by seasonal changes, and in Ohio it normally ranges between 50 and 55 degrees Fahrenheit.

The relatively high purity of groundwater in respect to biological quality and the ready availability at the point of use have made groundwater the major source of water in Ross County. The cool and relatively constant temperature is desirable for use in industrial cooling processes. Some of the mineral constituents of groundwater may give undesirable characteristics; examples include hardness from dissolved calcium and magnesium salts and undesirable tastes from iron. These properties can usually be remedied by softening and water treatment.

The filtering effect of rocks and soils above the zone of saturation provide a high degree of natural protection of groundwater from surface-derived pollutants. Exceptions occur in critical recharge areas where the water table is close to the surface or the soil is coarse and water quickly drains through it without much filtration. In these areas, polluting substances associated with surface drainage can be rapidly carried into an aquifer.

The pollution of groundwater can be far more complex and damaging than the pollution of surface water since the pollutants migrate slowly underground. Long periods of time may pass before pollutants from point sources appear in nearby wells. This makes it hard to determine the source and estimate the extent of pollution. It then may take years after the pollution source is stopped before the water quality is restored by natural rejuvenation or artificial control.

Serious local problems may result where on-lot sanitary facilities are not adequate. On-lot facilities which discharge waste water diffusely into the soil depend on the soil to absorb, filter, and purify by naturally occurring physical and biological processes. Many septic tanks in Ross County may be on soils that are not adequately performining these functions, thereby permitting insufficiently treated waste water to filter into the adjacent groundwater. This can be a health hazard where water supply wells are close to septic tanks or privies. Unfortunately, the Ross County Health Department does not have enough funds and manpower needed to periodically inspect water supplies and septic tanks.

The latest available information from the Ohio EPA on groundwater quality at various well sites in Ross County is summarized in Table 2. This data can in turn be compared with normal ranges registered at the statewide level. An analysis and comparison of the data suggests that groundwater quality in the county is generally good. However, as with most underground water supplies, the water from all the wells tested is hard and must therefore be softened. Softening removes the minerals that cause scale formation in pipes and increases the sudsing ability of soap. Except for Bainbridge, the iron content of the tested wells was high enough to cause objectionable taste and stains.

Since the areas tested do not get their water from shale bedrock, none of the water is acidic or high in sodium. There is no pollution from the brine of strip mines and oil fields which usually causes high chloride, sodium, and sulfate concentrations and high acidity. Contamination from sewage, road salt, or water softening backwash is evidently negligible since the chloride content of the groundwater is low. None of the wells have enough dissolved solids (except iron) to give bad tastes, laxative effects, or corrosiveness.

Clarksburg has more than the amount of fluoride needed in the water for prevention of tooth decay. If the amount increases to 2.5 mg/l, it could discolor tooth enamel.

Frankfort and Kingston water supplies have the correct amount of fluoride that is recommended for decay prevention. The rest of the wells tested had less than the recommended amount. Chillicothe and the Ross County Water Company add fluoride to the water to bring it up to the standard concentration.

The water from the well at Bainbridge had a high concentration of nitrates. Nitrate contamination is usually caused by seepage of surface water into shallow wells.

IDAHO

Idaho Division of Budget, Policy Planning, and Coordination, _Agricultural Land in Idaho: What is it? Should it be Protected? If so, How?_, 1979, pp. 37-41.

Agricultural Land Retention in Idaho

Why and Where is it Needed or Desired?

Without being able to visit all 44 counties in Idaho, the need or public desire for preserving agricultural land must be determined through means similar to the questionnaire mailed to each county. It

Table 2 Water Analysis of Tested Wells in Ross County

Location	Well Number 16 Chillicothe	Well Number 13 Water Works Chillicothe	Adelphi	Well Number 2 Bainbridge	Clarksburg	Well Number 1 Frankfort	Well Number 3 Kingston
Use	Public Supply	Public Supply	Public Supply	Public Supply	Public Supply	Public Supply	Public Supply
Water Bearing Formation	Sand and Gravel	Sand and Gravel	Sand and Gravel	Sand and Gravel	Sand and Gravel	Limestone	Sand and Gravel
Yield	1000 GPM	1500 GPM	12	400	5	100	75
Iron mg/l	1.2	1.1	4.0	0.04	3.1	1.7	2.2
Chloride mg/l	24.0	23.0	16.0	51.0	0.0	9.0	7.0
Dissolved Solids mg/l	461.0	440.0	433.0	512.0	738.0	462.0	504.0
Hardness mg/l	342.0	278.0	356.0	328.0	504.0	334.0	368.0
pH	7.7	7.8	7.6	7.3	7.6	7.6	7.7
Sodium mg/l	19.0	32.0	21.0	31.0	43.0	12.0	29.0
Sulfate mg/l	87.0	77.0	18.0	21.0	235.0	57.0	93.0
Flouride mg/l	0.31	0.18	0.6	0.14	2.08	1.08	1.15
Nitrates	0.1	0.3	0.4	11.2	0.1	0.0	0.09

is recognized that the opinions sought represent the views of only 27 elected officials, and depending upon their occupation, age, place of residency, etc., their attitudes may or may not coincide with the majority of their constituents. It is assumed that as elected representatives who assume land use decision-making roles in their respective counties, they are somewhat capable of expressing the attitudes of the citizenry, despite biases.

Of the 22 counties who responded to the questionnaire, most believed that "more than half" of the citizens are concerned about the conversion of their farmland to other uses. Others were equally divided between "about half" and "less than half," with one respondent conceding that only farmers are concerned.

In responding to the question, "Do most elected and appointed officials believe that agricultural land in your county should be protected?," 64 percent said "Yes--some of it" and 36 percent, "Yes--all of it." Although "No--none of it" could have been checked, no respondent did so.

In trying to discover why respondents feel any or all of their agricultural land should be protected, four reasons were supplied. These are listed below in order of the number of agreeable checks received:

Percent	Reasons
84.6	To maintain the local economy
73.1	To encourage farmers to keep it in production
53.8	To grow food and fiber for the future
42.3	To maintain a rural/scenic landscape

Other reasons offered include: development leads to more loss of agricultural land, needed for a natural resource base, keeps growth down, and keeps costs down.

It is important to note that respondents seemed to be more concerned about local economic stability than their contribution to the country's food supply. Note also that there is some interest in protecting agricultural lands for aesthetic purposes. This was supported by the responses to another question which asked if there is interest in protecting non-agricultural lands. Over half (55.5) percent responded "Yes," suggesting that "open space" also may be important to preserve. How well this report will meet the needs of these counties is questionable, although most techniques discussed are flexible enough to be used for preserving other kinds of land. In anticipation of this need, usefulness for open space has been included in the discussions.

It was also asked why land should not be protected; the reasons and responses follow:

Percent	Reasons
19.2	Because better money can be made by subdividing it
15.4	Because it isn't productive enough to be economically important
7.7	Because there's too much land regulation already
3.8	Because the U.S. has so much agricultural land, our counties don't need to be kept agricultural

Marginal land is better for residential use, we have little private land, and needs for locating industry and residences were given as other reasons.

The reason which scored the highest rating is perhaps one of the greatest obstacles to agricultural land preservation in areas of Idaho where farming and grazing have become marginal operations. It is in these areas where outright resriction of development will not be acceptable.

What is Politically Acceptable?

Relative to Idaho, techniques that are less restrictive, expensive, and complicated, that are within the existing legal framework, and that do not require mandatory compliance will have the greatest chance of success. However, with the dissemination of literature and facilitation of structured citizen participation workshops, public attitudes can be changed.

Based on this premise, techniques like quarter/quarter zoning, transfer of densities, transfer fee plan, and restrictve use tax agreements could be utilized in Idaho.

To give readers a generalized idea of how officials viewed certain techniques, their responses and the researcher's interpretations have been included in Table VIII. The response means and medians for each technique are listed on the graph. A range from one (1) to five (5) was possible with three (3) being a neutral response.

Interpretations of Table VIII:

1. There is strong sentiment against increasing taxes even if the generated revenues were used to retain agricultural land.
2. Those who approve of the farmer having to pay "back taxes" apparently believe that a rollback tax law is needed in Idaho's preferential taxing policies for agricultural landowners. It is surmised that the few who responded negatively may not understand the need for a rollback tax; or, that they feel farmers are already taxed too heavily.
3. Disapproving responses to prohibiting other uses on marginal agricultural land may be a reaction to "blanket zoning"--the zoning of land for preservation whether or not it's appropriate to zone all the land with one classification. Others may be negative because they believe marginal land is better suited for development. Still, some officials believe that even marginal land is important to protect.
4. The tendency toward approval of development rights could reflect two things: (1) that respondents believe compensation is needed and (2) that the flexibility implied by "so that agricultural land can be zoned for low density; other land, high density" may have influenced their responses.
5. There was a strong positive response as well for containing growth in periodically expanding city impact areas. A similar stronger response occurred with controlling growth through a public facilities

Table VIII Survey Results About Ways to Protect Agricultural Land[1]

TAXES	mean	median	approval
Increase taxes so the county can buy either agricultural land or easements	1.7	1.4	LOW
Enforce a sales tax on liquor and tourist accommodations so the county can buy either agricultural land or easements	1.6	1.3	LOW
Require the farmer to pay "back" taxes when he subdivides his agricultural land if he has been receiving tax relief	3.3	3.8	HIGH
ZONING ORDINANCES			
Prohibit other uses on agricultural land, even if it's only marginally productive	2.9	2.4	MED
Allocate transferable "development rights" that agricultural land can be zoned for low density; other land, high density	3.6	3.8	HIGH
Allow development only in city impact areas which would be periodically expanded as new land areas are needed	3.6	3.8	HIGH
Allow development on marginally productive land using strict development controls	3.9	4.1	HIGH

SUBDIVISION ORDINANCES	mean	median	approval
Prohibit traditional subdividing but allow "planned unit developments" (clustered housing)	3.0	3.2	MED
Require maximum lot sizes of 20 acres or more in agriculturally zoned areas	3.4	3.8	HIGH
Require the developer to give some amount of money to the county for buying agricultural easements or land	2.6	2.5	MED
Require the developer to protect some percentage of the land from any development	3.2	3.7	HIGH
Require minimum lot sizes of less than 20 acres in agriculturally zoned areas	2.1	1.9	LOW
MISCELLANEOUS			
Halt all development beyond city limits until some means of agricultural land protection can be adopted	2.8	2.8	MED
Control the location of development by following a plan for the expansion of public facilities	3.9	4.1	HIGH

[1]Means and medians are based on responses to the following question: "How do you feel about the following ways to protect agricultural land? (circle one): (1) don't know enough to comment; (2) strongly approve; (3) approve; (4) neither approve nor disapprove; (5) disapprove; (6) strongly disapprove." (Cases in which "don't know enough to comment" was circled were not included in the mean and median calculations.)

plan. This could be interpreted as a concern about the costs of sprawl. Local officials probably are more aware of this than the general public. Halting growth altogether, in the form of a moratorium, was not met with as much approval. This response may be due to (1) previous experience or familiarity with a moratorium, (2) resistance against "no growth" or (3) the desire to avoid having to work out an ordinance under the pressure of time.

6. Respondents were heavily in favor of using strict development controls compared to prohibiting development on marginal agricultural lands.

7. A fairly even distribution of responses to the planned unit development and resulting neutral mean concept may be a result of little experience with PUDs, or because respondents felt PUDs would have minimum impact either positively or negatively on the preservation of agricultural land.

8. There was strong opposition to relatively small minimum lot sizes in agricultural zones. The intent of another technique suggested was to find out if larger lot sizes are more desirable. While the responses indicated this, because the word "maximum" should have been typed "minimum" on the questionnaire, this conclusion cannot be validated.

9. Requiring the developer to "dedicate" money for agricultural easements or land received little support, but many were not sure how they felt about it. Perhaps most have never considered this option as it has not been used extensively in Idaho.

10. Requring the developer to provide agricultural open space received greater approval. Compared to monetary dedication, open space dedication probably has greater public support and therefore is favored by local officials.

Bibliography: Land Use

Calhoun, Cherokee, Cleburne, and Talladega, Alabama. East Alabama Planning and Development Commission, East Alabama Regional Land Use Plan, 1977 (136 pgs.).

Cherokee, Alabama. East Alabama Regional Planning and Development Commission, Cherokee County Land Use Plan, 1976 (121 pgs.).

Greene and Pickens, Alabama. West Alabama Planning and Development Council, West Alabama Region Land Development Plan (84 pgs.).

Henry, Alabama. Southeast Alabama Regional Planning and Development Commission, Prime Agricultural Lands Study: A Guide for Identifying and Preserving Long-Term Productive Lands in Southeast Alabama, 1978 (57 pgs.).

Limestone, Alabama. Top of Alabama Regional Council of Governments, "Land Use Plan" (map).

Mississippi, Arkansas. Land Utilization Plan: Blytheville-Osceola Development Corridor, 1979 (25 pgs.).

Merced, California. Merced County Planning Department, Merced County General Plan: Vol.1, Plan Introduction and Land Use Element, Vol. 2, Circulation Element, 1978 (37 pgs.).

Ouray, Colorado. Colorado Division of Planning, Ouray County Zoning Regulations, revised 1976 (44 pgs.).

Tri-County Development Department, Subdivision Regulations for Montrose-Ouray-San Miguel Counties, as Amended May 1976 (49 pgs.).

Litchfield, Connecticut. Northwestern Connecticut Regional Planning Agency, "The NWCRPA Land Use Policies Plan" (7 pgs.).

Monroe, Florida. Monroe County Commission, "Ordinance Regulating Development within flood Hazard Districts" (11 pgs.).

_______, "Ordinance Regulating Major Development Projects" (33 pgs.).

Monroe County Planning Department, Monroe County Land Use Plan, 1977 (48 pgs.).

Berrien, Brooks, and Echols, Georgia. Coastal Plain Area Planning and Development Commission, Areawide Future Land Use Plan, Coastal Plain Area, 1977 (164 pgs.).

Elbert, Georgia. Northeast Georgia Area Planning and Development Commission, Elberton Comprehensive Plan, Vol. 2: Zoning and Subdivision Regulations, 1976 (90 pgs.).

_______, Northeast Georgia Areawide Land Use Element, 1976 (198 pgs.).

Seminole, Georgia. Southwest Georgia Planning and Development Commission, 1978 Seminole County Land Use Plan (103 pgs.).

Seminole and Terrell, Georgia. Southwest Georgia Planning and Development Commission, Southwest Georgia Land Use Plan, 1976 (101 pgs.).

Troup, Georgia. Chattahoochee-Flint Area Planning and Development Commission, West Point, Georgia, Future Land Use Plan, Community Improvement Program, and Housing Assistance Plan, 1977 (133 pgs.).

Heard and Troup, Georgia. Chattahoochee-Flint Area Planning and Development Commission, Chattahoochee-Flint Areawide Land Use Policies Plan, 1977 (190 pgs.).

Upson, Georgia. McIntosh Trail Area Planning and Development Commission, Thomaston, Georgia, Future Land Use Plan, 1976 (59 pgs.).

Idaho. Idaho Division of Budget, Policy Planning and Coordination, Agricultural Land in Idaho: What Is It? Should It Be Protected? If So, How?, 1979 (74 pgs.).

Hancock, Illinois. Western Illinois Regional Council, Regional Land Use Plan, 1976 (61 pgs.).

_______, "Western Illinois Regional Land Use Plan, Supplement Number One: Floodplains," 1977 (8 pgs.).

_______, "Western Illinois Regional Land Use Plan, Supplement Number Two: Regional Environmental Analysis for Sanitary Land Fill Development," 1977 (14 pgs.).

Pike, Illinois. Two Rivers Regional Council of Public Officials, Land Use in Two Rivers Region: A Summary of the Regional Development Guide, 1979 (67 pgs.).

Allen, Indiana. Allen County Plan Commission, "The Future of Agricultural Land in Allen County: Here Today, Gone Tomorrow?" (11 pgs.).

Martin, Indiana. Blake, Brian, and Joe O'Leary, "The Forest Issue from the Citizens Viewpoint," Purdue Agriculture Reports, Vol. 8, November 1979 (2 pgs.).

Martin and Perry, Indiana. Cooperative Extension Service, Purdue University, "Residents' Views Toward Forest Land in Martin and Perry Counties," 1979 (9 pgs.).

Iowa. State of Iowa, Proposed Senate bill to establish and implement a land preservation policy, 1980 (20 pgs.).

Butler, Iowa. Iowa Northland Regional Council of Governments, Land Use Projections and Policies, 1978 (69 pgs.).

Lyon, Iowa. Northwest Iowa Regional Council of Governments, Lyon County Subdivision and Zoning Ordinances (108 pgs.).

Washington, Maine. Washington County Regional Planning Commission, Land Use Element of the Regional Comprehensive Plan, 1977 (123 pgs.).

Baltimore, Maryland. Farmland Preservation Survey, "Rural Zoning in Baltimore County, February 1980" (6 pgs.).

Calvert, Maryland. Calvert County Planning Department, Community Living Areas Study of Calvert County, Maryland: A Study of the Pattern and Impact of Residential Land Use Within the County, 1979 (43 pgs.).

_______, "Agriculture Land Preservation Program Criteria for Transfer Zones" (12 pgs.).

_______, "Calvert County Maryland Agricultural Preservation Program," 1979 (7 pgs.).

Dickinson, Michigan. Dickinson County, "Dickinson County Zoning Ordinance," 1979 (24 pgs.).

Washtenaw, Michigan. Washtenaw County Metropolitan Planning Commission, Agriculture in Washtenaw County: Conditions, Policies and Approaches to Preservation, 1979 (46 pgs.).

_______, Washtenaw County Land Use Policies, 1978 (74 pgs.).

Becker, Pope, Stevens, and Traverse, Minnesota. West Central Regional Development Commission, Region IV Land Use Policy Plan (105 pgs.).

Lake, Minnesota. Agricultural Extension Service, University of Minnesota, Township Supervisors and Land Use in Eight Northeast Minnesota Counties (30 pgs.).

Martin, Minnesota. Martin County Planning and Zoning Advisory Commission, Land Use Survey and Analysis: Martin County, Minnesota, 1970 (31 pgs.).

_______, Martin County Minnesota Land Use Plan, Roads and Highways Plan, 1970 (35 pgs.).

Martin County Board of Commissioners, Martin County Minnesota Zoning Ordinance (96 pgs.).

Mower, Minnesota. Mower County, "Draft Proposed Amendment to the County Zoning Ordinance" (about agriculture land use policies) (4 pgs.).

Jackson, Mississippi. Jackson County Planning Commission, Jackson County Zoning Ordinance (as amended 1979) (49 pgs.).

_______, Jackson County Subdivision Regulations (32 pgs.).

Iron and Ste. Genevieve, Missouri. University of Missouri Extension Division, Lake Development Property: A Consumer's Buying Guide (29 pgs.).

_______, "A Checklist For Buying Property in Small Lake Developments" (34-pg. brochure).

Chouteau, Montana. Chouteau County Comprehensive Plan (85 pgs.). City of Fort Benton, City of Fort Benton Zoning Ordinance, 1978 (48 pgs.).

Broome, New York. Broome County Planning Department, Broome County Land Use Plan, 1977 (165 pgs.).

_______, "Agricultural District No. 1 Eight Year Review," 1980 (14 pgs.).

Cattaraugus, New York. Cattaraugus County Planning Board, Cattaraugus County Land Use Plan, Year 2000, 1977 (97 pgs.).

Columbia, New York. Columbia County Planning Department, Columbia County Land Use Plan, 1977 (157 pgs.).

North Carolina. Neuman, D.F., and E.C. Pasour, Jr. (Department of Economics and Business, N.C. State University), "Agricultural Use-Value Taxation in North Carolina," Economics Special Report No. 50, 1979 (16 pgs.).

North Carolina Agricultural Extension Service and Center for Rural Resource Development, Land-Use Planning in Rural Areas, Report No. 11, 1978 (53 pgs.).

_______, "Land Use Planning in Rural Areas: The Issues," Center for Rural Resource Development Report No. 9, 1978 (6 pgs.).

Rural Land Use Planning Committee, Schools of Agriculture and Life Sciences and Forest Resources, N.C. State University, Rural Land Use Planning Committee Report, 1978 (29 pgs.).

Ashe, North Carolina. Rash, James O., Jr., and Glenn C. McCann (Agricultural Research Service, N.C. State University), The Ashe County Airport: A Case Study of a Development Event, 1979 (45 pgs.).

Ashe, Avery, Buncombe, and Rutherford, North Carolina. North Carolina Department of Administration, A Balanced Growth Policy for North Carolina: An Agenda for Discussion and Appalachian Regional Commission Investment Policy for FY 1978, 1977 (207 pgs.).

Carteret, Columbus, Dare, Edgecombe, Harnett, Hertford, Northampton, Onslow, and Scotland, North Carolina. North Carolina Department of Administration, North Carolina Coastal Plains Regional Public Investment Plan, 1979 (59 pgs.).

Caswell, North Carolina. Piedmont Triad Council of Governments, Caswell County Land Use Development and Community Facilities Plan, 1977 (56 pgs.).

Hertford, North Carolina. Hertford County Planning Board, Hertford County-Ahoskie Land Use Plan, 1976 (155 pgs.).

Hertford County Board of Commissioners, Zoning Ordinance, Hertford County North Carolina, 1979 (111 pgs.).

Union, North Carolina. Union County, Land Use Plan, Union County, North Carolina (77 pgs.).

North Carolina Department of Natural and Economic Resources, Updated Land Use Survey and Development Plan, Union County, N.C., 1975 (49 pgs.).

Ross, Ohio. Ross County-Chillicothe Planning Commission, Optimum Land Use Policy and Plan: Ross County and Chillicothe, Ohio, 1978 (134 pgs.).

Ohio Department of Natural Resources, Division of Water, Land Capability Analysis in Ross County, Ohio, 1979 (45 pgs.).

USDA and Ohio Department of Natural Resources, "Important Farmlands - Ross County, Ohio," 1979 (map).

Yamhill, Oregon. Yamhill County, "Revised Goals and Policies: Yamhill County Comprehensive Land Use Plan," 1979 (37 pgs.).

Potter, Pennsylvania. Potter County Land Policy Committee, "Potter County Land Policy Committee Report" 1977 (9 pgs.).

Providence, Rhode Island. League of Women Voters and Cranston Conservation Commission, West Cranston Farmland Survey and Report, 1979 (23 pgs.).

__________ "Saving Cranston 'Farms,'" approximately 1978 (14 pgs.).

South Carolina. Budget and Control Board, Division of Research and Statistical Services, An Economy in Transition: South Carolina and Its Ten Planning Districts: The Next Decade, 1979 (101 pgs.).

South Carolina Land Resources Conservation Commission, 1978-79 Annual Report (118 pgs.).

McCormick, South Carolina. McCormick County Council, "McCormick County Land Use Update: An Implementation Tool" (15 pgs.).

Oconee and Spartanburg, South Carolina. South Carolina Appalachian Council of Governments, Proposed Regional Land Use Element: The South Carolina Appalachian Region, 1977 (61 pgs.).

Shelby, Tennessee. Memphis and Shelby County Office of Planning and Development, Memphis 2000: Land Use, 1979 (33 pgs.).

_______,"Shelby County 1978 Urban Development Report: Building Permits, Subdivisions, Rezonings" (9 pgs.).

Charlotte, Virginia. Piedmont Planning District Commission, Areawide Land Use Policies for the Piedmont Planning District, 1975 (122 pgs.).

Henry, Virginia. West Piedmont Planning District Commission, Regional Land Use Plan, 1975-2000 (20-pg. excerpt).

Sheboygan, Wisconsin. Sheboygan County Planning and Resources Department, Sheboygan County Farmland Preservation Plan, 1979 (335 pgs.).

Crook, Wyoming. Crook County Planning Commission, Crook County Land Use Plan, 1977 (38 pgs.).

Hulett Planning Committee, Land Use Policy Plan for the Town of Hulett, Wyoming, 1977 (29 pgs.).

Moorecroft Planning Commission, Town of Moorecroft Land Use Policy Manual, 1978 (58 pgs.).

Sundance Planning Commission, Sundance Land Use Plan, 1977 (35 pgs.).

Hot Springs, Wyoming. Hot Springs County Planning Office, Hot Springs County Land Use Plan, 1978 (57 pgs.).

Teton, Wyoming. Blundell, William, "Peril in Paradise - Jackson Hole Worries that Developers' Plans Threaten Its Beauty - Community Splits Over How to Manage Local Boom, Elk Herd is Endangered - What Role for the 'Feds'?," Wall Street Journal (Western ed.), December 10, 1979 (1 pg.).

Hocker, Jean, "Jackson Hole: Are We Loving It to Death?," Sierra Club Bulletin, August 1979 (3 pgs.).

Jackson Hole Projects, "Jackson Hole," 1979 (2 pgs.).

_______, "A Proposal for Selected Land Conservation in Jackson Hole," 1979 (2 pgs.).

_______, "A Private Land Trust for Jackson Hole: Could It Offer Choices for Preserving Open Space?," 1980 (1 pg.).

Strain, Peggy, "Subdivisions vs. Open Space: Tug of War on for Jackson Hole's Rustic Lands," Denver Post, May 11, 1980 (1 pg.).

COMMUNITY FACILITIES

Most community facilities and capital improvements plans are financed by HUD. Contents vary depending on the topic, e.g., fire protection, sewage systems, waste collection, public buildings, or general public budgeting.

The first example uses a question and answer format to explain some aspects of the revenues and expenditures of King and Queen County, Virginia. The answers are illustrated with various types of graphs.

The second example, from North Dakota, contains an analysis of two methods of solid waste collection and disposal. Various aspects of efficiency and financing are presented for the two methods.

The third example, from the Ozark region of Missouri, presents information obtained from a survey of several city and rural fire protection groups in the area. Information has been obtained for each group on its organization, water supply, and equipment.

The fourth example, from Cattaraugus County, New York, contains county income projections. These are presented in a table and a graph and include property tax, sales tax, and off-track betting revenues.

KING AND QUEEN, VIRGINIA

Middle Peninsula Planning District Commission, Financial Analysis and Capital Improvements Program, King & Queen County, Virginia, 1979, pp. 1-5.

Questions and Answers
About Finances in King and Queen County

QUESTION: What share of the County Budget goes for various County Functions?

ANSWER: From 1974 through 1979 about three-fourths of all outlay went for schools: operations, instructions, Capital and Debt Service. The remaining share of the County governmental cost was split about evenly between Public Welfare and all other general County departments.

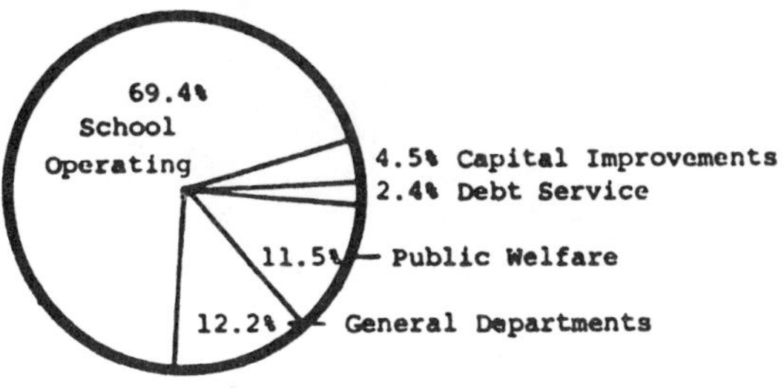

Distribution of County Expenses 1974-1979

QUESTION: What changes are occurring in County expenditures?

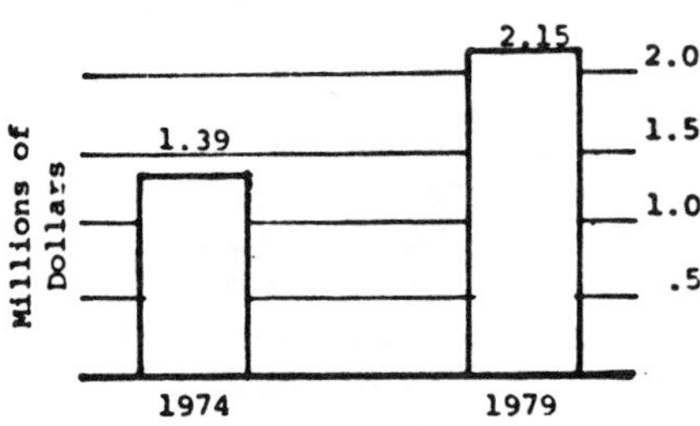

Trends in
Operating Budgets

ANSWER: As everywhere else, County costs have been pushed up because of two major forces: First, new services required by the State have been added, such as kindergartens and other special programs. Also, new projects made possible by special Federal or State grants have accounted for some of the increases. Second, inflation which has been at an all time high during the 1970's continues to contribute to higher costs at all levels, public and private. The net effect of new programs and inflation has been to increase the County Operating Budget about 11% per year since 1974.

QUESTION: How are these services paid for?

ANSWER: More than half of the County's income during the past five years has been from a combination of State and Federal sources. About one-third of the budget was financed by local property taxes. Other local sources such as licenses and fees provided the remainder of the revenue.

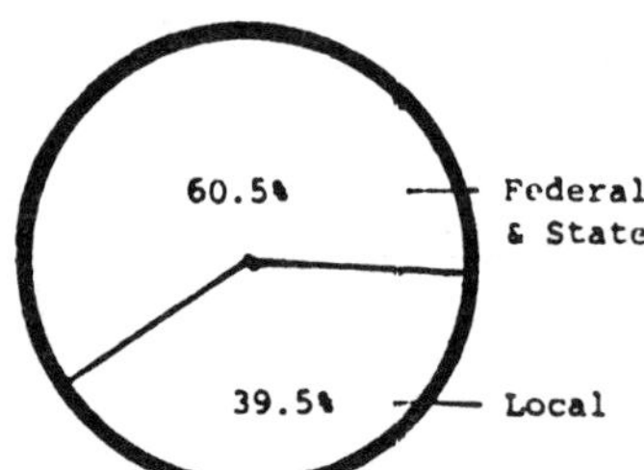

Sources of County Revenue
1974-1979

QUESTION: What is happening to State and Federal sources?

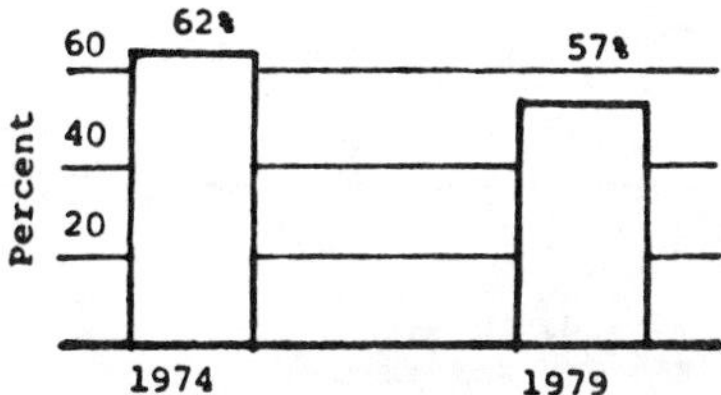

Trends in Revenue From State and Federal Sources

ANSWER: Unfortunately, the State and Federal sources have not kept pace with rising costs and a larger share of County government costs falls on local sources. One factor causing this situation is that several Federal Programs initiated during the early 1970's, such as revenue sharing, have not been increased consistent with rising costs. Also, State revenue sources have not generally kept up with additional requirements for school services mandated by the State.

QUESTION: How has this affected County taxes?

ANSWER: For the most part it has meant higher taxes mostly for real estate. The 1979 tax levy was slightly more than double the 1974 levy and the average for the period was about 22% per year. Part of this was accounted for in a reassessment in 1974 and part in increased tax rates.

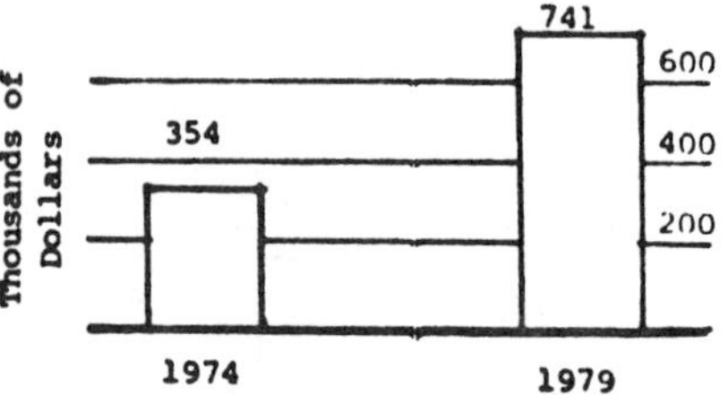

Trends in Real Estate Tax Assessments

QUESTION: With the present situation, how can the County undertake a Capital Improvements Program?

ANSWER: The County has some experience in financing capital projects which accounted for 4.5% of all expenditures between 1974 and 1979. Expressed in current budget terms, this percentage would be about $100,000 per year. These have been "out of pocket" costs for general maintenance, school bus replacement, etc.

For purposes of taking on additional capital programs it is convenient to think of a share of the Real Estate tax as a Capital Improvements tax. Using the $100,000 per year example eight cents of the 1978-79 tax rate would go for capital projects. As a general rule then every $25,000 added to the budget for capital outlay adds two cents to the tax rate. In Chapter 3 of this report two trial Capital Improvements programs are presented. Both are very modest. The first would require an additional Capital Improvements tax of nine cents over the next five years and the second would require five cents.

It is possible to arrange any combination of projects that the County desires and to express them in terms of a Capital Improvements tax rate.

QUESTION: What Capital Improvements are proposed over the next five years?

ANSWER: The only major improvement proposed during the period is a Vocational School at Central High to satisfy State Board of Education requirements for additional classroom space and vocational training facilities. In addition a required reassessment in four years and accumulation of a sinking fund for courthouse complex improvements after 1984 are included. Restoration of an Operating Reserve to avoid reliance on Temporary Loans for operating costs has been included in one alternative program.

QUESTION: What will happen to the Real Estate Taxes with this program?

ANSWER: Unless new grants become available or inflation can be reduced, real estate taxes will increase. Estimated required tax rates for Operations and Capital Improvements using the most conservative Capital Improvements Program would be increased from $.65 in the current year to 1.01 by 1984.

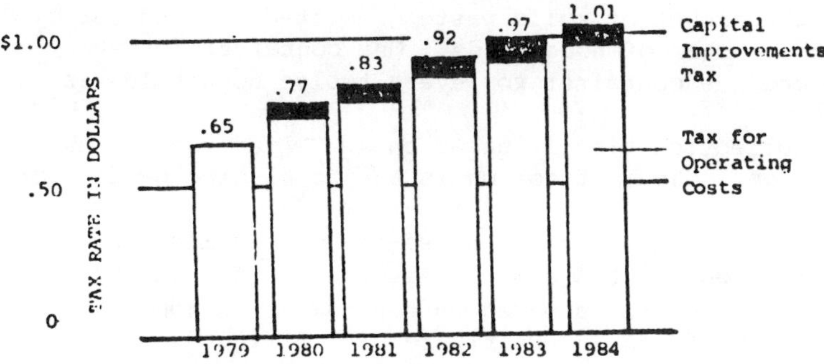

Projected Impact of Operating and Capital Costs on Property Taxes.(1979 - 1974

CAVALIER AND TOWNER, NORTH DAKOTA

North Central Planning Council, Comprehensive Plan, Volume III: Solid Waste Systems Analysis, 1977, pp. 81, 85, 86, 170-173.

IX. Analysis of Solid Waste in the North Central Region

Knowledge of the amount of solid waste generated in the region is necessary in order to plan for collection and disposal. Figures for the amount of solid waste generated can be used to determine the necessary level of service. The level of service can be itemized to determine the costs for the service. Finally, the cost figures will provide the information needed to determine the rates and area to be serviced by a system.

Tables 11a-f* are route designs for centralized "container system" collection of the communities pinpointed on the maps. This system uses three cubic yard containers strategically placed throughout each town. The truck leaves from the landfill site for collection of solid waste. The first column is the towns that will be collected according to the most feasible routes. The criteria used are the distance between towns (second column) and a truck capacity of 16 cubic yards. The average speed is the third column. This is based mainly on weather and road conditions. Travel time in the next column is the distance to the community divided by the average speed times 60 to get a figure in minutes. The next column is the compacted volume of solid waste collected in that community. The number of three cubic yard containers used is based on the amount of solid waste generated, the number of businesses, and the number of households. One container for every three businesses and one container for every twelve households is a reasonable yardstick.[10]

The container collection time is based on an EPA average of two minutes for each stop. The last column is the total time needed for the collection point.

Tables 12a-f are route designs for house-to-house collection. The travel time between towns is the same as Alternative I. The number of residential collection points is based on the number of households and the time required is based on an EPA figure of 1.5 minutes per stop in small communities and .8 minutes in larger communities. The non-residential points are the total number of three cubic yard containers. One container is used for every three non-residential sources.

Table 13a-f are budget sheets of collection costs for the centralized collection system. The amounts are based on current figures supplied by other studies,[3,5] interviews,[1,2] and EPA figures[14] for personnel, maintenance, and equipment. The major

---

*Tables for six jurisdictions (a-f) were included in the original text; data on only one jurisdiction (f) are presented here.

Table 11F Alternative I Container System (Towner)

Collection Point	Distance (Mi.)	Avg. Speed (Mi./Hr.)	Travel Time (Min.) (D x 1.5)	Compacted Volume Collected (Cu. Yd.)	Volume Generated (Cu. Yd.)	Number of Containers (3 Cu. Yd.)	Container Collection Time (Min.)	Total Collection Time (Min.)
ROUTE 1								
Hansboro	37	40	56	3.9	17.9	3	6	62
Perth	23	40	35	2.5	11.2	2	4	39
Bisbee	9	40	14	9.5	42.7	7	14	28
Cando	18	40	27	--	--	--	--	27
Total	87	40	132	15.9	71.8	12	24	156
ROUTE 2								
Bisbee	18	40	27	9.0	40.5	6	12	39
Egeland	13	40	20	7.3	32.9	5	10	30
Cando	15	40	10	--	--	--	--	10
Total	46	40	57	16.3	73.4	11	22	79
ROUTE 3								
Rock Lake	41	40	62	16.7	78.3	12	24	86
Cando	41	40	62	--	--	--	--	62
Total	82	40	124	16.7	78.3	12	24	148
ROUTE 4*								
Cando	60	40	90	93.4	420.7	96	192	282

*These figures are for six truck loads.

variables on the budget sheet are the number of three cubic yard containers used in the system and the mileage costs.

Tables 14a-f are budget sheets for each house-to-house collection system. Containers are still used for non-residential collection under this system.

Notes

[1]Andrick, 1977. Charles Andrick, information provided on Langdon sanitary landfill and collection systems (City Auditor, Langdon, N.D., May, 1977).

[2]Britsch, 1977. Derrel Britsch, information provided on Devils Lake sanitary landfill and collection systems (City Auditor, Devils Lake, N.D., May, 1977).

[3]Crowe, 1974. Stephen Crowe, "A Study in Regional Disposal of Solid Wastes in the North Central Planning Region - An Interim Report (unpublished, North Central Planning Office, August, 1974).

[5]Hall and Jones, 1973. J. Patrick Hall and Lonnie L. Jones, "Costs of Solid Waste Management in Rural Communities in Texas" (Abstract).

[10]PEDCO - Environmental Specialists, Inc., 1975. Proposed Solid Waste Management System for Turtle Mountain Reservation of North Dakota (March, 1975).

[14]U.S. Environmental Protection Agency, Sanitary Landfill Design and Operation.

Table 12F Alternative II House-to-House Collection System (Towner)

Collection Point)	Travel Time (Min.)	Compacted Volume Collected (Cu. Yd.)	Residential		Non-Residential		Total Collection Time (Min.)
			Number of Collection Pts.	Collection Pt. Time (Min.)	Number of Collection Pts.	Collection Pt. Time (Min.)	
ROUTE 1							
Hansboro	56	3.9	16	24	2	4	90
Perth	35	2.5	13	20	1	2	57
Bisbee	14	9.5	74	111	--	--	125
Cando	27	--	--	--	--	--	27
Total	132	15. 9	103	155	3	6	299
ROUTE 2							
Bisbee	27	9.0	--	--	7	14	41
Egeland	20	7.3	24	36	4	8	64
Cando	10	--	--	--	--	--	10
Total	57	16.3	24	36	11	22	115
ROUTE 3							
Rock Lake	62	16.7	68	102	7	14	178
Cando	62	--	--	--	--	--	62
Total	124	16.7	68	102	7	14	240
ROUTE 4*							
Cando	90	93.4	517	420	46	92	602

*These figures are for six truck loads.

Table 13F Towner County--Alternative I Collection Costs--Service to 7 Communities

EXPENSE ITEM	Initial Cost	Salvage Value	Annual Principle		Annual Interest		Annual Loan Amortization		Annual Operation Cost
Salaries, Wages and Fringe Benefits									
1. Personnel									
a. Refuse Truck Personnel (2)									22,700
SUBTOTAL									22,700
Operation and Maintenance									
1. Fuel, Lubrication (@22¢/mile)									3,146
2. Repairs									2,650
3. Insurance									1,125
SUBTOTAL									6,921
Equipment									
1. 1-16 yd. Packer Truck	27,500	8,000	2,750						
SUBTOTAL	27,500	8,000	2,750	+	2,200	=	4,950		
2. Containers (3 cu.yd., 131 @ $350/unit)	45,850	11,463	4,585		3,668				
SUBTOTAL	45,850	11,463	4,585	+	3,668	=	8,253		
TOTAL							13,203	+	29,621 = 42,824

Table 14F Towner County--Alternative II Collection Costs--Service to 7 Communities

EXPENSE ITEM	Initial Cost	Salvage Value	Annual Principle	Annual Interest	Annual Loan Amortization	Annual Operation Cost
Salaries, Wages and Fringe Benefits						
1. Personnel						
a. Refuse Truck Personnel (2)						22,700
SUBTOTAL						22,700
Operation and Maintenance						
1. Fuel, Lubrication (@22¢/mile)						3,718
2. Repairs						2,675
3. Insurance						1,150
SUBTOTAL						7,543
Equipment						
1. 1-16 yd. Packer Truck	27,500		2,750	2,200		
SUBTOTAL	27,500		2,750 +	2,200 =	4,950	
TOTAL					4,950 +	30,243 = 34,193

CARTER, MISSOURI

Ozark Foothills Regional Planning Commission, An Analysis of Fire Protection and Fire Prevention Systems within the Ozark Foothills Region, May 1979, pp. 3, 7-8, 18-19.

Survey Format and Results

There are three basic components or parts of any fire protection system: organization, including organizational structure; personnel and training; water supply, including water mains, hydrants, and water storage; equipment, including vehicles, communications equipment, safety equipment, and fire fighting apparatus. By utilizing this format, a survey form was prepared and transmitted to all cities and rural fire protection organizations within the region. The questionnaires were followed up by personal interviews with those individuals active in rural fire protection, as well as discussion with representatives of the State Fire Marshal's office, the Insurance Service Organization, various insurance companies, and local elected officials.

The tabulated results of this survey are presented in the following charts which divide each system into the three categories previously discussed.

The information shown in the following charts was current to the year 1977.

Carter County

The 1970 Census found 3,878 persons residing in Carter County and found 1,605 dwelling units of which 338 were constructed prior to 1940. The county encompasses 506 square miles with a population density of eight persons per square mile. Public ownership of land within the county is extensive with 67 percent of the land in forest cover. Only 33 percent of the county's population live within the incorporated areas of the county. In addition to the residents who live in the cities of Van Buren, Ellsinore, and Grandin, the remaining population is concentrated within the unincorporated communities of Fresmont, Hunter, South Van Buren, and Eastwood, and along U.S. Highway 60.

The following presents an analysis of the county's fire protection capabilities.

City of Ellsinore The City of Ellsinore has an adequate water supply system with fire hydrants which operate on 45 p.s.i. with 4" water mains. The city's equipment consists of one pumper with 300' of 2" hose. The pumper can carry 500 gallons of portable water which is seriously inadequate if hydrant or main failure should occur. The department is manned by a fire chief and twelve (12) volunteer firemen. Training and drills are below those Insurance Service Organization standards necessary for effective fire protection. The alarm system consists of an outside siren only, which is inadequate in the instance of power failure.

Chart 3 Carter County Fire Protection System Organizational Component

Location	Full-Time Firemen	Volunteer Firemen	Alarm System	Fire Station	Regular Drills & Training	Interest In Fire Training	Organi-zation
Ellsinore	0	12	Siren	Yes	Yes	Yes	Chief
Van Buren	0	11	Siren Phone	Yes	Yes	Yes	Chief
Grandin	0	6	Phone	yes	Yes	Yes	Chief

Source: Ozark Foothills Regional Planning Commission Survey.

Chart 3a Carter County Fire Protection System Equipment Component

Location	Pumper Trucks	Booster Trucks	Hose Size	Hose Length	Nozzle Size	Ladder	Foam Extin-guisher	Pump Pressure
Ellsinore	1	1	2 1/2"	300'	2"-2 1/2"	28'	Yes	N/A
Van Buren	1	1	1 1/2"- 2 1/2"	1,000'	2 1/2"- 3 1/2"	28'	Yes	250 lb.
Grandin	1	0	1 1/2"- 2"	1,500'	N/A	28'	Yes	50 lb.

Source: Ozark Foothills Regional Planning Commission Survey.

Chart 3b Carter County Fire Protection System Water Supply Component

Location	Portable Water (Gallon)	Hydrant Pressure	Hydrant Gallon per Minute	Hydrant Connection Size	Fire Codes	Rating
Ellsinore	500	45 lb.	N/A	4"	Yes Enforced	10
Van Buren	300	65 lb.	300	4"	Yes Enforced	10
Grandin	3,000	60 lb.	500	4"	Yes Enforced	10

Source: Ozark Foothills Regional Planning Commission Survey.

The following activities are recommended for the City of Ellsinore to meet Insurance Service Organization Class 8 equipment and organizational standards:

1. Begin regular meetings for the purpose of training and drills;
2. Purchase additional equipment to meet Insurance Service Organizaton apparatus and appliance standards;
3. Enact and enforce a fire protection ordinance;
4. Increase hydrant p.s.i. to a minimum of 50 pounds p.s.i.
5. Improve organizational structure within the department with the adoption of bylaws and designated responsibilities.

City of Van Buren The City of Van Buren has an adequate water supply with 4" water hydrant connections and hydrant producing 60 p.s.i. with a flow of 500 gallons per minute. The department has one new pumper truck which operates at 250 p.s.i. and has a portable water capacity of 750 gallons; carries 1,200' of 2 1/2" hose, 600' of 1 1/2" hose, 150' of 1" hose, and is manned by eleven (11) volunteer firemen. At present time, there is no housing for the new truck. An older model pumper is used as a back-up truck and operates at 250 p.s.i. with a portable water capacity of 300 gallons; and carries 1,200' of 2 1/2" hose. The alarm system is of the telephone/siren variety.

The following action is recommended for the City of Van Buren to meet the Insurance Service Organization Class 8 Standards in the areas of oranization and equipment:

1. Increase volunteer personnel to include an assistant chief;
2. Purchase additional equipment to meet Insurance Service Organization apparatus and appliance standards;
3. Enact and enforce fire prevention ordinances;
4. Begin regular training and drill meetings;
5. Survey existing fire hydrant distribution to assure total coverage;
6. Housing for new truck.

City of Grandin The City of Grandin has an adequate water supply system with fire hydrants which operate on 60 p.s.i. at a 500 gallon per minute capacity with 4" lines. The city has one pumper with a portable water capacity of 3,000 gallons. The department consists of six (6) volunteer members with limited training and organizational structure. The city is deficient in various safety equipment and operates a telephone/siren alarm system.

The following actions are recommended to be taken by the City of Grandin to meet the Insurance Service Organization Class 8 Standards in the categories of organization and equipment:

1. Increase trained personel to twelve (12) members; elect an assistant chief; increase the number of meetings, drills, and training; and adopt bylaws;
2. Purchase additional equipment to meet Insurance Service Organization apparatus and appliance standards;
3. Enact and enforce fire prevention ordinances;
4. Survey existing fire hydrant coverage area to identify deficiencies.

CATTARAUGUS, NEW YORK

Cattaraugus County Planning Board, Cattaraugus County Fiscal Trends and Capital Improvements Program, 1978, pp. 14, 24-25.

Projections

Future capacities, both legal and practical, of the county for financing capital projects will be determined by the amounts of revenue available after other obligations have been met. This requires projectons of both revenues and expenditures, based on extensions of current trends plus knowledge of any extraneous factors which may tend to modify these trends.

Revenues

The following tables and graphs contain projections as prepared by the County Planning Board for real property values, amount of sales, sales tax revenues, and off-track betting revenues. Real property taxes will continue to produce the largest return, with sales tax in second position. These tables assume that county sales tax rate would remain at 3 percent, while three alternates are shown for the property tax rates.

At present, the county would only be able to legally increase property tax rates. The three percent sales tax rate is the maximum currently permitted by state law. Due to present indicators of a leveling off in our national economy, there may be added popular pressures to keep taxes at present rates or to reduce them.

Projections of tax revenues from retail sales and services in Cattaraugus County indicate increases in yields of about 135 percent between 1977 and 1980. This would compare favorably with an expectation of only 116 percent increase in property tax revenues if the same assessment and tax rates should continue. By 1990, total retail sales would have reached $556 million in Cattaraugus County and sales of services would have reached $55 million.

The sales tax has provided a means whereby the county is better able to balance its revenues with expenditures in an inflationary economy. Retail sales have moved upward at a very rapid pace. The county sales tax has increased 121 percent from $1,676,813.09 in 1968 to $3,714,875.00 in 1978. It is anticipated that the rapid pace will continue and that the county will be drawing approximately $8,750,000.00 by 1990. This figure assumes that inflationary trends will continue, an increase in the county population to approximately 96,000, and an increase of approximately 3 percent more area devoted to commercial activity to accommodate the increasing population.

Total Projections of Income from County Sources--Cattaraugus County (Based on no Increase of Tax Rates)

Category	1976*	1980	1982	1990	Percent of Increase 1976-1990
Real Property Tax (including re-levies and penalties)	$ 6,104,123.27	$10,041,528	$11,597,964	$17,823,712	192.0
Sales Tax	3,287,209.57	4,925,000	5,675,000	8,750,000	166.2
Licenses, Fees, Reimbursements & Other Charges	4,622,340.08	5,546,808	6,101,488	8,320,212	80.0
Off-track Betting	85,290.00	182,500	231,500	422,500	395.4
Other	756,627.37	1,034,791	1,180,206	1,765,821	133.4
Subtotal	14,855,590.29	21,730,627	24,786,158	37,082,245	149.6
Revenue Sharing	1,184,476.00	1,200,000	--	--	--
TOTALS	$16,040,066.29	$22,930,627			

*Actual amounts received

PROJECTIONS OF INCOME FROM COUNTY SOURCES

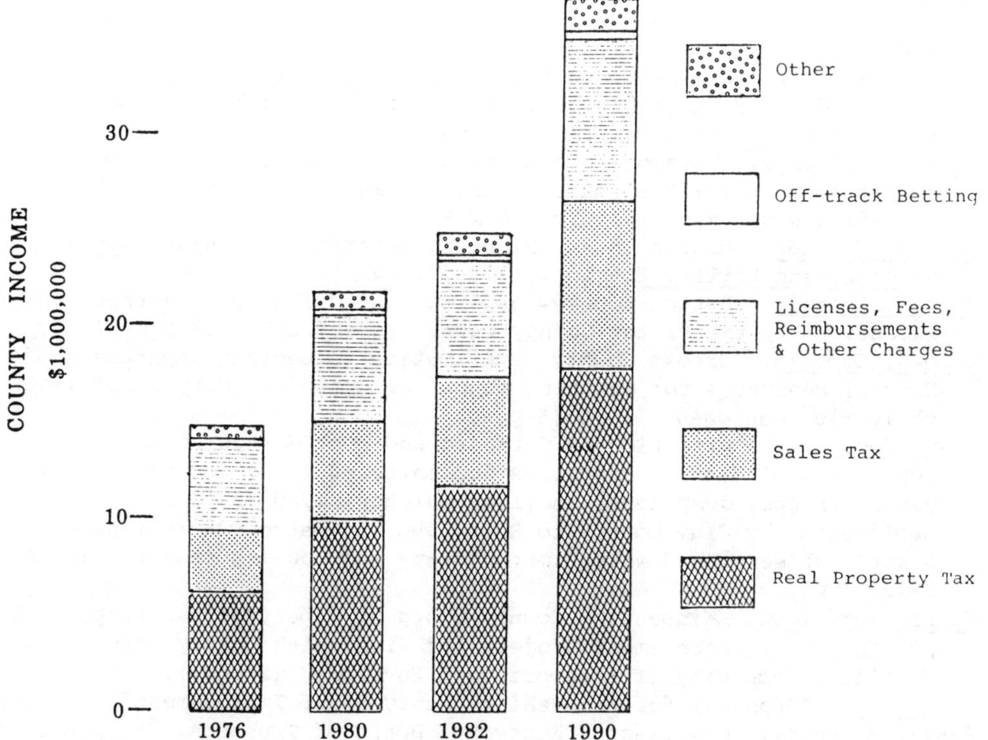

Bibliography: Community Facilities

Henry, Alabama. Southeast Alabama Regional Planning and Development Commission, "Community Center Implementation Plan: A Study for the Utilization of Vacant Public Buildings to Meet Critical Space Shortages," 1978 (17 pgs.).

_______, Proposals for Rural Fire Protection: A Study Detailing Ways to Improve Fire Protection in Rural Communities, 1977 (32 pgs.).

_______, "A Proposal for Secondary Libraries: A Study for the Expansion of Library Services to Unserved Areas," 1978 (13 pgs.).

_______, Recreation Implementation Plan: A Study for the Utilization of School and Church Facilities for Public Recreation, 1978 (33 pgs.).

Lowndes, Alabama. South Central Alabama Development Commission, Lowndes County Community Facilities Plan, Public Improvements Program, Capital Improvements Budget, 1979 (103 pgs.).

Fairbanks, Alaska. Fairbanks Town and Village Association for Development, Inc., Community Facilities Summaries, 1979 (187 pgs.).

Boone, Marion, and Searcy, Arkansas. Northwest Arkansas Economic Development District, Inc., "Housing Needs Surveys," 1980 (2 pgs.).

County Development Committee, "County Facilities and Services Survey" (5 pgs.).

Searcy, Arkansas. McGoodwin, Williams and Yates, Inc., "Water Supply and Facility Needs: Marshall, Leslie, and Searcy County Arkansas" (7 pgs.).

Northwest Arkansas Economic Development District, Inc., "Water, Sewer and Solid Waste Disposal Charges in the Northwest Arkansas Economic Development District" (5 pgs.).

Sussex, Delaware. Town of Bethany Beach, Application to FmHA (Water and Waste Disposal Systems for Rural Communities) for funds for upgrading water system, 1979 (88 pgs.).

Monroe, Florida. Monroe County Planning Department, Monroe County Services and Utility Element, 1978 (61 pgs.).

Bartow, Georgia. Bartow County, Application to EDA for construction of extensions to the Bartow County water system, 1976 (23 pgs.).

Brooks, Georgia. Brooks County, Application to Georgia Department of Natural Resources for matching funds for upgrading city solid waste collection equipment, 1975 (6 pgs.).

Clay, Georgia. Application by Cuthbert and Fort Gaines to Georgia Department of Natural Resources for matching funds for solid waste packer trucks, dumpsters, and limb mulcher, 1980 (1 pg.).

Application by Clay County to HUD (CDBG Non-Metro Discretionary Grant) for sewer and water improvements and housing rehabilitation 1979 (1 pg.).

Winneshiek, Iowa. Winneshiek County Board of Supervisors, "Proposal to EDA for water improvement project for Winneshiek County Care Facility, Community of Freeport, and Environs" (8 pgs.).

_______, "Proposal for Winneshiek County Sewer Improvement" (3 pgs.).

Henry, Kentucky. New Castle, Kentucky, Board of Trustees, "Proposal to EPA for Wastewater Treatment Construction Grant" (20 pgs.).

Marshall, Kentucky. Marshall Sanitation District No. 1, Application to FmHA for wastewater treatment facilities and wastewater collection system, 1979 (116 pgs.).

Ohio, Kentucky. Ohio County Park and Fair Board, "Request for funding assistance for two major exhibit buildings" (13 pgs.).

Acadia, Louisiana. Acadia Parish Policy Jury, "Proposal to FmHA for a multi-purpose livestock-meeting-show-facility" (9 pgs.).

Delta and Dickinson, Michigan. Central Upper Peninsula Planning and Development Regional Commission, Regional Water Supply Plan 1980 (85 pgs.).

Dickinson, Michigan. "Communities in the Region which operate or are served by Public Water Supply Systems" (36 pgs.).

Livingston, Michigan. Rural Development Planning Program for Western Livingston County, Open File Report: Essential Community Services (62 pgs.).

Adair and Schuyler, Missouri. Northeast Missouri Regional Planning Commission, Northeast Missouri Areawide Development Assistance Plan, 1979-1980. Vol. 1: Water and Sewer (171 pgs.).

Carter, Missouri. Ozark Foothills Regional Planning Commission, Bridge Survey, Ozark Foothills Region, October 1978 (43 pgs.).

_______, An Analysis of Fire Protection and Fire Prevention Systems within the Ozark Foothills Region, May 1979 (64 pgs.).

Jasper and Lawrence, Missouri. Agricultural Experiment Station, University of Missouri-Columbia, Analyzing the Feasibility of Domestic Rural Water Supplies in Missouri with Emphasis on the Ozarks Region, 1980 (57 pgs.).

Valley, Nebraska. "Rural Energy Initiative-Small Scale Hydro," 1979 (1 pg.).

Lea, New Mexico. Lea County, Application to DOT/FAA Airport Development Aid Program for funds for correcting surface deficiencies on runway, 1979 (12 pgs.).

Town of Tatum, Application to Department of Interior, Heritage Conservation and Recreation Service, for funds for development of existing park to include tennis court improvements, picnic area, and playground, 1979 (9 pgs.).

Cattaraugus, New York. Cattaraugus County Planning Board, Cattaraugus County Fiscal Trends and Capital Improvements Program, 1978 (60 pgs.).

North Carolina. North Carolina Agricultural Extension Service and Center for Rural Resource Development, "Rural Fire Protection in North Carolina," Center for Rural Resource Development Report No. 2, 1977 (15 pgs.).

Cavalier and Towner, North Dakota. North Central Planning Council, Comprehensive Plan, Vol. III: Solid Waste Systems Analysis, 1977 (228 pgs.).

McCormick, South Carolina. Upper Savannah Council of Governments, McCormick County Fire Protection Study and Plan, 1979 (57 pgs.).

Custer, South Dakota. City of Custer, Application to the Bureau of Outdoor Recreation for funds for construction of a restroom, 1979 (5 pgs.).

Sixth District Council of Local Governments, Application to FmHA for fund for Water and Waste Disposal System for Rural Communities for Custer City, 1980 (11 pgs.).

Hanson, South Dakota. Planning and Development District III, Wastewater Treatment: A Survey of Needs in Planning and Development District III, 1978 (348 pgs.).

Shannon, South Dakota. Shannon County School District, Application to EDA for funds for shower and dressing room facilities for high school gymnasium, 1977 (43 pgs.).

Benton, Tennessee. Northwest Tennessee Development District, Fire Protection Plan, Benton County, Tennessee, 1979 (36 pgs.).

Henry, Virginia. Piedmont Planning District Commission, Metropolitan Regional Comprehensive Water and Wastewater Disposal Plan: Update, 1977 (107 pgs.).

______, Regional Capital Improvements Needs Study, 1978-1988 (24 pgs. - contents and excerpts).

Mathews, Virginia. Mathews County, Analysis of Public Building Needs, 1977 (31 pgs.).

Middle Peninsula Planning District Commissin, "Financial Analysis and Capital Improvements Program, Mathews County Virginia," 1977 (21 pgs.).

Mecklenburg, Virginia. Southside Planning District Commission, Water Quality Management Plan, 1974: Vol. 1: Introduction and Planning

Studies (306 pgs.); Vol. 2: Existing Facilities and Water Quality (384 pgs.); Vol. 3: Water Quality Management Plan (143 pgs.).

King and Queen, Virginia. Middle Peninsula Planning District Commission, Financial Analysis and Capital Improvements Program, King & Queen County, Virginia, 1979 (22 pgs.).

Marquette and Waushara, Wisconsin. East Central Wisconsin Regional Planning Commission, Community Facilities in East Central Wisconsin, 1979 (59 pgs.).

Crook, Wyoming. Town of Hulett, Application to HUD for water system improvements (CDBG-small cities program), 1980 (12 pgs.).

Town of Moorcroft, application to FmHA for site acquisition and development of a municipal complex (Rural Development Section 601 Energy Impacted Area Development Assistance Program), 1979 (6 pgs.).

_______, "Application to the Wyoming Farm Loan Board for a Grant from the Mineral Royalties Tax Account" (for water supply improvements), 1979 (18 pgs.).

_______, "Application to the Wyoming Farm Loan Board for a Grant from the Mineral Royalties Tax Account" (to relocate town's sewer lagoon), 1978 (13 pgs.).

Town of Sundance, "Application to the Wyoming Farm Loan Board for a Grant from the Mineral Royalties Tax Account" (for water well, storage tanks and pumps), 1978 (12 pgs.).

NATURAL RESOURCES

Various kinds of natural resource plans are funded by EPA, USDA, HUD, and state agencies. The contents vary depending on whether the focus is on clean water, clean air, soil retention, or preserving flora and fauna.

The first data example shows the nesting and range areas of the bald eagle in Teton County, Wyoming. It also describes some of their habitat requirements.

The second example describes the problem of groundwater contamination from chemicals used on the blueberry barrens in Maine. The location of blueberry and surface water areas are mapped.

The next example describes the pollution of Maine clamflats by sewage from shoreland development. Clamflat productivity by town is presented to make clear that this important economic activity should be protected.

The last example, from Maryland, makes projections about the number of acres of land that will be used in various ways (e.g., agricultural, forest, urban) under different long-term planning assumptions. Economic, social, and environmental implications are considered.

TETON, WYOMING

Izaak Walton League of America, Wildlife in Jackson Hole, Wyoming: Private Lands as Critical Habitat, 1979, pp. 12, 18-20.

IV. Species by Species Analysis

It is important to specify what benefits will accrue to particular wildlife species with the protecton of private lands in Jackson Hole. Too little is known to give equal consideration to all species. Because of their importance within the ecosystem, many species may be used as indicator species. Changes in their populations drastically alter the entire ecosystem and give insight into the condition of all species.

Bald Eagles

The riparian community is essential to bald eagles. For nesting, they require large trees with strong crotches, usually within 50 yards (46 m) of open water. During the breeding season, fish are their most important food source, especially cutthroat trout. Presently three nests are located on private land along the Snake River (Figure 7). The South Park portion of the Snake River is essential winter habitat for bald eagles; approximately 20 winter there now. Wintering bald eagles also have specific requirements and are especially sensitive to human disturbance.

Tall, dead deciduous trees, such as cottonwoods, are important daytime roosts and need to be within 50 yards (46 m) of streams. At night, dense stands of conifers are preferred, also close to the river. Thus, in South Park, maintenance of dead trees and a buffer strip of dense vegetation is needed along the river. Feeding bald eagles appear to be particularly sensitive to human disturbance, but this can be mitigated by dense vegetation. Vegetative buffer zones of 270 yards (250 m) would be important protection for the wintering eagles.

WASHINGTON, MAINE

Washington County Regional Planning Commission, 208 Water Quality Management Plan: Agriculture and the 208 Water Quality Plan for Washington County, Agricultural Chemical Use and Disposal 1979, pp. 11-12.

Implications for Water Quality

Washington County has been blessed with large resources of clean fresh water. Surface water alone constitutes over 12 percent of the county's areas, and large aquifers and groundwater recharge areas have been mapped in just the coastal areas. Inland groundwater resources are as yet unmapped and may have great potential.

FIGURE 7

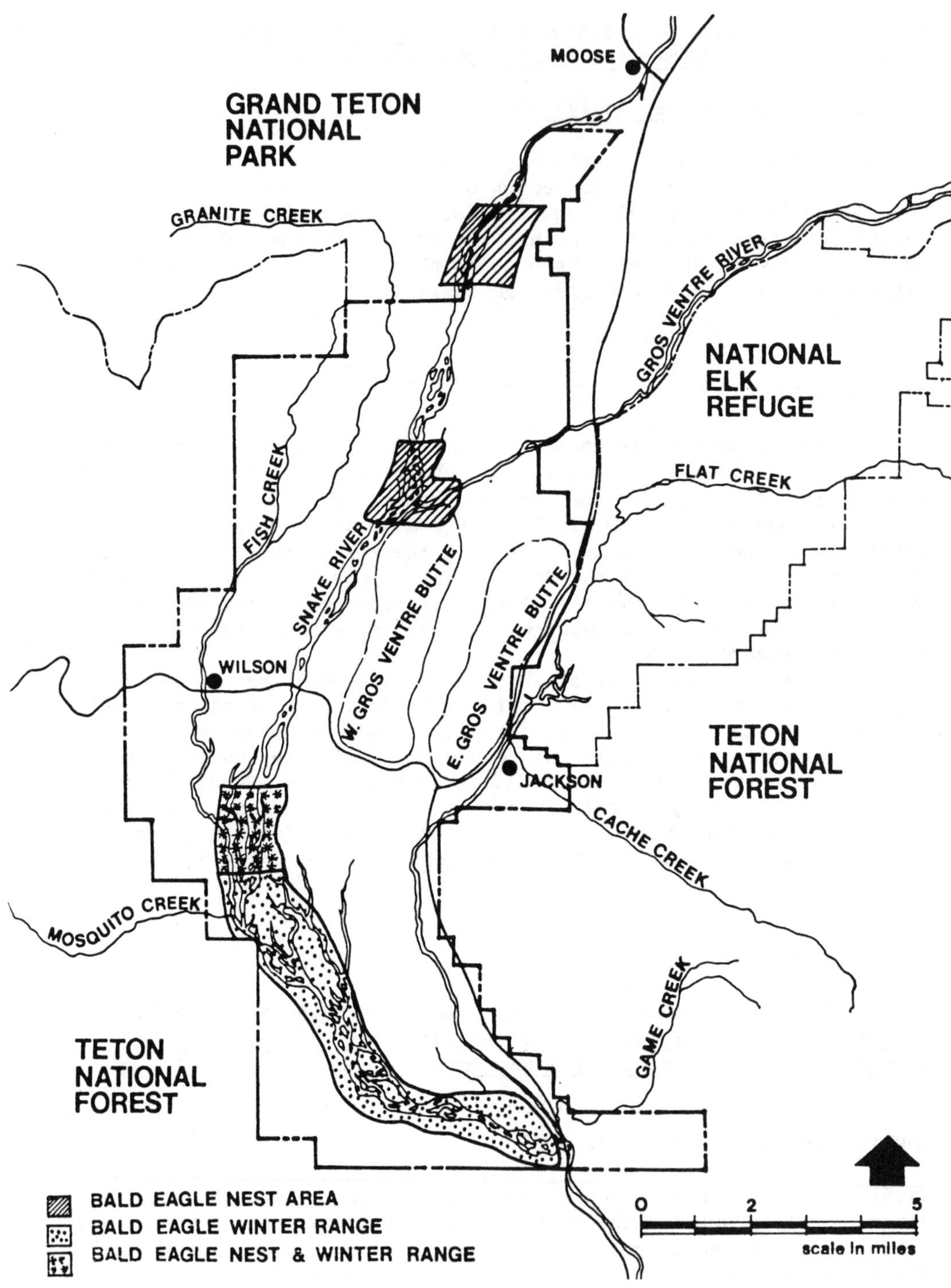

MOOSE
GRAND TETON NATIONAL PARK
GRANITE CREEK
GROS VENTRE RIVER
NATIONAL ELK REFUGE
FISH CREEK
SNAKE RIVER
FLAT CREEK
W. GROS VENTRE BUTTE
E. GROS VENTRE BUTTE
WILSON
TETON NATIONAL FOREST
JACKSON
CACHE CREEK
MOSQUITO CREEK
GAME CREEK
TETON NATIONAL FOREST
BALD EAGLE NEST AREA
BALD EAGLE WINTER RANGE
BALD EAGLE NEST & WINTER RANGE
0
2
5
scale in miles

Portable drinking water supplies are becoming scarcer in the nation and the world, which may make water supplies in this county an important resource for the Northeast. It is not unfeasible to consider that sometime in the not-too-distant future, Washington County may have the opportunity to ship fresh drinking water to other parts of Maine or New England. At present, growing metropolitan areas are building pipelines to reservoirs more than a hundred miles away to meet their water demands. Metropolitan areas aside, future development in Washington County may rely heavily on sources of clean water for industrial and commercial use, as well as private domestic supplies. It would be well not to jeopardize the future of these resources by careless activities today.

The county map below shows important aquifers and superimposes available information on large blueberry tracts on the map as well. As discussed in the WCRPC report, "Assessment of Existing Information," the highly permeable soils on which blueberries are managed increase the chances of groundwater contamination from chemicals used on the blueberry barrens. Precipitation close on the heels of an application of spray may wash off the chemical and carry it rapidly into the groundwater before it has a chance to break down. This may be a particular hazard with chemicals that, in order to degrade, 1) require sunlight, 2) must be adsorbed by the soil, or 3) require certain amounts of oxygen, which is less prevalent in groundwater than in exposed surface water. Besides this, many pesticides, mixed with a petroleum base for application, are insoluble in water.

Pesticide contamination has occurred in Washington County waters. A University of Maine at Orono report by Borns, Dimond, and Norton in 1971 showed that the groundwater supply in the Cherryfield area often approaches maximum pesticide limits for human consumption after fields have been treated.

WASHINGTON, MAINE

Washington County Regional Planning Comimssion, <u>208 Water Quality Managemet Plan: Assessment of Existing Information</u>, 1978, pp. 14-16.

<u>Private Sewage Disposal Systems</u>

2. Washington County's Situation

With a population the size of Bangor living in an area of over a million and a half acres, Washington County is considered rural. About 75 percent of the population lives in towns of less than 2,500 persons, most of it in the coastal zone. Calais, Machias, and Baileyville all have sewage collection and treatment serving their urban areas. Peter Dana Point in Indian Township also has a sewage treatment facility. The federal government operates two small treatment plants, one in Bucks Harbor and one in Cutler, to handle wastes from their military housing developments. And the Georgia-Pacific Corporation, a pulp and paper manufacturer in Baileyville, has built a large secondary

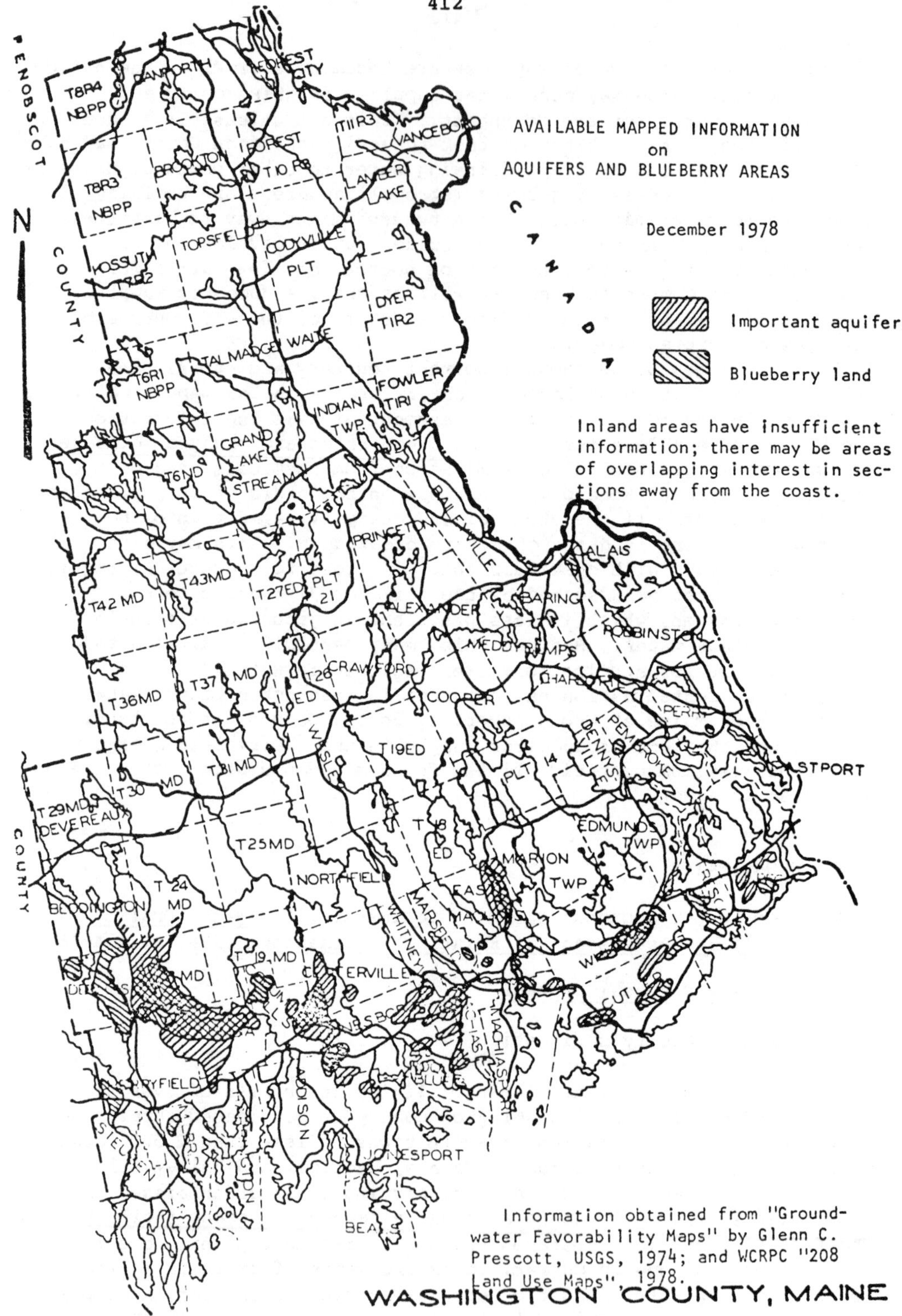
AVAILABLE MAPPED INFORMATION
on
AQUIFERS AND BLUEBERRY AREAS
December 1978
Important aquifers
Blueberry land
Inland areas have insufficient information; there may be areas of overlapping interest in sections away from the coast.
Information obtained from "Groundwater Favorability Maps" by Glenn C. Prescott, USGS, 1974; and WCRPC "208 Land Use Maps", 1978.
WASHINGTON COUNTY, MAINE
PENOBSCOT COUNTY
CANADA
N
DANFORTH
FOREST CITY
T8R4 NBPP
T8R3 NBPP
BROOKTON
FOREST
T10 R3
T11 R3
VANCEBORO
LAMBERT LAKE
KOSSUTH
TOPSFIELD
CODYVILLE
PLT
DYER TIR2
TALMADGE
WAITE
T6R1 NBPP
FOWLER TIR1
INDIAN TWP.
GRAND LAKE STREAM
T6ND
BAILEYVILLE
PRINCETON
CALAIS
T43MD
T27ED
PLT 21
T42 MD
ALEXANDER
BARING
ROBBINSTON
MEDDYBEMPS
T37 MD
T26 ED
CRAWFORD
T36MD
COOPER
PERRY
PEMBROKE
DENNYSVILLE
T31 MD
T19ED
PLT 14
STPORT
T30 MD
T29MD
DEVEREAUX
T25MD
T18 ED
EDMUNDS TWP
MARION TWP
NORTHFIELD
WHITNEY
T 24 MD
BEDDINGTON
MARSHFIELD
T 19 MD
MD
ERVILLE
CUTL
CHERRYFIELD
ADDISON
JONESPORT
BEALS

treatment facility to handle its industrial wastes. Danforth, Eastport, Jonesboro, Lubec, and Milbridge have sewer collection without treatment. Milbridge is in the process of designing a collection and treatment system. All other towns depend upon private means of disposal.

A variety of problems beset sewage treatment plants. In Machias, for instance, average daily flow often exceeds the capacity of the treatment plant of 300,000 gallons per day. Overflows at the plant must be released and can only be treated with chlorine, though the effectiveness of chlorination is unknown.[4] A hydrographic study of the Machias River in 1976 showed a rapid travel time and wide dispersal area from the point of discharge to productive mudflats, giving little chance for a significant die-off of microbials and increasing the likelihood of high coliform bacteria counts.[5] Other treatment plants in the county tend to have fewer, less complex problems.

Malfunctioning sewage treatment plants cannot take all the blame for coastal pollution in Washington County. They handle sewage disposal for only a small percentage of the population. Overboard discharges and malfunctioning private sewage systems within shoreland areas have led to the closure of almost 10 percent of Washington County's clamflats (see Table below). Compared to the rest of the state, our county proves to be fairly clean. This is mostly because of the sparse population. The polluted clamflats, however, all occur adjacent to shoreland development--subdivisions, towns, villages, and thickly settled areas. Increasing pressure to develop shorelands by our growing population will tend to aggravate this situation, and unless protective measures are taken, more clamflats will be closed because of domestic wastes.

Clams are the second-most economically important fisheries resource in the county, lobsters being first.[6] Washington County supplies nearly 40 percent of the entire state's landed value of soft-shell clams.[7] Increased pollution of clamflats will therefore take a more and more sizable chunk out of the pockets of local fishermen. The mathematical estimates presented below, though perhaps not totally accurate, give some idea of the value of clams that could be harvested if the closed flats were opened for harvest. The figures were derived from estimates made after two years of study by the Department of Marine Resources. (The average price per bushel of clams in 1976 was fourteen dollars.)

A. Total value of clams in flats in Washington County:
   (total # bushels) x (average price/bushel)
   1,570,450 x $14 = $21,986,300

B. Total potential value of clams on closed flats:
   (# bushels on closed flats) x (average price/bushel)
   126,825 x $14 = $1,775,550

C. Estimates that the digger harvests about 30 percent of crop yearly:
   (value of clams in closed flats: B) x (0.30)
   $1,775,550 x 0.30 = $532,665

Survey of Washington County Clamflats and Productivity

TOWN	Total # Acres	Total # Bushels in Flats	Average Bushels Acre	# Acres Closed	# Bushels on Closed Flats	% Acres Closed	% Bushels on Closed Flats	# Clean Acres
Robbinston	153	12,225	79	61	4,575	39.8%	37.4%	92
Perry	647	38,150	59	56	2,800	8.6	7.3	591
Eastport	323	19,025	58	234	12,350	72.4	64.9	89
Pembroke	652	32,650	50	0	0	0.0	0.0	652
Dennysville	20	500	25	0	0	0.0	0.0	20
Edmunds	465	12,000	26	0	0	0.0	0.0	465
Lubec	2126	172,350	81	48	3,600	2.2	2.1	2078
Trescott	957	38,950	41	0	0	0.0	0.0	957
Cutler	1296	108,850	84	229	15,275	7.6	14.0	1067
Whiting	375	28,125	75	133	9,975	35.4	35.5	242
Machiasport	1396	116,450	83	523	46,700	37.5	40.0	873
East Machias	112	6,600	59	112	6,600	100.0	100.0	0
Roque Bluffs	574	38,465	67	0	0	0.0	0.0	574
Jonesboro	313	22,325	71	0	0	0.0	0.0	313
Jonesport	859	43,720	51	33	3,050	3.8	7.0	826
Beals	223	13,400	60	36	1,800	16.1	13.4	187
Addison	1558	157,850	101	0	0	0.0	0.0	1558
Harrington	2154	364,955	169	0	0	0.0	0.0	2154
Milbridge	1425	193,085	135	112	19,775	7.8	10.2	1313
Steuben	1133	150,775	133	13	325	1.1	0.2	1120
TOTALS	16,761	1,570,450	94	1590	126,825	9.5%	8.1%	15,171

These figures were calculated after two years of study (1972 - 1974) by the Department of Marine Resources and are estimates. They do not reflect closing of flats due to periodic red tide.

These figures serve to illustrate the value of clams only as they are harvested. Clams increase greatly in value as they are sold to restaurants and other food-serving businesses. The value of a bushel of raw clams may multiply 13 to 17 times when it is converted into fried clams. Steamed clams experience an even greater magnification in value, multiplying up to 27 times over the fresh-off-the-flats value.[8]

It is obvious that clams represent a great source of income to residents of Washington County and serious efforts should be made to keep the remaining open flats open through water pollution control.

Footnotes

[4]Information from Dennis Purington, Municipal Services, Department of Environmental Protection, Augusta, Maine, September 14, 1976.

[5]Santo Furfari and Virgil E. Carr, "Report on the Machias River, Maine: Hydrographic Studies," Shellfish Sanitation Branch, U.S. Food and Drug Administration, May 11-13, 1976.

[6]"Maine Landings, Annual Summary 1976," U.S. Department of Commerce, Maine Department of Marine Resources, April 21, 1977.

[7]Ibid.

[8]"A Multiplier for Computing the Value of Shellfish," U.S. Department of the Interior, Needham, Massachusetts, October 1969; also, telephone conversation with Ed Wong, Region I, Environmental Protection Agency, Lexington, Massachusetts, November 2, 1977.

KENT, MARYLAND

USDA, Maryland Department of Natural Resources, Maryland Department of Agriculture, Delaware Department of Natural Resources and Environmental Control, and Virginia Soil and Water Conservation Commission, Delmarva River Basins Survey, 1978, pp. IV-1 - IV-5.

Chapter IV - Future Without Plan Conditions

Introduction

This chapter describes expected future conditions without a comprehensive plan of resource development. These projections are simply estimates of future conditions under carefully defined circumstances. Future without plant conditions assume that there will be no new starts in federal or state assisted projects and no change in federal or state programs which are not already scheduled. These conditions are described in order to assist in identification of future needs, and formulation of alternative plans and comparison of alternatives.

Assumptions

General. Projected conditions are based on long-term trends and ignore cyclical fluctuations which characterize the short-term paths of our economy. It is assumed that present industries will continue to be a part of Delmarva's economy, that land treatment programs such as soil and water conservation district programs with technical assistance will remain at their present levels, that state and other programs will remain at present levels, and that technology will result in higher per acre yield.

Economic Considerations. Projections of agricultural production at the national level (OBERS Projections) have been made by the U.S. Department of Agriculture. These projections are based on requirements for domestic consumption and estimated exports. When disaggregated to the state and river basin level, they estimate the study area's expected share of a steady flow of products to meet domestic and export demands. Year to year fluctuations in production induced by weather conditions or transitory price differentials are not estimated.

Social Considerations. The composition of age and sex within the Peninsula population has important implications for individual resource demands and economic potential. Trends indicate that most young adults will continue to migrate from the farm population into the non-farm sector. This migration will continue to reduce the labor force for existing and potential rural employers and aggravate some existing economic and social conditions.

Environmental Considerations. Future without plan activities will include environmental enhancement practices from ongoing projects such as 208 water quality improvement plans. Programs for wetland preservation, federal cost sharing for water treatment plants, forestry incentive programs, wildlife enhancement programs, and others will increase the protection of the environment.

Ongoing Programs. The state agencies' programs should not be affected by the "without development" assumption. The roles of federal agencies will only be altered after about ten years because of projects already approved for operation. Additional assumptions were that there would be no new watershed flood prevention and drainage projects constructed, no group projects installed with federal assistance, and no acceleration of ongoing programs.

Other programs necessary to sustain agricultural production are assumed to continue as part of the future conditions without a plan. Included are the traditional soil and water conservation and erosion control programs of the soil and water conservation districts, with the technical assistance provided by the Soil Conservation service and U.S. Forest Service. The U.S. Department of Agriculture, colleges, universities, and private enterprise will continue to carry out agricultural research activities.

Table IV-A - Historical and projected land use, Delmarva Peninsula.

	1975	FWOP[1] study projections 1990	FWOP[1] study projections 2000	OBERS Series Projections 1990	OBERS Series Projections 2000
	Thousand acres				
Agricultural					
Harvested cropland and pasture	1,531.4	1,585.6	1,546.7	1,481.3	1,759.3
Cropland failure	61.3	63.4	61.9	59.3	70.4
Planted cropland and pasture	1,592.7	1,649.0	1,608.6	1,540.6	1,829.9
Double cropped	162.4	244.4	223.6	136.0	444.9
Cropland and pasture (net)	1,430.3	1,404.6	1,385.0	1,404.6	1,385.0
Idle cropland and pasture	84.5	77.2	74.8	77.2	74.8
Other agricultural use	32.7	32.7	32.7	32.7	32.7
Total agricultural uses	1,547.5	1,514.5	1,492.5	1,514.5	1,492.5
Forest land	1,257.9	1,262.0	1,266.1	1,262.0	1,266.1
Wetlands	370.6	370.6	370.6	370.6	370.6
Urban land	223.4	252.3	270.2	270.2	270.2
All other uses	165.6	165.6	165.6	165.6	165.6
Total land area	3,565.0	3,565.0	3,565.0	3,565.0	3,565.0

1 FWOP - Future without project.

Programs designed to minimize increases in non-agricultural flood-water damage such as the flood insurance program administered by the U.S. Department of Housing and Urban Development and land use planning by all levels of government are assumed to continue.

Ongoing programs concerned with supply, distribution, and quality of water, recreation resources, fish and wildlife, economic and human resources, historical resources, and wetlands will continue at all levels of government and private enterprise.

General Description of Future W/O Plan Conditions

Land Use. The land base for production of agricultural products will diminish over time as more land is converted to highways, homesites, industries, ponds, and other uses. More pressure will be placed on the remaining acres for production. Accordingly, idle land will be brought into production and some forest land will be cleared for crops and pasture, particularly in areas where timber value offsets clearing costs. Some areas will be planted to trees and other areas will revert to forest uses. Estimated land use under without plan conditions is shown in Table IV-A.

The levels of crop production forecast for 1990 and 2000 imply a substantial increase in double cropping as the cropland base decreases due to the conversion of land to urban and forest uses. Some idle crop and pasture land will be brought into production. Idle land was only 5.5 percent of available cropland and pasture in 1974. This probably reflects conditions such as isolation, changes in ownership, death of operator, etc. rather than a lack of economic incentives for production. Consequently, a similar proportion of idle land is expected to remain in future years. While a slight increase in forest land is expected because of the permanent conversion of cropland to forest on steep slopes subject to erosion (particularly in the northern part of the Peninsula), conversion of land to and from forest uses is expected to be essentially equal with no increase or decrease in forest land. Urban land use is expected to increase by 13 percent by 1990 and by an additional 7 percent by 2000, reflecting continuing growth of the population and economy and continued use of local recreation resources by an increasing proportion of the surrounding area's population. No substantial changes are expected in other land uses which are primarily wetlands, beaches, and transitional areas.

Bibliography: Natural Resources

Alabama. Alabama Cooperative Extension Service, "Land and Water Resource Management Issues," 1980 (8 pgs.).

Calhoun, Alabama. Soil Conservation Service, "Long-Range Program for Calhoun County Soil and Water Conservation District" (23 pgs.).

Searcy, Arkansas. "Application, Water Quality Special Project, Chief Wiley's Watershed Area, Searcy County, Arkansas, 1979 (13 pgs.).

Litchfield, Connecticut. Northwestern Connecticut Regional Planning Agency, Lake Waramaug Watershed Management Plan, 1978 (52 pgs.).

______, "Housatonic River Management Plan," 1978 (10 pgs.).

Shepaug/Bantam River Board, "Shepaug/Bantam River Management Plan Summary," 1979 (6 pgs.).

Monroe, Florida. Monroe County Commission, "Ordinance Providing for Shoreline Protection" (6 pgs.).

______, "Ordinance Providing Site Clearing and Tree Protection" (6 pgs.).

Monroe County Planning Department, Monroe County Coastal Zone Protection and Conservation Element, 1978 (164 pgs.).

Bartow and Dade, Georgia. Coosa Valley Area Planning and Development Commission, Coosa Valley Regional Environmental Process Atlas, 1979 (91 pgs.).

Oneida, Idaho and Cache, Utah. Bear River Resource Conservation and Development, Action Plan, 1977 (48 pgs.).

Jasper, Indiana. Kankakee-Iroquois Regional Planning Commission, Arrow Head Country Resource Conservation and Development Area Natural Resources Plan, 1970 (66 pgs.).

Indiana Department of Natural Resources, Report on the Water and Related Land Resources, Kankakee River Basin, Indiana, 1976 (250 pgs.).

Bath, Menifee, and Morgan, Kentucky. U.S. Forest Service, Technical Planning Workshop for the Licking River Unit, Daniel Boone National Forest, 1976 (118 pgs.).

Washington, Maine. Down East Resource Conservation and Development Council, Down East Resource Conservation and Development Area Framework Plan, 1977 (74 pgs.).

Washington County Regional Planning Commission, 208 Water Quality Management Plan, 1978 (104 pgs.).

______, 208 Water Quality Management Plan: Agriculture and the 208 Water Quality Plan for Washington County, 1979 (60 pgs.).

______, 208 Water Quality Plan, 1977 (22 pgs.).

______, 208 Water Quality Management Plan: Assessment of Existing Information, 1978 (33 pgs.).

Maryland. Maryland State Soil Conservation Committee, "Definition of Terms Relative to Soil Conservation and Water Quality Plans for Farms in Maryland," 1978 (4 pgs.).

______, "How to Select Critical Areas for Nonpoint Sources of Soil Erosion and Animal Wastes on Farms in Maryland," 1978 (24 pgs.).

______, "Best Management Practices for Controlling Soil Erosion or Animal Wastes in Maryland," 1978 (12 pgs.).

______, "Guide for Soil Conservation and Water Quality Plans," 1978 (10 pgs.).

Kent, Maryland. USDA, Maryland Department of Natural Resources, Maryland Department of Agriculture, Delaware Department of Natural Resources and Environmental Control, and Virginia Soil and Water Conservation Commission, Delmarva River Basins Survey, 1978 (175 pgs.).

Dickinson, Michigan. Central Upper Peninsula Planning and Development Regional Commission, Natural Features, 1978 (27 pgs.).

Minnesota. Dorf, Ronald, and Gordon Rose (Agricultural Extension Service, University of Minnesota), "An Operational Information System for Natural Resource Management in West Central Minnesota," 1978 (9 pgs.).

Martin, Minnesota. Minnesota Department of Natural Resources, Division of Waters, Soils and Minerals, "Shoreland Management: Classification Scheme for Public Waters," 1971 (23 pgs.).

Pope, Minnesota. Water Conservation District, "Groundwater Study" (brochure).

Jackson, Mississippi. Jackson County Planning Commission, Geographic Areas of Particular Concern in Jackson, Mississippi for Mississippi Water Continental Shelf Impact Study, 1976 (4 pgs.).

______, Geographic Areas of Particular Concern and Priorities of Use in Jackson County, Mississippi for Mississippi Coastal Zone Management Program, 1976 (61 pgs.).

______, Generalized Siting Criteria for Onshore Outer Continental Shelf Related Impacts for Mississippi Outer Continental Shelf Impact Study, 1976 (26 pgs.).

Chariton, Missouri. Soil and Water Conservation District of Chariton County, Missouri, "Long Range Program of the Soil and Water Conservation District of Chariton County, Missouri," Revised 1979 (27 pgs.).

Hitchcock, Nebraska. Middle Republican Natural Resources District, Middle Republican Natural Resources District Master Plan, 1979 (58 pgs.).

Carteret, Dare, Hertford, and Onslow, North Carolina. Center for Rural Resource Development, North Carolina State University, Raleigh, Overview: Agricultural and Forest Land Drainage in North Carolina's Coastal Zone. Report No. 8, 1978 (66 pgs.).

______, Proceedings: 1978 Workshop on Coastal Land Drainage for Agriculture and Forestry, Report No. 13 (64 pgs.).

Beaufort, South Carolina. Beaufort Conservation District, Long-Range Plan of Work of the Beaufort Soil and Water Conservation District, Beaufort County, South Carolina, 1977 (33 pgs.).

Hanson, South Dakota. Lower James Resource Conservation and Development Council, "Lower James RC&D Short-Term Plan, FY1980" (35 pgs.).

Floyd, Texas. South Plains Association of Governments, Regional Land Resources Management Plan, 1977 (69 pgs.).

Marquette and Waushara, Wisconsin. East Central Wisconsin Regional Planning Commission, Environmental Characteristics, 1978 (pgs. 81).

Teton, Wyoming. Isaak Walton League of America, Wildlife in Jackson Hole: Private Lands as Critical Habitat, 1979 (27 pgs.).

HEALTH

Most of the health items received are miscellaneous proposals and studies. Health planning is not done by local or regional general purpose agencies but by separate bodies, thus few full plans were received. Those received are financed by HEW and include data on physical, mental, and environmental and occupational health, along with health status, health service, and health education goals.

The first example from a health plan is a discussion from the Central Georgia Health Plan of the problems of obtaining health data.

The second example, also from the Central Georgia Health Plan, presents some data from a utilization analysis of hospital services. Number of beds and various measures of hospital use are compared.

The next example, from New Mexico, analyzes the availability of health care. The main indicator of availability, physician/population ratio, is examined. Medical shortage areas, designated by various measures are shown in tables and maps.

The fourth example, also from New Mexico, examines several indicators of the lack of financial access to medical care, including poverty, private insurance coverage, and Medicaid coverage.

The last example is the questionnaire from a health care survey done in South Dakota. The survey questioned people about their access to and satisfaction with medical care.

WILKINSON, GEORGIA

Health Systems Agency of Central Georgia, Inc. Central Georgia Health Plan, Vol. II, 1980, pp. 6-8.

Interpretation of Health Data

Data are the backbone of any health planning effort. However, quite often the data which are presented in planning documents are difficult to interpret--especially for those who are not involved in the provision of health services or other technical or professional fields of endeavor using statistics.

Data are collected by nearly every health and health-related agency. The more comprehensive a plan is to be, the more diverse and complete the data to be collected should be--and the more different agencies need to be requested to provide data. The multiplicity of data sources causes numerous technical problems. Some of the data difficulties experienced by this Agency in developing the Central Georgia Health Plan as follows:

Misleading Rates. Rates are commonly used to compare frequencies of any specific occurrence because they are based upon a common denominator. However, rates may be misleading when comparing counties with larger populations to counties with smaller populations. For example, one death in Muscogee County (the area's most populous county with 171,264 residents*) raises its death rate by 0.6 deaths per 100,000 residents, whereas one death in Quitman County (the area's least populated county with 1,900 residents*) raises its rate by 52.6 deaths per 100,000 residents. A single death is not a large number of deaths, but the rate which results from the one death in a county with few residents could lead a reader to believe that an unusually large number of people in the county died. There is no way to avoid using rates to compare counties, and in most cases they provide a valid means of comparing two or more counties. However, to avoid being misled, when considering comparisons, the reader must take into account not only the rates themselves, but also the total number of occurrences, and the populations of the counties involved.

Age of Data. In some cases in the Plan, data collected during the 1970 Census are used because more current comparable data are not available. Much of the information provided by the decennial census figures, prepared by the U.S. Bureau of the Census, is not available from any other source. Thus, the latest data available at any point in time are data collected during the last census--in this case, the 1970 Census. Most likely there have been substantial changes in many census data figures since 1970, making the use of the 1970 figures marginally appropriate. However, census data can be used in a valid manner for comparing counties as long as the year of collection is the same for all counties being considered, and the reader understands that the figures may be somewhat out of date.

Lack of Common Source and Standardization. This Health Systems Agency serves a bi-state health service area, thus the Agency must obtain data not only from Georgia state sources, but also from Alabama state sources. Since the two states do not presently collaborate in health data gathering and analysis activities, comparable data have been difficult to obtain. On many occasions, it was necessary to manipulate data to make Alabama and Georgia data comparable. In every case, a double effort had to be made by Agency staff to work with two sets of data sources to obtain an adequate data base for 37 Georgia counties and one Alabama county.

Nonexistent Data. In some cases, the Agency was unable to acquire desired baseline data, especially health status data related to morbidity (illnesses or injuries). For example, specific data on the amount of dental disease present in the population, and the number of residents with hypertension within the Health Service Area were not

---

*Population totals derived from Georgia Office of Planning and Budget estimates.

available. Instead, general data estimates based upon experience elsewhere in the state or nation were used. For a number of categories where specific data were needed but not available, the Agency has recommended in the Annual Implementation Plan portion of the Central Georgia Health Plan that data gathering and analysis efforts be undertaken to make such data available for use in future planning efforts.

Questionable Data Quality. Many data efforts rely upon local data generation and statewide compilation and analysis. An example of this occurs when county coroners complete death certificates and then send them to a State office for compilation and aggregation with the figures from other counties. In cases such as these, the reliability of the data depend upon consistency and uniformity in completing the forms. During the Agency's data gathering and analysis activities, there have been occurrences when reliability and validity of data have been doubted but used since there was no other source of the needed data.

Inconsistency Among Data Sources. Frequently, more than one agency collects data on any particular subject and quite often the result is as many different outcomes as there are agencies collecting the data. A good example is data on fluoridation of community water supply systems. Three agencies collect statistics regarding the number of Georgia systems which are fluoridated and estimate the number of people served by those systems: the Georgia Department of Human Resources, the Georgia Department of Natural Resources (Environmental Protection Division), and the National Center for Disease Control. Each provided different figures when asked for information regarding fluoridation, thus generating both confusion and concern over which set of data to use in the Agency's planning efforts.

WILKINSON, GEORGIA

Health Systems Agency of Central Georgia, Inc., Central Georgia Health Plan, Vol. I, 1980, pp. S6-S9.

Utilization Analysis

Several factors should be considered in the development of long range plans for hospital services. Among them are specific measures of need based on health status indicators, socio-economic information about the service population, and assumptions about the future, including projected population changes. One of the most important, however, is the historic use of hospital facilities and services.

Hospital use is expressed by several different measures. Occupancy rate is the most commonly employed measure. When occupancy rate is used along with other indicators of hospital use and hospital bed capacity, several reasonable and logical conclusions can be reached about the historic use of the facilities in the Area and also about projected future use.

Hospital use can be thought of as a continuum beginning with an admission to a hospital. Each admission generates a length of stay, or the number of inpatient days provided. Several admissions over time generate several patient days of care which are then translated into an average length of stay for that hospital for that period of time. Average length of stay is an important measure of use since an unusually long length of stay might indicate inappropriate hospitalization. This would result in unnecessary costs to the patients.

Another important measure of hospital use is the average daily census. Average daily census, on an annual basis, is the average number of inpatients who used a hospital on any given day during the year. With heavy use, the average daily census would approach the number of beds the facility has available for patient care. Occupancy rate is derived directly from average daily census and, on a yearly basis, indicates what percentage of a facility's beds were being used on any given day during that year.

Historical utilization of hospitals in Area V (based on data obtained from the Georgia Joint Hospital Questionnaires for the years 1973-1978 and from the Alabama State Department of Public Health) indicate that they were underused and/or overbedded. They had a significant overcapacity to meet the demand which was generated by the residents of their service areas. Use data are not yet available for 1979, but indications are that this areawide overcapacity extended through 1979 as well.

As the following table illustrates, the number of surveyed hospital beds in Area V increased steadily from 1973 through 1977. Coincident

Area V Hospital Beds and Measures of Hospital Use, 1973-1978

Measure	1973	1974	1975	1976	1977	1978
Number of Surveyed Hospital Beds	3,297	3,441	3,584	3,812	3,819	3,804
Number of Admissions	96,799	110,334	111,354	126,485	126,877	125,832
Number of Patient Days of Care	717,315	724,505	726,082	789,558	806,108	799,699
Annual Average Daily Census	1,965.2	1,925.8	1,989.2	2,163.3	2,208.5	2,191.0
Average Annual Occupancy Rate	67.5%	62.9%	60.9%	59.4%	57.8%	57.6%

Source: 1973-1978 Georgia Joint Hospital Questionnaires and State of Alabama Department of Public Health.

with the capacity increases were more admissions, more patient days of care, and a larger areawide average annual daily census through 1977. All measures of use showed a decrease in 1978. However, when these indicators are compared with hospital surveyed capacity, despite gradually increasing utilization through 1977, the percentage of total capacity which was actually used as reflected by the average annual occupancy rate steadily declined throughout the 6-year period.

In 1978, the Area's average annual occupancy rate for the 29 general and limited service hospitals was 57.6 percent. That means that out of every 100 inpatient hospital beds available for use in the Area in 1977, only about 58 of them were being filled on a full-time basis by patients. The following graph compares surveyed bed capacity and average annual occupancy rate for Area V for 1973 through 1978 and illustrates the long-term nature of the Area's problem with excess hospital bed capacity.

In area V in 1978, eight of the twenty-nine hospitals operated at less than a 50 percent average annual occupancy rate while more than one-half (17 of 29) operated at less than a 60 percent rate. By comparison, the national hospital average annual occupancy rate in 1977 was 75 percent. Hospitals averaged 58.8 percent occupancy in Georgia in 1978. Among other health service areas in the state, the rates changed from 52.9 percent (Area IV) to 77.9 percent (Area I).

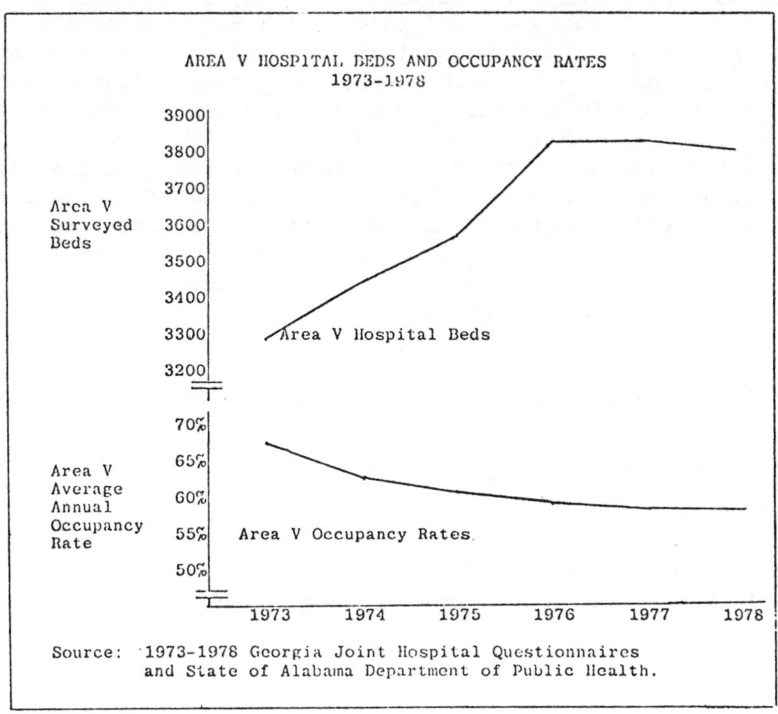

Source: 1973-1978 Georgia Joint Hospital Questionnaires and State of Alabama Department of Public Health.

NEW MEXICO

New Mexico Health Systems Agency, Health Systems Plan, 1979, 1978, pp. 6-13, 18.

IV. Problems

National attention has been focused on the problems of primary care. Increasing health care costs and a shift to specialized care are causing a reassessment of the role of primary health care in the United States.

A. Perceived Problems

In the New Mexico Health Systems Agency (NMHSA) survey of public concern about health care problems, the subarea councils rated problems of primary health care high on the list of health service problems. Primary health care has also been identified as a problem through community workshops and in several state and areawide plans.

The most important perceived primary health service problem was the inability of the consumer to afford services. Concern was also expressed for the lack of prevention services. While this component relates to diagnostic and treatment services, it is important to be aware of the public concern and potential benefit of promotion and protection services. Other problems that ranked high include the lack or poor distribution of health manpower, inadequate outpatient care services, and problems related to transportation to and from health care.

While the lack of services was a concern throughout the state, it was mentioned most often in Districts II, V, and VII. Problems relating to health manpower came most often from Districts IV, V, VI, and VII. Transportation problems were most prevalent in Districts I, II, V, and VII. The problem of coordination between resources was largely a problem in District III.

B. Problem Measurement

Availability Problems

Problem Statement

1. Lack of primary health care services.
2. Lack of sufficient primary medical care manpower in non-urban areas.
3. Lack of sufficient dental care manpower in non-urban areas.

Indicator 1. Critical Manpower Shortage Area, Primary Care Physician-to-Population Ratio

The Department of Health, Education, and Welfare designates an area as a "critical medical shortage area" if it has a primary physician-to-population ratio of less than 1 to 3,500 people (or 1 to 3,000 when there are problems in access to care). For purposes of this indicator, the number of physicians is a proxy variable for the availability or supply of services while the demand for services is assumed to remain constant. Information on primary physician/population ratios in New Mexico can be found in Exhibit 1 for:

1. Primary Physicians
2. General and Family Practitioners
3. Internists
4. Pediatricians
5. Obstetricians and Gynecologists.

The information shows that many counties do not have primary physician manpower. This is particularly important when looking at the distribution of manpower in the fields of pediatrics, ob/gyn, and internal medicine. The distribution of the categories of manpower shows a concentration of manpower in urban areas and in the larger counties.

"Critical medical manpower shortage area" designation qualifies an area for placement of National Health Service Corps and loan replacement personnel and grants under various other government health care programs. A listing of the counties in New Mexico that qualified as shortage areas can be seen in Exhibit 2. According to this index, 128,000 people, or 11.35 percent of the population in New Mexico, live in critical medical manpower shortage areas. These figures will be revised when new designations are made based on the new criteria.

Except for Bernallillo, Santa Fe, and Los Alamos counties, most of the state has a lower ratio (population/physician) for the various types of primary manpower than the state as a whole. When looking at the distribution of internists, pediatricians, and ob/gyns, it is obvious that much of the work of this manpower in non-urban areas is being performed by general/family practitioners.

The availability of primary health care manpower is particularly important in non-metropolitan areas where the loss of one physician can be crucial. Since the data in this component were developed, for example, DeBaca County has gone from three physicians to one, while Quay County has gone from six physicians to three.

Indicator 2. Medically Underserved Areas (MUA)

1. Primary care physician per 10,000 population
2. Infant mortality rate
3. Percentage of the population which is age 65 and over
4. Percentage of population with family incomes below the poverty level

Exhibit 1 Summary of Primary Health Care Manpower/Population Ratios, 1976

DISTRICT	County	PHYSICIANS No.	PHYSICIANS Ratio	AGE: 65 & OVER No.	AGE: 65 & OVER %	PRIMARY CARE No.	PRIMARY CARE Ratio	PRIMARY CARE %	GEN/FAMILY PRACTITIONERS No.	GEN/FAMILY PRACTITIONERS Ratio	INTERNISTS No.	INTERNISTS Ratio	PEDIATRICIANS No.	PEDIATRICIANS Ratio	OB/GYN No.	OB/GYN Ratio	NURSE PRACTITIONERS No.	NURSE PRACTITIONERS Ratio	PHYSICIANS ASSISTANTS No.	PHYSICIANS ASSISTANTS Ratio
I																				
	McKinley	100	512	12	12%	50	1,024	50%	26	1,969	9	5,689	11	4,655	7	7,314	1	51,200	13	3,938
	San Juan	57	1,145	6	10%	35	1,866	61%	25	2,612	3	21,767	3	21,766	3	21,767	3	21,767	4	16,325
	TOTAL	157	74	18	11%	85	1,370	54%	51	2,284	12	9,708	14	8,321	10	11,650	4	29,125	17	6,853
II																				
	Colfax	15	860	1	6%	9	1,433	60%	6	2,150	2	6,450	-	-	1	12,900	-	-	-	-
	Los Alamos	26	612	1	4%	16	994	61%	2	7,950	7	2,271	5	3,180	2	7,950	-	-	-	-
	Mora	1	4,900	0	-	1	4,900	100%	1	4,900	-	-	-	-	-	-	2	2,450	-	-
	Rio Arriba	23	1,117	1	4%	17	1,647	74%	14	2,000	2	14,000	-	-	1	28,000	4	7,000	7	4,000
	San Miguel	23	1,021	2	9%	13	1,808	56%	6	3,917	4	5,875	3	7,833	2	11,750	1	23.500	3	7,833
	Santa Fe	121	512	24	20%	60	1,033	49%	24	2,583	20	3,100	7	8,875	4	15,500	4	15,500	2	31,000
	Taos	24	804	2	8%	20	965	83%	14	1,379	3	6,433	1	19,300	1	19,300	1	19,300	4	4,825
	TOTAL	223	714	31	13%	136	1,244	58%	67	2,485	38	4,382	16	10,406	11	15,136	12	13,875	16	10,406
III																				
	Bernalillo	997	326	115	11%	438	748	44%	153	2,361	188	1,921	30	12,040	45	8,027	36	10,741	17	21,482
	Sandoval	11	2,054	3	27%	10	2,260	91%	8	2,825	1	22,600	1	22,600	-	-	5	4,520	4	5,650
	Torrance	3	2,133	0	-	2	1,600	67%	4	1,600	-	-	-	-	-	-	1	6,400	-	-
	Valencia	21	2,190	5	24%	19	2,421	90%	16	2,875	4	11,500	1	46,000	1	46,000	-	-	3	15,333
	TOTAL	1032	589	123	12%	469	845	45%	181	2,410	193	2,260	32	13,631	46	9,478	42	10,393	24	18,175
IV																				
	Curry	31	1,393	5	16%	16	2,444	52%	7	5,586	4	9,775	3	13,033	2	19,550	2	21,600	-	-
	De Baca	3	866	2	66%	3	867	100%	3	867	0	-	-	-	-	-	-	-	-	-
	Gaudalupe	3	1,633	1	33%	3	1,633	100%	2	2,450	1	4,900	-	-	-	-	-	-	-	-
	Harding	0	-	0	-	0	-	-	-	-	0	-	-	-	-	-	-	-	-	-
	Quay	6	1,900	2	33%	6	1,900	100%	5	2,280	0	-	1	11,400	1	-	-	-	2	5,700
	Roosevelt	9	1,588	2	22%	8	2,038	89%	7	2,329	1	16,300	-	-	-	16,300	1	16,300	2	8,150
	Union	4	1,225	1	25%	3	1,633	75%	3	1,633	0	-	-	-	3	-	-	-	-	-
	TOTAL	56	12,343	13	23%	39	2,061	70%	27	2,978	6	13,400	4	20,100	-	26,800	3	26,800	5	20,100
V																				
	Catron	1	2,300	1	100%	1	2,300	100%	1	2,300	-	-	-	-	-	-	-	-	-	-
	Grant	21	1,171	3	14%	12	2,050	57%	8	3,075	4	6,150	1	24,600	1	24,000	-	-	4	6,150
	Hidalgo	3	1,900	2	66%	3	1,900	100%	3	1,900	-	-	-	-	-	-	-	-	1	5,700
	Luna	5	2,900	2	40%	4	3,625	80%	4	3,625	-	-	-	-	-	-	-	-	-	-
	TOTAL	30	1,570	8	27%	20	2,355	67%	16	2,944	4	11,775	1	47,100	1	47,100	-	-	5	9,420
VI																				
	Chavez	56	860	12	21%	25	1,928	45%	15	3,213	4	12,050	4	12,050	4	12,050	4	12,505	-	-
	Eddy	36	1,177	2	5%	20	2,120	55%	13	3,262	3	14,333	1	42,400	4	10,600	-	-	-	-
	Lea	39	1,313	8	20%	27	1,896	69%	21	2.438	2	25,600	2	25,600	1	51,200	-	-	-	-
	Lincoln	8	1,186	2	25%	7	950	87%	9	1,056	-	-	1	9,500	-	-	-	-	-	-
	Otero	29	1,472	3	10%	18	1,083	62%	10	3,750	4	9,375	2	18,750	3	12,500	-	-	-	-
	TOTAL	168	1,155	27	16%	97	1,888	58%	68	2,776	13	14,523	8	23,600	12	15,733	4	47,200	-	-
VII																				
	Dona Ana	79	1,014	10	13%	48	1,635	61%	20	3,925	13	6,038	3	26,167	4	19,625	2	40,000	-	-
	Sierra	18	472	18	100%	7	1,214	39%	6	1,417	-	-	1	8,500	-	-	-	-	-	
	Socorro	7	1,400	3	43%	5	1,960	71%	5	1,960	-	-	-	-	-	-	-	-	1	
	TOTAL	104	945	31	30%	60	1,613	58%	31	3,122	13	7,446	4	24,200	4	24,200	2	48,400	1	96,800
NEW MEXICO		1,780	644	235	13%	956	1,184	54%	441	2,568	279	4,058	81	13,979	86	13,166	65	17,648	67	17,121

SOURCE: The New Mexico Health Resources Registry, UNM, January, 1977.

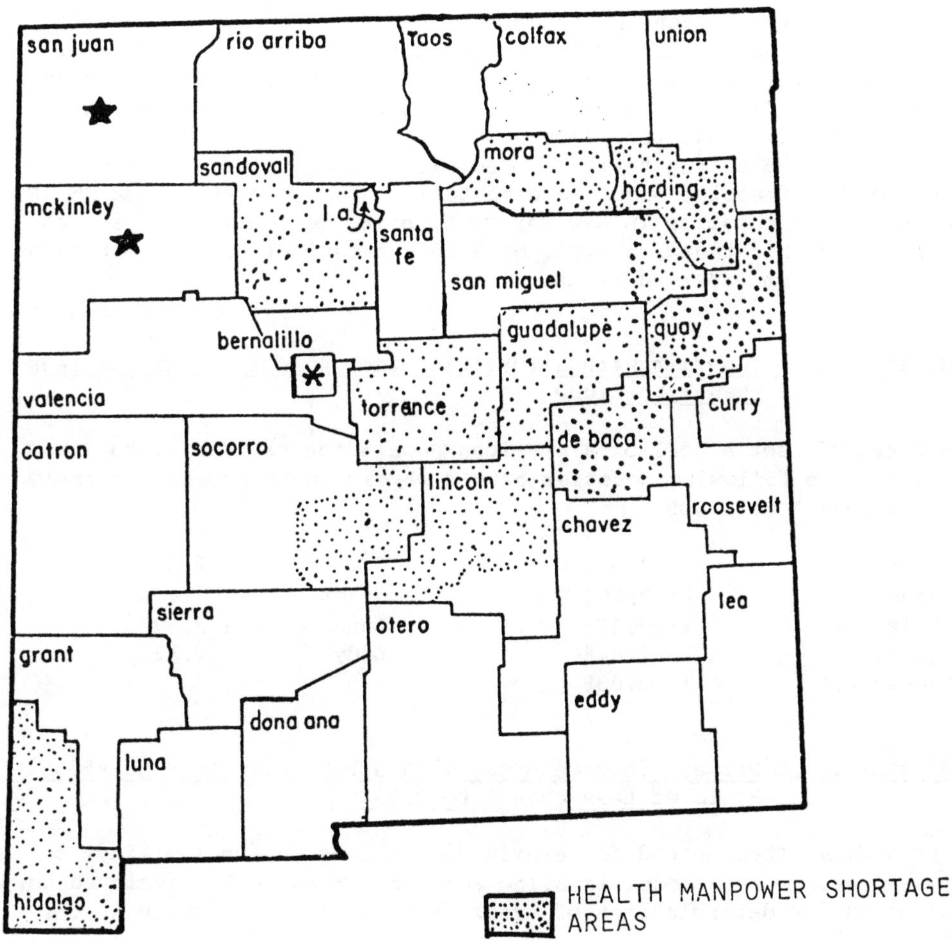

Designated by Secretary of Health, Education, and Welfare

PURPOSE: Placement of National Health Service Corps personnel; placement of loan repayment personnel.

CRITERIA:

1. Population to primary-care physician ratio 3500:1 or 3000:1 (See text)
2. Existence of neighborhood health center(s)
3. Existence of organized hospital outpatient department(s)
4. Other pertinent factors.

SOURCE: The New Mexico Health Resources Registry, UNM, January, 1979.

*SW Vallejos, Los Padillas, Bernalillo Co. Census Tract 4.
★Part of Navajo Reservation (Mexico Springs, Navajo and Crystal Chapters).

Exhibit 2 Critical Medical Shortage Areas, New Mexico

The Department of Health, Education, and Welfare has combined the above four indicators to develop an index of "medical underservice." The counties in New Mexico that are included in this index can be seen in Exhibit 3. Exhibit 4 gives the indicator values and index scores used to determine underservice by county.

When compared to the "critical medical shortage areas," the introduction of socioeconomic and mortality data into the index shows almost all the counties in New Mexico as being medically underserved. According to this index, 575,800 or 50.85 percent of all New Mexicans are living in underserved areas.

Indicator 3. Counties with a Physician-to-Population Ratio of Less than 1 to 2,000

The first HSP set a goal of a physican/population ratio of 1 to 2,000 by 1982. The following counties have a physician-to-population ratio of less than 1 to 2,000:

Mora	1: 4,900	Catron	1: 2,300
Sandoval	1: 2,260	Grant	1: 2,050
Valencia	1: 2,421	Luna	1: 3,625
Curry	1: 2,444	Eddy	1: 2,120
Roosevelt	1: 2,038		

Indicator 4. Primary Service Areas with a Physician-to-Population Ratio of Less than 1 to 2,000

To provide another method for examining problems in availability, a primary service area model is being adopted. When fully developed this will allow for determination of areas of medical underservice at the subcounty level.

Indicator 5. Travel Time to Care in Excess of 30 Minutes

One way to view the availability of health care services to to look at the distribution of those services. The National Health Guidelines contain a standard that primary health care should be available within 30 minutes travel time one way, except under extraordinary circumstances. While access to care for rural populations continues to be a problem in New Mexico, no specific information on the distance to primary care is currently available. An attempt will be made to plot travel time upon completion of the primary service model.

Analysis of Indicators

While the presence or absence of health manpower is not itself an indicator of a service delivery problem, it can serve as a proxy

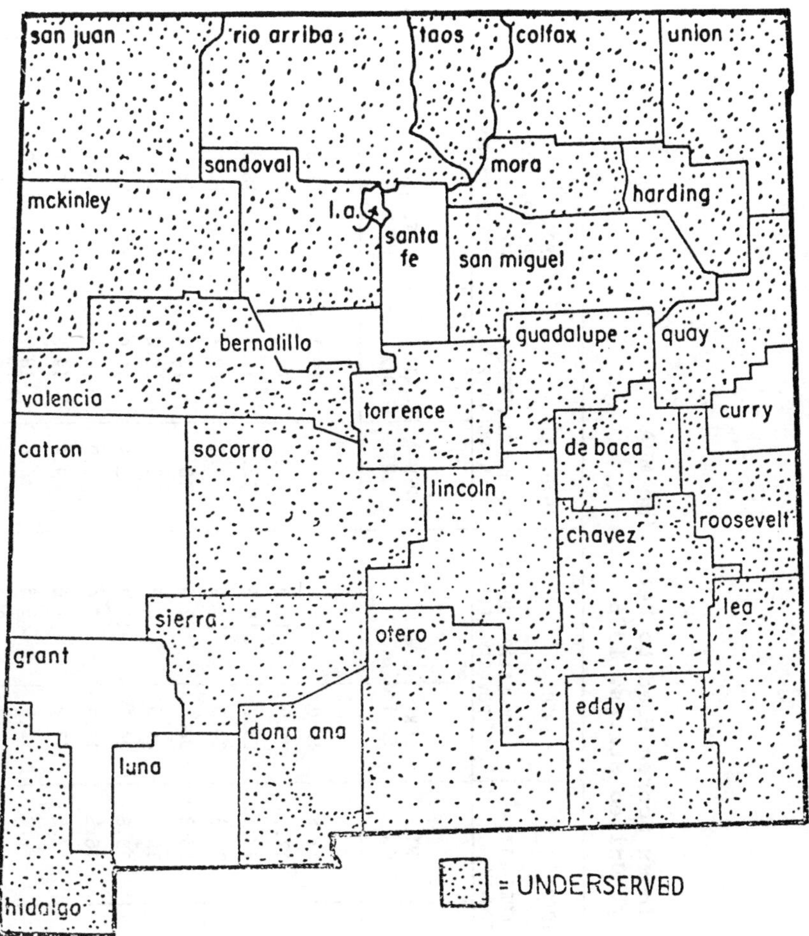

Source: Federal Register

Designated by Secretary of Health, Education, and Welfare

PURPOSE: To determine eligibility for Health Maintenance Organizations (HMO) funding.

INDICATORS USED:

1. Primary care physicians per 1,000 population
2. Infant mortality per 1,000 live births
3. Percent population below poverty level
4. Percent population 65 and over
5. Other pertinent factors

SOURCE: The New Mexico Health Resources Registry, UNM, January, 1977

Exhibit 3 Medically Underserved Areas, New Mexico

Exhibit 4 Indicator Values and Index Scores Used to Determine MUA Status by Non-Metropolitan County, United States, 1976

STATE AND COUNTY	MUA INDEX'	1969/1973 INFANT MORTALITY-FOR COUNTY		1970 POPULATION BELOW-POVERTY LEVEL		1970 POPULATION AGED-65 AND OVER		1973 PRIMARY CARE PHYSICIANS FOR COUNTY
		PLR 1000 BIRTHS	WT. INDEX	PER-CENT	WT. INDEX	PER-CENT	WT. INDEX	WT. INDEX
NEW MEXICO								
CATRON	83.4	15.8	21.5	17.0	16.2	12.3	19.1	26.8
CHAVES	60.9	19.1	17.5	25.9	10.9	9.0	19.9	12.6
COLFAX	60.0	23.1	13.1	25.2	10.9	12.3	19.1	18.9
CURRY	61.5	19.2	17.5	20.0	14.9	7.4	20.1	9.0
DE BACA	63.3	21.1	15.3	30.8	6.6	18.1	12.8	28.6
DONA ANA	63.2	17.2	19.5	24.3	10.9	5.3	20.2	12.6
EDDY	54.2	25.3	10.8	24.2	10.9	8.9	19.9	12.6
GRANT	72.9	18.3	18.5	14.4	17.4	7.9	20.1	16.9
GUADALUPE	44.0	19.7	17.5	42.2	1.0	9.4	19.8	5.7
HARDING	24.3	51.7	.0	32.5	5.6	14.6	18.7	.0
HIDALGO	52.4	19.1	17.5	27.3	9.3	8.8	19.9	5.7
LEA	57.4	25.8	10.8	15.4	17.4	5.4	20.2	9.0

LINCOLN	60.3	27.0	9.6	26.9	9.3	11.6	19.4	28.0
LOS ALAMOS	89.3	17.7	19.5	2.2	23.7	2.1	20.2	25.9
LUNA	63.2	25.4	10.8	26.0	10.9	10.2	19.6	21.9
MCKINLEY	37.8	28.8	7.3	40.1	1.3	4.4	20.2	9.0
MORA	31.2	29.9	6.1	64.3	.0	11.9	19.4	5.7
OTERO	60.8	22.1	14.2	14.8	17.4	4.1	20.2	9.0
QUAY	55.0	20.5	16.4	23.2	12.2	12.5	19.1	7.3
RIO ARRIBA	53.6	19.8	17.5	36.5	3.4	7.4	20.1	12.6
ROOSEVELT	59.3	17.2	19.5	26.4	9.3	9.9	19.8	10.7
SANDOVAL	34.1	29.0	7.3	43.9	1.0	7.2	20.1	5.7
SAN JUAN	48.2	30.0	6.1	26.5	9.3	4.9	20.2	12.6
SAN MIGUEL	48.4	22.0	15.3	44.8	.7	9.9	19.8	12.6
SANTA FE	74.5	15.8	21.5	22.1	12.2	7.8	20.1	20.7
SIERRA	18.1	35.5	3.6	33.0	5.6	24.7	6.1	2.8
SOCORRO	50.2	20.3	16.4	34.4	4.7	7.7	20.1	9.0
TAOS	42.4	24.6	11.9	37.6	3.4	9.3	19.8	7.3
TORRANCE	46.0	15.9	21.5	42.2	1.0	11.9	19.4	4.1
UNION	42.1	29.2	6.1	32.9	5.6	15.4	17.8	12.6
VALENCIA	53.0	24.4	11.9	20.9	13.6	5.6	20.2	7.3

*A score of 62.0 or below does not indicate that the area is an MUA, since changes resulting from health planning agency recommendation for additions and deletions are not reflected on this list.
SOURCE: DHEW, 1975.

indicator. A phsyician/population ratio alone, however, may not be the best method for determining need in an area. The ratio deals only with the supply but not the demand or need for services. Instead, the ratio of manpower-to-population is constant, with scarcity defined when the ratio is below set standards.

Use of the medically underserved area index is more sophisticated than the physician/population ratio in that it factors in the need for services as determined by infant mortality, the percent of population over 65, and the percent of population below the poverty level. The index, however, fails to account for several additional factors that influence the demand for services.

The population over 65 and the low income population increases the need in that they use services more frequently than the total population. However, the population under 17 uses services less often than the total population, and in New Mexico this can have a significant impact on the need for services.

In addition to these deficiencies, neither index takes into account the mid-level practitioner as an alternative to physician manpower, nor the potential of organizational settings such as group practices and HMOs to enhance physician productivity. Improved transportation and technological advances such as telemedical communications are also ignored. Although the medically underserved index attempts to more clearly define need for primary medical services, there is no adjustment in the definition of supply. Despite their deficiencies, the component will continue to use "medical shortage areas" and "medically underserved areas" pending further development of the demand- and need-based methods for determining availability.

NEW MEXICO

New Mexico Health Systems Agency, Health Systems Plan, 1979, 1978, pp. 22, 24-26.

Affordability Problems

Before looking at the cost of health care at the local level and problems in financial access, it is necessary to provide an overview of the increasing costs of primary health care nationally, and how this has affected the ability of people to afford health services.

Nationally, total expenditures for health have increased from 5.9 percent of the gross national product in 1966 to 8.3 percent in 1975. During this period, the per capita expenses for health increased from $256.58 to $476.40. At the same time, the public share of the total health care bill increased from 25.7 percent to 42.7 percent while the private share went down from 74.3 percent to 57.8 percent. Of the $118 billon spent on health, $22 billion went for physicians' services with $16 billion from private funds and $5,855 billion from public funds. A further breakdown shows that 34.5 percent of the physicians' services are covered by direct payment, 39 percent by private health insurance, and 26.5 percent by public, principally Medicare and Medicaid, funds.

The cost of physicians' fees has generally been increasing at a faster rate than total prices as indicated by the Consumer Price Index.

In New Mexico, a recent study by Rudolph Pendall found that the cost of physicians' services has been estimated to be $94,733,000, of which 24 percent is public funds, 31 percent is insurance pay, and 51 percent is direct pay.[1]

---

[1] "The Financing of Health Care in New Mexico," 1977.

Problem Statement

1. Lack of financial access to care.

Indicator 1. Percentage of Population Covered by Third Party Primary Health Care Insurance

Nationally, 70.3 percent of the population has some form of health insurance for individual physician visits, however, Pendall estimates that only 59 percent of the population in New Mexico has this coverage. Specific information is not available on the nature and scope of the insurance available, although insurance usually requires some form of a deductible. Information also does not exist on which ages or income groups have insurance for primary health care. Since fewer people are covered by this type of insurance in New Mexico than in the nation as a whole, the problems of financial accessibility would appear to be greater in New Mexico than in the remainder of the nation.

Indicator 2. Percentage of Low Income Population
•Percentage of population below the poverty level

The percentage of the population below the poverty level is a good estimate of the number of people who might have problems with financial access. In New Mexico, an estmated 22.6 percent of the population is below the poverty level (see Exhibit 10).

Indicator 3. Percentage of Population Medically Indigent
•Percentage of population below poverty level not eligible for Medicaid (see Exhibit 10)

Another way to measure the extent to which financial access can be a problem is to estimate the medically indigent population in the state. The low income population eligible for Medicaid theoretically have no problems in financial access since they participate in the Medicaid program. For purposes of this component, the "medically indigent" population is assumed to be the population below the poverty level that is not eligible for Medicaid benefits.

Exhibit 10 Medically and Medically Indigent Population, 1976

DISTRICT	COUNTY	POPULATION						
			BELOW POVERTY					
		TOTAL POPULATION	NO PERSONS BELOW POVERTY LEVEL[2]	% PERSONS BELOW POVERTY	NO. MEDICAID BENEFICIARIES[3]	% TOTAL POPULATION WHO ARE MEDICAID BENEFICIARIES	NO. MEDICALLY INDIGENT*	% POPULATION WHICH IS MEDICALLY INDIGENT
. I	McKinley	51,600	17,389	33.7	5,540	10.8	11,849	23.0
	San Juan	65,000	14,105	21.7	5,176	8.0	8,929	13.7
	TOTAL	116,600	31,494	27.0	10,716	9.2	20,778	17.8
II	Colfax	13,000	2,613	20.1	819	6.3	1,794	13.8
	Los Alamos	16,800	353	2.1	34	.2	319	1.9
	Mora	4,200	2,407	57.3	757	18.0	1,650	39.3
	Rio Arriba	29,100	9,981	34.3	3,681	12.6	6,300	21.7
	San Miguel	23,500	9,212	39.2	3,776	16.1	5,436	23.1
	Santa Fe	63,400	11,539	18.2	4,385	6.9	7,154	11.3
	Taos	19,600	7,036	35.9	2,632	13.4	4,404	22.5
	TOTAL	169,600	43,141	25.4	16,084	9.5	27,057	15.9
III	Bernalillo	376,600	48,958	13.0	22,531	6.0	26,427	7.0
	Sandoval	25,000	9,375	37.5	2,324	9.3	7,051	28.2
	Torrance	6,800	2,217	32.6	632	9.3	1,585	23.3
	Valencia	47,200	8,732	18.5	3,529	7.5	5,203	11.0
	TOTAL	455,600	112,423	24.7	29,016	6.6	83,407	17.2

IV	Curry	44,700	6,750	15.1	2,525	5.6	4,225	9.5
	DeBaca	2,500	613	24.5	179	7.2	434	17.3
	Guadalupe	5,100	1,933	37.9	688	13.5	1,245	24.4
	Harding	1,300	368	28.3	44	3.4	324	24.9
	Quay	11,800	2,277	19.3	746	6.3	1,531	13.0
	Roosevelt	17,500	3,763	21.5	1,053	6.0	2,710	15.5
	Union	5,000	1,310	26.2	299	6.0	1,011	20.2
	TOTAL	87,900	17,014	19.4	5,534	6.3	11,480	13.1
V	Catron	2,100	1,300	14.3	103	4.9	1,197	9.4
	Grant	23,700	2,820	11.9	1,538	6.5	1,282	5.4
	Hidalgo	5,300	1,150	21.7	446	8.4	704	13.3
	Luna	14,900	3,054	20.5	957	6.4	2,097	14.1
	TOTAL	46,000	8,324	18.1	3,044	6.6	5,280	11.5
VI	Chaves	49,400	10,078	20.4	3,285	6.6	6,793	13.8
	Eddy	43,000	7,654	17.8	2,489	5.8	5,165	12.0
	Lea	53,000	6,625	12.5	2,485	4.7	4,140	7.8
	Lincoln	9,200	1,904	20.7	561	6.1	1,343	14.6
	Otero	43,800	5,384	12.3	1,572	3.6	7,812	8.7
	TOTAL	198,400	31,648	15.9	10,392	5.2	21,256	10.7
VII	Dona Ana	82,000	16,810	20.5	4,650	5.7	12,160	14.8
	Sierra	8,000	1,912	23.9	641	8.0	1,271	15.9
	Socorro	9,300	2,743	29.5	1,183	12.7	1,560	16.8
	TOTAL	99,300	21,465	21.6	6,474	6.5	14,991	15.1
NEW MEXICO	TOTAL	1,173,400	265,509	22.6	81,260	6.9	184,249	15.7

1) Bureau of Business and Economic Research
2) 1970 Estimates applied to 1976 population projections
3) December, 1976, HSSD
*The "medically indigent" are considered here to be persons who live below the poverty level, and who do NOT receive Medicaid.

SOURCE: HSSD Statistical Report.

In New Mexico, 22.6 percent of the population is estimated to be below the poverty level. Thirty percent of this population, or 6.9 percent of the total population, is covered by Medicaid. The population with possible problems in financial access is estimated to be 70 percent of all persons who live below the poverty level, or 15.7 percent of the total population. The 15.7 percent figure is a conservative estimate since many of the people who are eligible for Medicaid still encounter problems in access to care as discussed in the next indicator.

Indicator 4. Number of Unserved Medicaid Beneficiaries
- Physician visits per Medicaid beneficiary
- Patient flow

There is no way to accurately measure the extent to which Medicaid beneficiaries are unable to receive care. The information in Exhibit 11 gives the average number of visits of beneficiaries by county of residence. The information shows that utilization by Medicaid beneficiaries is lowest in Districts IV and V. The counties of McKinley, San Juan, and Sandoval have the lowest percentage of beneficiaries served indicating that the largely Indian population in these counties is using the Indian health services. This information shows that equal financial access does not necessarily result in equal utilization of services, but, at the same time, the information does not necessarily show that Medicaid beneficiaries are underserved, either.

Another way to view the problem is to examine the patient flow of Medicaid beneficiaries. Information from 9-1-71 through 9-31-75 shows that some areas of the state experienced significant patient flow, for example, from the Las Cruces area to El Paso, Lordsburg to Silver City, Harding County to Colfax County, and Torrance County to Albuquerque. This would tend to indicate problems in availability of primary health care for Medicaid beneficiaries in these areas. In the Las Cruces area, which has physician manpower, the excessive outward patient flow may be a result of physicians' unwillingness to take Medicaid patients.

HANSON, SOUTH DAKOTA

McCook-Hanson Health Care, Inc., Rural Health Initiative Applications, 1978, pp. 92, 103-104.

This is a report of a consumer study of McCook and Hanson counties, South Dakota, in regard to health care. Its purpose is to provide the information which will guide the McCook/Hanson Counties Rural Health Initiative Steering Committee in its decisions about priorities. While the information contained in this report cannot in itself determine direction for the committee, when the information is combined with information gathered from health care professionals and others, the committee should be in a better position to judge where and when to put its emphasis on different facets of health care in its area.

Exhibit 11

UTILIZATION OF PHYSICIAN SERVICES MEDICAID BENEFICIARIES

JULY 1, 1976 - JUNE 30, 1977

DIST.	COUNTY	BENEFICIARIES NUMBER(1)	PATIENTS(2)	% RECEIVING CARE	VISITS NUMBER	PATIENT	MEDICAID POPULATION
I	McKinley	5,540	728	13	3,699	5.08	.66
	San Juan	5,176	1,054	20	4,923	4.67	.95
	TOTAL	10,716	1,782	17	8,622	4.83	.90
II	Colfax	819	866	100	4,694	5.42	5.73
	Los Alamos	34	27	79	118	4.37	3.47
	Mora	757	735	97	4,640	6.31	6.12
	Rio Arriba	3,681	3,162	86	19,809	6.26	5.38
	San Miguel	3,776	3,387	90	19,700	5.81	5.21
	Santa Fe	4,385	3,559	81	21,122	5.93	4.81
	Taos	2,632	2,426	92	16,185	6.67	6.14
	TOTAL	16,084	14,162	88	86,268	6.09	5.36
III	Bernalillo	22,531	18,914	84	125,793	6.65	5.58
	Sandoval	2,324	1,036	44	6,032	5.82	2.59
	Torrance	632	609	96	4,166	6.84	6.59
	Valencia	3,529	2,932	83	16,214	5.53	5.53
	TOTAL	29,016	23,491	81	152,205	6.47	5.24
IV	Curry	2,525	2,446	97	12,127	4.95	4.80
	De Baca	179	195	100	967	4.95	5.40
	Guadalupe	688	623	90	3,430	5.50	4.98
	Harding	44	48	100	232	4.83	5.27
	Quay	746	703	94	3,268	4.64	4.38
	Roosevelt	1,053	988	94	4,013	4.06	3.81
	Union	299	310	100+	1,746	5.63	5.83
	TOTAL	5,534	5,313	96	25,783	4.85	4.65
V	Catron	103	81	79	370	4.56	3.59
	Grant	1,538	1,578	100	9,076	5.75	5.90
	Hidalgo	446	342	77	1,293	3.78	2.89
	Luna	956	708	74	3,000	4.23	3.13
	TOTAL	3,044	2,709	89	13,739	5.07	4.51
VI	Chaves	3,285	3,344	100	21,195	6.33	6.45
	Eddy	2,489	2,421	97	12,660	5.22	5.08
	Lea	2,485	2,546	100	14,990	5.88	6.03
	Lincoln	561	514	92	2,510	4.88	4.47
	Otero	1,571	1,480	94	7,539	5.09	4.79
	TOTAL	10,392	10,305	99	58,894	5.71	5.66
VII	Dona Ana	4,650	4,014	86	22,316	5.55	4.79
	Sierra	641	663	100	4,518	6.81	7.04
	Socorro	1,183	984	80	5,990	6.31	5.06
	TOTAL	6,474	5,635	87	32,824	5.83	5.07
	New Mexico	81,260	61,659	76	378,335	6.13	4.65/ 5.51

SOURCE: New Mexico Health and Social Services Department

(1) December, 1976.
(2) Number of patients may exceed number of beneficiaries as the number of patients is a cumulative figure and number of beneficiaries is only for the month of December.
(3) Without McKinley, Sandoval, and San Juan Counties.

APPENDIX
QUESTIONNAIRE SAMPLE -- PARTIAL SUMMARY OF DATA

MC COOK/HANSON COUNTIES RURAL HEALTH INITIATIVE STEERING COMMITTEE

Chairmen: Ed Franz, McCook County - Harold Naser, Hanson County

Your household is one of those chosen at random to represent your township. This questionnaire will aid your Rural Health Steering Committee to evaluate health needs and plan health services for Hanson and McCook Counties. It wants to start with what it learns from you and your neighbors so that it can plan practical programs that fit your needs.

Any adult in your household may fill out this questionnaire. Please take a few minutes today or tomorrow or as soon as you can to answer our questions. Return the questionnaire in the enclosed, self-addressed, stamped envelope.

Thank you for your time and effort.

1. How many people, including you, live in your household? aver. 3.20

The figures below are for 3 or more persons. Lone: aver:67M+

2. How old is the youngest? 12.49 3. How old is the oldest adult? 47.21M+ 2 Pers:ave:57½ Av.Range:54-61

4. How old are you? 51½ M+ 5. Check one: Male 35% Female 65%

6. Write your township ______ 7. Check one: McCook County 33% Hanson County 67%

8. Write in the town you would go to for each of the following services:

General Medical Care Mitch:28% Salem:21% Bridg:22% S.F.:13%
Specialized Medical Care Sioux Falls:78% Mitch:15%
Dental Care Mitch:28% Salem 19% S. F.:21% Bridg 10%
Mental Health Care S. F.:76% Mitchell:13%: Yankton 8%
Back Trouble Mit:25% S.F.:25% Canstot:15% Marion:14% Freeman: 9%
Hospital Care Sioux Falls: 50% Mitch: 30% Freeman: 14%

9. Where do you or members of your household go for health service? (CHECK ALL THAT APPLY)

21% Nurse
86% Dentist
95% Doctor (M.D.)
62% Chiropractor
M+ 69% Druggist
M+ 57% Hospital Emergency
1% Midwife
H+ 79% Eye Doctor (Optomestrist)
33% Eye Doctor (M.D. Specialist)
82% Hospital

____ Other (Specify) ______

10. In receiving medical care, which of the following problems are you and members of your family faced with? (CHECK ALL THAT APPLY)

M+ 40% Must travel too far to receive medical care
H+ 20% Medical people are too impersonal or independent
H+ 27% Medical people don't spend enough time with us
H+ 22% Medical people don't tell us anything
H+ 41% Have to wait too long for appointments
H+ 44% Have to wait too long in doctor's office
8% No specialist that I need
M+ 8% Too many referrals to specialists
68% Medical care is too expensive
H+ 26% Not sure that medical care is thorough
11% None of the above
____ Other (Specify) ______

* H+ = Hanson Sample more than 5% higher than McCook, or significantly older.
M+ = McCook Sample more than 5% higher than Hanson, or significantly older.

APPENDIX

11. Are you and the members of your household satisfied with the medical and health care you receive? (CHECK ONE ONLY)

M+ 35% Very Satisfied   H+ 8% Somewhat Dissatisfied

H+ 56% Somewhat Satisfied   1% Very Dissatisfied

12. Do you have health insurance? Yes 86% No 14%

13. Are you on Medicare? Yes 27%M+ No 73%H+ If you are on Medicare, what, if any, additional help do you need that it does not cover? Write in below:

Medicine; Portion of Doctor Bills; Glasses; Hearing Aid.

14. Are the financial means (insurance, savings, etc.) available to your household for health care enough for: (CHECK ONE ONLY)

31% Extended illness, hospitalization   11% Day-to-day health needs, occasional office calls

52% Brief illness, some office calls, a week or so in hospital   6% We can't afford health services

15. Do you believe that pap smears are important? Yes 84% No 2% Don't Know 1[illegible]

16. In each of these next items, just give your immediate reaction about health care in your area. Check under the column that best fits your reaction.

In our area we need:	AGREE	DISAGREE	NOT SURE
More health services	68%H+	14%	18%
Closer health services	64%M+	22%	14%
Better health services	61%H+	19%	20%
Better Emergency service	58%	19%	23%M+
Better Ambulance service	35%H+	34%	31%
More Home Care	54%	11%	35%
Better Stroke Care	47%	9%	44%
Better Heart Care	51%M+	11%	37%M+
Better Back Care	41%	17%	42%M+
Better Children's Care	50%H+	16%	34%
Better Care for Aged	55%	14%	31%
In our area we need little or no improvement in health care services	23%	58%	19%

17. Please add any ideas you have about health and medical care in your area which would help the committee do its job of planning better. You may also use this space and the back of this page to answer more fully any questions we did not give you enough space or opportunity to answer above.

46% of the resondents wrote some response. Common themes were: Need more doctors or closer doctors or druggist or emergency services, (depending upon which type of service absent in respondent area). Need home care for those who are ill and shut in. Doctors overworked, too unavai[illegible] Health care costs are out of line (or sight or reason).

We thank you very much for you kind assistance. Please remember to mail your questionnaire in the self-addressed, stamped envelope.

* H+ = Hanson Sample more than 5% higher than McCook.
M+ = McCook Sample more than 5% higher than Hanson.

Bibliography: Health

Alabama. Alabama Cooperative Extension Service, "Health Facilities and Services," 1980 (5 pgs.).

Ashley, Arkansas. University of Arkansas Medical School, "Arkansas Physician Distribution" (10 pgs.).

Kit Carson, Colorado. Colorado East Central Council of Governments, "Emergency Medical Technician Meeting Minutes," February 1980 (6 pgs.).

Sussex, Delaware. Delmarva Rural Ministries, Application to DHEW for continuation of funding for Delmarva Migrant Health Project (primary care services to migrant farmworkers on Delmarva Peninsula), 1980 (77 pgs.).

Mid-Sussex Health Center, Inc., Proposal to Public Health Service, HEW, for funding of "Rural Health Initiative Project" to increase primary care capacity in the county, 1978 (53 pgs.).

Baldwin, Bleckley, Chattahoochee, Clay, Putnam, Taylor, Telfair, Webster, and Wilkinson, Georgia. Health Systems Agency of Central Georgia, Inc., Central Georgia Health Plan, 1980, Vol. I (386 pgs.); Vol. II (301 pgs.).

Dade, Georgia. Hospital Authority of Walker, Dade, and Catoosa Counties, "Primary Medical and Health Care Center for Dade County" (application to Office of Planning and Budget), 1977 (2 pgs.).

Kentucky. East Kentucky Health Systems Agency, Inc., "Executive Summary: The Health Systems Plan, 1979-1983" (19 pgs.).

Spencer, Kentucky. Two articles from the Spencer Magnet (Taylorsville, Kentucky), 1979, concerning the Spencer County Rural Development Committee's preliminary application for funding of a new Primary Health Care Facility and the "community health assessment" they are conducting (4 pgs.).

Tensas, Louisiana. Projects and Planning Associates, Inc., An Ambulatory Health Care Directory of the State of Louisiana (7 pgs.--excerpt).

Washington, Maine. Washington County Health Plan, 1980 (44 pgs.).

Kent, Maryland. Upper Shore Mental Health, Inc., "Regional Mental Health Services-Upper Shore," 1979 (24 pgs.).

Minnesota. Agricultural Extension Service, University of Minnesota, "Analyzing the Adequacy of Health Services in Rural Areas," Minnesota Agricultural Economist, May 1975 (6 pgs.).

Lake, Minnesota. Agricultural Extension Service, University of Minnesota, "A Summary of the Home Interview Survey of 219 Community Health Center Members Regarding their Perceptions of the Community Health Center Services, Facilities, Benefits, Goals, and Philosophy" (20 pgs.).

New Mexico. New Mexico Health Resources Registry, University of New Mexico, Health Resources Registry, 1977--New Mexico Statistical Summary (42 pgs.).

New Mexico. New Mexico Health Systems Agency, Health Systems Plan, 1979 (397 pgs.).

Colfax, McKinley, and Valencia, New Mexico. New Mexico Emergency Medical Service Bureau, Emergency Medical Service Systems, Region

I: Expansion and Improvement of an Emergency Medical Services System 1980-1981 (480 pgs.).

Lea, New Mexico. Emergency Medical Services Bureau, Health Services Division, Emergency Medical Services System Plan, New Mexico Emergency Medical Services Region III Summary, 1980 (121 pgs.).

Columbia, New York. Columbia County Planning Department, An Evaluation of the Health Services in Columbia County, 1975 (98 pgs.).

Hanson, South Dakota. McCook-Hanson Health Care, Inc., Rural Health Initiative Application (application to PHS, HEW for funds for clinics), 1978 (130 pgs.).

Shelby, Tennessee. Memphis and Shelby County Office of Planning and Development, Preliminary Analysis of Alternatives for Shelby County Ambulance Service, 1979 (28 pgs.).

Charlotte, Goochland, Greensville, and Mecklenburg, Virginia. Rural Health Study Group, Report of the Rural Health Study Group to the Plan Development Committee, Central Virginia Health Systems Agency, 1979 (84 pgs.).

TRANSPORTATION

Most of the transportation plans are financed through the Urban Mass Transportation Administration. The contents of the plans are similar, including the following sections:

- Population and the Economy
- Existing Transit Service
  - Elderly and Handicapped
  - Education
  - Social Service Agencies
  - Taxis
  - Buses
- Needs Assessment
  - Elderly and Handicapped
  - General Public
- Analysis and Evaluation of Transportation Alternatives
- Area Coverage
  - Origins and Destinations Served
  - Eligible Uses
  - Methods of Payment
  - Fares
  - Fixed Route/Fixed Schedule
- Dial-a-Ride Demand Response
- Point Deviation
- Shared Taxis
- Carpool/Vanpool

The first example of transportation data contains ridership estimates from a rural area in northern Utah. Two transit options (fixed-route and dial-a-ride) are then analyzed in regard to these ridership needs.

The second example is an assessment of transit needs for several counties in eastern Colorado. Ridership is calculated on the basis of national multipliers, estimated and current ridership figures, and average ridership figures from other regions. It is broken down by general public and elderly and handicapped. Also presented are the results of a survey which identified transportation as a primary concern.

The third example, from Harnett County, North Carolina, examines the transportation provided by local human service agencies. Number and type of vehicle, cost, current client transportation use, and transportation need are described.

CACHE, UTAH

Bear River Association of Governments, Transportation Development Plan of the Bear River District, 1979, pp. 10-11, 14-15.

Estimating Demand

Traditionally, people who reside in rural areas have characteristics of individualism and independence. They are dedicated to the use of the automobile as their primary mode of transportation. Many surveys, conducted to ascertain if people would ride public buses, have consistently over-estmated potential ridership for a proposed bus system. It is easy for the people to respond "yes" to a question about riding the bus, but if conditions are not right for individuals then it is quite a different matter for them to actually use bus service. Factors that influence bus ridership are weather conditions, the need for a multi-purpose trip, illness, season of the year, economic status, quality of service, and lack of service. They all have a bearing on prospective ridership. If the mental attitude of the public toward transit is negative, then the rider will decide on the use of another mode of transportation.

One method used to estimate ridership in a rural area is to use estimated levels which would give a range of possible ridership. The base population of 21,250 which is 85 percent of Logan's population is used to derive the estimated levels of ridership. (Note: 15 percent

TABLE 30 Nine Use Levels for Logan City

Nine Use Levels for Logan City									
Levels of Use	1%	1½%	2%	2½%	3%	3½%	4%	4½%	5%
Daily Ridership	215	318	430	531	637	743	850	956	1062
Yearly Ridership (307 days)	66,005	96,900	122,010	161,955	194,285	228,101	260,950	293,568	326,187
Average Passenger Per Hour	15	23	30	38	45	53	60	68	75

of the population is considered inaccessible to a transit system because of age or location.)

Option 1 Fixed-Route, Fixed-Schedule: The fixed-route, fixed-schedule has traditionally been the service most transit companies use as it is easy to administer. It is a system that benefits the worker and "captive riders," for the system is designed to transverse areas containing known users and accommodate high volume of traffic along densely developed corridors.

An established route network and a regular service schedule will encourage repeated use of the transit service. Efficiencies in operation are realized early as drivers and the ridership become familiar with the system.

It should be noted, however, that despite these advantages, there are constraints on the traveler which might be reasons why there was a national decline in transit ridership. A fixed-route, fixed-schedule does not meet the needs of those people hampered by physical defects or where a special service provision is required.

A reference manual Analyzing Transit Options for Small Urban Communities, Figure V-4, published by the Urban Mass Transportation Administration, was used to obtain the following estimated ridership. It should be noted that these estimates do not take into account any variables and that all data are based on averages derived from their transit systems.

For the ridership to meet the low estimate of 148,750 would require 2 1/4 percent of the Logan population to become customers of the transit system, whereas it would require 4 percent of the population to equal the high estimation. The revenue from 239,060 riders (medium estimate) for a $.25 fare would cover about 26 percent of the yearly operating cost.

TABLE 31 Fixed Route, Fixed Schedule Estimated Ridership and Revenue[1]
(122,500 miles per year)

Factors: 4 vehicles (19 passenger van)
Operating 12 hours per day (7 am - 7 pm), 307 days (Sundays excluded)

Ridership		Revenue Fare					
		.25	.30	.35	.40	.45	.50
Low	148,750	37,970	45,560	53,160	60,750	68,340	75,940
Medium	239,060	59,675	71,720	83,670	95,625	107,580	119,530
High	255,000	53,750	76,500	89,250	102,000	114,750	127,500

Estimated operation cost: U.S. average $1.83/mile[1] = $224,175

Source[1]: UTA, 1977 Supply and Demand Characteristic Table 19 as projected.

The routes would be subject to further review and refinement by the transit operator before actual implementation. Should longer hours be required to cover night or Sunday operation, it would be possible to add a demand response system.

Option 2 Demand Response Transportation (DRT or Dial-a-Ride)

General

DRT systems are particularly suitable for low-density areas where buses on fixed routes and schedules have traditionally been unable to operate successfully. Logan's population density of approximately 4,000 per square mile and geographic features would enable the system to feature short trips which is the hallmark of the DRT system. All aspects of scheduling many-to-many, or many-to-few destinations can be effectively handled. DRT services are particularly appropriate during off-peak periods when the demand for travel is lighter and more diffuse. The DRT system can also be used in conjunction with a fixed-route and schedule should demand warrant such a combined system. It is possible to make the DRT services available 24 hours a day, 7 days a week.

DRT Estimates

Table 32 gives estimates of ridership and revennue that could be expected from a responsive system.

TABLE 32 DRT System Estimates of Ridership and Revenue

Factor: Population of 21,250; 307 days and 12 hours daily except Sunday; fleet of four vans

Ridership	per day	per year	Fare .25	.30	.35	.40	.45	.50
Low	122	37,454	9,360	11,110	13,110	14,980	16,850	18,730
Medium	204	62,628	15,660	18,790	21,920	25,050	28,180	31,320
High	322	98,854	24,710	29,660	34,600	39,540	44,480	49,430

Source: Figure V-9, UMTA Manual.

KIT CARSON, COLORADO

Colorado Department of Highways, Division of Transportation Planning, Transit Development Program (TDP), East Central Colorado, 1979, pp. 17-20, 38-39.

V. Assessment of Transit Needs

It is important to evaluate transit needs on the basis of several techniques to obtain a comprehensive view of the needed transit and the possible alternatives for satisfying the unmet need.

One of these variables examines what is a "reasonable utilization" of a transit system. Planners at the Colorado Department of Highways have determined that a 46-person per day ridership, in a 15-passenger van, running 8 hours a day, at half hour trip length, have reasonable utility for a demand responsive system (see Table 7).

Another technique deals with data that show as closely as possible the actual demand and need for service. This section examines transit needs for the general public, elderly and handicapped in Region 5 on the basis of national multipliers, estimated and current ridership figures and average ridership figures from other regions. The demand and need figures are explained in depth with explanatory tables in the following pages. In general, the estimated demand presently exceeds the supply of transportation services for elderly and handicapped. The expansion of service to the general public will somewhat increase the gap between demand and supply.

Table 7

CDH REASONABLE UTILITY:		
46 trips per day 15 passenger van 8 hours a day service demand responsive = 20% utilization	Cheyenne:	10 riders per day 80 miles per day demand responsive and regular route 1 12-passenger van 1 station wagon
	Elbert:	7 riders per day 75 miles per day regular route 2 12-passenger vans
	Kit Carson:	15.4-riders per day 91 miles per day 4 demand responsive and regular route 4 12-passenger vans
	Lincoln:	10 riders per day 30 miles per day demand responsive 2 12-passenger vans

Other variables to consider are the needs expressed by the populace. Two regional planning and needs surveys were recently conducted in Region 5. The results identified transportation as a primary concern of the populace in Region 5. The survey results are summarized in Appendix A.

Table 7 demonstrates that there is a significant low level of utility of all of the transit vehicles listed, since ridership is low in relation to the high level of demand and needs of the transportation disadvantaged. This further supports the need for coordination of existing services to provide a better utilization and service level of transit systems.

The following tables and narrative discuss the variables which influence the actual demand for transit in Region 5.

Transportation Assessment of Transit Nedds

Narrative for Table 8: Table 8 shows the present and projected four-county population and resultant trip demand utilizing the 3 percent multiplier, which is the average ridership for similar county operations. The elderly and handicapped figure was taken from data based on CDH summaries.

Narrative for Table 9 Table 9 shows the current elderly and handicapped population by county, the national multiplier estimate of transit demand (.09 transit trips per day for elderly and .55 transit trips per day for handicapped), and the need for additional service. The greatest need is in Kit Carson County, which has the largest elderly and handicapped population. The unmet demand for the entire region totals 354 one-way trips per day.

Narrative for Table 10 Table 10 shows the projected elderly and handicapped populations for each county along with their estimated transit trip demand through 1983, based on the national multipliers. These figures show that population increases will be minimal; therefore, future planning options can easily be accommodated for.

Table 8 Estimated Ridership by General Public

Cheyenne County	Estimated Estimated Population	Estimated Population Minus Elderly and Handicapped	Estimated Daily Transit Needs by General Public*
1980	2000	1661	50
1981	2000	1661	50
1982	2000	1661	50
1983	2000	1661	50
1984	2000	1761	53

Table 8 (continued)

Cheyenne County	Estimated Estimated Population	Estimated Population Minus Elderly and Handicapped	Estimated Daily Transit Needs by General Public*
Elbert			
1980	6600	5734	172
1981	6800	5934	178
1982	6900	6034	181
1983	7100	6234	187
1984	7200	6334	190
Lincoln			
1980	5200	4398	132
1981	5600	4798	145
1982	6000	5198	156
1983	5900	5098	153
1984	5900	5098	153
Kit Carson			
1980	7900	6829	205
1981	8100	7029	211
1982	8400	7329	220
1983	8400	7329	220
1984	8500	7429	223

*Based on a 3 percent multiplier

Table 9 Current Transit Needs 1980

	Elderly Population	Estimated Handicapped	Total Elderly and Handicapped	Elderly and Handicapped Transit Demand	Trips in 1979	Need for Additional Service
Cheyenne	299	40	339	49	20	29
Elbert	780	86	866	117	15	102
Lincoln	722	80	802	109	8	101
Kit Carson	948	123	1071	153	31	122
TOTALS	2749	329	3078	428	ONE-WAY 74	ONE-WAY 354

Table 10 Projected Transit Need for Elderly and Handicapped

Cheyenne County	65+	Handicapped	Elderly and Handicapped	Elderly and Handicapped Demand
1979	299	40	339	49
1980	299	40	339	49
1981	299	40	339	49
1982	299	40	339	49
1983	299	40	339	49
1984	299	40	339	49
Elbert County				
1979	780	86	866	117
1980	781	86	867	118
1981	782	86	868	119
1982	783	86	869	120
1983	784	86	870	121
1984	785	86	871	122
Lincoln County				
1979	722	80	802	109
1980	723	80	803	110
1981	724	80	804	111
1982	725	80	805	112
1983	726	80	806	113
1984	727	80	807	114
1979	948	123	1071	153
1980	949	124	1073	155
1981	950	125	1075	157
1982	951	126	1077	159
1983	952	127	1079	161
1984	953	128	1080	162

APPENDIX A
SENIOR SPEAK-OUT III
SENIOR CONCERNS SURVEY RESULTS

Regional Results

#1 High Energy Cost
#2 Inadequate Transportation
#3 Legal Assistance
#4 Tax Relief
#5 Housing Repairs
#6 Inadequate Health Care
#7 Health Costs
#8 Dental Problems
#9 Income Assistance
#10 Personal Care
#11 Nutritional Needs
#12 Housing Costs
#13 Loneliness
#14 Employment

Kit Carson County

#1 High Energy Cost
#2 Inadequate Transportation
#3 Housing Repairs
#4 Health Costs
#5 Legal Assistance
#6 Housing Costs
#7 Inadequate Health Care
#8 Income Assistance
#9 Dental Problems
#10 Tax Relief
#11 Nutritional Needs
#11 Loneliness
#12 Personal Care
#13 Employment

Cheyenne County

#1 High Energy Cost
#2 Tax Relief
#3 Inadequate Health Care
#4 Inadequate Transportation
#5 Income Assistance
#6 Housing Repairs
#7 Health Costs
#8 Dental Problems
#9 Legal Assistance
#10 Personal Care
#10 Housing Costs
#11 Loneliness
#12 Employment
#13 Nutritional Needs

Lincoln County

#1 High Energy Cost
#2 Health Costs
#3 Tax Relief
#4 Nutritional Needs
#5 Legal Assistance
#6 Inadequate Transportation
#7 Housing Costs
#8 Income Assistance
#8 Housing Repairs
#9 Dental Problems
#10 Loneliness
#11 Inadequate Health Care
#12 Personal Care
#13 Employment

Elbert County

#1 High Energy Cost
#2 Inadequate Transportation
#3 Inadequate Health Care
#4 Housing Repairs
#5 Tax Relief
#6 Housing Costs
#7 Loneliness
#8 Legal Assistance
#9 Personal Care
#10 Dental Problems
#11 Health Costs
#12 Income Assistance
#13 Employment
#14 Nutritional Needs

APPENDIX A (continued)

In August of 1978, the ECCOG conducted a random sample needs survey. The following areas were listed as areas of concern:

1. Transportation
2. Homemaking Assistance/Home Health Care
3. Financial Assistance
4. Home Repairs
5. Telephone Reassurance
6. Recreation
7. Nutrition
8. Information and Referral

In June of 1979, a survey of approximately 150 people was conducted as part of the planning effort for Senior Speak-Out III. The following areas were identified as problems:

1. High Energy Costs
2. Inadequate Transportation
3. Legal Assistance
4. Tax Relief
5. Housing Repair

Based upon this information, Region 5's major areas of concern in planning efforts for Older Americans Act programs are:

I. Income
(including income-related problems such as: taxes, costs of housing repair, and high energy costs)

II. Health and Nutrition
(including long term care)

III. Transportation

IV. Supportive Services
   A. Basic Services (I&R, legal services, visiting, telephone reassurance, shopping assistance, and escort)
   B. Life-Enrichment (recreation programs, volunteer opportunities, and education)

HARNETT, NORTH CAROLINA

Region "M" Council of Governments, Transportation Development Plan, Harnett, North Carolina, 1979, pp. 13, 18-19, 21, 26-27.

Human Services Agency Providers

In order to understand the scope of transportation services being offered by human services agencies, the TDP Steering Committee surveyed eighteen of the county's public agencies. Sixteen agencies responded to the survey.

Of the sixteen responding agencies, only five indicated that they own transit vehicles: Lee-Harnett Mental Health, Council for Senior Citizens, Sheltered Workshop, Henley Roberts Civic Organization, and the Board of Education. Although only five of the agencies own transit vehicles, five additional agencies assist their clients with transportation problems. Table 6 illustrates the degree to which these agencies are in the transportation business. Although the sheriff's department owns and operates 27 vehicles, all of which are patrol cars, they are not included in the data analysis because of the nature of that agency.

Agency Needs

The survey of human services agencies in Harnett County resulted in the identification of several agency needs. Table 11 lists the agencies surveyed, the number of clients served, and the number experiencing transportation difficulties. Percentages of the agencies' clients needing transportation services range from 5 percent to 100 percent. Of all clients served, it is estimated that 65 percent of them experience difficulty getting around.

Cost of Transportation in Harnett County

It is obvious from the information given that Harnett County is in the transportation business. Over $835,000 is spent annually on transportation by human services agencies in Harnett County. The largest portion of the expenditures, $760,000, is attributed to the school system. Almost $75,000, then, is spent by "other" human services agencies in the county. Including the schools, Harnett County government contributes almost $60,000 to transportation programs. Figure 4 generally illustrates a typical breakdown of costs that a human services transportation program can expect to incur.

Table 6 Existing Vehicle Data

Agency/Group	Equipment Type of Vehicle	Current Mileage	Seating Capacity	Type Client Restriction	Average Weekly Ridership	Operating Schedule	Method of Operation	Equipment
Lee-Harnett Mental Health	1976 Van	72,000	15	Elderly, Low Income, Handicapped	45	M-F 8:30-10:30 2:30-4:30	Fixed Route	None
Senior Citizens	1977 Van	15,000	15	Elderly, Low Income	45	M-F 9:00-5:00	Request	None
Workshop	1) 1977 Van	11,000	12	Handicapped	55	M-F 6:30-9 AM 3:30-5 PM	Fixed Route	Vehicle to Base Radio
	2) 1977 Van	40,000	15	Handicapped	70	8:00-9 AM 3:30-5 PM	Fixed Route	Vehicle to Base Radio
	3) 1974 Van	100,000+	12	Handicapped	55	8:00-9 AM 3:30-4:30 PM	Fixed Route Radio	Lift &
	4) 1974 Van	100,000+	12	Handicapped	60	7:45-9 AM 3:30-5 PM	Fixed Route	Radio
Headstart	1975 Ford Van	70,000	12	Headstart Clients	28	8:00-10 AM 2:30-4 PM	Fixed Route	None
Harnett County Schools	3 Special Needs Buses		20 ea	Children (Handicapped)		7:00-8:20 AM 2:45-4:30 PM	Fixed Route	
	2 Vans		15 ea	Children				
	18 Activity Buses		45 ea	Children				
	153 Public School Buses		36-62 ea	Children				

TABLE 11 Agency Clients Experiencing Transportation Difficulties

Agency Name	Clients/Week	Clients/Week with Transportation Problems	Percent with Transportation Problems
Agricultural Extension	150	8	5
Parks and Recreation	Varies with Seasons		30
Vocational Rehabilitatin	25 - 75	9 - 26	35
DHR - Manpower	160	72	45
Social Services	1130	565	50
County Library	1500	1050	70
Health Department	155	140	90
Association for Retarded Citizens	89	85	95
Mental Health	45-50	43 - 48	95
Senior Citizens	116	116	100
Sheltered Workshop	58	58	100
	3426 - 3483	2146 - 2168	Approx 65

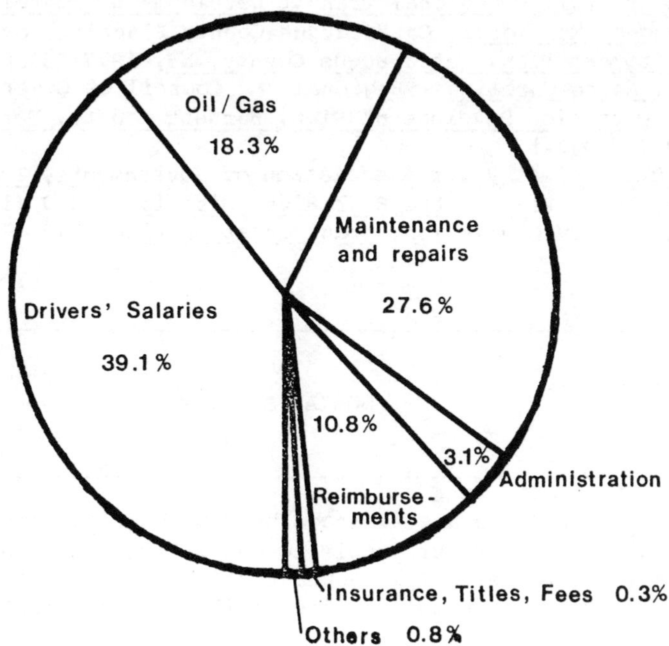

Figure 4 Breakdown of expenditures for providing transportation services.

Bibliography: Transportation

Alabama. Alabama Cooperative Extension Service, "Public Passenger Transportation in Rural Alabama 1980" (3 pgs.).

Lowndes, Alabama. South Central Alabama Development Commission, Lowndes County Land Use Plan and Transportation Plan, 1976 (359 pgs.).

Searcy, Arkansas. Northwest Arkansas Economic Development District, Inc., "Rural Public Transportation Project" (23 pgs.).

Kit Carson, Colorado. Colorado Department of Highways, Division of Transportation Planning, Transit Development Program (TDP), East Central Colorado, 1979 (39 pgs.).

Elbert, Georgia. Northeast Georgia Area Planning and Development Commission, Northeast Georgia Areawide Transportation Plan, 1979 (186 pgs.).

Jefferson, Indiana. Indiana University Institute of Mass Transit, Madison Transit Feasibility Study, 1980 (30 pgs.).

Butler, Iowa. Iowa Northland Regional Council of Governments, Regional Transit Development Program Update 1979-1983 (56 pgs.).

Carter, Missouri. Ozark Foothills Regional Planning Commission, Regional Transportation Plan for Ozark Foothills Regional Planning Commission, 1980 (63 pgs.).
Ozark Foothills Regional Transit Development Program, September 1978 (54 pgs.).

Chariton, Missouri. Missouri Valley Regional Planning Commission, Missouri Valley Regional Transit Development Program, 1979 (46 pgs.).

Cattaraugus, New York. Cattaraugus County Planning Board, Mass Transit Development Plan, Cattaraugus County, NY, 1977 (51 pgs.).

Harnett, North Carolina. Regional "M" Council of Governments, Transportation Development Plan, Harnett County, North Carolina, 1979 (67 pgs.).

Cache, Utah. Bear River Association of Governments, Transportation Development Plan of the Bear River District, 1979 (161 pgs.).
Cache County Commission, Transportation Plan 1979 (21 pgs.).

SOCIAL SERVICES

Social services plans are financed by HUD, HHS, and FmHA. There are not enough of them in our sample to generalize, but there seems to be an emphasis on the elderly. Population characteristics, population needs, and existing social service facilities are usually covered in the plans.

The first example of social service data is a social and demographic profile of the clients of programs for the aged in southwestern Indiana. Theseneeds assessments data were obtained through a survey.

The second example maps the location of the aged population in southwestern Minnesota. There are also comparisons of the change in numbers through time of this age group with other age groups.

The third example presents data from a sample survey of the elderly in five counties in northern Nebraska. The questions were about the limitations of living alone and the types of social activities respondents would like.

The next example, from the same area of Nebraska, concerns daycare. Selected census data are used to delineate the need for daycare services in the area.

The last example, from Columbia County, New York, is from a survey of 213 human service agencies. The agencies were asked about the type of service they render and the type of client they serve.

DUBOIS, GREEN, KNOX, MARTIN, AND PIKE, INDIANA

Cooperative Extention Service, Purdue University, Title XX Statistical Report No. 2: Needs Assessment of Older Americans, 1979, pp. 1-4.

Introduction

The purpose of this report is to summarize the preliminary results of the needs assessment of clients in the Title XX "Personal Care Assessment" program of the Area 13A Agency on Aging in Vincennes, Indiana. Area 13A Agency on Aging is jointly sponsored by Vincennes University and the Indiana Cooperative Extension Service, Purdue University.

The personal care assessment program as developed in Area 13A consists of a two-fold effort to develop a data base on the status of older Americans with respect to a series of need areas, and to provide personal care services where appropriate. Services included within the personal care assessment program are transportation, friendly visitor, and home meals. Their purpose is to assist the older American to achieve self-sufficiency and thereby prevent or reduce institutionalization.

The personal care assessment program is funded through Title XX of the 1975 Social Security Act. The Indiana Office of Social Services purchases personal care services from a local provider as established by the Indiana law for Title XX. The local provider in this case is the Area 13A Agency on Aging.

This preliminary report includes the results of information collected from the short form which is a brief survey instrument used by the personal care assessor during the initial visit to the Title XX client. Five counties are included in the analysis.

Profile of the Title XX Clients

Nearly three-quarters of the Title XX clients were female, and over 98 percent were white. Average age was slightly over 75 years. Ages ranged from a low of 59 to five persons who were 99 years old.

Approximately 30 percent of the Title XX participants were less than 70 years old, and 29 percent were 80 years and over (Table 1).

Average total monthly family income was $258.61. Monthly income ranged from as little as $100 to $717. Forty-six percent of the Title XX participants had total monthly incomes below $200. Twenty-seven percent had monthly incomes between $200 and $299, and an equal percent received incomes greater than $300. Eighty-nine percent received social security payments. Other frequently mentioned sources included job pension (9.8 percent), interest/dividends (15.8 percent), public aid/food stamps (7.0 percent), veterans' benefits (6.3 percent). Nearly half (48.4 percent) of the Title XX participants listed only one source of income: social security.

About 62 percent of the households were single member. Only 17.0 percent were composed of a married couple without children or other persons residing in the household. Slightly over 7.0 percent of the households consisted of a married couple with offspring still residing at the parental home. The remaining households had other types of arrangements.

Nearly 62 percent of the households were owned by the occupants. About 27 percent rented a house or apartment, and another 0.3 percent rented a trailer. About 5 percent either lived in a retirement home or a nursing home.

The county breakdown of Title XX clients included in this report by both participating persons and households is as follows: Dubois, 129 persons, 115 households; Greene, 126 persons, 114 households; Knox, 115 persons, 105 households; Martin, 61 persons, 51 households; and Pike, 85 persons, 71 households.

JACKSON, PIPESTONE, AND ROCK, MINNESOTA

Minnesota Board on Aging, 1980 Area Plan for Programs on Aging for the Southwestern Area Agency on Aging, pp. 20-21, 59.

Planning and Service Area: Southwestern

Analysis of Needs of Older Persons in the Southwest Planning and Service Area

The planning and service area of the Southwestern Area Agency on Aging is large and diverse. It comprises nine southwest Minnesota counties, 163 townships, and 80 incorporated municipalities. It is the home of 28,100 persons age 60 years and over, who are 19.8 percent of the area's total population.

The population of southwest Minnesota peaked in 1940, has declined since then, and is projected to remain relatively stable thereafter. Southwest Minnesota has declining numbers while the state as a whole continues to increase. It may come as a surprise then to find that the Minnesota State Planning Agency estiamtes that five of the nine counties in Region VIII show population increases from 1970 to 1975. A close look at the demographic data shows that although all five

TABLE 1 Social and Demographic Profile of Title XX Participants (Report #1)

DESCRIPTION	FREQUENCY	PERCENT
(A) Sex		
(1) Female	371	73.6
(2) Male	133	26.4
(3) Total	504	100.0
(B) Race		
(1) White	496	98.4
(2) Black	8	1.6
(3) Total	504	100.0
(C) Age		
(1) 59 - 69	148	29.6
(2) 70 - 79	206	41.3
(3) 80 and over	145	29.1
(4) Total	499	100.0
(5) No Information	5	-----
(D) Total Monthly Family Income		
(1) Less Than $200	185	46.0
(2) $200 - $299	108	27.0
(3) $300 and over	108	27.0
(4) Total	401	100.0
(5) No Information	55	-----
(E) Source of Income (N = 456)		
(1) Working Part-Time	17	3.8
(2) Social Security	404	88.6
(3) Job-Related Pension	45	9.8
(4) Interest/Dividends	72	15.8
(5) Rental Income	20	4.4
(6) Disability	9	1.9
(7) Public Aid/Food Stamps	32	7.0
(8) Farming Part-Time	11	2.5
(9) Veteran's Benefits	29	6.3
(10) Hobby/Arts and Crafts	3	0.6
(11) Support from Non-Household Members	1	0.3
(F) Household Composition		
(1) Single Person	284	61.7
(2) Two Persons/Married	78	17.0
(3) Husband/Wife With One or More Children	33	7.2
(4) Single Person or Married Couple Residing at Home of Offspring	5	1.1
(5) Three Persons, Of Whom Two Are Related	17	3.7
(6) Two or More Persons/Not Related	17	3.7
(7) Nursing Home/Retirement Home	22	4.8
(8) Total	456	100.0
(G) Tenure Status		
(1) Homeowner	273	61.5
(2) Home Rental/Apartment Rental	121	27.3
(3) Trailer Rental	1	0.3
(4) Nursing Home/Retirement Home	22	4.8
(5) Total	444	100.0
(6) No Information	39	-----

MAP #6 Concentration of Population Age 65+

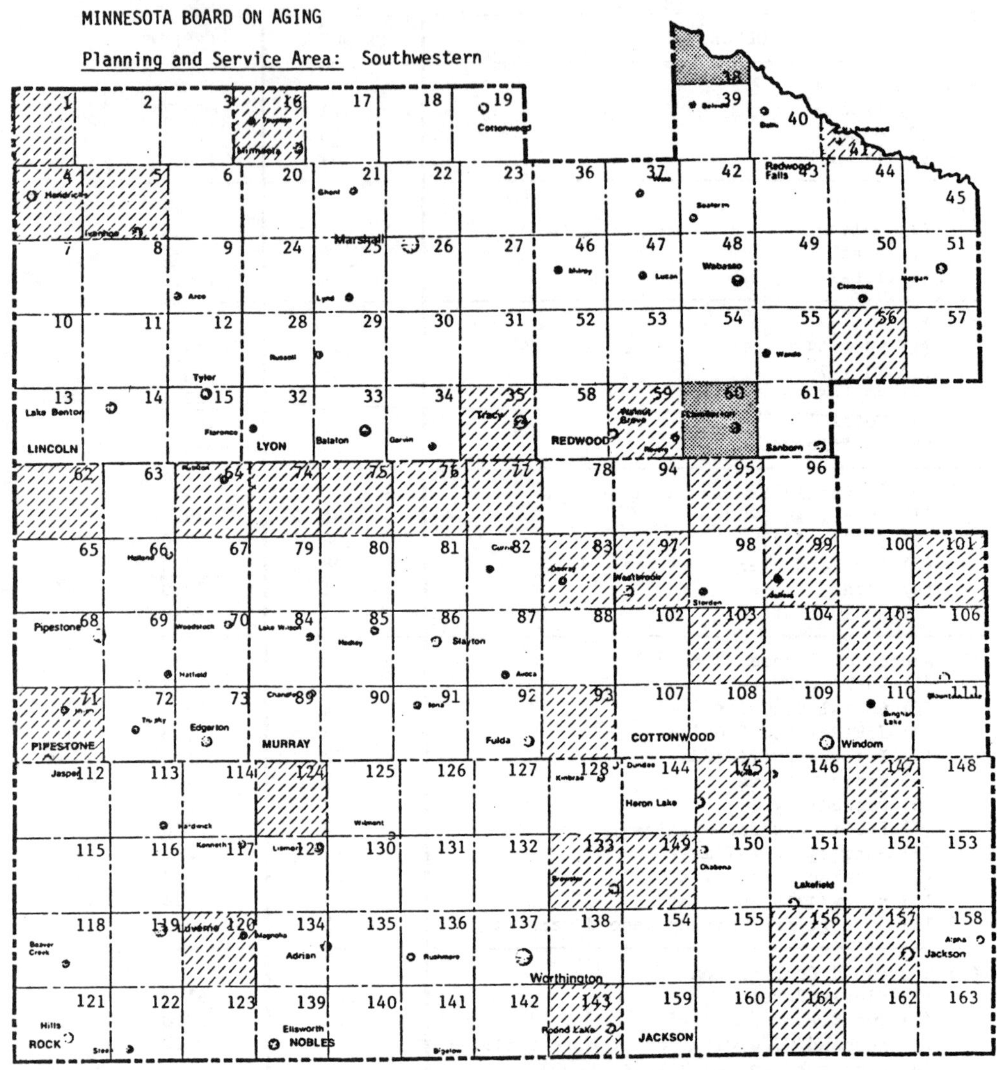

SOURCE: U.S. CENSUS

Southwest Minnesota

6 CONCENTRATION OF POPULATION AGE 65+

- 15 % + OF TOTAL POP.
- 10 % - 14.9 %
- LESS THAN 10 %

barton aschman associates, inc.

NORTH

miles 0 5 10 15

counties which showed population gains sustained dramatic declines in the number of children age 17 and under, the same counties displayed large increases in the age 18-29 group and consistent growth in the age 65 and over category. While the five counties showed a modest growth in population of 1.6 percent on the average from 1970 to 1975, the elderly population increased in the same period by an average rate of 6.2 percent--nearly four times the rate of growth of the population as a whole. Even in the four counties which sustained an estimated loss in population of -3.6 percent on the average from 1970 to 1975, the elderly population grew by an average rate of 6.1 percent during the same time. Cottonwood County's elderly population showed the most striking gain, 12.2 percent within these five years--double the average rate of growth of the elderly population in southwest Minnesota.

One might suspect that a large proportion of southwest Minnesota's elderly would live on isolated farmsteads in the county. U.S. Census data (1970) were examined by township to find the concentration of persons aged 65 and over in the area. Map #6 indicates that only 33 of the 163 townships (20 percent) showed a concentration of older people of 10 to 14.9 percent. This is not a very high proportion considering that the concentration of elderly 65 years and over region-wide is 13.7 percent by 1970 data. Only two townships, both in Redwood County, showed a 15 percent or over concentration of elderly.

To explain the relatively low proportion of eldery in the area, rural community data were found to record a trend toward a steady and sharp drop in rural farm residences, consistent and sizeable growth in communities of 2,500 people or more (nearly all county seats), and a slight decline in the proportion of population which lives in rural communities under 2,500 population (see Graph #5).

ROCK AND KEYA PAHA, NEBRASKA

Region 24 Council of Governments, Comprehensive Human Service Plan for Boyd, Brown, Hold, Keya Paha, and Rock Counties in Nebraska, 1979, pp. 10-16.

Elderly and Socialization

I. Problem Statement

There is a need for more senior citizen centers and social activities for many elderly persons (aged 60 and over) in the five counties.

A. Exact Nature of the Problem

1. There is a high percent of persons 65 and over in the five-county area, only one senior center, and limited social activities.

2. Many elderly persons are isolated, both physically and socially, from the rest of the population.

3. Feelings of loneliness are experienced by many elderly persons.

GRAPH 5 Projected Urban/Rural Population 1970-2000

MINNESOTA BOARD ON AGING
Planning and Service Area: Southwestern

Exhibit C-1 Part II
Page 5 of 29

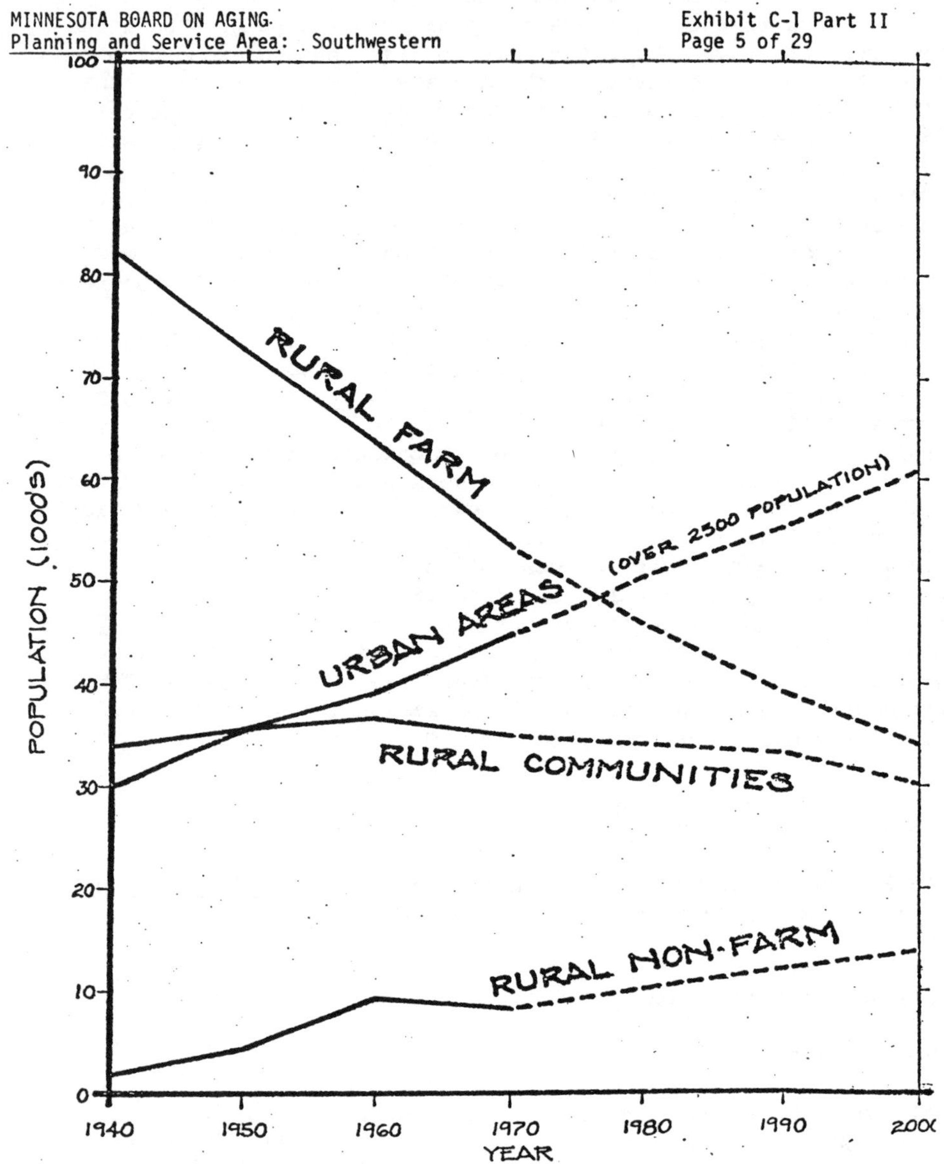

5 PROJECTED URBAN/RURAL POPULATION 1970-2000

SOURCES: U.S. CENSUS
MINNESOTA PLANNING AGENCY, "MINNESOTA POPULATION PROJECTIONS, 1970-2000," 1975.

Elderly and Socialization Tables and Sources of Documentation

1

1975 NEBRASKA POPULATION PROJECTIONS (65 & OVER)

	Boyd	Brown	Holt	Keya Paha	Rock
#:	751	694	2024	191	414
%:	21.2	17.9	16.3	14.4	19.2

*Nebraska Population Projections II, Bureau of Business Research, University of Nebraska-Lincoln, July 1976.

2

ELDERLY LIVING ALONG, RETIRED, WIDOWED AND LIMITATIONS ON PARTICIPATION

	Live Alone	Retired	Widowed
Boyd	69%	76%	60%
Brown	48%	93%	45%
Holt	49%	74%	22%
Keya Paha	22%	70%	22%
Rock	70%	87%	73%
Average	52%	80%	49%

*Prepared by the Gerontology Program, University of Nebraska at Omaha in cooperation with the Nebraska Commission on Aging, November 1977. (Surveyed the following persons aged 60 & Over: Boyd: 45; Brown: 40; Holt: 70; Keya Paha: 23; Rock: 30)

3

HOW OFTEN DO YOU FEEL LONELY?

	Frequently	Sometimes	Very Rarely or Never
Boyd	44.4%	28.9%	26.7%
Brown	15.0%	42.5%	42.5%
Holt	20.0%	41.4%	38.6%
Keya Paha	-----	56.5%	39.1%
Rock	6.7%	46.7%	46.7%

*Prepared by the Gerontology Program, University of Nebraska at Omaha in cooperation with the Nebraska Commission on Aging, November, 1977. (Surveyed the following persons aged 60 & Over: Boyd: 45; Brown: 40; Holt: 70; Keya Paha: 23; Rock: 30)

4

ARE THERE ANY RECREATIONAL ACTIVITIES THAT YOU WOULD LIKE TO PARTICIPATE IN?

	Boyd	Brown	Holt	Keya Paha	Rock
Yes:	44.4%	2.5%	17.1%	17.4%	10.0%

*Prepared by the Gerontology Program, University of Nebraska at Omaha in cooperation with the Nebraska Commission on Aging, November, 1977. (Surveyed the following persons aged 60 & Over: Boyd: 45; Brown: 40; Holt: 70; Keya Paha: 23; Rock: 30)

4. There are some elderly persons who would like to participate in recreational activities.

5. Many elderly persons have problems associated with such things as finances, health and nutrition, transportation, and housing, which services provided by a center could help alleviate.

B. Amount

1. The average percent of persons aged 65 and over in the five-county area in 1975 was 18 percent.

a. Keya Paha is the only county that currently has a senior citizen center, but Boyd County is presently in the process of establishing one.

2. Of 208 elderly persons in the five-county area who were surveyed in 1977, an average of 52 percent live alone, 80 percent are retired, and 49 percent are widowed.

3. When asked, "How often do you feel lonely?", an average of 17 percent of those surveyed said frequently; 43 percent said sometimes; and 18 percent said very rarely or never.

4. In response to the question, "Are there any recreational activities that you would like to participate in?", an average of 18 percent of those surveyed responded yes.

5. Specific problems, such as finances, health and nutrition, transportation and housing, which affect the elderly are discussed in more detail elsewhere in this plan.

C. Who and Where

Those affected by these problems are elderly persons (age 60 and over) in the five counties of Boyd, Brown, Holt, Keya Paha, and Rock.

II. ACTIVITY STATEMENT

To set up senior citizen centers in the five counties so that all senior citizens have reasonable access to them and to develop more social activities for the elderly.

A. Senior citizen centers could be established in Brown, Holt, and Rock counties, where no previous facility exists.

1. Programs and services offered by the centers in Boyd and Keya Paha counties should be reviewed and updated and new programs added as needed.

2. Additional or satellite centers could be established if needed to assure that all elderly persons have reasonable access to the facilities.

B. Senior citizen centers could provide many services and functions that would be useful for many elderly persons.

1. The following is a list of just a few of the social and recreational functions a center could offer:

a. library and reading services;

b. companionship;

c. Bible study;

d. cards;
e. birthday parties;
f. painting;
g. quilting;
h. dinners;
i. volunteer community services.

2. This list suggests some services a center could provide to elderly persons:
a. social security representative;
b. Department of Public Safety--driver's license;
c. State Commission for the Blind;
d. public health nurse;
e. housing counseling;
f. counseling;
g. referral services;
h. employment;
i. services to the homebound;
j. adult education;
k. telephone reassurance;
l. day care;
m. Meals-On-Wheels;
n. chore services;
o. legal aid;
p. transportation.

C. There are numerous programs and services that pertain to the elderly that could be utilized.

1. The <u>Retired Senior Volunteer Program</u> is for anyone 60 and over who wants to use his or her experience and talents in useful service to others in the community.

2. The <u>Service Corps of Retired Executives</u> is retired business men and women who offer counseling in management and business to small business and other community groups, serving the general public on a volunteer basis.

3. Three other programs: <u>Green Thumb</u>, <u>Foster Grandparent Program</u>, and <u>Senior Companion Program</u>, offer employment opportunities to the elderly and will be discussed thoroughly elsewhere in this plan.

D. Brown, Holt, and Keya Paha counties should be persuaded to join the Northeast Nebraska Area Agency on Aging.

1. Boyd and Rock counties are presently the only counties participating in the Northeast Nebraska Area Agency on Aging.

2. Participating in the Area Agency on Aging will qualify Brown, Holt, and Keya Paha for funds from the Nebraska Commission on Aging, as well as from the Area Agency on Aging.

3. The programs provided by the Nebraska Commission on Aging are:
a. supportive services;
b. nutrition;
c. multi-purpose senior centers;
d. employment;
e. training;
f. advocacy and volunteer activities.

III. RECOMMENDATIONS

A. The Committee fully supports having senior citizen centers in each county.

B. The Committee recommends that all the counties join the Northeast Nebraska Area Agency on Aging.

C. The Committee suggests having the Council of Governments check on and try to implement the following programs:

1. Retired Senior Volunteer Program;
2. Service Corps of Retired Executives;
3. Green Thumb;
4. Foster Grandparent Program;
5. Senior Companion Program.

II. ACTIVITY STATEMENT

To see that families who need daycare service are provided with it.

A. There should be a push for more licensed family daycare homes, which provide care for up to seven children.

B. Licensed daycare centers which provide care for eight or more children, could be started in Ainsworth and O'Neill if shown to be economically feasible.

1. Some of the funds which could be used toward a daycare center are:
    a. Department of Agriculture's Child Nutrition Division;
    b. U.S. Department of Health, Education, and Welfare, Division of Social and Rehabilitation Services;
    c. Small Business Administration;
    d. General Revenue Sharing;
    e. Housing and Community Development Act.

C. Another idea for low-income and handicapped children would be the Head Start Program.

1. Head Start is a child development program providing comprehensive educational and social services, parent involvement, and health services to pre-school children of low-income families.

III. RECOMMENDATIONS

A. The Committee recommends that the city councils and Village boards or planning commissions in interested towns develop a survey to determine the need for daycare services.

COLUMBIA, NEW YORK

Columbia County Planning Department, Columbia County Human Services Study, 1976, pp. 6-7, 10, 23, 27.

Potential human service agencies were sent a comprehensive questionnaire with instructions that included the definition of the services and agencies of concern, asking the agency to return the questionnaire without filling it out if they felt that their services did not fall within the guidelines.

The questionnaire was designed to elicit specific information about the agency, including the organization's purpose, service area, personnel, fiscal information, interactions with other service agencies, the delivery of services, the services provided, the clientele served, and the problems and needs identified by the agency.

Fifty-three of the 115 human service agencies (excluding religious organizations) responded to the questionnaires; of these, 7 agencies responded with a blank questionnaire explaining that this study did not apply to them. Excluding the 7 blank questionnaires, it should be stated that 46 out of 115 agencies who were contacted responded with information applicable to this study. While at first glance this may appear to be a poor ratio, there is a major factor which contributed to this which, when considered in the proper light, indicates that the 46 agencies represent a true picture of the human service delivery system in Columbia County. The point is that the 115 agencies were identified only as potential human service agencies in the first place, many chosen by their name only in the effort to be comprehensive. The figure of 115 agencies is therefore inflated: the total human service delivery system is really made up of fewer agencies.

To organize the information from the returned questionnaires into a usable form, the following methods were applied. The 41 services listed in the questionnaire were grouped according to 4 headings based upon the functional thrust of each service. The 4 headings are: reinforcement of self-maintenance (which includes those primary care services such as education, daycare, etc.), services to persons under special stress (including counseling services and temporary shelter care), services re: a substitute environment (including adoption and foster care services), and social-administrative services (i.e., services geared towards the administration of the delivery system, such as fund raising and community planning). (The New York State Temporary Commission To Revise The Social Services Law reports were used as a basis for the development of these main service groupings.)

Persons of all age groups appear to be served fairly equitably. Although at the time of the completion of the questionnaire, there were no agencies offering a temporary substitute environment to those aged under 18, this service is now being provided by the Columbia County Department of Social Services in the form of a nonsecure detention home.

Chart IX shows that the agencies generally serve the lower income groups and persons receiving welfare, as is expected when assessing the nonprofit human service delivery system. At the same time, no income group is excluded from the services; income level is used as an eligibility requirement only by four agencies. Most of the agencies which have age as an eligibility requirement are concerned with recreational activities. One exception is the Family Planning Service, which cannot serve youths under age 18 except under special circumstances.

CHART IX Clientele Characteristics: Average Percentage of Clients Served, Classified by Income Groups, by Functional Group

Total Responses - 21

FUNCTIONAL GROUP	TOTAL AGENCIES RESPONDING	BELOW $3000/yr.	$3000-8000/yr.	$8000-12,000/yr.	$12,000-15,000/yr.	$15,000-20,000/yr.	OVER $20,000/yr.	RECEIVING WELFARE
I - Reinforcement of self-maintenance	9	39%	39%	13%	4.5%	3%	1.5%	44%
II- Services to persons under special stress	3	15%	53%	22%	5%	3.5%	1.5%	28%
III- Services re: a Substitute Environment	2 (1)* (1)	100%						54%*
IV- Social-Administrative Services	2 (1) (1)*	10%	35%	50%	3%	2%	0%	10% 80%*
V- Multi-Functional Agencies	5 (4) (1)	22.5%	42.5%	28.75%	5%	1%	.25%	34%

* These agencies reported percentages on welfare only and are therefore considered seperately.

NOTE: Information on this chart is an average percentage derived from percentages reported for each income bracket by each agency reporting.

Bibliography: Social Services

Lowndes, Alabama. South Central Alabama Development Commission, Social Services Directory for Bullock, Butler, Crenshaw, Lowndes, Macon, and Pike Counties, 1979 (16 pgs. on Lowndes).

Graham, Arizona. Citizens Advisory Planning Committee, "Citizens Task Force on the Elderly: A Report to the City Council of Safford," 1978 (8 pgs.).

Sussex, Delaware. Delaware Department of Community Affairs and Economic Development, Office of Economic Opportunity, Proposal to Community Services Administration for funds for training and technical assistance for community groups to work on behalf of the poor, 1979 (41 pgs.).

Sussex County Community Action Agency, Inc., Proposal to CSA for funding of projects for low-income people in nutrition, energy, and housing, 1980 (116 pgs.).

Sussex County Community Action Agency, Inc., Proposal to CSA (Small Town Emphasis Program) for funding for developmental activities of community organizations in poverty areas, 1979 (37 pgs.).

Bacon, Georgia. Alma-Bacon County Community Development Agency, Application to HUD (small cities program) for funds for a mental retardation training center, 1979 (58 pgs.).

Glascock, Georgia. Glascock County, application for multipurpose senior center award under Title V of the Older Americans Act, 1980 (10 pgs.).

Glascock Redevelopment Cooperative, Inc., Application to DOT for capital assistance to provide transportation services for the elderly and handicapped, 1977 (7 pgs.).

Jefferson, Indiana. Madison-Jefferson County, "Madison-Jefferson County Senior Citizens' Center Older American Program" (brochure).

Dubois, Greene, Knox, Martin, and Pike, Indiana. Cooperative Extension Service, Purdue University, Title XX Statistical Report No. 2: Needs Assessment of Older Americans, 1979 (21 pgs.).

Saginaw, Michigan. Saginaw County Planning Commission, A Report on the Transportation Problems and Recommendations for Improving Services for Senior Citizens and the Handicapped, 1979 (27 pgs.).

Minnesota. Agricultural Experiment Station, University of Minnesota, "Planning Transportation Systems for Older Rural Americans," Station Bulletin 519, 1977 (17 pgs.).

Jackson, Pipestone, and Rock, Minnesota. Minnesota Board on Aging, 1980 Area Plan for Programs on Aging for the Southwest Area Agency on Aging (97 pgs.).

Rock and Keya Paha, Nebraska. Region 24 Council of Governments, Comprehensive Human Service Plan for Boyd, Brown, Holt, Keya Paha, and Rock Counties in Nebraska, 1979 (52 pgs.).

Lea, New Mexico. Jal Public Schools, Application to Office of Education for funds for Bilingual Education Program (Spanish-English), 1979 (42 pgs.).

Columbia, New York. Columbia County Planning Department, Columbia County Human Services Study, 1976 (65 pgs.).

Karnes, Kendall, and Kerr, Texas. Alamo Area Council of Governments, Resource Directory for Alcohol, Drug Abuse, and Mental Health Services, 1979 (41 pgs.).

Kendall, Texas. Alamo Area Council of Governments, Kendall County Social Services Guide, 1979 (23 pgs.).

Kerr, Texas. Alamo Area Council of Governments, Kerr County Social Services Guide, 1979 (29 pgs.).

Cache, Utah. Bear River Association of Governments, Bear River District Comprehensive Human Services Plan for Program Year 1979 (87 pgs.).

Henry, Virginia. West Piedmont Planning District Commission, Directory of Social Services in the West Piedmont Planning District, 1976 (16 pgs.-excerpt).

RECREATION

Recreation plans, frequently financed by HUD, typically include the following sections:

- Facility standards
- Existing facilities
- Demand
- Needs analysis
- Goals

The first example of recreation data is from a recreation demand study in the Florida Keys. Local residents were surveyed about their recreational preferences, and tourist recreational preferences were computed from various formulas.

The next example, from Marquette County, Wisconsin, is a projection of future active and passive recreation land needs. The land needs are based on population projections and recreation standards.

The last example is from a plan which outlines the existing outdoor recreation facilities in the Missouri Valley region. There is a comparison of existing facilities to accepted standards in order to determine local needs.

MONROE, FLORIDA

Monroe County Planning Department, Monroe County Recreation and Open Space Element, 1978, pp. 21-24.

Demand for Recreational Facilities

Demand for recreation opportunities is generated by people's preferences and desires to particiate in recreational activities. The tangible and intangible factors which influence people's desires and preferences relate directly or indirectly to a wide range of socio-economic characteristics such as: income, occupation, education, sex, age, family composition, place of residence, changing technology, spatial mobility, leisure time, and social values. The combined influence of these factors which results in a particular demand pattern can best be understood by conducting a survey of citizens' recreational preferences. Although such a survey is highly desirable for assessing a community's recreational needs, no effort was made to conduct a special survey for this recreation plan due to the following reasons: first, the available time, staff, and financial resources were inadequate to conduct such a comprehensive survey; and second, it was realized that a reasonable inference could be drawn conerning user preferences on the basis of the studies and surveys conducted in recent years.

The most prominent of these surveys was conducted during the spring of 1978 by the Monroe County School District and deals with people's interests and leisure time activities. In an effort to determine community education needs, 450 households were surveyed by telephone according to methods recently validated by the Rand Corporation. In order to maintain the level of precision needed to make the rankings useful in community planning, samples were stratified by geographical location and race. The major limitation of this survey lies in the fact that it deals in a broad sense with people's interests and leisure time activities but not so much with supply and demand of outdoor recreation facilities. Also, it excludes those who do not have phones and a large number of those who live in the county on a seasonal basis, since the survey was conducted in late spring. The survey, nevertheless, does reveal some interesting facts which could be interpreted as having implications for planning recreation facilities. More than sixty different activities and interests were ranked on the basis of the percentages of people indicating their interest in these activities. Table 1 indicates rankings on this survey among fifteen selected outdoor recreation activities.

Population estimates and projections represent the combined permanent and seasonal resident taxpayers population who may reasonably be expected to demand neighborhood and community parks and special recreational facilities in a given year. Tourists or transients should not be treated as requiring similar user-oriented recreation facilities. Tourists to the Keys, attracted as they are by the Keys' natural resources and amenities, engage primarily in resource-based outdoor recreation such as beach activities, fishing, swimming, diving, camping, picnicking, nature study, etc. Demand for these recreation activities should be established on the basis of total resident and tourist population as is reflected in user occasions in Table 3. User occasions were calculated by applying 1975 per capita participation rates for various activities for Region X and the methodology described in "Outdoor Recreation in Florida 1976."

TABLE 1

Activity	County-wide Rank	%	Lower Keys Rank	%	Middle Keys Rank	%	Upper Keys Rank	%
Picnicking	1	50	1	50	3	55	2	42
Fishing	2	49	3	46	1	63	3	41
Swimming	3	49	2	49	4	54	1	44
Diving	4	37	7	31	2	55	5	32
Boating	5	36	8	30	5	53	4	32
Tennis	6	36	4	35	7	50	7	22
Baseball or Softball	7	34	5	34	8	44	8	22
Track & Field	8	33	6	32	9	44	9	19
Sailing	9	32	12	24	6	52	6	26
Volleyball	10	30	9	28	10	43	11	18
Football or Soccer	11	27	10	25	11	36	10	19
Handball or Racketball	12	25	11	25	13	34	14	13
Basketball	13	25	13	23	12	36	12	17
Shuffleboard	14	17	14	14	15	26	13	16
Golf	15	17	15	13	14	26	15	12

NOTE: (%) refers to the percentage of people interested in a particular activity.

Source: Monroe County Community Education Needs Survey, 1978.

MARQUETTE, WISCONSIN

Marquette County Rural Planning Committee and the East Central Wisconsin Regional Planning Commission, Marquette County Outdoor Recreation Plan, 1977, pp. 17-18

Recreational Needs

Marquette County has had a relatively constant population for the past century. Recent trends, however, indicate a shift in growth from urban to rural areas. Marquette County is projected to grow from 9,915 in 1976 to 14,230 by the year 2000. This growth will have an impact on all kinds of development including the demand for recreational facilities. In addition, the already substantial seasonal population is projected to increase from 20,000 in 1975 to 28,000 by the year 2000, placing further pressure on county recreational facilities.

To determine how much land is necessary to meet recreational demand and what specific recreational facilities for specific recreational activities need further development, various standards were applied to the population projections. These standards were developed by the East Central Wisconsin Regional Planning Commission after researching

TABLE 3

RESOURCE-BASED OUTDOOR RECREATION
1978 USER-OCCASIONS
MONROE COUNTY (KEYS)

ACTIVITY	RESIDENT USER-OCC.	TOURIST USER-OCC.	COMBINED USER-OCC.	MAXIMUM PEAK DAY USER-OCC.
Beach Activities	452,187	1,998,556	2,450,743	12,143
Fishing	166,559	226,324	392,883	1,947
Boating	149,352	187,416	336,768	1,669
Picnicking	70,890	167,140	238,030	1,179
Nature Study	46,113	31,784	77,897	386
Hiking	9,636	38,360	47,996	238
Camping (RV Sites)	5,506	161,112	166,618	826
Camping (Tent Sites)	8,259	132,616	140,875	598
Visiting Arch. & Hist. Sites	9,636	132,068	141,704	702
Boat Ramp Usage	55,749	37,812	93,561	464
Bicycling	522,389	90,968	613,357	3039
Water Skiing	9,636	120,560	130,196	645
Sailing	7,571	104,120	111,691	553

standards used by other regions and adjusting them according to the characteristics of counties in East Central Wisconsin.

Recreational Land

To determine the overall county need for park and recreational land, the following standard was adopted:

For every 1,000 persons, a minimum <u>total</u> of 100 acres of outdoor recreational open space should be provided, comprised of:

70 acres of passive recreational open space per 1,000 population	- includes forests, wildlife areas, hunting preserves, and portions of regional parks suitable for uses such as hiking, nature study, cross-country skiing, and hunting.

30 acres of active recreational - open space per 1,000 population	includes portions of state parks, regional parks, and community parks with facilities such as play areas, ball fields, swimming, and campsites.

Applying this standard to population projections indicates a substantial increase in demand for recreational land by the year 2000:

Marquette County Recreational Demand*

	Population			Demand (Acres)****		
Year	Resident**	Seasonal***	Total	Passive	Active	Total
1975	9,692	20,000	29,692	2,078	891	2,969
1977	10,088	20,200	30,288	2,120	909	3,029
1980	10,610	21,000	31,610	2,213	948	3,161
1990	12,650	25,000	37,650	2,636	1,130	3,766
2000	14,230	28,000	42,230	2,956	1,267	4,223

* Source - East Central Wisconsin Regional Planning Commission.
** Wisconsin DOA population estimates and projections.
*** Derived from Wisconsin DNR Recreation Economic Barometer indices by the ECWRPC.
**** Based on total resident and seasonal demand.

Comparing projected demand with existing supply of recreation open space suggests that Marquette County will continue to have a surplus in passive recreation land through the year 2000. However, a deficiency of 770 acres of active recreation land already exists and this deficiency will worsen unless supply is increased:

Marquette County Recreation Land Needs*

	Demand**			Supply**(Public)			Need(-) or Surplus (+)**		
Year	Passive	Active	Total	Passive	Active	Total***	Passive	Active	Total
1975	2,078	891	2,969	7,775	139	7,914	+5,697	- 752	+4,945
1977	2,120	909	3,029	7,775	139	7,914	+5,655	- 770	+4,885
1980	2,213	948	3,161	7,775	139	7,914	+5,562	- 809	+4,753
1990	2,636	1,130	3,766	7,775	139	7,914	+5,139	- 991	+4,148
2000	2,956	1,267	4,223	7,775	139	7,914	+4,819	-1,128	+3,691

* Source - East Central Wisconsin Regional Planning Commission.
** - in acres.
*** Forest croplands not included.

It should be noted that these county needs are in addition to local open space needs. The recommended local open space standard is 10 acres per 1,000 population in the form of rec-lots, neighborhood parks, or community parks. Local units of government are responsible for providing such facilities.

CHARITON, MISSOURI

Missouri Valley Regional Planning Commission, Missouri Valley Regional Outdoor Recreation Plan, 1979, pp. 19, 48-49.

Existing, Needed, and Desired Facilities

The following section outlines the existing outdoor recreation facilities in the towns within the Missouri Valley Region. It compares the existing facilities to accepted standards to determine local needs. The local desires for outdoor recreation facilities are also listed for each community. The local desires were obtained through discussions with city councils and/or local park boards. The prioritized desires represent what the local officials stated their citizens want for outdoor recreation. In many cases the listed items are not presently within financial reach of the town. However, if money were available, the town has the desire to construct and maintain the specified facility.

MARSHALL

The City of Marshall operates one large park that contains a variety of facilities. There are no neighborhood parks other than the school facilities. Through a professional parks and recreation staff, the city maintains its facilities and offers activity programs throughout the year.

Existing Outdoor Recreational Facilities					Needed Facilities
	City	School	Private	Other	
Picnic shelters	9	0	0	0	0
Picnic tables	88	0	0	0	8
Playground/pieces	6/48	5/35	0	0	6/42
Tennis court	0	2	3	0	0
with lights	4	0	0	0	4
Baseball field	0	0	0	0	0
with lights	1	0	0	0	1
Softball field	1	4	0	0	0
with lights	4	0	0	0	1
Multipurpose court	1	6	0	0	3
Restrooms	3	0	0	0	0
Swimming pools	1	0	2	0	0
Golf course	1	0	0	0	0
Shuffleboard courts	1	0	0	0	3
Band stage	1	0	0	0	0
Moto cross track	1	0	0	0	0
Football field	0	2	1	0	0
Track	0	1	1	0	0

Existing Outdoor Recreational Facilities	City	School	Private	Other	Needed Facilities
Archery range	1	0	0	0	0
Fishing lake	1	0	0	1	0
Croquet court	1	0	0	0	0
Ice rink	0	0	0	1	0

The first five projects in the five-year plan deal with existing facilities that need improvement or maintenance. This is a strong indication that the Marshall Park Board has a commitment or at least senses a need to maintain and care for existing facilities before adding additional ones. The highest ranking "new" project in the five-year plan is the addition of one neighborhood park.

Within the long range plan, there seem to be two major groupings according to the priority assigned to them. It appears there is a stronger sense of need for neighborhood parks, a new picnic shelter, an activity lake, and a nature trail than for the remaining five projects. The first priority was one or two neighborhood parks.

Expressed Desires for Outdoor Recreation	5 Year Plan	Long Range Plan
Improved pool parking	1	0
Purchase existing golf course	1	0
Renovate shelters	9	0
Baseball lighting	1	0
Clean fishing lake	1	0
Neighborhood park	1	2
New shelterhouse	1	1
Tennis court lighting	1	0
Additional park land	43 acres	0
Additional tennis courts	2	0
Softball improvements	1	0
Improve lower lake	0	1
Exercise trail	1	0
Nature trail	0	1
Additional golf course land	0	9 holes
Additional restroom	0	1
Tennis courts (high school)	2	0
Bike trails	0	1
Play equipment	1	0
Renovate archery range	0	1
Lakes on golf course	2	0
Ball fields (high school)	0	2

Bibliography: Recreation

Calhoun, Cherokee, Cleburne, and Talladega, Alabama. East Alabama Regional Planning and Development Commission, Recreation and Open Space Analysis (72 pgs.).

Monroe, Florida. Monroe County Planning Department, Monroe County Recreation and Open Space Element, 1978 (70 pgs.).

Clay, Georgia. Application by Fort Gaines for matching grant for recreation equipment for city park, 1979 (1 pg.).

Elbert, Georgia. Northeast Area Planning and Development Commission, Northeast Georgia Areawide Recreational Trails Study, 1977 (75 pgs.).

______, Northeast Georgia Areawide Recreation and Open Space Plan and Program, 1976 (177 pgs.).

Webster, Georgia. Webster County Extension, Recreation survey, 1978 (1 pg.).

Dickinson, Michigan. Dickinson County Planning Commission, Dickinson County Recreation Plan, 1977 (47 pgs.).

Montmorency, Michigan. Montmorency County Board of Commissioners, "Montmorency County Recreation Plan," 1976 (20 pgs.).

Chariton, Missouri. Missouri Valley Regional Planning Commission, Missouri Valley Region Outdoor Recreation Plan, 1979 (89 pgs.).

Custer, South Dakota. Sixth District Council of Local Governments, "Custer Outdoor Recreation Assessment," 1979 (10 pgs.).

Floyd, Texas. South Plains Association of Governments, Recreation and Open Space for the South Plains: A Comprehensive Plan, 1978 (124 pgs.).

Marquette, Wisconsin. Marquette County Rural Planning Committee and the East Central Wisconsin Regional Planning Commission, Marquette County Outdoor Recreation Plan, 1977 (109 pgs.).

Marquette and Waushara, Wisconsin. East Central Wisconsin Regional Planning Commission, Snowmobile Trail Plan for East Central Wisconsin, 1979 (32 pgs.).

Waushara, Wisconsin. East Central Wisconsin Regional Planning Commission, "Snowmobile Element-Waushara County," 1975 (17 pgs.).

______, "Waushara County Outdoor Recreation Plan--Plan Amendment," 1978 (9 pgs.).

APPENDIX E

DATA SET DESCRIPTIONS

This appendix contains descriptions of 34 data sets that contain data relevant to the rural development issues discussed in the report. The order of the data sets follows the order of Chapters 5-11 of the report, from data sets that contain primarily population data through those that contain environmental data. However, many data sets contain items relevant to more than one of those chapters. The data sets are described in this appendix in the following order:

National County Data Base
Census of Population and Housing
Current Population Survey
Donnelley Marketing's Residential Data Base
Basic Vital Statistics
Annual Housing Survey
Health Interview Survey
Health and Nutrition Examination
Hospital Discharge Survey
National Ambulatory Medical Care Survey
Area Resource File
Master Facility Inventory
National Nursing Home Survey
Merged Data File (data on school districts)
National Assessment of Education Progress
Census of Governments
Federal Assistance Programs Retrieval System
Federal Information Exchange System
National Rural Community Facilities Assessment Study
BEA Regional Economic Information System
Statistics of Income: Individual Income Tax Returns
Statistics of Income: Small-Area Data
Continuous Work History Sample
Current Employment and Unemployment Analysis
Census of Agriculture
Survey of Income and Education
County Business Patterns
Census of Manufactures
Federal-State Cooperative Program for Local Population Estimates

Second National Water Assessment
STORET (data on water quality)
National Emissions Data System
Storage and Retrieval of Aerometric Data

Insofar as possible, the descriptions of the data sets describe the unit of analysis, the types of variables collected, and the types of publications or other output available. Since the data sets differ widely in purpose, a common format cannot be used in all the descriptions. An attempt was made in the descriptions to ascertain what levels of disaggregation were available since data for small rural areas is a focus of the report. Throughout, we have quoted and paraphrased material from the listed sources.

NATIONAL COUNTY DATA BASE

CENTER FOR SOCIAL DATA ANALYSIS, MONTANA STATE UNIVERSITY

Unit of Observation

County.

Purpose

This is a combination of several existing data sets that can be accessed with one software system. The establishment of this large data base was stimulated by the research investigating the nonmetropolitan migration turnaround. This research demanded answers to questions concerning what kinds of people were moving to and from what kinds of places. While much research could be done using the existing discrete data sets, the merged data allow for more comprehensive analyses of rural populations and socioeconomic change.

Contents

Continuous Work History Sample
1960 Census
1970 Census
City-County Data Book
Area Resource File
Area Measurement File (provided by Census Bureau to append coordinates of county population centroids to county characteristics)
BEA employment and income data
County Business Patterns

Population and net migration estimates (prepared for the Census Bureau under the Federal-State Cooperative Program for Local Population Estimates)
Net migration (prepared by Bowles for 1950-1960 and 1960-1970)

Other data sets under active consideration for addition to the NCDB include 1976 and 1977 Medicare enrollment data to provide estimates of retirement-age migration to nonmetropolitan counties, data from the Census of Governments on county-level revenues and expenditures to examine fiscal and service impacts of migration-induced growth, county-level 1980 census products as they become available, and establishment of city files nested within the county data with information from the cities portion of the Consolidated County-City Data Book and matching information from the revenue sharing population and per capita income estimates. Other types of information are being sought to expand the applicability of the NCDB to questions of land use, energy consumption, and educational enrollments.

Access

The software system is not transferable to other computer installations at this time, so the Center for Social Data Analysis provides a variety of services to researchers interested in using the NCDB. The simplest of these services is the creation of custom files based on subsets of the data items in the NCDB. More frequently the Center performs data analyses according to user specifications.

Source

Wardwell, John M., C. Jack Gilchrist, and Celia A. Allard (1980) Notes: A national county data base for rural research. Newsline 8(July):22-32.

CENSUS OF POPULATION AND HOUSING

BUREAU OF THE CENSUS

Unit of Observation

Housing units and persons within housing units. The tabulations will be made in terms of individuals and also in terms of families and households.

Periodicity

Decennial.

Universe Description

Population of the United States. For some information, a sample is used.

Subject Matter Description

Housing items available include availability of telephone and plumbing facilities, tenure, rent paid or value of property, type of fuel, and detailed information concerning presence of such items as air-conditioning, automobile, washing machine, clothes dryer, and television set.

Information is available about the housing units in each area, showing how many units are single family dwellings and how many are in multiunit structures. Information is also gathered on whether the housing unit is owned or rented, and the value of owner occupied units and the rent for those for which rent is paid. This information is collected for all housing units for which cash rent is paid, and for owner-occupied units if they are not located on a place of ten acres or more and if they are not used partially for commercial purposes.

Mobile homes or trailers are separately identified. Data are available to show to what extent mobile homes are occupied by older or younger persons, by couples and families or by persons living alone. No information is gathered about the value of mobile homes or trailers.

One measure of the quality of housing is supplied through the question on whether the housing unit includes complete plumbing facilities for the exclusive use of the household. In rural areas there would be special interest in the units which have no plumbing facilities in the living quarters.

Information about living conditions is also obtained through the several housing questions collected on a sample basis. These include age of housing unit, whether it is connected to a public sewer, and whether water comes from a public system, an individual drilled well, an individual dug well, or some other source. The method of heating and the fuel used are included, as is the fuel used for cooking and for water heating. Cost of utilities obviously is a matter of growing concern. Automobiles, vans, and small trucks are counted, and there are questions on presence of air conditioning, number of bedrooms in the unit, and existence of complete kitchen facilities. Real estate taxes and mortgage payments provide additional information on how families live.

Household information includes household size, household type (*e.g.*, whether the family is a one- or two-parent family), and number of generations living in one household. The number of rooms, in relation to the number of occupants, provides a measure of crowding.

Person data include relationship in household, sex, race, age, marital status, years of school completed, children ever born, occupation, industry, total income, place of residence five years ago, and means of transportation to work.

Information available for the smallest areas is that which is collected on a 100 percent basis. This includes the count of persons by age, sex, and marital status. It also includes whether respondent is white, black or Negro, Japanese, Chinese, Filipino, Korean, Vietnamese, American Indian, Asian Indian, Hawaiian, Guamanian, Samoan, Eskimo, or Aleut. On this question there is a provision for a person who is not identified with any of these groups to list the applicable identification. The Hispanic population is identified by asking those individuals to specify the appropriate sub-group, i.e., Mexican, Mexican-American, Chicano, Puerto Rican, Cuban, or other Spanish/Hispanic.

The information to be collected on a sample basis, and thus not available for the smallest areas, includes the occupation and industry of each individual in the labor force, the money income of each member of the family, and the family (or household) money income. Income is listed by source, and thus it becomes possible to specify whether families who have self-employment income from farming also have other types of income, such as wages or salaries; other self-employment income; income from dividends, royalties, or rents; from commissions, tips, etc; or from Social Security, unemployment compensation, etc.

The occupation shown is that which took up the majority of the working time during the week preceding the Census. This may mean that a part time farmer would report a non-farm activity as his occupation. In that case, information about the extent of such part-time activity becomes available by a tabulation showing the persons reporting self-employment income from farming, which ideally would include all cases of farm operation. The combination of data for occupation and for income provides a great deal of information about the extent to which families engaged in farming are drawing part of their income from other sources, including non-farm earnings by members of the family.

Other information collected on a sample basis includes the number of years of school completed by each individual; the ethnic group with which each person identified; veteran status; whether the person is a citizen; country of birth (if foreign born); and movement within the country during the preceding five years. Information is also collected on the method of getting to work and where the job is located in relation to the worker's residence.

Information is collected separately about persons who have a physical or mental handicap which prevents job holding, or which limits the kind or amount of work which the person can do. Women are asked how many children they ever had. This information assists in understanding the growth of populations and the contributions of rural and urban populations to the increase in the national population.

Geographic Coverage

In recent years, data on certain characteristics of the population have been gathered and tabulated for areas as small as a city block, while other statistics have been collected on a sample basis and published for larger geographic areas, such as census tracts (about 4,000 people), cities, counties, SMSAs, and states. In regard to local rural use, results are tabulated for every municipality and, where they exist, every township or similar governmental unit.

State governments were invited to make their needs for data by specific areas known in advance of the Census in order to enable the Bureau to take these special needs into account. Because of the fine-grained geographic detail, it is not particularly difficult to secure some population data for areas defined in terms of special purposes, such as river basins, conservation districts, rural development districts, and other areas with boundaries which may not conform entirely to political units.

Information gathered through the sample questions cannot be made available for the very smallest areas, but generally would be useful for areas with a population of 2500 persons or more. Here too, it might be possible to provide information for special areas which are made up of places, none of which has a population sufficiently large to be the base for tabulations of the sample data.

More generally, metropolitan/nonmetropolitan, urban/rural, and central city/noncentral city partitions are available.

Access

The Census tabulations are published in considerable detail, in printed volumes, or on computer tape. Whatever appears in a printed report can also be had on computer tape, and in many instances the computer tape will provide some detail which is not shown in the printed reports. If space for storage of data is a problem, the information could be secured in microfiche.

There is one other source of information which is availabe for any user who has access to computers. That is in the form of microdata tapes, i.e., the detailed information for a sample of households, without names or other information which would permit identification of the individual or the family. One limitation on the use of these data is that there is no geographic information for any place or area with less than 250,000 inhabitants. Nevertheless, many useful special tabulations can be prepared from these tapes, focused on special problems or special constituencies. The user wishing information which can be supplied through the means of such sample tapes is likely to find within the state that there are a number of offices which have the relevant tapes and are prepared to provide special tabulations on request.

CURRENT POPULATION SURVEY

BUREAU OF THE CENSUS

Unit of Observation

Individuals, families, and households.

Periodicity

Monthly.

Universe Description

The universe consists of the civilian noninstitutional population of the U.S. living in housing units, and the male members of the armed forces living in housing units for families on a military base or with their families not on a military base.

Currently, two probability samples are used in selecting housing units. The national sample, approximately 55,000 households, was originally designed to provide estimates at the U.S. level, but also has been used to make estimates for some of the larger states and SMSAs. The present CPS national sample consists of households and persons in group quarters in 461 primary sampling units (PSUs) where each PSU consists of an independent city or county or two or more contiguous counties. The sample of 461 PSUs comprises 923 counties and independent cities.

The state supplement, instituted in 1975, comprises additional samples selected within the District of Columbia and several of the smaller states and is designed to improve the reliability of estimates made for these areas from the national sample. This supplement includes approximately 11,000 units.

A characteristic of the sampling design is sample rotation. This is the partial replacement of respondents in successive months in accordance with a planned, continuing design. There is also occasional replacement of the primary sampling areas. The rotation of the sample and the replacement of PSUs are carried out in such a way that each month's sample is a probability sample of the population covered by the survey.

The rotation system was incorporated in the design to avoid the undue reporting burden of survey respondents, if they were to constitute a permanent panel. Substantial reductions in sampling costs could result if it were feasible to conduct interviews of the same sample of households every month. However, it was believed that asking the same respondents to supply information once every month for an indefinite period might create administrative problems due to complaints and, by substantially increasing the refusal rate, introduce biases and reduce the sampling efficiency.

Beginning in the 1930's, the CPS has over the years greatly improved its methods of sample selection and estimation. This increase in efficiency, which has had the effect of enlarging the sample, but at a much smaller cost, has been greatest in the estimates of agricultural employment. The current reliability in this labor force category is equivalent to that of a sample more than two and one half times as large, using the method employed in 1943.

Subject Matter Description

The CPS was initially designed primarily to produce timely estimates on a sample basis with measurable reliability for labor force data at the U.S. level every month. Although this summarizes the major objectives considered in designing the original sample program, the CPS is now used for purposes well beyond those originally envisioned. Expanding needs for additional current data by government and other users have been met by adding additional questions to the monthly interview, and by occasional supplementary inquiries.

The CPS provides a large amount of detail not otherwise available on the economic status and activities of the population of the U.S. It is the only source of monthly estimates of total employment, both farm and nonfarm; of nonfarm self-employed persons, domestics and unpaid helpers in nonfarm family enterprises, as well as wage and salaried employees; and of total unemployment, whether or not covered by unemployment insurance. It is the only intercensal comprehensive source of information on the personal characteristics of the total population (both in and out of the labor force), such as age and sex, race, marital and family status, veteran status, eduational background, and ethnic origin.

It provides the only available distributions of workers by the number of hours worked (as distinguished from aggregate or average hours for an industry), permitting separate analyses of part-time workers, workers on overtime, "moonlighting," etc., as well as being the only comprehensive current source of information on the occupation of workers and the industries in which they work.

Information is available from the survey not only for persons currently in the labor force but also for those who are outside the labor force. The characteristics of such persons--whether married women with or without young children, disabled persons, students, older retired workers, etc.--can be determined. Information on their current desire for work, their past work experience, and their intentions as to jobseeking are available from a subsample. Information on school enrollment and the number of children women expect to have is also obtained.

The CPS is being used increasingly to meet legislative requirements for data to administer public programs. For example, sample estimates of labor force data for the states are used to allocate federal funds to the states under the CETA program. For other programs, the Bureau of the Census uses special statistical techniques to prepare various income and poverty estimates for the states from special tabulations of the CPS and estimates from administrative data.

Geographic Coverage

Data have been provided at the national level since the inception of the CPS. After a few years, data for the census regions were also provided. More recently, the sample has been expanded to increase the reliability of data for states and the larger SMSAs. To improve the reliability of estimates tabulated at levels below the census regions, some of the monthly estimates are cumulated for publication as quarterly and annual averages. Each household record includes information on SMSA/nonSMSA, central city/noncentral city, farm/nonfarm, and SMSA size.

Data for rural areas have not been of high priority, except for the annual joint release by the Census Bureau and the Department of Agriculture on the size of the farm population and changes in that population. The CPS could become a more important source of information for rural areas than it has been. Some redesign of the sample might be needed if the full potential in respect to rural development were to be realized. These needs should be made known in time to be taken into account when the redesign is undertaken following the 1980 Census.

Access

National estimates from the CPS of the size, composition, and changes in the composition of the labor force are published each month by the Bureau of Labor Statistics in *Employment and Earnings*. Estimates of the total and civilian labor force are produced in considerable detail at the national level, in most instances by race, sex, and age. Unemployment rates are given, in addition, by marital status and relationship to the household head and by occupation and industry, duration of unemployment, job search methods used, etc. The number of persons employed is shown by agriculture and nonagricultural industries, full or part-time status, and hours worked by major industry group and major occupational group. Seasonally adjusted data are provided for many of these series. Several subsets of these estimates are published in less detail as annual averages for the larger SMSAs and for states.

In addition, the CPS is the source of periodic studies of personal and family income, migration, educational attainment, and other demographic, social, and economic topics. For example, the Farm Wage Workers Survey is published annually by USDA and includes total farm days and wages, total nonfarm days and wages, chief activity during the year, migratory status of hired farm workers, when workers migrated, and the states in which they worked.

Since 1968, the individual sample records from the CPS have been made available in the form of computer tape files for public use.

These public use files contain all of the demographic and economic information for each person in every interviewed household in the survey. Sufficient geographic information is removed, however, to insure the confidentiality of the respondent households. These microdata files have been increasingly used by private and government researchers for a variety of purposes.

Source

Bureau of the Census (1978) The Current Population Survey: Design and Methodology. Technical Paper 40. Washington, D.C.: U.S. Department of Commerce.

DONNELLEY MARKETING'S RESIDENTIAL DATA BASE

DUN'S MARKETING SERVICES

Description

This proprietary residential data base contains approximately 65 million names and addresses, covering almost 85 percent of U.S. households. While not a complete census in itself, it can measure some trends within individual census tracts. Historical data provide a longitudinal measurement of the rate of household growth and decline on a census tract basis. Before using the data base, consideration should be given to the effects of bias stemming from incomplete coverage of all households, the quality of the various estimates used in updating the data base, and the problems that arise when matching techniques are used. For some purposes these considerations are not important but for others they could impair the utility of the data.

The data base uses more than a dozen proprietary demographic elements and associates them with the 476 pieces of information from the U.S. census. The system uses three major types of data:

1. 1970 census data;
2. intercensal federal government estimates, including revenue sharing, population and per capita income figures, Current Population Survey estimates of persons per household, and Bureau of Economic Analysis income estimates;
3. disaggregated income and household trend data from proprietary Donnelley Marketing files.

Donnelly Marketing's proprietary data is the main component in making small area estimates. A portion of the data is a national file of residential telephone listings supplemented by a list of owners of privately registered passenger vehicles. Individual records are consolidated to the household level. Household records are then coded to census tracts. It is possible to assign zip codes or census tract designations to known addresses.

Updating

Current estimates of populations, households, and family incomes are done by a statistical modeling technique to update census tract data.

Rate of household change is applied to 1970 household counts to yield current per year household estimates. Household counts are controlled at the county level based on extrapolated revenue sharing data. Persons per household is taken from the 1970 data for each census tract and adjusted to the current year based on state-level rates of change as observed between the 1970 census and the 1978 current population survey. Current persons per household is multiplied by current households to yield current population. Population is controlled at the smallest local area possible (county or minor civil division) using revenue sharing estimates projected forward to the current year.

Estimates of current income are made using a multivariate statistical model applied to individual household data. The model is calibrated using data collected from a large, independently conducted nationwide probability survey. Income is predicted from a number of factors largely associated with patterns of vehicle ownership. As with household data, income estimates of identified households are intermediate input into the final calculations. Income distributions over time are measured and rates of change are applied against the 1970 census distribution. Total income is controlled at the county or minor civil division level using the latest data from the Bureau of Economic Analysis and the extrapolated revenue sharing data. Income estimates are for families and unrelated individuals, a category used by the Census Bureau.

Occupancy in single and multiple family dwelling units is based on 1970 census data. Trends in single family occupancy rates in the data based have been applied against census data to provide updated estimates.

Residential mobility is computed through analysis of the 55 million households having a listed telephone. The sample is sufficiently large to serve as a representation of flux within a neighborhood (census tract) for some purposes, but not for cases in which the population without telephones is important.

An Example of Updating: Mobility Measurements

The following seven measurments of neighborhood mobility can be made for census tracts, enumeration districts, and counties.

1. The newcomer factor describes a neighborhood in terms of the percent of telephone households that are new listings.
2. The stability factor describes a neighborhood in terms of the percent of telephone households that are repeat listings.
3. The change factor describes a neighborhood in terms of the percent increase or decrease in the number of telephone households during the past year.

4. The exodus factor describes a neighborhood in terms of the percent of last year's telephone households that have moved out of the area.

5. The churn factor blends inward and outward mobility to describe a neighborhood in terms of an overall mobility ratio. This ratio is formed by comparing households that have moved into or out of an area against all households resident in that area at any point in the directory cycle.

6. The mobility 1970 to 1975 factor describes a neighborhood in terms of the percent of 1975 telephone households that moved during the preceding five-year period.

7. The mobility last five years factor describes a neighborhood in terms of the percent of current telephone households that moved to their present addresses during the last five-year period.

Access

Donnelley Marketing, of Washington, D.C., sells its services to governments and businesses.

Sources

Donnelley Marketing (n.d.) Donnelley Marketing's Residential Data Base. Washington, D.C.: Donnelley Marketing.

Donnelley Marketing (1979) An Overview of Mobility and SESI. Washington, D.C.: Donnelley Marketing.

BASIC VITAL STATISTICS

NATIONAL CENTER FOR HEALTH STATISTICS

Unit of Observation

Event: birth, death, marriage, divorce, etc.

Periodicity

Continuing.

Universe Description

Nationwide, total population of the U.S. This is a census, not a sample.

Data Collection

Basic vital statistics provided through the registration system come from records of live births, deaths, fetal deaths, induced terminations of pregnancy, marriages and divorces or dissolutions of marriages. Registration of these events is a local and state function, but uniform registration practices and use of the records for national statistics have been established over the years through cooperative agreements between the states and the National Center for Health Statistics (NCHS) and its predecessor agencies. Both provisional and final vital statistics are derived from the registration system. The provisional data are obtained from counts of vital records registered without reference to the date the event occurred and the final data are obtained from the record and its contents, processed by date of occurrence of the event.

The civil laws of every state provide for a continuous and permanent birth, death, and fetal death registration system. In general, the local registrar of a town, city, county, or other geographic place collects the records of births and deaths occurring in the area, inspects, queries, and corrects if necessary, maintains a local copy, register, or index, and transmits them to the state health department. There the vital statistics office inspects the records for promptness of filing and for completeness and consistency of information; queries if necessary; numbers, indexes, and processes the statistical information for state and local use; and binds the records for permanent reference and safekeeping. Microfilm copies of the individual records or machine-readable data are transmitted to the National Center for Health Statistics for use in compiling the final annual national vital statistics volume.

The system for collecting national data on marriages and divorces is not as well developed as the system for births and deaths. All states have marriage and divorce laws but, as of January 1, 1980, three states did not have a central file of marriage records and four states did not have a central file of divorce records. For states without central registration, final counts are collected from individual counties either by the state vital statistics office or by NCHS. In these instances some counties report only marriage licenses issued and divorce petitions filed rather than marriages performed and divorces granted.

Subject Matter Description

To promote uniformity in the statistical information collected from states and local areas for national statistical purposes, the National Center for Health Statistics recommends standard certificates or reports for birth, death, fetal death, induced termination of pregnancy, marriage, and divorce. The standard certificates and reports are developed cooperatively with the states and local areas and the federal agency, taking into account the needs and problems expressed by the major providers and users of the data. They are reviewed about every ten years to assure that they meet to the fullest extent feasible current needs as legal records and as sources of vital and health statistics. However, the use of standard certificates and reports by states is voluntary and their form and content may vary according to the laws and practices of each state. The certificates and reports in most states closely follow the standard.

Access

Vital statistics data reach the public through the Monthly Vital Statistics Report (MVSR); supplements to the MVSR; Vital Statistics of the United States (VSUS), bound volumes issued annually; micro-data tapes (issued annually); and Vital and Health Statistics Series reports and special reports. Unpublished tabulations may also be available upon request. The MVSRs containing provisional monthly counts are published within 60 days following the end of the data month. Provisional cause-of-death information from the Current Mortality Sample are published a month later; the advance supplements to the MVSR releasing final annual statistics are published within 12 months of the data year; data tapes and unpublished tabulations are released at the same time as these advance MVSR supplements and thus, have a corresponding lag; series and special reports are issued as resources permit; and the annual VSUS's are expected soon to be distributed with about an 18-month lag.

For vital records, names and addresses are not coded and never appear on data tapes or tabulations; certificate numbers are never released without written permission from the states whose records are involved; and data tapes including data from localities having less than 250,000 population are classified to reflect population size but do not reveal specific geographic areas.

Source

U.S. Department of Health, Education, and Welfare (1980) Data Systems of the National Center for Health Statistics. Office of Health Research, Statistics, and Technology, National Center for Health Statistics. DHEW Publication No. (PHS) 80-1247. Washington, D.C.: U.S.Department of Health, Education, and Welfare.

ANNUAL HOUSING SURVEY

BUREAU OF THE CENSUS

Unit of Observation

Housing units. Census Bureau interviewers visit the households of occupied houses, and obtain information from landlords, rental agents, or neighbors on vacant units.

Periodicity

Yearly, since 1973.

Universe Description

The sample of housing units used is drawn from units enumerated in the 1970 census and updated to include units constructed since 1970. Except for new construction and losses, the same housing units remain in the sample from year to year.

The total housing supply is sampled in two different ways. The first is a national survey of a sample of housing units. The first survey was a sample of approximately 60,000 units, including 16,000 rural units. In 1974, the size of the rural sample was doubled in order to increase the reliability of estimates of rural housing characteristics. The designated sample consisted of 78,000 to 82,000 housing units for each of the 1974-1976 surveys. In 1977, as a consequence of cost considerations, the sample size was reduced to 76,000 units and is expected to remain at that level in subsequent years.

Subject Matter Description

Data are collected on type of unit, location, and whether a unit is owner- or renter-occupied or vacant. Housing unit data include whether the houses have kitchens, heating units and electrical systems, and, if so, how well they work. Information on the costs incurred for mortgage payments, real estate taxes, property insurance, utilities, and garbage and trash collection permit comparisons of housing costs from one year to another or between geographic areas. Data collected on income are used in conjunction with annual housing expenditures to estimate the average (median) percentage of families' and primary individuals' income spent on housing. Households which have moved in the twelve months prior to enumeration are asked to provide comparative information on the current and previous residences of household heads. Information is collected on whether employment, family, or other factors such as changes in neighborhood or financial conditions influenced the decision to move.

Approximately one-third of the households included in the 1973 and 1974 enumerations were asked a supplemental series of questions concerning the purchases and ownership of selected household items. Data were collected for cars and licensed 4-wheel vehicles, washing machines, clothes dryers, dishwashers, refrigerators, freezers, and kitchen ranges. Subjects covered included availability and ownership, purchases, and expenditures. Purchases of and expenditures for television sets and room air conditioning units were also surveyed.

Beginning in 1975, a group of questions on travel to work was added as a supplement. This supplement provides data on principal means of transportation to work, use of an automobile as a secondary mode, carpool occupancy, time of departure for work, travel time and distance, changes in principal means within the past year, satisfaction with mode, and place of work for persons 14 years or older who were working.

A series of questions on energy facilities and conservation has also been included as a supplement to the AHS. Data pertaining to occupied single family homes, mobile homes and trailers, on the presence of storm doors, storm windows, and attic and roof insulation have been included since 1974.

Two supplementary surveys to the AHS have also been proposed. The "Housing Adjustments of Older People" supplement is a longitudinal study which will be conducted in two or three SMSAs annually over a 10-year period with a sample size of abut 2,500 in each metropolitan area. This study will focus on households with householders or spouses 55 years of age or older to determine the major factors contributing to housing changes of the elderly and measures which could be implemented to prevent or postpone institutionalization. The "Housing Modifications" supplement is designed to determine for households with physically disabled persons, whether certain modifications have been made or would be useful to make the unit more accessible to the disabled individuals.

Geographic Coverage

Individual units in the survey can be examined by the following cuts: urban/rural, census region, central city residence, urban status (urban, rural farm, rural nonfarm), place size (outside SMSAs, 5,000-19,000, 20,000-49,000, all others, SMSA status (inside SMSA, outside SMSA), SMSA code.

Access

Major results of the AHS national sample are published each year in six reports. Data are shown at the national level and separately for each of the four census regions by type of residence (total metropolitan, inside central cities, inside SMSAs but not in central cities, and outside SMSAs). Characteristics are also published for black and Spanish-origin households. One publication, Part E, contains housing characteristics for urban and rural areas. These statistics update the 1970 census. Data include items such as tenure, race, occupancy status, rooms, units within structure, and household composition. Characteristics of newly constructed housing units, units removed from the housing inventory and occupied mobile homes and trailers are also shown. In addition, some indicators of housing and neighborhood quality are included.

A large number of tabulations have been prepared to meet special needs which have not been included in published reports. These tabulations range from distributions of single variables to detailed cross-classifications and concern such subjects as housing needs of the elderly, differentials in average utility costs by selected demographic and structural characteristics, and selected structural characteristics by year built.

In addition, the entire AHS data base, by individual units, is made available for public use. Certain modifications are present to avoid identification of individual households.

Source

Bureau of the Census (1979) Data from the Annual Housing Survey. Data Access Description No. 43. Washington, D.C.: U.S. Department of Commerce.

HEALTH INTERVIEW SURVEY

NATIONAL CENTER FOR HEALTH STATISTICS

Unit of Observation

Person and Household.

Periodicity

Continuous, since 1957.

Universe Description

The survey covers the noninstitutionalized civilian population of the United States living at the time of the interview. Because of technical and logistical problems, several segments of the population are not included in the sample or in the estimates from the survey. Persons excluded are: patients in long-term care facilities for the handicapped (data are secured on patients in some of these facilities through the Nursing Home Survey of NCHS); persons on active duty with the Armed Forces (though their dependents are included); and persons who have died during the calendar year preceding the interview. The result is that the Health Interview Survey data somewhat underestimate levels of disability and health services utilization when the total population is considered.

The sample is a multistage probability design which permits a continuous sampling of households. The first stage consists of a sample of 376 primary sampling units (PSUs) drawn from approximately 1,900 geographically defined PSUs that cover the 50 states and the District of Columbia. A PSU consists of a county, a small group of contiguous counties, or a Standard Metropolitan Statistical Area. Within PSUs, smaller units called segments are defined in such a manner that each segment contains an expected four households.

Each calendar year the sample is composed of approximately 40,000 households containing about 120,000 persons. The households in each week's sample are a probability sample representative of the target population. Since the design of the survey is a complex multistage probability sample, it is necessary to use complex procedures in the derivation of estimates.

The annual response rate of HIS is usually at least 95 percent of the eligible households in the sample; the 5-percent nonresponse rate is divided equally between refusals and households where no eligible respondent could be found at home after repeated calls.

Data Collection Procedures

Data are collected through a personal household interview conducted by interviewers employed and trained by the Bureau of the Census according to procedures specified by the National Center for Health Statistics. Interviews are conducted each week throughout the year.

Nationally there are approximately 110 interviewers, trained and directed by health survey supervisors in each of 12 Census Bureau regional offices. The supervisors are career civil service employees whose primary responsibility is the Health Interview Survey. The interviewers are part-time employees, selected through an examination and testing process. Interviewers receive thorough training in basic interviewing procedures and in the concepts and procedures unique to the Health Interview Survey.

All adult members of the household 19 years of age and older who are at home at the time of the interview are invited to participate and to respond for themselves. The mother is usually the respondent for children. For individuals not at home during the interview, information is provided by a responsible family member (e.g., spouse, parent, or adult son or daughter) residing in the household. Between 65 and 70 percent of the adults aged 19 or older are self-respondents. Upon occasion a random subsample of adult household members is selected to respond to questions on selected topics. There are also instances in which followup supplements are completed for either the entire household or for individuals identified as having particular health problems. As required, these supplements are either left for the appropriate person to complete and return by mail, or the interviewer calls again in person or by telephone to secure the information directly.

Subject Matter Description

The structure that has evolved for the questionnaire is one of a relatively stable nucleus of questions, approximately 70 percent of the questionnaire, complemented by one or more supplements on topics which vary from year to year.

Each year's questionnaire contains questions in the following areas:

Basic demographic characteristics of household members, including age, sex, education, and family income;

Disability days, including restricted activity, bed, work and school-loss days, occuring during the two-week period prior to the week of interview;

Physician and dental visits occurring during the same two-week period;

Acute and chronic conditions responsible for these days and visits;

Long-term limitation of activity and the chronic conditions related to the disability;

All hospital episodes, including the reason for entering the hospital, whether surgery was performed, and the length of stay, during the 12 months prior to interview;

Interval since the last doctor and dental visit.

Each year's questionnaire also includes a set of questions related to chronic conditions. The questions are designed to obtain information on the prevalence of specific conditions and on the disability and use of health services associated with them.

The supplements to the questionnaire change every year. There are two kinds of supplements, rotating and one-time. Rotating supplements include health insurance coverage, hearing ability (1963, 1971), loss of income, nursing care and/or special aids, personal health expenses, prescribed and nonprescribed medicines, smoking habits, vision impairment and use of corrective lenses, and X-ray visits.

One-time supplements have included acute conditions (1974), arthritis (1969), blood donorship (1973), diabetes (1965), hypertension (1974), medical care availability (1974), motor vehicle accidents (1968), orthodontic care (1974), pregnancy (1973), preventive care (1973), specialists' services and routine checkups (1964).

In 1978, there were supplements on health insurance coverage, usual source of health care, blood donations, immunization, smoking, military service, and for households in the first quarter sample, health expenditures in calendar year 1977. During 1979 the immunization and smoking supplements were continued and supplements on home health care, eye care, residential mobility and retirement income were added. In 1980 the supplements on home health care, residential mobility and retirement income are being continued and a supplement on health insurance has been added.

On the average the interviews require about 45 minutes in the household. Depending upon the family size and the nature and extent of its health conditions the length of interview usually runs between 15 and 90 minutes.

The content of the Health Interview Survey questionnaire reflects both the results of survey research and requests for data. For example, the recall period for many questions is the two weeks prior to the week of interview, but for some items for which the memory loss is known not to be excessive, recall extends over the year prior to interview or for some other period specified according to topic, such as three months for X-ray visits. The body-systems approach to chronic conditions was adopted in 1968, after several years in which there was instead a standard set of questions focused around a list of diverse chronic conditions. Limiting questions to one body system at a time has been found to secure more thorough reporting of conditions from a targeted list and to increase the number of conditions for which estimates of prevalence can be made.

Suggestions and requests for special supplements are received from many sources, including a panel of leading members of the health professions, university-based researchers, administrators of national organizations and programs in the private and public health sectors, and other parts of the Department of Health and Human Services (e.g., the National Institutes of Health and the Center for Disease Control). Although it is not possible to include all of the suggested topics, every effort is made to be responsive to the data needs of such groups. A lead time of at least one year is required to develop and pretest questions for new topics to be included as special supplements.

Geographic Coverage

In published analyses, the data are available for four regions and for place of residence: SMSA (by central city/outside central city) and outside SMSA (by farm/nonfarm). Since much of the information is technical, many special tabulations are run for individual researchers, but there are strong confidentiality restrictions which would limit any type of small area analysis.

Access

Data release occurs in several forms. The earliest reports containing survey data were issued in Series B and C, Health Statistics from the U.S. National Health Survey. About 50 reports were published in these series before they were replaced by the Vital and Health Statistics Series. More than 130 reports have been published in Series 10 of the Vital and Health Statistics Series. Publication of a year's data begins in about October of the year following completion of data collection. The first report, "Current Estimates," is followed by between 8 to 10 other publications.

Since not all possible cross-tabulations can be analyzed and published in Series 10 reports, many unpublished tabulations are routinely made available upon request. In addition, within budgetary and other limitations, special tabulations are prepared upon request.

The other medium for data release is public use computer tapes. The tape is usually availabe for distribution within about two years after completion of data collection. Primarily this time lag is due to the need for staff to work with the data in order to insure completeness and reliability of data secured on the supplements and to permit development of adequate documentation. About one month is required after receipt of a tape order to process the request and deliver the tape.

Data from the Health Interview Survey have been used in a number of major government programs. Estimates of health problems and resultant utilization of health care services were used in formulating the legislation for both the Medicare and Medicaid programs and for making preliminary estimates of the likely costs of the programs. Statistics on health characteristics of smokers and non-smokers provided one basis for the 1964 reports of the Surgeon General entitled Smoking and Health. Special compilations on particular population groups have also been developed and provided to various White House conferences and for other special purposes. Data requests from government agencies usually account for approximately one-fourth of each year's inquiries.

Almost 40 percent of the data requests come from private industry and foundations, and an additional 10 percent are from individuals affiliated with educational institutions. In addition to general research, these users have relied upon Health Interview Survey data for estimates of persons with particular health problems for whom advertising campaigns or new products are being designed. The potential demand for special aids or devices for persons with limitations of mobility and for various types of drugs is often assessed using data from the Health Interview Survey.

Edited micro-data tapes of data from the annual survey, beginning with the 1969 data collection year, have been available for several years. Universities and federal, state, and local governmental agencies have been the main purchasers of the tapes.

Sources

U.S. Department of Health, Education, and Welfare (1975) Health Interview Survey Procedure, 1957-1974. Public Health Service, Health Resources Administration, National Center for Health Statistics. DHEW Publication No. (HRA) 75-1311. Washington, D.C.: U.S. Department of Health, Education, and Welfare.

U.S. Department of Health, Education, and Welfare (1980) Data Systems of the National Center for Health Statistics. Public Health Service, Office of Health Research, Statistics, and Technology, National Center for Health Statistics. DHEW Publication No. (PHS) 80-1247. Washington, D.C.: U.S. Department of Health, Education, and Welfare.

HEALTH AND NUTRITION EXAMINATIONS

NATIONAL CENTER FOR HEALTH STATISTICS

Background

The first Health and Nutrition Examination Survey, referred to as the HANES I, was initiated in 1970, with data collection beginning in April 1971. HANES I was a modification and expansion of the earlier Health Examination Survey (HES) which had been initiated a decade earlier and had carried out three separate programs. The restructuring and modification of the HES reflected the assignment to NCHS of an additional specific responsibility--the measurement of the nutritional status of the population and the subsequent monitoring of changes in that status over time. Upon completion of HANES I, a second Health and

Nutrition Examination Survey (HANES II) began, with data collection for HANES II beginning in February 1976 and finishing in February 1980.

The HANES and its predecessor program, the HES, share a common purpose--the collection and utilization of data which can be obtained only by direct physical examination, clinical and laboratory tests, and related measurement procedures. This information, which cannot be furnished by the people themselves or by the health professionals who provide their medical care, is of two kinds: (a) prevalence data for specifically defined diseases or conditions of ill health; and (b) normative health-related measurement data which show distributions of the total population with respect to particular parameters such as blood pressure, visual acuity, or serum cholesterol level.

Unit of Observation

Person and household.

Periodicity

Continuous (in some form) since 1959; approximately every five years. One cycle takes several years to complete.

Universe Description

The samples for all of the HES and HANES programs have been multi-stage, highly clustered probability samples. All of the samples were stratified by broad geographical region and by population density grouping. Within the strata, the sampling stages employed have been the primary sampling unit, the Census enumeration district, the segment, the household, and lastly the individual person. Until the household stage is reached, all sampling is carried out centrally in conjunction with the Bureau of the Census.

The next stage of the sampling is conducted in the field in the particular chosen area. It involves interviewer visits and questionnaire completion at each one of the selected households, with the final selection of individuals included in the sample being dependent upon information elicited by the household interview questionnaire. The size of the sample in the survey program has varied. In each of the three HES programs, the sample size was approximately 7,500 persons. In HANES I the sample selected for the major nutrition components of the examination contained approximately 28,000 people and yielded about 21,000 examined persons. A comparable sized sample for HANES II again yielded approximately 21,000 examined persons.

In the HES and HANES program there has always been and continues to be much attention devoted to the question of the response rate, which is the proportion of sample persons who are actually examined. In the HANES there have been, as anticipated, problems in the area of response. The difficulties faced have led to a variety of innovative measures, including a policy of remunerating examined persons. While response rates from HANES II are not yet available, the first HANES program succeeded in obtaining household interview data on 99 percent of the sample population. More detailed health data appear in the medical history questionnaires, and these were completed for 88 percent of the selected sample persons. Finally, in HANES I, 74 percent of the sample persons selected for the nutrition component and 70 percent of the persons for the detailed health component were given the standard examinations and tests. There is considerable ancillary information on most of the non-examined persons in the sample population, and it is possible to make use of those data in the process of imputation. There is, moreover, some evidence that data obtained through examinations, tests, and measurements such as used in these surveys are less susceptible to potential bias from a given rate of nonresponse than data provided by the individuals themselves.

Data Collection Procedures

Household interviewing during HANES II was conducted by Bureau of the Census personnel. NCHS employees do the rest of the interviewing, history taking, examining, testing, and measuring that provide the data. Data collection is done by specially trained teams of interviewers and examiners including physicians, nurses, dentists, dietitians, and medical, laboratory and x-ray technicians. The examinations take place in the survey's mobile examination centers. These are sets of specially constructed units, each consisting of three truck-drawn trailers which are interconnected and which provide a standardized environment and equipment for the performance of specific parts of the examination.

The time required for the examination varies, of course, with the content of the examination and the age of the examinee. The time constraint included among planning factors has been that the total examination time not exceed 2-1/2 hours. Much attention is given in the planning process and in the actual pretests of a survey to the actual flow of examinees through the examination center and every effort is made to streamline this process in order to reduce the time burden on the sample person. Additional respondent burden arises from the interview and the completion of forms and questionnaires in the household, and from the varying time required by the sample person to travel to the examination site.

Subject Matter Description

The kinds of information collected in the HANES and other examination survey programs are so varied and extensive that they are only illustrated here. With respect to nutrition, four types of data are included: (1) information concerning dietary intake--the mechanisms used have included 24-hour recall interviews and food frequency questionnaires, both administered by an interviewer who has been a trained dietitian; (2) hematological and biochemical tests--a sizable battery of such tests has been performed, at the mobile examination centers where necessary, but for the most part at a central nutrition laboratory established at the Center for Disease Control; (3) body measurements--the battery used is especially important in connection with infants, children, and youths where growth may be affected by nutritional deficiencies; and (4) various signs of high risk of nutritional deficiency, based on clinical examinations.

The health component of the HANES program includes detailed examinations, tests, and questionnaires, which have been developed to obtain a measure of prevalence levels of specific diseases and conditions. These vary with the particular program and have included such conditions as chronic rheumatoid arthritis and hypertensive heart disease. Important normative health-related measurements, such as height and weight are also obtained. A major element in the health component in the HANES I program was an assessment of unmet health needs through the use of index conditions.

Here, for example, the examination established the presence or absence of emphysema or another chronic respiratory disease. At the same time, information was obtained from the examined person with respect to his self-perceived health needs in this regard and the actions he had taken with respect to seeking medical care. Analytic plans call for the interrelating of these two kinds of information to produce measures of unmet health needs.

In HANES II the nutrition component remained nearly identical to that fielded previously. From an early analysis of the HANES I data, it was decided to focus the nutritional examination elements around an anemia-related assessment approach. This involved the addition of certain medical history items and a more tailored set of laboratory determinations. Less was done in the area of health care needs with an emphasis that will probably continue in future programs being placed on the effects of the environment upon health. Data were gathered to measure the effects of pesticide exposure, the presence of certain trace elements in the blood, and the amounts of carbon monoxide present in the blood. In the medical area, primary emphasis in HANES II was placed on diabetes, kidney pathology, liver function, allergy and speech pathology.

The general pattern of data collection has meant that each survey has been conducted over a period of three or four years. This is due to the constraints which limit the number of persons examined in a given time span (e.g., the number of field teams). This imposes a limitation on the kinds of data to be collected by this mechanism, since conditions which might show marked year-to-year variation or seasonal patterns cannot be included. However, many important chronic diseases and health-related measurements are not subject to such changes in prevalence within short-run periods.

Geographic Coverage

No explicit information is given in survey design publications. It is unlikely that published analyses will provide data for rural areas other than at the national level. Since most of the information is technical, many special tabulations are used by individual researchers.

Access

Findings from HANES programs traditionally are presented primarily through publication of individual reports in NCHS Vital and Health Statistics, Series 11. In order to make HANES findings more rapidly available to consumers, a program was initiated to release basic descriptive summary tables in what is called "basic data publications." These publications are an adjunct to the other Series 11 reports for selected topics. Additionally some HANES data appear in abbreviated preliminary reports in the NCHS Advance Data series.

Data are also released through appropriate scientific journals, separate monographs, special reports, and data tapes. Due to the voluminous amount of data collected in HANES I, and to the need for disseminating these data as expediently as possible, a policy shift was made which allows the release of data tapes to in-house analysts and the sale of these tapes to the public simultaneously as soon as final editing has been performed and documentation has been prepared. Data tapes from HANES II are expected to become available in approximately one year from the completion of the field operations.

Published reports are not issued on a set frequency, but rather made available as completed. The reports are organized on a topical basis with, for example, one report presenting data on peridontal disease, another on auditory acuity, etc. Generally the first reports produced are descriptive in nature while later reports become more analytic and may be interdisciplinary in approach.

The sale of data tapes from this survey has increased greatly in the past few years. Known data users number in the hundreds. Projects currently under way using HANES data tapes include small scale or local area health surveys that use the HANES data as norms and epidemiological studies that examine geographic patterns in morbidity.

Source

U.S. Department of Health, Education, and Welfare (1980) Data Systems of the National Center for Health Statistics. Office of Health Research, Statistics, and Technology, National Center for Health Statistics. DHEW Publication No. (PHS) 80-1247. Washington, D.C.: U.S. Department of Health, Education, and Welfare.

HOSPITAL DISCHARGE SURVEY

NATIONAL CENTER FOR HEALTH STATISTICS

Unit of Analysis

Hospital discharge.

Periodicity

Continuous since 1964.

Universe Description

The scope of HDS is limited to discharges from nonfederal hospitals in the 50 states and the District of Columbia. Only short-stay hospitals with six or more beds and an average length of stay for all patients of less than 30 days are included in the sample.

The sample plan is basically a two-stage stratified design. The first stage is a sample of about 10 percent of the hospitals, excluding federal hospitals, listed in the Master Facility Inventory (sampling frame). The primary stratification variables are number of beds and geographic region. Hospitals are selected in direct proportion to size such that hospitals with 1,000 or more beds are sampled with a probability of approximately 1/40. Growth in the inventory of hospitals is represented in the survey by a sample of hospitals selected from a special universe of new hospitals.

The second stage of the design is a systematic sample of the discharges from the sampled hospitals. The sampling frame in nearly all hospitals is the daily listing of discharges. The size of the within-hospital sample varies inversely with the size of the hospital from about 1/100 in hospitals with 1,000 or more beds, to 4/10 in hospitals with less than 50 beds. The overall sampling rate for each bed-size group is about 1/100, the product of the first and second stage sampling rates.

In 1978 the sample consisted of 535 hospitals from a universe of approximately 7,900 short-stay hospitals. Of the 487 in-scope hospitals, information was collected from 413 participating hospitals (approximately an 85 percent response rate) on approximately 219,000 discharges.

The Bureau of the Census, acting as the data collecting agent for NCHS, inducts sample hospitals into the HDS. After induction, hospitals are visited at least once a year by a representative of the Bureau of the Census, at which time survey procedures are reviewed and information about the hospital is updated.

Discharge data are collected throughout the year. Sample discharges are systematically selected, usually on the basis of the final digit(s) of the patient's medical record number. For each sample discharge, an abstractor records personal, administrative, diagnostic, and surgical information from the face sheet of the patient's medical record onto a Medical Abstract Form. Data collection frequency depends upon the arrangement made with the hospital. In about 35 percent of the participating hospitals, a representative of the Bureau of the Census visits the hospital bimonthly, completes the abstract forms for records selected during the previous visit, and selects records for abstracting at the next visit. This allows time for records to be completed and properly filed (or pulled from file) prior to the visit. In about 65 percent of the hospitals, the same forms are completed by members of the medical record department.

Subject Matter Description

The Medical Abstract Form contains items relating to the personal characteristics of the patient including birthdate, sex, race, and marital status but not name and address; administrative information including admission and discharge dates, discharge status, and medical record number; and medical information including diagnoses and surgical operations or procedures. It is estimated that medical record personnel can sample and complete each form, on the average, in about five minutes.

The contents of the Medical Abstract Form did not change from the inception of the survey until 1977 when modifications were made so that it more nearly parallels the Uniform Hospital Discharge Data Set. The items added to the abstract at that time are residence of patient (zip code), expected source of payment, disposition of patient, and dates of procedures. In 1968-1970, actual hospital charges by service and payments by source were recorded on a Ledger Abstract Form for approximately one-third of the sample discharges.

Access

Annual data are published in Advance Data reports and in the NCHS Vital and Health Statistics Series, Series 13. The publication program is, at a minimum, to update the nonmedical, the medical, and the surgical data for characteristics of patients and hospitals. Special reports on average length of stay, patient charges, geographic utilization, hospital ownership, and methodology are also published.

Unpublished data are available on request from the Hospital Care Statistics Branch, which receives about 500 requests per year, usually for specific diagnostic and surgical listings in the International Classification of Diseases. In addition, data for years since 1969 are available on magnetic tape.

The names of the participating hospitals and all information related to individual patients are confidential. No data are released in published, unpublished, or tape form that could identify hospitals or patients.

The HDS is the principal source for national data on the characteristics of patients discharged from short-stay hospitals. The data are used for a variety of planning, administrative, and evaluation activities by governmental, professional, scientific, educational and commercial institutions as well as by private citizens.

Source

U.S. Department of Health, Education, and Welfare (1980) Data Systems of the National Center for Health Statistics. Office of Health Research, Statistics and Technology, National Center for Health Statistics. DHEW Publication No. (PHS) 80-1247. Washington, D.C.: U.S. Department of Health, Education, and Welfare.

NATIONAL AMBULATORY MEDICAL CARE SURVEY

NATIONAL CENTER FOR HEALTH STATISTICS

Unit of Analysis

Ambulatory care patient visits and physicians.

Periodicity

Continuous from 1973.

Universe Description

The NAMCS target population consists of all office visits within the conterminous United States made by ambulatory patients to nonfederal physicians who are in office-based practice and engaged in direct patient care. Excluded are visits to hospital-based physicians, visits to specialists in anesthesiology, pathology, and radiology, and visits to physicians who are principally engaged in teaching, research or administration. Telephone contacts and non-office visits are also excluded. Since about 70 percent of all direct ambulatory medical care visits occur in physicians' offices, the current NAMCS design provides data on the majority of ambulatory care services.

The most objective and reliable sources of data about physicians' services rendered to ambulatory patients during office visits are the physicians themselves and members of their office staff. The sampling frame is a list of licensed physicians in "office-based, patient care" practice compiled from files that are classified and maintained by the American Medical Association (AMA) and the American Osteopathic Association (AOA). These files are continuously updated by the AMA and the AOA, making them as current and correct as possible at the time of sample selection.

The NAMCS utilizes a modified probability-proportional-to-size sampling procedure using separate sampling frames for Standard

Metropolitan Statistical Areas (SMSAs) and for nonmetropolitan counties. After sorting and stratifying by size, region, and demographic characteristics, each frame is divided into sequential zones of one million residents, and a random number is drawn to determine which primary sampling unit (PSU) from each zone is included in the sample. The NAMCS final first-stage sample contains 87 PSUs, corresponding to individual counties or small groups of contiguous counties across the country.

The second-stage sample is selected from the list of physicians located in the sample PSUs ordered by major specialty categories so that the overall probability for including any individual physician is the reciprocal of the number of physicians in the frame at the time of selection. The present annual sample of approximately 3,000 physicians is randomly distributed across the 52 weeks of the year so that the resulting data reflect any seasonal variations. Since the assignment of the reporting week is an integral part of the sample design, each physician is required to report during his predetermined period, and no substitute reporting periods are permitted. Approximately 75 percent of the eligible physicians in the sample participate in the survey. From this size physician sample, information is secured from about 50,000 patient visits a year. Samples for subsequent years exclude with certainty sample physicians included within the previous two years of the study.

The final stage involves sampling patient visits within a physician's practice. The sampling rate, which is determined at the time of the interviewer's appointment, is dependent on the number of days during the reporting week that the physician is in practice and the number of patients he expects to see. In actual practice, the sampling procedure is handled through the use of a patient log.

Data Collection

To maximize participation levels and minimize data reporting burden in the physician's office, NAMCS field procedures have been designed to accommodate the circumstances of individual physicians. Each physician is contacted by several means, including mail, telephone, and personal interview. Initially, each physician in the sample is sent an introductory letter from the director of the Center, followed by a letter of endorsement from the AMA or AOA. The physician is then telephoned by an informed and trained interviewer who explains the survey briefly and arranges a personal appointment to relate more detailed instructions. During this appointment, the interviewer verifies the physician's eligibility for participation in the survey, delivers survey materials with printed instructions, provides detailed verbal instructions, and assigns a predetermined seven-day (Monday through Sunday) reporting period.

The actual data collection for the National Ambulatory Medical Care Survey is carried out by the participating physician, aided by his office assistants when possible. The physician completes a patient record for a sample of his patients seen during his assigned reporting week. Based on the physician's own estimate of patients expected to visit during the survey period, the physician is assigned to use an "every-patient" or a "patient-sampling" procedure. These sampling procedures are designed so that patient records are completed each day of practice for at most ten patient visits. Physicians expecting 10 or fewer visits per day record data for all of them, while those expecting more than 10 visits per day record data after every second, or third, or fifth visit, observing the same predetermined sampling interval continuously. These procedures minimize the workload of data collection and maintain equal reporting levels among sample physicians regardless of the size of their practice. Each form requires one to two minutes to complete, so that approximately 15 minutes are required on days when patients are attended in the physician's office.

Subject Matter Description

Two data collection forms are employed by the participating physician; the patient log and the patient record. The patient log is a sequential listing of patients that serves as a sampling frame to indicate for which visits data should be recorded. The patient record contains 14 items of information about the visit: date and duration of the visit; patient's birthdate, sex, race, and problem; whether the patient was referred by another physician; length of time since onset of the problem; diagnoses; diagnostic and therapeutic services; seriousness of the condition; and disposition. Periodically, ad hoc supplementary items are added to the basic Patient Record to investigate specific health conditions or other aspects of ambulatory care. Also, data concerning basic practice characteristics, such as the physician's specialty and makeup of his staff, are collected.

Access

NAMCS results in the form of summary statistical tabulations of national and regional estimates for number of visits, percent distributions, and population rates of use are published as soon as possible after each annual cycle is complete. More detailed tabulations and analyses follow, which present visit characteristics by major physician specialty groups, patient groups, diagnostic categories, treatment provided, and disposition. Cross tabulations of less common visit characteristics are published when sufficient data about them are available to meet practical standards of precision. These data are released through the Center's Advance Data reports, and the Vital and Health Statistics Series, Series 13. Other modes of publication, including the various journals and newsletters of the NAMCS endorsing organizations, also provide a means of releasing data to the medical community. In addition, data tapes are made available approximately one year after the end of data collection when documentation of the data is complete and its validity is checked.

As part of the procedures designed to protect the identity of the patients, the patient log containing the names of the patients is detachable from the patient records. At the end of the reporting period, the patient logs, and thus the names of the patients, are retained by the physician. Sample physicians are further assured that "all information which would permit identification of an individual, a practice or an establishment will be held confidential, will be used only by persons engaged in and for the purposes of the survey, and will not be disclosed or released to other persons or used for any other purpose." All findings are released in the form of summary statistics which preclude any individual identification.

Source

U.S. Department of Health, Education, and Welfare (1980) Data Systems of the National Center for Health Statistics. Office of Health Research, Statistics, and Technology, National Center for Health Statistics. DHEW Publication No. (PHS) 80-1247. Washington, D.C.: U.S. Department of Health, Education, and Welfare.

AREA RESOURCE FILE

BUREAU OF HEALTH MANPOWER, HEALTH RESOURCES ADMINISTRATION, HHS

Unit of Observation

County.

Periodicity

Began in 1971. Some data are updated periodically.

Universe Description

All counties. The county is used as the basic geographic unit primarily because it is the smallest unit for which the range of data necessary for health system analysis is available.

Subject Matter Description

ARF contains data organized into eight broad categories:

Health Manpower. Included are the most current data available for health professions as well as some historical data. Data for one year (1975) are available for physicians by specialty, activity, sex, age, specialty board certification, and country of graduation. In addition, there is information on sites designated for National Health Service Corps personnel, sites staffed/approved but not staffed/terminated, and current staff level for five manpower types, and on areas designated as having shortages of health manpower for purposes of Health Professions and Nursing Loan Repayment programs.

Health Facilities. Included is information on the characteristics and services offered of hospitals. Limited data are also included for nursing homes.

Health Training. Included is information on the number of schools, enrollments, and graduates for major health professions as well as limited data on allied health training. The number of 2-year colleges, 4-year colleges, and universities is also included.

Population Characteristics. Included are age, race, and sex for the 1970-1975 population as well as total population for earlier and more recent years. Also included are mortality, infant mortality, natality, crime, and housing statistics.

Economic Data. Included are total, per capita, and median income; distribution of families and individuals by income class; and number of recipients of Aid to Families With Dependent Children (AFDC) for recent year.

Utilization. Included are hospital utilization levels.

Expenditures. Hospital expenditure data are included. Medicare enrollments and reimbursements data, and Medicare prevailing charges screens for fifty commonly performed medical procedures for general practitioners and for specialists are also included.

Environment. This category includes land area, large animal population, elevation, latitude and longitude of the population centroid, water hardness index, and climatic data such as mean temperature, precipitation, and humidity. Also included are population and percent of population served with fluoridated water.

The data which are updated on an annual basis are shown below:

SMSA codes
Active non-federal M.D.s
All hospital data
Total population estimates
AFDC recipients
Health professions schools, enrollments, graduates
Per capita income (updated biannualy)
Medicare reimbursements and enrollment
Medicare prevailing charges screens
Mortality
Natality

Geographic Coverage

The use of the county as the basic geographic unit permits aggregation of the data in various ways for analysis. A number of geographic areas have been defined in the system:

SMSAs
Ranally Major and Minor Trading Areas
Office of Business Economics (OBE) Economic Areas
Federal Regions
Comprehensive Health Planning (CHP) Areas
Health Service Areas (HSAs)
Professional Standards Review Organization (PSRO) Areas
Census County Group Codes
Primary Sampling Unit numbers used to link to the Physician Capacity Utilization public use files.

In addition, each county has codes attached to it which indicate the state in which the county is located, the metropolitan/non-metropolitan nature of the county, and its population size as follows:

Government Services Administration state codes
American Hospital Association state codes
Human Resource Profile county adjacency codes
American Medical Association county group codes
City size codes
County group urbanization codes

Access

The available printed reports are of two types. The first are the Basic Area or Summary Profiles, and the second are the Ranking Profiles.

Basic Area Profile from ARF provides a compact profile of selected data for a particular area or set of areas, which serves to bring together the major data on an area. Such a tabulation can be prepared for any county, state, or group of counties, as well as for the OBE areas, Ranally Areas, HSAs or SMSAs. Not only can the data be provided for the individual counties comprising such areas, but totals for any of the areas can also be provided.

National Summary Profile is provided with each report requested. Its format is the same as the Basic Area Profile and presents totals for the entire United States.

The Ranking Profile ranks selected geographic areas (counties or county groups) on the basis of 36 variables or ratios of variables contained in the ARF. In this profile, all counties in a state, or all states in the United States, may be ranked numerically in either ascending or descending order. For example, a printout may be provided which ranks physician-population ratios in each county in the United States, starting with the lowest ratio in any county and proceeding through all counties to the county with the highest ratio. Another standard printout of this type provides selected data elements in a state and that state's numerical ranking vis-a-vis other states. Thus, on a single page, one can identify how a particular area ranks on each of a number of variables.

There is also a master ARF tape, a county-specific data file from which other tabulations and analyses can be done.

Source

U.S. Department of Health, Education, and Welfare (1979) The Area Resource File: A Manpower Planning and Research Tool. Public Health Service, Health Resources Administration. DHEW Publication No. (HRA) 80-4. Washington, D.C.: U.S. Department of Health, Education, and Welfare.

MASTER FACILITY INVENTORY

NATIONAL CENTER FOR HEALTH STATISTICS

Unit of Observation

Facility.

Periodicity

Continuous since 1963.

Universe Description

The Master Facility Inventory (MFI) is a comprehensive file of the 33,000 facilities in the United States which provide medical, nursing, personal, or custodial care to groups of unrelated persons on an "inpatient" (at least overnight) basis. Facilities in the MFI are categorized into three broad types: hospitals, both short- and long-stay; nursing and related care homes; and other custodial or remedial care facilities including homes or resident schools for the deaf, blind, mentally retarded, emotionally disturbed, other neurologically impaired, or physically handicapped; resident treatment centers for alcohol and drug abusers; orphanages or homes for dependent children; and homes for unwed mothers. It is the most comprehensive file of inpatient health facilities available in the United States, and serves as the universe from which probability samples are selected for conducting sample surveys.

Data Collection Procedures

The MFI was first assembled in 1962-63, by collating the files of four federal agencies which contained the names and addresses of facilities, directories of national associations and organizations, and state licensure files.

Two mechanisms are used to keep the data in the MFI as current as possible. For all facilities except hospitals, NCHS conducts a series of mail surveys to (1) insure that the data on file on the basic characteristics of the facilities are accurate, and (2) identify and then delete those facilities that have gone out of business or are no longer eligible for inclusion. These surveys are conducted on an approximately biennial basis. In addition, at regular intervals state licensure agencies, national voluntary associations, and other appropriate sources send to NCHS their most recent directories or lists of new facilities. These lists are then clerically matched with the most current MFI file and facilities not already included are added. For hospitals, NCHS has arrangements with the American Hospital Association to obtain their data tapes.

In order to measure statistically the extent of its scope of coverage, a Complement Survey was developed. It is an application of a general technique often called "multiframe survey." In this application there are two frames--the Master Facility Inventory and a geographic area sample list. From a probability area sample, all institutions found in the sample areas are identified and the probability with which each comes into the sample is determined. Those inpatient health facilities found in the area sample survey (the Complement Survey) are matched against the MFI list of facilities for that area. Any in-scope facility discovered in this sample survey but missed by the MFI constitutes undercoverage and an appropriate weight is assigned to the missed facility.

Data for nonresponding facilities, as well as data for questions not answered on the returned questionnaires, are obtained through various types of imputation procedures. Whenever possible, data from the previous MFI survey are used to replace missing data. For those responding facilities that omitted data which are not available from a previous survey, an imputation method is used. In this method, all facilities of the same type are stratified by predetermined variables such as bed size groups, ownership categories, and major type of service. Missing data for a facility are then supplied by using the data from a facility of like characteristics. When a responding facility fails to answer any of the major questions (e.g., bed size, ownership, type of facility, number of patients), a followup questionnaire containing the omitted questions is sent with a request that the information be provided.

Subject Matter Description

The following types of data are collected for the three categories of facilities:

<u>Hospitals:</u> Ownership; major types of service offered; whether various facilities and services are offered; number of beds, admissions, inpatient days of care, and discharges; patient census; number of bassinets, live births, and newborn days of care; out-patient utilization; number of surgical operations; revenue, expenses, and assets; and staffing.

<u>Nursing Homes:</u> Ownership; major type of service; licensed and staffed beds; beds certified for Medicare and Medicaid, admission policy with regard to age, sex, and various conditions; patient by age and sex; inpatient days of care; number of admissions, discharges, and deaths; staffing; who is in charge of nursing care; number of patients receiving nursing care; services routinely provided; basic monthly charge; and operating expenses.

<u>Other Facilities</u>: Ownership; major type of service; licensed and staffed beds; beds certified as intermediate care beds; admission policy regarding age and sex; patient census by age and sex; inpatient days of care; number of admissions, discharges, and deaths; staffing; basic monthly charge; and operating expenses.

Access

Data from the MFI surveys are published in various NCHS reports. The biennial editions of <u>Health Resources Statistics</u> contain the most current available data (often preliminary estimates) from these surveys. Final data are published in Series 14 of <u>Vital and Health Statistics</u> and in a special series reporting data by county and SMSA (one for hospitals and one for nursing homes). Directories of facilities for the mentally retarded and of nursing homes have been published from the MFI survey data. Methodology reports appear in Series 1 and 2 of <u>Vital and Health Statistics.</u>

The MFI data also are released in the form of (1) special tabulations prepared specifically for individual requests; (2) computer tapes available through the Center's micro-data tape release program; and (3) special printouts or listings from the data tapes.

Approximately 45-50 tape copies are purchased annually by such organizations as drug companies, state agencies, other federal agencies, private contractors working on projects for other government agencies, universities, and national health care organizations.

Only the financial data from the hospitals data tapes prior to 1977 are confidential; all other information is available for individual hospitals. However, beginning with the 1977 hospital data tape, all the information is confidential. Portions of the nursing home and other health facility data are collected under a pledge of confidentiality and can only be released in statistical aggregates, or with all identification items stripped.

Source

U.S. Department of Health, Education, and Welfare (1980) Data Systems of the National Center for Health Statistics. Office of Health Research, Statistics, and Technology, National Center for Health Statistics. DHEW Publication No (PHS) 80-1247. Washington, D.C.: U.S. Department of Health, Education, and Welfare.

NATIONAL NURSING HOME SURVEY

NATIONAL CENTER FOR HEALTH STATISTICS

Unit of Observation

Nursing homes, staff, residents.

Periodicity

Continuous since 1973 (approximately every 4 years).

Universe Description

For the initial survey conducted in 1973-74, the universe included only those nursing homes which provided some level of nursing care, regardless of whether or not they were participating in the Medicare or Medicaid programs. Thus, homes providing only personal or domiciliary care were excluded. Beginning with the 1977 survey, the universe was expanded to include all nursing, personal care, and domiciliary care homes, regardless of their participation in Medicare or Medicaid. Homes which provide room and board only are excluded. In both surveys, homes in the universe included those which were operated under proprietary, nonprofit, and government auspices. The universe included homes which were units of a larger institution (usually a hospital or retirement center).

The Master Facility Inventory (MFI) listing is the universe from which the sample homes are selected. The MFI listing, maintained by NCHS, contains basic information about the home (such as name, address, size, ownership, number of residents, and number of staff) that is needed to design efficient sampling plans.

The initial survey, conducted from August 1973 to April 1974, had a nationally representative sample of 2,100 nursing homes, with a subsample of 25,000 staff and 20,000 residents. The second survey, conducted from May to December 1977, had a total sample of 1,700 nursing homes, with a subsample of 18,900 staff, 8,000 residents, and 5,900 discharged residents.

The response rates for the surveys differed according to the type of questionnaire, as presented below.

Questionnaire	Response Rate 1973-74 Survey	1977 Survey
Facility	97%	95%
Expense	88%	85%
Staff	82%	81%
Resident	98%	99%
Discharges	-	97%

Data Collection

The survey is given to a number of respondents in a home and is a combination of personal interview and self-administered questionnaires. Facility information is secured through a 20 minute personal interview with the administrator. Expense data are collected on a self-administered questionnaire, requiring about 30 minutes to answer, completed by the facility's accountant under authorization from the administrator. Sampled staff members fill out a brief form that requires about five minutes to complete. Information on sample current residents is secured by the interviewer in a personal interview with the nurse who provides care to the resident and who refers to information from the medical record. Residents are not interviewed directly. About 15 minutes is required for each sample resident.

For the 1977 survey, information on the sample discharged residents was secured by the interviewer in a personal interview with the nurse who was most familiar with the medical records and who referred to them for replying to all questions.

Subject Matter Description

The purposes of the surveys are:

To collect national baseline data on characteristics of the nursing home, its services, residents, and staff for all nursing homes in the nation, regardless of whether or not they are participating in federal programs such as Medicare or Medicaid.

To collect data on the costs incurred by the facility for providing care by major components such as labor, fixed, operating, and miscellaneous costs.

To collect data on Medicare and Medicaid certification (such as utilization of certified beds and the health of residents receiving program benefits) so that all data can be analyzed by certification status.

To provide comparable data for valid trend analyses on a variety of topics. Such analyses can, for example, identify the impact of legislative changes in standards and reimbursement on the growth of facilities and the impact of institutionalization on the health of the aged.

To interrelate facility, staff, and resident data to reveal the relationships that exist between utilization, services offered, charges for care, and the cost of providing care.

The survey system uses several questionnaires. The facility questionnaire includes questions on number of beds and residents, services provided, certification status, and various utilization measures. The expense questionnaire includes questions on the facility's expenses by major components, such as labor, fixed, operating, and miscellaneous expenses. The staff questionnaire includes questions on training, previous experience, salary, duties performed, and fringe benefits. The current-resident questionnaire includes questions about the resident's demographic characteristics, health status, functional status, participation in social activities, monthly charge, and source of payment. Included in the 1977 survey was the discharged-resident questionnaire, which included some of the same questions as the current-resident questionnaire, selected on the basis of their availability in the medical record.

The 1977 survey included several modifications of the 1973-74 survey design and methodology:

Collecting data on discharged residents, especially in the areas of health status, length of stay, and where the resident goes after discharge.

Collecting data on the revenues of the facility as well as on its expenses.

Producing estimates for five states with the largest proportion of nursing home residents.

Limiting respondent reporting by limiting subsamples of residents and discharges to a maximum of eight per facility, and of staff to 23 per facility.

Access

National estimates are available to requesters in the form of tabulations, NCHS publications, and data tapes. Tables are aggregated so that no one respondent can be identified. Similarly, no identifying information concerning the facility, staff, or residents is contained on the data tapes, although a pseudo identification number allows linkage of data among the various files.

A report analyzing provisional tabulations is available six months after data collection ends. Selected final tabulations are released six months later. Data are analyzed and presented in the NCHS *Advance Data* reports and in *Vital and Health Statistics*, Series 13. These reports present data on the facility (utilization, expenses, services), residents (demographic characteristics, health status, services received, charges), and the staff (number, training, experience). Once data have been reviewed and analyzed, data tapes are available for release to requesters.

Source

U.S. Department of Health, Education, and Welfare (1980) Data Systems of the National Center for Health Statistics. Office of Health Research, Statistics, and Technology, National Center for Health Statistics. DHEW publication No. (PHS) 80-1247. Washington, D.C.: U.S. Department of Health, Education, and Welfare.

MERGED DATA FILE FOR SCHOOL DISTRICTS

NATIONAL CENTER FOR EDUCATION STATISTICS

Unit of Observation

School district.

Periodicity

Biennial (planned--the component surveys have generally been conducted on a continuing basis).

Universe

All school districts.

Subject Matter Description

Variables include revenue, expenditure, investment, enrollment (including racial/ethnic), grant, staff, poverty/welfare, and property value information are included.

The following seven component surveys make up this new merged file of 289 variables per school district:

File Name	Collecting Agency	Number of Records
ELSEGIS School District Universe (School year 1976-77)	NCES	16,720
F-33-Survey of Local Government Finances (School year 1976-77)	Bureau of Census	16,194
OCR-Elementary and Secondary School Civil Rights Survey (Fall 1976)	Office of Civil Rights	15,675
437 State Administered Programs (School year 1976-77)	Office of Education	14,902

File Name	Collecting Agency	Number of Records
EEO-5 Elementary Secondary Staff information (Fall 1976)	Equal Employment Opportunity Commission	7,137
NIE Special Tabulations of Census Data by School District (1970 Census, 1973-74 School District Boundaries)	National Institute of Education	16,661
Equalized Property Value (School Year 1976-77)	Killalea Associates	15,792

Variables include revenue, expenditure, investment, enrollment (including racial/ethnic), grant, staff, poverty/welfare, and property values.

Geographic Coverage

In addition to identifying school districts as central city, suburban, or non-SMSA, there is another breakdown based on whether district population is primarily urban or rural. This is called the population metro code. Population counts were extracted from the NIE Special Tabulations of Census Data by School District. This yielded three counts for each district: rural population, central city population, and other population. Depending on the location of a district, one or more of these variables could be zero. Population metro codes were assigned according to the following rules:

- If the rural population is greater than the sum of the central city and other populations, the population metro code equals 3.
- If the rural population is less than the sum of the central city and other populations, and other population is greater than central city population, the population metro code equals 2.
- If a district does not fall into either of the above two categories (e.g., central city population is greater than the sum of rural and other populations), the population metro code equals 1.

Population data were not available for districts with less than 300 enrollment, so this location variable cannot be described for such districts.

Access

Educational Equity Profiles for the 50 states are planned.

Source

National Center for Education Statistics (1980) Data Base Documentation: Merged Files. Unpublished document. National Center for Education Statistics, U.S. Department of Health, Education, and Welfare, Washington, D.C.

NATIONAL ASSESSMENT OF EDUCATIONAL PROGRESS (NAEP)

NATIONAL INSTITUTE OF EDUCATION

Unit of Observation

Individual school child and young adult.

Periodicity

Annual, starting in 1970.

Universe Description

A national sample of 100,000 persons per year was drawn from the universe of 9-, 13-, and 17-year-olds. The sample was stratified by region and size of community. After 1973, young adults aged 26-35 were sampled on a periodic basis.

Subject Matter Description

Sex, race, parental education, size and type of community, region, response range to tests on mathematics, science, social studies, music, reading, and literature. After 1973, career and occupational development, and citizenship.

Geographic Coverage

Results are reported by size and type of community. The following categories are used:

Size of Community

Big cities. Students in this group attend schools within the city limits of cities having a population over 200,000.

Fringes around big cities. Students in this group attend schools within metropolitan areas served by cities having a population greater than 200,000 but outside the city limits.

Medium cities. Students in this group attend schools in cities having a population between 25,000 and 200,000 not classified in the fringes-around-big-cities category.

Smaller places. Students in this group attend schools in communities having a population less than 25,000 not classified in the fringes-around-big-cities category.

Type of Community

Advantaged-urban (high-metropolitan) communities. Students in this group attend schools in or around cities with a population greater than 200,000 where a high proportion of the residents are in professional or managerial positions.

Disadvantaged-urban (low-metropolitan) communities. Students in this group attend schools in or around cities with a population greater than 200,000 where a high proportion of the residents are on welfare or are not regularly employed.

Extreme-rural communities. Students in this group attend schools in areas with a population under 10,000 where most of the residents are farmers or farm workers.

Access

Tape and publications available.

Sources

National Assessment of Educational Progress (1979) Attitudes Toward Science: A Summary of Results from the 1976-77 National Assessment of Science. Denver, Colorado: Education Commission of the States.

U.S. Department of Health, Education, and Welfare (1979) Directory of Federal Agency Education Data Tapes. National Center for Education Statistics. DHEW Publication No. (NCES) 79-426. Washington, D.C.: U.S. Department of Health, Education, and Welfare.

NATIONAL LONGITUDINAL STUDY (NLS) OF THE HIGH SCHOOL CLASS OF 1972

NATIONAL CENTER FOR EDUCATION STATISTICS

Unit of Observation

Individual high school student.

Periodicity

Periodic: 1972, 1973, 1974, 1976 (longitudinal).

Universe Description

The respondents were sampled as 1972 12th graders from a national probability sample of 1,318 public, private, and church-affiliated high schools in 50 states and the District of Columbia. The school sampling frame was stratified into 600 final strata based on: type of control of school, geographic division, grade 12 enrollment, proximity to institutions of higher education, percent minority group enrollment, income level of the community around the school, and degree of urbanization. Two schools with known probabilities were chosen from each of the strata, and within each school a simple random sample of 18 students was selected. Students in low-income areas or with high minority group populations were oversampled.

Subject Matter Description

Each student record contains 2,471 variables including: birthdate, sex, ethnicity; test scores, grades, class rank; courses of study, income, work experience and relation to studies; plans for further education and financial aid; parents' education, socioeconomic status; perceived influence of friends, parents, counselors on plans and aspirations; feelings of self-worth and locus of control; importance of family, community life, job success; changes in activities and plans 1-1/2 years and 2-1/2 years after high school graduation.

Geographic Coverage

Cannot be accessed at state level, but can be accessed by region and by community type. Can be accessed below state level at individual level only.

Access

Data tape, special tabulations, and publications are available.

Source

U.S. Department of Health, Education, and Welfare (1979) Directory of Federal Agency Education Data Tapes. National Center for Education Statistics. DHEW Publication No. (NCES) 79-426. Washington, D.C.: U.S. Department of Health, Education, and Welfare.

CENSUS OF GOVERNMENTS

BUREAU OF THE CENSUS

Unit of Observation

Governmental unit (includes state governments, counties, muncipalities, townships, school districts, and other special districts).

Periodicity

Every 5 years (in years ending in 2 and 7).

Universe Description

All units.

Subject Matter Description (1977)

Volume 1 consists of 2 separate reports on governmental organization:

Number 1. Governmental Organization: national summary data for states, and for SMSAs, on county, municipal, and township governments by size classes; on school districts and other public school systems by size of enrollment, by kind of area served, by grades provided, and by number of schools operated; and on special districts by function performed and by area served. Also shown is the number of local governments, by type, in each county in the nation.

Number 2. Popularly Elected Officials: data on elected officials by state, inside and outside SMSAs, by type of government and by type of office.

Volume 2: Taxable Property Values and Assessment/Sales Price Ratios: amounts of assessed value officially determined in 1976 for local general property taxation, for counties and for each city having a July 1973 estimated population of 50,000 or more, with totals for states and their SMSA and non-SMSA components. Also included for a group of large assessing jurisdictions are estimates of locally assessed realty distributed among major use categories.

The volume provides statistics, based on a sampling within 1,939 of the 7,805 county based or equivalent primary assessing jurisdictions throughout the United States, on real properties involved in measurable sales during a 6-month period of 1976. Statistics include effective tax rates, assessment/sales price ratios, and dispersion coefficients applicable to single-family (non-farm) houses and certain other realty, for states, local assessing jurisdictions classified by type, and selected (over 50,000 population) local areas.

Volume 3. Public Employment: three separate reports on public employment, payroll, selected benefit coverage for full-time employees and labor-management relations.

Number 1. Employment of Major Local Governments: statistics on October 1977 employment and payrolls of individual major local governments. Data are presented individually for all county governments, municipalities (and townships in selected states) with 10,000 or more population, school systems with 5,000 or more enrollment, and special districts having 100 or more full-time employees. Data include total, full-time, and full-time equivalent employment as well as payroll and average October 1977 earnings of full-time employees. Full-time equivalent employment of individual counties and municipalities is shown for selected governmental functions.

Number 2. Compendium of Public Employment: a comprehensive summary of public sector employment, payrolls, and selected benefit coverage for full-time employees as of October 1977. National and state-by-state summaries are provided for state and local government (by type of local government) employment and payrolls by function, average October 1977 earnings of full-time employees, and coverage of full-time employees by selected benefits. Additionally, data on local government employment, payrolls, and average October 1977 earnings of full-time employees are summarized by county area; by population-size groups for counties, municipalities, and townships; by enrollment-size groups for school districts; and by employment-size groups for special district governments.

Number 3. Labor-Management Relations in State and Local Governments: a national and state-by-state summary of labor-management relations in state and local governments as of October 1977. Statistics include information on the number and percent of full-time employees who belong to an employee organization; number of governments with a labor relations policy, by type of policy; number of employees covered by contractual agreements; number of bargaining units with distributions by size groups (number of employees represented) and by major types of employees represented; and work stoppages. Additional national summaries are presented for counties and municipalities (including townships in selected states) by population-size groups and for school districts by enrollment-size groups.

Volume 4. Governmental Finances: five separate reports on government finances.

Number 1. Finances of School Districts: statistics on revenue, expenditure, debt, and financial assets of school districts for the fiscal year 1976-77. Figures are shown in detail for each state and, as to selected financial items, for enrollment-size groups of school districts and individual school districts with enrollment of 5,000 or more pupils.

Number 2. Finances of Special Districts: data for fiscal 1976-77 on finances of special districts, by state, and for selected large districts.

Number 3. Finances of County Governments: statistics for the United States and for each state on revenue, expenditure, debt, and financial assets of county governments. Selected financial items are shown for groups of counties, classified by size of population, and for individual county governments.

Number 4. Finances of Municipalities and Township Governments: data on revenue, expenditure, debt, and financial assets of municipalities and townships for fiscal 1976-77. Detailed statistics are given for states. Selected financial items are reported for population-size groups of these governments, and for individual municipalities and townships having 10,000 or more inhabitants.

Number 5. Compendium of Government Finances: a comprehensive summary of the census findings on governmental finances for fiscal 1976-77, showing data for the federal government, individual states, and local governments by type of government, and data for state and local governments by states, including a breakdown by type of government.

Volume 6. Topical Studies: separate reports on selected subjects, for example:

Number 3. State Payments to Local Governments: description of programs for financial grants and reimbursements to local governments in each state, indicating the basis of allocation and amounts paid under each program during fiscal 1976-77.

Number 5. Graphic Summary of the 1977 Census of Governments: charts and maps first issued in other reports of the census, with a brief explanatory text and a reference guide to the subject matter reports where the underlying statistics appear.

Number 6. Regional Organizations: information, for the first time, on the number, types, organizational character, financial transactions, and employment and payrolls of selected multijurisdictional organizations. These organizations are closely associated with the government sector, but in the past have been excluded from the Census Bureau's governmental statistics program. Characteristics for the following three types of organizations are presented: general purpose, community action agencies, and special purpose.

Volume 7: Guide to the Census of Governments: samples of tables published in 1977 Census of Governments.

In addition to the 1977 census reports, there are several annual and quarterly reports made available since the 1972 census, most of which are updates of census information. There are also several intercensal special reports, some of them on topics not covered in the census, and some of them on longitudinal coverage of census variables. These include:

Land Title Recording in the United States: A Statistical Summary

Governing Boards of County Governments, 1973

Property Values Subject to Local General Property Taxation in the United States: 1973, 1978, 1980

Environmental Quality Control

Governmental Finances and Employment: Fiscal Years 1971-72, 1972-73, 1973-74, 1974-75, 1975-76, 1976-77

State and Local Ratio Studies and Property Assessment

Expenditures of General Revenue Sharing and Antirecession Fiscal Assistance Funds, 1976-77

Source

Bureau of the Census (1980) 1977 Census of Governments, Volume 7: Guide to 1977 Census of Governments. Washington, D.C.: U.S. Department of Commerce.

FEDERAL ASSISTANCE PROGRAMS RETRIEVAL SYSTEM (FAPRS)

DEPARTMENT OF AGRICULTURE

Purpose

The system catalogs all federal domestic aid programs that can be used to meet specific development needs of communities and of individuals. Programs whose basic eligibility requirements have been met by the requester and that are funded for the fiscal year may be listed after the requester submits a descriptive profile to the computerized FAPRS. The system enables someone who is unfamiliar with the federal aid process to employ a single source of program eligibility information rather than conducting extensive research. The system is carried nationwide by private time sharing networks and is available in almost all State Cooperative Extension Service offices for a small fee.

Input

The system is interactive in nature, requesting the user to make choices from 37 subcategories of need. A data base of counties (by state) is used to assist the requester in answering eligibility questions concerning the county in which the aid program is to be applied. The requester must supply the applicant type and population of the area in which the program is to take place.

Content

The information consists of a list of the agency numbers and names of funded aid programs for which the requester has met the eligibility requirements. All program titles and number identifications are keyed to the Catalog of Federal Domestic Assistance which is used in the initial screening of programs. At the user's request, the system will provide a modified text of a specific program as it appears in the catalog. Coding of each program as to appropriate subcategories and eligibility criteria is verified by each program's manager prior to entry in the FAPRS data base. Program eligibility criteria are updated a minimum of every six months concurrent with the publication of the catalog and the catalog update. Additional updates are made when necessary on a program by program basis. County eligibility updates are made through listings provided by the federal agencies involved.

Output

The frequency and amount of output are determined by the individual user. On an overall basis, usage has averaged 3,000 queries monthly.

Source

U.S. General Accounting Office (1976) Federal Information Sources and Systems: 1977 Congressional Sourcebook Series. PAD-77-71. Washington, D.C.: U.S. Government Printing Office.

FEDERAL INFORMATION EXCHANGE SYSTEM

COMMUNITY SERVICES ADMINISTRATION

Purpose

The system is to disseminate information on federal outlays by geographic location in the U.S.

Input and Content

Each federal agency submits information on all 1,300 program categories listed in the Catalog of Federal Domestic Assistance by county, independent city, city over 25,000 population, and state. These submissions are updated annually. Outlays are distinguished by type of assistance: formula grants, project grants, other grants, direct payments, direct loans, insurance, contractual procurement, salaries and expenses, donations of property, goods or commodities, and guaranteed/insured loans.

Qualifications

1. There are inadequacies in the estimation methods used to obtain county-level data. Various (approximately 25) proration and allocation

methods are used. These methods include the following examples which are applied to selected programs:

a) To obtain city estimates, the county figures are prorated on the basis of the portion of the population in the city relative to the county population.

b) Funds are allocated to the location of the state agency receiving the money.

c) Funds are allocated to the location of the prime contractor's main office.

d) State totals are based on average monthly annuities applied to the national figure. Proration to counties and cites is based on population.

e) The monies assigned to a state are allocated within the state to counties and cities on the basis of the proportion of population in the given locality.

f) Funds are reported for the largest city in the state and the county where it is located.

g) Funds are prorated to localities on the basis of the fraction of the state's special group population in a locality.

h) Prorated to state, county, and city by size of geographic area.

2. There is difficulty in identifying individual program categories listed in the outlays report.
3. There are problems of accomodating year-to-year changes in the outlays reports (and in federal programs themselves) when attempting to compare federal spending over time.

Access

Geographic Distribution of Federal Funds Reports (called Federal Outlays before 1979) are available for the U.S. (state-level breakdowns only) and for each state (local breakdowns). Where appropriate, outlay entries are accompanied by a code for the proration method used.

Sources

Community Services Administration (1976) Instructions for Reporting Federal Outlays by Geographic Location. Memo. Community Services Administration, Executive Office of the President, Washington, D.C.

Community Services Administration (1980) Geographic Distribution of Federal Funds in Iowa, Fiscal Year 1979. Executive Office of the President. Washington, D.C.: U.S. Government Printing Office.

Reid, J. Norman, W. Maureen Godsey, and Fred K. Hines (1978) Federal Outlays in Fiscal 1976: A Comparison of Metropolitan and Nonmetropolitan Areas. Rural Development Research Report No. 1, Economics, Statistics, and Cooperatives Service. Washington, D.C.: U.S. Department of Agriculture.

NATIONAL RURAL COMMUNITY FACILITIES ASSESSMENT STUDY

(BY ABT ASSOCIATES FOR FARMERS' HOME ADMINISTRATION)

Unit of Observation

Rural community.

Periodicity

1980 only.

Universe Description

All incorporated or unincorporated places which are located outside urbanized areas and which have a population of less than 50,000. A sample of from 500 to 2,346 communities will be randomly selected, stratified by region and population size. Data will be gathered by field interviews and mail surveys.

Subject Matter Description

The objective of this study is to guide future investment actions of the national and state governments in rural areas. The inventory and assessment of rural community facilities will produce baseline data against which future capital trends in rural areas can be measured. Shortfalls in the inventory will be identified and measured and the costs of remedying them through new construction, rehabilitation, or alternative service provision (e.g., new technology, noncapital solutions, or substitution of one kind of capital for another) will be estimated. Relative priorities, in light of national goals and community preferences, for closing the identified gaps in the inventory will be established. An intergovernmental rural community facilities inventory system to be used by federal, state, and local officials will be established.

Information is to be gathered on service facilities and production facilities. Each facility is to be assessed for accessibility, capacity, condition, diversity, and quality. The following facilities are to be included:

I. SERVICE FACILITIES
- A. Education
  1. Elementary Schools
  2. Middle Schools
  3. Secondary Schools
  4. Post-Secondary Schools
  5. Public Libraries
- B. Health
  1. Hospitals
  2. Nursing Homes
  3. Ambulatory (Outpatient) Care Facilities
  4. Ambulatory Dental Care Facilities
  5. Ambulatory Mental Health Facilities
  6. Residential Facilities for:
     - a. orphans & dependent children
     - b. the emotionally disturbed
     - c. alcoholics & drug abusers
     - d. physically handicapped
     - e. mentally retarded
     - f. blind & deaf
  7. Emergency Vehicle Services
- C. Industrial Parks
- D. Justice
  1. Law Enforcement Facililities
  2. Courthouses
  3. Jails
- E. Recreation
  1. Community Recreation Facilities
  2. Recreation Centers
- F. Transportation
  1. Railroad Facilities
  2. Airports and Related Facilities
  3. Streets and Highways (including bridges)
  4. Public Transit Terminals
  5. Intercity Bus Terminals
  6. Intercity Truck Terminals
  7. Waterway Facilities

II. PRODUCTION FACILITIES
- A. Energy
  1. Direct Power Suppliers
  2. Indirect Power Suppliers
- B. Fire Safety
  1. Fire Stations
  2. Vehicles
  3. Communications System
  4. Water Supply and Storage
- C. Solid Waste
  1. Collection Facilities and Equipment
  2. Disposal Sites
  3. Resource Recovery Plants
- D. Telecommunications
  1. Telephone
  2. Cable Television
  3. Over-the-Air Television
  4. Radio
  5. Disaster Preparedness
  6. Postal Service
- E. Waste Water
  1. Sewer Mains and Collector Systems
  2. Treatment and Disposal Systems
- F. Water Supply
  1. Community Systems
     - Storage Facilities
     - Treatment Facilities
     - Delivery Facilities
  2. On-Site Wells and Cisterns

Geographic Coverage

The entire sample is from rural areas. It is not yet set up as a data set, so geographic categories for which data can be made available are not known.

Access

The data base developed in this study will be integrated into the following national data sources:

Facility or Jurisdiction	Source	Title	Date
COMMUNITY	DOC/Bureau of the Census	Census of Population Characteristics of the Population	1970
		Current Population Reports (P-25 Series)	1977, 1978
		Census of Agriculture	1974
		County Business Patterns	1974, 1979
		Census of Governments, Revenue Sharing Detail File	1978, 1979
		Census of Governments, Finance Data, File A and File B	1977
		Sampled Communities	
	NOAA	Climatic Data by Community	1930-1978
	USGS	Topographic Maps of Communities	1955-78
EDUCATION	DOC/Bureau of the Census	Census of Governments; Finances of School Districts	1977
	Market Data Retrieval	School Enrollments, Administration and Special Services	1980

Facility or Jurisdiction	Source	Title	Date
ENERGY	DOE	Forms 12, 12A, 12D Inter-Utility Electricity Sales	1979
	DOE	Form 67 Pollution Control Characteristics	1979
	DOE	GURF (Generating Unit Reference File)	1978
	DOE	Form 4 Monthly Operation and Fuel Availability	1979
HEALTH	AHA	Guide Issue Tapes	1977
	HEW/HCFA	Medicare, Medicaid Automated Certification Reporting System	1979
	DHEW/NCHS	Master Facility Inventory	1976
		Area Resource File	1979
		National Inventory of Ambulatory Health Clinics	1980
JUSTICE			
Jails	DOC/Bureau of the Census	1978 National Jail Census	1978
TRANSPORTATION			
Highways	Individual Counties	County Road Maps	1979-1980
Railroads	Amtrak	Train Earnings Report	1980
	Amtrak	Station On/Off Reports	1980
Railroads	Amtrak	Advance Reservation Ticketing System	1980
Airports	DOT/FAA	Airport Master Record FAA Form 5010-1	1979
	CAB	Form 41, Schedule T3	1977, 1979
	Jeppeson-Sanderson Co.	Notice to Airmen of Airport Closings	1980
WASTEWATER	EPA/Office of Water Program Operation	Wastewater Needs Survey	1978

Sources

Abt Associates, Inc. (1980) National Rural Community Facilities Assessment Study: Pilot Phase, Final Report. Cambridge, Mass.: Abt Associates, Inc.

Abt Associates, Inc. (1980) National Rural Community Facilities Assessment Study: Supporting Statement for OMB Clearance Request, National Survey. Cambridge, Mass.: Abt Associates, Inc.

BEA REGIONAL ECONOMIC INFORMATION SYSTEM

BUREAU OF ECONOMIC ANALYSIS

REIS is the term applied to the data file, computer programs, and staff established for the maintenance, management, and distribution of the personal income regional data base. The system currently contains 22 million separate estimates covering 3,500 local areas.

Definitions

Personal Income Personal income is the income of residents of an area from all sources. It is measured after deduction of personal contributions to old age and survivors insurance, government retirement, and other social insurance programs, but before deduction of income and other personal taxes. It includes income received from business, governments (federal, state, local, and foreign), households and institutions. It consists of wages and salaries (in cash and in kind), various types of supplementary earnings termed "other labor income" (the largest item being employer contributions to private pension, welfare, and workmen's compensation funds), proprietors' income (farm and nonfarm, the latter including the income of independent professional and producer cooperatives), rental income of persons, dividends, personal interest income, and government and business transfer payments (in general consisting of disbursements to persons for services not currently rendered).

Per Capita Personal Income Another measure of income presented by BEA in its tables is per capita income. This is the total personal income of the residents of a given area divided by the resident population of the area. In computing per capita income for the counties, BEA uses Bureau of the Census county population totals as of July 1, which are available for each year beginning with 1971. Midyear county population for the years preceding 1971 were estimated by BEA (based on a combination of Census midyear state population data, the Census April 1970 benchmark county population, and county population data supplied by the individual states).

Per capita personal income serves as an indicator of the quality of consumer markets and of the economic well-being of the residents of an area. This measure, however, can vary widely from county to county and should be used with caution for several reasons.

In many instances, an unusually high (or low) per capita income is the temporary result of unusual conditions, such as a bumper crop, a major construction project (e.g., a defense facility, nuclear plant, or dam), or a catastrophe (e.g., a tornado or drought). In some cases, a high per capita income is not representative of the standard of living in an area. For example, a construction project may attract a large number of highly paid workers who are included in the population but who send a substantial portion of their wages to dependents living in other areas. Conversely, a county with a large institutional population (e.g., residents of a college, correctional institution, or domiciliary medical facility) may show an unusually low per capita income, which is not necessarily indicative of the economic well-being of the noninstitutional population.

Moreover, population is measured at midyear whereas income is measured as a flow over the year. Therefore, a significant change in population during the year, particularly around midyear, can cause a distortion in the per capita figures.

In counties where farm income predominates, additional considerations should be taken into account. Farm proprietors' income, as measured for personal income, reflects returns from current production; it does not measure current cash flows. Sales out of inventories, though included in current gross farm income, are excluded from net farm income since they represent income from a previous year's production. Additions to inventories are included in net farm income at current market prices. Therefore, farmers' attempts at regulating their cash flows by adjusting inventories are not reflected in BEA's farm proprietors' income estimates. Yet it is this regulation of cash flows by farmers that extends their earnings cycle and aids them in adjusting to losses or lowered income for two or three years.

In counties that are characterized by small population and almost total dependence upon farming, the per capita income will react more sharply to the vagaries in weather, world market demand, and changing government policies related to agriculture than for counties where the sources of income are more diversified.

The substantial differences between BEA estimates of per capita income and Census Bureau estimates are due to differences in definition of income, collection mode, and method of computation. For example, the Census Bureau computes 1976 per capita income by dividing 1976 total money income by April 1977 total population, whereas BEA derives its 1976 per capita income by dividing 1976 total personal income by July 1976 population.

Resident Individuals actually residing in a state or county, civilian and military personnel alike, are counted as residents. This generalization does not mean that the personal income estimates for a particular state or county include the income of tourists or others in similar temporary status (such individuals are not counted as residents). The concept of residence is based essentially on physical rather than usual permanent, or legal residence. It differs from the

Census Bureau concept mainly in the treatment of seasonal and short-term workers. The Census Bureau includes many such workers at their usual place of residence (rather than where they were on April 1). BEA assigns the wages of these workers to the area where they resided while performing the work.

Place of Measurement For regional economic measurement, income is recorded either by place of work (where earned) or by place of residence (where received). Personal income, by definition, is a measure of income received. Therefore BEA's estimates of total personal income (TPI) reflect the state, county, and SMSA of residence of the income recipients.

The measure of labor and proprietors' income that BEA presents in industry detail for states, counties, and SMSAs reflects place of work. These individual industry estimates are useful for the analysis of the industrial structure of a given area.

The bulk of the income data basic to preparing the estimates of labor and proprietors' income is reported by industry in the state and county in which the business establishment is located. These data are subsequently adjusted to a place of residence for inclusion in the personal income measure.

Rental income of persons, dividends, personal interest income, and transfer payments are estimated from data that are reported where they are received. There is no relevance to a where-earned classification for transfer payments.

The Allocation Procedure

The estimates of state and local area personal income are characterized by the systematic use of allocation procedures in their preparation. The state estimates are made by allocating the U.S. total for each income item (estimated for the national personal income series) to the states proportional to each state's share of a related economic series. In a similar manner the state estimates are allocated to the counties proportional to each county's share of a related economic series. In some cases, national, state, and county estimates are constructed from the same basic source, as for example, wages and salaries reported under the various state unemployment insurance programs. In other cases, data that are available at the national and state levels are not available at the county level and allocators prepared from related, but indirect, data are used to reflect the geographic distribution of the income item among the counties. An example of this is veterans' payments. At the national and state levels direct information is available on payments to veterans under various government programs, but for many of these programs, such information is not tabulated at the county level. Where the direct data are not available, county veteran population, an indirect allocator, is used to distribute the state total to the counties.

Occasionally, direct information is available for SMSAs as a unit that is not available for counties. In such cases, amounts for single-county SMSAs are assigned to the appropriate county and amounts for multicounty SMSAs are allocated to the constituent counties proportional to some indirect, but related, series that is available by counties. The SMSA counties are grouped by states (some SMSAs cross state lines) and summed. The difference between the state estimate and the sum of the selected SMSA counties is allocated to the remaining counties within the state proportional to the indirect, but related, county series.

The use of the state estimates as control totals in conjunction with the allocation procedure imparts additional reliability to the county estimates because most components of personal income can be estimated more reliably for states than for smaller geographic areas. It also permits, if necessary, the use of a different allocator, in each state, to distribute income items to the counties without impairing the interstate comparability of the estimates.

Data Sources

The estimates are constructed from nearly 400 individually estimated income items based on data gathered from diverse sources. The bulk of the materials used to prepare the estimates is data generated as the byproduct of federal and state government programs (administrative records data). The remainder comes from the various censuses and from nongovernment sources. Among the more important sources of the administrative record data used by BEA are the state unemployment programs of the Employment and Training Administration of the Department of Labor, the insurance programs of the Social Security Administration, and the federal tax program of the Department of the Treasury. The two most important censuses utilized are the censuses of agriculture and population. The information obtained from administrative records and censuses yields more than 90 percent of the data needed for the preparation of the state and local area income estimates.

BEA supplements these basic statistics with data of lesser quality, scope, and relevance. In order to adjust for gaps and deficiencies in the poorer quality data, indirect procedures and value judgments are sometimes employed. The impact of these indirect procedures on the reliability of the individual state and local area estimates has varied over the 50-year estimating span because of regional differences and changes in industrial composition. It is not possible, therefore, to provide measures of the error introduced into the income estimates by the indirect procedures.

Because the estimates are made from existing statistical information they can be prepared annually and in considerable detail at relatively low cost. However, because the data are generated from programs not primarily designed for income measurement, it is necessary for BEA to adjust the data for definitional differences and for deficiencies in the data. The alternative would be for BEA to collect the necessary information in surveys of income recipients. The surveys would provide data directly suited for the measurement of personal income, eliminating the necessity of adjusting the inputs for definitional and other previously mentioned reasons. The costs associated with this approach, however, would be prohibitive because a very large sample would be necessary to permit reliable local area estimates. The use of administrative record data has the additional advantage that it does not add to the reporting burden of businesses and households.

Geographic Structure

Estimates are developed independently for states and counties only. Estimates for all other geographic areas below the state level are made by aggregating the county estimates in the appropriate combinations. This building block approach provides BEA with the flexibility necessary for meeting the needs of the wide variety of users of local area data. It also permits estimates for areas whose boundaries change over time--such as SMSAs--to be presented on a consistent geographic definition for all years for analytic purposes. Because estimates are made only for local areas that can be defined in terms of counties, the metropolitan areas for the New England states in BEA's local area personal income series are not the officially designated SMSAs but rather the alternative NECMAs developed by OMB. New England County Metropolitan Areas are approximations of SMSAs in terms of counties.

Access

The REIS includes an active information retrieval service, which provides a variety of standard and specialized analytic tabulations for counties and specified combinations of counties. All of the tabulations are available on magnetic tape. The REIS data base currently includes the following data sets.

Quarterly state personal income These estimates, available approximately 4 months after the close of the subject quarter, are published regularly in the January, April, July, and October issues of the *Survey of Current Business*. As of April 1980, quarterly estimates are available from the first quarter of 1958 through the fourth quarter of 1979.

Annual state personal income Annual estimates for states are published twice each year. Preliminary estimates of total and per capita personal income, derived from the quarterly estimates, are published in the April issue of the *Survey* (4 months after the close of the subject year). A revised set of estimates, based on more complete data and therefore more reliable, is presented in greater detail in the August issue of the *Survey*.

Annual county personal income These estimates become available approximately 16 months after the close of the subject year. Summary statistics are published in the April issue of the *Survey*. Estimates are available for 1959, 1962, and 1965-78.

Gross farm flows These estimates of gross receipts and expenditures of farms, which underlie the net farm income estimates in the state and county personal income series, are unpublished. However, tabulations for the years corresponding to the personal income series are available upon request from REIS.

Average annual employment for states and counties These unpublished estimates are a companion series to the personal income estimates. They are constructed from similar sources using the same concepts and definitions. Tabulations are available from REIS for 1967-78.

In addition to responding to specific data requests addressed to it, REIS distributes estimates through a group of universities and state agencies officially designated as BEA users. This group was created by a congressional directive to provide BEA's personal income and related series to university bureaus and state agencies on a no-cost basis. Each of these users, currently 189 in number, receives a full set of standard tabulations for the relevant state, its counties, and its metropolitan areas. The congressional directive encourages utilization by universities and state agencies of data that are comparable for all states and counties and consistent with national totals. This enhances the uniformity of analytic approaches taken in economic development plans and programs and improves the ability of the recipient agencies to assess sub-state economic developments and to service their local clientele.

Source

U.S. Department of Commerce (1980) Local Area Personal Income, Vol. 1: Summary. Bureau of Economic Analysis. Washington, D.C.: U.S. Department of Commerce.

STATISTICS OF INCOME: INDIVIDUAL INCOME TAX RETURNS

INTERNAL REVENUE SERVICE

Unit of Observation

Individual taxpayer.

Periodicity

Annual.

Universe

Data are estimated from a stratified systematic sample of unaudited individual income tax returns, Forms 1040 and 1040A, filed by U.S.

citizens and residents in a calendar year. In 1977, 155,299 returns were selected from a population of 86,759,093 returns. Returns are stratified into sample classes based on state groups, the presence or absence of a Schedule C (profit or loss from a business or profession), and combinations of adjusted gross income or deficit and business or farm receipts.

Subject Matter Description

A wide range of information entered in various types of tax returns is gathered, including items of personal income, exemptions and deductions, age, marital status, geographic location, personal wealth, items of business receipts, business deductions, profits and losses, items of assets and liabilities, types of business organization, industry, estate value, tax credits, and tax liability.

Geographic Coverage

Published tabulations are available at the national level and for individual states.

Access

Three annual publications are available: *Individual Income Tax Returns*, *Corporation Income Tax Returns*, and *Business Income Tax Returns*. An abbreviated preliminary report is issued for each of these three publications. Various special reports are occasionally issued, for example, *Personal Wealth* (1972). There is no on-line query capability.

Source

U.S. Department of the Treasury (1980) *Statistics of Income--1977, Individual Income Tax Returns*. Internal Revenue Service. Washington, D.C.: U.S. Department of the Treasury.

STATISTICS OF INCOME: SMALL AREA DATA

INTERNAL REVENUE SERVICE

Unit of Observation

Individual Taxpayer.

Periodicity

Available for 1972 and 1974, and planned for 1976 and 1979.

Universe

Statistics are based on the complete Internal Revenue Service's Individual Master File (IMF) rather than on the sample of returns used for *Statistics of Income, Individual Income Tax Returns* described elsewhere in this appendix.

Subject Matter Description

The following items are computed for each geographic reporting unit (see below) by class of adjusted gross income (under $5,000, $5,000-$9,999, $10,000-$14,999, $15,000 or more, and totals, are the income classes in the report for 1972): number of returns, number of joint returns, number of exemptions, dependent exemptions, and adjusted gross income. In addition, the number of returns and the dollar amount for each of the following items are computed by geographic reporting unit and income class: salaries and wages, interest, dividends, and total tax.

Geographic Coverage

The statistics noted above are available for the United States, individual states, the 125 largest SMSAs, and 3,141 counties and county equivalents.

Access

IRS publications containing the 1972 and 1974 data are available from the U.S. Government Printing Office. The data are also available on magnetic tape.

Source

U.S. Department of the Treasury (1977) *Statistics of Income, Small Area Data, 1972*. Internal Revenue Service. Washington, D.C.: U.S. Department of Treasury.

CONTINUOUS WORK HISTORY SAMPLE

SOCIAL SECURITY ADMINISTRATION

Unit of Observation

Individual (Social Security number).

Periodicity

Continuous from 1937.

Universe

Various samples are drawn from the universe of social security numbers (these numbers are stratified by state and chronology). In general, 9 out of 10 workers are in employment or self-employment which is covered. Relevant workers who are not covered include agricultural employees who neither receive $150.00 from one farm employer during the year nor work for pay on a part-time basis for 20 days or more for one farm employer during a year.

The various general purpose research files include the following:

One-percent sample annual Employee-Employer (Ee-Er). This is a one-percent sample of social security numbers for which wage and salary employment was reported in the reference year. It contains one record for each employee-employer combination in the year.

One-percent sample annual Self-Employed (SE). This is a one-percent sample of social security numbers for which self-employment earnings subject to social security coverage were reported in a reference year.

One-percent sample Longitudinal Employee-Employer Data (LEED). This file was assembled from the Ee-Er records which are prepared annually. In this file, the original records from the various annual files have been merged so that all of the records associated with an employee over the time span of the file appear together.

One-percent 1937-to-date CWHS. This is a one-percent sample of social security numbers issued through the cutoff date of the file reflecting entire work experience in covered employment.

One-tenth of one-percent 1937-to-date CWHS. This is a 0.1-percent sample of social security numbers issued through the cutoff date of the file reflecting entire work experience in covered employment. It contains more detailed earnings information.

Subject Matter Description

Data for the CWHS are obtained from records derived from reporting and informational forms that are used in administering the retirement, survivors and disability programs of the SSA. The date of birth, sex, and race of the person is obtained from the application for a Social Security number. Geographic and industry information is obtained from the employer's application for an identification number and other related forms that are used periodically to update this information. Initially, employers are assigned geographic and industry classifications based on the location and nature of business information supplied. Information not satisfactorily reported is obtained by mail or phone.

Employers who operate more than one place of business and have a total of 50 employees with at least 6 in a separate location are asked to use the Establishment Reporting Plan (ERP). Under this plan, the employer gives SSA a list showing the location, industrial activity and approximate number of employees of each establishment. This arrangment allows SSA to classify the employees by geography and industry.

One factor which may influence the wage data available in the CWHS is the change to annual, rather than quarterly, wage reporting by employers (begun in 1978).

Geographic Coverage

The SSA has developed its own set of state and county codes to classify employers, workers, and self-employed persons according to geographic location. However, the Tax Reform Act of 1976 has prevented employee residence information from being available. Before 1976, IRS was regarded as a conduit through which information on earnings and contributions was channeled to SSA for program administration purposes. Under the Tax Reform Act, it is not clear whether the IRS, because of new confidentiality interpretations, can release certain information to SSA. This affects the CWHS in that it no longer receives the residence information (and certain other variables) contained in tax returns. Thus, since 1976 all information obtained from tax returns has been suppressed in the CWHS. There is currently some interest in using the addresses reported on the W-2 forms to replace this IRS residence data.

Access

CWHS microdata files are available to outside users on a restricted basis. This means that certain limitations concerning confidentiality and purpose are agreed to beforehand by the user.

Sources

Alexander, Lois A., and Thomas B. Jabine (1978) Access to social security microdata files for research and statistical purposes. Social Security Bulletin 41(August):3-17.

Buckler, Warren, and Creston Smith (1980) The Continuous Work History Sample (CWHS): Description and Contents. Paper presented at the American Statistical Association meeting, Houston, Texas.

U.S. Department of Health, Education, and Welfare (1980) Research Publications and Microdata Files, Spring 1980. Social Security Administration. SSA Publication No. 13-11925. Washington, D.C.: U.S. Department of Health, Education, and Welfare.

CURRENT EMPLOYMENT AND UNEMPLOYMENT ANALYSIS (CEUA)

BUREAU OF LABOR STATISTICS

This system supports analysis and publication of data on the U.S. labor force. It features information on employment, unemployment, and nonparticipation, classified by a variety of demographic, social, and ecomomic characteristics. The input is derived from the Current Population Survey conducted by the Bureau of the Census for the Bureau of Labor Statistics. the aggregated (MACRO) estimates from the CPS comprise the CEUA data base. Data in the CEAU system are available at the national level only. Reports output include The Employment Situation (monthly, press release); Employment and Earnings (monthly, periodical); The Monthly Labor Review, various articles and tables (monthly, periodical); and Special Labor Force Reports (periodic reports).

Source

U.S. General Accounting Office (1976) Federal Information Sources and Systems. 1977 Congressional Sourcebook Series. PAD-77-71. Washington, D.C.: U.S. Government Printing Office.

CENSUS OF AGRICULTURE

BUREAU OF THE CENSUS

Farm Definition

The definition of a farm for census purposes has changed several times since 1850. In all censuses, however, the essential features of the farm definition have been that the land should be operated under the day-to-day control of one person or management and should be used for or connected with agricultural operations. Control may be exercised by the owner or a manager, or through a lease, rental, or cropping arrangement, and the tracts of land operated as a farm need not be contiguous.

Agricultural operations are defined as those that include the growing of crops, the raising of livestock and poultry and their products, and the production of other agricultural items such as honey and greenhouse or nursery products. Such operations may vary in size from a small truck garden to the operation of diversified enterprises including thousands of acres of cropland harvested, extensive orchards, large livestock feedlots, and sizable dairy and poultry operations.

It has been necessary since the first agriculture census to specify some minimum limits for inclusion of agriculture operations in the Census. The minimum criteria have included measures of land areas, land use, agricultural resources, and agricultural output or sales. For 1978, the final published statistics include any place operated under the control of an individual management on which the sales of agricultural products amounted, or would normally amount, to $1,000 in the census year.

Periodicity

The census, taken every 10 years from 1840 to 1920 and every 5 years from 1925 through 1974, is undergoing a reference year change. Two 4-year censuses, taken for 1978 and 1982, will adjust the data-reference year to coincide with the censuses of business and industry for 1982. Thereafter the agriculture census will revert to a 5-year cycle.

Data Collection

The 1969 and 1974 censuses were taken by mail; most prior censuses were conducted by personal interview. The 1978 census was taken by a combination of both.

The mailing list comes from a variety of sources, including the previous agricultural census, Census Bureau special lists (e.g., of farms large enough to receive special handling), previous economic censuses, Agricultural Stabilization and Conservation Service (a file of landlords and farm operators enrolled in ASCS programs), and the IRS (name and address only).

The data collection process is lengthy, and involves various mailout, telephone, and personal interview phases. The standard data collection form is considered by many respondents to be too long and complex, and there is particular resistance to providing data about off-farm income. County agents help many respondents fill out their forms and are provided with a lengthy reference manual for this task.

A review prior to the 1978 census had the objectives of reducing the reporting burden, simplifying the report form, increasing promptness of response, and reducing the time between data collection and publications. Only essential basic items were asked of all farms; additional items for which county-level data are urgently needed were asked on a 20-percent sample basis. Data for which state or national estimates are sufficient to meet the needs were obtained through small sample surveys (10,000 to 50,000 farms).

Subject Matter Description

In the first censuses of 1840 and 1850, farmers were asked only about livestock in terms of the number of cattle, milk cows, and working oxen. Items such as production of Indian corn, pounds of cheese made, pounds of silk cocoons, and gallons of wine produced were also enumerated.

As agriculture expanded westward, the number of farms and ranches grew and gradually increased in mechanization, specialization, and complexity. The scope of the census of agriculture also had to expand to meet the needs for data to measure these rapid developments.

Changes in report form content since 1910 reflect interest in (1) the degree to which agriculture is affected by technological change, and (2) the socioeconomic characteristics of farm operators and their families. While some of these characteristics could be obtained from the population and housing censuses, collecting data on them in the agriculture censuses allows cross-tabulation with farm data as well. Since 1950 there has been an increasing emphasis on the measurement of farm versus nonfarm employment and income, farm expenditures, and (in 1969) the type of organization (individual partnership, corporation, etc.) operating the farm.

In 1974, specific areas of emphases were (1) inclusion of various areas not previously considered, such as grain and fuel storage and farm accidents and (2) expansion of the coverage of food and fiber production and of nonagricultural activities conducted by farm operators to supplement income.

For 1978, the principal categories of data collected were:

Acreage
Crops
Fruit and nut production
Vegetables
Nursery and greenhouse products
Value of sales
Land Use
Irrigation
Organization
Livestock and poultry
Animal specialties
Characteristics and occupation of operator
Foreign ownership of farmland in 1978
Use of fertilizers, pesticides, and other chemicals
Selected production expenditures
Expenditures for energy

Machinery and equipment
Market value of land and buildings

Special surveys In addition to the regular census, there are a number of special censuses and surveys. Foremost is the Cotton Ginnings Survey, taken annually since 1905. In 1935 special studies were done of part-time farming and farm mortgage indebtedness. Since 1890 there have been surveys on selected aspects of agricultural finance. The latest agricultural finance survey covers 1970, but the principal finance questions were included on the all-farm report form for later censuses.

In the 1969 census, data were collected on agricultural services. These include establishments primarily engaged in performing soil preparation services, crop services, veterinary and other animal services, farm labor and management services and landscape and horticultural services, for others.

In earlier years, most of these agricultural services were performed by the farmers themselves. However, the great technological, scientific and economic changes in the agricultural system over the past few decades encouraged the development of a separate, specialized industry that can deliver the services farmers can no longer provide for themselves. The enumeration of these services began as a special census in 1969 and was incorporated into the regular census in 1974. For census purposes, an agricultural service establishment is defined as an economic unit primarily engaged in (50 percent or more of gross receipts) certain industries.

Access

Data on agriculture in the U.S. have been published periodically for every census from 1840. Most of the statistics are issued in printed reports.

Preliminary reports Prior to publication of the final 1978 census figures, a separate 4-page report for each county in the U.S. with 10 or more farms was released, giving statistical highlights on basic data items, including the crops and livestock for each county, along with comparable data for 1974. An 8-page preliminary report was published for each state. For agricultural services, a preliminary 2-page state report was issued showing the number of agricultural service establishments, gross receipts and payroll.

Final Volumes. Volume I: State and County Data For each state, a separate report was published, divided into four sections:

1) Tables showing detailed data at the state level;

2) Tables of selected data for states and counties, organized by subject;

3) County data, by subject, for miscellaneous crop and livestock items found in relatively few counties, and

4) Tables of detailed data for each county.

Volume II: Statistics, by Subject This report presents statistics, by subject, for the U.S., regions, geographic divisions, and states. It also includes some data tabulated in greater detail than shown in Volume I.

Volume III: Agricultural Services The volume covers agricultural service establishments at the U.S., state, and county level.

Volume IV: Special Reports This is a series of reports including the Procedural History, Coverage Evaluation, Ranking Counties and States, and the Graphic Summary. The latter offers a profile of the U.S. agricultural system in a series of U.S. maps, a number of them in color. The graphic summary and the ranking counties report are two of the most widely used census of agriculture publications.

Summary data, available on computer tapes, contain much of the information from Volume I.

Sources

Bureau of the Census (1979) Agricultural Statistics. CFF No. 3, revised. Factfinder Series. Washington, D.C.: U.S.Department of Commerce.

Bureau of the Census (1979) 1974 Census of Agriculture, Volume IV, Special Reports, Part 4, Procedural History. Washington, D.C.: U.S. Department of Commerce.

SURVEY OF INCOME AND EDUCATION

BUREAU OF THE CENSUS

Unit of Observation

Household.

Periodicity

1976 only.

Universe Description

The survey used 51 independently selected state samples in almost 1000 sample areas rather than one national sample. The number of households interviewed was 151,170. The SIE sample was selected from three different sampling frames: housing units, new construction units, and mobile home parks. The largest portion of the sample was selected from the 20 percent sample basic records from the 1970 Census of Population and Housing. Samples of new housing units and new mobile home parks were also taken.

Subject Matter Description

The SIE was conducted in order to furnish a more current estimate of the number of school-age children living in poverty families for each state, and to estimate the number of persons who are in need of bilingual education. It is the largest available demographic/socioeconomic micro data base covering the reference period between the 1970 and 1980 censuses. While many of the same kinds of data are included on the Annual Demographic Files derived each year from the March CPS, the SIE sample size for almost all states is substantially greater than in CPS.

The March CPS questions formed the core of SIE questions asked for persons 14 years and older. These questions covered labor force status, work experience and income in 1975 for those individuals aged 14 and over, and basic demographics such as age, race, sex, educational attainment, and ethnic origin.

Additional items included cover a wide range of subjects such as school enrollment, bilingualism, nonmoney income and monetary assets, 1975 and 1976 food stamp recipiency and public assistance, disability conditions, health insurance coverage, costs of institutional care paid for by household members, and various housing characteristics for persons aged 14 and older. Only questions on basic demographics, school enrollment, bilingualism, disability conditions, and health insurance coverage were asked for children under 14.

Geographic Coverage

Tabulations can be made for the nation, census regions and divisions, states, and selected SMSAs. Each state and most SMSAs of 250,000 or more population are identified. Outside of identified SMSAs, there may be identification of the remaining population of a state in terms of metropolitan/nonmetropolitan and inside central city/outside central city. For some states, however, the outside SMSA population can only be identified as state remainder. It is not possible to prepare national tabulations from the file on the characteristics of metropolitan and nonmetropolitan or central city and noncentral city populations since these components are not identified for all states. The SIE data do not include any identification for urban or rural residence.

There are two further limitations to the geographic content of the SIE data. First, the sample design of the SIE limits its applicability for obtaining small area data other than for states and large SMSAs.

Even with a sample quite large relative to other household surveys, the SIE is not large enough to support tabulations for small areas such as counties or small metropolitan areas. Second, a limitation on geographic detail is required by the Census Bureau's confidentiality restrictions.

Access

Various publications using SIE data have been released in the Current Population Reports Series. These reports contain national totals and also data broken down by region, census division, and state. No publications contain data below the state level. However, the SIE household data are available on computer tape organized into files by census geographic region.

Source

Bureau of the Census (1979) Microdata from the Survey of Income and Education. Data Access Description No. 42, revised. Washington, D.C.: U.S. Department of Commerce.

COUNTY BUSINESS PATTERNS

BUREAU OF THE CENSUS

Units of Observation

County.

Periodicity

Annual.

Universe

Reporting is on an establishment basis, consistent with other economic censuses.

Subject Matter Description

Data on detailed economic activity for the full range of 2-, 3-, and 4-digit SIC codes, except for farm workers, railroad transportation, private household (domestic) service, and public administration (government). Contains statistics on mid-March employment, first quarter payroll, annual payroll, and number and employment-size of establishments for private non-farm organizations. Reports are useful in updating county data from the various economic censuses conducted by the Census Bureau and also providing coverage for activities not included in the censuses, such as construction activity by county; transportation (except railroads); finance, insurance, and real estate; and religous organizations.

Access

Available in County Business Patterns and public use computer tapes.

Source

Bureau of the Census (1979) Mini-Guide to the 1977 Economic Censuses, revised. Washington, D.C.: U.S. Department of Commerce.

CENSUS OF MANUFACTURES (AND ANNUAL SURVEY OF MANUFACTURES)

BUREAU OF THE CENSUS

Unit of Observation

Statistics are collected and published primarily in terms of the establishment--a single physical location at which a manufacturing activity, as defined by a standard industrial classification (SIC), takes place. Manufacturing industries and their products are classified according to the SIC coding system, and the data for establishments are tabulated in the same manner.

Periodicity

The first census of manufactures for the United States was taken in 1810, and all of the decennial censuses through 1900, except the one for 1830, included questions on manufacturing activities. From 1905 through 1919, a census of manufactures was taken every 5 years, and then every 2 years through 1939. Following World War II, 5-year censuses were resumed, beginning with 1947. The census of manufactures is now included in the economic censuses taken for years ending in 2 and 7. In addition, the Annual Survey of Manufactures (ASM) provides census-type information for the years between censuses. Based on a sample from the census, this survey has been conducted for most years since 1949.

Universe Description

Full enumeration of establishments in 20 major SIC industry groups.

Data Collection

Two different data collection procedures are used in the census. All multi-establishments and large, single-establishment companies receive and return questionnaires by mail. Diversity of activities necessitates using more than 200 different report forms on about 13,000 separate products. Data for small, single-establishment firms with under 20 employees are extracted from federal administrative records. This relieves approximately 140,000 companies from filling out census returns.

Survey statistics are collected by mail. They are currently obtained for about 5,000 of the 11,000 products manufactured in the United States, supplementing the data collected in the census. ASM data are compiled from a mail sample of about 70,000 establishments, representing the complete range of products and industrial activities.

Subject Matter Description (1977)

Censuses The principal categories for which data are collected in the censuses are employment, payrolls, worker-hours, inventories, assets, capital expenditures, and the cost of materials, resales, fuels, electricity, and contract work. Through the use of almost 200 specialized report forms that are designed for specific industries, detailed information is collected on materials consumed, supplies used, and products made and shipped. In selected industries, supplemental information is also obtained on characteristics of the plant, for example, the type of operation, processing of metals, and types of equipment used.

Surveys The ASM carries forward the key measures of manufacturing activity that are covered in more detail every 5 years in the census and provides annual national estimates of the value of product shipments for each of approximately 1,100 classes of manufactured product. The ASM also collects details not requested of all manufacturing establishments, even in census years, such as the type of fuel and energy consumed.

The monthly, quarterly, and annual Current Industrial Reports (CIRs) supply information on the output of manufactured products in the following major categories:

- All manufacturing industries
- Processed foods
- Textile mill products
- Apparel and leather
- Lumber, furniture, and paper products
- Chemicals, rubber, and plastics
- Stone, clay, and glass products
- Primary metals
- Intermediate metal products
- Machinery and equipment
- Electronics and instruments

The CIRs provide current information on detailed commodities (e.g., confectionery, including chocolate products; inorganic fertilizer materials and related acids; and major household appliances) that otherwise are covered only at the much broader product-class levels in the ASM. As part of the CIR series, the Bureau conducts an overall monthly survey of manufacturers' shipment, inventories, and orders (series M3). These statistics, shown for 38 detailed industry categories and 6 market classifications, provide sensitive indicators of short-run changes in business conditions. In addition to the M3 survey, there are overall surveys of pollution abatement, plant capacity, defense-oriented industries, and research and development.

Geographic Coverage

Census data on manufacturing are available for the United States, census divisions, states, counties, standard metropolitan statistical areas (SMSAs) and cities. Current Industrial Reports from the surveys, present primarily national data, with a few reports at the state level. The ASM provides statistics for states and SMSAs.

Access

Censuses Preliminary reports are issued for industries and geographic areas. The final data appear in such volumes and computer tapes as the following:

Subject Series: Volumes include, among others: Fuels and Electric Energy Consumed, Size of Establishments, Water Used in Manufactures, and Distribution of Sales by Class of Customer.

Industry Series: Consists of 82 reports that present final statistics for each of 452 manufacturing industries (value of shipments, value added, capital expenditures, employment, and payrolls), by geographic regions and states, by employment-size class of establishment, and by degree of primary product specialization.

Geographic Area Series: Consists of a series of 51 reports (each state and the District of Columbia) presenting general statistics for industries and industry groups. Similar totals are shown for all manufacturing industries for counties, SMSAs and their central cities, and other cities with significant manufacturing activities.

Location of Manufacturing Plants: This series, available only on computer tapes, covers either state and county, or state and place, by industry. Data cover the number of establishments by employment size code by 4-digit SIC industry codes for states, counties, and places of 2,500 or more inhabitants.

1977 Census of Minority-Owned Business Enterprises: This consists of four reports, Black, Spanish Origin, Asian American, American Indians and Others, and Minority-Owned Businesses, extracted from the 1977 data.

Surveys: There are two major series of reports issued from the surveys:

Annual Survey of Manufactures: Includes such titles as Fuels and Electric Energy Consumed; Expenditures for New Plant and Equipment, Book Value of Fixed Assets and Rental Payments for Building and Equipment; Statistics for States, Standard Metropolitan Areas, Large Industrial Counties, and Selected Cities; Industrial Profiles; and Survey of the Origin of Exports of Manufactured Products. These reports are available for the U.S. and for states.

Current Industrial Reports: results are published in over 100 series for major categories.

Data from both the censuses and current surveys are the principal sources of facts about the structure and functioning of the manufacturing sector of the U.S. economy. At the federal level, for example, the data are used extensively by the Bureau of Economic Analysis in compiling the gross national product, by the Federal Reserve Board in producing its monthly index of industrial production, and by the Department of Labor in its measure of productivity and price change. The Department of Energy relies on the Census Bureau's data when assessing the probable impact of fuel shortages on industry. States and local governments and chambers of commerce also use census data in studying the economic structure and changes occurring in their areas. Individuals, manufacturers, and distributors take the statistics into account in establishing measures of their potential markets, forecasting their sales, analyzing sales performance, and locating plants or warehouses. Trade associations use census information to evaluate changes in their industries.

Source

Bureau of the Census (1980) Statistics on Manufactures. CFF No. 15, revised. Factfinder Series. Washington, D.C: U.S. Department of Commerce.

FEDERAL-STATE COOPERATIVE PROGRAM FOR LOCAL POPULATION ESTIMATES

BUREAU OF THE CENSUS

Purpose

The Federal-State Cooperative Program for Local Population Estimates was initiated in 1967 to develop an annual series of county population estimates prepared jointly by the Bureau of the Census and the state agencies designated to work with the Bureau. The specific goals of the program were to construct a consistent series of estimates with comparability from area to area, to extend the coverage of ongoing estimating programs for a nationwide comprehensive system, to insure the quality of the estimates by improved estimating methods, data collection procedures, and data editing and review techniques, and to reduce the confusion surrounding current population estimates by discouraging competing estimates.

Since the program's inception in the late 1960's, and after extensive testing of methods against the results of the 1970 census, the nature of the program has shifted to a somewhat broader focus. This occurred largely as a result of two developments: the enactment of general revenue sharing legislation in 1972 requiring population estimates for civil jurisdictions below the county level, and a diversification of interest on the part of the cooperating agencies away from concentration on total population. More recently, the Government Division of the Census Bureau has developed and implemented a cooperative program to obtain tax and intergovernmental revenue data for counties, municipalities, and townships.

Data Collection and Estimation Procedures

Data are collected at the county and state levels by the cooperating agencies, with data for municipalities and minor civil divisions collected by the Census Bureau for tabulation with the series for other geographic areas.

The Administrative Records method is used to make estimates of the population below the county level. In general, these estimates are developed using a component technique in which each of the components of population change--births, deaths, and migration--is estimated separately. For the period from the census until the estimate date, resident births and deaths are taken from recorded information or are estimated. Immigration from abroad is developed from data provided by the Immigration and Naturalization Service and other sources. Internal net migration rate is estimated by developing a net migration rate from exemptions on matched individual federal income tax returns for successive periods between the base date and the estimate date. This rate is multiplied by a household population base to yield net migrants in households for the entire period. Change in special groups (e.g., college, military) is added separately. The final estimate of the resident population is obtained by adding natural change (births minus deaths), immigration from abroad, net internal migration, and change in special groups to the last census count. Estimates for subsequent years begin with the last estimate as a base point.

Estimates of the population of counties are made independently of the estimates developed for sub-county areas. For most counties, the revised estimates are based on an average of estimates developed from Component Method II (which employs vital statistics to measure natural increase and school enrollment to measure net migration), the Regression Method (which uses a multiple regression equation to relate changes in a number of different data series to population change), and the Administrative Records Method.

The state estimates are used as independent controls for the corresponding county estimates. They are also developed by averaging the estimates provided by three methods.

As in the case of the population estimates, per capita income estimates are developed using base year census estimates and rates of change developed from various administrative record sets and compilations, mainly from the IRS and BEA.

Evaluation of the Estimates

At the state and county levels the Administrative Records Method does not have significantly different results from the results of other estimating techniques. Comparisons of the estimates developed through the Administrative Records technique to county special census counts indicate that this method has an acceptable error level, even against counties which are not representative and are difficult to estimate. For areas below the county level, comparisons of results using the Administrative Records Method to special census counts reveal that these estimates have the same problems as other types of estimates, i.e., difficulty in estimating very small areas and those that experience extreme growth.

There are fewer independent estimates of income with which to compare the Administrative Records income estimates. At the state level there is a favorable comparison of the Administrative Records estimates with CPS data. There are no independent estimates of total money income for all counties. At the sub-county level, there were 82 special censuses conducted by the Census Bureau in 1973 which collected income data. The absolute average difference between the 1972 estimate and the census value for these places is 14.5 percent, with larger places being less and smaller places being larger.

Use of the Estimates

State and Local Fiscal Assistance Act of 1972 Distribution of federal funds under this act (known as general revenue sharing) are generally made on the basis of three factors: population, per capita income, and tax effort. The first two of these data elements are derived from the intercensal estimates.

Comprehensive Employment and Training Act of 1972 Under CETA, federal funds are distributed to prime sponsors for establishing and implementing employment training programs. In order to qualify as a prime sponsor, an area must contain at least 100,000 persons. The Census Bureau every year documents which areas have reached or dropped below this requirement.

Housing and Urban Development Act of 1972 HUD uses current population estimates both in determining areas eligible to receive community development funds and in distributing such funds. Areas with populations of 50,000 or more qualify.

Access

The areas covered by the estimates are all states, counties (or county equivalents), incorporated places, and active minor civil divisions (towns and townships). Separate income and population volumes are available for each state for every couple of years since the 1970 census.

Sources

Bureau of the Census (1980) Population and Per Capita Money Income Estimates for Local Areas: Detailed Methodology and Evaluation. Current Population Reports, Series P-25, No. 699. Washington, D.C.: U.S. Department of Commerce.

U.S. Department of Commerce (1978) A Framework for Planning U.S. Federal Statistics in the 1980's. Office of Federal Statistical Policy and Standards. Washington, D.C.: U.S. Department of Commerce.

SECOND NATIONAL WATER ASSESSMENT

U.S. WATER RESOURCES COUNCIL

History

The Water Resources Planning Act of 1965 directs the U.S. Water Resources Council to maintain a continuing study of U.S. water and related land resources and to prepare periodic assessments to determine the adequacy of these resources to meet present and future water requirements. In 1968, the Water Resources Council reported the results of its initial assessment. The Second National Assessment came out in 1978.

Data Sources

Data are collected on various subjects from several federal agencies, including Corps of Engineers, Environmental Protection Agency and the Departments of Commerce, Energy, Agriculture, and Interior.

Data Collection Units

Regions The first level of classification divides the United States into 21 major geographic areas - 18 in the conterminous United States and one each for Alaska, Hawaii, and the Caribbean. These hydrologic areas contain either the drainage area of a major river, such as the Missouri Region; or the combined drainage areas of a series of rivers, such as the South Atlantic-Gulf Region, which includes a number of rivers draining directly into the Atlantic Ocean or the Gulf of Mexico.

Subregions The second level of classification divides the regions into 222 planning subregions. A planning subregion includes that area drained by a river system, a reach of a river and its tributaries in that reach, a closed basin(s), or a group of streams forming a coastal drainage area. These planning subregions are delineated on Hydrologic Unit Maps for each of the states.

To simplify analysis of information for the Second National Water Assessment, the U.S. Water Resources Council reclassified the 222 planning subregions into 106 assessment subregions. These assessment subregions are groupings (larger drainage areas) of the planning subregions. Socioeconomic data collected for the assessment subregions were based on groupings of counties to approximate the subregion boundaries. These groupings are called assessment subareas.

Subject Matter Description

Social, economic, and environmental data include:

Population, employment and per capita income
Earnings by major sector
Surface area land use
Cropland and irrigated farmland
Sheet erosion by source
Flood damages by land use
Recreation requirements
Designated wilderness areas
Electric power generation by fuel source
Steam electric generating plants
Commercial navigation.

Annual water supply and use data include:

Mean streamflow
Existing surface storage
Water imports and exports
Net evaporation of reservoirs
Withdrawals and consumption for: agriculture, manufacturing, domestic, commercial, minerals, public lands.

Access

The final report of the Second National Water Assessment consists of four separate volumes:

Volume 1, Summary, gives an overview of the nation's water supply, water use, and critical water problems for 1975, 1985, and 2000 and summarizes significant concerns.

Volume 2, Water Quantity, Quality, and Related Land Considerations, consists of one publication with five parts:

Part I, Introduction, outlines the origin of the Second National Water Assessment, states its purpose and scope, explains the numerous documents that are part of the assessment, and identifies the individuals and agencies that contributed to the assessment.

Part II, Water-Management Problem Profiles, identifies the 10 general water-problem issues and their implications and potential consequences

Part III, Water Uses, focuses on the national perspectives regarding existing ("1975") and projected (1985 and 2000) requirements for water to meet offstream, instream, and flow management needs. State-regional and federal perspectives are compared.

Part IV, Water Supply and Water Quality Considerations, analyzes the adequacy of freshwater supplies (ground and surface) to meet existing and future requirements. It contains a national water budget; quantifies surface- and ground-water supplies, reservoir storage, and transfers of water within and between subregions; describes regional requirements and compares them to supplies; evaluates water-quality conditions; and discusses the legal and institutional aspects of water allocation.

Part V, Synopses of the Water Resources Regions, covers existing conditions and future requirements for each of the 21 water resources regions. Within each regional synopsis is a discussion of functional and location-specific water-related problems; regional recommendations regarding planning, research, data, and institutional aspects of solving regional water related problems, a problem issue matrix, and a comparative-analysis table.

Volume 3, Analytical Data, describes the methods and procedures used to collect, analyze and describe the data used in the assessment. National summary data are included with explanatory notes. Volume 3 is supplemented by five separately published appendices that contain data for the regions and subregions:

Appendix I, Social, Economic, and Environmental Data, contains the socio-economic baseline ("1975") and growth projections (1985 and 2000) on which the water-supply and water-use projections are based. This appendix presents two sets of data. One set, the National Future, represents the federal viewpoint; the other set, the State-Regional Future, represents the regional sponsor and/or state viewpoint.

Appendix II, Social, Economic, and Environmental Data, contains baseline water-supply data and baseline and projected water-withdrawal and water-consumption data used for the assessment. Also included are a water-adequacy analysis, a natural-flow analysis, and a critical-month analysis.

Appendix III, Monthly Water Supply and Use Analysis, contains monthly details of the water-supply, water-withdrawal and water consumption data contained in Appendix II and includes an analysis of monthly water adequacy.

Appendix IV, Dry-Year Conditions Water Supply and Use Analysis, contains both annual and monthly baseline and projected water-withdrawal and water-consumption data for dry conditions. Also, a dry-conditions water-adequacy analysis is included.

Appendix V, Streamflow Conditions, contains detailed background information on the derivation of the baseline streamflow information. A description of streamflow gauges used, correction factors applied, periods of record, and extreme flows of record are given for each subregion. Also included is the State-Regional Future estimate of average streamflow conditions.

Volume 4, Water Resources Regional Reports, consists of separately published reports for each of the 21 regions. Synopses of these reports are given in Volume 2, Part V.

Sources

Water Resources Council (1978) The Nation's Water Resources, 1975-2000. Second National Water Assessment. Vol. I: Summary and Vol. 3: Analytical Data Summary. Washington, D.C.: U.S. Government Printing Office.

STORET (DATA ON WATER QUALITY)

Description

The Federal Water Pollution Control Act Amendments of 1972 provided for the collection and dissemination of basic water quality data by EPA in cooperation with other federal departments and agencies and with public or private institutions and organizations concerned with water pollution control.

STORET is the name given to the computerized data base system maintained by EPA for the storage and retrieval of data relating to the quality of the waterways within and contiguous to the United States. The system encompasses not only the centralized data base of water quality data, but also the associated software for storing and retrieving data on water quality, water quality standards, point sources of pollution, pollution-caused fish kills, waste abatement needs, implementation schedules, and many other water quality related items. The system is used by federal, state, and local water quality agencies to solve such problems as defining the causes and effects of water pollution, measuring compliance with water quality standards, checking the status of waste treatment plant needs, and determining pollution trends.

Data Files

The Water Quality File is the largest file within STORET in terms of amount of data stored. Many individuals and organizations actively participate in the collection, storage, retrieval, and analysis of the data in the WQF. Information is gathered through cooperative programs involving EPA, state water pollution control authorities, and other governmental agencies covering over 3.5 million miles of rivers and streams, the Great Lakes, and coastal areas.

The WQF is a collection of data relating to the quality of the waterways within and contiguous to the United States. These data are gathered by a process called water quality monitoring whereby samples are taken of water from streams, rivers, lakes, and other bodies of water. These samples are then analyzed within a laboratory to determine the presence, and if present, the amount of pollutants and other particulates within the samples. The findings of these analyses are stored as data in the WQF.

The information on the results of the sample analyses within the WQF consists of two basic types of data: station data, which describe and categorize the geographical location of where a sample has been taken; and parametric data, which describe the conditions under which a sample was taken (such as date, time, and depth).

The number of unique collection points, or stations, in the WQF has grown significantly over the years, from about 150 in 1964 to over 200,000 in 1976. Station data may include the following types of station description information: a unique station identification number; the latitude and longitude of a station's location; the state and county codes identifying the stations political location; a River Mile Index identifying the station's hydrologic location; the major and minor river basins in which the station is located; as well as other station identification codes and descriptive information.

All toxic substances for which water quality analyses have been performed are also defined within this file.

The Waste Facilities/Municipal Waste Inventory File is the depository for data on municipal waste sources and disposal systems. It includes data from all communities and/or municipal waste facilities, including those privately owned, in the U.S. The Fish Kill File provides nationwide information on major pollution-caused fish kills which result from a variety of industrial, municipal, agricultural, and transportation-related operations. A fish kill is usually first noticed by a fisherman, camper or sportsman who, as an interested and concerned private citizen, reports the kill to a state official. In most instances, the state agency sends trained specialists to investigate and identify the size and cause of the kill. These specialists sometimes request the help of Environmental Protection Agency field personnel to assist in on-site investigations, or to make laboratory analyses of dead fish tissue samples. When water pollution is determined to be the cause of the kill, the state submits a report to the Environmental Protection Agency. Information from these reports is entered into the Fish Kill File, which contains fish kill data back to 1960.

Uses

STORET is utilized by a variety of governmental agencies and other organizations to achieve numerous objectives relating to water quality assessment and management, such as the following:

To detect changes in pollutants that could change ambient criteria/standards.

To help promote water quality programs by substantiating the effectiveness of other similar programs.

To help justify budget requests for water quality programs.

To help cut sampling costs by coordinating efforts with other organizations.

To provide a repository for data collection efforts.

To help identify where monitoring efforts are needed, thereby determining where funds need to be allocated.

To help design overall programs based upon the successes of others.

To help complete water quality management basin plans.

To help prepare fact sheets required for permit processing.

To detect changes in pollutants that could change existing permits.

Access

The utilization of computer technology has been an integral part of the design, growth, and use of the STORET system, tracing back to the initial development of the system in the early 1960s. Today, the STORET system runs on a large-scale, third generation IBM computer system which can easily accommodate the many observations of water quality data available in the system, and which can support a large number of users who are simultaneously utilizing the system from remote terminals located in their offices. The computer system is offered by a commercial time sharing service company whose primary business is to provide remote processing services to its subscribers or clients.

Representatives from state agencies and from other federal, interstate, and local government agencies may become users of STORET. The regional STORET representative can advise as to what monitoring activities are currently underway within the new user's area of interest; he can provide information on the amount and type of water quality data already present in the system that might be of interest to the user; and often, he can identify other users within the region who are pursuing an effort like or similar to that being considered by the potential user.

Data reported can reflect the most current information available, or it can draw upon the historical depth of the data, going back as far as the 1950s. Output alternatives include tabular listings of data values, statistical summaries of parameter values, and a number of plotting techniques, including line printer or precision plots of sample values or statistical analyses. Plotting capabilities also include station location plots which readily illustrate monitoring coverage over a selected geographical area. Violations to established water quality standards, on an individual or summary basis, may be reported.

Station selection options are extensive. An area of interest can be defined by a set of latitude-longitude coordinates (thereby describing a polygon enclosing the desired area), or by state, county or basin designations. One or more individual stations can be selected by specifying their station identification numbers. And stations may be chosen based upon the presence or absence of one or more specific parameters, or on prescribed values of the designated parameters.

Source

U.S. Environmental Protection Agency (n.d.) STORET User Handbook, Part OV: Overview. Office of Water and Hazardous Materials. Washington, D.C.: U.S. Environmental Protection Agency.

NATIONAL EMISSION DATA SYSTEM

ENVIRONMENTAL PROTECTION AGENCY

Background

The National Emissions Data System is a computerized data handling system which accepts, stores, and reports on information relating to sources of any of the five criteria pollutants (particulates, SO_x, NO_x, CO, and hydrocarbons). The development of NEDS was initiated in late 1971. Previously source-emissions data had been collected by various agencies but had usually not been stored in any common format. Thus, it was very difficult to relate the emissions data from one location to those for another location and produce meaningful reports that could be made readily available to interested individuals. NEDS was created to provide a centralized source-emissions data bank for which standard input forms would be used and output reports could be quickly and efficiently generated to meet user requirements.

Data Types and Collections

In NEDS, major distinction is made between two types of sources: point sources and area sources. Point sources, in the broadest sense, are stationary sources large enough to be identified and tracked individually. Through NEDS reporting requirements, they are any plants with a potential of emitting more than 100 tons/year of any of the criteria pollutants. Area sources, on the other hand, are those stationary and mobile sources which individually emit much less than 100 tons/year and are too small and too numerous to keep individual records on. In NEDS, area sources are considered collectively on a county basis. A large boiler within a power plant would be an example of a point source, whereas a single automobile is an example of the type of source considered collectively as an area source.

The point source data are collected by state and local air pollution control agencies utilizing state questionnaires and plant visits. These data are coded onto the point source form and submitted for inclusion in NEDS through the EPA regional offices. The states are required to update the data as new sources are constructed, and when existing sources are modified or cease operation.

The current NEDS point source file reflects the latest data reported by state agencies. Since annual reporting is not required for all sources, all point sources in NEDS do not have a common year of record. It is assumed that no significant changes have occurred for those sources whose reported year of record is older than the current year.

Data reported for point sources in NEDS may be categorized according to the following groups:

General source information: name, address, type(s) of source(s), Standard Industrial Classification, year of record, and comments

Emissions data: operating or production rates and capacities, estimated emissions, estimation method, and type and efficiency of control device for each pollutant.

Modeling parameters: UTM coordinates of source, stack height and diameter, exhaust gas temperature, and gas flow rate.

Compliance information: allowable emissions compliance status, and compliance schedules.

NEDS point source data are organized into three hierarchical levels.

1. Plant level data apply to an entire facility defined as a point source.
2. Point level data apply to individual emission points within a plant

A plant may contain any number of emission points. A point is that portion of a facility that may be considered individually for emission purposes. A point may contain one or more processes or pieces of equipment that are related in contributing to the emissions from the point. In most cases, a point emits pollutants through a single confined location such as a stack, but it may emit pollutants at more than one location or at no clearly defined location within a plant.

3. Process Level data apply to individual processes within a point and are utilized to calculate emissions.

Each process is defined by a Source Classification Code (SCC). In general, for each SCC there are emission factors, which relate the quantity of pollutants generated by a process to annual process operating rate. These emission factors are used to compute emissions. Multiple processes and multiple SCCs may be grouped under one emission point, as in the case of boilers using two fuels or two separate processes sharing the same stack. The point source file provides for the use of alternative methods for determining the emissions being reported.

The point source data are routinely submitted by states to the regional offices and by the regional offices to the National Air Data Branch (NADB). These data are updated on a regular update schedule and are then available for generation of publications or computerized reports.

Area source data are developed mainly by NADB, but may be supplemented by data voluntarily submitted by state agencies. NEDS area source data are grouped as follows:

General source information: name and location of area (county) source, year of record.

Activity levels: countywide activity level of each area source category (e.g., tons of coal burned in all domestic space heating equipment in a county).

Emissions data: emissions estimates for the entire county for each pollutant as well as for each source category for each pollutant.

Activity levels are derived primarily from related information published by other federal agencies, supplemented by special data developed by EPA for the purpose of developing NEDS area source inventories. Published data such as fuel use by state, motor vehicle miles of travel by state and county, and forest fire acres burned by state are used with related data such as employment, population, and miscellaneous geographic or economic data available on a county-by-county basis to derive annual estimates of the activity levels for each of the NEDS area source categories. The activity levels derived are adjusted to account for point source activity (such as fuel use by point sources) so that the area source data reflect only the activity levels (and resulting calculated emissions) that are not accounted for by point sources.

The area source emission estimates are calculated for each source category utilizing emission factors which are contained in the NEDS area source emission factor file. For many categories, the same emission factors are used for all counties; however, for some source categories, state or county specific emission factors account for local variables that affect emissions. These more specific emission factors are used in NEDS calculations for all highway motor vehicle categories, fugitive dust categories, and for selected other categories in a few counties where data are available to develop more applicable emission factors than the national emission factors.

The area source data are updated on an annual basis by the National Air Data Branch. All area source data in the file at any given time therefore reflect a common year of record. Currently in NEDS, information is being maintained on approximately 175,000 point sources and about 3,200 area (county) sources in the 55 states and territories of the United States. The point sources total will fluctuate as additional sources are reported, new sources come into operation, or old sources cease operations, whereas the number of area sources is fixed by the number of counties.

Access

Published annually by EPA, the National Emissions Report contains a NEDS emission summary table for each of the 55 "states" and each of the 247 Air Quality Control Regions (ACQRs) in the United States. The tables that constitute the body of the document are as follows:

1. Summary for the United States
2. Summary tables for each state
3. Tables for each AQCR or portion of an (interstate) AQCR lying within that state.
4. Tables for all of the interstate AQCRs, each one in its entirety.

The individual tables are organized according to the major categories of sources of emissions of the five pollutants. The five major source categories are:

1. Fuel combustion
2. Industrial processes
3. Solid waste disposal
4. Transportation
5. Miscellaneous

Each annual report reflects data determined to be the most representative of actual emissions for a particular calendar year. Thus, the 1975 NEDS National Emissions Report, based on area source data for 1975, and point source data best representing 1975, provides the best available data from NEDS on actual air pollutant emissions for calendar year 1975.

The NEDS Fuel Use Report is published annually, concurrent with the NEDS National Emissions Report. This publication contains a fuel summary for the nation and for each state in both English and metric units. The publication contains fuel use totals for each fuel for major source categories such as area sources (stationary and mobile) and point sources (external combustion, internal combustion, and in-process fuel).

Computerized Reports

These can be broadly classified as raw data reports and summary reports. The raw data reports list the actual stored data or a subset of the data based on specific location and data options. The summary reports provide various geographical summaries of emissions and fuel consumption. The following table summarizes some of the reports available at their various retrieval options.

SUMMARY OF NEDS RETRIEVALS

Report	General Selection Capability	Nation (All Records in File)	State	EPA Region	AQCR	State Portions of Interstate	All Counties in a State	All Counties in an AQCR	County
Raw Data Reports									
Point Source Report	X								
Condensed Point Source Report	X								
Allowed vs. Computed Emissions Report	X								
AQDM Data Tabulation Report		X					X	X	X
Quick Look Report	X								
Area Source Report		X	X		X	X	X	X	X
Area Source Cards		X					X		X
Area Source File on Tape		X					X		X
Point Source Cards	X								
Point Source Subfile on Tape	X								
Summary Reports									
Emission Summary Report		X	X	X	X	X	X		X
Annual Fuel Summary Report		X	X		X	X	X		X
Potential Emissions Report	X	X	X		X	X	X		X
Plant Emissions Report	X								
SCC Emissions Report		X							
Plant Name Report	X								
Emissions by SCC Report	X								
SIC Emissions Report	X	X	X		X	X	X		X
County Point and Area Source Emissions Report	X						X		
Modeling Parameters Report		X							
Management Reports									
Plant-Point-SCC County Report		X							
Missing Item Report	X	X	X		X	X	X		X
Highest Plant Number in County Report		X							

Sources

U.S. Environmental Protection Agency (1976) AEROS Overview, Volume I, AEROS Manual Series. EPA-450/2-76-001. Research Triangle Park, N.C.: U.S. Environmental Protection Agency.

U.S. Environmental Protection Agency (1978) Update Number 1, AEROS Overview, Volume I, AEROS Manual Series. EPA-450/2-76-001-1. Research Triangle Park, N.C.: U.S. Environmental Protection Agency.

U.S. Environmental Protection Agency (1980) NEDS: National Emissions Data System Information. Office of Air Quality Planning and Standards, EPA-450/4-80/03. Research Triangle Park, N.C.: U.S. Environmental Protection Agency.

U.S. Environmental Protection Agency (1980) Update Number 2, AEROS Overview, Volume I, AEROS Manual Series. EPA-450/2-76-001-2. Research Triangle Park, N.C.: U.S. Environmental Protection Agency.

STORAGE AND RETRIEVAL OF AEROMETRIC DATA (SAROAD)

ENVIRONMENTAL PROTECTION AGENCY

Background

SAROAD is a computerized data handling system that accepts, stores, and reports on information relating to ambient air quality. Development of SAROAD was preceded by early programs for the collection of air quality and associated meterological data. The National Air Sampling Network (NASN) was developed in 1953 as the first nationwide air monitoring system. In 1955, the present policy that state and local governments have the fundamental responsibility for dealing with community air pollution problems was established. Subsequently the scope of NASN broadened tremendously, both in geographical and pollutant coverage. The passage of the Clean Air Act of 1963, authorizing the awarding of grants directly to state and local agencies for maintenance of their own control programs, produced an additional need for dissemination of air pollution data. This need generated the idea for creation of a national air quality data bank and by 1966, the SAROAD computer system had been developed.

Data Types and Collection

There are two distinct classes of information that are accommodated in SAROAD: ambient air quality data and sampling site information.

Ambient air quality data This information must be supplied to SAROAD in order to completely characterize the air quality at a site over a specified time interval. This includes the location of the sampling site, the pollutants which are monitored at that site, the methods of collection and analysis of each pollutant monitored, the magnitude of each pollutant concentration, and the time interval over which the measurements are made.

Site information Site information includes detailed descriptive information about the location and environment of the sampling site. This includes the state, a county, and city wherein the site is located, the latitude and longitude of the site and its elevation above the local terrain and mean sea level. It also includes a description of the site location (center city, suburban, rural, or remote) as well as the dominating influence on the sampler within approximately a 1-mile radius of the sampling site (industrial, residential, commercial, or mobile).

Air quality data are supplied continuously to the National Air Data Branch of EPA by state and local agencies as well as a number of federal air quality networks. Site information, on the other hand, is submitted only once for each location, although it must be updated whenever the site environment changes.

Because SAROAD, like NEDS, is a large computerized system, and must handle data from all the states and territories, all information submitted to SAROAD must be in a standardized format. To facilitate this, special SAROAD input formats have been defined, and an elaborate system of codes has been established to ensure standardization and ease of data submission on the part of any contributing agency. In addition, a number of edit checks have been instituted to screen all data being submitted to the system.

Currently, air quality information is being submitted by over 6,000 air monitoring sites across the nation. The number of aerometric data values stored in SAROAD is approaching 100,000,000, with approximately 20,000,000 values being added to the system annually.

Access

Air Quality Data - Annual Statistics Published annually by EPA, this report contains summary statistics for the air quality data generated by state and local agencies as required by EPA regulations. This publication makes particulate, carbon monoxide, sulfur dioxide, nitrogen dioxide, hydrocarbons, and oxidant data available to all agencies and the public. It provides a one-line summary for each site-pollutant combination and is sorted by pollutant, method of collection and analysis, state, Air Quality Control Region, area, and site. This is the only routine air quality data publication published by the National Air Data Branch.

Directory of Active Air Monitoring Sites Published annually by EPA, this publication contains the complete site description for any site that has reported data to SAROAD for the specific year. In addition to the site description, the pollutants, method of collection and analysis, time interval, units, and number of observations are also listed for each site. The sites are listed in alphabetical order by state and alphabetically within each state.

Computerized Reports Both raw data and summary reports can be obtained from the computer. In most of these reports, various selection criteria can be employed which allow the user to limit the number of records the system will process in generating a particular report. For instance, most of these reports have geographical selection criteria which allow the user to obtain records for certain areas of interest such as a particular state, AQCR, etc. In some reports, the user can select by pollutant or a specific pollutant/method or pollutant/interval combination. Still others allow the user to select only data pertaining to specified years.

Raw data reports list the actual stored data on pollutant concentrations in the ambient atmosphere. They give the geographic location of the site, as specified by the Site Code; the times and averaging periods of the data; and the method of data collection and analysis. Raw data reports include the following:

1. Raw data for less than 24-hour averaging periods.
2. Raw data for sampling periods equal to or greater than 24 hours.
3. Standards-violations reports.
4. Site description inventory.
5. Raw data in SAROAD format.
6. Meteorological raw data report.

Summary reports list quarterly and annual summary statistics for individual sites and provide summaries of available data on a state or national basis. Summary reports include the following:

1. Yearly frequency distribution.
2. Quarterly frequency distribution.
3. Yearly report by quarters.
4. Inventory reports.
5. Summary report of valid data.
6. Summary of monitoring activities.
7. Active site report.

Sources

U.S. Environmental Protection Agency (1976) Aeros Overview, Volume I, Aeros Manual Series, EPA-450/2-76-001. Research Triangle Park, N.C.: U.S. Environmental Protection Agency.

U.S. Environmental Protection Agency (1978) Update Number 1, Aeros Manual Series, Volume I, EPA-450/2-76-001-1. Research Triangle Park, N.C.: U.S. Environmental Protection Agency.

U.S. Environmental Protection Agency (1979) SAROAD (Storage and Retrieval of Aerometric Data) Information. Office of Air Quality Planning and Standards EPA-450/4-79-005. Research Triangle Park, N.C.: U.S. Environmental Protection Agency.

APPENDIX F

HEALTH SERVICE AREA DATA COLLECTION

While the health service agencies (HSAs) are not yet functioning in their data collection efforts, several presentations at a recent health statistics conference concerned actual and potential types of data collection that HSAs might usefully perform. This appendix presents three examples.

POPULATION-BASED DATA

The executive director of the Cooperative Health Information Center in Vermont has suggested several data needs and uses from his experience in providing data to an all-rural statewide HSA (Dorsey 1979). Before the HSA, several facilities requested renovation and expansion permits based on data that reflected only institutional utilization. As a consequence, decisions were made that added facilities, equipment, and staff at particular sites without regard to the availability of similar resources in nearby communities. The HSA requested an extensive data set that tabulates the rate of utilization of health resources not by institution but by subgroups of the population. Such information, reflecting consumption of resources by where people live rather than by where they are served, will be the basis for the Vermont Health System Plan. The use of such data in resource allocation decisions will add a dimension to the planning and regulation process that will address over-utilization and underutilization by population subgroups as well as by institutions. This approach also has caused others to ask how many cases came from a particular area rather than how many cases a particular institution handled last year.

This approach argues for the availability and utility of population-based data, both with respect to utilization and to resource availability. Population basing requires the definition of several areas for various types of health care resources. If the records (i.e., encounter forms) of various types of providers include patients' place of residence, historical patterns can be used to establish these areas. To generate rates for these defined areas additionally requires small-area population estimates. To make appropriate comparisons between areas also requires adjustments for age and sex, so detailed age and sex information is required on the encounter forms and detailed population age and sex breakdowns are needed. Similar encounter data for ambulatory cases would also be needed.

EXPENDITURE DATA

Another local planner, representing the HSA in northeast Florida, has developed several information sources for estimating local health expenditures (a primary interest of the HSA legislation is cost containment). The following are some examples of the types and sources of information he has collected (Bredenberg 1979):

Hospital expenditures. The American Hospital Association's annual guide lists expenses for most hospitals.

Physician expenditures. Local agencies receive from the Health Care Financing Administration a listing showing Medicare expenditures by county. Using national data from the Social Security Administration, an index was developed that produced a good estimate of expenditures for physician services.

Dentists' services. The same index used for physicians' services was used for dentists' services, supplemented by IRS data showing the average receipts for dentists by state.

Nursing home care. In Florida, this is provided by the state office that administers Medicaid. This can be supplemented by a phone call to a nursing home about their charges and bed count and/or patient days.

Drugs. Each year *Sales Marketing Management Magazine* computes information on drugstore sales by county. However, the proportion of this that goes for drugs is estimated differently in two Department of Commerce estimates.

Eyeglasses. The planner made the assumption that a greater number of eyeglass expenditures will result from a greater number of optometrists and opthalmologists. The AMA and IRS give rates of these specialities per 100,000 people nationally. The planner compared the local count with national data and developed an expenditure estimate. If the state forbids eyeglass price advertising and the national discount eyeglass chains do not operate in the area, the price per unit may be 25 percent higher.

Expenses for prepayment and administration. A source for this information is an article, "Private Health Insurance in 1975," published in the *Social Security Bulletin* in June 1977. For governmental costs, use national per-capital data and make modifications based on local conditions, e.g., the percentage of persons on Medicare in the area compared to national averages.

Research and construction. Most of the information on this can be obtained from HSA files on Certificate of Need actions and from the agency that does the A-95 reviews.

Who pays the bills. There are six sources of data for this information: Medicare statistics by county for 1976; Medicaid data from the appropriate state agency; budget data from local government; *The Source Book of Insurance Data*, for insurance coverage by state for various health expenditures; spot check of hospitals for sources of payment; and estimates of sources of payments from local medical and dental societies.

ENVIRONMENTAL ILLNESS DATA

Another author has noted the importance of gathering environmental data and has suggested that one important rural data problem to be handled by HSAs is to gather data on rural water supplies and individual sewage disposal systems, which are found mostly in rural areas. Because of the potential health problems these facilities can cause, he suggests that the following data be collected (Lisella 1979):

- Prevalence of water-borne diseases and gastrointestinal disorders in the area.
- Expenditures for treatment of gastrointestinal disorders.
- Extent of hospitalization by persons consuming water from private supplies or by persons disposing of sewage through private systems.
- The extent of the area and population covered by existing water and sewage systems.
- Adequacy of laws or ordinances relating to water supplies and sewage disposal systems.
- Extent of past expenditures and plans for future development and maintenance of water supply and sewage disposal systems in a HSA.

REFERENCES

Bredenberg, K. (1979) Estimating health expenditures at the local level. Pp. 188-190 in The Public Health Conference on Records and Statistics: The People's Health: Facts, Figures, and the Future. National Center for Health Satistics, Public Health Service. DHEW Publication No. (PHS) 79-1214. Washington, D.C.: U.S. Department of Health, Education, and Welfare.

Dorsey, F.C. (1979) Data needs for health resource policy: a local view. Pp. 257-259 in The Public Health Conference on Records and Statistics: The People's Health: Facts, Figures, and the Future. National Center for Health Satistics, Public Health Service. DHEW Publication No. (PHS) 79-1214, Washington, D.C.: U.S. Department of Health, Education, and Welfare.

Lisella, F.S. (1979) Data aspects of a strategy for linking environmental criteria into health planning. Pp. 357-359 in The Public Health Conference on Records and Statistics: The People's Health: Facts, Figures, and the Future. National Center for Health Satistics, Public Health Service. DHEW Publication No. (PHS) 79-1214. Washington, D.C.: U.S. Department of Health, Education, and Welfare.

APPENDIX G

REGRESSION ESTIMATION FOR SMALL AREAS

WAYNE A. FULLER and GEORGE BATTESE

METHOD

In this appendix we present a method of constructing estimates for small areas. We assume that current estimates are desired for the variable Y for N areas. The census value for the preceding census and values of a vector of explanatory variables are assumed to be available for each of the N areas. The vector of explanatory variables might contain, for example, the change in retail sales between the census year and the current year and the change in school attendance between the census year and the current year. Also available are sample estimates of the current value of Y for a random sample of n of the areas. Let

Y_i denote the current census value for the i-th area,

$$i = 1,2,\dots,N;$$

Y_i^* denote the prior census value for the i-th area,

$$i = 1,2,\dots,N;$$

$\underset{\sim}{X}_i$ denote a k-dimensional row vector of explanatory variables for the i-th area, $i = 1,2,\dots,N$; and

$\tilde{Y}_i$ denote an unbiased estimator for the current census value in the i-th sample area, $i = 1,2,\dots,n$.

We assume that

$$\tilde{Y}_i = Y_i + u_i\ , \quad i = 1,2,\dots,n \tag{1}$$

and

$$Y_i - Y_i^* = \underset{\sim}{X}_i\underset{\sim}{\beta} + e_i\ , \quad i = 1,2,\dots,n,\ n+1,\dots,N, \tag{2}$$

where

$$u_i \ , \ i = 1,2,\ldots,n, \text{ are N.I.D.}(0,\sigma_u^2);$$

$$e_i \ , \ i = 1,2,\ldots,N, \text{ are N.I.D.}(0,\sigma_e^2);$$

and u_i and e_i are independently distributed. We also assume that $\underset{\sim}{X}_i = (1,\underset{\sim}{W}_i)$, where $\underset{\sim}{W}_i$, $i = 1,2,\ldots,N$, are N.I.D. $(\underset{\sim}{\mu},\underset{\sim}{V})$ and are independent of the u_i and e_i.

The model representation (2) assumes that the changes in the census values can be treated as a sample from a superpopulation. Note that the sample areas are represented by the subscripts $i = 1,2,\ldots,n$, and the nonsample areas are represented by the subscripts $i = n+1,n+2,\ldots,N$. The assumption of constant error variance, σ_u^2, is to simplify the presentation. The assumption of normal $\underset{\sim}{X}_i$ permits us to obtain an exact expression for the error of prediction. Both of these two assumptions can be relaxed.

From the sample data, the parameters of the model are estimated from the linear model involving the observable variables,

$$\tilde{Y}_i - Y_i^* = \underset{\sim}{X}_i\underset{\sim}{\beta} + (e_i + u_i), \quad i = 1,2,\ldots,n \ , \tag{3}$$

and the least-squares estimator for $\underset{\sim}{\beta}$ is

$$\hat{\underset{\sim}{\beta}} = (\sum_{i=1}^{n} \underset{\sim}{X}_i'\underset{\sim}{X}_i)^{-1} \sum_{i=1}^{n} \underset{\sim}{X}_i'(\tilde{Y}_i - Y_i^*). \tag{4}$$

It is easily verified that, under the model (1)-(2), the conditional expectations of the current census values, given the sample data, are

$$E[Y_i|(\tilde{Y}_i, \underset{\sim}{X}_i)] = Y_i^* + \underset{\sim}{X}_i\underset{\sim}{\beta} + \sigma_e^2(\sigma_e^2 + \sigma_u^2)^{-1}(\tilde{Y}_i - Y_i^* - \underset{\sim}{X}_i\underset{\sim}{\beta}) \ ,$$

$$i = 1,2,\ldots,n, \tag{5}$$

and

$$E[Y_i|(\tilde{Y}_j, \underset{\sim}{X}_j) \ , \ j = 1,2,\ldots,n] = Y_i^* + \underset{\sim}{X}_i\underset{\sim}{\beta} \ , \quad i = n+1,n+2,\ldots,N \ . \tag{6}$$

We consider the following predictions for the current census values,

$$\hat{Y}_i = \begin{cases} Y_i^* + \underset{\sim}{X}_i\hat{\underset{\sim}{\beta}} + w(\tilde{Y}_i - Y_i^* - \underset{\sim}{X}_i\hat{\underset{\sim}{\beta}}) \ , & i = 1,2,\ldots,n \quad \text{(7a)} \\ Y_i^* + \underset{\sim}{X}_i\hat{\underset{\sim}{\beta}} \ , & i = n+1,n+2,\ldots,N \quad \text{(7b)} \end{cases}$$

where $w = \sigma_e^2(\sigma_e^2 + \sigma_u^2)^{-1}$. It is assumed above that the variances σ_e^2 and σ_u^2 are known. (Extensions are discussed in the latter part of this appendix.) The mean squared errors for the predictors (7a), (7b) for the sample and nonsample areas are given in Theorem 1.

Theorem 1. Let the assumptions of the model (1)-(2) hold with σ_e^2 and σ_u^2 known, and $n > k + 1$. Then the predictor (7a) has mean squared error for the sample areas given by

$$\sum_{i=1}^{n} E(Y_i - \hat{Y}_i)^2 = (n - k)[(1 - w)^2 \sigma_e^2 + w^2 \sigma_u^2] + k\sigma_u^2 , \tag{8a}$$

and the predictor (7b) has mean squared error for the nonsample areas given by

$$\sum_{i=n+1}^{N} E(Y_i - \hat{Y}_i)^2 = (N - n)\sigma_e^2$$

$$+ (nk - 2)(N - n)[n(n - k - 1)]^{-1} (\sigma_e^2 + \sigma_u^2) \quad . \tag{8b}$$

Proof. Given the predictors (7a) for the sample areas, it follows from the model assumptions (1)-(2) that

$$Y_i - \hat{Y}_i = \underset{\sim}{X}_i\underset{\sim}{\beta} + e_i - \underset{\sim}{X}_i\hat{\underset{\sim}{\beta}} - w(\underset{\sim}{X}_i\underset{\sim}{\beta} + e_i + u_i - \underset{\sim}{X}_i\hat{\underset{\sim}{\beta}}) , \quad i = 1,2,\ldots,n,$$

$$= (1 - w)e_i - wu_i - (1 - w)\underset{\sim}{X}_i(\hat{\underset{\sim}{\beta}} - \underset{\sim}{\beta}) .$$

Thus

$$\sum_{i=1}^{n} E(Y_i - \hat{Y}_i)^2 = \sum_{i=1}^{n} \{(1 - w)^2 \sigma_e^2 + w^2 \sigma_u^2 - 2(1 - w)^2 E[\underset{\sim}{X}_i(\hat{\underset{\sim}{\beta}} - \underset{\sim}{\beta})e_i]$$

$$+ 2w(1 - w)E[\underset{\sim}{X}_i(\hat{\underset{\sim}{\beta}} - \underset{\sim}{\beta})u_i] + (1 - w)^2 E[\underset{\sim}{X}_i(\hat{\underset{\sim}{\beta}} - \underset{\sim}{\beta})(\hat{\underset{\sim}{\beta}} - \underset{\sim}{\beta})'\underset{\sim}{X}_i']\} .$$

We have

$$\sum_{i=1}^{n} E[\underset{\sim}{X}_i(\hat{\underset{\sim}{\beta}} - \underset{\sim}{\beta})e_i] = \sum_{i=1}^{n} E\{\underset{\sim}{X}_i E[(\sum_{j=1}^{n} \underset{\sim}{X}_j'\underset{\sim}{X}_j)^{-1} \sum_{j=1}^{n} \underset{\sim}{X}_j'(e_j + u_j)e_i | \underset{\sim}{X}_i]\}$$

$$= \sum_{i=1}^{n} E\{\underset{\sim}{X}_i (\sum_{j=1}^{n} \underset{\sim}{X}_j' \underset{\sim}{X}_j)^{-1} \underset{\sim}{X}_i' \sigma_e^2\}$$

$$= E\{\sum_{i=1}^{n} \underset{\sim}{X}_i (\sum_{j=1}^{n} \underset{\sim}{X}_j' \underset{\sim}{X}_j)^{-1} \underset{\sim}{X}_i' \sigma_e^2\}$$

$$= E\{tr[(\sum_{j=1}^{n} \underset{\sim}{X}_j' \underset{\sim}{X}_j)^{-1} (\sum_{i=1}^{n} \underset{\sim}{X}_i' \underset{\sim}{X}_i) \sigma_e^2]\}$$

$$= k\sigma_e^2 \ .$$

Similarly,

$$\sum_{i=1}^{n} E[\underset{\sim}{X}_i (\hat{\underset{\sim}{\beta}} - \underset{\sim}{\beta}) u_i] = k\sigma_u^2$$

and

$$\sum_{i=1}^{n} E[\underset{\sim}{X}_i (\hat{\underset{\sim}{\beta}} - \underset{\sim}{\beta}) (\hat{\underset{\sim}{\beta}} - \underset{\sim}{\beta})' \underset{\sim}{X}_i'] = k(\sigma_e^2 + \sigma_u^2) \ .$$

Therefore,

$$\sum_{i=1}^{n} E(Y_i - \hat{Y}_i)^2 = n[(1 - w)^2 \sigma_e^2 + w^2 \sigma_u^2] - 2(1 - w)^2 k\sigma_e^2 + 2w(1 - w)k\sigma_u^2$$

$$+ (1 - w)^2 k(\sigma_e^2 + \sigma_u^2)$$

$$= (n - k)[(1 - w)^2 \sigma_e^2 + w^2 \sigma_u^2] + k\sigma_u^2 \ .$$

For the predictors 7(b) for the nonsample counties, we have

$$Y_i - \hat{Y}_i = e_i - \underset{\sim}{X}_i (\hat{\underset{\sim}{\beta}} - \underset{\sim}{\beta}) \ , \quad i = n+1, n+2, \ldots, N$$

and

$$\sum_{i=n+1}^{N} E(Y_i - \hat{Y}_i)^2 = \sum_{i=n+1}^{N} \{\sigma_e^2 - 2E[\underset{\sim}{X}_i (\hat{\underset{\sim}{\beta}} - \underset{\sim}{\beta}) e_i]$$

$$+ E[\underset{\sim}{X}_i (\hat{\underset{\sim}{\beta}} - \underset{\sim}{\beta}) (\hat{\underset{\sim}{\beta}} - \underset{\sim}{\beta})' \underset{\sim}{X}_i']\} \ .$$

But for $i = n+1, n+2, \ldots, N$,

$$E[(\hat{\beta} - \beta)e_i | X_i] = E[(\sum_{j=1}^{n} X_j' X_j)^{-1} \sum_{j=1}^{n} X_j'(e_j + u_j)e_i | X_i] = 0 .$$

Now

$$\sum_{i=n+1}^{N} E[X_i(\hat{\beta} - \beta)(\hat{\beta} - \beta)' X_i'] = \sum_{i=n+1}^{N} E[X_i(\sum_{j=1}^{n} X_j' X_j)^{-1} X_i'](\sigma_e^2 + \sigma_u^2)$$

$$= E\{ \sum_{i=n+1}^{N} X_i(\sum_{j=1}^{n} X_j' X_j)^{-1} X_i')(\sigma_e^2 + \sigma_u^2)\} .$$

Because

$$X_i = (1, W_i) , \quad i = 1,2,\ldots,N ,$$

$$(\sum_{j=1}^{n} X_j' X_j)^{-1} = \begin{pmatrix} n^{-1} + \bar{W}_n A^{-1} \bar{W}_n' & -\bar{W}_n A^{-1} \\ -A^{-1}\bar{W}_n' & A^{-1} \end{pmatrix} ,$$

where

$$\bar{W}_n \equiv n^{-1} \sum_{j=1}^{n} W_j \quad \text{and}$$

$$A = \sum_{j=1}^{n} (W_j - \bar{W}_n)'(W_j - \bar{W}_n) .$$

Further, it can be shown that

$$\sum_{i=n+1}^{N} X_i(\sum_{j=1}^{n} X_j' X_j)^{-1} X_i' = (N - n)n^{-1}$$

$$+ (N - n)(\bar{W}_n - \bar{W}_{N-n})A^{-1} (\bar{W}_n - \bar{W}_{N-n})'$$

$$+ \sum_{i=n+1}^{N} (\underset{\sim}{W}_i - \overline{\underset{\sim}{W}}_{N-n}) \underset{\sim}{A}^{-1} (\underset{\sim}{W}_i - \overline{\underset{\sim}{W}}_{N-n})',$$

where

$$\overline{\underset{\sim}{W}}_{N-n} \equiv (N-n)^{-1} \sum_{i=n+1}^{N} \underset{\sim}{W}_i .$$

By the assumptions of the model (1)-(2), $[n^{-1} + (N - n)^{-1}]^{-\frac{1}{2}}(\overline{\underset{\sim}{W}}_n - \overline{\underset{\sim}{W}}_{N-n})$ is distributed as a $N(\underset{\sim}{0}, \underset{\sim}{V})$ independent of $\underset{\sim}{A}$, where $\underset{\sim}{A}$ has the same distribution as

$$\sum_{i=1}^{n-1} \underset{\sim}{Z}_i' \underset{\sim}{Z}_i ,$$

and $\underset{\sim}{Z}_i'$, $i = 1,2,\ldots,n-1$, are N.I.D. $(\underset{\sim}{0},\underset{\sim}{V})$. Therefore, the quadratic form,

$$[n^{-1} + (N-n)^{-1}]^{-1} (\overline{\underset{\sim}{W}}_n - \overline{\underset{\sim}{W}}_{N-n}) \underset{\sim}{A}^{-1} (\overline{\underset{\sim}{W}}_n - \overline{\underset{\sim}{W}}_{N-n})'$$

$$[(n-1) - (k-1) + 1](k - 1)^{-1} ,$$

has a central F-distribution with k-1 and n-k+1 degrees of freedom (see Anderson 1958:6). Hence, the expectation of the quadratic form is $(n - k + 1)(n - k - 1)^{-1}$.

Further, $[1 - (N - n)^{-1}]^{-1}(\underset{\sim}{W}_i - \overline{\underset{\sim}{W}}_{N-n})\underset{\sim}{A}^{-1}(\underset{\sim}{W}_i - \overline{\underset{\sim}{W}}_{N-n})' (n - k + 1)(k - 1)^{-1}$ has a central F-distribution with $k - 1$ and $n - k + 1$ degrees of freedom. Thus,

$$E\{ \sum_{i=n+1}^{N} \underset{\sim}{X}_i (\sum_{j=1}^{n} \underset{\sim}{X}_j' \underset{\sim}{X}_j)^{-1} \underset{\sim}{X}_i' \}$$

$$= (N - n)n^{-1} + (N - n)[n^{-1} + (N - n)^{-1}](n - k + 1)^{-1}(k - 1)$$

$$[(n - k + 1)(n - k - 1)^{-1}] + (N - n)[1 - (N - n)^{-1}]$$

$$(n - k + 1)^{-1}(k - 1)[(n - k + 1)(n - k - 1)^{-1}]$$

$$= (N - n)\{n^{-1} + n^{-1}(1 + n)(k - 1)(n - k - 1)^{-1}]$$

$$= (N - n)(n - k - 1)^{-1} n^{-1}(nk - 2) .$$

Therefore,

$$\sum_{i=n+1}^{N} E(Y_i - \hat{Y}_i)^2 = (N - n)\sigma_e^2$$
$$+ (N - n)(nk - 2) [n(n - k - 1)]^{-1}(\sigma_e^2 + \sigma_u^2) .$$

Note that the assumption that σ_e^2 and σ_u^2 are known was used in proving result (8a) but was not needed to obtain result (8b).

The results of Theorem 1 are basic for a comparison of the efficiency of the regression predictors (7a)-(7b) with the prior census values. A sufficient condition for the regression predictors to have smaller mean squared error than the prior census values is stated in the following theorem.

Theorem 2. Let the assumptions of Theorem 1 hold and let

$$k(\sigma_u^2 + \sigma_e^2) < (n - k - 1)E[(\underset{\sim}{X}_i\underset{\sim}{\beta})^2] , \tag{9}$$

then

$$\sum_{i=1}^{N} E(Y_i - \hat{Y}_i)^2 < \sum_{i=1}^{N} E(Y_i - Y_i^*)^2 .$$

Proof: By equation (8b),

$$\sum_{i=n+1}^{N} E(Y_i - \hat{Y}_i)^2 < (N - n)\sigma_e^2 + k(N - n)(n - k - 1)^{-1}(\sigma_e^2 + \sigma_u^2)$$

$$= (N - n)\{\sigma_e^2 + k(\sigma_e^2 + \sigma_u^2)(n - k - 1)^{-1}\}$$

$$< (N - n)\{\sigma_e^2 + E[(\underset{\sim}{X}_i\underset{\sim}{\beta})^2]\}$$

$$= \sum_{i=n+1}^{N} E(Y_i - Y_i^*)^2 .$$

However, by equation (8a) and the fact that

$$(1 - w)^2\,\sigma_e^2 + w^2\sigma_u^2 = \sigma_e^2\,\sigma_u^2(\sigma_e^2 + \sigma_u^2)^{-1} ,$$

it follows that

$$\sum_{i=1}^{n} E(Y_i - \hat{Y}_i)^2 < (n - k)\sigma_e^2 + k\sigma_u^2$$

$$< (n - k - 1)\sigma_e^2 + k(\sigma_u^2 + \sigma_e^2)$$

$$< (n - k - 1)\{\sigma_e^2 + E[(\underset{\sim}{X}_i\underset{\sim}{\beta})^2]\}$$

$$< \sum_{i=1}^{n} E(Y_i - Y_i^*)^2 .$$

Therefore,

$$\sum_{i=1}^{N} E(Y_i - \hat{Y}_i)^2 < \sum_{i=1}^{N} E(Y_i - Y_i^*)^2 . \qquad \square$$

Provided the vector $\underset{\sim}{\beta}$ is not zero, it is possible to select a sample design for which the inequality (9) is true. That is, by choosing a design with a sufficiently large sample size, n , and a sufficiently small variance, σ_u^2 , of measurement error, it is possible to construct predictors superior to the preceding census values.

We developed the estimators for the areas under the assumption that the area means are normally distributed and that the variances σ_e^2 and σ_u^2 are known. If σ_u^2 , but not σ_e^2 , is known, it is possible to use the estimator of James and Stein (1961) discussed by Efron and Morris (1973, 1975) for the n observed areas. The James-Stein estimator has been applied to the small area problem by Fay and Herriot (1979). The estimators for the $N - n$ areas that are not observed remain unchanged if σ_e^2 is unknown. That is, the conditions necessary for the regression estimators to be superior to the preceding census values for the $N - n$ areas that are not observed are not dependent upon knowledge of σ_e^2 and σ_u^2 . If σ_u^2 is known, the modified James-Stein estimator for the n observed areas is

$$\dot{Y}_i = Y_i^* + \underset{\sim}{X}_i\hat{\underset{\sim}{\beta}} + \hat{w}(\tilde{Y}_i - Y_i^* - \underset{\sim}{X}_i\hat{\underset{\sim}{\beta}}) ,$$

where

$$\hat{w} = \max\{0, 1 - \sigma_u^2(n - k - 2)[(n - k)s^2]^{-1}\}$$

$$s^2 = (n - k)^{-1} \sum_{i=1}^{n} (\tilde{Y}_i - Y_i^* - \underset{\sim}{X}_i\hat{\underset{\sim}{\beta}})^2 .$$

The following theorem demonstrates that there is a modest increase in the mean squared error associated with the estimation of σ_e^2 .

Theorem 3. Let the assumptions of model (1)-(2) hold with σ_u^2 known and $n > k + 2$. Then the mean squared error for the sample counties satisfies

$$\sum_{i=1}^{n} E\{(\dot{Y}_i - Y_i)^2\} < \sum_{i=1}^{n} E\{(\hat{Y}_i - Y_i)^2\} + 2\sigma_u^4(\sigma_e^2 + \sigma_u^2)^{-1} ,$$

where $\hat{Y}_i$ is the predictor constructed with known σ_e^2 .

Proof. Because $\hat{w}$ is a function of s^2 , $\hat{\beta}$ is independent of $\hat{w}$. Furthermore,

$$\begin{aligned}(\hat{\beta} - \beta)'X'e &= (\hat{\beta} - \beta)X'X(X'X)^{-1}X'e \\ &= e'X(X'X)^{-1}X'e + u'X(X'X)^{-1}X'e ,\end{aligned}$$

where we have used

$$e = X(X'X)^{-1}X'e + (I - X(X'X)^{-1}X')e ,$$

$$e' = (e_1, e_2, \ldots, e_n) ,$$

and

$$X' = (X_1', X_2', \ldots, X_n') .$$

Therefore,

$$E\{\hat{w}(1 - \hat{w})(\hat{\beta} - \beta)'X'u\} = k\sigma_u^2 E\{\hat{w}(1 - \hat{w})\} ,$$

$$E\{(1 - \hat{w})^2(\hat{\beta} - \beta)'X'e\} = k\sigma_e^2 E\{(1 - \hat{w})^2\} ,$$

and

$$\begin{aligned}&E\{(1 - \hat{w})^2(\hat{\beta} - \beta)'X'X(\hat{\beta} - \beta)\} \\ &\quad = k(\sigma_e^2 + \sigma_u^2)E\{(1 - \hat{w})^2\} .\end{aligned}$$

Also, again using the orthogonal partition of $\underset{\sim}{e}$ and $\underset{\sim}{u}$,

$$E\{(1-\hat{w})^2\, \underset{\sim}{e}'\underset{\sim}{e} - 2\hat{w}(1-\hat{w})\underset{\sim}{e}'\underset{\sim}{u} + \hat{w}^2\, \underset{\sim}{u}'\underset{\sim}{u}\}$$

$$= E\{(1-\hat{w})^2\, \underset{\sim}{e}'(\underset{\sim}{I} - \underset{\sim}{X}(\underset{\sim}{X}'\underset{\sim}{X})^{-1}\underset{\sim}{X}')\underset{\sim}{e}$$

$$- 2\hat{w}(1-\hat{w})\underset{\sim}{e}'(\underset{\sim}{I} - \underset{\sim}{X}(\underset{\sim}{X}'\underset{\sim}{X})^{-1}\underset{\sim}{X}')\underset{\sim}{u}$$

$$+ \hat{w}^2\, \underset{\sim}{u}'(\underset{\sim}{I} - \underset{\sim}{X}(\underset{\sim}{X}'\underset{\sim}{X})^{-1}\underset{\sim}{X}')\underset{\sim}{u}\}$$

$$+ k\, \sigma_e^2\, E\{(1-\hat{w})^2\} + k\, \sigma_u^2\, E\{\hat{w}^2\} .$$

By the results presented in Efron and Morris (1973), the expectation of the sum of the first three terms on the right of the equality is less than

$$(n-k)\sigma_u^2\{1 - \sigma_u^2(n-k-2)[(n-k)(\sigma_u^2+\sigma_e^2)]^{-1}\}$$

$$= (\sigma_e^2+\sigma_u^2)^{-1}\, \sigma_u^2[(n-k)\sigma_e^2 + 2\sigma_u^2] .$$

The variance of $\hat{w}$ is finite because $\hat{w}\, \varepsilon[0, 1]$. It follows that

$$E\{\sum_{i=1}^{n}(Y_i - \dot{Y}_i)^2\} = E\{(1-\hat{w})^2(\hat{\underset{\sim}{\beta}} - \underset{\sim}{\beta})'\underset{\sim}{X}'\underset{\sim}{X}(\hat{\underset{\sim}{\beta}} - \underset{\sim}{\beta})$$

$$- 2(1-\hat{w})^2(\hat{\underset{\sim}{\beta}} - \underset{\sim}{\beta})'\underset{\sim}{X}'\underset{\sim}{e}$$

$$+ 2(1-\hat{w})\hat{w}(\hat{\underset{\sim}{\beta}} - \underset{\sim}{\beta})'\underset{\sim}{X}'\underset{\sim}{u}$$

$$+ (1-\hat{w})^2\, \underset{\sim}{e}'\underset{\sim}{e} - 2\hat{w}(1-\hat{w})\underset{\sim}{e}'\underset{\sim}{u} + \hat{w}^2\, \underset{\sim}{u}'\underset{\sim}{u}\}$$

$$= k(\sigma_e^2 + \sigma_u^2)E\{(1-\hat{w})^2\}$$

$$- 2k[\sigma_e^2\, E\{(1-\hat{w})^2\} - \sigma_u^2\, E\{(1-\hat{w})\hat{w}\}]$$

$$+ E\{(1-\hat{w})^2\, \underset{\sim}{e}'\underset{\sim}{e} - 2\hat{w}(1-\hat{w})\underset{\sim}{e}'\underset{\sim}{u} + \hat{w}^2\, \underset{\sim}{u}'\underset{\sim}{u}\}$$

$$< (\sigma_e^2 + \sigma_u^2)^{-1} \sigma_u^2[(n - k)\sigma_e^2 + 2\sigma_u^2] + k\sigma_u^2$$

$$= (n - k)[(1 - w)^2 \sigma_e^2 + w^2 \sigma_u^2] + k\sigma_u^2$$

$$+ 2(\sigma_e^2 + \sigma_u^2)^{-1} \sigma_u^4 .$$

ILLUSTRATION

To illustrate the use of the regression estimator for small areas, we use a constructed data set. The data were constructed using some data analyzed at Iowa State University under a Cooperative Agreement with the Department of Agriculture. The Economics and Statistics Service of the Department of Agriculture determined the area in soybeans in a sample of area segments in several Iowa counties in 1978. By satellite imagery the number of pixels classified as soybeans in each area segment and in the county as a whole was determined. (A pixel is an area approximately one acre in size.) In the actual analysis the segment data were used to estimate the regression relationship between estimates constructed from satellite imagery and estimates constructed from low-level photography and personal interview. For the purposes of this illustration we generated a set of 10 county observations, $\tilde{Y}_i$, with smaller variances than those observed in the study. We assume that estimates are desired for six counties in which no observations are made.

The regression procedure has been extended to data sets with an unequal number of sampling units per county, but we present results under the simpler assumption of one unit per county. We also present the mean squared errors under the assumption that σ_e^2 and σ_u^2 are known.

Let Y_i and Y_i^* represent the mean soybean hectares per segment for the ith county in 1978 and in the 1974 Agricultural Census, respectively; let $\tilde{Y}_i$ represent the estimated soybean hectares for the ith county in 1978; and let X_{2i} represent the mean number of pixels of soybeans per segment for all segments in the ith county.

The model for the 16 county means is

$$\tilde{Y}_i = Y_i + u_i$$

$$Y_i - Y_i^* = \underset{\sim}{X}_i \underset{\sim}{\beta} + e_i , \quad i = 1,2,\ldots,16 , \qquad (10)$$

where

$$\underset{\sim}{X}_i = (X_{1i}, X_{2i}, X_{3i}) = (1, X_{2i}, Y_i^*) .$$

We have given the model in the form (3) discussed earlier. The form (3) explicitly includes the census values into the model. In the soybean example one could fix the coefficient of Y_i^* at -1 and work with the reduced model

$$\tilde{Y}_i = \beta_1 + \beta_2 X_{2i} + u_i + e_i .$$

For illustrative purposes we retain model (10).

The data are given in the first three columns of Table G-1. For the purposes of this illustration, the variances of the random errors, e_i and u_i, are assumed to be $\sigma_e^2 = 25$ and $\sigma_u^2 = 18$. (These values are about one-tenth of the between-county component and the between-segment component estimated in the study.)

TABLE G-1: Constructed Data and Prediction for Soybean Area

County i	Reported Hect. $\tilde{Y}_i$	Mean Pixels X_{2i}	1974 Census Hect. Y_i^*	Predicted Hect. $\hat{Y}_i$
1	86.2	189.7	76.8	86.5 (3.0)
2	79.2	188.1	75.6	82.1 (3.1)
3	90.7	196.6	89.9	91.3 (3.0)
4	93.6	198.7	84.4	92.8 (2.9)
5	85.3	177.0	70.7	83.5 (3.2)
6	89.1	220.2	99.2	94.8 (3.0)
7	107.7	204.6	96.0	102.9 (3.0)
8	113.8	247.1	102.4	113.5 (3.2)
9	116.0	247.1	96.7	114.3 (3.3)
10	88.9	185.4	91.8	88.7 (3.2)
11	--	205.3	76.7	92.6 (6.6)
12	--	221.4	99.8	103.2 (5.9)
13	--	199.2	76.8	90.4 (6.2)
14	--	217.9	96.0	101.1 (5.6)

TABLE G-1 (Continued)

15	--	190.3	84.4	88.7 (5.6)
16	--	209.7	89.9	96.9 (5.4)

The least-squares estimate of $\underset{\sim}{\beta}'$ is

$$\hat{\underset{\sim}{\beta}}' = (\hat{\beta}_1, \hat{\beta}_2, \hat{\beta}_3) = \begin{pmatrix} \underset{(19.0)}{2.4} , & \underset{(0.14)}{0.36} , & \underset{(0.32)}{-0.79} \end{pmatrix} ,$$

where the numbers in parentheses are estimated standard errors. The covariance matrix, conditional on the observed $\underset{\sim}{X} \equiv (\underset{\sim}{X}_1', \underset{\sim}{X}_2', \ldots, \underset{\sim}{X}_{10}')'$, for the least-squares estimator is

$$\underset{\sim}{V}(\hat{\underset{\sim}{\beta}} | \underset{\sim}{X}) = \begin{pmatrix} 360.4 & -0.9643 & -1.7881 \\ & 0.0204 & -0.0366 \\ \text{sym.} & & 0.1053 \end{pmatrix} .$$

The predictor for the mean hectares of soybeans per segment in the sample counties is

$$\hat{Y}_i = Y_i^* + \underset{\sim}{X}_i \hat{\underset{\sim}{\beta}} + w(\tilde{Y}_i - Y_i^* - \underset{\sim}{X}_i \hat{\underset{\sim}{\beta}}) , \quad i = 1,2,\ldots,10 ,$$

where

$$w = \sigma_e^2(\sigma_e^2 + \sigma_u^2)^{-1} = 25(25 + 18)^{-1} \doteq 0.58 .$$

The mean squared error for this predictor, conditional on $\underset{\sim}{X}$, is

$$E\{(\hat{Y}_i - Y_i)^2 | \underset{\sim}{X}\} = w\,\sigma_u^2 + (1 - w)^2[\underset{\sim}{X}_i(\underset{\sim}{X}'\underset{\sim}{X})^{-1}\underset{\sim}{X}_i'](\sigma_e^2 + \sigma_u^2) .$$

The predictions for the sample counties are the first ten values in the last column of Table G-1. The estimated standard errors of the predictors are given in parentheses below the predictions. It can be verified that the sum of the mean squared errors of the predictors for the ten sample counties is

$$\sum_{i=1}^{10} E\{(\hat{Y}_i - Y_i)^2 | \underset{\sim}{X}\} = 127 \equiv (10-3)w\,\sigma_u^2 + 3\sigma_u^2 .$$

The predictor for the mean hectares of soybeans per segment in the nonsample counties is

$$\hat{Y}_i \equiv Y_i^* + \underset{\sim}{X}_i \underset{\sim}{\hat{\beta}} , \quad i = 11,12,\ldots,16 .$$

The mean squared error for this predictor, conditional on $\underset{\sim}{X}$, is

$$E\{(\hat{Y}_i - Y_i)^2 | \underset{\sim}{X}\} = \sigma_e^2 + [\underset{\sim}{X}_i (\underset{\sim}{X}' \underset{\sim}{X})^{-1} \underset{\sim}{X}_i'](\sigma_e^2 + \sigma_u^2) .$$

The predictions for the nonsample counties are the last six values in the last column of Table G-1. The sum of the estimated conditional mean squared errors of the predictors for the six nonsample counties is

$$\sum_{i=11}^{16} E\{(\hat{Y}_i - Y_i)^2 | \underset{\sim}{X}\} = 210 .$$

This estimate cannot be obtained by substitution in (8b). The reason for the difference is that we have used a conditional estimator for the mean squared error of the predictor for nonsample counties, which does not utilize the assumption of normality of the $\underset{\sim}{X}_i$ vectors. Expression (8b) is the expectation of our estimator over possible $\underset{\sim}{X}$ values under the assumption of normality.

By the model assumptions, the mean squared error of the prior census predictor, Y_i^* , for the mean hectares of soybeans per segment in the ith county is

$$E\{(Y_i^* - Y_i)^2\} = E\{(e_i + \underset{\sim}{X}_i \underset{\sim}{\beta})^2\} .$$

An unbiased estimator of the sum of squared errors of the prior census predictor is

$$\sum_{i=1}^{16} \hat{E}\{(Y_i^* - Y_i)^2\} = \sum_{i=1}^{16} \{\sigma_e^2 + (\underset{\sim}{X}_i \underset{\sim}{\hat{\beta}})^2 - \underset{\sim}{X}_i (\underset{\sim}{X}' \underset{\sim}{X})^{-1} \underset{\sim}{X}_i' (\sigma_e^2 + \sigma_u^2)\}$$

$$= 13\sigma_e^2 - 3\sigma_u^2 + \sum_{i=1}^{16} (\underset{\sim}{X}_i \underset{\sim}{\hat{\beta}})^2$$

$$- \sum_{i=11}^{16} \underset{\sim}{X}_i (\underset{\sim}{X}' \underset{\sim}{X})^{-1} \underset{\sim}{X}_i' (\sigma_e^2 + \sigma_u^2)$$

$$= 1287 .$$

This is considerably larger than the sum of the estimated mean squared errors for the predictor $\hat{Y}_i$, which is

$$127 + 210 = 337 .$$

REFERENCES

Anderson, T.W. (1958) *An Introduction to Multivariate Statistical Analysis.* New York: Wiley.

Efron, B., and Morris, C. (1973) Stein's estimation rule and its competitors--an empirical Bayes approach. *Journal of the American Statistical Association* 68:117-130.

Efron, B., and Morris, C. (1975) Data analysis using Stein's estimator and its generalizations. *Journal of the American Statistical Association* 70:311-319.

Fay, R.E., and Herriot, R. (1979) Estimates of income for small places: an application of James-Stein procedures to census data. *Journal of the American Statistical Association* 74:269-277.

James, W., and Stein, C. (1961) Estimation with quadratic loss. Pp. 361-379 in *Proceedings of the Fourth Berkeley Symposium of Mathematical Statistics and Probability, Vol. 1.* Berkeley: University of California Press.

APPENDIX H

USE OF SOME STATISTICAL TECHNIQUES IN DEVELOPMENT STUDIES

WALTER T. FEDERER

Many variables being studied in surveys are cross-classified, that is, classified on several dimensions. For example, the variable "income" could be classified in the two dimensions of sex and age to give a two-way table. A third classification could be level of education. This process could be carried out for a number of classification variables, and one would have an n-way cross-classified division (factorial arrangement) of the variable income. If there were k_1 levels of the first classification, k_2 levels of the second classification, etc., up to k_n levels of the nth classification, there would be $k_1 \times k_2 \times . . . \times k_n = N$ possible combinations. Depending upon n and the number of levels in each classification, N could be a very large number. For example, ten levels of each of six factors (classifications) would result in an N of one million.

In practice, some of the combinations may not be present in the population, or one may wish to sample a subset of these combinations. A subset of the N combinations is known as a *fractional replicate* of the complete factorial arrangement (n-way classification). There are many ways to select a fractional replicate and many possible fractional replicate plans, but it would be desirable to have one that had the smallest variance for the effects estimated from the fraction. However, it should be emphasized that certain fractional replicates will arise because the combinations do not exist in the population or did not exist in the sample survey. In this case one does not worry about good properties but only about what effects can be estimated. In certain instances, it may be desirable to select a relatively small fraction of N. For the example of $10^6 = 1,000,000 = N$, one might select an n of 55 combinations, which would allow one to estimate the population mean and the nine single degrees of freedom for the main effects of each of the six classifications used. This might be done because of budget and time restrictions on the sampling procedure and because one believes interactions of classifications are less important. Fractional replication has been used extensively in industrial investigations and especially in quality control studies.

To develop the idea of fractional replication further, consider an example with four factors and several levels for each:

Factor 1. Education, with the five levels: 8th-grade diploma, high-school diploma, 4-year college diploma, masters degree, and doctoral degree.
Factor 2. Income, with the ten levels (in thousands of dollars): 10 or less, 11-20, 21-30, 31-40, 41-50, 51-70, 71-100, 101-150, 151-300, and more than 300.
Factor 3. Sex, with two levels: male and female.
Factor 4. Ethnic background, with the six levels: Caucasian, African, Hispanic, Oriental, Arabic, and others.

This would result in 600 combinations (5 × 10 × 2 × 6). If one adds other factors or more levels of the given factors, the number of combinations increases rapidly. Some of the combinations may not exist or may have a very low occurrence in a population, so that getting the information would be impossible or, if it is available, very costly. When one is allowed to design the combinations, one can select a fractional replicate plan with the desired properties.

In the above example, one could use a main effect plan with 20 combinations such as:

1111	1211	1121	1112
1211	1311		1113
1311	1411		1114
1411	1511		1115
1511	1611		1116
	1711		
	1811		
	1911		
	1011		

where the first digit refers to level of education (1,2,3,4,5), the second to level of income (1,2,3,4,5,6,7,8,9,0(10)), the third to sex (1,2) and the fourth to ethnic background (1,2,3,4,5,6). Thus, the combination 1211 designates the first level of factor one, the second level of factor two, the first level of factors three and four; the combination 1116 designates that factors one, two and three are each at level one and factor four is at level six. It should be noted that this plan is easy to construct but has poor statistical properties. Better plans can be constructed.

If one wants information on sex by education interaction and some information on other interactions, a 60-combinations plan has good statistical properties (see Table 1). From this fraction one can obtain an analysis of variance table (see Table 2).

Another plan, which has main effects of sex, ethnic background, and income levels orthogonal to each other and has income levels and education levels in a partially balanced block arrangement is given in Table 3.

The first design was obtained by taking six rows of a cyclical 10×10 Latin square design in an appropriate manner to achieve as much balance as possible. One may alter the above design slightly to improve the

TABLE 1

Ethnic background	Sex 1 Education 1	2	3	4	5	Sex 2 Education 1	2	3	4	5
	(income levels)									
1	0	1	2	3	4	5	6	7	8	9
2	1	2	3	4	5	6	7	8	9	0
3	4	5	6	7	8	9	0	1	2	3
4	5	6	7	8	9	0	1	2	3	4
5	8	9	0	1	2	3	4	5	6	7
6	2	3	4	5	6	7	8	9	0	1

TABLE 2

Source of variation	d.f.
Total	60
Correction for mean	1
Sex	1
Education	4
Sex × education	4
Ethnic levels	5
Income levels	9
Remainder (interactions)	36

TABLE 3

Ethnic background	Sex 1 Education 1	2	3	4	5	Sex 2 Education 1	2	3	4	5
	(income levels)									
1	0	1	2	3	4	8	9	5	6	7
2	5	6	7	8	9	0	1	2	3	4
3	4	0	1	2	3	6	7	8	9	5
4	7	8	9	5	6	3	4	0	1	2
5	2	3	4	0	1	5	6	7	8	9
6	9	5	6	7	8	1	2	3	4	0

balance property a little for symbols 0, 1, . . ., 9 and the ten columns. One such plan is Table 4. This plan was obtained from the preceding one by interchanging 5 and 6 in row 1, 0 and 9 in row 2, 7 and 8 and 1 and 2 in row 4, and 3 and 4 in row 5. One could probably increase the balance with further manipulations. Thus, it can be seen that there are many fractional replicate plans for any given situation.

In studies that can be planned, these combinations can be used as stratification categories. One should note that a fractional replicate is any fraction of a complete factorial or n-way classification. Unfortunately, this idea is not conveyed in textbooks, but it is important in the statistical analysis of survey and observational data.

In most surveys and observational studies, the fractional replicate will not be planned beforehand. One will need to take the fraction obtained and obtain whatever main effects and interactions that are estimable. Whether in the planned design case or in the unplanned case, one may use concepts from factorial design theory in the statistical summarization. Also, from this theory one can determine which effects are confounded with other effects. It should be pointed out that little work has been done on this aspect of fractional replication (or in the equivalent situation of an n-way classification with missing subclasses).

When relatively few subclasses are empty, a statistical procedure known as "the missing plot technique" may be used rather than treating the situation as a fractional replicate. Here one obtains some idea of the values for the missing categories, depending upon the validity of the assumptions made in computing values for the empty cells. In surveys and observational studies, there will often be missing combinations in two-way three-way, . . ., n-way tables, and one wants to obtain some information or estimates for the missing categories. If one can assume that interactions are absent or negligibly small, then one can use the "missing plot" or "borrowing on strength" techniques. The border totals are used to estimate the missing combinations (see Table 5). Data are not available for combinations of factor 1 level 1 with factor 2 level 3 and of factor 1 level 2 with factor 2 level 2. Denote these as X_{13}

TABLE 4

	Sex									
	1					2				
	Education									
Ethnic background	1	2	3	4	5	1	2	3	4	5
	(income levels)									
1	0	1	2	3	4	8	9	6	5	7
2	5	6	7	8	0	9	1	2	3	4
3	4	0	1	2	3	6	7	8	9	5
4	8	7	9	5	6	3	4	0	2	1
5	2	4	3	0	1	5	6	7	8	9
6	9	5	6	7	8	1	2	3	4	0

TABLE 5

Factor 2 level	Factor 1 level 1	2	3	Sum
1	6	5	4	15
2	15	?	8	23
3	?	15	12	27
Sum	21	20	24	65

and X_{22}. Then, missing plot formulas (see Federer 1955:133-4) would give the following estimates $\hat{X}_{13}$ and $\hat{X}_{22}$ as:

$$\hat{X}_{13} = \frac{4(21+27) - (20+23) - 65}{5} = 16.8$$

$$\hat{X}_{22} = \frac{4(20+23) - (21+27) - 65}{5} = 11.8$$

Even if interaction were present, this would give some information, even if not very reliable, on the missing combinations.

It should be pointed out that the above procedure holds for a linear, additive model with no interaction. If the model is one of multiplicative effects with additive error terms such as used in a chi-square contingency table, then the use of logarithms of data and of a linear, additive model is inappropriate. One could obtain the estimated row ($\hat{\mu}_{i\cdot}$), column ($\hat{\mu}_{\cdot j}$), and grand ($\hat{\mu}$) means for a two-way analysis of variance with no interaction. Then, one forms the estimate $\hat{\mu}_{i\cdot}\hat{\mu}_{\cdot j}/\hat{\mu}$ as the value for the item missing in row i and column j. Note that one uses the model

$$Y_{ij} = \mu_{i\cdot}\mu_{\cdot j}/\mu + \varepsilon_{ij},$$

where $\mu_{i\cdot}$, $\mu_{\cdot j}$, and μ are the population means for row i, column j, and the overall mean, and ε_{ij} is a random error component. When all the cells are filled, one uses the row ($\bar{y}_{i\cdot}$), column ($\bar{y}_{\cdot j}$), and grand ($\bar{y}_{\cdot\cdot}$) arithmetic means to compute the "expected value", $y_{i\cdot}y_{\cdot j}/y_{\cdot\cdot}$, for the ith row and jth column. The estimated residuals are

$$\hat{\varepsilon}_{ij} = Y_{ij} - \bar{y}_{i\cdot}\bar{y}_{\cdot j}/y_{\cdot\cdot},$$

and

$$\bar{y}_{\cdot\cdot}\Sigma_{i=1}^{r}\Sigma_{j=1}^{c}\hat{\varepsilon}_{ij}/\bar{y}_{i\cdot}\bar{y}_{\cdot j}$$

is used as a chi-square statistic with (r-1)(c-1) degrees of freedom.

Another technique that is useful for handling missing subclasses, especially when there are relatively many of them, is that of collapsing levels of a factor. In the above example, if one combined levels 2 and 3 of factor 2, there would be no missing combinations. In more extreme cases, one may need to collapse levels in several ways in such a manner as to maximize the number of combinations and/or the number of levels of a factor. For example, consider the two-way array of 10 levels of income (1, 2, . . ., 9, 0) and 6 levels of ethnic background (1, 2, . . ., 6) where the X means data are available (see Table 6). To maximize levels of income, one could collapse levels 1 and 2 or levels 5 and 6 or both of ethnic background. To maximize both levels of ethnic background and income, one could leave the table as it is, but one would have to contend with several empty cells. In order to have no missing cells, one could combine income levels 4 and 5, and income levels 6, 7, 8, 9, and 0. Also, one could combine levels 4 and 5, 6 and 7, and 8, 9, and 0 and then estimate three values for ethnic background levels 3, 4, and 5, each with income levels 8, 9, and 0.

In addition to the above analytical procedures, one could set up some form of experimental design (sometimes called a quasi-experimental design when used in a survey or observational situation) involving various levels of a factor. For example, one could use a random selection of ten states for the blocks and a set of five different record-keeping procedures as treatments of a randomized complete blocks design to study the effect of treatments on farm income over a period of 10 years. One could perform all the usual statistical analyses for these data that one performs for a randomized complete block design in a nutrition or fertilizer experiment. Likewise, other types of experimental designs, such as a Latin square, Youden, incomplete block, repeated measures, etc., could be used if conditions warranted.

TABLE 6

	Income level									
Ethnic background level	1	2	3	4	5	6	7	8	9	0
1	X	X	X		X		X		X	
2	X	X	X	X		X		X		X
3	X	X	X		X	X				
4	X	X	X	X		X				
5	X				X	X	X			
6	X	X	X	X		X		X	X	X

REFERENCE

Federer, W.T. (1955) *Experimental Design--Theory and Application*. New York: McMillan.